VALLE-INCLÁN

VALLE-INCLÁN

The Theatre of His Life

ROBERT LIMA

University of Missouri Press
Columbia, 1988

Library of Congress Cataloging-in-Publication Data

Lima, Robert.
  Valle-Inclán : the theatre of his life.
  Bibliography: p.

  Includes index.
  1. Valle-Inclán, Ramón del, 1870–1936—Biography. 2.
Authors, Spanish—19th century—Biography. 3. Authors, Spanish—
20th century—Biography. I. Title.
PQ6641.A47Z734   1988   868'.6209   [B]   87–19119
ISBN 0–8262–0661–1 (alk. paper)

∞™ This paper meets the minimum requirements of
the American National Standard for Permanence of Paper
for Printed Library Materials, Z39.48, 1984.

Frontispiece portrait of Valle-Inclán by Keith E. Lima.

To
My Aunts
Dª Vicky Millares, Viuda de Canoura
Dª Otilia Millares, Viuda de Arbona
and
My Friend
D. Severiano Loroño Viazcoechea

and
Our Galicia,
Celtic Homeland
of the ancestors,
of my own Sons of Breogan,
Mark, Keith, Michele, Debra,
and of my wife Sally.

Preface

The year 1986 marked the fiftieth anniversary of the death of Ramón del Valle-Inclán (1866–1936),[1] noted playwright, novelist, poet, and aesthetician of Spain's highly influential "Generation of 1898." In conjunction with this significant event, I completed *Valle-Inclán: The Theatre of His Life*. This is a biographical study in English, with Spanish quotations in an Appendix. All translations are mine. It is my objective to present a full biographical study by focusing on all aspects of Valle-Inclán's reality—as Man, Artist, Mask, the three dimensions that he himself emphasized.

Idiosyncrasy has characterized the lives of many noted writers. Indeed, interest in some of these individuals is sustained more by their colorful behavior than by their literary achievements. During his lifetime, it was the unfortunate lot of Ramón del Valle-Inclán to be viewed largely as an eccentric because he cultivated an individuality that was forceful and unyielding, argumentative and cynical, founded on a subjective approach to ethics, aesthetics, and metaphysics. He was not alone among his contemporaries in the creation of a personal lifestyle, however. Benavente, Unamuno, Azorín, Baroja, Machado, and others who are grouped with Valle-Inclán in the *Generación de 1898* possessed an arrogant individualism (*egolatría*, as Unamuno termed it) that went to the extreme of ferocity. These men from different provinces of Spain came together in turn-of-the-century Madrid and began to issue their dissimilar works. But despite the divergence of their writings they came to know of each other through the periodicals in which they published; they became acquainted through conversations in the *tertulias* convened daily in the cafés of the capital. Yet neither of these concurrences suffices to explain their grouping as a generation. The reason why Azorín created the generation concept is that these writers coincided in a vociferous concern over "the problem of Spain": the erosion of national prestige and power since the seventeenth century. It was the ignominious defeat of Spain by the United States in 1898 that catalyzed Valle-Inclán and his generation into a formidable voice of dissent. In their opinion, the crisis of the times demanded a complete reassessment of national and personal values.

Valle-Inclán reacted to these needs in a decisive manner. His attitude toward life and art was marked by his abandonment of mercenary occupations, disdain for pettiness and hypocrisy, aloofness from the mainstream of politics, religion, and literature, dissatisfaction with the social order, impatience with the self-serving role of public and elite institutions, passionate reaction to injustice, personal purification through privation and fasting, independence on all levels, . . . and just pride.

His life and works reflected these negations and commitments. And although he realized that the achievement of perfection was impossible in the human context, he knew as well that unless the attempt was made life would have little meaning. Recognizing this truth, he carefully molded everything that concerned him so that the totality he sought, in the Aristotelian sense, might be approached in a complete lifetime.

Insofar as it is possible to categorize the creative foundation of an author who produced twenty-four plays, thirteen novels, seven collections of stories, three poetry books, and assorted other titles, not to mention numerous translations and adaptations from the French, Italian, and Portuguese, it can be said that Valle-Inclán's literature, like his life, was conceived and crystallized under self-imposed aesthetic parameters. The full exposition of his ideas on creativity is found in *La lámpara maravillosa* (*The Lamp of Marvels*),[2] subtitled "Spiritual Exercises." In this 1916 apologia Valle-Inclán develops fully the travails of the artist in rising above his humanity, in breaking the bondage of the body to set his creative spirit free, to the end of reaching the heights of beauty. In Valle-Inclán's version of the agon, the artist becomes a mystic through a threefold aesthetic initiation: "There are three transits through which the soul passes before it is initiated into the mystery of Eternal Beauty. The first transit, painful love; the second transit, joyful love; the third transit, love with renunciation and quietude." Serving his apprenticeship in the teachings of Miguel de Molinos and Pico della Mirandola, Valle-Inclán underwent the process described in *La lámpara maravillosa*. His commitment to the search for creative fulfillment is visible in the concerted effort he made to energize aesthetic principles into kinesis in his literature. This process can be traced back to the stories first issued in Spanish and Mexican periodicals prior to 1895. These early works disclose their author's dedication to stylistic perfection, the first hallmark of his aesthetic stance, for, as he believed, "Literary men will live in future anthologies because of a well-written page. Beauty resides only in form. Whoever fails to carve and polish his style will be no more than a poor writer." This approach was carried through in all his writings.

Similarly, his life was committed to an aesthetic integration which would parallel that in his works. This book follows a traditional biographical pattern. The text presents a chronological panorama of Valle-Inclán's life, featuring his own words—culled from his creative writings, interviews, lectures, correspondence, articles, book prologues, among other sources—in order to have his "voice" speak autobiographically as much as possible. To the end of emphasizing this self-presentation, only his words are quoted in the text. The assessment by contemporaries and others—the anecdotes, reminiscences, opinions, reviews, and other data—is fully documented in the Notes; this procedure creates a parallel biography. It is my intention through the parallelism of "voices," with my commentary in the text and in the notes as guide, to provide the reader a full, detailed account of the Man-Artist-Mask that was Ramón del Valle-Inclán.

R. L.
August 1987

Acknowledgments

Over many years, grants from The Pennsylvania State University's Vice-President for Research, the College of the Liberal Arts Associate Dean for Research, the Department of Spanish, Italian and Portuguese, as well as the Institute for the Arts and Humanistic Studies have helped in financing the release time and research travel requisite for the completion of this book.

In Madrid, the Fundación Juan March provided me with a study, staff support and the facilities of its library during several months. The Ateneo de Madrid, the Biblioteca Nacional and the Hemeroteca Municipal were also generous on numerous occasions in rendering their services, including the careful microfilming of time-worn holdings.

In Galicia, I have worked at the Museo de Pontevedra, at the library of the Universidad de Santiago de Compostela, at the Instituto "Padre Sarmiento" de Estudios Gallegos, at the Museo do Pobo Galego, and at the Real Academia Galega, La Coruña.

In the United States, the Library of Congress, the New York Public Library, the libraries of Columbia University, the University of Pennsylvania, and, in particular, The Pennsylvania State University, have proved very useful.

I am grateful to these institutions and their staffs for having eased the burden of compiling the voluminous data that must be processed in the preparation of a biography such as this.

Contents

"Cuando se haga un día la verdadera epopeya de Valle-Inclán, se empleará el copioso anecdotario de su vida, no para enterrar al escritor bajo un diluvio de hechos insignificantes—como se hace hoy—, sino para llevar un poco de luz a la más honda raíz de su personalidad."

Someday, when the real epic of Valle-Inclán is written, the copious anecdotes of his life will be used, not to bury the writer under a deluge of insignificant deeds, as is the case today, but to cast light on the depths of his personality.

> Antonio Machado, "Prólogo,"
> *La corte de los milagros*
> (Barcelona, 1938)

"Nuestro buen amigo don Ramón de Valle-Inclán—séale la posteriorídad aficionada—seguirá por mucho tiempo nutriendo más los anecdotarios que las antologías. Algo así le pasó a Quevedo. Se hablará de él más que se estudie su obra. Aunque su obra cardinal ¿no fué él mismo, el actor más aún que autor? Vivió—esto es, se hizo—en escena. Su vida, más que sueño, fué farándula. Actor de sí mismo.

My good friend don Ramón del Valle-Inclán—may the future recognize his worth—will continue to appear more often in collections of anecdotes than in anthologies. Something similar happened with Quevedo. More so than his work, he will be the topic of conversation. Although, isn't it true that he, the actor, rather than the author, was his principal work? He lived, that is, he created himself on the stage. More than a dream, his life was histrionics. Interpreter of himself.

> Miguel de Unamuno,
> "El habla de Valle-Inclán,"
> *Ahora* (28 January 1936)

I THE EARLY YEARS

1866–1897

1 Origins

In his maturity, the Man-Artist-Mask that was Valle-Inclán envisioned many moments of his early life in terms that range from the whimsical to the macabre. Refusing to disclose the facts of his birth, he substituted the fantasy that he was born aboard a sailboat in the middle of the *ría* (fjord) of Arosa; at other times he gave his place of birth as Puebla del Caramiñal or elsewhere. Such pronouncements were to be taken seriously by many, including journalists and biographers, and so the "legend" of his birth was created, to the chagrin of some and to the delight of others. Valle-Inclán thrived on such controversy, for he loved to obfuscate. In his poems from *El pasajero* (The Traveler), he depicts his birth and youth, sometimes employing the vocabulary of the fantast, as in "Rosa de pecado" (Rose of Sin):

The cat that bristles! The door that creaks!
The gutter dripping glu glu glu!
Alone in the house! At the door the howl
of the beast aborted when I was born.

That night in October! They say of the Full Moon,
with a vehement wind and choppy seas;
under its stars my destiny surged,
strong sea and winds beheld my birth.[1] (A1)

While in "Rosa del paraiso" (Rose of Paradise), from the same collection, he identifies the emotional context of his life in terms of his youth:

This divine emotion's from one's youth
when happily we tread the path
and everything's dissolved within
the fragrance of Palm Sunday's branch.[2] (A2)

Thus, Valle-Inclán traces to his youth many of the feelings and attitudes of his maturity, proving once again that "the child is father to the man." The reticence of the Man in communicating his reality is supplanted by the willingness of the Artist to give added value to his work through auto-biographical references and by the intent of the Mask to create an anecdotal personality. In so doing, he provides keys to the first doors that must be opened in the process of discovering the Man-Artist-Mask that was Valle-Inclán.

Don Ramón María del Valle-Inclán was in fact the literary and vital pseudonym of Ramón Valle y Peña, who was born on 28 October 1866 (under the sign of Scorpio)[3] in Villanueva de Arosa, a colorful Galician village on the Atlantic coast of Spain, near its provincial capital of Pontevedra. In the master bedroom of the traditional stone house of the Peña family, with the nautical name of Cuadrante, on the Calle del Priorato, Dolores de la Peña Montenegro Cardecid y Saco Bolaño delivered a son at six o'clock in the morning while her husband, Ramón del Valle Inclán y Bermúdez, waited to hold the child that he knew would bear his name but never suspected would bring it international renown. The register of the parish records the baptism of the infant the following day.[4] The child was given the middle names of José and Simón, the first in honor of the god-mother's patron saint and the second in reverence for the saint on whose feastday he was born. The celebration that normally accompanies such an occasion was not held because the birth had been a difficult one for the mother and she was still in serious condition at the time of the christening. Although she would recover eventually, she was unable to care for this second of her four offspring,[5] and the charge was given to a servant.

Ramón Valle y Peña was born and grew up in the turbulent nineteenth century. This dramatic era witnessed the domination of Spain by France, first through the *afrancesado* Bourbon monarch Carlos IV and thereafter through the direct Napoleonic conquest. Spanish resentment against France became fury on 2 May 1808 when the populace of Madrid marched in open rebellion. French troops under the leadership of Murat, Napoleon's brother-in-law, faced the rebels' valiant but badly armed attack; the slaughter of that day was followed by the mass executions of May 3. Francisco Goya, who viewed the atrocities, portrayed the horror and despair of those days in his unforgettable series of etchings *The Disasters of War* and the oils entitled "Fusilamientos de la Moncloa" (Executions at the Moncloa) and "Lucha de los patriotas con los Mamelucos" (Battle of the Patriots against the Mamelukes). Goya's grotesque interpretation in these works was to have a profound impact on Valle-Inclán's work, from the *Comedias bárbaras* (Savage Dramas) through the *Esperpentos* (Grotesques).

With the expulsion of the Bonapartist regime, Spain regained her national integrity in 1814. Fernando VII returned from his French exile to claim the throne he had barely possessed in 1808. But Fernando was an inept monarch who ruled capriciously. The life of the king was marked by personal ineptitude as well. He had been married three times, but none of his wives had provided him with an heir. On the death of his third wife in 1829, he married his niece María Cristina de Borbón. Out of this last union was born Isabel. The child was declared heir to the throne in spite of the "Ley Sálica" (Salic Law, 1713) that had been promulgated to prevent the feminine succession under such circumstances where another male claimant might exist. The decree of Isabel's stature challenged Don Carlos, Fernando's brother, who expected to inherit the kingdom. From this moment the king had an ardent enemy, and Spain began to take sides on the difficult issue. Fernando's death in 1833 led to the proclamation of his child as Isabel II and of María Cristina as her regent.

Don Carlos rebelled openly against Isabel's succession. The First Carlist War began immediately and lasted until 1839 when the pact of Vergara pronounced the defeat of Don Carlos, even though he had not given his consent to General Maroto to sign such a peace agreement. The majority of the Carlists accepted the treaty, but a few continued to fight and even followed their sovereign into exile in France. Nonetheless, Carlism had been effective. Its strongly conservative position—supported by the clergy, the Basque and Catalonian provinces, absolutists, traditionalists, and peripheral groups—forced the regency into dire straits and instability. The internal strife kept the hopes of the Carlists strong despite the military defeat of the movement. They took up arms periodically thereafter.

Valle-Inclán was to find in the struggles of "The Cause" material for his two series of historical novels, *La guerra carlista* (The Carlist War) and *El ruedo ibérico* (The Iberian Cycle), among other works. He was also highly critical of Queen Isabel II, satirizing her most strongly in *Farsa y licencia de la reina castiza* (Farce and Licentiousness of the Noble Queen).

Isabel's reign continued to reflect the instability of the nation. Externally, there were two wars. The most important was the Moroccan War of 1859–1860. The War of the Pacific, fought against the new republics of Chile and Peru, took place in 1866 and gave the Spanish Navy, still suffering the humiliation of Trafalgar, a much needed boost. General Prim, hero of the Moroccan War, led an unsuccessful revolt that same year against the increasingly dictatorial stance of the government, but the end came in 1868 when he and other military leaders overcame the forces of Isabel and entered Madrid. The queen, who was vacationing in San Sebastián, fled to the protection of France. The Bourbon succession was halted once more.

The ouster of Isabel II led first to the formation of a provisional government and then to the accession of Amadeo of Savoy, son of Victor Emanuel II, the king of Italy. But Amadeo's reign, too, was fraught with internal strife, and he soon gave up the crown.

On his departure, the Cortes established the First Republic (February

1873), in which the provinces of Spain were joined in a federal concept. By the end of 1874 the Republic was dissolved and replaced by a military junta that decreed the restoration of the Bourbons. Alfonso XII returned to Spain on 10 January 1875 to assume the throne his mother Isabel had vacated.

The young Ramón Valle y Peña lived the history of that period in his native region. Galicia, a northwestern sector of the Iberian Peninsula where sea and earth meet to create dramatic contrasts, nurtured the youth with its own history, traditions, and spirit, all of which were exalted in the separatism of the era.

The topography of Galicia is rugged and varied, the vegetation lush, the sky a melancholy gray whose burdened clouds grant the land an abundance of rain. The *rías*, inlets of the Atlantic that cut into the coastline, provide peaceful, almost idyllic, harbors for the fishing communities that populate so much of the shoreline. Its interior, patterned by pine and eucalyptus forests, as well as an infinite number of rivers and streams, yields rich harvests of grains and provides rolling grazing lands for the shepherd's flocks. The sea and the earth—net and scythe, fish and grain— form a partnership engendering a hardy people and providing a backdrop for the drama that is Galicia.

The region has a mixed and relatively obscure history. Other than the so-called Iberians, who are supposed to have dwelt throughout the peninsula, and the various trading peoples of the Mediterranean, who may have made forays into Galicia, the most identifiable inhabitants were the Celts. This people left enduring physical traits on both land and populace. Remains of that distant period[6] are commonplace in Galicia—curious round houses of gray stone, dolmens, menhirs, hillforts, tombs, jewelry, the traditional granaries called *hórreos*, statuary, iron weapons, artifacts. Even the physical makeup of the *gallego* certifies his kinship with the Celtic people, reflecting shadings of two principal strains.[7] Beyond this evidence there exist the varied substantiations of language, tradition, superstition: elements Valle-Inclán was to employ in poems, novels, and plays that have Galicia and *gallegos* as subjects.

It was in the era of the Reconquest, the crusade against the Moors, that Galicia emerged as a leading factor in peninsular life. The reason behind the rise of Galicia's influence was a simple and yet important one. Early in the ninth century (813) the body of St. James the Greater, an Apostle of Christ, was believed to have been discovered in the ancient city of Iria Flavia. Through this purported miracle, Galicia was transformed from an isolated and unimportant kingdom into the bastion of European Christianity. The church built to venerate the saint by housing his bones in time became the holy Cathedral of Santiago de Compostela.[8] As a center of religious pilgrimage second only to Rome, Galicia also became one of the focal points of a Europe threatened by Moslem power. Rivaling St. Peter's in grandeur and prestige, Santiago became the seat of Western hopes in the face of the Islamic onslaught. The holy city was to play an important role in Valle-Inclán's life and works as well.

The flowering of Galicia in the early Middle Ages was due to the growth of the cult of Santiago. Her religious importance led to the establishment of several routes to the city of the Saint; these extended throughout Europe and brought Santiago de Compostela into contact not only with the rest of the peninsula but also with the rest of the continent and the British Isles. While Galicia profited from the economic and cultural advantages of her position, she contributed as well by exporting her native heritage. Particularly influential was her lyric poetry, which gave peninsular literature its first non-epic, non-didactic verse in romance. *Gallego* was to remain the literary language of the peninsula until the fifteenth century when the cultural supremacy of Galicia declined with the rise of Castile as the dominant political power. The language of Galicia was thereafter relegated to a provincial role, its cultural impact reduced to an echo. It was not until the eighteenth century, with the encyclopedic writings of Benito Jerónimo Feijóo y Montenegro (1676–1764) and Martín Sarmiento (1694–1791), that Galicia emerged from seclusion to claim a rightful place in the nation's literature, becoming an important influence on its native authors who wrote in Castilian. In the late nineteenth century and afterward, the spirit of Galicia was reflected amply in the works of Manuel Murguía, Rosalía de Castro, Eduardo Pondal, Manuel Curros Enríquez, Emilia Pardo Bazán, and Ramón Menéndez Pidal, among others.

In the twentieth century, Valle-Inclán carried on the tradition of Galician contribution to Spanish literature. The rapport of the Man, the Artist, and the Mask with the native soil of Galicia is one of the most distinguishing elements in the life of Valle-Inclán. Galicia is the place of his birth and of his death, as well as his haven from the difficulties of his career. On the intellectual level, it is foundation, cornerstone, and buttress of his work. Galicia imprinted its image on the physical, creative, and social aspects of Valle-Inclán. Therefore, he is the epitome of Galician contribution to the literature of Spain and the inheritor of the treasure trove of an ancient culture. Among the projects that Valle-Inclán seems not to have undertaken was a *Historia de Galicia* (History of Galicia), in which he envisioned classifying the region's evolution by focusing on three distinct figures of its rich past: the great heretic Priscillian, the great archbishop Gelmírez, and the great encyclopedist Feijóo.

Ramón Valle y Peña's ancestral heritage had important implications in his totality. Both the maternal and paternal sides of the family contributed patents of nobility. Each had a distinctive Galician background. The mother's family traced its ancestry, through the Montenegro name, to long-established clans[9] among whose more prominent figures were Tristán de Montenegro (Capitán de las Torres de Pontevedra, Payo de Montenegro, Señor de Mourente), Alonso de la Peña Montenegro (Obispo de

Quito), the poet Amador Montenegro, and the architects José Peña and Domingo Luis Montenegro, whose works are evident in Santiago de Compostela. A hand-hewn coat-of-arms of the Peña family still graces the doorway of the house in which Ramón Valle y Peña was born. The motto that accompanies the coat-of-arms, "Mi sangre se derramó / por la caza que cazó" (My blood was shed / for the game it bled), was incorporated by Valle-Inclán into the composite arms with which he adorned his editions. His esteem for the Montenegro name and tradition is evidenced in one of the author's principal creations—Don Juan Manuel Montenegro, protagonist of the *Comedias bárbaras*—and in the words uttered by this character in *Sonata de otoño* (Autumn Sonata):

We, the Montenegros of Galicia, are descended from a German empress. Ours is the only Spanish heraldic shield that has metal on metal: Golden spurs on a field of silver.[10] (A3)

The paternal side of the family had roots elsewhere in Spain: the Valle branch in Torrijos, province of Toledo, and the Inclán in Concejo de Pravia, province of Asturias. But the ancestors of Ramón Valle y Peña had arrived in Galicia very early. In choosing to cast his name in the paternal onomatology Valle-Inclán was acknowledging his descent from the ancient family that had settled in Rua Nova at Sobrán, a short distance from Villanueva de Arosa.[11]

The statues of Don Miguel and Doña Rosa still perch atop their high pedestals guarding the entrance to the inner garden at Rua Nova and overseeing the ruin into which their *pazo* (estate) has fallen. But while the grandeur of the family declined in an economic sense, its intellectual prowess began to emerge. The advent of Francisco del Valle-Inclán, born in 1736, marked this direction. He practiced law on graduating from the Universidad de Santiago de Compostela, became rector of several schools, and served the Real Audiencia de la Coruña; his public-spiritedness was manifested in the founding of Santiago de Compostela's first public library and its Academia de la Lengua Gallega. The journal that he published beginning 1 May 1800 became the cornerstone of the Galician press.

Don Francisco's brother, Miguel, was the direct ancestor of Ramón Valle y Peña. Don Miguel's son, Carlos Luis de Valle-Inclán y Malvido, married Juana Bermúdez y Castro, owner of a Renaissance estate in nearby Puebla del Caramiñal. The marriage brought together two of the noblest families of Galicia. From this union was born Ramón del Valle Inclán y Bermúdez, the father of the subject, who would continue the intellectual pursuits begun by his great-uncle.

In 1835 another of these ancestors, Joaquín Domínguez del Valle, asked for and received official proof of the family's lineage and its hereditary arms. But by the time of Ramón Valle y Peña's birth the patents of nobility had become obscured and the family wealth had dissipated. It was through the earlier confirmation that, years later, Ramón Valle y Peña became convinced of his noble heritage. In time, he himself petitioned the Ministerio de Gracia y Justicia in Madrid asking that the ancient titles, long vacant, be bestowed on his person so that he could be rightfully recognized as "Marqués del Valle, Vizconde de Viexín, y Señor del Caramiñal." But the petition was denied and he had to be satisfied with the sonority of his chosen name and with the ironic motto, "El que más vale / no vale tanto / como vale Valle" ("The person most valued / is not valued / as is valued Valle"), of an impoverished family distinguished only by an exalted past. Ramón Valle y Peña chose to ignore the obvious sarcasm in the application of the motto to his family's present state. He patterned his behavior by signorial attitudes, his imagination by quixotic thrusts, his work by personalized styling. He adopted his inheritance as if it could clothe and feed more than his spirit, sensing the necessity of such commitment.[12] All his life he maintained the spirit of true nobility as Man, Artist, and Mask.

Establishing the relationship of Ramón Valle y Peña to his immediate household is more difficult than tracing his lineage. The scarcity of facts in this regard makes it impossible to fathom the extent of his activity within the family unit. What was his relationship with his brothers and sisters? With his father? With his mother? With the servants who cared for him?

While his private world in the years of youth has proved indecipherable, due largely to Valle-Inclán's reticence to speak of his relatives and the reluctance of the family to discuss him, some evidence may be extracted from the works of the author if his statements therein are interpreted in a loose autobiographical sense, New Criticism notwithstanding. Thus, in the prologue to *Jardín umbrío* (Shadowed Garden) he refers to a servant who influenced his imagination:

My grandmother had an old servant named Micaela la Galana. She died when I was a child. I remember that she spent long hours spinning in the recess of a window and that she knew many stories of saints, souls in Purgatory, goblins, and thieves. I now narrate those that she told me while her wrinkled fingers spun the spindle. Those tales full of ingenuous and tragic mystery frightened me at night throughout my childhood and that is why I haven't forgotten them. From time to time, they still well up in my memory and, as if a silent cold wind were passing over them, they possess the long murmur of dried leaves. The murmur of an old abandoned garden! Shadowed Garden.[13] (A4)

Besides the value that the revelation adds to the stories collected in the volume (not unlike the realistic base that Socrates "invented" with his references to Diotima), the evocation of the fictional Micaela serves to fill a biographical void, for she is the literary counterpart of "La Pexeja," a sometime seller of fruit who told the young Valle many tales of the vicinity when she worked for the family. Other servants in the household also stirred his imagination with impressive tales and songs of America; these, too, were influential in his later writings.

In "Mi hermana Antonia" (My Sister Antonia), one of his best short stories, the author's fictional narrative uncovers possible sketches of relatives. Speaking of his sister, the narrator says,

Antonia was much older than I. She was tall and pale, with dark eyes and a somewhat sad smile. She died while I was a child. But how I remember her voice and her smile and the iciness of her hand when she would take me to the Cathedral in the afternoons.[14] (A5)

Antonia may be the fictionalized portrait of his stepsister Ramona; if so, it is the only tangible evidence of the real-life relationship of brother and sister. In the same tale, the narrator speaks of his mother:

Our mother was very pious and didn't believe in omens or witchcraft, but she sometimes acted as if she did in order to excuse the passion that consumed her daughter. . . . My mother was very beautiful, fair and blonde, always dressed in silk, with a black glove on the hand that was missing two fingers, while the other, which was like a camelia, was covered with rings. It was this hand that we kissed and it was the one with which she caressed us.[15] (A6)

Similarly, the author creates portraits of mothers in many of his works; of particular note are those in the stories "Del misterio" (On Mystery) and "Hierbas olorosas" (Fragrant Herbs) as well as in the novels Los cruzados de la causa (Crusaders of the Cause) and the Sonatas. Again, it is possible to derive from these fictionalized figures a plausible interpretation of the author's relationship to his own mother.

Looking further into Valle-Inclán's writings, there may be discerned another real figure in the slightly fictionalized autobiographical references of La lámpara maravillosa. In this aesthetic treatise the author presents, among other things, a word picture of his godmother who, as the baptismal records affirm, was also his grandmother:

I knew a saintly woman when I was a child, and I have never been granted a greater boon. . . . I still remember feeling the penetration of grace from her ideal and candid gaze. To this day I evoke and relive that sacred emotion. On many other occasions I had seen my Godmother in a similar posture . . . but only on that evening, seemingly out of a pious legend, did I experience such ineffable joy on contemplating her. Under the shade of the old cypresses my child's soul entwined aesthetic and mystical emotions, much like color and fragrance are mingled in the grace of a rose. That may have been my first literary intuition: I had succeeded in incarnating the pious histories and tales of princesses told me by my Godmother in the very stuff of life and in its most beautiful shadings.

That evening in the rose garden I underwent an initiation through which all things revealed their mystical and beautiful eternity to me. . . . At nine I became enamored of my Godmother. . . . But from that moment on all her deeds were full of divine significance for me.[16] (A7)

This woman brought beauty to his imagination; she became the touchstone of his youthful aspirations and the focus of the mature man's remembrance of things past.

Fictional decorations aside, these various characters from the stories, novels, and aesthetic treatises of Valle-Inclán could be drawn from his reality, as is the case with many writers. Fantasy stirred in with experience has been a leading pigment for the artist since the earliest manifestations. It is not absurd to state that Valle-Inclán is no exception; it is more ridiculous to dismiss such internal evidence. In the case of Valle-Inclán, the Artist benefited greatly from the experience of the Man.

It is disappointing not to find in the works of Valle-Inclán characters who fit into the mold of his brothers Francisco, nicknamed Farruco, and Carlos. But this omission is somewhat mitigated in one case by a few scattered biographical facts. Carlos, after whom Valle-Inclán named his second son, was a journalist who founded several periodicals and wrote some literary pieces that were collected in 1894 and published in Pontevedra. His prize-winning book, *Escenas gallegas*[17] (Galician Scenes), was serialized in 1891. The fourteen sketches of regional life undoubtedly influenced various of Valle-Inclán's first writings, but that they were only a point of departure was evident after the publication of his own first book. However, Carlos abandoned literary pursuits in favor of the study of law, later becoming the notary in Cangas de Morrazo, near Vigo.

Portraits of fathers proving as satisfactory as those of other relatives are also missing from Valle-Inclán's writings. Certainly the paternal figure of Don Juan Manuel Montenegro recommends itself, particularly in the *Comedias bárbaras* where he is the protagonist, but the author does not portray him evoking any of the intuitive sympathy and love that the sister, mother, and godmother figures did. Nor does Valle-Inclán refer to him in the personal way he employed with the other three characters. Fortunately, facts about the father of Ramón Valle y Peña fill this lacuna.

Ramón del Valle Inclán y Bermúdez (1822–1890) was a man of varied talents and low economic status. He earned his living as a coastguardsman on the cutter "Atalaya," as a minor governmental functionary in Pontevedra, and as a journalist of provincial repute. In the latter capacity, he founded *La Opinión Pública*, a weekly newspaper in Santiago de Compostela that expressed strong Republican views during its brief existence between 1864 and 1865. Later, he established another newspaper, the weekly *La Voz de Arosa* in Villagarcía de Arosa, and went on to collaborate in the magazine *La Ilustración Gallega y Asturiana*, published in Madrid under the direction of Manuel Murguía. His small inheritance apparently was spent on these unrewarding journalistic ventures and for much of his life he and his family had to exist on very limited means. Nonetheless, he cultivated his literary inclinations and achieved a substantial reputation in Galicia as a poet and a historian, becoming a correspondent of the Real

Academia Gallega. He won several literary prizes, among them one on 28 July 1875 in Santiago de Compostela for his poem "A la ría de Arosa" (To the Ría of Arosa), which competed against the entry by the young Emilia Pardo Bazán, then at the start of her distinguished career as a writer. His contemporaries often spoke warmly of the man and his literary gifts. Manuel Murguía, an important political and literary figure in Galicia as well as the husband of the major poet Rosalía de Castro, expressed his admiration of Ramón del Valle Inclán y Bermúdez in the prologue to the son's first book.[18] This son not only surpassed the father as a writer but also experienced greater hardships in his life. Yet it is doubtful that Valle-Inclán would have developed as he did without the influence of his father. Murguía tied the two men prophetically in an indelible bond forged out of their similarity of character and talent.

Among the few preserved incidents of Ramón Valle y Peña's youth are three that give indications of later character traits. The first, which took place around 1877, concerns the eleven-year old being cast in the role of Don Ramiro in Zorrilla's *El puñal del Godo* (The Dagger of the Goth), to the chagrin of the parish priest of Villagarcía. Not only did the priest forbid the boy to play the part, but he also tried to censure him publicly. As the anecdote has it, the young Valle, arrayed in the armor of his role, pursued the priest with his mock sword into the church proper. The result was that Valle did perform his role, perhaps relishing this victory as much as he would relish later triumphs in his encounters with the establishment.

The second, and probably the earliest, anecdote concerns his father. According to Murguía's account,[19] the father had salvaged a human skull of anthropological interest from an excavation for a dock in the *ría* of Villagarcía; the construction work quickly destroyed the other remains and the skull became the only clue to the mystery. Valle Inclán y Bermúdez informed his friend Murguía of the find and promised to keep it in a safe place for his examination. But his children, finding the box in which he had secreted the skull, proceeded to enlist it in their games. Shortly, it was in fragments too small to be reconstructed. The incident presents an early example of the grotesquery that underscores Valle-Inclán's later interest in the macabre and may be a source for his story "El miedo," in which a skull plays an important role.

The third anecdote is more personal because it concerns the young Ramón's reaction to the killing of a wolf. In his maturity he related the occurrence to an interviewer, but his words still conveyed the deep impression the incident made on the child, who may have been exposed to one or another of the numerous nineteenth-century treatises on hunting wolves:

The only event in my youth worth mentioning is the assassination of a wolf. It was a brave wolf who used to devour our sheep. With my grandfather, who set the trap, I lay in hiding, fired point blank, and had the unfortunate luck to pierce his heart. Unfortunate because, then as now, I believed that even wolves shouldn't be killed treacherously. . . . The animal, which was excessively large, had snout and paws smeared with the blood of his young victim; furious over the red evidence of his crime, I grabbed his tail and dragged him home. But he was massive and I made frequent stops, to the great amusement of my grandfather, a male with a somewhat mocking sense of humor. "So, you coward, you can't drag him because you're afraid!" Afraid! . . . He knew very well that I wasn't afraid of wolves. Now if he'd been talking about mice! . . . There's nothing more I care to say about my youth. I was proud, mischievous, noisy, a dreamer, indolent.[20] (A8)

Four years earlier, he had published a self-assessment in *La lámpara maravillosa* that associated him with the wolf of his youth:

Around the dawn of manhood I was full of violence and disaffection. I was a wolf among sheep.[21] (A9)

The predatory nature of the wolf also served the playwright in his *Comedias bárbaras*, most notably in *Romance de lobos (Wolf Song)*.

Father and son also shared interests in history, *galleguismo*, and literature. The twelve-year old boy worked alongside his father producing the weekly editions of *La Voz de Arosa*, thus encountering the various aspects of journalism that prepared him for newspaper work in Madrid and Mexico in the early phase of his career. Together, they complemented the family's intellectual tradition begun by Francisco del Valle-Inclán. This ancestor's library had passed into the possession of Ramón del Valle Inclán y Bermúdez, who added books and periodicals of his own era. The collection contained the works of the foremost regional authors as well as those of important writers of Spain, France, Italy, and England. Through this impressive library, and under the tutelage of his father, the young Ramón was able to transcend the relative seclusion of rural life; his imagination was free to wander the vast landscape a good book can divulge.

He grew up reading the classics of Spanish literature. In the library were the works of Cervantes and Quevedo—whose distinct views of the human condition (hope, in the case of the first; pessimism, in that of the second)—were to influence Valle-Inclán's own *Esperpentos*. He read Góngora and was fascinated by the intricacies of his language, although in later years he would excoriate his frivolities and excesses.[22] The *Poema de Mio Cid* (Poem of the Cid) and romances on the epic hero stirred his sense of adventure. The works of Spanish and French romanticism, particularly those of Zorrilla, proved very influential in the early development of Valle-Inclán as Man, Artist, and Mask. Still, the principal attraction to reading lay in the classic treatises of history, where his imagination found satisfaction at the same time that he trained himself:

I never experienced that irresistible love, that determined vocation of those pre-
destined for the cultivation of literature. I read to educate my spirit—classical
books, especially; history titles, generally.[23] (A10)

While his readings were often haphazard, the wealth of the library holdings made it unlikely that his choice of books would be inconsequential.
There was also the living lesson of the history of his times.

By the beginning of 1876, under the vigorous efforts of Alfonso XII and
his Prime Minister Antonio Cánovas del Castillo, the Carlist opposition
was temporarily quelled through an amnesty, and the *Constitución de 1876*
was drafted in an attempt to unify leading political factions. With cessation
of major internal hostilities, both political and military, a large segment of
the army was freed to take care of more pressing matters in Cuba, where
insurgents were demanding greater self-rule. By 1878 the Cuban problem,
too, had been settled, if only temporarily.

Within Spain the attempt to establish dictatorial rule by the conservative
Cánovas led to friction with Práxedes Mateo Sagasta's Liberal Party and,
more markedly, with socialists, federalists, and regionalists. Because of
such conflicts and the danger that Spanish national integrity would be
impaired, after 1881 the leadership of the government was alternated
between conservatives and liberals in mock elections devised by Cánovas.
The plan (*Turno Pacífico*) kept the nation intact and free from revolutionary
activity of any importance. Nonetheless, such constitutional abuses and
growing social unrest, fanned by leftist organizations, caused disturbing
reactions. Periodically there erupted serious cases of civil disobedience and
crime that, in turn, led to increasingly stronger governmental retorts.

On 5 November 1885 Alfonso XII died. Six months afterward his second
wife, Maria Cristina, gave birth to his only son. The queen became the
regent for Alfonso XIII and fostered liberal reforms under the premiership
of Sagasta. Moves to implement the liberal *Constitución de 1869*, which had
largely been set aside by Cánovas, made Spain the ideal example of democ-
racy in Europe, if only on paper.

Besides the experience of literature and history garnered throughout his
boyhood, the young Valle received the formal education typical of a small
Spanish town. His first teacher was José Soto Campos, who had arrived in
Villanueva de Arosa in December 1873 to take charge of the school. The
parish priest of Villajuan, Reverend Rafael Torrón, first instructed him in
the classical tongue of Rome. He was also to study Latin with Cándido
Pérez Noal, the schoolmaster of Puebla del Caraminal, a town across the *ría*
of Arosa. Years later, Valle-Inclán recalled the torturous process in *La lámpara maravillosa*:

I still recall the anguish I would feel while studying Latin under the harsh tutelage
of a village cleric. All the events of that time hark back in the half-light of evening

and the mist of rain. We would gather in the kitchen; the housekeeper roasting chestnuts with the cat on her lap, the cleric reading his breviary, and I, languishing over Nebrija's grammar.[24] (A11)

At other times the recollection of his early studies of Latin is stated in a fictional context, as in the story "Nochebuena" (Christmas Eve) from *Jardín umbrío*:

It was in the Galician mountains. I was then studying Latin grammar with the Archpriest of Céltigos, experiencing my punishment in the rectory. I can still see myself in the window well, crying and sighing. My tears fell silently on Nebrija's grammar, open atop the ledge. It was Christmas Eve and the archpriest had condemned me to fasting until I learned that terrible conjugation: "Fero, fers, tuli, latum."[25] (A12)

In *Los cruzados de la causa*, Bradomín and an old sacristan recall their study of Latin in a convent under "aquel bendito Fray Ambrosio" (that saintly friar Ambrose).[26] There are countless other references in the works of Valle-Inclán to the hardship of studying the classical tongue; these are derived from the experience of the Man. Yet, despite the despondent tone of most of these references, Latin provided the Artist with one of the best tools in the formulation of his highly personal writing style.

Once his studies had progressed beyond the level obtainable in the immediate vicinity of his home, Ramón Valle y Peña was sent to the Instituto de Santiago, whose entrance examinations he had passed 27 July 1877. During the 1877–1878 academic year he was successful in Latin and Castilian, but he did not take the examination in geography; in the following year he failed both Latin and Castilian. In his third year at the Instituto, he passed world history, arithmetic, and algebra, but he no longer appears on the records as a student in the 1880–1881 academic year.

Later, in 1881, he attended the Instituto de Pontevedra. There he came under the guidance of his father's friend Jesús Muruáis,[27] whose residence (known as "Casa del Arco") was a center of activity for Pontevedra's intellectuals. This early contact with Muruáis led to the later participation of the young writer in his teacher's *tertulia*. Valle y Peña continued his studies at the Instituto until their completion on 29 April 1885, when he received the title "Bachiller." He graduated without distinction, having received notable grades only in "Historia de España" and "Retórica y Poética." He had failed "Aritmética y Algebra" and "Latín y Castellano," having to re-take them; the latter course, taught by Muruáis, reinforced the anti-Latin attitude of the young man.

Although Ramón Valle y Peña was not an outstanding student, he had a record that permitted his parents to aspire to his admission to the Universidad de Santiago de Compostela. In 1887, after two years in the Preparatorio de la Facultad de Derecho, he began to study law at the prestigious university, looking toward a career in politics, a field to which he was directed by his father. There is a letter to the "Exm. Sr. Rector de esta Universidad," dated "Santiago, 10 de Enero de 1888," and signed by Ramón del Valle y de la Peña, in which the student requests permission to be examined:

Excellent Sir: The student Ramón del Valle y de la Peña from Villanueva de Arosa, province of Pontevedra, begs of your excellency that, having studied privately the subjects of general and Spanish literature and statistical economics, he be granted permission to be examined in them through independent studies. It is a favor hopefully to be granted through your excellency's well-known fairness to Ramón del Valle y de la Peña.[28] (A13)

He passed these and other examinations during his stay at the university, but his caliber as a student was not distinguished. What is already evident, however, is his predilection for the archaic word (e.g., "alugno"), which characterizes his later writing.

While in Santiago, Ramón Valle y Peña lived at 45 Calle del Franco with the family of Joaquín Díaz de Rábago, another of his father's friends.[29] Although this permitted him to live without many cares, the student found that his personal means were limited. To supplement the small income his father sent him, Valle began to tutor the children of various noble families.[30] This activity not only brought him monetary rewards but also put him in contact with socially prominent and artistic individuals who were to become influential in his personal and creative lives.

Increasing his finances through employment made it possible for Valle to participate in the social and literary life of Santiago de Compostela. The city itself proved of enormous interest to him; the impression it made on the youth remained with him all his life and manifested itself in many of his works, as in *La lámpara maravillosa*:

Among vintage Spanish cities, Santiago de Compostela is the only one that seems to be immobilized in a dream of granite, immutable and eternal. . . . A mystical rose of stone, a rustic and romantic flower, it preserves the ingenuous grace of old rhymed Latin as in the bygone days of its great pilgrimages. . . . The concept of Time disappears in this petrified city. Santiago seems to be eternal rather than ancient. It has the solitude, sadness, and strength of a mountain. . . . Compostela, immobilized in the ecstasy of pilgrims, amasses all its stones in a single evocation, and the chain of centuries always had the same resonance in its echoes. All hours are one and the same hour there, eternally repeated beneath the rainy sky.[31] (A14)

The sensitivity expressed in these words of his maturity began in his days as a student and resident in the Holy City, which had been called the second Jerusalem because of its importance as a pilgrimage center in the Middle Ages.

It was during this extended stay in Santiago de Compostela that his artistic and social personalities began to evolve. Disdaining the lecture halls of the university, he preferred to participate in the activities at the Ateneo Compostelano, to frequent the gatherings at the Café del Siglo, to haunt the Librería Galí, and to tour the ancient streets of the city in the company of a select group of friends. In short, he led the type of hectic and disorganized life that inspired Alejandro Pérez Lugín to write *La casa de la Troya* (The House of Bedlam), the popular insider's novel on student life at the university. Although he is not discernible as a character in the novel, Valle-Inclán had among his intimates of this period two who figured in the book: Camilo Bargiela ("Casimiro") and Enrique Labarta Pose ("Barcala"). Other friends were Salvador Cabeza de León, Manuel Casas Fernández, Vázquez de Mella, Pedro Seoane,[32] and Augusto González Besada. The last two played roles in later attempts to resolve the economic distress that plagued Valle-Inclán during most of his mature life.

González Besada filled yet another role when he became Valle's competitor for the affections of a young woman from a prominent family of Santiago. Valle lost the cause,[33] but the two men remained friends. It is quite probable that "Mi hermana Antonia" was inspired by Valle's own experience. In the story, the student Máximo Bretal, who tutors in a noble house of the city, becomes enamoured of his pupil's sister, Antonia. Of course, the story has too many departures from the author's reality to be taken literally; nonetheless, it seems correct on the basis of the evidence to relate the real and the fictional events. Generally, the works of Valle-Inclán reflect some aspects of the life of the Man.

The political, sociological, and economic acuity that Valle-Inclán demonstrated during his career began to develop during this period through exposure to ideas and ideologies of regional, national, and international scope. Against the closed view of Galicia espoused by his teacher and friend Alfredo Brañas in his book *Regionalismo* (Regionalism), Valle promoted an enlightened monarchy that would unite Spain spiritually as well as physically in an attempt to regain its past greatness. He saw Carlism as the ideology that could effect this end and from this time espoused its cause with intellectual fervor. Clearly to him, provincial self-rule would only bring about deterioration of the national spirit and eventual collapse of the political entity that was Spain.

The portrait of the Artist during this period also includes the process toward self-discovery that Joyce portrays in Stephen Daedalus. The young Valle underwent the frustration of love, resented the unsatisfactory economic status of his family, awakened to political and social reality, resolved to free himself from his regional life, showed little interest or ability in formal studies, and sought out life through experience. The university atmosphere provided opportunities, if limited ones, to expand along new lines of interest. The impact of academic life was not restricted to the classroom (most of Valle-Inclán's university education was under independent study); it was felt also in activities of a less formal nature. Important among these were associations and friendships, conversations and arguments, intellectual and creative activities. However, Valle, who read voraciously during this period, despite infrequent attention to school texts, could not tolerate the naïveté of his fellow students toward the writing in the press:

In those days all the students read *Los Lunes de El Imparcial* with relish, and several of my companions were amazed by the merit of its writers. "Marvellous, aren't they?" While I, with the arrogant disdain of a young iconoclast, cast my vote against them: "Anyone can write that nonsense. My articles would be worth much more." And to prove my point, I wrote a short story—"A media noche" (At Midnight)—which was published recently in *Jardín sombrío[sic]*.[34] (A15)

The periodic exposure to important men of letters and to political figures was also a bonus to the impressionable student. José Zorrilla, the great lyric poet and playwright who had been elected to the Real Academia Española in 1885, was one of the visitors to the university during Valle's residency. Recalling his emotion at meeting Zorrilla, Valle-Inclán stated in a lecture entitled "Semblanza de literatos españoles" (Commentary on Spanish Writers):

The almost religious veneration that I felt toward Don José Zorrilla, poet of long hair and lordly beard . . . increased in my youthful perplexity before the presence of my idol when he arrived in Santiago like a pilgrim out of fantasy, prestigious in his white hair and melancholic air. I was one of a column of students who went to greet him. I was among the first, and when Zorrilla asked me, "You. Are you a poet?" I felt the phrase touch my spirit as if it were a veritable consecration. A Poet? Yes; I had already beheld in the depths of things the distinctiveness of sadness, had spoken with the moon, and was starting to discover that roses possess the charm of once having been women.[35] (A16)

In the same lecture he viewed the life of Zorrilla with sympathy and sadness:

Zorrilla spent his final days in the most tragic misery. Taking advantage of the poet's situation, a publisher with few scruples convinced him to write a geography in verse, and so he wrote some poems about Madrid, Barcelona, Cádiz, Alicante, etc. . . . Another publisher asked him for a poem to accompany Gustave Doré's illustrations for *The Divine Comedy*. That's how *Los ecos de la montaña* (Echoes of the Mountain) came to be. Zorrilla lived between despair and hunger. . . . In due time death came, as did his burial, replete with people and local color. . . . Yet, despite the greatness of the poet and his contributions to Spain, the government refused to render him honors "because there were no precedents," as the President of the Council stated in such a picturesque way.[36] (A17)

Valle-Inclán's own life was similar in many respects to Zorrilla's; it was undoubtedly because he felt such a rapport that from his very beginnings as a writer Valle-Inclán used the great poet as the subject of stories and lectures,[37] and made a pilgrimage to his Mexican home:

When I was in Mexico, I visited Zorrilla's hacienda on the plains of Apam and pored over many of the poet's manuscripts. In *La siesta*, for example, as well as in the piece dedicated to the Medinaceli woman, one could discern that talent which the poet possessed of uniting two words for the first time and thus converting them into a new aesthetic category. . . . And, above all, I dreamed about the birth of Don Juan Tenorio in that very same Mexican abode.[38] (A18)

Zorrilla became a literary and vital touchstone for Ramón del Valle y Peña. The student who was making discoveries found in the great romanticist the dignified bearing that appealed to him as Man, the sensibility that impressed him as Artist, and the unforgettable figure that attracted him as Mask.

Inspired by Zorrilla, Valle exercised his own creative talent. That he may have written before entering the Universidad de Santiago de Compostela is quite probable considering his family background, but it was during these university years that he published his first known works. The poem "En Molinares" and the short stories "Babel" and "A media noche," all signed by Ramón del Valle de la Peña, appeared within a short time of each other.[39] Also from this era is the holograph poem "Era el postrer momento" (It Was the Final Moment), which bears the date 6 December 1889 but was published only many years after he died.[40] The manuscript is signed "Ramón del Valle-Inclán y de la Peña," an important indication of its author's tentative first known usage of the name Valle-Inclán in a literary context. Little else is known of his writings during this time. The devotion to writing, however, was problematical; the demon of literature had not captured him completely:

How could it conquer me! I despised literature with my entire being! . . . And so, in order to meditate seriously and choose a path in life, I retired to a ruined mansion that, having been abandoned by my family, was crumbling serenely in the forest.[41] (A19)

But the dedication to his real calling—literature—was resolved through the process of elimination, as he stated in *La lámpara maravillosa*:

When I was a boy the glory of literature and the glory of adventure tempted me equally. It was a time full of dark voices, replete with a vast murmur, ardent and mystical, to which my being responded by becoming sonorous like a conch-shell. I felt the breath of that great atavistic and unknown voice like the blast from a furnace; its sound, like the murmur of the tide, filled me with restlessness and perplexity. But my dreams of adventure, lustrous with the colors of emblazoned shields, fled like birds from a nest.[42] (A20)

In another instance, he presented the dilemma in a less formidable context:

When the matter of having to choose a way of life arose, I thought immediately, "I have to seek a profession without a boss." And it was difficult. I considered becoming a soldier, and despotic generals appeared giving me stupid orders. I thought about becoming a priest, and the bishop and the pope came up instantly. If I ever entertained the idea of being a civil servant, the thought of the director began to preoccupy me. . . . The only one without a boss is the writer.[43] (A21)

Regardless of the methods he said he employed to reach the decision, the writer had been launched. Thereafter, his assurance of having made the right choice met with another obstacle: his law career. In this regard he stated,

I wasn't born to be an ambulance chaser, nor a court recorder, nor a judge, nor a notary. . . . Defending undistinguished bandits and troublesome workers, having to be a fox at the service of other foxes . . . no, no![44] (A22)

Having crossed the first barrier, he faced the greater dilemma of whether to continue his law studies and write occasionally or to forsake a career that held no attraction and give himself completely to a creative life as a writer. The choice would be clear in 1890.

2 Emergence

The death of his father on 14 January 1890 acted as a catalyst on the life of Ramón Valle y Peña. The influence that had strongly guided the young man to the pursuit of a career as a lawyer was removed and he saw himself freed of that obligation. Furthermore, a legal career seemed precarious in light of recent politics. With the automatic return to power (*Turno Pacífico*) of Cánovas in 1890, the true bankrupt nature of the Spanish government was disclosed. Economic disability and social discomfiture at home were complicated by external conflicts in Morocco and Cuba. Thus, the reluctant student deserted the university and began to dedicate himself to other interests.

However, the increased financial difficulties that his family experienced as a result of the death of its patriarch prevented the young man from total commitment to his artistic calling. In light of this reality, Ramón Valle y Peña chose to pursue his livelihood in journalism. Never a provincial in his views, he forsook the facile job offerings that Galician periodicals might have made to the son of a respected journalist. Instead, he moved to Madrid, the literary center of Spain, and took up residence in a boarding house of the old bohemian quarter. Like Don Quixote, he had set out alone.

The date of his arrival in the Spanish capital is not established. There is a possibility that on his departure from the university he made a trip to Italy, perhaps from a seaport in Galicia or on the Mediterranean, perhaps overland. This conjecture is founded on a statement in an article published by Valle in 1892. In it he writes,

In another article I'll discuss the phenomena produced by mediums, in particular by Eusepia Palladino, the "medium" used by Lombroso in his experiments, at which I had the honor to be present in Naples.[1] (A23)

If true, the last phrase indicates that Valle spent some time in Italy when he has been placed in Madrid by his biographers. But his visit has been neither corroborated nor refuted. Valle's name is not included in the list of those who witnessed two of Professor Lombroso's experiments in Naples with Eusapia Palladino as medium.[2] The two seances in question took place on 2 March and 21 March 1891. However, the exclusion of Valle's name is not conclusive; those mentioned were considered authorities on the subject of spiritualism or in some recognized science, while Valle, if he was present, was merely a curious twenty-five year-old observer without credentials or reputation and, therefore, not a creditable witness. It may also be that in citing names, Lombroso's daughter forgot an unimportant young man. Another possibility is that Valle could have attended a session or sessions other than those cited in the book.

Since Valle's whereabouts between the time he left Santiago de Compostela (sometime after his father's death in 1890) and the publication of his first item in Madrid (7 June 1891)[3] are not established, it is very possible that he was in Italy and, as he claimed, attended Lombroso's psychic demonstrations. Further, Valle hints that he studied in Italy when, in "Psiquismo," he states, "Dijo mi ilustre amigo y maestro Enrico dal Pozo de Mombello" ("As was said by my friend and mentor Enrico dal Pozo de Mombello"). In naming Pozzo di Mombello, Valle could be referring to having been tutored by him during his stay in Italy. Perhaps it was through Mombello that he gained entry into the select group that witnessed Lombroso's seances.

Even if Valle did not go to Italy in 1891, he could have done so in 1892 before setting out for America. Allowing the accepted theory that he went directly to Veracruz from Marín, a port near Pontevedra, there are several months between his last public appearance on 6 February in Pontevedra and his arrival in April. In that space of time he could have been in Italy and witnessed the further demonstrations of Eusapia Palladino that took place in 1892 and in which Lombroso was also involved.

Just as the trip to America influenced his work (*Sonata de estío* [Summer Sonata], *Tirano Banderas* [The Tyrant Banderas], for example) so it is reasonable to assert that the Italian current in stories (such as "Octavia Santino" and "X") and novels (*Sonata de primavera* [Spring Sonata]) is traceable to an Italian journey made at the start of his literary career, either in 1891 or 1892.

The beginning of Valle's public life, like its continuation, was fraught with uncertainties. The young author, searching for a particular form of expression, turned to writing stories and articles; but these found limited acceptance in sophisticated Madrid. Between July 1891 and February 1892, Valle published various pieces in *El Globo*, one of the capital's newspapers, whose editor, Alfredo Vicenti, was a friend from Santiago de Compostela. The first piece was signed Ramón del Valle de la Peña and subsequent ones were signed Ramón del Valle.[4] In Galicia the *Diario de Pontevedra*, headed by Andrés Landín, who would years later publish Valle's first book, printed selections from his unfinished novel, *El gran obstáculo* (The Great

Obstacle),[5] and issued "En tranvía" (By Trolley),[6] a piece dealing with an encounter between the author and Zorrilla. On the same day that "En tranvía" appeared, Valle gave a lecture, "El ocultismo" (Occultism), in an event at the Recreo de Artesanos de Pontevedra that also included presentations by Eleodoro F. Castañaduy, Torcuato Ulloa, and Gerardo Alvarez Limeses.[7] This modest success was an important factor in the formulation of the young writer's decision to continue in his chosen field; his self-assurance had begun to take root.

Thereafter, Valle made a decision concerning a matter he had considered since his student days. The sense of adventure that his readings had inculcated grew larger with his increasing independence. That his career had borne encouraging results from the start led Valle to think of satisfying his thirst for travel by plying his trade elsewhere. Since childhood's exposure to stories of foreign lands, Valle had felt a desire to visit America. The dream became reality in the spring of 1892 when he embarked for Mexico. The land of the *Conquistadores* was the only nation whose name contained the mystic letter "X"; the intermingling of the spirit of history and an aura of mystery proved irresistible to the fledgling itinerant:

And, while reflecting in my bed-hammock, I decided to abandon my studies and set out for America. There were many reasons, and one of them was of great romantic importance for a young man of twenty who wanted to get involved in a revolution and become a general. You'll see why. I had a tower in Santa María del Caramiñal from which had set out to conquer the Indies my ancestor Gonzalo Domínguez, Captain of Cavalry, who, during the battle of the Sorrowful Night died in sight of Cortés, whom he had defended. The Indians grabbed his lance, threw him off his horse, and, while he was still alive, ripped his heart out, later casting it down from the Teocalli as an offering. According to Bernal Díaz, Cortés "was horrified and disgusted by this" because Domínguez was as formidable a captain as Gonzalo de Sandoval and Pedro de Alvarado. So, reading about that barbarous and glorious death, and desiring to know the country that witnessed the most heroic enterprise ever undertaken by men, I planned the trip to Mexico. That's how it's written: Mexico. No need to substitute the harshness of the j for the sonority of the x.[8] (A24)

Of this decision to visit Mexico he said in another interview,

While I was in Spain my parents wanted me to join the bar, that is, to complete that dreadful preparation for which I had no inclination, despite the fact that only the last examination remained to be taken. So, to avoid finishing my studies, I moved to Mexico with the money my parents had given me to begin my career.[9] (A25)

A penchant for oversimplification characterized Valle's statements about his life, which he sought to keep mysterious by revealing very little; time, too, often distorted past reality and made his statements seem less real. At other times he spiced essential reality with touches of fantasy, as in "Rosa hiperbólica" (Hyperbolic Rose) from his book *El pasajero*:

I entered the world with a crazy leap;
I became a pilgrim upon the seas,
and in every port, sinning a bit,
I left my soul as if a chantey.

I wasn't afraid; I was a whirlwind;
I looked on heights as into light.
I cast word and soul to the wind.
I bear my cross just like a sword.[10] (A26)

   Valle's impressions on first sight of continental America—the view of
the Mexican landscape, with the interpolation of Veracruz—are recorded
in "Bajo los trópicos" (In the Tropics):

We have just anchored. The horizon smiles beneath the gorgeous sun. Voluptuous
vibrations can be felt in the air. Gusts from the virgin jungles . . . deeply moved, I
contemplate the scorching beach where the Spanish adventurers landed before any
other people of old Europe . . . I remember readings that even as a child have made
me dream of this land, daughter of the sun. . . . It was true that I was going to set
foot on that sacred beach! . . . Veracruz, seen from the sea . . . is a smiling city . . .
somewhat strange . . . [11] (A27)

Disembarking, Valle went in search of the history and romance that Mexico
represented.

I landed in Veracruz and, as if on a pilgrimage, went on horseback from Antigua,
where Cortés made his men burn their ships, to Mexico. . . . The tree of the
Sorrowful Night. Yes. And I have never felt a sharper, more ironic, fiercer, or more
tender emotion than the one that took hold of me in front of that colossus. It was in
the afternoon. . . . From its branches, which are of a melancholic dark green, like
those of cypresses, hang something like cobwebs that give the effect of thick and
silky dirty beards. The Indians call these webs "beards of Spaniards." Beards of
Spaniards! I experienced such a great emotion before that decrepit giant, wounded
by lightning and dressed in old Spanish beards, that I have never been able to
describe it.[12] (A28)

Valle also referred to another historical landmark he had visited, the
hacienda of Zorrilla.
   After a short stay in Veracruz, Valle proceeded to Mexico City where he
found employment as a journalist.[13] What had been started in Spain with
the publication of a few articles and stories gained momentum in the Mexican capital. Between April and August 1892, Valle published thirty-six,
including poems, in El Correo Español[14] and in El Universal,[15] the only two
newspapers known to have issued his work in Mexico during this time.
   Valle began to find his identity in Mexico. First, he discovered the name
that suited him both as man and as writer.[16] The past signatures were put
aside in April 1892 with the publication of "En el tranvía," signed Ramón
del Valle-Inclán, and "Los últimos versos del Duque de Rivas" (The Last

Verses of the Duke de Rivas), to which he appended the last name in the familiar hyphenated form. Thereafter, "Valle-Inclán" was the autonym affixed to all his work, either alone or with his first name.

The style of his stories and articles, too, began to evolve toward those characteristics that particularize the author's mature writing. The works published in Mexico can be noted for their fictionalization of personal reality, increasing use of double (a la Zorrilla) and triple adjectivism, less derivative content, marked preference for archaic and obscure terms, quaint or archaic spelling, economy achieved through precise phrasing, inventive relationship of words and ideas, and a tendency toward aesthetic statements.[17] Valle-Inclán later acknowledged this evolution and the role played in it by Mexico:

> . . . where I found my own freedom to choose a vocation. Therefore, I owe Mexico, indirectly, my literary career. . . . It was here that I began to find my own path, that is, the literary one.[18] (A29)

As he cultivated his art Valle-Inclán also concerned himself with his public image. Through deliberate accents he created the figure of the serious and mature man out of the youthful original. In caricatures and drawings[19] of this period, he appears older than his twenty-six years. He is depicted with a full mustache curled up at the ends and his hair neatly combed back. He is well-dressed and in style, and wearing pince-nez. The impeccable and correct figure denies the shabby and eccentric image that biographers have painted for this period.

While Valle's physical appearance was conservative, even distinguished, his personality began demonstrating an inclination toward the hyperbolic. A dreamer of adventures since his youth, Valle-Inclán found in Mexico the ideal setting for his imagination. To his later public he presented the fictional autobiography created therein:

> The early years of my life were full of risks and hazards. I was a lay brother in a Carthusian monastery and a soldier in the lands of New Spain. . . . I had hardly reached that age called youth when, as the result of a love gone awry, I embarked for Mexico on "The Dalila," a frigate that went down off the coast of Yucatan the next day. . . . It was on board "The Dalila"—I remember it with pride—that I assassinated Sir Robert Yones. It was an act of revenge worthy of Benvenuto Cellini. . . . It was on the very day that the frigate dropped anchor in the waters of Veracruz . . . One of my ancestors, Gonzalo de Sandoval, had established the reign of New Galicia in those lands. Following the impulse of a nomadic life, I sought to lose myself as he had in the vastness of the ancient Aztec empire, whose history is unknown, buried forever with the mummies of its kings . . . [20] (A30)

Throughout his life Valle-Inclán referred to this initial visit to the land of Montezuma and the usurper Cortés in terms of his personal fantasy. He even created the impression among his contemporaries that he had gone so far as to enlist in the Mexican army:

I was a soldier for five years in the 7th Cavalry. I could not help but be a soldier in Mexico. Everything there smells of war, of death, and of adventure, and that perfume enchanted me.[21] (A31)

Valle-Inclán cultivated the friendship of military men. Among these was Sóstenes Rocha, a general who had fought beside Benito Juárez and had published several books on military tactics. In spite of the relative calm during Valle-Inclán's stay in Mexico due to the strong government of Porfirio Díaz, the adventurer in him attached itself to Rocha:

He was a man with the face of a lion, who drank liquor with gunpowder, and who would go into the streets on horseback at the slightest hint of a commotion. . . . Those were the days in Mexico when a fair-haired man named Poucel bit off the finger of the giant Zetina; when we set off in pursuit of Catarino Garza, a member of Hipólito Cuellar's gang . . . [22](A32)

Such associations led to the fabrication of countless anecdotes about Valle-Inclán's heroic deeds in Mexico, some created by himself, adding to the mythos of the Mask. In time, Valle-Inclán enhanced his militaristic dreams by presenting himself to the gullible as "Coronel-general de los ejércitos de Tierra Caliente" (Colonel-General of the Armies of Tierra Caliente).[23] One anecdote describes how Porfirio Díaz invited him to a private audience on learning of his sympathetic views on dictatorships,[24] and he was introduced to the president as "El gachupín Valle-Inclán. Un león en dos pies" (The Spaniard Valle-Inclán. A Lion on Two Feet).[25] He admired Porfirio Díaz throughout his life, as evidenced in a later interview:

I believe that the two greatest diplomats of the 19th century have been Leo XIII and Don Porfirio. Porfirio Díaz put his conscience above the law, not like Julius Caesar, who affirmed the legality of violating the law, but in order to better it.[26] (A33)

It was also in Mexico that the first manifestations of Valle-Inclán's eccentric temper were recorded. One incident received much publicity at the time. Being an avid newspaper reader, Valle would obtain local periodicals on arriving in a city to acquaint himself with its tempo and life. Paging through a newspaper of the capital, Valle-Inclán came across a long and bitter anonymous letter (signed by "Oscar") in which the character of Spaniards in Mexico was attacked vehemently. The entire letter proved repulsive to Valle-Inclán, but he was particularly struck by a passage[27] directed at all Spaniards in Mexico. He took the accusations personally, the letter having named several individuals whose names were omitted by the newspaper. Suspecting that he was one of those mentioned, Valle-Inclán proceeded to the office of Victoriano Agüeros, the publisher, and demanded to be given both the identity of the writer and the deleted names. Even though a disclaimer had appeared with the letter, Valle-Inclán held the publisher responsible when this information was denied him. The only other means of satisfaction that he would consider was a duel. Agüeros was intimidated neither by the resolve of his adversary nor by the archaic challenge; attempts by the seconds to arrange a duel were fruitless.[28] Finally, however, Agüeros acceded to the advice of the seconds, Juan Miguel Sancho and Manuel Larrañaga Portugal, and sent an explanatory letter that sought to reassure Valle-Inclán, which was later published in part within a public communication.[29] Since the duel never took place, it is plausible that the explanation satisfied Valle-Inclán. Nothing further was ever said by either party, but Valle-Inclán had made his point. Undoubtedly, the incident was responsible for the hiatus in Valle-Inclán's literary activity; there was nothing published between 8 May ("Zan el de los osos" [Zan of the Bears]) and 20 May ("Ecos de la prensa española" [Echoes of the Spanish Press]).[30] The incident delineated Valle-Inclán's emerging temperament and indicated a haughty manner that attended him throughout his life.

Mexico's exotic ambience intrigued Valle-Inclán. His desire for knowledge led him even to the more obscure traditions of that nation.[31] Excursions to villages containing remnants of Indian civilizations made him aware of folkways traceable to antiquity. Impressed by the mystic quality of the life he observed, Valle-Inclán took up the search for the reasons behind it. In the pronounced use of marijuana he found what he had sought. Through it he interpreted the national character of Mexicans:

. . . marijuana, which makes it possible for them to live in an extraordinary religious exaltation. . . . That's how their indifference to death, which gives them a superhuman quality, can be explained.[32] (A34)

Such was the import of this discovery that Valle-Inclán became a convert to the use of marijuana. Whether he first employed the herb in Mexico or after his return to Spain is debatable; beyond the peripheral accounts of his contemporaries[33] stand the declarations he made in his writing and in his lectures. Convincing evidence is the panegyric "La tienda del herbolario" (The Shop of the Herbalist), from La pipa de kif (The Pipe of Kiff):

Poisons of green! Lethal grasses
Coming forth from False Paradises.

Everyone falls before marijuana,
Which gives the knowledge of the Ramayana.

Oh, marijuana, green pneumonic,
Cannabis Indic et Babylonic.

To sesame's joy you hold the key,
Green Indic hemp, the kiff of Turkey.

Grass of the Old Man of the Mountain,
The Inquisition found you in Spain.

Grass that initiates all the fakirs,
Full of great pleasures and Dies Iraes.

The emerald green of the Persian poet—
The green also donned by the Prophet!

(Kiff—the green grass of the Persian—is
The same achisino bhang of the Bengalese.

Charas are smoked upon the divan,
Among odalisques, by the Grand Sultan.)[34] (A35)

The poem by the mature artist reveals his familiarity with narcotics and related stimulants. Like Coleridge and De Quincey, Valle-Inclán sought these means as transportation into the realm of unhindered imagination and unfettered insight. But in "Breve noticia" (Brief Note), which prefaced *La media noche* (Midnight), he indicated the failure of his narcotic to provide the vision he desired:

Clumsy and vain as I was, I desired to become centered and possess an astral vision of the war, one beyond geometry and chronology, as if the soul, already diverted, looked at the Earth from its star. I have failed in my desire, my Indic drug having denied me its marvellous effluvium on this occasion. The pages that now come to light are nothing more than the stutter of that imagined ideal.[35] (A36)

But the most direct admission of the influence of hallucinogens in both his aesthetic and physical lives is found in his lecture "Los excitantes" (The Stimulants):

Let us now consider the influence of hashish, the Indic hemp, on literature and, particularly, on my work. I confess to having used it extensively without knowing its consequences and with a medical prescription. The physiological effects produce a long-lasting interior coldness, voracious hunger, and symptoms akin to poisoning; but let us now analyze the anemic effects of the hallucinogenic. . . . My individuality split into two distinct aspects. I began to see new qualities in things: disharmony was created in one instance, while a chimerical affinity was evident in another. It was somewhat akin to "the harmony of opposites." . . . Later, all things acquired the prestige of mystery, as do the sounds of the night; my thoughts returned to my youth and I arranged strange relationships such as that of a flower to a hill. The most terrifying thing in those hallucinations was the remembrance of all the dead, filing past my memory like a film. It was this phenomenon that made me decide to abandon hashish.[36] (A37)

Despite the final declaration, the abandonment was only periodic. Instances of marijuana usage between the time of this lecture-confession and his death are frequent, as his acquaintances have attested. In later life,

Valle-Inclán found in marijuana the tranquillity that his real life did not permit him.

It is difficult to trace Valle-Inclán's whereabouts and activities between August 1892, when his last-known article published in Mexico appeared in *El Universal*, and July 1893, when he returned to Spain.[37] It seems that the termination of his association with *El Universal* was due to his departure from Mexico City, though the reasons for this move are not known.

Between the publications of his last verifiable article in Mexico and the first after his return to Spain, there is a hiatus of nearly a year. What occurred from 7 August 1892 to 8 July 1893? Where was Valle-Inclán during this extended period? Did he write or publish anything? The obvious resource for answers to these questions has been skirted carefully by biographers; Valle-Inclán's own work suggests the possibilities about his life during this period.

Several months can be accounted for, if inadequately, by accepting the dating of "La Condesa de Cela" (The Countess of Cela) in Veracruz, January 1893. From this it appears that Valle-Inclán left Mexico City (in August?) and returned to Veracruz where he was in residence from January on, as attested by his letter to Murguía, dated 2 March 1893:

My ever dear friend and respected mentor:
 On writing to you it seems as if I'm addressing our entire Galicia—poor, pensive, alone, as the poet said—so totally do you incarnate the region's spirit in my eyes, along with the love of the land, which, though the deepest nostalgia, those of us in America feel like a sacred inheritance, preserving through the centuries a remnant Celticism that leads us to love the decaying oaks and venerable rocks of our wild land. Bewitching sensations, which are inhaled on reading your *Historia* (History), and which emit the soft clarity of a full moon on the ancient peoples who lit the first fire in the great Galician hearth.
 Yes, my dear friend, you are our great Bard, in the most archaic and pure sense of the term, and it is for this reason that I request of you a few lines to put at the front of my first book.
 The affection you have always shown me leads me to believe that, despite your numerous literary commitments, you might find a moment of leisure in which to present to the public the humblest of your admirers, but perhaps the most loyal and enthusiastic.
 My brother will give you the originals, along with further comments, if, as I trust, you will acquiesce to my request.
 Through these lines, dear friend and mentor, I forward the testimony of my respectful affection; you may order, when it pleases you, this errant disciple who, wheresoever the winds of fortune, inclement and adverse, may blow him, preserves ever glowing, among many ashes, the feelings of respect and affection toward you.
  Ramón del Valle-Inclán
  Villa Rica de la Veracruz, 2–3–93.[38] (A38)

As the use of the imprinted stationery implies, Valle-Inclán may have had a working relationship with *La Crónica Mercantil*, but it was probably not as a writer, since there are no known articles by him in that publication. The dating of "La Niña Chole"[39] in Paris, April 1893, conflicts with the probability that Valle-Inclán visited Cuba at that time, residing there for an unknown period in the company of Antonio González de Mendoza.[40] The last gap, between his supposed departure from Cuba and his arrival in Spain, can be explained in terms of the suggested visit to Paris.

Valle-Inclán returned to his native Galicia, choosing to live in Pontevedra from 1893 to 1896, although he spent frequent intervals in nearby Villanueva de Arosa and Puebla del Caramiñal. It was a period of adjustment, both for the author and for Spain. The Rif tribes bordering Spanish Morocco increased their subversive activities in 1893. The reaction in Spain was immediate to a swift attack against Melilla that defeated the Spanish forces in the autumn of that year. But by the time the expeditionary force of 25,000 men arrived in Melilla a treaty had been signed in Fez. The Sultan further sought to pacify Spain by agreeing to pay an indemnity of 20,000,000 pesetas. At home, the affair angered the citizenry and added to the general discontent.

The Cuban situation presented another point of contention. After repeated attempts in the Cortes to pass a strong reform law providing greater autonomy for the island met with no success, José Martí sparked the spirit of rebellion on the island with his words; his call for an uprising went out in February 1895. The subsequent revolt impeded the vote on a compromise proposal made by Maura's successor. The inability of Spain to concede greater autonomy at this stage led to the disillusionment of the Autonomists.

It may be that Valle-Inclán sought in Galicia a refuge from such turmoil. In the first months after his return from Mexico, he published four stories in Pontevedra's Extracto de Literatura,[41] but these were mainly re-elaborations of earlier works.[42] The heightened journalistic activity that typified his stay abroad was no longer in evidence; Valle-Inclán was in a moment of transition, as was the nation.

Encouraged by his friendships with Jesús Muruáis, his former Latin professor at the Instituto de Pontevedra, and Torcuato Ulloa,[43] a writer of some distinction in the province, Valle-Inclán began to delve into the rich libraries these men possessed. Ulloa, who was conversant with contemporary Parisian life that he depicted in his column in Galicia Moderna, possessed an interesting collection of newspapers and periodicals from France; Muruáis, an avid reader of French and Italian literature, had an important collection of classic and contemporary works in both languages.[44] The accessibility of these cultured men and their libraries was an important factor in the continuing evolution of Valle-Inclán,[45] as Man, Artist, and Mask.

It was during this relatively obscure period that Valle-Inclán's appearance began to change from the neat and orderly visage of his Mexican days to the bohemian and anarchistic look inspired in the French romantics and Parnassians he had begun to read. His supposed stay in Paris certainly could have inflamed the personal association he made with those traditions, rekindling the interest he had manifested earlier in José Zorrilla and the Duque de Rivas, two of the great figures in Spanish Romanticism. It was at this time and not before that Valle-Inclán adopted a physical framework for his emerging personality, a mask cast in the mold of romanticism.[46] From this period on Valle-Inclán was a composite: the blending of Man, Artist, and Mask never ceased thereafter.

The transition was also manifest in his writing. Already showing what was to be a characteristic of his technique, Valle-Inclán began to revise his stories with an eye toward their collection. To the product of his journalistic work was added the new sensibility gained abroad; the result was Valle-Inclán's first book. *Femeninas. Seis historias amorosas* (Of Women. Six Amorous Tales)[47] was published in Pontevedra by his friend Andrés Landín in 1895. The book, dedicated to his university friend Pedro Seoane, was prefaced by the laudatory words of Manuel Murguía. Originally requested by Valle-Inclán in March 1893, the preface was not completed until May 1894.

Femeninas, a first book by an obscure journalist, did not attract much attention. The only known critical reaction to it at the time of publication was an anonymous mention in a magazine issued by Navarro Ledesma,[48] even though Valle-Inclán had written to the renowned critic "Clarín" on 9 May 1895, sending a copy of *Femeninas* in the hope that he would review it:

Most Respected Sir and Maestro:
Our mutual friend Luis París told me yesterday that you must by now have heard of my *Femeninas*, the book of a disheartened beginner who, through the workings of fate, has always lived apart from men of letters. I am fully aware of the little that my book is worth, but to keep the matter in perspective one should consider my inexperience and youth. It is with great pleasure that I forward a copy to you today, one whose pages I have cut; not that it may be easier for you to read it—I don't impute that you have either time or patience—but that you may leaf through it.
I am aware that *first* books rarely have intrinsic worth. The critic who mentions them does so as something of a prophet. My book could be seen as a *hope*, which is yet to be *realized*, as I know better than anyone. How could I not know it when I possess—and keep to show my friends—a copy of *Femeninas* where there isn't a single page without a deletion. It's a book that troubled me even before its publication.
If only I had the time and some stimulus, I believe I could do something somewhat better. . . . But for God's sake don't judge definitively by those *six amorous tales*.
My aspiration is solely that my name may have some meaning for you when I send you another book—provided I don't put aside my pen, convinced at last that God hasn't called me to follow the path of writing.
I take pleasure in using this occasion to offer, most respected maestro, the most enthusiastic testimonial of my admiration and friendship.
    Yours affectionately,
    Ramón del Valle-Inclán.[49] (A39)

Although the artistry of Valle-Inclán's later work would be traced to *Femeninas* by Juan Ramón Jiménez,[50] the collection passed unnoticed by "Clarín" as well as others, and sales were extremely poor.

I could sell only five copies of my first book . . . five readers. My entire public. Well then, I continued to write for those five readers. I didn't seek out those who joined their number later. I was not about to write like this or that one simply because my writing style did not suit some people. . . . That would be tantamount to robbing the readers of your colleagues and I am not a thief. One must establish oneself with what one has to give. If one fails, it's a sign of lack of personality.[51] (A40)

This integrity had already been noted by Manuel Murguía in his incisive preface.[52]

Excessive attention to so-called influences has plagued the study of many authors. The case of Valle-Inclán is no exception. Critics are willing to concede that the education of the writer in his craft usually has a point of departure in some movement or author that appeals to him; what they will not accept as readily is that soon after his initiation the artist strikes out on his own in the search for personal fulfillment. In the case of a controversial figure like Valle-Inclán, criticism never retires from such an enticing battleground. Consequently, there has been a proliferation of comments in this equivocal area. Critics have "discovered" in his work the "clear" influence of such disparate writers as Casanova, Prosper Mérimée, Edgar Allan Poe, Eça de Queiroz, Guy de Maupassant, Gabrielle d'Annunzio, Charles Baudelaire, José Maria de Hérédia, Paul de Kock, René Ghil, Arthur Rimbaud, Théodore de Banville, and Paul Bourget.

Like any author exposed to the historic and contemporary currents of world literature, Valle-Inclán could not help but assimilate what was compatible with his own artistic nature, often manipulating elements to give texture to a period he was recreating. But for him integrity is paramount. While Currita, the protagonist of "La Generala" (The General's Woman), may prefer the novels of Daudet over those of López Bago, and her admirer Sandoval may introduce her to the work of Barbey d'Aurevilly, that is hardly enough evidence to claim that *Femeninas* is modeled on French novels or, more particularly, that its six stories with female protagonists are derived from the six tales in *Les Diaboliques*.

Valle-Inclán found in Jules Barbey d'Aurevilly the admirable quality of detachment from the social vulgarity of his time, together with a royalist attitude and an aesthetic stance apart from the naturalistic excesses of Zola. Valle-Inclán indicated his preference, in "La Generala," for the sense of values espoused by "le Connétable des Lettres," as Rubén Darío noted.[53] But preference does not imply imitation or plagiarism. *Femeninas* is a book of beginnings, and if it uses *Les Diaboliques* as the inspiration for its own format it is to the author's credit that he rises to his own individuality, establishing themes and characters embryonic to his later work.

By late 1895 three of Valle-Inclán's stories—"Un cabecilla" (A Ring-leader), "X," and "Ivan el de los osos" (Ivan of the Bears)—had been published in Madrid.[54] The following winter its author returned to the capital with *Femeninas* as his principal literary credential. The trip was encouraged by Torcuato Ulloa, who arranged a political appointment for Valle-Inclán in the Ministerio de Fomento.[55] This was done through the influence of Augusto González Besada, the same fellow law student who had successfully competed against Valle-Inclán for the affection of a young lady; at this time, he was a rising young lawyer and a member of the Partido Conservador (Conservative Party).[56] The circumstances that pre-vented the fruition of this appointment are not clear. It is generally con-ceded that Valle-Inclán refused the post on his own account, perhaps disappointed by the necessity of transferring himself to León when Madrid was the center of intellectual and cultural activity. But it is also likely that the sinecure was denied him because of his radical appearance and man-ner.[57] The fact is that he never undertook the duties.

The possibility of economic stability disappeared as swiftly as it had come, and Valle-Inclán was channeled into the uncertain life of the strug-gling artist, although he never succumbed to the dark aspects of bohemian life.[58] Faced with harsh reality, the author of *Femeninas* denounced the mediocrity of the social order and devoted himself exclusively to the search for creative fulfillment. Fired with the zeal of the artist, Valle-Inclán fumed against suggestions made by friends that he continue as a journalist—the employment held by many of his literary compatriots. Having run the gamut of that professional life, Valle-Inclán retorted with authority,

Journalism debases style and shrivels the aesthetic ideal. Reputations created by the press are abhorrent. One must work in isolation, without alienating any part of spiritual independence.[59] (A41)

While this outlook fed his spirit with great aesthetic rewards, his body endured many hardships, not least of which was living in a small room with the barest essentials at 3 Calvo Asensio, near the Cárcel Modelo (Model Jail).[60] But more responsible for the commencement of his physical deterioration was the interminable fast that his penury forced on him.[61] In spite of his privation or, perhaps, because of it, Valle-Inclán adapted him-self admirably. Superseding its negativity, he created an advantageous situation out of adversity; fasting became the means toward aesthetic com-pleteness:

There are stimulants that have a moral prestige, such as fasting. . . . Among the ancients, fasting was considered to be the path toward exaltation, as well as mental and moral perfection. The individual who understands the most is the one who loves the most, and love is the flower of morality. To that end Jesus fasted in the desert, while fakirs fast to develop their almost miraculous powers.

The fasting of the writer consists in abstaining from all worldly passions and ambitions, contrasted with days of searing sun and nights of humid dew always apart from living beings. Fasting in the desert, on the shore of a lake, or at the edge of the sea. In those places where the eye can sink into the curve of the horizon and sense the suggestion of the infinite. It is a divining of the pleasure inherent in great monotony, taking this word in its highest meaning, which is equivalent to eternity.

Second sons, condemned to perpetual fasting, conquered America; if not, they would not have become heroes.

Today, fasting is a way of life only for bohemian artists whose pockets are empty.

I see the regeneration of Spain through fasting, but of a voluntary nature, given that without such conviction there would be no virtue. Rather, it would be the seed of rebellion and anarchy everywhere.

Fasting in the solitude of the cell is the source of that supreme excitation that has eight prior states, namely: prayer, meditation, edification, contemplation, aridity, transition, trance, ecstasy.[62] (Á42)

Such opinions were formulated during Valle-Inclán's bohemian years. But his later attitude can be noted even in such early writings as his review of *Angel Guerra* by Galdós:

There exists a *higher realism* that the Spanish public, eating well and enjoying excellent health, cannot comprehend. It would be necessary to subject these happy readers to fasts such as those experienced by Angel Guerra . . .[63] (Á43)

Because of such foundations the stoic attitude toward privation developed into the positive outlook declared by his lecture. The aesthetic rewards, therefore, permitted Valle-Inclán to confront the daily onslaughts of misery and pain. He bore his poverty with an admirable dignity. While to the world he presented a frail figure ornamented with the trappings of bohemia, the "son of Jules Verne," as he came to be known on the streets of Madrid, pushed aside the drab reality of his life and replaced it with the mysterious and the fantastic; he escaped through his imagination into a world of supernal beauty.

During the lengthy daily periods Valle-Inclán spent in bed to preserve his strength, his bony hand held the quill that plodded over the paper, devising the difficult script that expressed his thoughts. At night there were other directions for the creative intuition. Salon and café served as arenas for the intellectual ferment that typified fin-de-siècle Madrid. The café was a public place where anyone might enter and be drawn to the conversations at hand; the salon was private, and elegant or comfortable according to the means of the proprietor. Luis Ruiz Contreras, an important patron-publisher to young writers of that era, provided his ample study and library as the setting for the Wednesday *tertulias* that originated in 1896 and continued over a period of years. Valle-Inclán was introduced into his *tertulia* by Antonio Palomero, as Ruiz Contreras reports,[64] becoming a regular participant, along with Joaquín Dicenta (who had written the naturalistic play *Juan José* in 1895), Jacinto Benavente (whose *El nido ajeno*

[Another's Nest] in 1894 marked his first important statement in drama), José Martínez Ruiz (the future "Azorín," who had arrived in Madrid on 25 November 1896), the journalists Ricardo Fuente and Antonio Palomero (both with *El País*), Ramiro de Maeztu (the essayist who would produce *La crisis del humanismo* [The Crisis of Humanism]) and Manuel Bueno (with *El Globo*), Rubén Darío (who had published *Azul* [Blue] in 1888 and *Prosas profanas* [Profane Prose] in 1896, the principal Modernist books and was on his first visit to Spain), and Pío Baroja (whose first writings included *Estudio sobre el dolor* [Treatment on Pain]); Miguel de Unamuno (who would publish *Paz en la guerra* [Peace in War] in 1897) attended whenever he was in Madrid. Other emerging literary figures frequented the study-library of Ruiz Contreras as well, among them Adolfo Luna, Emilio Fernández Vaamonde, Rafael Delorme, and Luis Gabaldón.

Other salon gatherings were held periodically at the home of the Barojas.[65] Valle-Inclán, Maeztu, and Pío Baroja formed the nucleus of this group, joined later by Martínez Ruiz. It was through this affiliation that an unusual project came into being: the proposed joint authorship of *Los misterios del Transvaal* (The Mysteries of the Transvaal). The work was to be divided into parts, one each assigned to Valle-Inclán, Maeztu, Baroja, and Camilo Bargiela.[66] But the group could not interest the publisher they approached, a man who was normally attentive to the projects of young writers. The failure of the joint venture caused its abandonment by all but Maeztu, whose work entitled "La guerra del Transvaal y los misterios de la banca de Londres" (The War in the Transvaal and the Mysteries of London Banking), was published in installments in *El País*, under the pen name Van Poel Krupp.[67]

By 1897, Valle-Inclán had become established as an imposing mask in Madrid, vying with La Dama de Elche, the enigmatic pre-Roman bust that had been discovered that year, and with the Cuban situation as the subject of controversy and conjecture. The outlandish character he fostered went before him everywhere and anecdotes about him circulated throughout the city with pronounced frequency. Yet, the notoriety of the Man did not help the Artist. Only a curious few purchased his book and eventually the edition of *Femeninas* had to be consigned to the bookdealer-publisher Fernando Fe for the price of the paper.[68] However, Valle-Inclán's real fame did not rest upon his physical appearance or his scant writings, but rather, like that of the ancient *juglares*, on his vocality.[69] His vital personality and intellectual prowess evoked awe and respect in those who listened to him make aesthetic pronouncements or relate fantastic stories at the stimulating reunions in the cafés[70] he frequented some afternoons and most evenings. Like the salon, but on a larger scale, the café provided the framework within which Valle-Inclán acted out his self-imposed role of aesthetician and fantast.

The Café de Madrid was a principal rendezvous of novelists, poets, painters, playwrights, journalists, publishers, and assorted bohemians, all of whom joined the vociferous expression of personal views to the din of coffee-cups and brandy glasses. Valle-Inclán, the Barojas, Benavente, and Martínez Ruiz attended with frequency; others who did likewise were the painters Francisco Sancha Lengo, Ricardo Marín, Leal da Camara, and the Solana brothers; the young playwright-to-be Gregorio Martínez Sierra; aspiring politicians Portela Valladares and Bargiela; the journalists Luis Bello, Bernardo Gómez de Candamo, and Palomero; the poets Darío, Lozano y Angulo, and Ramón de Godoy; as well as Pedro González Blanco, Aldolfo Luna, Tomás Ors y Ramos, José de Campos, Enrique (Henri) Cornuty, Rafael Urbano, Manuel and Alejandro Sawa, Delorme del Salto, and Enrique Gómez Carrillo, among others.[71]

The gatherings at the Café de Madrid were centered on Valle-Inclán and Jacinto Benavente. But the great mass was not homogeneous; there were too many individualists for any one faction to be supreme.[72] The conflict of ideas and personalities eventually brought about a separation.[73] Benavente led his group to the Cervecería Inglesa on the adjoining Carrera de San Jerónimo; Valle-Inclán took his followers to the Horchatería de Candelas to meet at ten every night; another sector, led by Pío Baroja, Ramiro de Maeztu and Martínez Ruiz (known as "Los Tres"), remained at the Café de Madrid. Benavente attracted the theatrically inclined, Valle-Inclán drew the aesthetically oriented, and the third group kept those whose interests were in social, economic, and political discussions. However, the three factions were not mutually exclusive or hostile; rather, they were complementary. There was a free flow between the congregations and an exchange of impressions through "messengers."

Valle-Inclán thrived in his role. He moderated, listened, concurred, attacked, questioned, proposed. . . . In effect, his was the voice that guided his listeners but, unlike Dr. Samuel Johnson, Valle-Inclán had no James Boswell to systematically preserve his vocal genius. As a consequence, most of his profound utterances have been lost; only in sparse instances have his contemporaries preserved an unusual quip or pronouncement in their memoirs and biographies. Other than these verifiable statements there are countless anecdotes,[74] many of which are spurious.

But Valle-Inclán did not permit the prestigious stature he had achieved among his contemporaries in the artistic world to rest solely on the spoken word. In spite of public indifference to *Femeninas*, he decided to cultivate the small readership which had purchased his first book. The incentive of the immediate publication of a second book by Antonio Marzo, to whom he had been introduced by Ruiz Contreras, fanned his hopes.[75] But the process of writing was drawn out in an attempt by the author to polish his style and make precise his creation in the spirit of his increasingly demanding aesthetics.[76] *Epitalamio* (Wedding Song),[77] finally appeared on 7 March 1897. The small volume represented the concentrated labor and care that were to characterize all of Valle-Inclán's works thereafter; design and content were fully integrated, thus demonstrating a new awareness of the writer as artist, and of his work as the totality of thought, expression, and design:

In the future, writers will live in anthologies because of a well-written page. Beauty exists only in form. Whoever fails to hone and polish his style will be nothing more than a hack.[78] (A44)

However, despite its intrinsic value, the book was not well received; booksellers whom Valle-Inclán and his friends approached showed little interest in *Epitalamio*,[79] while critical reaction was scant and scathing, as in the unequivocal rejection of the book by Leopoldo Alas[80] and the earlier disapproval by Navarro Ledesma.[81] The only extant notice of Valle-Inclán's reaction to the crushing critical reception occurs in a letter to "Clarín" dated four days after the critic's review:

Señor Don Leopoldo Alas.
Sir, who merits my greatest and most distinctive admiration and respect:
    I offer my sincere thanks for the "Palique" that you dedicated to my book *Epitalamio* in *Madrid Cómico*. I accept and thank you for noting the faults you found in the book and the suggestions made to its author. Even more, I appreciate the generous frugality with which you point to defects in style and language. I'm not unaware that you could have taken me to task much more, much more indeed. . ..
If you could only see how I have marked corrections and changes on a copy of *Epitalamio* . . .
    You state that I could still repent and work in the real vineyard—I was grateful to you with my entire being for that final encouragement. Insofar as "repenting," I have already done so; as to the other . . . it is extremely difficult! . . .
    Through these lines I send you the sincerest expression of my acknowledgment, my admiration, and my friendship. The honor of placing himself at your disposal at Madrid, s/c Calvo Asensio, 4 is that of
        Ramón del Valle-Inclán.[82] (A45)

Valle-Inclán's humble acceptance of the master's chastisement in the "Palique" led to a second published comment by "Clarín," this time as an open letter to Valle-Inclán on 9 October 1899.[83] Closing out the "Clarín" affair, Valle-Inclán wrote yet another letter on the stationery of the Ateneo de Madrid, dated 18 October 1897:

Sr. Don Leopoldo Alas.
My Distinguished Friend and Maestro:
    Thank you for your kind letter. I couldn't respond earlier because *influenza* had me in bed for fifteen days. Even today it is difficult to handle the pen.
    The publication of your letter in *El Heraldo* has stuck in the throats of certain gentlemen who took great delight in affirming that your "Palique" in *Madrid Cómico* left me without a sound bone. Those poor people fail to realize that a bit of justice

administered by you can be more pleasant than the anonymous write-up of the press or the praises of Burell.

You advise me to flee from a certain type of socialist literature now in style. I've already fled from it. Better stated, I never desired to belong to that *school*. The rationale that has so advised me is almost the same that you detail in your letter.

Believe in my friendship and call on the services of your affectionate friend,

Madrid-18-X-97.

Ramón del Valle-Inclán.[84] (A46)

It may be that the negative commentary by Navarro Ledesma and "Clarín" led Valle-Inclán to claim in later years, as a belated *apologia*, that:

. . . on arriving in Madrid, I saw that everything being written was very bad. I said as much to my friends. And since they, incredulous, attributed my attitude to an immoderate desire to criticize, I replied by making it quite clear that anyone could write those detestable books. And so I wrote one: *Epitalamio*, which I published at my own expense.[85] (A47)

Such statements were typical of the mature author viewing his youthful work. But his apparent disdain for his second book must be considered feigned since it was later refurbished and reissued as "Augusta" in various collections of his stories.[86] Another example of the continuity of his interest in past stories is manifest in the re-issuance of "El rey de la máscara" (The King of the Mask) in *Germinal*,[87] which listed Valle-Inclán on the editorial staff of the magazine founded by his friend and Zolaphile Joaquín Dicenta.[88] He was also publishing prose vignettes in a small periodical with the curious title *Almanaque de Don Quijote*.[89] All in all, he was beginning to amass a respectable number of publications in newspapers, magazines and avant-garde periodicals.

But 1897 was not just a pivotal year in Valle-Inclán's literary career. The nation, too, was undergoing a critical evaluation which kept it under the international limelight. Led by Gómez and Maceo, the Cuban rebels gathered momentum as well as the open sympathy and arms support of the United States of America. Cánovas, faced with the inability of General Martínez Campos to adopt drastic measures against the insurgents, placed General Weyler in charge of the Cuban campaign. Almost immediately Weyler became the target of the U.S. press, which accused him without foundation (as shown upon unbiased investigation) of employing "concentration camps" as a war policy. Reports of "excesses" in the treatment of prisoners colored American opinion and the public began to think of Weyler and Spain as conspirators against humanity in the tradition of the infamous Inquisition. It was a revival of the "Black Legend." The threat of American intervention on behalf of the rebels loomed ever larger.

Cánovas made only token gestures in an attempt to placate the powerful United States. Whether or not he would have succeeded is a moot question because he was assassinated on 8 August 1897. The months that followed saw a series of ministries which proved ineffective. Finally, in October, Sagasta returned to power and began a rapid movement toward rectification. After dismissing Weyler, and without waiting for the consent of the Cortes, he declared Cuban autonomy. But even his decisiveness was to no avail. Factional riots in Cuba greeted the declaration of autonomy; Unionists saw the action by Sagasta as a betrayal and set out to express their discontent with acts of terrorism which, in turn, brought about equal retaliation. Seeing this state of affairs, the United States dispatched its cruiser *Maine* to protect American citizens on the island. The matter was brought to a head on 15 February 1898 with the mysterious destruction of the ship in Havana's harbor. Valle-Inclán, like all Spaniards, awaited the consequences that the tragic act was certain to bring.

II THE MIDDLE YEARS

1898–1929

3 Absorption

The American public clamored for war on the basis that the *Maine* was lost due to overt Spanish action. President McKinley did not favor a war with Spain, but the pressure of the press, along with lobbyists and public opinion, left him no alternative. His ultimatum resulted in the ouster of the American legation from Madrid; the intervention of the United States was a fact in April 1898. Events moved quickly thereafter. Having traveled under secret orders before the declaration of war, Admiral Dewey reached the Philippines and forced the surrender of the Spanish Pacific Fleet in the so-called battle of Manila Bay, which technically lasted one hour. Elsewhere, Admiral Cervera, ordered against his judgment to proceed to Cuba, saw his fleet outclassed and destroyed in the bay of Santiago de Cuba on 3 July. American and Cuban troops joined in assaults on Spanish garrisons and won successive victories. By the end of July the war was officially ended.

This was the most disastrous year in Spanish history since the destruction of the Armada. Forces beyond the military had a powerful effect on the belligerence of that year, on its outcome, and on the subsequent reaction within the defeated nation. While Spain had remained an international power after the 1588 Armada fiasco, the later defeat brought an end to Spanish colonial power in America and in the Orient.

As a consequence of having lost the Spanish-American War, Spain forfeited Cuba, Puerto Rico, the Philippine Islands, and other Pacific possessions to the United States. The treaty marking the end of Spain's vestigial colonialism in the Americas and the Pacific was signed in Paris on 12 December 1898.

The cataclysm of 1898 forced Spain's confrontation with modernity. The destiny of empire having come full circle, the nation had to redefine its purpose. Traditionalists felt indignation and resentment at the abandonment of previous commitments, but others saw an opportunity for national renewal.

Among no group was the reaction to events leading to the debacle of 1898 more heated than within the current generation of young Spanish intellectuals, many of whom made forceful public statements in newspapers and magazines on the condition of Spain. Miguel de Unamuno noted gravely and with shame the crisis of Spanish life in "Sobre el marasmo actual de España" (On the Current Atrophy in Spain),[1] and José Martínez Ruiz contrasted Spanish laggardness and European progressiveness in "El tema de España" (The Theme of Spain).[2] While the future Azorín made a bitter denunciation of social, political, moral, and economic conditions, Ramiro de Maeztu qualified the theme with the phrase "Parálisis progresiva" (Progressive Paralysis), the title of one of his articles.[3] Pío Baroja in "Vieja España, Patria Nueva" (Old Spain, New Nation)[4] claimed that current problems growing directly out of Spain's history as a colonial power were well deserved.

Valle-Inclán did not publicize his views on "the problem of Spain" in the obvious ways of his co-generationists.[5] While his contemporaries expressed themselves in articles and pamphlets, he chose to maintain his writing on the level of art—his principal concern always. To have subjected his prose to the dissection of the national chaos would have meant deserting his aesthetic commitment and returning to the journalistic expression he had abandoned earlier as demeaning. But because he elected not to expound his reaction in writing at that time does not mean that he lacked opinions on the subject. Vocal exclamations in cafés, interviews, and lectures, as recorded in his biographies, indicate his great concern with Spain's political development. In the matter of the Cuban insurrection, there is even the frail evidence of his anecdotal statement:

The Cuban War was won by the Cubans on their soil and by me on the streets of Madrid.[6] (A48)

The anecdote giving rise to this declaration may or may not be true, but it is characteristic of Valle-Inclán. It is said that Valle-Inclán encountered a group of students shouting anti-American slogans on the streets of Madrid during the Spanish-American War. Enraged, he approached them, saying,

Cowards! Those things should be said from Cuban soil . . . To battle, to battle . . . Why don't you go there? (A49)

The demonstrators turned on Valle-Inclán, but with typical bravado he stood his ground and faced them with a stick. No one came to his assistance and, nonetheless, he was able to defy their threats. He emerged triumphant in his account of the incident, as much a hero of the war for Cuban independence as if he had fought valiantly on the island.

Valle-Inclán's view was largely historical. Throughout his work there is a subtle but constant insight into past events and their effect on contemporary life. This is evident in his knowledge of Spanish character (*Comedias bárbaras, Voces de gesta* [Epic Voices], *Sonatas*), social problems (*Esperpentos*), religiosity (*Flor de santidad* [Flower of Sanctity], *Divinas palabras* [Divine Words]), and socio-political history (*La guerra carlista, El ruedo ibérico*). In *La lámpara maravillosa* he even made reference to the decadence of Spain in a tone worthy of his contemporaries:

We are no longer a race of conquerors and theologians, yet our romance tongue always fosters that illusion. We no longer master the routes to the Indies nor are the Popes Spaniards, yet our tongue retains Baroque hyperboles in imitation of ancient Latin when it was sovereign of the world. Gone is that Hispanic vigor in which fortune in war, the Catholic faith, and the call to adventure throbbed like three hearts; but the deceit of the throbbing continues in bland echoes . . . No longer is our posture for the world. We must once again live in ourselves . . . We must exile that high-flown mode, which is but a commentary on a posture which disappeared along with our conquests and our wars. We must love tradition, but only in its essence, attempting to decipher it as an enigma which stores the secret of the Future.[7] (A50)

Trenchant analyses by the young intellectuals of the "problem of Spain" was devoid of any proposals that might solve the dilemma. Their awareness of the need to renovate was dressed only in hope. It was typical of the anarchistic fervor of these individuals to clamor for change, even upheaval, but not to suggest what might replace the decadent society they wished to exterminate. Rightly or wrongly, this vocal group came to be known as the "Generación del '98."

The concept of generation is difficult to establish under most circumstances. Only through redefining the term is it possible to place this group of highly individualistic creative men in such a category. In the case of Valle-Inclán and his colleagues, the process requires establishing common ground in spite of vast character, stylistic, and artistic differences among them.

It was Azorín who baptized the group of writers and continued to refer to Valle-Inclán, Benavente, Antonio Machado, Unamuno, Maeztu, Pío Baroja, and himself as the "Generación del '98,"[8] acknowledging at the same time that lesser figures among their contemporaries also belonged in that generation. This concern with classification is reflected in many of the essays that Azorín wrote throughout his career. He pointed to the factors and situations that joined these individuals in an intellectual bond despite their differences.[9] Similarly, he stated the physical ties that united the group in his article "Dos generaciones,"[10] written in 1910. In "La generación de 1898,"[11] a collection of essays, he provides further support for this classification.

Maeztu and Unamuno also contributed to the concept of generation, the first by clarifying the points made by Azorín[12] and the second by his incisive defense of the *egolatría* of his contemporaries.[13] But a great dissident voice emanated from the very core of the group when Pío Baroja rejected the banding together of such diverse writers under one rubric. In his lecture "La supuesta generación de 1898" (The Supposed Generation of 1898),[14] read at the Sorbonne, he chided Azorín for having fomented what he considered an untruth. He denied his own place in the scheme of things and proceeded toward a strict interpretation of the term *generation*.

Valle-Inclán's position within the Generation proposed by Azorín seems ambiguous because he did not voice frequent or strong sentiments in regard to the affiliation. But Valle-Inclán did recognize the Generation as valid and his place in it as a fact:

My generation has made History through culture. Literature is much more operative than people suppose. And Azorín, the Baptist of the group—was very insightful in naming us "The Generation of '98."[15] (A51)

At a banquet in his honor on 7 June 1932, Valle-Inclán responded to Unamuno's address with words clarifying even further his own acceptance of membership in the Generation:

I have been placed in the Generation of '98. What does the Generation of '98 represent and what is its value? Don Manuel Azaña has spoken of a monstrous digression in the history of Spain. Well then, the Generation of '98 came on the scene to fight against it and all that it stood for in terms of the language. Up to the XV century, written and spoken Castilian had the same rhythms and the same pattern of breathing. Came the Renaissance and, through the fashion of the time, written Castilian began to deviate from the spoken language. The Generation of '98 desired to reunite them, fleeing from the long paragraph that came down from Cervantes to Ricardo León. We of '98 were called Modernists because we didn't follow the Castilian of the XV century. Rubén Darío and I wanted to return to the Castilian language the traditional norms that lay behind that fortunate couple known as the Catholic Kings.[16] (A52)

Moreover, he saw clearly the role played by the Generation in the interpretation of Spanish reality:

In literature, Unamuno, Benavente, Azorín, Ciges Aparicio, Baroja, the Machados, Marquina and Ortega y Gasset possess a new sense of patriotism. They love the regional novel for its tradition, eschewing those authors who are of little worth and represent nothing. Patriotism consists in imposing that which is great and not in permitting a vain audacity to take hold. Such is the force that motivates and animates the works of the new writers. They emerge at an agitated moment in Spain and bear a sense of patriotism, not that boastful, quarrelsome patriotism which hides defects and covers itself with a shawl, but rather the attitude of those who set about attaining greatness through their self-imposed criterion. Their patriotism is not one of exaltation. . . . Peoples are great because they share a mutual sentiment in History.[17] (A53)

These observations apply as well to their author. Valle-Inclán matured and began to publish during a critical period in Spanish history. He saw his art through the emerging concepts of his age, as Azorín has pointed out in the prologue to Valle-Inclán's complete works.[18] In that sense, he was very much a part of the "Generación del '98."

Whether or not such a phrase as "Generación del '98" is admissible is academic. The fact remains that the creative writers, painters, musicians, journalists, critics, and politicians, among others, joined under such a heading were indeed acting out their roles on the same stage in the same epoch, and expressing similar opinions. Although they embraced the idea of intellectual individuality, this neither excluded similar influences nor deterred sociability; rather, it enhanced them with the shadows and lights cast by the diverse personalities. The friendships and antagonisms that resulted through interaction in café and salon, recorded so fully in the voluminous literature on the Generation, are the best indication that there was a continuous and mutually influential contact.

The group was also brought together through periodicals, many of which were founded during this era of unrest. *Germinal*, whose first issue is dated 30 April 1897, was one of the first periodicals to encompass the young writers' works,[19] but other journals of greater significance in the unification of individuals who made up the "Generación del '98" followed. Valle-Inclán and his colleagues observed rapid changes heralded by the approaching century. The mutuality of their lives in such an era shaped the intellectual force of the new century.

When the weekly *Vida Nueva* was initiated in Madrid on 12 June 1898, its front page espoused newness and modernity.[20] The rallying cry of its editors—Vicente Blasco Ibáñez, Benito Pérez Galdós, and Eugenio Sellés, luminaries of an older generation—attracted not only "Clarín," Echegaray, and Valera, but also writers of another ilk. Both Unamuno and Maeztu contributed, as did Darío, Juan Ramón Jiménez, Dicenta, Ricardo Fuente, and Angel Ganivet, whose suicide shortly after cast him in the role of patron of the "Generación del '98." Although Valle-Inclán did not publish in *Vida Nueva*, perhaps due to a growing aversion to Blasco Ibáñez and Echegaray, perhaps because his work was not well-received, his picture did appear over an article dealing belatedly with *Femeninas*.[21]

Other magazines and newspapers sponsoring the new generation appeared during this period. *La Vida Literaria*, a weekly founded by Bernardo Rodríguez Serra, lasted from 7 January to 10 August 1899. Edited by Benavente, its early issues were not concerned with political topics; instead, *La Vida Literaria* concentrated on Modernism, the regional literature of Spain, and European literary currents. "Clarín" and Palacio Valdés were among the contributors, but more characteristic of the new magazine were contributions by Darío, Gregorio Martínez Sierra, Manuel Machado, Camilo Bargiela, Unamuno, Maeztu, and Baroja. Two stories by Valle-

Inclán, "*Tierra Caliente. Impresión*" and "La Reina de Dalicám" (The Queen of Dalicam), appear in *La Vida Literaria*.[22] The latter story is accompanied by a full-page caricature of Valle-Inclán by Leal da Camara in which he's presented with arms crossed above plant tendrils that form his lower extremities; above the caricature is the heading "Nuestros Colaboradores" (Our Contributions). His story "Del libro *Tierra Caliente*" (From the Book *Tierra Caliente*) was also published in *Don Quijote* that year.[23]

Revista Nueva, founded by Luis Ruiz Contreras and devoted exclusively to the new writers, made its first appearance on 15 February 1899. Its editorial offices in the publisher's home at 24 Madera were the same quarters that accommodated the Wednesday *tertulias*. Its first editorial, addressed "A la juventud intelectual" (To the intellectual youth), set forth the disdain felt toward the established order in a declaration of self-sufficiency.[24] Valle-Inclán later expressed the motivation behind the founding of the magazine:

All the dailies had shut their doors in my face. My articles were seen as strange . . . In light of that blockade, Azorín, Baroja, Benavente and I, indeed all of us who were excluded from publishing in newspapers, decided to found *Revista Nueva*.[25] (A54)

Baroja contributed consistently to the first ten issues, often using the pseudonyms "S. Paradoxa," "Doctor Baroja," and "J. Nessi"; Martínez Ruiz had only one article published, in one of the final issues; Unamuno, Darío, Benavente, Maeztu, Martínez Sierra, Francisco Villaespesa, and Dicenta were among others whose work appeared in print from time to time in the magazine before it ceased publication on 5 October 1899.

In the sixth issue of *Revista Nueva* on 5 April 1899, Valle-Inclán contributed the first chapter of a novel, *Adega (Historia milenaria)* (Adega. An Age-Old Tale). Unable to complete the work, Valle-Inclán had asked Ruiz Contreras to publish it in installments as an incentive. But this was not sufficient, and Valle-Inclán failed to supply more than six chapters.[26] The reason stated publicly was that he was dissatisfied with the slipshod editing of the magazine.[27] But there was also an underlying annoyance with Ruiz Contreras for his attempt to force contributors to finance the magazine.[28] For these various reasons, the friendship of the two men came to a temporary halt. *Adega* reached a similar impasse not overcome until 1904 when the completed novel appeared with the revised title *Flor de santidad*.[29]

The birth and death of periodicals was sporadic. After *Revista Nueva* there was a hiatus of several years before another important magazine was created by members of the Generation. *Juventud—Revista Popular Contemporánea* was founded by Pío Baroja and Azorín, fresh from their collaboration in the short-lived *Arte Joven* (whose artistic director had been Pablo Ruiz Picasso). *Juventud* published a total of twelve issues between October

1901 and 27 March 1902. Among its prominent contributors were Unamuno, Maeztu, Francisco Giner de los Ríos (who had founded the innovative Institución Libre de Enseñanza in 1876), "Silverio Lanza" (Juan Bautista Amoros, author of *El año triste* [The Sad Year]), Ciro Bayo, Palomero, Martínez Sierra, Manuel Machado, and Salvador Rueda (often considered the creator of *Modernismo*). Valle-Inclán contributed two stories, "Hierba santa" (Sacred Herb) and "Corazón de niña" (A Girl's Heart), to the journal.[30]

Most significant among the periodicals of this period was *Alma Española*, founded late in 1903. Its singularity lies in that it is the only publication uniting all the writers of the "Generación del '98" within its covers.[31] Valle-Inclán's contribution appeared on 27 December 1903 in the eighth issue. Placed beneath a picture of him, "Autobiografía" was a compound of fact and fiction produced from the cauldron of its creator's imagination. The supposedly factual account of Valle-Inclán's life contained generous extracts from his "Bajo los trópicos," "La Niña Chole"[32] and *Sonata de estío*. But a few facts were discernible:

The one before you, with a Quevedesque and Spanish countenance, black *quedeja* and long beard, is me: Don Ramón del Valle-Inclán. . . . I have a motto which, like me, is proud and resigned: "Have disdain toward others and no love of self." . . . It's time that I admitted never having felt the love of family. . . . I had hardly reached that age called youth when . . . I embarked for Mexico . . . I was something of a poet in those days, having no experience and a head full of romantic notions. I held in good faith many things that I now doubt and, free from skepticism, I rushed to enjoy life. Although I didn't avow it, perhaps unknowingly, I was happy: I dreamed of accomplishing great things, like an adventurer of old, and I despised literary laurels. (A55)

Traces of the young Ramón Valle y Peña are visible through the mask he superimposed on his biography. The autocriticism is no less severe than the outward-directed censure that marked his public life. He had toward himself the same attitude he had toward others. In creating his autobiography in terms that mix the real and the imaginary, Valle-Inclán was doing exactly what each member of his generation had done with his public image in his own way.

4 Early Stages

The period 1898–1899 framed Valle-Inclán's first theatrical activity. The histrionic atmosphere of the cafés and the success of his role as head of several *tertulias* led him to consider a career in acting. Ambitiously, he took advantage of evening walks through Madrid in the company of friends, making an entire plaza his stage; he impressed his companions by loudly reciting, with grandiose gestures, the most dramatic moments of Hartzenbusch's *Los amantes de Teruel* (The Lovers of Teruel), or excerpts from other romantic plays.[1] These frequent performances would sometimes bring the whole group before a police official or a magistrate; then, too, Valle-Inclán acted out the fictitious career of the mask he was creating: he paraded his resounding name and listed his occupation as Colonel-General of the Armies of Tierra Caliente. His deadpan expression and tenacious insistence on his prestige riled the official and entertained his fellow "prisoners." In all these situations Valle-Inclán demonstrated his inventiveness, humor, and picaresque character. His native sense of drama was always in evidence.

It was not surprising therefore that he actually set out to fulfill his desire to act on a professional stage. However, with typical evasiveness, and with a sarcastic view of the theatre that thereafter characterized his attitude, Valle-Inclán disguised his reasons:

Seeing that literature doesn't provide adequate means to live, I'm thinking of working as an actor . . . I have no other recourse but to tread the boards . . . When all is said and done, that's what anyone in Spain does who isn't capable of doing anything else.[2] (A56)

To that end, he wrote to Pérez Galdós on 5 September 1898, using the stationery of the Ateneo de Madrid, of which he was a member,

Sr. D. Benito Pérez Galdós.
My Dear Friend and Maestro:
    I have, for a long time, been harboring the idea of dedicating myself to the theatre as an actor, to which end I have studied some, and I believe that I have some ability. But you know the difficulties one encounters here in attempting anything. I need the support of a great Authority and so beg you to lend me yours by recommending me to Carmen Cobeña, Emilio Thuiller, and Donato Giménez—of the brilliant new company which La Comedia has taken on. If you use your respectable position, I know that your recommendation will be a *hukasse* to them.
    Forgive my having to bother you, Don Benito, and let your amiabilities to me be my excuse.
    Thanking you in advance, I remain your respectful admiring friend,
        Ramón del Valle-Inclán[3]
        Madrid, 5-IX-98
        S/c Calvo Asensio, 4 (A57)

It is not clear if it was Galdós who made his wish come true, but the opportunity to implement this decision came through Jacinto Benavente. Already a rising playwright after the productions in Madrid of *El nido ajeno* and *Gente conocida* (Well-known People) in 1894, Benavente was preparing to open a new play, *La comida de las fieras* (The Banquet of the Beasts). He invited Valle-Inclán to take a minor role, that of Teófilo Everit, in the company of Emilio Thuiller and Carmen Cobeña, whom he had aspired to join. As a reading of the play attests,[4] the role of Teófilo Everit was closely patterned on Valle-Inclán himself. Benavente had transferred the wit, appearance, and mannerisms of Valle-Inclán to his creation. The part may have been small, but Benavente was excited about the prospect of having the original create the characterization on stage.

    There was a problem to be resolved, however, before the aspiring actor could be accepted into the theatrical company of Emilio Thuiller, the director and principal actor. Valle-Inclán had openly denounced Thuiller as a bad actor and a worse director on many public occasions, as well as in an article on Thuiller, published in 1898 in *Madrid Cómico*. Clearly, Thuiller had to be placated before he would admit Valle-Inclán to the group. To accomplish the task, Benavente sought the intercession of Ruiz Contreras, a good friend of Thuiller. The ploy was effective.[5] Shortly thereafter Valle-Inclán became affiliated with the company and began to rehearse his part in October 1898.

    The magnanimity of both Thuiller and Valle-Inclán was shown in the cordial relationship that existed between them during their association in the play. But Valle-Inclán did not change his opinion of Thuiller; rather, as the rehearsals progressed, he saw his opinion justified. He communicated his feeling to Benavente:

One can't work like this . . . Don Emilio directs as if this were a funeral procession . . . The actors lose vivacity . . . You can't allow your play to fail because of the director.[6] (A58)

Rather than instigate an argument with Thuiller, Benavente and Valle-Inclán again worked through Ruiz Contreras. He subtly conveyed their criticism, and this led to an improvement in the play's tempo.

As rehearsals progressed, Valle-Inclán's inherent theatricality asserted itself. Benavente enhanced his role many times, and as the importance of Teófilo Everit increased, so did the character's eccentricity. Valle-Inclán wore a costume that reflected this: cane in hand, he sported a top hat, knee-length coat with a boutonniere, tight pants, pointed shoes, a Lord Byron collar with a broad bow, and an outlandish vest. Valle-Inclán's own beard and long hair completed the "decadent" mannequin that was Teófilo Everit.[7] Tirso Escudero, the producer, provided the money with which Valle-Inclán obtained the wardrobe from a second-hand store; Ruiz Contreras supplied the unique vest.

Benavente's *La comida de las fieras* premiered at Madrid's Teatro de la Comedia on 7 November 1898. The opening was not without incident. Henri Cornuty, an anarchistic French writer and friend of Paul Verlaine, attended the performance in the company of Martínez Ruiz. Compelled to react upon hearing some disdainful comments against Benavente by apparently wealthy spectators, Cornuty stood on his seat and shouted back insults in his colorful Spanish.[8] The audacious Cornuty added the necessary note of absurdity that would always appear whenever a project by a member of the Generation faced public reaction. But in spite of the misbehavior, the incident passed unnoticed in the generally favorable reviews, and the three-act play was the playwright's first commercial success.

Valle-Inclán acquitted himself admirably in his debut[9] and looked eagerly for criticism of his performance, but he found only a passing reference to "el aplomo y la discreción del debutante" (the poise and discretion of the debutant) in the review by "Zeda."[10] Sensitive to the snub of his first professional performance, Valle-Inclán was alternately depressed and enraged. He had lived the part as only the original could live it, but the critics had not taken notice. The personage that anyone could see and hear on the streets of Madrid or in its cafés had not been singled out in its personification. As a consequence, Valle-Inclán gave notice that he was vacating the role:

It seems that I performed badly yesterday and so have decided never to act again. . . . I can't act. I did very badly. And I don't wish to tempt fate again. One shouldn't persist in doing things over; when badly done, they shouldn't be repeated.[11] (A59)

Benavente succeeded in entreating him to remain until a replacement could be found. But Valle-Inclán's assurance was based solely on friendship and not on a change of attitude:

Very well. I will perform because you want me to do so and in order to avoid causing a financial blow to the company. I don't like to harm anyone. But let it be clear that you have very little concern for your plays. I would never tolerate mine being ruined by bad actors. It's between you and your conscience.[12] (A60)

After three performances in the role of Teófilo Everit, Valle-Inclán closed the doors on his first theatrical venture. He left with the bitter taste of having been ignored by the press, but he took with him something positive as well. Through his association with the company he had become friendly with Josefina Blanco, the young actress who played the role of Anita. Many years later, she would become his wife.

Disappointed by the blow to his acting aspirations, Valle-Inclán sought solace at the café tables and in his writing, publishing stories in various new literary periodicals. But the appeal of the boards was not so easily denied. Early in 1899 Valle-Inclán again entered the lists as an actor, if only for a single performance and in a small role, in *Los reyes en el destierro* (Kings in Exile). The drama was presented at the Teatro de la Comedia in a belated commemoration of Alphonse Daudet's death in 1897. The French novelist's *Les Rois en exil* had been adapted for the stage by Alejandro Sawa, the fabled bohemian novelist whose intimate knowledge of French literary life disclosed many new avenues to the Spanish writers of his generation. Undoubtedly, Sawa, who was a close friend of Valle-Inclán, convinced him to participate in the production. But Valle-Inclán's portrayal of the old general was not a success.[13]

Another example of his growing interest in the theatre was his association with the production of Shakespeare's *The Taming of the Shrew*. Translated by Manuel Matoses with the title *La fierecilla domada*, it was presented in the Teatro de las Delicias in the Carabanchel Alto sector of Madrid by Benavente's "Teatro Artístico." While Valle-Inclán did not act in this instance, he was artistic director of the group whose producer was Antonio Vico. Benavente as Petruchio, Concha Catalá as Tarasca (Katharina), Barinaga as Vincentio, Pedro González Blanco, Alonso y Orera, and Gregorio Martínez Sierra made up the cast.[14]

On 7 December 1899 the same "Teatro Artístico" premiered Valle-Inclán's first play, *Cenizas* (Ashes), to a sold-out house at Madrid's Teatro Lara.[15] The cast of the melodrama, which was rehearsed at the studio of Saint-Aubin, included Rosario Pino as the protagonist Octavia Santino, Jacinto Benavente in the co-starring role of Pedro Pondal, Gregorio Martínez Sierra as the righteous Padre Rojas, and Moreno as Don Juan Manuel. In conjunction with the opening, the same group financed the publication of the play;[16] Valle-Inclán's third book was dedicated to "Jacinto Benavente, en prenda de amistad" (Jacinto Benavente, as a token of friendship).

Cenizas ended Valle-Inclán's first period of theatrical activity. Its premiere was not completely auspicious due to a great misfortune occurring in

July 1899 that forever altered Valle-Inclán's life. At that time he frequented the Café de la Montaña, situated between Calle de Alcalá and Carrera de San Jerónimo, in the company of Benavente, Barinaga, Rodríguez Serra, Bargiela, Cornuty, José de Campos, Palomero, Marín, Ricardo Baroja, and other so-called *Modernistas*. On one occasion the topic of discussion was a duel pending between the Portuguese caricaturist Leal da Camara and López del Castillo. Manuel Bueno, one of the members of the *tertulia*, asserted that the duel could not be held because Camara was not of legal age; Valle-Inclán opposed that view with characteristic vehemence in spite of the fact that he and Bueno were friends. Words alone did not resolve the argument between such volatile individuals, and blows were exchanged. Bueno's cane struck Valle-Inclán so forcibly that a cuff link he was wearing became embedded in his wrist. Valle-Inclán's version differs somewhat:

Manuel Bueno grasped my hand and on squeezing it, drove my cuff link into the flesh, at the very edge of the wrist.[17] (A61)

The confrontation with Manuel Bueno had grave repercussions. Valle-Inclán dismissed the wound as inconsequential and refused to have it attended properly in spite of attempts by Benavente and Ruiz Contreras to convince him that medical examination was necessary:

I didn't pay any attention to the wound, but a week later the hand began to swell, producing horrible pains.[18] (A62)

By that time gangrene had set in. The verdict of the physician to whom Valle-Inclán finally went was that the left arm had to be amputated. Valle-Inclán agreed:

One evening I read in the *Heraldo de Madrid* that the torero Angel Pastor had died from an infection similar to mine; and when I met with the doctor, I told him to cut.[19] (A63)

What was to be the first of many operations over his long life was performed immediately.[20] Despite anecdotes to the contrary, Valle-Inclán's reaction to the amputation was highly human: he felt all the anguish, pain, and fear that such a traumatic experience can evoke, yet, he bore it well. After the surgery he asked to be left alone:

Would you like to know why I wanted to be alone? Because I felt like crying. And I did, yes, I cried, as would any man over a lost arm; I cried over the shoulder orphaned by the arm . . . That's why I didn't want anyone to see me . . . Once my tears were over, the drama ended. There was no need to involve others in my sorrow.[21] (A64)

For a time, Valle-Inclán's attitude toward Manuel Bueno was understandably violent. He could not wait, he said to daily visitors such as Martínez Ruiz, to rise from his bed and revenge himself on his malefactor. His friends circumvented such an occurrence by entreating Manuel Bueno to approach Valle-Inclán. The reconciliation was completed at Valle-Inclán's bedside. Their renewed friendship was never severed again; indeed, so uncommon was Valle-Inclán's generosity that it prompted an illustrated entry in "Ripley's Believe It or Not."[22]

Baroja, for one, could not comprehend the complexity of a man who would forgive a personal injury of such magnitude yet vociferously attack someone who would question his pronouncements. But then Baroja was never able or willing to penetrate the psychological depths of his contemporaries. In this case, he could not see the dual aspect of Valle-Inclán's personality—the man could be generous under the most adverse conditions, but the artist could be relentless in the pursuit of his beliefs and in the defense of his aesthetics against detractors. Clearly, these stances were separate and distinct. Those who were aware of this seldom resented for very long Valle-Inclán's barbed words; consequently, as Baroja observes enviously, no one spoke against Valle-Inclán, even though he spoke badly of almost everyone at one time or another. The fact was that Valle-Inclán's comments on his contemporaries were never vicious; often they were made to entertain his audience.

The proceeds from the presentation of *Cenizas* and its publication in book form were used to buy Valle-Inclán an orthopedic arm that replaced an awkward piece improvised by a local carpenter. The new mechanical arm served to bridge the time between psychological distress and stoic acceptance. Eventually, Valle-Inclán tired of the pretense and relative uselessness of the contraption. He abandoned it completely, with a sense of satisfaction at how well his changed condition suited the mask he was creating. Through accident he had achieved a closer relationship to the author of *Don Quixote*, in whom, as one of Valle-Inclán's characters would state,[23] he had always envied the results of his career of arms more than his creation of a masterpiece. As he saw it, destiny had sardonically underlined his claim to identification with Cervantes:

Gentlemen, I've been known to have said that I was worth more than Cervantes. Perhaps that wasn't true . . . But from now on you can't deny that, one-armed as I am, at least I resemble him greatly.[24] (A65)

The one-armed man took full advantage of the situation to augment his singularity. While his career as an actor had to be abandoned, his accidental deformity was turned from a handicap to an asset. His figure had been quite suddenly and unexpectedly endowed with an even greater aura of mystery, and the near-legendary stature he was achieving was further vitalized. Valle-Inclán relished the mythical being that emerged in the fanciful anecdotes then making the rounds of cafés, salons, and newspapers.[25]

The real-life event is reflected throughout the work that followed. In *Sonata de invierno* (1905), the Marqués de Bradomín is wounded in his left arm during a skirmish and has it amputated in a convent, showing his bravery by withstanding the surgeon's process without a sign of pain.[26] Bradomín's sole reaction was:

. . . I concerned myself only with the attitude I would adopt hereafter toward women in order to make the loss of my arm more poetic.[27] (A66)

In *Una tertulia de antaño* (A Tertulia of Yesteryear; 1908) the same Bradomín recalls the loss of his arm in different terms:

I regret having lost it in an obscure encounter. It would have been magnificent to have seen the hand fall on reaching for the sword in defense of the small Princes and their mother, the Queen.[28] (A67)

This point of view was characteristic not only of Bradomín but of Valle-Inclán himself. The dreams of military glory he had entertained had to be abandoned with the occurrence of his loss:

On reaching the age of thirty, one of my arms was amputated, and I don't quite know whether the dreams took flight or simply became mute. The love of the Muses consoled me in my anguish! I aspired to drink from the sacred fountain, but first I wished to listen to my heartbeat, and I allowed my senses to express themselves. With the murmur of their voices I created my Aesthetics.[29] (A68)

Turning to literature as opposed to merely tolerating it, Valle-Inclán transferred his sense of adventure; his characters would do for him what he had hoped to do before the loss of his arm. To better identify himself with his favorite character, he made Bradomín undergo the same privation. But the heroic attitude of the protagonist of the *Sonatas* is not the only expression of Valle-Inclán's view. Another attitude is evident in *Tragedia de ensueño* (Dream Tragedy), a playlet in which the ringed hand of a beautiful damsel is mercilessly severed by a bandit chieftain taken with her jewels; there, the horror of his act is immediate and damning. Still another attitude is reflected in "Mi perro" (My Dog), a poem in which the loss of the arm is made pathetic:

I have a dog,
His name's Carabel,
A fond remembrance of Marquina.
Nothing pleases him more
Than to sleep underfoot.

When he upsets me
And I send him away,
He comes back meekly
And licks my hand.
Knowing that he likes it, I oblige,
Then he seeks my missing hand
And searching my sleeve, gives a yelp.
He cries for a hand to lick,
While, my Lord, I cry desiring to give
A part of my very self![30] (A69)

Physical deformity occurs with sufficient frequency to note it as an important subtheme in Valle-Inclán's works. It is possible to argue that this event
in Valle-Inclán's life shifted his vision from the purely romantic channels of
such works as *Femeninas*, *Epitalamio*, and *Cenizas* into an increasing recognition of life's grotesqueness. This recognition shaped the *Comedias bárbaras*
and eventually led to the production of that series of works known as
Esperpentos (Grotesques). But while Valle-Inclán's artistic vision led him to
a cynical exposure of life in the latter plays and novels, he was not cursed
with the personal hatred that marred the existence of such deformed
writers as Alexander Pope or, closer to his own tradition, the lame
Quevedo and the hunchbacked Ruiz de Alarcón.

With the beginning of the twentieth century Valle-Inclán still found himself in financial distress. He was forced to leave his poor quarters on Calvo
Asensio Street to take up residence in an attic on 9 Calle Argensola, in the
building where his friend Dr. José Verdes Montenegro lived. Wanting to
alleviate his poverty somewhat, but not willing to submit to the deadlines
and routines of newspaper work, he undertook various literary projects.
Among these was the translation for the stage of a work by Alexandre
Dumas, done in collaboration with Ruiz Contreras. Entitled *La condesa de
Romani* (The Countess of Romani), the play was prepared for director-
playwright Ceferino Palencia and his wife, the actress María Tubáu, who
had met Valle-Inclán through Ruiz Contreras.[31] The play was produced at
the Teatro Novedades, then a center in Madrid for foreign melodramas. A
second project was the adaptation into a novel of the successful play *La cara
de Dios* (The Face of God) by Carlos Arniches.[32] In this novel are manifested
many of the themes, treatments, and characteristics that found full expression in later works by Valle-Inclán.[33] He also employed his talents as a
versifier in creating advertising slogans for a new medicine, "Harina Plástica" (Plasticized Flour):

While braiding a nautical cord,
The maker of rope became ill;
yet, quickly, returned to his skill
With Plasticized Flour aboard.[34] (A70)

He composed his lines in the Horchatería de Candela where he was "assisted" by his friends. The results of the collaboration were other verses that could never be employed in advertisements:

Do nightmares beset you
And trouble your hibernal sleep?
Take this, you clod, it'll mend you,
Plasticized Flour just wends through
And sets stomach juices at ease![35] (A71)

Such trivialities brought out his humor and helped maintain his histrionic image when he was away from a real stage.

Whether or not he was connected with a play, Valle-Inclán was always attracted to the theatre. In it, he thought, his personal authority could not be denied; since the theatre was an arena for the spoken word, he had as much right as anyone to be heard. At the premiere of Benavente's *La gata de Angora* (The Angora Cat), Valle-Inclán defended the playwright against an unappreciative public.[36] In that defense he expressed his pent-up fury and frustration at the constant derision he himself had experienced at the hands of audiences. At the premiere of *La tempranica* (The Early Bloom), a *zarzuela*, Valle-Inclán, Luis Bello, Pío and Ricardo Baroja, and several others caused a great commotion in the theatre and were arrested.[37] At other times he attacked a playwright to whom the public had given ready acceptance in spite (or because) of inconsequential writing, and he often led a group in stomping during a performance.[38] There were many events, where, as a member of the audience, he turned the house into yet another stage.

But not all the reactions of Valle-Inclán and his friends to theatrical productions in Madrid were negative. In many instances the group set out to assist one of their own, like Benavente, as a *claque*, and on other occasions they sponsored the cause of an older playwright. On 30 January 1901, a new play by Benito Pérez Galdós opened at the Teatro Español in Madrid. Valle-Inclán, who had shown great admiration for the master novelist in his review of *Angel Guerra* years before, attended the opening with others of his generation, many of whom were prepared to defend Galdós's play, *Electra*, with great enthusiasm.[39] The anticlerical tone of the work instigated Maeztu to stand during a fitting moment of the action and shout, "¡Abajo los jesuítas!" (Down with the Jesuits!). But Maeztu was the only one whose candor lasted after the performance.[40] His impassioned support of Galdós's *Electra* led to friction with Martínez Ruiz who had published a very cold review of the play. The only member of the Generation whose reaction to *Electra* was not recorded in his own words was Valle-Inclán; however, he is reported to have cried during the performance.[41] Although in 1913 Galdós rejected Valle-Inclán's *El embrujado* (The Bewitched) for the Teatro Español, which he was directing at the time,

Valle-Inclán still held him in esteem. In an interview in 1915, he referred to Galdós as a genius of the Spanish theatre.[42] As late as 1918, he thought of him sympathetically as "Ciego como Homero, pobre como Belisario" (Blind like Homer, poor like Belisarius).[43] Years later, however, he was to turn a neat phrase in having one of his characters refer to the author of the *Episodios Nacionales* (National Episodes) as "Don Benito el Garbancero" (Don Benito the Chickpea Man).[44]

Besides the cafés, salons, theatres, and streets of Madrid, there were other stages on which Valle-Inclán performed. Having developed the habit of walking, he and his friends often took to the road to visit nearby towns and historical sites. Impressed by El Greco and the city he immortalized, Valle-Inclán went to Toledo many times. His impressions of the city were best expressed in *La lámpara maravillosa*:

Toledo is an old haunted city. . . . Toledo is haunting in its evocativeness. . . . For me, these old stones have the marvelous power of marijuana which, creating the illusion that life is a mirror we encounter along the way, flashes in an instant the faces seen through the years. Toledo has that same mystic power. It raises the slabs of her sepulchres and allows phantoms to file out in a procession more anguishing than life. . . . Toledo is like a sepulchre. . . . Toledo can prompt only literary evocations, being as full of anguish to eyes as of enchantment to memory.[45] (A72)

Cities like Toledo and Santiago de Compostela interested Valle-Inclán because of their perfect settings for his budding mysticism.

Equally fascinating as a stage were the several cemeteries in the environs of Madrid. This was exemplified during the public homage to the great romantic Mariano José de Larra, in which the members of the "Generación del '98" participated, at his tomb in the city's abandoned San Nicolás cemetery on 13 February 1901. Valle-Inclán was among the celebrants of the rites described by Azorín in *La voluntad* (Will) and elsewhere.[46] The works of Baroja, Azorín, and Unamuno display fully the affinity for forgotten resting places typical of the members of the Generation.[47] In Valle-Inclán the aura of death is present in much of his work; the function of cemeteries and places, things, and situations associated with death are particularly notable in the *Comedias bárbaras* and the *Esperpentos*. The conversation between Rubén Darío and the Marqués de Bradomín in the Cementerio del Este is framed with Shakespearean gravediggers readying the grave of Max Estrella, the protagonist of *Luces de bohemia*. The cemetery is the final stage and the most fascinating and as such it holds the interest of Valle-Inclán. And, indeed, it would be at his own gravesite that Valle-Inclán would "participate" in his last stage appearance.

5 Recognitions

Achieving public notoriety came easily to the theatrical nature of Valle-Inclán. The exotic figure on the streets of old Madrid and the authoritative voice in the cafés attracted immediate attention. The anecdotes that appeared in the press added to a growing reputation extending beyond the capital to artistic circles in other Spanish cities. The fame of his *tertulia* attracted such young writers as Juan Ramón Jiménez, whose *Ninfeas* (Nymphead) was entitled by Valle-Inclán.[1]

Although the café remained a principal stage for the man, more and more, since the loss of his arm, Valle-Inclán turned to literature. He began to devote himself seriously to writing. The same year the first books by Juan Ramón Jiménez and Pío Baroja were published,[2] Valle-Inclán began his first concerted effort toward attaining literary recognition. In January 1900 the Madrid newspaper *El Liberal* held one of its periodic literary contests, and Valle-Inclán entered his story "Satanás." The 667 entries were judged by a distinguished panel composed of Juan Valera, José Echegaray, and Isidoro Fernández Flóres. The first prize was awarded to José Nogales Llovet, while the second award went to Emilia Pardo Bazán.[3] Valle-Inclán's work was not singled out for honors, but it created controversy among the judges, as the author stated later at the Café Lion d'Or:

Valera refused to sign the certificate in the first contest, believing that mine is the one that should have been given the prize . . . [4] (A73)

Valera's objection to the exclusion of "Satanás" from the awards was made public in his letter to *El Correo de España*, a Buenos Aires periodical.[5] But high praise from the author of *Pepita Jiménez*, the Spanish critic who first recognized the poetic genius of Rubén Darío, and laudatory remarks by a few discerning men of letters did not overcome public indifference to and press ostracism of Valle-Inclán. His reaction to this period has survived in a prologue he wrote years later:

Grotesque Spanish times, when everything sounds like fake coins! All the values are suspect: History, Politics, Militarism, Academies. Never has there been such commercialism in what was then starting to be called the Great Press: G. P. Foul suggestion that of the anagram![6] (A74)

Such a prize would have increased not only his literary stature but also would have helped ease Valle-Inclán's penury for a time. But it was not his destiny to find an easy solution to his financial problems. So he listened attentively to any possibility of an honorable but quick way of securing wealth. Fascinated by accounts of buried treasures in the ancient mines of Almadén, in La Mancha, which produced a third of the world's mercury, Valle-Inclán set out inconspicuously with Ricardo Baroja on horseback. They were armed, ready to uncover some secret trove and to protect it with their lives:

Like all adventurers, I felt the allure of gold . . . Seeing that literature wasn't providing enough to live on, I devoted myself to searching for mines . . . Balzac had done the same, dreaming of silver mines, and so had our own Gustavo Adolfo Bécquer, who believed that a treasure was buried in the monastery of Veruela . . . I thought that mining would be a fabulous business and took it up. The Romans, lacking the means that modern industry and science have made available, abandoned those mines in which the desired mineral—sulfur, phosphorus, or any other—was bonded to the ore extracted . . . I made a careful study of the matter and deduced that there were such mines in La Mancha. On a cold January night, a very cold night when I rode alone on horseback through snowy fields, my pistol went off accidentally. I shot myself in the arm and foot. I was far from the train station at Valdecampo. I provided a provisional cure with snow; not giving in to the pain of the wounds, I crossed the fields to Almendralejo. I reached the station and waited for the train, which seemed forever in coming. I spent twelve hours in that unsheltered place. When the train finally arrived, it had mostly cargo cars and some miserable second-class cars. "Where are the first-class cars?" I asked. "There aren't any, sir," was the reply. I complained about the omission and when my indignation was at its peak, a tall slim gentleman wearing a fur coat appeared. He asked about my condition and, on telling him, I was invited to his private compartment. It was Don Segismundo Moret. The political leader took care of me. I was consumed by fever and tortured by pain, but not a sound escaped my lips. On arriving in Madrid, I put myself in the hands of that saintly man who was Dr. Alejandro San Martín, who performed the first painful cures . . . At the time his assistant was Dr. Goyanes . . . I spent three months in bed, forgetting about the mines of La Mancha . . .[7] (A75)

One-armed like Cervantes, lame like Lord Byron,[8] Valle-Inclán told his visitors that the only other requisite to greatness he had yet to attain was to be blind like Homer. While he was never to suffer loss of sight, his concern with blindness is, nonetheless, evident in his later works.[9]

Valle-Inclán spent the months of his confinement in his attic quarters on 9 Calle Argensola writing. He was contracted by the Barcelona publisher Maucci to translate several novels by the noted Portuguese author José

María Eça de Queiroz, whose death on 16 August 1900, during his tenure as consul in Paris, instigated renewed interest in his work. *El crimen del Padre Amaro* (Father Amaro's Crime)[10] was the first of the series undertaken by Valle-Inclán. Also in Barcelona, "Un cabecilla," one of his earliest stories, was reprinted,[11] thus continuing the pattern of re-issuing earlier pieces.

By far the most significant literary activity of Valle-Inclán during his lengthy recuperation was the creation of a new work:

. . . I wrote *Memorias* . . . I read them to Antonio Machado and Francisco Villaespesa. I had hardly finished the last page when the latter exclaimed: "It's similar to D'Annunzio's *Le Vergini delle Rocce*." And Machado added: "It's magnificent!" Antonio counseled me to publish the manuscript as soon as possible. Those *Memorias* became *Sonata de otoño*. I wrote easily. I possessed a literary sensibility and felt great disdain for those who wrote without technique and were called "maestros" by the press.[12] (A76)

The facility of the writer stemmed from his "creative patience:"

Before starting to write, I need to visualize the characters in great detail. I need to see their faces, figures, dress, walk. I see their entire life prior to the moment at which they appear in the novel. Out of that total life that I first visualize in my mind, I use very little when the character is developed on the page, where, perhaps, he appears only in one scene. Having once seen the character, I "insert" him, I "wedge" him into the novel. Thereafter, the task of writing is very easy.[13] (A77)

On the advice of Machado and Villaespesa, Valle-Inclán prepared *Memorias* for publication in periodicals. His neighbor Verdes Montenegro, perceiving the need of the man and the talent of the writer, introduced him to José Ortega Munilla, the influential editor of *Los Lunes* (the literary supplement of the newspaper *El Imparcial*) and the father of José Ortega y Gasset, who would later become an important philosopher and the founder of *Revista de Occidente*. Another source for publication was *Juventud*, a magazine newly established by Baroja and Martínez Ruiz, who asked Valle-Inclán to contribute. Through these contacts he was able to place various "excerpts"[14] from what became *Sonata de otoño*.[15] Valle-Inclán's gratitude to Ortega Munilla was expressed a few years later in the prologue to the first novel in the series:

Less than three years ago, I was making a living by writing episodic novels, which I signed with pride, whether out of disdain or out of defiance. I wallowed painfully in the obscurity of my name and in the oblivion in which I existed. It would have been my desire then that books be written in the Lombard script, as were the old patents of nobility, and that only a few initiates be able to read them. This fantasy has been a talisman for me. It has kept me from entering base competitions, as well as from feeling the cruelties of a sorrowful life. Alone, haughty, and poor, I've come to literature without having sent my books to the so-called critics, and without once having sat at their feet in the daily upholding of their egos by the hussies and eunuchs of Art.

And yet, I have received such generous and noble patronage from someone that without it I would never have written *Memorias del Marqués de Bradomín*. That patronage, the only one in my life, came from a great literary figure and a man with a great heart: I have described Don José Ortega Munilla. Today I offer this book to him with that same unaffected and loving respect which, when I was a child, the shepherds from the vicinity showed when they brought the whitest of their lambs to my father's house.

V-I. Real Sitio de Aranjuez. May 1904.[16] (A78)

Sonata de otoño. Memorias del Marqués de Bradomín[17] was published as a book in March 1902, through the intercession of several enthusiastic friends. Ruiz Contreras donated the paper for the edition and Ricardo Calvo financed its processing.[18] The faith of his supporters was rewarded in the success of the work, and through the novel Valle-Inclán achieved the first real literary recognition of his career. In homage to Galicia, which had produced such a writer, the young Ortega y Gasset published "Glosa," dedicated to Ramón del Valle-Inclán.[19]

Sonata de otoño was only one of four novels concerned with the autobiography of the fictitious Marqués de Bradomín. The tetralogy, beginning with *Sonata de primavera* and continuing with *Sonata de estío*, *Sonata de otoño*, and *Sonata de invierno*, relates the romantic life of the protagonist by allying each episode to one of the four seasons. The autumnal sequence takes place in Galicia, a fitting setting for the funereal tone of the novel; the other works are set respectively in Italy, Mexico, and Carlist Spain.

The tomes comprise a masterly tale whose plot is subservient to the sensations of the principal character, the same who inspired Darío to compose his "Soneto autumnal al Marqués de Bradomín" (Autumnal Sonnet to the Marquis of Bradomín).[20] The splendid, if anachronistic, figure of Bradomín recounts his amorous exploits from the spring of his life to the winter of his years. In the process of the narrative, the classic concept of Don Juan (who was concerned solely with passion and death) is enhanced by Bradomín's sensibility in appreciating his surroundings and relating them to himself. Bradomín moves within society as it permits or condones, not with the satanic fury that directs Don Juan to raze its commandments with every act. Bradomín samples life with the gusto of the wine taster; Don Juan downs the draught, finds it wanting, and seeks desperately after another. Bradomín lives fully. It is perhaps a life full of delusion, but he lives nonetheless.

The personage created by Valle-Inclán has many interesting features, aesthetically and realistically, that distinguish him from Don Juan.[21] He is described in a note that accompanies the tetralogy as "feo, católico y sentimental." Valle-Inclán has explained his particular selection of these adjectives:

But if, besides the material sensation, it is necessary to convey a more or less psychic image of this or that individual . . . perhaps it would be best to proceed as I did in stating that my Marquis of Bradomín was a Don Juan who was ugly, catholic and sentimental, a scheme in which the first adjective defines, in a picturesque way, the physical exterior of the character, while the second and third signal, in order of importance, the fundamental aspects of his interior being.[22] (A79)

Bradomín has been equated with Valle-Inclán ever since the publication of *Sonata de otoño*. The author, never one to miss an opportunity to confuse his critics, agreed to the equation by not denying it. But later, in a lecture, he added sardonically,

And I confess that my Marquis of Bradomín is inspired in Campoamor, and that many of his traits are not at all autobiographical, as some believe, but pertain to the author of the *Doloras*.[23] (A80)

The complication of the matter suited Valle-Inclán. The possibility that Bradomín was an interpretation of Chateaubriand, the author of the voluminous *Memoires d'outre-tombe*, or Leonardo Sánchez Deus, a Galician adventurer who, among other things, was an officer in Italy and aide-de-camp to Garibaldi,[24] did not take away from the character but added veracity to Valle-Inclán's conception.

Sonata de otoño was the first work in which Valle-Inclán consolidated his style. The technique of the novel shows a marked change from the predominantly romantic expression of his early stories. The tenets of *Modernismo* matured in the novel to become the guiding aesthetic of the literary activity of this period. But the creed was expressed not only in action; while the work itself represented the success of the ideology, Valle-Inclán formulated the guidelines elsewhere. In his article "Modernismo," published in the same year as *Sonata de otoño*, he stated,

If there is anything new in contemporary literature that could be justly given the name of "Modernism," it isn't grammatical and rhetorical extravagance, as some guileless critics believe, perhaps due to the fact that the term "Modernism," as with all oft-repeated words, has come to have a meaning as ample as it is doubtful. For that reason, I don't think it superfluous to attempt to posit what it means or could mean. The characteristic condition of all modern art, and especially of literature, is a tendency to refine sensations and increase their number and intensity. There are poets who dream of giving their stanzas the rhythm of dance, the melody of music, and the majesty of sculpture.[25] (A81)

He continued by aligning his life and creativity along these parameters:

Believing only in beauty, I already harbor in my soul, obstinate rose, the mockery of all that is divine and all that is human. I love music above all beautiful things because it is the fragrance of emotion . . . Oh, emotion! It is a book in which everything—idea, sentiment, rhythm, rhyme—may be intimate and tepid, without needless decor and verbiage. I detest the cold palace of the Parnassians. Let the phrase be touched by soul, let it evoke blood, or tears, or a smile; let there always be a subword in the word, a word shadow, secret and tremorous, an enchanting mystery, as with dead women or sleeping children. . . . Although I'm an ultralyrical poet, I don't believe in the supernatural; I have tried solely to create garden and valley in my work; and I know that a few colors, a few sounds, some basic truths of this life are more than sufficient. Harmonies, melodies: everything is there. If you give me a woman, a fountain, distant music, roses, the moon—beauty, crystal, rhythm, essence, silver—I will promise an eternity of beautiful things. I have been child, woman, man; I love exterior order and spiritual restlessness; I believe that there are two corrosive things: sensuality and impatience; I don't smoke, I don't drink wine, I hate cafés and the bulls, religion, militarism, the accordeon and the death penalty; I know I was born to write poetry; I don't like numbers; I admire philosophers, painters, musicians, poets—in short, my mind is as one with their idea and my heart with their sentiment.[26] (A82)

Another verbose statement of his position on *Modernismo* was also made in 1902, in the prologue to a friend's book:

The young ought to be arrogant, violent, impassioned, iconoclastic. . . . This world has many wretched people, victims of the Devil, who argue against the parables of Christ but fail to attack a bad play by Echegaray or Grilo . . . Such adulation for whatever is considered to be hallowed, such admiration for whatever bears the dust of antiquity, always typify intellectual servitude, which is, unfortunately, quite extensive in this land. Nevertheless, such attitudes have merited their place in a way because they served to kindle that iconoclastic fury that possesses all young spirits today. In art, as in life, to destroy is to create. Anarchy is ever a desire for regeneration; for us, it is the only regeneration possible. . . . The author of *Sombras de vida* has made his profession of Modernist faith: seeking oneself within rather than in others. For that is what the embattled literary school is all about. . . . That is why young writers demonstrate a greater determination to express sensations than ideas. Never have ideas been the exclusive patrimony of an individual, but sensations have. . . . The characteristic condition of all modern art, and especially of literature, is a tendency to refine sensations and increase their number and intensity. . . . This analogy and equivalency of sensations is what constitutes Modernism in literature. . . . Today we perceive gradations of color, gradations of sound, and distant relationships among things that certainly were not perceived by our ancestors hundreds of years ago. Primitive languages seldom possess words that convey the concept of color. . . . And it is well-known that a dearth of words is always the result of a paucity of sensations. . . . Today, there are artists who endeavor to find a strange correspondence between sound and color . . . [27] (A83)

Valle-Inclán was one of those *Modernistas*, as his further definition shows:

I believe that a good dictionary of synonyms would have established the parallel, the intimate relationship between Modernist youth and Jewish dog. . . . The Modernist is the one who disturbs . . . the one who seeks to give his art the interior emotion and mysterious expression that all things manifest to the one who knows how to see and understand. He is neither the one who breaks the old rules, nor the one who creates new ones, but rather the one who, following the eternal norm, interprets life in his own way: he is the exegete.[28] (A84)

Skillfully and masterfully applying these ideas in *Sonata de otoño*, Valle-Inclán created for himself a singular style that made him the exemplary prose writer of the movement. On par with the poetry of Darío stands the prose of Valle-Inclán. *Sonata de otoño* was only one of the early works that enhanced Valle-Inclán's position not only among his contemporaries but also for the generations to follow.

In 1902 other works by Valle-Inclán were published that brought him increasing recognition. There was a total of sixteen stories and three articles,[29] among them refurbished stories such as "A media noche" and "Tierra Caliente. Los tiburones,"[30] this last being a version of "La Niña Chole." And in addition to his own works, Valle-Inclán had published several translations commissioned by different houses. From the French he did a version of a novel, entitled in Spanish *Las chicas del amigo Lefèvre*, by Paul Alexis, who had died in 1901.[31] From the Portuguese he translated a novel, entitled in Spanish *La reliquia*, by Eça de Queiroz.[32]

In November 1902 Valle-Inclán again submitted to the pressures of a literary contest. He entered "¡Malpocado!" to be judged by the panel convened under the auspices of *El Liberal*. The judges, including Eugenio Sellés, José Nogales, and Echegaray, could not agree unanimously on granting the first prize to Valle-Inclán's entry, and it was consequently given the second prize of two hundred and fifty pesetas. The first prize was not awarded at all.

I triumphed with my story "¡Malpocado!" but a great mixup resulted . . . over the absurd decision of the jury, which gave the story I entered and which had won first prize, half of the amount advertised . . . It should be noted that I won in a contest in which there were over seventeen hundred entries.[33] (A85)

While Valle-Inclán's interpretation may seem one-sided, he could consider his story the winner, which indeed it was, since the first prize was not awarded. As he had done in the earlier contest, Valera again protested the underhanded treatment of Valle-Inclán, as did Juan Ramón Jiménez.[34] Although there was no rectification of the inequity, the story was published in *El Liberal*. Ironically, the loss of the first prize created enough controversy that Valle-Inclán's literary prestige increased rather than diminished; with the publication of the story he gained added stature.[35]

Partly because of Echegaray's participation in both juries that denied him first prize in the contests run by *El Liberal*, partly because Valle-Inclán could not accept Echegaray's theories of writing, partly because of the public's adulation of that author, which he saw as unwarranted, Valle-Inclán became the sworn enemy of Echegaray and his ilk. Earlier, he had expressed an admiration for the popular dramatist:

The journey to Marín—which I made a few days ago to visit the renowned author of *El Gran Galeoto*—is what in a popular and somewhat hackneyed phrase is said to be charming. . . . I don't recall another author who, seen in person, is less in accord with his works. While the maestro spoke, I listened in awe, unable to comprehend how such an amiable and affectionate man—who seems so set against bloodshed and in whom mildness appears to be the principal trait—could be the forger of the most sorrowful, bloody encounters, as well as the most tragic passionate conflicts. This, in my opinion, is the most obvious proof of the artist that Echegaray is when it comes to feelings. His is a privileged, multiple nature that knows how to indulge in auto-suggestion at will and evoke in himself the most distinct and contradictory personalities, which, through the phenomenon of *psychic polarization* and the very power of what is known as *the law of contrasts*, tend to be as dissimilar as possible from the normal personality of the poet.[36] (A86)

Under the circumstances and according to his own sense of aesthetics, Valle-Inclán now found Echegaray wanting. Youthful admiration became passionate hatred. He never missed an opportunity to attack his adversary vocally, as various anecdotes demonstrate.[37] Seeing Echegaray exit from the Ateneo, for example, Valle-Inclán referred to him as "a bit of a brute." When one of Echegaray's admirers told Valle to retract the statement, he replied, "Well, I'll only retract the word 'bit.'" On another occasion, addressing a letter to Nilo Fabra who lived on Calle de Echegaray, Valle-Inclán wrote on the envelope, "Calle del Viejo Idiota, 16" ("Street of the Old Idiot, 16"), and marveled at the intelligence of the postman who delivered the letter. On yet another occasion, he said, "That Don José is obsessed with marital infidelity. All his dramas are autobiographies of a deceived husband." Hearing Valle-Inclán attack Echegaray, a young man ordered him to stop, declaring himself to be the son of the defamed, to which Valle-Inclán replied, "Are you certain, young man?"

More than the man he was attacking the writer. In this attitude he was supported by his own generation of artists who saw in the public and critical acceptance, even deification, of Echegaray the hypocrisy that characterized contemporary Spain. Echegaray, greatly revered in his own day, has today fallen to near anonymity. The judgment of Valle-Inclán has been seconded.

From 1902 on, Valle-Inclán's literary output increased steadily, fostered by the recognition he was finally receiving and by the subsequent improvement of his economic situation. The contract with the Barcelona publisher Maucci brought a welcome income. The prize money from *El Liberal* and the small but constant sales of *Sonata de otoño* also contributed to his income, as did the publication of his stories in newspapers. These tithes paid by a small sector of society permitted the author to live with less pressure than in previous periods of privation, when he had been forced to fast. His current income allowed Valle-Inclán to move to the Hotel Pastor in 1903, where life was more comfortable though no less humble.

In 1903 the evening *tertulias* began to meet at the Nuevo Café de Levante, situated on Calle del Arenal, near Puerta del Sol, the hub of Madrid. Valle-Inclán was the dominant figure of the gatherings, which continued until the closing of the café after the outbreak of hostilities in Europe. Throughout these many years the *tertulia* changed in character as it drew groups with specific leanings or interests. At first, it was largely a center for writers. Framed by the classical strains of Abelardo Covino's violin and the piano artistry of Enguita, a group of men, including Luis Bello, Pío Baroja, Martínez Ruiz, Benavente, Ricardo Baroja, Manuel and Antonio Machado, Alejandro Sawa, Nogales, Candamo, Urbano, Bargiela, Palomero, Ciro Bayo, "Silverio Lanza," Villaespesa, among others, met and conversed. Foreign writers often attended the sessions when they visited Madrid; among them were Darío, Paul Schmitz, Jacques Chaumié, Amado Nervo, and Santos Chocano. But in time the reunion became more the haven of painters, sculptors, and caricaturists, as well as an occasional architect, who found in Valle-Inclán's aesthetics the principles they sought.

Around him gathered a vast group of artists that included Ricardo Baroja, Pablo Ruiz Picasso, Anselmo Miguel Nieto, Antonio Vivanco, Victorio Macho, Darío de Regoyos, José Moya del Pino, Ricardo Marín, José Gutiérrez Solana, Francisco Sancha, Ignacio Zuloaga, Aurelio Arteta, Juan de Echevarría, Julio Romero de Torres, Sebastián Miranda, Rafael de Penagos, and Santiago Rusiñol; they, too, were joined by visiting foreign artists, among them Henri Matisse and Diego Rivera. It was the Valle-Inclán of these gatherings that Villaespesa captured in a celebrated poem.[38] The most emphatic acknowledgment of Valle-Inclán's extensive influence over the artists of his time came from Moya del Pino,[39] while Ricardo Baroja has written a fine analysis of the meetings at the Levante.[40] Valle-Inclán himself made frequent reference to the *tertulias* and to their importance in the nation's cultural life:

The Café de Levante has had a greater influence on contemporary Art and Literature than several Universities and Academies.[41] (A87)

The reason the *tertulias* were so influential was Valle-Inclán. His sympathy was with the struggling artists, no matter what their medium. Having experienced rejection at the hands of the powerful, he could comprehend the difficulties faced by painters and sculptors in their attempts to breach the conservatism prevalent among juries. Valle-Inclán read the names of the panel for one exposition and exclaimed:

. . . it reads like a racing form . . . Two or three well-known names and then one could write, as of those lists, "four or five other animals will also take part."[42] (A88)

Besides the cynicism was the insight. Through his pronouncements he opened doors and established guidelines. His words are memorable, now as then:

Art is a game—the supreme game—and its norms are dictated by numerical chance, wherein resides its peculiar charm. Fourteen verses are said to make a sonnet. Art is, therefore, form.[43]

Art requires waiting. One could be waiting an entire lifetime only to achieve one's farewell verse, a sincere and simple goodbye.[44]

Art is always an abstraction. If my gatekeeper and I see the same thing, she doesn't know what she has seen because she lacks prior knowledge.[45]

In art, when one is not a genius, it is best to imitate the populace.[46]

Art is asking heaven for alms at the church door.[47]

Paintings should be viewed by looking down at them so that the subject doesn't infringe on the perception of color itself.[48]

Art never ends, and it is endless because art is useful in getting through Winter, since art is always Spring.[49] (A89)

Valle-Inclán could speak authoritatively. His concern with aesthetics is evident throughout the body of his work, both in content and in physical appearance. His conception is essentially sensual, and consequently word (with its form, sound, and musicality) and color (with its hue, light, and tonality) are fundamental to the structure of his works. Word and color are interrelated on two planes. The first—outward style—manifests the intimacy of audial and visual recourses:

There are poets who dream of giving their stanzas the rhythm of dance, the melody of music, and the majesty of sculpture. Théophile Gautier, author of *Symphonie en blanc majeur*, affirms in his preface to *Les fleurs du mal* that Tertulian's style has the black splendor of ebony. According to Gautier, through sound, words attain a value that dictionaries cannot determine. Through sound some words are like diamonds, others are phosphorescent, others float like fog. When Gautier speaks of Baudelaire, he says that he knew how to capture in his stanzas the vague tonality that stands indecisively between sound and color; those thoughts that resemble arabesque motifs and themes from musical phrases. Baudelaire himself says that his soul rejoices with perfumes, as other souls with music. For this poet, aromas are equated not only to sound but to color: "Il est des parfums frais comme des chairs d'enfants, Douces comme les haut bois, verts comme les prairies" (It is from perfume fresh like the skin of infants, mellow like the oboe, green like the meadows). But if Baudelaire speaks of green perfumes, Carducci has called the silence green, and Gabriel D'Annunzio has stated in beautiful rhythm: "Canta la nota verde d'un bel limone in fiore" (The green note of a beautiful lemon in flower sings out). There are those who consider all such images as extravagant, when, in reality, they are nothing more than the logical consequence of the progressive evolution of the senses. Today, we perceive gradations of color, gradations of sound, and distant relationships among things which certainly were not perceived by our ancestors hundreds of years ago. Primitive languages seldom possess words to convey the concept of color. In Basque, the hair of certain cows and the color of the sky are indicated with the same word: "Artuña." And it is well-known that a dearth of words is always the result of a paucity of sensations. Today, there are artists who endeavor to find a strange correspondence between sound and color. One of these was the great poet Artur Rimbaud, who defined the colors of vowels in a celebrated sonnet: "A— noir, E—bleu, I—rouge, U—vert, O—jaune" (A—black, E—blue, I—red, U—green, O—yellow). More recently, Renato Ghil, in another sonnet, assigns the vowels not only color but also orchestral values: "A. claironne vainquer en rouge flamboiement" (A. victorious clarion call in flamboyant red). This analogy and equivalency of sensations is what constitutes Modernism in literature. Its origin should be sought in the progressive development of the senses, which tend to multiply their different perceptions and make correspondences among them, thus forming a single sense, as they did in Baudelaire:

Oh! Mystical metamorphosis
of all my senses blended into one:
its breath makes music,
as its voice makes perfume.[50] (A90)

The second plane—conceptual attitude—establishes an interplay of masses of color as the prerequisite to literary activity. Accordingly, creative intuition begins with abstracted pigmentation aswirl before the mind's eye in suggestive kinesis. Slowly, or at least at a fitting pace, there is an evolution from fluidity toward definition. As this occurs, the composition of colors achieves greater precision and poignancy; the improved focus permits shades, hues, and tints to become visible. Ultimately, the panorama is identifiable as character, plot, setting, mood. The association of word with color, making the first subservient to the latter, takes place at this stage. Word transmits the painterly view to the canvas of the page. Vision becomes visible, audible when read aloud.

Through ideas such as these Valle-Inclán captured the intellects of his listeners and influenced their artistic techniques. Thus, he helped forge a broad aesthetic foundation for the art of his and subsequent generations. The painters and writers who participated in the discussions he led recognized the genius of Valle-Inclán and did not let his words go unheeded. This, in a sense, was the most important of his recognitions.[51]

6 Continuation

Spurred by the recognition of the previous year, Valle-Inclán continued to publish at a feverish pace in 1903. *El Globo*, where Martínez Ruiz was an editor, published several of his articles, for each of which he received fifty pesetas. Other articles appeared in *El Liberal* and *Album Americano*, [1] while "Antes que te cases," based on "La Generala" from *Femeninas*, was anthologized, leading a long list of stories.[2] Dissatisfaction with his first two books led to the preparation of new editions of his tales under different titles and revised style. But the motivation to publish was also founded on his precarious economic situation. During this period he was living in a garret on Calle de la Visitación, near the Teatro Español, suffering such privation that he had to resort to using newspapers for bed cover as protection against the Madrid cold. Nonetheless, he considered his art superior to the physical comfort that payment for his work could assure, as is shown in his reply to a publisher who offered a substantial amount if Valle-Inclán would permit the "adaptation" of four texts previously issued:

Did I hear you correctly? . . . Reduce it, cut forty-eight pages from my works? . . . Do you know what you're saying? Cutting, mutilating solely for the purpose of having a book in a size that pleases you! No! No! That's the end of it, sir! Please leave immediately! . . . I'd die of hunger before I'd mutilate a single page on a publisher's whim![3] (A91)

Particularly in this part of his literary career the author imposed rigid standards on his work belying the apparent facility his numerous publications demonstrated.

Jardín umbrío was one of the new collections of stories.[4] In it were "¡Malpocado!" "El miedo," "El rey de la máscara," "Un cabecilla," and "Tragedia de ensueño." All but the last had been published earlier. "Tragedia de ensueño," a prose piece in dialogue form, had marked dramatic leanings that made it the first original work since *Cenizas* (1899) to be conceived

71

dramatically. Its importance, of course, stems from the indication it gives of Valle-Inclán's reconsideration of dialogue as a form of expression. From this slight exercise the dramatist would again emerge slowly and in time create an impressive drama.

Corte de amor. Florilegio de honestas y nobles damas was a second collection of stories in the modernistic vein.[5] In it, too, Valle-Inclán revised some earlier writings. *Epitalamio* found new vitality, both in plot and character development, as "Augusta," while the controversial "Satanás" reappeared as "Beatriz;" the other two tales in the new book were "Rosita" and "Eulalia." The book was well received, as the review by Juan Ramón Jiménez makes clear.[6]

Despite the hectic pace of his literary life, Valle-Inclán always had time to honor the achievements of his colleagues. One such occasion was a banquet given that year for Enrique Gómez Carrillo, the journalist. Not a formal or expensive affair (the price was three and a half pesetas), it was held at the Buena Vista Café. It was a typical gathering of friends celebrating the accomplishments of one of their own. Among the numerous celebrants were Melchor Almagro, Antonio de Hoyos y Vinent, Azorín, Ramón Pérez de Ayala, Antonio Palomero, Mesa, Luis de Tapía, and Benito Pérez Galdós.[7]

Another gesture by Valle-Inclán toward a friend was in his prologue to *Sombras de vida* by Melchor Almagro, published in 1903.[8] Based on an article that Valle-Inclán had published earlier,[9] the prologue gave new insights into its author's view of style and content in contemporary writing:

All his pages possess an intangible, joyous palpitation of life, a springlike sprightliness, a charming welling up of antiquated images, at once ingenuous, daring, stunning. I confess my love for such books when I find exuberance and emotion in them. I love them as much as I detest that other literature, sanctimonious and prudent, by some ancient young writers who never learned how to join two words for the first time. . . . Sheltered in the glorious tradition of the seventeenth century, they judge themselves to be great solely because they imitate the great, presuming that they have accomplished what the divine Lope and the very human Cervantes did. When some youthful spirits seek new orientations, they turn themselves inside out invoking rancid, sterile precepts. Incapable of understanding that life and art consist of eternal renovation, they hold as heretical all that has not been consecrated by three centuries of routine. . . . This shouldn't be taken to mean that I promote the disappearance and death of classical literature, or the bonfire for its immortal books; not at all. They have been my mentors so often that I revere them as if they were noble ancient progenitors. I always study them and try to imitate them, but to this moment it hasn't occurred to me to hold them as inviolable and infallible.[10] (A92)

Such criticism was not gratuitous; that Valle-Inclán felt deeply about these concerns is evident in his social and creative lives. His own work of this period bears out his commitment to the aesthetic premises he promoted in this prologue. This is very obvious in his most important publication of the year: *Sonata de estío. Memorias del Marqués de Bradomín*. The novel entered the public lists first in a serialized version and subsequently as a book.[11] Second in publication as well as in the series depicting the seasons in the romantic life of the protagonist, the novel places Bradomín in Mexico where La Niña Chole weaves the web of love enmeshing him. This novel possesses a rare vibrancy and color. The tropical atmosphere creates an exoticism not found in the rest of the series; the ambient, too, becomes a protagonist, although not in the sense of *La Vorágine* (The Vortex) and other works of that nature. Instead, the setting becomes poetic and unforgettable, both to the Marqués and to the reader.

The popular acceptance of the new *Sonata*, perhaps due to its salacious subject matter, might have distracted another author and brought him to the world of *folletines*. Valle-Inclán, however, subjugated his subject matter to his aesthetic goal and, consequently, could not subject his work to the lower requisites of the popular novel. Among critics who recognized the author's intent and its execution were José Ortega y Gasset, then a young essayist writing his first articles. His analysis of *Sonata de estío* contains many appreciative remarks concerning the author's accomplishments, founded on recognition of Valle-Inclán's historicity, aesthetic sense, literary technique, and character.[12] But Ortega also points out what he considers a failure—Valle-Inclán's modernistic leanings.[13] He concludes by envisioning some future work wherein Valle-Inclán would rid himself of decoration and other deficiencies.[14] But Ortega himself came to realize that art was headed toward separation of the author's reality from the reality of his characters, as the publication of his *La deshumanización del arte* (The Dehumanization of Art, 1925) made evident. What he did not realize in 1904 was the precursory nature of Valle-Inclán's work.

In that year Valle-Inclán was publishing stories and serialized novels in a variety of periodicals in rapid sequence.[15] He was also under contract to the Barcelona publisher Maucci to provide the prologue to a book on a theme of Galician folklore and to translate Eça de Queiroz's two-volume novel *El primo Basilio*.[16]

Two important novels of his own were published in 1904. *Flor de santidad. Historia milenaria*[17] was the completion of *Adega*, whose first installments had appeared in *Revista Nueva* in 1899. Likewise, the novel incorporated the prize-winning story "¡Malpocado!"[18] (with variants) into its powerful plot played against the mountainous landscape of Galicia. In the mind of the country-girl protagonist, a deep sense of piety is transformed into sensuality when, convinced that the pilgrim before her is Christ, she gives herself to him in mystical abandon. Through the physical result of her action, Adega sees herself as the mother of Christ's son. Holy enthusiasm urges her to divulge the tale and reveal her pregnancy to the superstitious folk around her. Yet, in the end, pregnant and deserted, she permits herself to be exorcised in a Mass for the possessed and to be led naked to the seven waves of the sea required to cleanse her soul. Unlike the raving women who accompany her through these unsavory proceedings, Adega remains calm and pensive. The holy visions following her sexual initiation, along with a Messianic hope she harbors in her deepest recesses, sustain her and make her rise above social convention. Led by ignorance to accept a common physical act as divinely instigated, Adega acquires an unshakeable, if mistaken, faith. Her devotion makes her heroic; she inspires less pity than sympathy or even admiration, as evidenced in the sonnet dedicated by Antonio Machado to the novel.[19]

The second novel was *Sonata de primavera*, first in the sequence of the *Memorias del Marqués de Bradomín*. The author places the protagonist in Italy and installs him in the magnificent *palazzo* Gaetani where, as in *Sonata de otoño*, interiors provide an important aspect of the atmosphere required by the plot.[20] Such concern with decor and furnishings demonstrate yet another facet of Valle-Inclán's artistry.[21] The man who could not afford more than basic furniture of nondescript style in his own dwelling expressed his ideals through the artist and found satisfaction in the knowledge that his concepts were influential.

Sonata de primavera delineates the virile voluptuosity of the young Bradomín, a Papal knight with the mission of conferring the cardinal's biretta on Estefano Gaetani, Bishop of Betulia. To that end he journeys to the Gaetani palace, only to find the old cleric at death's door. Bradomín remains at the side of the bereaved princess, the bishop's sister, on his demise. But his thoughts are only on María Rosario, one of the five daughters of the princess. He is drawn to her by her beauty, but his desire of her goes beyond the physical. With satanic purpose he seeks to snatch from the grasp of God the girl who is about to enter the convent. Bradomín begins his systematic seduction with words spoken into her ear and an attempt to kiss her hand. But the virginal María Rosario resists, although the torture of love is evident on her face and in her nervous hands. Driven by his passion, Bradomín enters her room through a window; yet when she faints he does no more than place her on the bed and contemplate her innocent figure. The harmless but rash act of breaching her bedchamber causes complications in the household, and those within it react with severity, attempting to employ witchcraft to cause Bradomín's death. Bradomín scoffs and continues his game of seduction. In a final attempt to convert María Rosario to his pagan love he fails only because fate decrees the accidental death of her younger sister, left unattended because of Bradomín's overtures. María Rosario, already half-mad with the fever of denied passion, turns crazedly on her adversary. Blaming him for the girl's death, she shouts incessantly, "¡Fué Satanás!" (It was Satan!). Bradomín departs with great sadness. He has seduced not the body of María Rosario but her mind. And she will remain always before him to torture his imagination with might-have-beens and to condemn his heart to remorse.

Sonata de primavera contains echoes of Gabriel d'Annunzio's *La vergini delle rocce* (The Virgin of the Rocks)[22] and Gian Giacomo Casanova's *Mémoires*.[23] In each case Valle-Inclán has adapted a situation or scene for his own novel. But the author did not view his action as plagiarism; he chose to explain it in terms that today we would define as intertextuality and see as valid:

> The major difficulty in my historical narratives lies in grafting documents and episodes from the period. When the plot permits the introduction of a phrase, a poem, a song, or some writing from the time of the action, I know that all goes well. That usually occurs in all literary works. When I wrote *Sonata de primavera*, whose setting is Italy, I embedded a Roman episode of Casanova to convince myself that the atmosphere of the work was suitable and that everything was following the proper path. The episode fit perfectly into my narrative. Shakespeare has his Coriolanus utter speeches and sentences taken from historians of antiquity; his tragedy is admirable because, rather than reject those texts, it demands their inclusion. Add speeches and documents of the period to any of those historical dramas presented nowadays and you'll see how well it suits them.[24](A93)

Such a statement verifies what his works reveal: a primary concern with sensation and a lesser involvement with plot, the latter being the vehicle for the former. For this reason, Valle-Inclán can employ derivative material without the stigma of plagiarism; such material furthers an aesthetic end, not a story line.

The last of the *Memorias del Marqués de Bradomín, Sonata de invierno*, appeared in 1905[25] with the dedication, "Para unos ojos tristes y aterciopelados," (For a Pair of Eyes That Are Sad and Velvety) which was probably meant for the actress Josefina Blanco. The novel, which depicts the final season in the romantic life of Bradomín, is set in the Basque and Navarre regions of Spain, particularly in the court of Don Carlos VII, the Carlist pretender to the Spanish throne. Bradomín, now grown old, begins his narrative with a plaintive recognition of his state. All the women he has loved have preceded him to death, and he is alone. He finds, ironically, that having loved many and often he has entered old age without love. His eyes fill with tears as he combs white hair that was once the proud mane of the romantic lion.

Against the background of the Carlist conflagration Bradomín fights his last battle with characteristic bravado. But, as if to herald the end of his adventurous career, a musket ball smashes into his left arm. At a nearby convent he watches clinically as the arm is amputated and finds in the loss a possible gain: the advantage of sympathy. Testing what he terms a new attitude toward women, Bradomín begins the seduction of the young girl caring for him in the convent. Slowly, he comes to suspect that she is his daughter by an early afffair, but this does not deter him; the possibility of an incestuous relationship adds spice to his imagination, especially when it appears to be his last opportunity for love. His words disrupt the serenity of the inexperienced but fascinated girl. He extracts words of love from her, but the girl, shaken by the ordeal, flees to her convent cell. She "confesses" to the Mother Superior, who then faces Bradomín with accusations and reprimands. She orders him to leave the convent he has desecrated with his pagan words and desires. He leaves it as he has so many other places. But now he lacks the knowledge that other intrigues await him; alone, old, and without his left arm, he attempts to find solace in a reunion with the girl's mother. But circumstance prohibits even that satisfaction. Defeated but heroic in his acceptance of fate, Bradomín sets out from the court city of Estella. He knows that he has become old and pitiable; he knows that his only future lies in recalling his past through the compilation of his memoirs.

The rapid succession of the *Sonatas* did not prevent Valle-Inclán from other literary endeavors. Stories were issued in 1905 as well, typically in many different periodicals,[26] and in *Jardín novelesco. Historias de santos, de almas en pena, de duendes y ladrones* (Novelesque Garden. Tales of Saints, Souls in Purgatory, Goblins, and Thieves).[27] This collection of stories enlarged the contents of *Jardín umbrío* with nine additional titles: "La adoración de los Reyes," "La misa de San Electus," "Don Juan Manuel," "Un ejemplo," "Del misterio," "A media noche," "Nochebuena," "Geórgicas," and "Comedia de ensueño," a dialogue piece similar to "Tragedia de ensueño" in dramatic tendency. The year 1905, the tercentenary of the publication of *Don Quijote*[28] brought with it many studies on Cervantes and on the masterpiece he created. Valle-Inclán did not contribute to this growing volume of books and articles. He chose to remain silent at this time, although any contribution he would have made would have been remunerative. Valle-Inclán shunned the obvious. Perhaps, too, he felt that commentaries on such occasions should be made by critics and not by creative writers. When he did speak, on his own terms, his words were precise and unequivocal:

The *Quijote* is an admirable example of the reaction of society, of a people, in the face of a fact, in the face of the divine madness of "The Lord of the wretched"; it is a reaction of mockery and disdain, of deceit and laughter. It is a picaresque reaction. It is hard to find in the book's pages some compensation, some tenderness for the idealism of the knight. Spain is not a nation of Quijotes because Don Quijote was defeated. That cannot be his country because in it—on its soil, among its people— the desire for justice and love innate in the *hidalgo* from La Mancha did not take root. No, the Spaniard is not Don Quijote, not even Sancho, who sometimes demonstrates an affectionate piety toward the dreams and adventures of his lord. The Spaniard is Ginesillo de Pasamonte, he is the galley slaves.[29] (A94)

Other and varied attitudes toward Cervantes and his novels are dispersed throughout works as diverse as the plays of the *Comedias bárbaras, La cabeza del dragón,* and such *Esperpentos* as *Los cuernos de don Friolera,* as well as the novel *La corte de los milagros.* His felicitous use of masses of beggars and other folk types reflects his apprenticeship in the *Novelas ejemplares* (Exemplary Novels) as well. Obviously, therefore, in spite of his silence during the tercentenary, Valle-Inclán participated in the spirit of Cervantes through the creativity conveyed by his works.

When the cause demanded, Valle-Inclán could be as active as the next individual. One such situation arose in regard to José Echegaray. The famed dramatist and academician had been awarded the Nobel Prize for Literature in 1904, along with Frédéric Mistral, the Provençal philologist and author of the epic poem "Miréio." Following the successful production of Echegaray's *A fuerza de arrastrarse* (By Dint of Will) in 1905, the newspaper *Gente Vieja* and the Sociedad de Escritores y Artistas promoted a national tribute to the dramatist. There was an attempt to unite the leading intellectuals in unanimous accord, but the younger generation, opposed to the hypocrisy, artlessness, and oratory Echegaray represented, took a firm stand against this inclusion, even by inference, in the tribute. Azorín, who had been attacking Echegaray's drama for several years in his columns, instigated the rebellion with a series of articles under the heading "El homenaje a Echegaray," which appeared in *España.*[30]

Azorín was the key to the attack as well as the intermediary for the group sharing his views.[31] Valle-Inclán wrote the formal protest:

Part of the Press has initiated the idea of a tribute to Don José Echegaray, and the representation of the entire intellectual community is abrogated. We, who are rightly included in that community—no need to discuss here the literary personality of Don José Echegaray—make it known that our artistic ideals are quite distinct and what we admire very different.[32] (A95)

The simple but implicatory statement was given efficacy by the long list of signatures collected. The first signature was that of Azorín; it was followed by the signatures of all the members of the "Generación del '98" except Benavente, who refused to participate in the protest. Thereafter came a list of Madrid theatre critics: Antonio Palomero (*La Lectura*), Luis París (*El Heraldo*), Ricardo Catarineu (*La Correspondencia*), and Angel Guerra (*El Globo*); also included was José Nogales (*Vida Española*—Buenos Aires). Among other prominent names were Rubén Darío, Luis Bello, Manuel Machado, Rafael Urbano, Manuel Ciges Aparicio, Jacinto Grau, Francisco Camba, Francisco Villaespesa, Enrique Diez Canedo, José María Salaverría, Bernardo G. de Candamo, Melchor Almagro, Pedro González Blanco, Francisco Grandmontagne, Pedro Mata, and Enrique Gómez Carrillo. These were joined by Antonio de Zayas, Emilio H. del Villa, Nilo Fabra, J.

López del Castillo, Félix Méndez, Enrique Rivas, Miquel Avellac, J. Flóres de Lemus, A. Alvarez Insúa, Luis de Tapía, Irineo Coca, Manuel Carretero, Joaquín López Barbadillo, Miguel A. Ródenas, J. Sánchez Díaz, Pedro de Répide, José Prieto, Isaac Muñoz Llorente, Juan Torrendell, Antonio Zazaya, Enrique de Mesa, Constantino Román Salamero, and Antonio Viérgol. Also notable by his refusal to sign was Joaquín Dicenta, who later criticized Azorín in the pages of *El Liberal*, creating a minor literary controversy.

Life in the café also had its continuity. Besides being a marketplace for ideas the café provided a social contact not possible elsewhere. It was a man's world where words were not minced. However, on occasion, women penetrated the inner sanctum. One woman who frequently availed herself of the privilege around 1905 was a beautiful model named Dora. Her attractiveness and worldliness merited the attentions of the entire group; but Dora was not satisfied with propositions. Her burning passion was for service in a domestic capacity to the artists she befriended. She began to frequent Valle-Inclán's apartment in order to cook, clean, and wash for him. Thinking her interest sexual, Valle-Inclán made intimate proposals. Her indignation was accepted at first as the female prerogative, but in time the two argued. Dora did not return again. Seeing her on the street one day afterward, Valle-Inclán found revenge for her disdain by shouting, "¡Mendiga indecente, que me has robado los cubiertos de plata que yo tenía en casa!" (Indecent beggar, you've stolen the silver utensils I had at home!).[33]

Through the café Valle-Inclán was involved in a situation of a more serious nature. On 31 May 1906 Alfonso XIII married Victoria Eugenia of Battenburg, niece of Edward VII of England, who had given his consent during Alfonso's visit to London in 1905. The Spain of that period viewed the marriage with mixed feelings; to some it was a welcome step reflecting the re-entry of the nation into international affairs, but to others it signified a hateful strengthening of the monarchy, with its unequivocal design against regional autonomy. Since the region of Cataluña was the most fierce in its nationalism, it was no surprise that the perpetrator of an attempted assassination of the royal couple during the nuptial festivities should be identified as a native of that area. Mateo Morral, the anarchist who threw the bomb at the ceremonial coach, did not achieve his end and fled with the Guardia Civil in close pursuit. With the certainty of imprisonment and execution before him, the fanatical youth committed suicide in Campos de Torrejón de Ardoz. Ironically, the body was identified not by political cronies but by Valle-Inclán and Ricardo Baroja, who had met the regicidal Catalan during the *tertulias* at the Horchatería de Candelas. Valle-Inclán would remember him in the candid portrait of the Catalan anarchist Mateo who shares a cell with Máximo Estrella, the protagonist of *Luces de bohemia*, while Pío Baroja would use him as the model for the anarchist Brull in *La dama errante* (The Errant Lady).

The royal wedding also provided the setting for another *entreacto* in which Valle-Inclán was involved—the romance between Anita Delgado, a fifteen-year-old dancer, and the Maharajah of Kapurthala, ruler of the Punjab state in India, who had come to Madrid to attend the ceremonies. Anita and her sister Victoria, billed as "Las Camelias," were among the supporting acts for stars such as La Argentina and Mata-Hari at the Central Kursaal, a music hall converted nightly from a ball court. The potentate fell in love with the young Anita and pleaded his cause through emissaries who offered the girl and her parents riches beyond their dreams. The painter Leandro Oroz, who knew French, acted as interpreter to the family and as informant to his colleagues at the Café Levante. The Maharajah's infatuation caught the fancy of Valle-Inclán and his group, and after much indecision Anita and her family placed the matter in the hands of Valle-Inclán, who, from the tables at the café, prepared a letter to the Maharajah in which the terms of Anita's capitulation were dictated in beautiful language.[34] The result, shortly thereafter, was further correspondence from Paris, where the potentate was staying before returning to England, indicating acceptance of Anita's demands of marriage. After two more letters written by Valle-Inclán, the details were clarified, and Anita set out for Paris in the company of Leandro Oroz and her mother. The romantic adventure had been successfully completed and Valle-Inclán, ever the dreamer, asked Anita to intervene on his behalf with her husband-to-be for a decoration with the right to wear a uniform.[35]

Valle-Inclán's involvement in the celebrated romance was not atypical. Love, which in its many facets forms the core of the author's work, was not alien to the man. Early in his life he had felt a strong attraction to the daughter of a prominent family from Santiago de Compostela and had courted her while he was a student at the university. She eventually rejected him in favor of his friend and fellow-student Augusto González Besada.[36] This turn of events was later crystallized in Valle-Inclán's statement:

I had hardly reached that age called youth when, as the result of a love gone awry, I embarked for Mexico . . . [37] (A96)

While the veracity of this revelation has been tainted by its use in *Sonata de estío* with reference to Bradomín, the real-life occurrence presents a good basis for its acceptance.

As is frequently the case, such rejections lead to wariness or even disentanglement. One or both attitudes must have been adopted by Valle-Inclán because his life does not disclose other youthful amatory concerns.

Instead, the sensitive young man transferred his romantic inclinations to visions fulfilled in the writer's work. The mask he was creating camouflaged his sentiments effectively. Love became a metaphor.

His defensiveness evidently decreased over the years. The process began when, prior to the loss of his arm, he had met Josefina Blanco, a young actress, in the theatrical circle of Ceferino Palencia and María Tubáu.[38] The process continued when they acted together in Benavente's *La comida de las fieras*. Over the years, and especially during the rehearsals of Valle-Inclán's play *El Marqués de Bradomín*, which the Francisco García Ortega—Matilde Moreno company premiered at the Teatro de la Princesa on 25 January 1906, the courtship became serious.

Relations with writers of his generation or with other generations, from Spain or abroad, were another important facet of Valle-Inclán's life. He maintained correspondence with many of them, but one with whom he frequently exchanged letters, particularly on matters pertaining to the theatre, was Benito Pérez Galdós. He had written to him in 1898 about his own ambitions as an actor and again in 1904 regarding the version of Galdós's *Marianela* that he had agreed to do. Now he wrote on behalf of a new friend, the Mexican Modernist poet Amado Nervo, who had come to Madrid in 1905 to take up a diplomatic post:

Dear Don Benito:
    If you're at home at two o'clock, I'll stop by with the secretary of the Mexican legation, the poet Armando Nervo, who would like to meet you.
      As ever your affectionate friend,
      Valle-Inclán[39] (A97)

Undoubtedly, Nervo had been introduced to Valle-Inclán by Rubén Darío, either in person or through a letter. Valle-Inclán's ongoing friendship with the great Nicaraguan poet was again evident in the dedication of the second edition of *Sonata de estío*: "A Rubén Darío: Con toda mi admiración y mi amistad" (To Rubén Darío: With my full admiration and friendship).[40] It was a way of acknowledging Darío's own gift of the "Soneto autumnal para el señor marqués de Bradomín," written in Paris on the publication of *Sonata de otoño* in 1902.

When Josefina joined the company of Ricardo Calvo as an actress and Valle-Inclán became its artistic director, he wrote again to Galdós while on tour:

Granada, 30–10–1906
Dear Don Benito:
    I came to say goodbye before leaving Madrid but you were out.
    We're rehearsing *Alma y Vida*, which will premiere on Sunday. Josefina and Ricardo Calvo are very good as the protagonists. The others are also compatible, and they'll all be costumed rather suitably since I had the outfits made to order according to designs *I drew*.

The set, on the other hand, is not coming along well; having just started, I haven't been able to have it painted. It would be wonderful to use the original set for the production in Las Palmas if you could arrange for us to rent it.

I'm close to finishing *Marianela*.

You'll be kept up to date by your affectionate and admiring friend,

Valle-Inclán.

Address: Cervantes Theatre—Granada.[41] (A98)

The following day, Valle-Inclán wrote again to Galdós, this time on a postcard, about a problem regarding the play:

To Don Benito Pérez Galdós.
Paseo de Areneros, 46. Madrid.
Teatro Cervantes. Granada.
Dear Don Benito:

Some of the pages from the prompt book of *Alma y Vida* have disappeared and I would appreciate it if you could send another.

Ever your affectionate friend,

Valle-Inclán.[42] (A99)

Valle-Inclán and Josefina had left Madrid for an extended tour with the Calvo troupe. After the production of Pérez Galdós's *Alma y Vida* in Granada, the company accepted an invitation from the theatre group "Los Doce" to produce the play in the Canary Islands. At a banquet in Las Palmas in January 1907, where Valle-Inclán spoke as the guest of honor, Josefina Blanco presented a monologue titled "Fea" and Ricardo Calvo recited a piece by Zorrilla.[43] Returning to the Iberian Peninsula, the troupe ended its tour in Barcelona, where Valle-Inclán published a translation of an Italian novel, *Flor de pasión* (Passion Flower) by Matilde Serao, the collection of stories titled *Historias perversas* (Perverse Tales), and the first play of the *Comedias bárbaras*, *Aguila de blasón*.[44] There is a letter to Rubén Darío, dated 6 February 1907, and sent from Barcelona, in which he casually mentions his marriage:

Dear Rubén:

Some time ago I learned through *El Imparcial* that you were in Mallorca, but I didn't have the exact address until this moment. I wanted very much to hear about you and to tell you something of my life. First of all, I must tell you that I got married and that I've been away from Madrid for six months. I've had no word about the people there and, truthfully, I don't regret it. What of your life? When will you give us the gift of new poems? I'll be in Barcelona until the middle of March . . .[45] (A100)

All records show 1907 as the year for Valle-Inclán's marriage. Since Valle-Inclán states in the letter that he is married and the facts show that the ceremony took place in the capital, from which he had departed six months earlier, the wedding would appear to have been in 1906. Perhaps the statement in the letter to Darío means that Valle-Inclán and Josefina had been living together since 1906 or that they were married on board ship during the trip to the Canary Islands. In point of fact, the only marriage of record took place on 24 August 1907 at a ceremony officiated by the Reverend Andrés María Mayor at Madrid's Iglesia de San Sabastián, Capilla de Nuestra Señora del Carmen,[46] where a modern plaque lists Valle-Inclán among the prominent individuals married there. It is possible they were married by the Church in 1907 in order to give the children that would be born a proper start. Luiz Ruiz Contreras, who had fomented the marriage as a stabilizing factor in the life of Valle-Inclán, was in attendance, although not as an official witness to the proceedings.

The couple took up quarters in an apartment on 23 Calle de Santa Engracia, filling its walls with the art of such friends as Santiago Rusinol, Julio Romero de Torres, Ramón Casas, and Ricardo Baroja. Valle-Inclán experienced the first taste of home since his youth, and to augment his new respectability he abandoned his bohemian garb and locks to become the crew-topped and well-suited figure portrayed in an oil portrait by Anselmo Miguel Nieto, and less flatteringly in a photograph.[47] But while his trappings changed, the Mask remained essentially what he had made it during his years of bachelorhood.[48] Neither did his wit dissipate under the new yoke; he often commented that he had married by proxy and delineated the role of woman in the perfect marriage:

. . . that marriage is perfect in which the wife accepts totally the husband's views on all political and literary matters.[49] (A101)

Marriage did not change his habits. Although during this period his economic stature improved as a result of royalties from works that were finding public acceptance, he continued to practice his fasting; his stomach had become accustomed to privation, his delicate health demanded a strict diet, and his aesthetic bent found in fasting a means to a higher end. More and more, too, he wrote in bed out of both preference and necessity. He continued to attend the café, always his first stage, although some of his time was taken up with the care of his first child, Margarita Carlota (Concha).[50]

While there were many and varied episodes emanating from his home and the café, Valle-Inclán's public life also had continuity through the stage of the rostrum. Because of his friendship with Segismundo Moret, the man who had rescued him after the accidental wounding of his foot, Valle-Inclán was introduced to the Ateneo de Madrid and accepted as a member. But when Moret made a controversial political speech in Zaragoza in November 1908, Valle-Inclán put personal considerations aside and attacked his friend and others of his ilk in "¡Dios nos asista!" (God Help Us!), an article published on 1 December in *El Mundo*.

The Ateneo, founded in 1835 by the great *costumbrista* of Madrid, Ramón de Mesonero Romanos, was the intellectual center of the Spanish capital; its salons, library, and liberal atmosphere attracted individuals of all castes and national origins, many of whom participated in the lecture series held there periodically. Valle-Inclán was invited to address the membership and guests on 2 May 1907.[51] The lecture, "¡Viva la bagatela!" (borrowing a phrase from Azorín's La voluntad [Will]), was very successful.[52] The theatricality involved in such public presentations was a source of great satisfaction to Valle-Inclán, as he stated:

I would like to be an orator. Calumny and debasement have been the lot of oratory, but unjustly so. The principal condition of oratory is generosity. And supreme beauty lies in disinterest. There are falsifiers who degrade it with their base ambition for personal gain, but the ideal orator is the one who speaks artistically and beautifully to the end of distracting his listeners and interlocutors. Notice how the orator, the true orator, convinces through expression, gesture, tone. An example is Saint Bernard preaching the Crusade in Germany, not knowing the language, yet moving the credulous, convinced masses. Eloquence is like the Eucharist, which needs nothing external. It is all spirit, sanctified and generous detachment. Hernán Cortés comes to mind. He was a marvelous orator. Downgraded by his vices and passions, he nonetheless always managed to capture the sympathy of whoever spoke with him, to the extent that Bernal Díaz del Castillo records that when some officers who were set against him went to see him, he captivated them, despite their being aware that Hernán Cortés was deceiving them. Such was his ability.[53] (A102)

Such ideas ultimately found full expression in La lámpara maravillosa. The power of oratory, as exemplified by figures he considered heroic, attracted Valle-Inclán all his mature life, and in later years he lectured throughout Spain and Latin America with increasing frequency and attendant satisfaction.

Between 1907 and 1910 Valle-Inclán continued to publish important books, articles, poems, and stories. Aromas de leyenda. Versos en loor de un santo ermitaño,[54] his first book of poetry, disclosed a new facet of Valle-Inclán's creativity, unheralded except by his youthful efforts in "En Molinares" (In Molinares, 1888), "Era el postrer momento . . . " (It was the Final Moment, 1889), and in "An una mujer ausente por la muerte" (To a Woman Absent in Death, 1892). The poems in this collection are the work of a poet who waited for maturity before divulging his designs. The poems reflect the modernistic influence of Darío, but this is tempered by thematic context. The poems, in simple verses often punctuated by an ageless folk refrain, mirror the life—faith, toil, play—of the poet's native region in terms that are universally meaningful. Galicia is abstracted in its intrahistory, drawn in epochal strokes, de-regionalized, and made vital. There is an intense longing for its completeness—man in a landscape—that the poet expresses in the first stanzas of the introductory "Ave":

Oh, distant memories of the distant land,
filled with aromas of fresh morning grass!
Land of humid and rustling cornfields,
where invisible choirs sing from the wind
as the sun depetals the rose of its gold
on mountain heights that bulls make shudder!

Oh, rutted paths with crosses and tales,
where old women babble in the failing light
under kindling loads stolen from pine groves,
the wood that at night will burn in the hearth
while a voice through the smoke tells secular tales,
and dogs in the distance bark on haystacks! (A103)

Replete with an epic quality, these poems of Galician tone are powerful in their simplicity. Themes within the book carry the soul of a people in conjunction with Man's common destiny. Like *Flor de santidad*, *Sonata de otoño*, and several early stories, these poems rise above mere local coloration to greater status in their concern with the human condition.

Also within this era, when Valle-Inclán's poetry emerges as an important facet of his creativity, are the poems "A Isabel Venegas (Colombiana)" (To Isabel Venegas [A Colombian]), and "Auto-retrato" (Self-portrait), both of which appeared in the same journal.[55] The latter poem gives an interesting self-assessment:

My dream as poet, flowering in a song,
gave to my Psyche dual wings for flight—
a wing of anarchist, the other that of saint—
and in my right, a fist of wheat to sow.

. . . I had been born to be a village sire,
with an estate, a horse, and hounds;
but this world's course attracted me
and I abandoned my estate's own solitude,
dreaming of resounding and grand deeds
echoing of Mexico or Flanders' own.

My soul, enslaved to lust, you yielded
your virginity, your mystery, to heed its call;
and lust made you the gift of melancholy's state,
which, soul of mine, is your divine obsession.
Soul that trembles in your own dark cave,
like the shimmer of some distant star's
mysterious rose upon black water in a cistern held,
that rose upon the blue is sister to your self!
. . . .
And of my love of soldiering, of writing verse . . .
I claim as the reminders of that restless life,
a scar that looms large on my right,
a severed arm, a foot that's half-destroyed.
And still, I have the virtue of submissiveness,
having lived as an ascetic after living as a beast. (A104)

With the abandonment of the worldly life came an ever-increasing commitment to the life of the spirit, and that which fostered it, including Art. Although he had published some few statements on aesthetics and applied his ideas to his own works, Valle-Inclán did not have a treatise on the subject. But 1908 brought the opportunity to set down in writing what he had previously expressed mainly in his *tertulia*. He was commissioned by *El Mundo*, the Madrid newspaper owned and edited by his friend Julio Burell, to write a series of articles on the Exposición Nacional de Bellas Artes. This important exhibit brought together the best works of art by contemporary Spanish painters. And Valle-Inclán gave a detailed exposition of its works and trends, excoriating much of what was presented and praising only those artists whose paintings could compare favorably with classical art in inspiration and technique. Of the ten articles, three dealt with artists individually, praising Julio Romero de Torres and Ricardo Baroja, but reassessing Santiago Rusiñol.[56]

Historias perversas[57] repeated the prologue that Manuel Murguía had written for Valle-Inclán's first book and contained the stories from *Femeninas* together with "Beatriz" from *Corte de amor* (Court of Love), and "Augusta" from the same collection. The re-issuance of the tales of *Femeninas*, together with the prologue, demonstrated once more Valle-Inclán's continuing interest in refurbishing his earlier work and in finding a more perfect context for it within his maturing aesthetic. Similarly inclined, he made new editions of *Jardín novelesco* and *Corte de amor*,[58] prefacing the latter with "Breve noticia acerca de mi estética cuando escribí este libro" (Brief Account of My Aesthetics When I Wrote This Book):

The stories that you'll encounter in this book are of the type that Spanish critics habitually term decadent, no doubt because theirs is not a brutish sensibility. Their misadventure, when first I tried to publish them, was due to that unusual mode of expression. With the exception of "Eulalia," all of them were condemned to the bonfire in one or another of those editorial offices where stupidity reigns. . . . "Augusta" did not suit them . . . "Rosita" caused a scandal . . . while "Beatriz" failed to win a contest held by *El Liberal*. (A105)

The publication of *Cofre de sándalo* (The Sandalwood Coffer),[59] including the prologue by Murguía and several tales from *Femeninas*, featured works worthy to be included in what the author envisioned in 1909 as the first volume of his complete works. Thus, the contents of *Femeninas*, *Epitalamio*, *Corte de amor*, and *Historias perversas* were distilled into the five tales of *Cofre de sándalo*. Selections of his stories and other works were also issued in *Las mieles del rosal (Trozos selectos)* (The Nectar of the Rose [Selected Petals]).[60]

As ever, Valle-Inclán's managed his social life with as much care as he did his creative activities. Since the importance of friendships was paramount in his life, he was always among the organizers of events to honor his colleagues. One such affair was held 15 February 1908 at the Hotel Inglés, ironically on Calle de Echegaray, in honor of the novelist Gabriel

Miró, whose book *Nómada* (Nomad) had won the annual prize given by *El Cuento Semanal*. Valle-Inclán took Miró to see Galdós and in his absence left an invitation to the banquet, along with a brief note:

Dear Don Benito:
  I came to see you accompanied by Gabriel Miró, who wanted to thank you for your letter.
  An embrace,
    Valle-Inclán[61] (A106)

Galdós himself would be the recipient of Valle-Inclán's congratulations on the very successful opening of one of his plays on 15 December 1908:

Dear Don Benito:
  I'll return tomorrow to give you my congratulations on *Pedro Minio*.
  An embrace,
    Valle-Inclán[62] (A107)

Through his frequent attendance at the Ateneo in Madrid, which served not only as a literary forum but also as a center for diverse activities from science to politics, Valle-Inclán became acquainted with many other leaders in their respective fields. Among these individuals were participants in the Carlist movement, a cause espoused by Valle-Inclán since his youth, although the last battles of Carlism had been fought during his early years. Valle-Inclán sought out these men and listened to their narratives with attentive mind. His own Carlism was of an elusive brand. While he was dedicated to it at this time, as his political candidacy evidenced, the maxims of the movement satisfied only a part of the man. The appeal of Carlism for Valle-Inclán was its high ethical ideals and its sacrificial position, both of which placed Carlism within the cause of righteousness and encouraged rebellion against the political hypocrisy of the established order. The combination of these elements made the movement aesthetically appealing to Valle-Inclán, and he could speak through Bradomín in *Sonata de invierno*, the first of his novels with a Carlist background:

I have always found fallen majesty to be more beautiful than that which sits enthroned, and I was a defender of tradition for aesthetic reasons. For me, Carlism has the same solemn enchantment as the great cathedrals and, even during the war, I would have been content to have it declared a national monument.[63] (A108)

On other occasions he reiterated his aesthetic commitment to Carlism more directly, through his own words:

I am a Carlist solely by aesthetics. I like the beret. It is a pompous crest that ennobles. The white cape of the Carlists takes me back to the sway of an archaic court. It is, without a doubt, the most beautiful political costume ever devised.[64] (A109)

Behind the facile words lies the truth of his dedication to the Carlist cause. Along with other Carlists, Valle-Inclán lamented the loss on 18 July 1909 of yet another unrecognized pretender to the throne of Spain—Don Carlos de Borbón y de Este, who, to his followers, was King Carlos VII. The sorrow of the loss was somewhat diminished with the succession of his son Don Jaime to the Carlist leadership. Shortly thereafter, the series of blunders in colonial policy toward Morocco and the need to repress the rebellious Rif tribes led to instability in Spain. The Carlists waited expectantly as revolutionary strikes in Barcelona between 26 and 30 July, the so-called "Semana Trágica," threatened to topple the government. But the ruling monarch, Alfonso XIII, remained in control even after the fall of Prime Minister Maura's conservative coalition on 21 October 1909. Once again, the Carlists' expectations had been dashed.

The literature that Valle-Inclán created on the theme of Carlism began with *Sonata de invierno* and its partial adaptation *Una tertulia de antaño*.[65] But most important in the evolution of his ideas on and insight into this subject are the epico-historical novels he published under the generic title *La guerra carlista: Los cruzados de la causa, El resplandor de la hoguera, Gerifaltes de antaño*.[66]

The first novel in the series has a clear parentage in *Sonata de otoño* (from which it derives its setting as well as the characters Bradomín and Don Juan Manuel Montenegro) and *Sonata de invierno* (in its Carlist theme). Likewise, the *Comedias bárbaras* serve as a reference point for characters, setting, and atmosphere. It is on the familiar landscape of Galicia, far from the battlefields of the Carlist wars, that Bradomín and his uncle Don Juan Manuel act together in the accomplishment of the former's secret mission on behalf of the cause. The plot centers on three actions—the governmental search of a convent containing a cache of arms for Carlist soldiers; the death of a young man, an inductee into the army, placed on guard at the convent as a result of his desertion when conviction and duty came into unbearable conflict; and the conveyance of the weapons away from the convent.

El resplandor de la hoguera and *Gerifaltes de antaño* have their setting in the Basque and Navarre regions of Spain, the centers of Carlist activity. The transference from Galicia to such a locale has a basis in Valle-Inclán's reality. Between the issuance of *Los cruzados de la causa* and *El resplandor de la hoguera*, their author made the first of several journeys to the traditional stronghold of Carlism. With his mounting interest in the history of the movement, he recognized the necessity of becoming personally acquainted with the geographic area on which it flourished and bled. His desire to visit the scene was gratified by Joaquín Argamasilla de la Cerda, a young Carlist noble, who invited him to stay at his estate in Aoíz, near Pamplona in the province of Navarre. During this period he was also the guest of the Count of Rodezno in Villafranca, and traveled extensively in the company of former Carlist generals Amador del Villar and Fernando Adelantado de

Aragón. With these intimate friends of Don Carlos and Don Jaime, Valle-Inclán crisscrossed the Carlist country from 23 June through 3 July 1909 as reported in the press and elsewhere.[67] Awed by all he saw and heard, he confided to his host:

Had I come earlier, my dear Argamasilla, I would have given *Los cruzados* a different atmosphere![68] (A110)

The sequels to that novel show the mastery of detail, history, and landscape that Valle-Inclán learned during this sojourn.[69]

El resplandor de la hoguera is less a plotted novel than a sequence of episodes set against the hostilities, and although it contains only one battle scene the presence of the war is unavoidable. Everywhere in the work there is evidence of the bloody history of Carlism. Everywhere, too, is visible the impartiality of the author in recounting events or depicting individuals.[70] Valle-Inclán writes his novel without recourse to fatiguing series of occurrences, results, and dates. His view penetrates to the core and results in a sensation of the war seen in the characters and in minor events portrayed. The vision and its interpretation are largely poetic. Rather than a protagonist acting his role with the backdrop of the war, the author has brought the war itself into the foreground and made the human beings involved in it part of the overall scheme.

Gerifaltes de antaño is centered on the imposing figure of a priest, D. Manuel Santa Cruz, treated with great psychological and social insight. The ferocious warrior-priest, more a bandit than a patriot in the eyes of both government and Carlist forces, is depicted by Valle-Inclán with sympathy born out of recognition of the legendary stature of Santa Cruz. The cruel, despotic figure is interpreted as a fanatic with a holy cause—his ideal—that makes him inflexible. Under Valle-Inclán Santa Cruz assumes epic proportions.

On its publication *La guerra carlista* became identified in comparisons with the *Episodios Nacionales* (National Episodes) of Pérez Galdós and, to a lesser degree, with some novels by Pío Baroja.[71] But Valle-Inclán's conception and treatment of the political unrest were radically different from both authors. While Galdós approached the reality of nineteenth-century Spain with the historian's prudent attention to external occurrences, Valle-Inclán eschewed such exclusive dedication to outward detail. Galdós captured the minutiae of the period, but Valle-Inclán selected only those events and personalities indispensable to his impressionistic interpretation. The external and precise photography of the *Episodios Nacionales* is at a pole opposite to the internal and diffused portraiture of *La guerra carlista*. But this is not to contrast the ability or preparation of the two authors before the task. Valle-Inclán was no less versed in the history of the nineteenth century than Galdós. However, the latter's scholarship and research are evident on every page of his series of novels, while Valle-Inclán's interpretative technique disguises the inborn knowledge of the period enhanced through extensive readings since his youth.[72] Valle-Inclán has written history, but with the touch of the artist and from an aesthetic viewpoint. He has gone beyond mere externals into that area Unamuno has designated *intrahistoria*, the real roots of history. Baroja, on the other hand, did not have in him either the historian that was Galdós nor the artist that was Valle-Inclán. His attention to the Carlist era stemmed simply from his interest in a remote ancestor who had participated in the movement. His concern, therefore, was highly personal and he could not tolerate any other reason for involvement. Since neither Galdós nor Valle-Inclán possessed credentials of that nature, Baroja disapproved of both in their roles as historians of Carlism.

Despite Baroja's objections, *La guerra carlista* is a vivid evocation of the history and the adventure of an important period in Spanish politics. The series, too, is the consolation of its author, who would have derived great personal satisfaction had he been able to participate in the intrigues of that recent past. Unable to do so, he had to content himself with visits to the historic sites of Carlist Spain.

Even abroad, as on a trip to Argentina, Valle-Inclán's Carlism came to the fore very notably. Thus, on 24 June 1910 the Círculo Tradicionalista de Buenos Aires gave a banquet in honor of Valle-Inclán at which he spoke of his Carlist affiliation:

Ladies and gentlemen, I affirm my traditionalist lineage and affiliation. My traditionalist lineage and affiliation were bred in circumstances adverse to the Carlist cause. . . . My first literary works were generally praised by the press, since they weren't Carlist; but no sooner did I begin to write as a Carlist than my previous readers abandoned me. I don't care. . . . Nonetheless, on becoming convinced that whoever has an ideal ought to work on its behalf, I put my pen at the service of mine . . . And I devote the only arm I have to writing in defense of my ideas, and, if necessary, that arm will be at the disposal of the cause wielding other weapons.[73] (A111)

At the conclusion of the dinner the president of the Círculo and Valle-Inclán prepared a telegram to *El Correo Español* in Madrid indicating their dedication to Carlism.[74] That these were not idle words was made evident that same year when Valle-Inclán attempted to enter the political arena by presenting himself as the Traditionalist candidate for *diputado* in the Monforte de Lemus district of Galicia, which had inspired him in his literary youth to write a glowing description.[75] While in Buenos Aires he explained further his political intentions:

I have pressing commitments in Spain. I don't know how I could have left them. Until the last moment, I wasn't certain that I could embark to accompany my friend García Ortega. My journey has had many setbacks. Those commitments that tied me to Spain were of a serious nature. Political commitments . . . I've become a candidate for deputy in the next session of the Cortes. It wasn't for personal reasons that I became a candidate to the national legislature. It was the result of a command mandated by one who has the right to ask it of me. On putting together the slate of candidates, Don Jaime de Borbón sought to reward my efforts by naming me the candidate for the Monforte district. But unexpected difficulties arose and in the revised list I was honored to be named for the Estella district. Naturally, I had to excuse myself for strong reasons; stating that my deepest desire was to visit Buenos Aires was not sufficient. I felt the duty of writing to the King . . . And he granted me permission to withdraw my name. Another will take my place more advantageously.[76] (A112)

While this first attempt to create a political life had failed, Valle-Inclán remained in the Carlist camp and, by employing his pen in the creation of novelistic histories of Carlism, earned the gratitude of its leaders. Among Valle-Inclán's proudest possessions were photographs dedicated to him and letters that Don Jaime had written to him; but most important was the Cruz de la Legitimidad Pospuesta, the highest Carlist decoration, which he wore proudly. He lived in his contemporaniety and was content with gatherings of Carlist dignitaries, such as the banquet held 8 January 1911 at Madrid's Frontón Jai-Alai in honor of parliamentary constituents who had defeated a bill prejudicial to the cause. During the banquet Valle-Inclán, who presided at the event, sat at the main table with such important party figures as the Marqués de Cerralbo, Vázquez de Mella, Bartolomé Feliú, Sánchez Marco, Díaz Aguado, Sallaberry, and Bofarull. Two years later he was to write the prologue to a Carlist friend's study of the cause.[77] Such associations continually renewed his interest in Carlism and instigated the creation of evocative portraits of a fascinating era.

7 Drama

The second period of Valle-Inclán's activity as a dramatist began in 1903.[1]
Its commencement was indicated, if meekly, by the publication of the
playlet *Tragedia de ensueño* (Dream Tragedy) in the guise of a story in *Jardín
umbrío*. This dramatic vignette casts a compassionate glance at a human
being whose life has been misshaped by the ironic and cruel machinations
of Fate. The tragedy lies not in the cumulative deaths of the old woman's
seven sons and their children but in the irony that this centenarian must
live on, alone and useless, without understanding the reason for her
endurance.

This playlet was a mere exercise showing that the writer had not totally
abandoned the dramatic concept of composition. The idea of a theatre of
his own was kept alive through the personal necessity of finding a means
of contributing to the stage after his acting career had terminated. He came
to recognize after the loss of his left arm that the best participation for him
in the theatre would be as a playwright.

Following his regenerated interest, he continued to frequent the theatre
and to associate with its leading exponents. He supplemented the *tertulias*
at the Café Levante with the gatherings at the salon of the Teatro Español
where María Guerrero and Fernando Díaz de Mendoza, who headed the
theatrical company, convened a select group. Valle-Inclán, Manuel Bueno,
and Maeztu[2] joined Ricardo de la Vega, Balart, Picón, José de Laserna,
Ricardo J. Catalinéu, Gomar, Duque de Tamames, Eusebio Blasco, Eugenio
Sellés, and Echegaray, among others.

Encouraged by his acceptance into this private circle, Valle-Inclán proposed to Manuel Bueno the adaptation of Lope de Vega's *Fuenteovejuna*.
The project met with the approval of the Guerrero-Díaz de Mendoza company and the play was premiered on 27 October 1903 at the Teatro Español
in Madrid. It was withdrawn shortly thereafter for revamping but was
returned to the repertory early in January 1904. The delay was occasioned
by the troupe's tour through Andalucia. Valle-Inclán joined the company

in its excursion to witness the presentation of his adaptation of *Andrea del Sarto*, to which he also invited Antonio Machado,[3] who had recently published *Soledades* (Solitudes), his first book of poetry. The renewal of Valle-Inclán's active participation in the theatre was indicated as well by his committal in 1904 to adapt *Marianela*, the novel by Pérez Galdós, for the stage. A letter from the Gran Hotel de Pastor in Aranjuez, dated 5 August 1904, states:

Dear and admired Don Benito:
  Having just returned to Aranjuez after an excursion through several towns of Castile, I find your letter waiting for me and I feel a natural shame for the delay. Don't think that I haven't worked on *Marianela*, but I was unhappy with what I'd written and tore it up.
  I've taken it up again now. I hope to send something to you very soon.
  Forgive my laziness, and feel free to call upon your admirer and affectionate friend,
        Ramón del Valle-Inclán[4] (A113)

Valle-Inclán continued to show leanings toward the theatre when, in 1905, he published another playlet: *Comedia de ensueño* (Dream Play).[5] In this work Man's search for his personal redemption is presented in an allegorical setting resembling those in *The Arabian Nights* in its exotic and mysterious emanations. A bandit chieftain, haunted by his evil act—the severing of a damsel's ring-laden hand—is transformed from the unflinching leader of brigands into a tearful wretch when the hand is snatched by a vagabond dog who runs into the night. He sets out on his steed risking sanity and life in a search that Fate has decreed must be futile. Again, Valle-Inclán has underlined the absurdity of Man's existence, which he depicts as a hurtling through life toward illusion. And again a severed limb plays a role.

It was with *El Marqués de Bradomín*, however, that Valle-Inclán made his official return to the theatre as a dramatist. The play, the first of his works to be staged since *Cenizas*, opened at Madrid's Teatro de la Princesa on 25 January 1906 to a favorable reception.[6] But unlike the extreme romanticism of his first play, *El Marqués de Bradomín* features a flagrant *Modernismo* in description and dialogue. Through this drama the playwright consolidates configurations of Bradomín manifest in episodes from the last two novels of the *Sonatas*, adding as well elements and characters appearing earlier in *Flor de santidad*. This process of amelioration indicates amply the turn that Valle-Inclán had taken in regard to his literary productivity: what had begun in several stories and found extension in four novels was finalized in the genre of drama. It is not only in the novels of the *Sonatas*, then, that Valle-Inclán had made his definitive statement on Bradomín but also in the play *El Marqués de Bradomín*. While this character appears again in later novels, stories, and plays, the last concentrated aspect of his definition has been secured in the play bearing his name, which Valle-Inclán saw fit to publish.[7]

Bradomín does not enter until the end of the first act. His visits to the castle of his childhood sweetheart and former mistress, Concha, are brief and full of the uneasiness brought on by a separation that has been not only temporal but circumstantial. Yet, it is he and not any other of the many characters—noble, ecclesiastic, or folk—who dominates the entire play. There are three moments that emphasize his dramatic importance. In the first act, his impending arrival after many years of absence gives rise to an ever-increasing intensity (uncertainty, impatience, yearning, fear, etc.); in the second act, his presence motivates the dialogue to eloquence and hope as the two lovers taste in memory their amorous past; in the third act, his departure creates a deeply pathetic mood. Interlaced with these movements that give the drama its impetus are episodes of varying importance and hue: sequences between Bradomín and Don Juan Manuel Montenegro[8] in which the latter shows great stamina as he recounts ancestral and personal glories, between El Abad and Concha in which her adultery is underlined with the priest's presence, between the innocence of Florisel the page and the worldliness of Bradomín, between the celestinesque Madre Cruces and the love-starved Concha. Throughout the play are theatrical sequences in which beggars are arrayed against the backdrop of field and castle in compositions that possess all the vicious humour, candor, and folk quality of a Breughel canvas painted by the elder Peter.

The theatricality of the patriarchal Don Juan Manuel Montenegro, who had made many small entrances in previous works, became self-evident in *El Marqués de Bradomín*. Soon Valle-Inclán set out to create a suitable vehicle for the figure that had become grandiose despite its minor roles. The result was the series of plays entitled generically *Comedias bárbaras: Cara de Plata, Aguila de blasón*, and *Romance de lobos*.[9] The trilogy is a biography of distorted lives ruled by medieval traditions, pagan superstitions, and animal passions. The playwright makes Don Juan Manuel the vertical pillar of a feudal order around whom are arrayed the dependents—his sons, mistresses, wife, servants, serfs, and countless beggars—in various horizontal and diagonal attitudes. These people, with their fears, hatreds, and peculiarities, are contrasted with the decadent assurance of the protagonist. But, ironically and realistically, it is they who share in the triumph that dethrones the masterful Don Juan Manuel; however, the triumph is relative because Fate makes inevitable the convulsiveness of the human condition. The three plays recreate the picture of this upheaval of feudal decadence in nineteenth-century Galicia:

My work reflects the life of a people near extinction. My mission is to annotate it before it disappears. In my *Comedias bárbaras*, I reflect the entailed estates that disappeared in 1833. I knew many first-born sons. They're the last expression of a concept, and, for that reason, my plays have a certain historical value.[10] (A114)

In another statement on the subject, he aligned the *Comedias bárbaras* with the vision of the grotesque:

In this *Comedia bárbara* (divided into three tomes: *Cara de Plata*, *Aguila de blasón*, and *Romance de lobos*), the concepts I've indicated have motivated the form as well as the slightest episode. I have witnessed the transformation of a society of castes (the hidalgos whom I knew as a child), and what I've seen no one will ever again see. I'm the historian of a world that ended with me. No one will ever again encounter such founders of families and first-born heirs. And in this world of clergymen, beggars, scriveners, whores, and pimps that I present, the best of that which has disappeared—despite their many vices—were the hidalgos.[11] (A115)

The concepts expressed in the letter coincide with his vision in the *Esperpentos*, and, while the earlier *Comedias bárbaras* do not belong to that designation in his work, they are highly indicative of an early tendency toward portrayal of life's grotesqueness; this is particularly evident in the scenes in which the mass of beggars becomes the protagonist. The progress of Valle-Inclán's attitude, from that evident in the first two published parts of the trilogy to that demonstrated in *Cara de Plata*, published in 1922, is marked by the advanced conception of relationships in the three works: the last published antecedes the other two to complete the triangle that has its apex in *Aguila de blasón*—the height of plot. Like the quadripartite segments of the *Sonatas*, the tripartite format of the *Comedias bárbaras* shapes distinct episodes into a related whole.

The lives of Don Juan Manuel Montenegro and his rapacious sons, laced with superstition and brutality, reflect the conflict of tradition and social ferment that eventually forces society to change drastically, convulsively. They reflect, too, more particular aspects of that struggle:

It's been my desire to restore that which is Galician to the legend of Don Juan, which I've divided into three moments: impiety, slaughter, and women. The one concerning women is the final one, that of Seville, the nostalgia of the Moor who lacks a harem. The one about the querulous brawler is that of Extremadura, the Galician frontier. The one concerning impiety is that of Galicia proper, where it has its origin, as our dear friend Said-Armesto explained it. The Stone Guest is, by virtue of his bulk, a Galician. This impiety is Galician impiety: it denies no dogma, nor belief in God, and is irreverent toward the dead. Fatally, irreligiosity is contempt for the dead. Such ideas guided me to greater awareness on putting the finishing touches to *Cara de Plata*. It is playing with death, a firing of pistols, irate confrontations, a grotesque act of handing over the soul performed by the sacristan. But by dint of playing the ghost, one becomes one. Death, having been mocked, provoked and faked, does arrive. Then *Romance de lobos* begins. Death enters with its funeral candles, omens, shipwrecks and destitution, punishment and remorse. This essence of the first Don Juan—Don Galán in the old ballad—is what I seek with the greatest determination because I see it as the final decantation of the Galician soul.

You make a very justifiable comment when you point to the tentativeness of the plot, which somewhat resembles the pattern of a dream, wherein larvae can converse with the living. Certainly. Contributing to this effect is what could be termed the compression of time. The effect is similar to that in El Greco's compression of space. Velázquez is replete with space. His figures are free to change position, spread out, and make room for extraneous elements. But only El Greco can fit so many figures in the narrow space of *The Burial of Count Ordáz*; should the pattern be broken, it would be necessary to call on a Byzantine mathematician to restore order. Such compression of space becomes compression of time in the *Comedias*. Scenes that seem to have been placed arbitrarily are the consequent ones in the chronology of events. *Cara de Plata* begins at dawn and ends at midnight. The other parts follow without interval. In something that I'm now writing, this idea of filling time the way El Greco filled that space—wholly—is what concerns me. Some Russian or other knew about this.[12] (A116)

From the world of the *Comedias bárbaras*, his first important contribution to the evolution of the Spanish drama, Valle-Inclán returned to the scene of his first play, *Cenizas*. More confident and mature as a dramatist after the production of *El Marqués de Bradomín* and the publication of the first two of the *Comedias bárbaras*, Valle-Inclán refurbished his earlier offering and issued it in book form under the new title *El yermo de las almas* (The Barrenness of Souls).[13] Changes included renaming the "Acts" to read "Episodes," in keeping with the tenets of the romantico-modernist aesthetic, and infusing more descriptive matter into the stage directions, thus enhancing their utilitarianism without disrupting the play's dramatic quality. In its definitive form as *El yermo de las almas*, the work, too, demonstrated a conjunction and amelioration of characters, themes, and plots that had appeared earlier as stories.

Valle-Inclán's dramatic credo during this second era of activity in the theatre is, of course, reflected in the plays of the period. But there is a more direct statement of his attitude in the words he spoke after attending the premiere of Benavente's *Señora Ama* (The Woman of the House) in 1908:

I don't like this kind of theatre. With the staging techniques that the theatre has available, chunks of reality are being thrown in our faces. Art exists only when it has become superior to its living models through an ideal elaboration. Things are not as we see them but as we remember them. In literary creations, the word must always be transferred to that plane on which the world and human life are idealized. There is no poetry without that process.[14] (A117)

This transformation from the commonplaces of life to the idealization of characters and events is traceable to *El Marqués de Bradomín*, the *Comedias bárbaras*, and *El yermo de las almas*; it is heralded in the vignettes *Tragedia de ensueño* and *Comedia de ensueño*, which opened the way for the works that followed. It is in these early plays that the dramatist first touches on the absurdity of human existence by delving into the enigmas of life: the instability of personality, the variance in types, the implausibility of complete relationships, the injustice of the social order, the reaches of experience, the subservience to occult beliefs, the reliance on oppressive traditions. His characters and situations are ambiguous, caricatural, mock-heroic, fantastic, folkloric, grotesque, colorful, sombre, cynical, and pathetic. These suggestive modifiers are the most indicative of the playwright's vision, and the most dependable in assessing the direction of his later theatrical production.

Two other of Valle-Inclán's plays were announced on the marquees of Madrid's Teatro de la Comedia in 1910, the first to be performed since *El Marqués de Bradomín*. The premiere of the puppet farce *La cabeza del dragón*, under the auspices of Benavente's Teatro de los Niños, with Fernando Porredón creating the lead role, was held on 5 March.[15] The second play, *Cuento de abril*, was produced under different management on 19 March with Juan Bonafé and Matilde Moreno in the cast. On the same bill were Benavente's *La escuela de las princesas* (The School for Princesses) and the Alvarez Quintero brothers' *El último capítulo* (The Final Chapter).

Cuento de abril was published in *Europa* prior to the premiere of the play without the subtitle *Escenas rimadas en una manera extravagante* (Scenes in Extravagant Verse), which was added to the subsequent book edition.[16] *La cabeza del dragón*, which did not appear in definitive book form until 1914, was printed in two acts in *Europa* shortly after its production.[17]

La cabeza del dragón is full of Swiftian overtones and Cervantine ingenuity. It depicts the plight of a princess who is to be devoured by a dragon in a traditional ritual until a prince appears to slay the monster and win her hand in marriage. The play is a farce and thus heralds later works in this vein. *Cuento de abril*, a verse play, deals with a haughty Infante of Castile who travels to Provence to woo a gentle princess; unable to wrest her love from a sentimental troubadour, he returns to his kingdom perplexed. It is an example of Valle-Inclán's Modernist mode in drama.

Valle-Inclán's wife, Josefina Blanco, who had returned to the stage after the birth of their first child, Concha, toured the provinces with the company of Francisco García Ortega during the 1909–1910 theatrical season. Valle-Inclán joined her in the spring, enrolling in the troupe as its artistic director. Shortly thereafter the players set out from Lisbon for Argentina to participate in the Centennial Year celebrations in Buenos Aires. En route the company made a stop in Las Palmas, Canary Islands, to present some of its repertory. Among those plays was Echegaray's *Mancha que limpia* (The Stain That Cleans, 1895), in which Josefina Blanco was cast as Enriqueta. By this time Valle-Inclán had become totally intolerant of Echegaray's drama, and he flew into a rage on learning the ironic news that his wife was to act in the play. To prevent her performance on opening night he locked her in the hotel room. Despite her entreaties, he remained adamant. It required the intervention of the authorities, on the supplication of García Ortega, to rescue the actress. Much to his chagrin, Valle-Inclán was detained until the presentation was completed.

The García Ortega company arrived in Buenos Aires on 22 April 1910 on the British steamship "Amazon."[18] Valle-Inclán, his wife, and his small daughter moved into the Hotel Madrid on the Avenida de Mayo where the author received frequent visits from local journalists and literary figures, as well as from Spanish friends who had traveled to Argentina for the centennial. During his many interviews he disclosed his impressions of the city:

The first reaction that Buenos Aires evokes in me is one of astonishment. I've been able to verify that it is a large city and, probably, a great city. . . . I sense, because of what I've been told and seen, that Buenos Aires will be the great center of the Latin people in the future. . . . It was a perpetual temptation to my spirit to get to know Buenos Aires, of which so much is spoken in Spain. And the occasion has been doubly favorable, permitting me to visit the great city when preparations are under way for the centennial. I'm pleased to know that there are millions of my compatriots here. Some hold me in esteem, and it is a pleasure to meet them in person. . . . I will tour Argentina as my position of artistic director with the theatre company permits, not as a would-be conqueror, but simply as another curious person. Don't you think I might find a down-and-out son of Don Juan Manuel Montenegro around here? In the meantime, the city is seductive and enchanting. I couldn't conceive of anything as inexhaustible and overpowering . . . The only thing that disappointed me was not hearing a single song when I arrived. . . . A part of my soul will also be left in this land.[19] (A118)

His schedule was hectic. From the moment of his arrival Valle-Inclán experienced the enthusiasm of a sophisticated public that recognized and admired the Man and the Artist, while the curious turned out to view the Mask. Consequently, he was the recipient of many tributes from diverse organizations. The Centro Gallego held a banquet in honor of the author of *Flor de santidad* and *Aromas de leyenda*; the members of the group "Nosotros" gathered at a restaurant to toast the creator of the *Sonatas* and *Comedias bárbaras*;[20] the Círculo Tradicionalista de Buenos Aires celebrated a feast on 24 June in obeisance to the novelist of *La guerra carlista*.[21]

One of the more important events during Valle-Inclán's stay in Buenos Aires was the Argentinian premiere of *Cuento de abril* on 9 May at the Teatro de la Comedia, under the playwright's direction. In the cast were Josefina Blanco in the male role of Pedro de Vidal, García Ortega as the Infante de Castilla, and La Nestosa as La Princesa de Imberal. Apparently the play was well-received by an enthusiastic public.[22] After its run in the Argentinian capital the work was taken to Montevideo where it opened on 15 June at the Teatro Cibils. Valle-Inclán, occupied with the preparation of a series of lectures he was to deliver in Buenos Aires, could not attend. The play, however, was defeated by adverse criticism. The attendance was extremely low and within a week *Cuento de abril* was not only retired from the Cibils but irrevocably dropped from the repertory of the troupe.[23]

When Valle-Inclán received the news in Buenos Aires his characteristic temperament flared up; but it was to no avail. Even more infuriating than the dismantling of his play was its replacement by *Las vengadoras,* once a controversial drama, by Eugenio Sellés.[24] The move by García Ortega had political motivations, for that minor playwright, then considered important, was among the socially prominent writers forming the entourage of the Infanta Isabel as official representatives of the Spanish government to the centennial festivities in Argentina.

The reception accorded this delegation was correct but less than enthusiastic. Indeed, in Valle-Inclán's accounts in two newspaper articles published in Madrid at the time,[25] the public reaction to the visit was strongly anti-monarchical:

I've seen her Ladyship the Infanta of Spain arrive with her retinue. . . . Greeted by the call for a general strike and the city in a state of siege. . . . There isn't a single educated person here who hasn't commented on the stupidity of the Spanish goverment in sending a lady of the royal line to the city with . . . more than 50,000 anarchists. (A119)

The implied threat to the royal person became real a few days later, as Valle-Inclán reported in the second article:

Yesterday, her Ladyship the Infanta escaped with her life in the cathedral through a miracle. . . . The police detained an anarchist who had secreted a dagger in an issue of *La Nación.* . . . It is said that Doña Isabel noticed the detention and demonstrated true royal spiritedness. (A120)

Valle-Inclán's cynicism targeted not only Doña Isabel but also the member of her entourage who most rankled him and by whom he was most resented. Sellés, elected to the Real Academia in 1894, was particularly irked by the greater attention given to Valle-Inclán, as the latter disclosed in a letter to Azorín:

He was a bit upset with me because, having left Spain unannounced and without the hoopla of the press, I was somewhat better known here than he was. Privately, I've been told, he protested the tribute given to me by the intellectual community of Argentina, when in Spain I was a nobody.[26] (A121)

In the same letter he tells of an encounter with Sellés. In typical humour Valle-Inclán made use of the information as he addressed the infuriated playwright.

What kind of a place is this? Those who are nobodies in Spain seem to be important here, while those who are eminent in Spain are totally unknown.[27] (A122)

Valle-Inclán had had the last laugh and that satisfied him in regard to Sellés. But he and his wife broke their association with García Ortega over the disposal of *Cuento de abril* and over the quarrel that ensued when Valle-Inclán refused to permit his wife to perform in the Sellés play. Immediately, they shifted their allegiance to the María Guerrero-Fernando Díaz de Mendoza troupe, which had come to Buenos Aires at the commencement of its Latin American tour.

While Josefina performed, Valle-Inclán delivered a series of lectures at the Teatro Nacional under the auspices of the Conservatorio Labardén:

I didn't plan on lecturing in Buenos Aires. I'm not an orator. An orator doesn't hesitate, and I do because I know that things have hundreds of aspects and that they can be expressed in a hundred different ways. Nevertheless, I will lecture. . . . I've signed an agreement with the Conservatorio Labardén. I hope to return to Buenos Aires, perhaps soon, at which time I'll bring from Madrid prepared lectures on heroes and saints of Old Spain, on Santiago, Patron Saint of that peninsula, on Fray Diego of Cádiz, on forgotten heroes of Galicia. For now, I'll improvise. Although I don't intend to do as did Blasco Ibáñez when he also improvised lectures here.[28] (A123)

Elsewhere, he referred to the calling of lecturer in more typical fashion:

When the musicality of verses and the jingle of bells aren't sufficient to fill the purse, buffoons and poets leave the country to lecture in the Indies.[29] (A124)

The first in the series of lectures was delivered on 25 June 1910. Entitled "El arte de escribir," it was an important statement on the contemporary attitude of Valle-Inclán toward the creative process. As such it merits extensive repetition, but even more so because as an important landmark it heralds the ideas expressed later in *La lámpara maravillosa*, that most impressive of his statements on aesthetics:

The art of writing is a long, sorrowful apprenticeship with two faces: the apprenticeship toward discerning the beauty that all things possess, and the apprenticeship toward its expression. Both ought to be accomplished jointly . . . The entire apprenticeship must be completed before devoting oneself to the work of art—so that the concept emerges effortlessly; so that its raiment becomes an integral part of its essence, as is light to a star. The effort must never be visible in the work of art, remembering that to hide one's power is to double it. . . . The artist must never undertake the imitation of a model, no matter how noble it may be. It is imperative to till one's own soil in order to gather one's own flowers, and never to copy that style known as "classic" because it is generally a misinterpretation of Latin literature. Always flee from that lengthy period, so prejudicial to our Castilian language . . . To labor on behalf of the language of Castile is for you and for us like raising a strong, impregnable bulwark in frontier nations. Beware the day when you lose your language or let it evolve solely to serve the needs of business! It may become more apt, but its beauty will be lessened. Remember that none of the romance languages born of Latin equaled the mother tongue; none of the languages that may be born of ours will have its noble and sonorous austerity, which is the austerity of the Castilian spirit. And you, ladies, love beautiful, sonorous words because they possess an august eternity. Baptize your children with sonorous names, christen your estates and your farms, your hamlets and your towns with sonorous names as well. Populate the pampas with high-sounding, meaningful names; recall that the ancients baptized rivers with the most sonorous words, which seem to flow from our lips as do crystals of water under the sky. Such was the way of the ancients, who held that the rivers were divinities. You should consider divine all that is born and merits a name.[30] (A125)

The complete lecture reveals the aesthetic level reached by Valle-Inclán. Supplementing the expression in his creative work, it confirms his passionate dedication to beauty as the supreme goal of the artist and reinforces his credo that the attainment of that end must be through an individualistic form of expression, not the least of whose qualities is a kinetic style that employs language to full advantage. Style, therefore, must result from inspiration rather than from ponderance. Through this and subsequent lectures Valle-Inclán began to codify his aesthetic.

On 28 June he spoke on "Los excitantes," discussing the influence of hashish and other mind stimulants on literature and on his own work. He also gave much attention to the subject of fasting and formulated the contemporary application of traditional concepts that made fasting a stimulus to creativity and mysticism. In the same conference he pointed to his mission in life as a concentrated effort toward the achievement of a personal aesthetic, one that would deny access to the sensual and the mundane; further, he set about defining a cosmological system within which the artist must place himself:

The void engenders time, from which the present is born, toward immutability. In another sense, time is the polarization of two infinites: that of negation and that of affirmation. These, in turn, give us the eternal notion of the center. All knowledge resides in God, who does not know evil, and since God is the center, approaching Him ought to be the supreme human ambition. He who most loves, enjoys the most. Let us universalize our consciousness in order to be better. On earth man can only be a center of love as was Glarís. This theory or feeling about the center makes me think that the artist ought to view the landscape with "airborne eyes" in order to encompass the whole rather than the mutable parts. When the collective view that marks popular literature is preserved in art, all things acquire that beauty which distancing evokes. For that reason, figures must be painted by removing whatever they were not. Thus, a beggar ought to resemble Job and a warrior Achilles.[31] (A126)

The third lecture, "Modernismo," was given on 5 July.[32] In it Valle-Inclán defined and discussed the movement of which he had become a leading exponent. But beyond the apologia was the further statement on his personal aesthetic stance:

I don't repulse tradition; but I accept it only in its potential vitality and utility, noting the necessity of an internal rhythm upholding the norms. . . . So many hearts, so many ways of expression. In art, rules and precepts may be as variable as essences, but the manner in which each intervenes changes according to the personal mode of sentiment. . . . Whatever the work of art, it contains the seed of another quite distinct, and everything is in everything.[33] (A127)

The last lecture was titled "La España antigua" and was delivered 11 July 1910. Only a brief segment of the contents was preserved in the newspaper accounts:

Spain has never been a nation of warriors. Only one was great: Don Gonzalo de Córdoba, nicknamed the great captain, who knew how to overcome powerful armies due to his talent in strategy. The Spanish conquerors were moralists rather than warriors. They came to America with an eagerness to lay foundations. Hernán Cortés and Pizarro were successful in their endeavors, less for their warrior spirit than for the knowledge the men possessed, for their perspicacity, and for their faith. The founding fathers were greater than the warriors and the chroniclers. Hence, the fact that all wars undertaken by Ancient Spain had a moral goal.[34] (A128)

When he had completed his lecture contract Valle-Inclán joined the Guerrero-Díaz de Mendoza company on their tour of Latin America, which took him to Chile, Paraguay, Uruguay, and Bolivia. The circuit lasted into November and, interspersed with his theatrical activities with the troupe, Valle-Inclán lectured at the invitation of organizations in the countries visited. While there is no known record of this activity, it is possible that many of the topics he discussed paralleled those in Buenos Aires. In November the first and only trip that Valle-Inclán made to South America came to an end. While there had been some negative aspects, the journey as a whole proved worthwhile in the eyes of Valle-Inclán. When the company returned to Spain, he and his wife remained with it on a tour that took in Valencia, Barcelona, Zaragoza, Pamplona, San Sebastian, and Bilbao. Once again the author of *La guerra carlista* was in the northern sector he so admired. His fondness for the Basque country again led to frequent outings on foot and to lengthier excursions by automobile.

Afterward, during his residency in Raparacea in the Valley of Baztán, province of Navarra, Valle-Inclán worked on two new plays: *Voces de gesta* and *La Marquesa Rosalinda*. The first, although its setting is not defined and its period is not stated, is easily interpreted in the light of Valle-Inclán's political preferences as a further treatment of Carlism. Written in verse, this *Tragedia pastoríl en tres jornadas* (Pastoral Tragedy in Three Acts), as it was subtitled, expressed lyrically the brave but ultimately futile efforts of a people, personified in the shepherdess Ginebra, to restore to his rightful throne their sovereign, Arquino in the first version but pointedly Carlino in later ones. In the end, her symbolic vengeance physically executed, the blind Ginebra presents her trophy—the head of the adversary—to her king. The encounter produces not the resurgence of hope she had come to expect but rather a disillusionment caused by the recognition that he has no expectation of success. The specter of death that the uncrowned monarch has become wanders alone into the mountains in search of his fate. Ginebra is no longer the symbol of a people striving on behalf of its rightful king because he is no longer a king striving and suffering for his people. The unanimity of the cause has become the single purpose of individuals, Ginebra and Carlino. In pointing to this situation within the tragedy Valle-Inclán has underscored the position of the Carlist movement. In reality, Don Carlos had abandoned Spain and his hopes, dying in Venice in 1909. In effect, the movement under his son Don Jaime became less a possibility than a historic memento. *Voces de gesta* declared this fact and transmitted anew the aesthetic commitment of the Artist and the Man to the cause of Carlism in terms that supplement Bradomín's attitude in *Sonata de invierno*.

The tragedy *Voces de gesta* premiered in Valencia in 1911, and was presented later in Madrid and Barcelona by the Guerrero-Díaz de Mendoza company, with which Valle-Inclán and Josefina Blanco were still associated. The Madrid debut took place at the Teatro de la Princesa on 26 May 1912. The public acclaim that greeted the play on opening night in the capital included the applause of the reigning monarch, Alfonso XIII.[35] The king did not invite the dramatist to his box after the performance as was customary, but he enjoyed the play and lavished praises on it. The Infantes Don Carlos and Doña Isabel attended on successive evenings because of Alfonso's enthusiasm. But unlike the king, the infanta invited Valle-Inclán to her box, sending the message that no matter who was King of Spain, she was still the infanta; he accepted her frank approach. The royal approval crowned the first real success that Valle-Inclán had experienced in the theatre.

Voces de gesta began to be published in the 1911 Christmas issue of the Parisian magazine *Mundial* through the intercession of Rubén Darío.[36] It was to him that the playwright sent each act of the tragedy as it was completed. In a telegram to Darío in Paris, he announced that the work was on its way:

Original entitled *Voces de gesta* will go out tomorrow. [37] (A129)

Later, he wrote to Darío:

Dear Rubén:
  By now you will have received the first act of *Voces de gesta*. The play is now finished. I will publish it as soon as you have done so in your magazine, and I would like an *Invocation* in verse from you. The edition will have illustrations, in imitation of old woodcuts, something like *Figlia di Iorio*, but in two inks. Since all of this takes time, and your verses must be in the first gathering, with a border on each page, they are in a maddening and demanding hurry.[38] (A130)

The correspondence in regard to *Voces de gesta* continued through 1911. A letter from Valle-Inclán, dated 8 September and written from 15 Villa Carmen, Mira-Concha, stated:

Dear Darío:
   By now you will have received the second act of *Voces de gesta*, which I sent some days ago. Don't fail to send me the proofs so that I can make those corrections that I couldn't remedy on the copy. And what of my prologue in verse?[39] (A131)

With this note he sent a signed receipt for payment with the amount left blank:

I have received from the administration of the magazine *Mundial* the amount of _____ francs for the first and second acts of the tragic poem *Voces de gesta*. Madrid, September 8, 1911. Ramón del Valle-Inclán. (A132)

The matter of the payment must have troubled Valle-Inclán and Darío, both having been victims of the low standards of reimbursement practiced by publishers, because the correspondence on the matter continued. In a letter written in San Sabastián dated 16 September 1911 Valle-Inclán reiterated:

Dear Darío:
   Don't forget my prologue. About the matter in your telegram, do what you think is best. You know the magazine's financial condition and its customary payments. Therefore, I leave matters to your judgment.[40] (A133)

In the postscript to that letter Valle-Inclán indicated that he was returning to Madrid. In the meantime, Josefina remained on tour and continued to forward material written by her husband to Darío.[41] The next communication from Valle-Inclán to Darío is dated 18 October 1911, written in Zaragoza:

Dear Darío:
   I've received a check for 150 pesetas, payment for the act published. I would appreciate it if, on publishing the second, you would send a money order to Madrid. It would be even better if the gentlemen of *Mundial* would deign to pay for the two pieces sent, even before they appear in print. An effort on your part to this end could smooth the way, and I would be very grateful because at the moment I'm rather short of funds, the summer trips having cost a great deal. Write me in Madrid. Don't forget my prologue.[42] (A134)

Early in 1912, at the start of the new year, Valle-Inclán again corresponded with Darío, this time from 23 Santa Engracia, his address in Madrid:

Dear Darío:
   I'm anxiously awaiting your introduction to *Voces de gesta*. The work has already

been printed and the only thing left to do is print the first gathering. I recently completed *La Marquesa Rosalinda*. The entire play is in rather eccentric rhyme, as you saw in the prologue printed in *Mundial*. You have certainly put together a very beautiful issue, both typographically and literarily. My best wishes for the New Year and an embrace.[43] (A135)

The introductory verses not sent by October 1911 must have reached him shortly thereafter because *Voces de gesta* was published in book form early the next year, and it was prefaced by Darío's "Balada Laudatoria que envía al Autor el Alto Poeta Rubén."[44] The poem again demonstrated the esteem in which Valle-Inclán continued to be held by Darío; it was the third such work he had written to honor his friend's creativity. The exclamation "¡Admirable!" the Modernist employed for praise was frequently on the lips of the Nicaraguan poet when he heard Valle-Inclán speak or read. The impression that *Voces de gesta* created on Darío must have been profound, for his own poem "Los motivos del lobo" (The Ways of the Wolf) has been shown to be inspired directly in the language of the play.[45] The admiration was not ill-placed; Valle-Inclán had succeeded in what he had set out to do:

It will be a book of legends, traditions, in the style of *Cuento de abril*, but more powerful, more important. It will contain the voice of an entire people. Only those books that enfold ample plebeian voices are great: the *Iliad*, the plays of Shakespeare . . . [46]

Voces de gesta is a Wagnerian libretto.[47] (A136)

Besides content, Valle-Inclán concerned himself with the design of the new book. His forceful commitment to the concept of a work of art as unified made him seek cohesiveness in its presentation. He overlooked no detail in the writing and he showed equal dedication to the designing and printing of the book. He sought the collaboration of the artists who met with him at the Café Levante in order to give the work comprehensive artistry, and the latinized names that appear therein[48] give evidence of the communal effort. The resultant edition was an aesthetically integrated one, the effectuation of Valle-Inclán's concept of unity.

The Guerrero—Díaz de Mendoza company gave the first performance of *La Marquesa Rosalinda*; it took place in March 1912 at its theatre in Madrid.[49] This *Farsa sentimental y grotesca* brought together elements as disparate as the *Commedia dell'Arte* and the court of the Sun King, Louis XIV, in a fortunate blending of rhythms and characters.[50] The direction Valle-Inclán took in this play was already evidenced in his poem "A la Luna: Monólogo de Pierrot," which had appeared in the 9 November 1911 issue of *Nuevo Mundo*, a Madrid periodical. The fifty-one line poem evokes the moon's mystic and magical powers as seen by the suffering lover. Although it is Pierrot's lament that the poem carries, the transformation of the poem in *La*

Marquesa Rosalinda echoed the sentiments of another *Commedia* character, Arlecchino.

The plot of the farce, like the scenarios of the *Commedia*, relies on the complex involvement of characters, both on the external level of physical action and on the internal stratum of subversive intent. The central plot pivots on Arlequín. He is at the shared apex of two triangles—one completed by El Marqués d'Olbray and his wife Rosalinda, the other by Pierrot and his wife Colombina. By this amorous involvement with both women, representing the upper and lower sectors of society respectively, Arlequín ultimately initiates all the action. El Marqués reacts to Arlequín's affair with Rosalinda by attempting to intimidate him; Pierrot, as another cuckolded husband, stages a fake duel to salve his clownish "honor"; Colombina jealously rants and raves against Arlequín's indifference; Rosalinda entices him with the promise of ideal love and the tender of real jewels. But in the end, Arlequín overcomes these outward ploys and continues, if disillusioned, his aimless wanderings with his troupe of comedians.

Ever so subtly Valle-Inclán enhances the double ménage à trois with the play-within-a-play presented by Arlequín's troupe in the garden of El Marqués. The courtly atmosphere of Aranjuez, where the farce is set, merges with the universality of the *Commedia*, and the personages watching the performance become inextricably bound into it as characters in the play-within-a-play. The interaction of fantasy and reality within *La Marquesa Rosalinda* is continuous. In this manner the playwright has integrated elements normally considered disparate. The farcical and the grotesque, the noble and the base, the social and the popular become as one in this outlandish and clever play.

While *La Marquesa Rosalinda* was well-received by the Madrid public, all was not ideal. Signs of dissension between the playwright and the leaders of the company began to appear. At first these were of a minor order, stemming from a disagreement between María Guerrero and Fernando Díaz de Mendoza with regard to the possible exclusion of passages that might prove disagreeable to the subscription audience. Valle-Inclán, of course, was concerned about such cuts being made and immediately joined the argument:

Not knowing to what it could be attributed, I was thinking how nice it is to be in Madrid on Saturday evenings . . . Now I know why: all the imbeciles have season tickets to the Princesa. But next Saturday I'm going to forgo my habit of not taking bows in order to tell the subscribers a thing or two; I'm fed up with having to listen to stupidities.[51] (A137)

The Saturday in question proved that María Guerrero's opinion—that the passages should not be altered—was correct. The scene received the usual applause and Valle-Inclán did not carry out his threat. María Guerrero confronted both her husband and the playwright, deriding the first for his unsuccessful opposition and the second for his lack of faith. Valle-Inclán could not let her victory pass without cynical commentary:

"Since it's obvious that you bolstered the *claque* . . ."[52] (A138)

But the real tension came in the summer of 1912 when the troupe went to Barcelona after its season in Madrid. *Voces de gesta* was in the repertory and this time problems of greater magnitude arose between playwright and actors. Valle-Inclán admired the style of María Guerrero as a tragedienne ("Tiene capacidad para el grito" [She Knows How to Shout])[53] but he was less than pleased by the characterization of Fernando Díaz de Mendoza, whose talent, he thought, lay primarily in the comic. This dissatisfaction was not kept a secret and it began to bother the actor. By the time the troupe arrived in Barcelona the decision to retire the play had been reached on the pretext of squelching political demonstrations planned by Traditionalists who saw the tragedy's propaganda value. Valle-Inclán reacted with more restraint, though no less ardor, than usual; he obtained guarantees and assurances from civil and police authorities that such disturbances would not be permitted. Faced with such evidence of good faith from the governor and the chief of police, Díaz de Mendoza allowed the play to be performed. But his ire peaked when the Barcelona critics, who reviewed the play favorably, failed to laud his interpretation of King Carlino. After the company moved to Pamplona *Voces de gesta* was no longer in the repertoire.

This time Valle-Inclán was not as congenial. The news reached him as he and a group of friends were preparing to set out on an extended excursion through the countryside. He had to be restrained when Salazar, the agent of the troupe, tried to explain the reason for the withdrawal of the successful play. Valle-Inclán was convinced finally to continue the journey, but not before he had impressed his adversary's representative with his fury. The group then resumed its trek to the Santuario de San Miguel in Excelsis, a national monument in Monte Aralar, twelve hundred meters above Huarte-Araquil. There, tradition holds, a penitential knight slew a dragon with the aid of Saint Michael; the Romanic church gracing the spot of the victory dates from the eleventh century and its altar panel, from the same period, is a masterpiece of enamel work in the Byzantine style. In the church, too, are the knight's penitential chains. Undoubtedly, this mixture of legend and art attracted Valle-Inclán to the secluded church on the mountain pinnacle just as local worshipers were drawn every 17 June in procession. He, too, had done battle with the dragon that his theatre adversary represented.

Soon the time came to return to Pamplona. On his arrival, the local journalist Raimundo García ("Garcilaso") arranged a reading of *Voces de gesta* in the Teatro Gayarre. This public recognition seemed to have quelled Valle-Inclán's indignation at the banning of the work by Díaz de Mendoza and so he continued with the company when it moved to San Sebastián. The final break, however, could not be postponed under such trying circumstances. It came in June as the result of an incident with the actor Allen Perkins in the Teatro Bulevar. Josefina Blanco, too, left her position to follow her husband back to Madrid.

There were worthwhile moments in the capital. One such was the Madrid debut of the dancer (Carmen) Tórtola Valencia at the Ateneo in 1912. So impressed was Valle-Inclán by the "Dancer of the naked feet" that he composed the sonnet "A Tórtola":

On walking, she has feline grace,
Her being echoes deepest things,
Her coral and her tassels heralding
An oriental dream of the divine.

Her eyes of jet, warm and astute,
Her smile is sad with ancient lore,
Her flowered skirt a gentle breeze
Of sacred teachings of the East.

She plucked the apple from the tree
Forbidden in a garden of the East,
While, twining round her breasts,

The snake, with sacred sense, bedecks her
Lust. In the transparent haze that is
Her eyes, the light implants a hiss.[54] (A139)

But such cultural encounters were mere distractions from his problems. The separation from the company had serious economic and artistic repercussions. Ironically, the most successful of his plays had brought Valle-Inclán more trouble than reward. The income that he and his wife derived from the theatrical association having been severed, Valle-Inclán lived meagerly once more.

The artistic effect of his break with the Guerrero-Díaz de Mendoza company was also severe. The separation ended plans for the premiere of a new play, *El embrujado*, which had been scheduled for the 1912–1913 season. According to one source, the play was conceived on 28 October 1912, on the day of Valle-Inclán's forty-sixth birthday, during an outing to a pilgrimage site in Galicia. There, amidst the pilgrims who approached the hermitage on their knees to pray for their various needs, Valle-Inclán heard a blind balladeer recount a recent homicide. The setting and the ballad are said to be the inspiration for *El embrujado*.[55] Set in the Galician Valle de Salnés, this powerful rural tragedy delves into the mystico-occult, exploring the carnal bondage that fetters the male protagonist to the woman who has bewitched and seduced him.

Recovering his balance after the play's rejection, the dramatist turned to other producers. Chief among these was Pérez Galdós, then director of Madrid's Teatro Español, to whom Valle-Inclán wrote on 22 November 1912 from Cambados:

My dear and admired Don Benito:
 I've started to publish in the magazine of *El Mundo* a *comedia bárbara* in the manner of others, such as *Romance de lobos*. If your work permits a respite, I would appreciate your reading the issues. Perhaps in that *comedia bárbara* of mine, *El Embrujado*, there's a play suitable for production by making some cuts. You be the judge.
 I've promised Matilde something for the end of the season. And so I'm doubly interested in your opinion on *El Embrujado*.
 As ever, receive the greetings and an embrace from your affectionate friend,
  Valle-Inclán[56] (A140)

Galdós' reply was dated 6 December 1912, as noted on the letter from Valle-Inclán.[57] That communique did not contain a rejection of *El embrujado*; indeed, Galdós must have given Valle-Inclán some hope that the play could be produced, for on 3 February 1913 he wrote again:

Very dear and admired Don Benito:
 I have twice visited your house in the morning only to realize that it was too late to find you in.
 I was told that it was impossible to see you after ten, so, since I live at a great distance from you, I'd have to get up the night before.
 I'm anxious to embrace you and talk to you about my *Embrujado*. Would you be kind enough to set a day and time, making it possible for Fuentes to be there? Although his presence isn't essential since he already knows the play.
 With an embrace and the affection of your admirer,
  Valle-Inclán[58]
  February 3
  23 S/c Santa Engracia (A141)

But Galdós apparently was not enthused over the play and rejected it shortly thereafter. Valle-Inclán reacted first by confronting his new adversaries, then by taking back his manuscript, and finally by writing a letter of protest to the Ayuntamiento de Madrid in which he excoriated Galdós, the principal actress Matilde Moreno, and the leading actor Francisco Fuentes. He took his cause to the liberal tribunal of the Ateneo on 26 February 1913, where he proceeded to introduce his planned reading of *El embrujado* with a bitter history of the play. However, Valle-Inclán's remarks were so inflammatory that the throng that had gathered to hear him became incensed; the speaker had to be reprimanded, but Valle-Inclán reacted with typical bravado before the rising objections of his public. He was removed forcefully by the police, and the event became one more celebrated scandal that, in fact, pleased Valle-Inclán.[59] The actual reading of the play took place at the Ateneo several days later without incident. It was a different public reaction that punctuated this event: Valle-Inclán was applauded avidly and carried outside on the shoulders of members to yet another rousing reception by those who could not get into the Ateneo's auditorium.[60] Through this affair the earlier sympathies Valle-Inclán had demonstrated for Galdós turned to bitterness. Nonetheless, in his generosity, he often expressed later the opinion that Galdós was the renovator of the Spanish drama.

These negative occurrences imposed on the sensitivity of the playwright a new disgust for the establishment theatre. So pronounced was his reaction that Valle-Inclán separated himself not only from the stage but also from the writing of plays over a considerable period. While he would eventually resume his playwriting and see the production of *El yermo de las almas* in 1915, he would not publish a new play again until 1920 (*Farsa y licencia de la reina castiza* (Farce and Licentiousness of the Noble Queen) and did not have another work produced until 1924 (*La cabeza del Bautista* [The Head of the Baptist]). Thus, the second phase of Valle-Inclán's theatrical career came to an abrupt and bitter end.

8 Panorama

Forced to leave the expensive life of the capital, Valle-Inclán and his family moved to Galicia in the autumn of 1912. Although he did not break completely with Madrid, whose intellectual climate he would always need,[1] he spent more and more time in the familiar surroundings of the Valle de Salnés, scene of many of his writings. The setting was charged with the emotions stirred in him by the death of his mother in 1911. He lived in a house owned by Lucila Fernández Soler, Vda. de Fraga, in signorial Fefiñanes, ancient seat of the family of that name and one of three principalities incorporated to form the district capital of Cambados. In the vicinity were the palaces of the Conde de Fefiñanes, the Marqués de Montesacro, and the Marqués de Figueroa; nearby were the ruins of the church of Santa Marina, a Galician martyr, and the monastery of Armenteira, seat of the legend in the poem "Flor de la tarde" in *Aromas de leyenda*. Nearby, too, was the sea. From the terrace of the house he could see the Ría of Arosa. Its presence was a source of enjoyment for Valle-Inclán all his life and an inspiration for his aesthetics. It was in this splendid setting that he welcomed his friends from Madrid and elsewhere. Among the more frequent guests at his house were Ramón Pérez de Ayala, Jacques Chaumié, Julio Romero de Torres, and Rafael de Penagos. He took great pride in showing them the sights of the region, usually on foot.

Galicia was also proud of its native son, as seen in a banquet held in honor of Valle-Inclán. The event took place in Santiago de Compostela on 29 March 1913 under the auspices of the Círculo Jaimista de Santiago, a Carlist group. The proceedings, directed by the poet Filomena Dato Muruais, included a talk on Valle-Inclán's life and works that, because of its laudatory nature, prompted attacks by the clergy, who saw in his writings many anti-clerical and anti-dogma attitudes.[2]

The spring of 1913 found Valle-Inclán in poor physical condition. In a letter to Manuel Murguía on the occasion of his mentor's eightieth birthday (17 May), Valle-Inclán revealed his own state:

Ill and failing, to the point of having to rely on another to write these lines, I send my greeting of admiration, of affection, and of respect to the patriarch of Spanish literature, who I always had as my mentor, to the first and the best, who, in the traditional aridity of pure prose, gave a gift to all by making lyrical larks sing. You were the first man of your era. There was a stellar distance separating you from the men and things of your time. And you could not be understood.[3] (A142)

In spite of his illness Valle-Inclán found the energy to repay the tutelage of Murguía with the sentiments in the letter. It was typical of him, detractors notwithstanding, to acknowledge his debts and to recognize the value of friendship.

That same spring his economic outlook improved when he negotiated a contract with Perlado, Páez y Compañía, a Madrid publisher, for a volume of his collected works under the rubric "Opera Omnia." Valle-Inclán projected the series to include works not yet completed and others to be revised or issued for the first time. The first volume designation was reserved for *La lámpara maravillosa* (which he did not complete until 1916), and the second volume was *Flor de santidad*. The series was enhanced by three more volumes, published in 1913: *La Marquesa Rosalinda*, *El embrujado*, and *Aromas de leyenda*. The first series of "Opera Omnia" was designed by José Moya del Pino under the signature "Joseph Moja-Ornavit."

The new contract brought not only renewed prestige but also economic relief with its advances on royalties. On its negotiation, he transferred his home to the Casal de "La Merced," a farm near Puebla del Caramiñal, which continued to be his base in Galicia for many years as well as the birthplace of two of his children, Carlos and Mariquiña.

But Valle-Inclán could not be satisfied merely with living in Galicia. The artist who had chosen to make his career in the larger world of Spanish letters imposed his views on the Man and he soon looked for ways to return periodically to the capital. Extensive stays in Madrid during these years were made possible by the generosity of friends such as Sebastián Miranda, the sculptor, who tendered him many invitations to be his house-guest over a period of years. These Valle-Inclán accepted from time to time, pleased to be in the pleasant surroundings of the spacious and well-appointed house. Juan Belmonte, who had made a sensational appearance on 26 March 1913 at Madrid's Plaza de Toros, and Ramón Pérez de Ayala were among the frequent visitors to Miranda's house on Calle de Montalbán. It was Miranda who had introduced Valle-Inclán and Belmonte; the writer and the bullfighter became fast friends. As he appreciated artistic achievement in the dancer Tórtola Valencia, so too did Valle-Inclán admire the matador Belmonte, whose performances in the Plaza de Toros elevated him to heights beyond the reach of ordinary men:

The bulls are our only education. And a bullfight is a beautiful thing indeed. For example, one must admire the process: Juan Belmonte. Juan is small, ugly, ungainly, and, if I'm pressed a bit, ridiculous. Well, then, let's place Juan in front of the bull, facing death, and Juan becomes the very image of Apollo. The Greeks left no better sculpture . . . than that of Belmonte in the Plaza, fixed in mid-air, along-side a brave bull. I have been saying for years in my classes on aesthetics that the true artist is characterized by that harmony of opposites. Belmonte typifies that better than any other artist. And that marvelous transfiguration has no comparison.[4] (A143)

The admiration was mutual since their first meeting at Fornos, the famed Madrid café-restaurant. Whenever he was in the capital Belmonte joined Miranda, Valle-Inclán, and the painter Julio Romero de Torres at their *tertulia*. On the occasion of one visit Pérez de Ayala and Valle-Inclán announced that a banquet for Belmonte would be held 28 June 1913 at the restaurant Ideal Retiro.[5]

From such gatherings and earlier encounters proceeded the intimate insight into the life of Valle-Inclán and his circle that Ramón Pérez de Ayala showed in the picturesque novel of bohemian life, *Troteras y danzaderas*, published in 1913. Under the slight cover of a pseudonym—Don Alberto del Monte-Valdés—he depicted Valle-Inclán faithfully. The novel reproduces events of his social and literary life, as well as the physicality of the Mask down to a slight limp reminiscent of the model's condition after his accidental self-wounding.[6]

Valle-Inclán continued to work on the book that he would title *La lámpara maravillosa* and to read excerpts of the aesthetic treatise to special listeners such as the poet Mauricio Bacarisse, who attests to such a reading in March 1914.[7] Valle-Inclán was also writing poetry, and he contributed four poems—"Versos de Job" (Verses on Job), "Nigromancia" (Necromancy), "Mi perro" (My Dog), and "Paisaje" (Landscape)—to an anthology of contemporary Spanish poetry[8] and issued two more titles of his collected works: *Jardín umbrío*[9] and *La cabeza del dragón*. Also during this period Valle-Inclán's friendship with Jacques Chaumié led to the French translation of several of his works by the French diplomat and critic. An undated letter by Valle-Inclán to Darío shows his interest in the publication of one of these:

Some time ago I wrote asking you to intercede with M. Remy de Gourmont regarding the publication of *Romance de lobos* in *Le Mercure*. Today, I have the pleasure of presenting to you the author of that incomparable translation—M. Chaumié, Consul General of France in Spain—whom you will find to have a profound knowledge of our literature, one who knows how to fathom the esoteric depths of your verse, which so many of our academics, critics and poets seem to find so arcane. M. Chaumié is the only man capable of promoting Spain's aesthetic worth in today's world. I have every hope that you will help us through your friendship with M. Remy de Gourmont to set the project in motion.[10] (A144)

The effectiveness of Darío's influence is avouched by the publication of Chaumié's translation in 1914.[11]

Not long after the fortuitous publication of *La geste des loups*, Valle-Inclán had an even better reason to be joyous.. During one of the family's stays in Madrid, Josefina gave birth to their second child—a boy, Joaquín María, born on 28 May 1914--named after his godfather Joaquín Argamasilla de la Cerda, Marqués de Santa Cara, the Carlist noble who was one of Valle-Inclán's closest friends. As his son, the boy was expected to bear Valle-Inclán's name into posterity, preserving it from extinction and perhaps bringing it renown.

But it was not to be. In four short months the child died as the result of an accident on the beach at Fefiñanes on 31 August, when a cabaña door struck him on the head. Meningitis set in within a few days and Joaquín María died on 29 September. The child's coffin, borne by children, was buried the following day in the presbytery of the ruined chapel in the cemetery of Santa Mariña de Dozo. Valle-Inclán was overheard saying to his wife tearfully as he sustained her with his only arm:

Josefina, my sins have caused the death of our son; I'm going to Santiago to prostrate myself in front of the Great Confessor![12] (A145)

But before undertaking the penitential journey to the shrine of St. James, he communicated his grief to José Ortega y Gasset in a letter dated 2 October 1914:

My dear Ortega:
I haven't written earlier due to my suffering and anxieties. Two days ago I buried my baby son. Our Lord took him to Himself. It has caused the greatest sorrow in my life. I don't know what it is about death that one can feel its approach: My child was healthy and yet, I had the premonition of something like a fatal blow. It came, and may no other follow it. I'm worn out. It's a terrible situation. May you never experience such sorrow! The house has become oppressive and yet, I don't want to return to Madrid, where my beautiful dead child was born. I would like to go to Italy, but with my family: my wife and daughter. But it's expensive. My poor Josefina, who is as shattered as I am, has given me an idea. She's prompted me to write to you to ascertain whether the Junta de Estudios could give me a grant to undertake some type of research in Italy. In a field that I could pursue in good conscience. On painting, on literature: A study of Cervantes, Lope, Quevedo in Italy; dialogs of soldiers, gamblers, women, Catalan and Valencian seafarers. An aesthetic vision of Italy. I don't know if any of this is feasible, or the time appropri-

ate. My dear friend (may my Lord Jesus Christ, in whom you don't believe, keep you from such sorrow), the matter is in your hands.
   Eternally grateful, your unfortunate
      Valle-Inclán[13] (A146)

It had been a terrible year for him, his wife, and his daughter. Yet, he could still focus on his intellectual concerns, as another letter to Ortega y Gasset from Cambados, dated 29 October 1914, makes evident:

My dear Ortega:
   I was extremely grateful for your letter. You know that you had my whole friendship from the moment of our first meeting. To your serenity and great talent, of which I took notice from the start, was added your family name. It was in *Los Lunes* that I did my entire apprenticeship, experiencing the warmth, effusiveness, and encouragement of the biggest-hearted man and writer I have ever encountered.
   I've seen mention in an issue of *El Imparcial* of a book you've published (perhaps the one promised in your letter) and I would like to read it. In an article in which Gómez Baquero flaunts his insignificance, I read these words of yours: "Philosophy is the general science of love." So in accord am I that in the same newspaper I wrote: "The love of all things is the summit of supreme beauty, and whoever attains it penetrates the meaning of the world, possesses Mystic Knowledge: But doesn't love, when our egoism is put aside, become divine intuition?" Send me your book. An embrace from your constant
      Valle-Inclán[14] (A147)

European politics were tumultuous in 1914, as in the previous year. The planned French premiere of *La geste des loups* was made impossible by the political events that transpired that year. After the assassination of Archduke Ferdinand on 28 June, the situation between nations deteriorated rapidly. The temper of the times enveloped the entire European intellectual community. With Germany's formal declaration of war against France on 3 August, the lines were drawn and sides chosen. The majority of Spanish intellectuals sided with the Allies. Valle-Inclán, too, made that choice. It could not be otherwise for the Man when the Artist identified more closely with the ideas, literature, and traditions of Italy, France, and England than with those of Germany. His dedication to the cause of the Allied powers was demonstrated in his signing of the document entitled "Palabras de algunos españoles" (Words of Some Spaniards), which the francophiles had promulgated first in Paris and then in Madrid as a statement of their sympathies. The "Manifesto de los intelectuales," as the document came to be known in Spain, bore the signatures of many prominent individuals, among them Unamuno, Azorín, Antonio Machado, Maeztu, Grandmontagne, Rusiñol, Enrique de Mesa, Gabriel Alomar, Ciges Aparicio, Romero de Torres, and Anselmo Miguel Nieto. Curiously, in joining his sympathies to the Allied cause Valle-Inclán was opposing the stance of Carlism, which saw its own advantage in the heralding of Germanic rights. This separation marks the beginning of Valle-Inclán's concern with international problems over strictly nationalistic ones.

Most members of the "Generación del '98" adopted the Allied cause. But Benavente and Pío Baroja refused to sign the declaration. Benavente, apparently, made a point of keeping apart from such mass pronouncements; he had abstained from the condemnation of Echegaray, whom he was later to laud as the "primer autor dramático de España del siglo XIX" (the leading Spanish dramatist of the nineteenth century), and now he was doing the same in regard to Germany. Baroja, in contrast, held an artistic attitude closer to Germanic tradition. This choice created many problems for Baroja, who was already disliked for his hydrochloric character. Baroja was forced to counter various attacks on his integrity as a result of his abstention. One of these onslaughts brought the intervention of Valle-Inclán on his behalf. A controversial banquet given in Paris just prior to Baroja's return to Spain from one of his trips elicited some untoward commentary from Enrique Gómez Carrillo in a Parisian newspaper for which he wrote regularly. The literary repartee was joined by others; finally, on a later occasion, Baroja himself added his retort while defending another journalist. Gómez Carrillo demanded satisfaction for the insult he thought he had received, sending his seconds to Baroja. The latter responded by naming Valle-Inclán and Azorín as his representatives. Valle-Inclán attempted to pacify the journalist, but his diplomacy failed; only by resorting to his characteristic temper was Valle-Inclán able to terminate the affair without Baroja's involvement.[15]

Such altercations, triggered by minor incidents, had their real cause in the antipathies created by the European hostilities. The war became the principal subject of discussion and argument in Madrid. The Café Nuevo Levante was one of many stages for minor confrontations between germanophiles and francophiles. Spain's political neutrality made possible the freedom to express views openly. Valle-Inclán was always among the most opinionated:

Through my rebelliousness, I think that I'm the most patriotic of my contemporaries. And I believe that with the present government being so detestable and abhorrent, to collaborate in the work of the State would be tantamount to adding our efforts to the ruin of Spain. Whenever one of my friends becomes a politician— a politician!—rising and prospering as such, I stop greeting him.[16] (A148)

However, the country prospered because of the war in spite or because of its neutrality. Economic prosperity touched many quarters and so the passionate discussions against the fact of war were merely superficialities. The war appeared to be good for Spain, until its vagaries touched a quarter close to the individual. The war forced the closing of the Café Nuevo Levante, and the famed *tertulias* known throughout European and American artistic circles became another casualty.

As if the times mandated change, Valle-Inclán terminated his contract with Perlado, Páez y Compañía and immediately negotiated for the continuation of "Opera Omnia" through the Sociedad General Española de Librería; his new publisher would issue his works from 1915 through 1922, assuring Valle-Inclán of a good income:

Thirty-five or forty thousand pesetas a year . . . And note that I get a better income from old works than from recent ones. This shows that time is the same for books as for gold: it increases their worth.[17] (A149)

In time Valle-Inclán could afford to return to Madrid on his own account. He moved his family to 5 Calle de Francisco Rojas, in the Luchana section of the city. Friends regaled him with furnishings, artistic works, and decorations. Settled in the spacious and comfortable quarters, the Man experienced another pleasant period of his life. He returned to the *tertulias*, then held at the Café Lion d'Or, with renewed vigor and once more the intellectual climate of the capital received the added measure of Valle-Inclán's genius.

As always, he continued to write diligently, although he remained fond of confounding the critics:

I don't like literature. I'm the sort who has to overcome inertia in order to write. Consequently, I'm not happy doing it. I think I chose the wrong path . . . Yes, I made a mistake. I would like to be an orator. Oratory! How often it is slandered and debased![18] (A150)

Besides the projection of his complete works under the new publisher, he took time to answer special requests for his pieces, as in the case of the magazine *Labor Gallega*, in Havana, for the right to reprint his poem "Cantigas de vellas" (Old Women's Canticle), which had been published first in La Coruña by *El Noroeste* in 1910; when re-issued it was accompanied by illustrations by Antonio Alenda. The importance of this work lies in that at forty-seven lines it is the single longest piece Valle-Inclán ever published in *gallego*, the tongue of his native Galicia. Other publications of 1915 included sections of *La lámpara maravillosa*, in various Madrid journals.[19] He also showed a return of interest in dramatic writing by beginning a new tragedy, *Pan divino*, which he planned to dedicate to Margarita Xirgu.[20] In the interview with López Nuñez early in 1915, he stated that his works were being readied for publication in France under the editorship of Jacques Chaumié. But the project must have been thwarted either by the fortunes of the war or by literary misadventure because the complete works never appeared. Finally, he reissued *Aguila de blasón* as the fourteenth volume of "Opera Omnia" under the aegis of his new publisher.

The artistic well-being of Valle-Inclán during this period, reflected in his literary activity, was accompanied by his economic independence. Both these factors contributed to the formulation of a new attitude toward his role in society. Considering himself a landed gentleman after the acquisition of "La Merced," he became interested in establishing his personal claim to family titles supposedly vacant. To the end of receiving official sanction, he petitioned the Ministerio de Gracia y Justicia.[21] But the involved process did not have a satisfactory conclusion. His appeal was denied, perhaps because others had stronger claims or because the titles were not really vacant, or perhaps because Valle-Inclán lacked sufficient credentials. The title may have been denied out of base prejudice against him. Nonetheless, the Man carried himself erect, the Artist wrote with true nobility, and the Mask displayed the enigma of greatness.

Even during this era of acceptance Valle-Inclán remained a highly controversial figure, in all three aspects. The most direct attack occurred in January 1916 when Julio Casares took aim at Valle-Inclán in *Critica profana*.[22] Writing the first extended criticism of the author's works, he recognized the manifest artistry of his subject but chastised unequivocally what he held were instances of direct plagiarism, intellectual laziness, or artistic deception. He condemned the *Sonatas* because Valle-Inclán had employed an episode derived from Casanova's memoirs; he worried that the publication of Valle-Inclán's works in France would reveal the novelist as a charlatan and would reflect badly on Spain and her intellectuals. Casares saw his mission as providing the exposure of a fraud by a countryman before foreign critics discovered it and relished the implications. He proceeded to castigate the forgery that he deduced in Valle-Inclán's works, all the more culpable in his sight because of the writer's undeniable ability. He even went so far as to deride what he saw as self-plagiarism and redundancy in earlier works, innovations in language and aesthetic preferences. In short, Casares failed to see the growth of the artist or to understand the reasons behind the unending purification of his work through newer versions. In his prologue he recognizes himself as a neophyte but proceeds anyway to judge harshly without the critical acumen necessary to validate his opinion. Years later, writing in the prologue to the second edition of the same book, included in his collected works, Casares recognized his youthful impetuosity and repealed its unfounded opinions.[23]

At this time, Valle-Inclán did not make a formal defense or rebuttal to the accusations of Casares. Instead, he concentrated on preparing the final draft of the aesthetic treatise that would be the crystallization of ideas he had expressed earlier in conversations, lectures, and writings.[24] The publication of *La lámpara maravillosa*[25] was more than sufficient an answer to the self-styled critic who had not bothered to inform himself on the aesthetic stance of the writer he had criticized with great vituperation. These "Ejercicios espirituales," as Valle-Inclán subtitled the book, formalize the tenets of his personal aesthetic. Through biographical references that serve as keys to the evolution of the artist, Valle-Inclán discloses the ways and means of meditation, which he has employed in his constant approach toward the contemplation of Beauty:

At the onset of my aesthetic initiation, I had eyes only to delight in and to love the divine crystal of the world, eyes like those of birds whose song greets the rising of the sun. All forms and all lives communicated the ineffable secret of paradise, disclosing their fraternal kinship with me. Nothing was alien to me, but I felt the distress of the mystic who intuits that his path is an erroneous one. . . . Seeking the plane on which to still my life, I tormented myself with this divine and human anxiety. To a degree, I became a disciple of Miguel de Molinos: I elaborated my aesthetics on the basis of his mystical teachings. . . . I was wandering in the dark night alone, without another soul to direct me. I was guided solely by my love of the Muses.

I was ambitious for my words to be like clear crystals—mystery, light, firmness. For me, the music and the idea of these crystalline words had the same symbolic prestige as the sacred letters of pentacles. . . . And I toiled long years with the fortitude, sorrow, and joy of an ascetic in order to give my words the emotion of stars, of fountains, of fresh grass. . . . I agonized over the birth pangs of each . . . It was a felicitous moment when I learned to purge the ephemeral from my intuitiveness and to experience the world through sanctified eyes. . . . Pico della Mirandola was my master during that period.[26] (A151)

While critical response to the new work was limited and only sporadically favorable, the enthusiasm of such friends as Antonio Machado[27] was very satisfying to Valle-Inclán. He had also sent a copy of La lámpara maravillosa to Unamuno, along with a letter dated 14 February 1916:

There have always been few men with whom I can discuss spiritual matters, but their number decreases daily. People are afraid to speak of death and are like children frightened by ghosts, who on going to bed at night pull the covers over their heads. It would suit me always to speak of the life of our souls beyond the stars, as well as of the sidereal meaning of our actions. The sorrow of having lived must be horrible. If remorse oppresses us now, imagine what it will do afterward! Is there any comparison between the purification of years with the purification of death?[28] (A152)

Another who would have shown great interest in La lámpara maravillosa was Rubén Darío, who died in Nicaragua on 6 February 1916 shortly before its publication. Valle-Inclán received the news while at the afternoon tertulia at El Gato Negro on Calle del Príncipe. Subsequently, he, Azorín, Maeztu and Ortega y Gasset met at the Ateneo to discuss Darío and his work. Valle-Inclán defined his personality:

Darío was a child. He was extremely good. He lived in a pious religious fear. Unceasingly, he saw things from the other world. Better said, he projected everything there. I repeat, he was a child. He wasn't proud, spiteful, or ambitious. He had none of the angelic sins. More distant than anyone from the Luciferian sins, his were only those of the flesh. He had a sweet tooth, at times to the point of gluttony, he was sensual, he was licentious. All of that perishes with the flesh. His soul was pure, extremely pure.[29] (A153)

Perhaps more characteristic of Valle-Inclán's view of Darío is the attitude evident in an anecdote set in a Madrid café around 1900. Darío had just concluded a monologue praising Unamuno when someone showed him a newspaper in which Don Miguel said of Darío's writing, among other negative things, that it still showed "the Indian feathers that he had inside him." Darío absorbed the article, along with numerous cognacs, in a separate corner until only Valle-Inclán and he remained in the café. Valle-Inclán tried to bring him out of his depression:

Don't pay attention to it. It . . . is not important. Today Unamuno says this and tomorrow he's capable of saying the opposite. Let's get some fresh air.[30] (A154)

Several days later, Darío returned to the café to read a letter he was sending to Unamuno with a glowing article about him written for La Nación in Buenos Aires. His friends applauded Darío's generosity. Unamuno's reaction became known a few months later when, on encountering Valle-Inclán, he expressed his consternation over the Darío affair. Valle-Inclán was quick to put the matter in proper perspective:

The situation, my friend Don Miguel, is not unusual, much less baffling. It is, quite simply, the result of a confrontation between two different and opposite people. It's a very natural occurrence. You weren't born to understand one another because Rubén and you are antipodes. Let me demonstrate: Rubén has all the faults of the flesh—he's a glutton, a drinker, a womanizer, indolent, etc., etc. And yet, he possesses all the virtues of the spirit: he's good, generous, simple, altruistic, humble, etc., etc. You, on the other hand, hoard all the virtues of the flesh—you're frugal, abstemious, chaste, untiring. And you possess all the vices of the spirit: you're arrogant, egotistic, avaricious, spiteful, etc., etc. Therefore, when Rubén dies and his flesh rots, which is what is bad in him, his spirit will remain, which is what is good in him, and he will be saved! But in your case, when you die and your flesh rots, which is what is good about you, your spirit will remain, which is what's bad in you, and you will be condemned! . . . From that moment on, Unamuno has been very preoccupied.[31](A155)

Stunned by the loss, the artistic communities of Latin America and Europe sought ways in which to pay homage to the great poet on his passing. In Spain tributes of varying degree were planned; Valle-Inclán himself announced in El Liberal the formation of a planning committee[32] for a commemorative event worthy of Darío's importance, following earlier suggestions by Federico Oliver and Luis Fernández Ardavín in the same newspaper.

But the most personal tribute of Valle-Inclán to his friend was in his memory. That Darío was always before him is evidenced by the dedication to him of the 1906 edition of *Sonata de estío* and by the countless references to him in Valle-Inclán's works, as for example in *Luces de bohemia* (where he appears first in conversation with the protagonist and later with Bradomín in a cemetery); in *Tirano Banderas* (where he is the "Cisne de Nicaragua" [Swan of Nicaragua]); in "Bestiario" (Beastiary) from *La pipa de kif*: ("Meditaciones erudites / Que oyó Rubén alguna vez" [Lofty meditations / Heard by Rubén at some time]), and in "¡Aleluya!" also from that collection of poems, where the reference is more personal:

Darío's hand to me in shade,
Mention of Poe's name is made.

Pentagram of Magian star
Heralds day upon this bard.

His white tunic of Essene
Gives the luster of Selene.

Shadow out of delta's mist,
Celtic pipes resound your gift.

You have loved the roses, wine,
and the women on the vine.

Bard of Life and Hope,
All my praise on you I dote.

For your golden dawn's hurrah,
Hallelujah! Hallelujah! Hallelujah![33] (A156)

Not long after Darío's death, Valle-Inclán had occasion to laud the work of yet another great writer, Cervantes, whose death three hundred years earlier was being commemorated throughout the Hispanic world in 1916. Among the tributes was the publication of Cervantes's *La guarda cuidadosa* in Madrid, with illustrations by José Moya del Pino and a brief prologue by Valle-Inclán:

On the twenty-third of April of the year 1616, Miguel de Cervantes died of a heart ailment. To commemorate that date and the three centuries that are fulfilled today, this edition of LA GUARDA CUIDADOSA has been issued. It was undoubtedly written for an ingenuous public and performed by players perhaps even more ingenuous. Players of golden paper crowns and beards of flax. It always stirs up in children the ingenuity of past centuries, and so, in order to understand and to capture the enchantment of old literature, there is nothing better than to become childlike. In order to preserve the crystalline virtue of this enchantment, there are no footnotes, glosses, or jottings in the *entremés* LA GUARDA CUIDADOSA. It is printed for children, and they can understand it better than adults. (A157)

An important event for Valle-Inclán in 1916 was an invitation by the government of France, through his long-time friend Jacques Chaumié, to visit the country and to view the fighting on the front. Having decided to undertake the journey, Valle-Inclán spoke of his plan to put the experience into words:

I will write a book that I have already conceived. That book will be published in parts as I write it, appearing in various French, English, and Argentine news-papers.[34] (A158)

Because of the importance of the invitation, Valle-Inclán was made a special correspondent of the newspapers *El Imparcial* and *La Nación*. But before he expressed his viewpoint based on the actual experience, he expressed certain preconceived notions:

I would like to present a total view of the war, as if we were allowed to contemplate it without the limitations of time and space. I know very well that the people who read newspapers have no idea of the destiny of this war: the continuation of history and not its interruption . . . War is unavoidable. It is fated so that love can exist. Friction engenders heat and light. Light is love. Man is nothing more than the product of the marriage of sun and earth; just as the sunflower obeys the rotational movement of the earth that maintains its fascination with the sun, so must human-ity follow the solar route from East to West, being reborn once more at the point of departure.[35] (A159)

As Valle-Inclán believed, the war was the continuation of history because it formed a segment of the circle that is Man's past, present, and future. As such, there was in it a hint of the entire cycle, visible to the trained mind's eye; as Valle-Inclán predicted:

In Greece, our civilization gathered to itself the full primitive force of India; the Mediterranean was the *civilized* sea of Rome, until Spain, inheritor of that Greco-Roman past, established the civilization of the Atlantic with the discovery of Amer-ica. The Atlantic civilization has its apogee in the splendor of England . . . England will perish as did the empires of Greece, Rome, and Spain . . . England will perish; but never at the hands of Germany. Rather, fatefully, it will be at the hands of the United States of America, which is on the route of the sun. And a new dawn will be kindled in Japan when the American sun sets; in the meantime, the civilizations of the Pacific will flourish, with Panama becoming the navel of the world and the pathway to India, that is, to the return to that quietude where movement is engen-dered.[36] (A160)

According to his rationale, every nation involved in the war had an impor-tant role in the evolution of this circular pattern; the part played by some, even if villainous, had its importance in the greater scheme of things. Germany was a case in point:

It has a role, and a very important one. The same role as ever: the characters are sustained throughout the human tragedy. Now as before, the German is the seminal Scythian. It has been shown that Mediterranean races lose vitality as original crossbreeding is diluted through the enervating action of time. Nature wisely arranges that from time to time barbaric invasions invigorate our blood. Thus, the German, the seminal Scythian, travels South, thrusting into the lands of the sun; and, at the same time that he purifies overly spiritualized races, he allows himself to be conquered and dominated by their own vitalizing spirit. In this war, Germany, symbol of Jehovah's materialism, will be overcome in its strength.[37] (A161)

In spite of the prognostication of defeat Valle-Inclán interprets the role of Germany as a valid one because it was fulfilling historical necessity. But Spain had failed to recognize the importance of the moment; its lesser demand that Gibraltar be returned to Spain had clouded its judgment and made it politically impossible for the nation to become the ally of Great Britain:

We should have gone to war with Germany. The Allies offered us a reward in the eastern Mediterranean; it would have meant a continuation of our history, the shout of Lepanto thus being more than a sonorous echo . . . But Spanish politicians are ignorant of the exact locale of Constantinople. Of course, it would still be possible to do something in Spain without taking politicians into consideration. The King . . . has good intentions; a king alone could save a country, of course; but . . . what of the dynasty?[38] (A162)

Finally, he dedicates his trip to the verification of his preconceptions and to the interpretation of the war in a new way:

I have a prior conception; I go to verify that conception, not to invent one. Art is always an abstraction. If my gatekeeper and I see the same thing, she doesn't realize what she's seen because she lacks a prior conception. The war cannot be viewed in terms of a few grenades falling here and there, nor as a few dead and wounded who end up as statistics. It must be seen as from a star . . . beyond time and space.[39] (A163)

Valle-Inclán traveled to Paris along with Pérez de Ayala, Unamuno, Manuel Azaña, and Santiago Rusiñol, all of whom had also received invitations of an official nature. While in Paris Valle-Inclán was the guest of the Chaumié family, which returned the earlier courtesy that had been extended to Jacques when he had visited "La Merced." During his stay in the "City of Lights" Valle-Inclán was accompanied by many Spanish and French acquaintances from the artistic world; he spent much time with Corpus Barga, Ciges Aparicio (then a Paris staffer for *El Imparcial*), and Pedro Salinas (recently appointed to lecture at the Sorbonne). He saw the city through the memory of words spoken by Darío, and one of the sights he elected to visit, in the spirit of pilgrimage, was the house on the Rue d'Herchelle where the poet had lived, although such places greatly saddened him. Nonetheless, Valle-Inclán eagerly accepted the invitation to attend a soiree in Darío's honor at the Sorbonne that Ernesto Martinenche, a professor of Spanish literature, had arranged. Valle-Inclán was the principal speaker at the event, where he met many literary and academic figures, among them Alfred Morel-Fatio, the French Hispanist who founded the *Bulletin Hispanique*.

During a visit to the Latin Quarter, he ate at the restaurant Médicis, the first and last he visited in Paris. He found to his surprise that he was feted by the proprietor, who recognized him from a picture in the Parisian newspaper *Le Matin*.[40] Memorable, too, were Valle-Inclán's forays into the battlefield, where he paraded his Carlist uniform—cloak and beret—as he passed authoritatively through French trenches mistaken for a General Fourand, who had also lost an arm. Many anecdotes arose from his visits to the front. A letter from Valle-Inclán to his wife, dated 23 May 1916 and written in Paris, reveals other activities:

Dear Josefina:
  I can only write a brief note because I'm expecting a visit from an American and I think he's at the door. It wasn't the American. Let's go on. This afternoon I'll be visited by an editor from *Les Temps* who wishes to publish an interview with me. I think the American is at the door now. He's waiting in the salon and I'll finish the letter. Tomorrow I will be received by Briand, president of the Council of Ministers and the man who carries the most weight in the destiny of the world. He's indicated a desire to meet me. On Tuesday of next week, I'll be welcomed at the Society of Theatre Persons, which has cordially invited me to attend one of their sessions. I think that they want to propose me for the Legion of Honor . . . I think that you are the one who should be decorated, since you find such things so appealing.[41] (A164)

Despite his denial of personal interest in honors (perhaps due to having been denied the vacant family titles), Valle-Inclán sometimes accepted recognition quite happily. Such was the case when his influential friend Julio Burell, formerly governor of Toledo and at this time Minister of Public Education, recognized the intellectual contribution that Valle-Inclán made in the cafés of Madrid and sought to make his ideas available to a greater public by creating an important post for his friend: the Chair of Aesthetics at the Escuela Especial de Pintura, Escultura y Grabado de Madrid. Although the formal appointment was made through two royal communiques dated 18 July 1916,[42] Valle-Inclán was already using the title "Catedrático de Estética" on his calling card during his visit to France. In an anecdote told by Leal da Camara, Valle-Inclán revealed that while on a flight over enemy lines he dropped a hundred of his calling cards to the German troops below.[43] That Valle-Inclán flew over the battlefield at Alsace is verified by Corpus Barga, who listened as he explained in the Médicis restaurant how he had been seeking the proper perspective for his impression of the war until he was taken on a flight:

The night flight has been a revelation. It will provide the point of view of my novel, the stellar vision.[44] (A165)

As Corpus Barga recounts it, Valle-Inclán stirred such enthusiasm among French aviators during his visit to an air base that they insisted on his staying overnight. They called to cancel his previous dinner engagement and proceeded to involve him in all their activities, including the dangerous night flying that had been initiated during the war.

After the satisfying visit to Paris and a confrontation with the reality of war at the front, in Verdun and elsewhere, Valle-Inclán returned to Spain. In Cambados, he began to compile his notes, writing the projected book during August and September of that year. Interrupting his pacific life in Galicia for periodic stays in Madrid, he would join Azaña, Bello, Araquistaín, Icaza, Canedo, and others at the Café Regina.

Valle-Inclán accepted the post at the Escuela Especial for the academic year 1916–1917. But as he had done with past sinecures, he eventually abandoned his formal duties altogether, claiming that he did not wish to be paid for what he did free in the café. It is more than likely, however, that the demands of the position were the real causes for the desertion of what might otherwise have been an ideal post. Rather than adhere to the protocol of the classroom, he lectured to his classes in the Prado and in other museums of Madrid; often, the sessions would continue during walks or in the cafés. Yet, even after Valle-Inclán gave up his scheduled classes, he periodically convened his pupils for impromptu lectures, and Burell continued to send his monthly salary. Valle-Inclán's pride would not let him accept Burell's gesture and he became indignant each time the money arrived at his house.

Toward the end of 1916 his articles on the war began to appear in *Los Lunes de El Imparcial*, preceded by reports on the hostilities from Armando Palacio Valdés in Paris and by Ricardo León in Berlin. Valle-Inclán's essays were published under the heading "Un día de guerra (Visión estelar)," a work consisting of nine segments published between 11 October and 18 December. A continuation, subtitled "En la luz del día," was published in *Los Lunes de El Imparcial* from 8 January through 26 February 1917. The essays of the first segment were collected and published in one volume on 30 June 1917 with the title *La media noche. Visión estelar de un momento de guerra*.[45] This work, the book that he had promised earlier, became the definitive edition of his overview of the war between France and Germany. In his introduction, the "Breve noticia," the author explains his purpose:

It was my intent to bring together in a book the various and diverse incidents of a day of war in France. As it turns out, on writing of the war, the narrator, who was a witness earlier, gives the events a chronological intertwining that is purely accidental, born out of the human and geometric limitations that prevent us from being in several places at the same time. . . . The narrator adjusts the war and its accidents to his pace of walking: the battles begin when his eyes behold them: The terrible sounds of war are extinguished when he distances himself from the tragic places, resuming when he approaches. All the narratives are limited by the geometric position of the narrator.[46] (A166)

Recognizing this limitation, the author seeks to overcome its impediments by proposing a larger, panoramic view:

But the individual who could be in diverse places at the same time . . . would certainly have a vision, feeling, and conception of the war totally different from that of the miserable witness who was subject to the geometric laws of corporal, mortal matter. . . . This thaumaturgic intuition of places and events, this comprehensiveness that appears to go beyond space and time is not, however, foreign to literature.[47] (A167)

In the possibility of such a stance outside the confines of time and space lies the answer to the problems of presenting the totality of an event such as the war:

When the soldiers of France return to their villages . . . each one will have a different story to tell, and there will be hundreds of thousands of stories, expressive of as many views, which will ultimately be reduced to one view, the sum of the parts. The sad glance of the soldier will then disappear in order to create the collective vision, the view of the entire populace that was in the war and beheld all the events at once from all the places.[48] (A168)

In the attainment of this vision lies the creation of the poet, who can capture in words the impact of the event's totality. Yet, in the final paragraph of his "Breve noticia," the author declares the frustration he encountered in his attempt to obtain the astral view he had envisioned. Despite his failure, he sees the promise of fulfillment in a new attempt. In this final commitment to hope Valle-Inclán proves himself a true artist.

It was this serenity that Anselmo Miguel Nieto captured in 1917 in his second oil portrait of Valle-Inclán. The seated subject is clothed in typical dark garments setting off his bright countenance and into which his long black beard disappears. He is portrayed in three-quarter face against the strong vertical thrust of a wall whose massiveness is broken by two arched windows overlooking the water and distant mountains of Cambados. It is a magnificent study reminiscent of Whistler in its simplicity, line, and color but evoking the Renaissance in its use of light and background. Entering through the arches and falling directly on the single gaunt hand resting on the dark chair, the light is directed toward the subject's tranquil face by his elongated lone arm. The triangular composition—window, hand, face—supplements the other planes—vertical, horizontal, diagonal—adding to the realistic conception a cubistic quality appropriate in the context of Valle-Inclán's multifaceted personality.

The diversity the painter captured so ably continued to be evident in the literary productivity of Valle-Inclán. He could always be counted on to write a prologue to a friend's book, be it a young poet such as Fernando de la Quadra Salcedo, for whom he penned "Emoción lírica,"[49] or an old mentor such as Armando Palacio Valdés, who had referred his *Epitalamio* to "Clarín"; in an appendix to an anthology, he stated:

I profess that, since my student days, long before I dreamed of being a writer, I have had a deep admiration for Don Armando Palacio Valdés, one that grows daily because with the years I have come to understand him better. But as great as is my admiration for the writer, it is almost surpassed by my esteem for the serious and reserved man who is faced with the fragile and commonplace applause of critic and press.[50] (A169)

In another context, he was always willing to help his friends through his personal influence, as seen in a letter written from Madrid to Ortega y Gasset dated 20 June 1917:

My dear Ortega:
   I don't know if it's an indiscretion on my part writing to you at a time when the matter of *El Imparcial* must weigh on you with that intense and ethical preoccupation that you give everything. I beg you to forgive me. First of all, my most cordial congratulations for the position all of you have taken. And now, to a request: Nilo Fabra, a very dear friend who worked for many years at *El Imparcial*, wishes to return when you do. I feel that it is justly his due; you will find him to be an intelligent colleague and a loyal man. I would greatly appreciate it, dear Ortega, if you could help him in this matter.
   Again, my most effusive salute for your stance. An embrace from your old
      Valle-Inclán[51] (A170)

His generosity to young and old colleagues alike was rewarded with their respect and, not infrequently, with a tangible token of appreciation, through portraits done of him or through dedications of books. One dedication was by the occultist Mario Roso de Luna, who had been drawn to the author of *La lámpara maravillosa*.[52] Valle-Inclán's influence continued to spread through the varied promulgation of his own books, as with the continuation of the "Opera Omnia" series of his complete works.

   Uppermost in the minds of Europeans in 1917, Valle-Inclán among them, was the changing pattern of continental politics that World War I made inevitable. While the battles raged on many fronts, internal changes were occurring within various nations. Most important of these was the great turbulence within Russia; building over a period of years and fanned by misfortunes in the war, discontent soon erupted into open civil strife. With the overthrow of Czar Nicholas II in March 1917, the Russian Revolution became a fact from which there was no reprieve. By the official end of the war on 11 November 1918, the royal family of Russia had been annihilated. The imagination of the world was caught up in the fantastic push of Russia's belated upheaval. *Das Kapital* became increasingly important reading among intellectuals, particularly in Europe, as Marx and Lenin began to emerge as contemporary heroes. The impact of the proletarian revolt, much more so than the American or French revolutions, was felt everywhere.

In Spain, a general strike led by the socialists showed the growing demand for reform in many areas; it was to be one of many such acts in defiance of the established order. From this moment, the socialist movement gained momentum in Spain. In the elections of 1918, six socialist deputies were voted into the Cortes. For years thereafter socialism made inroads into the monarchical structure of the nation, ultimately achieving the forced, but peaceful, exile of the king and the establishment of the Second Republic.

Valle-Inclán, never indifferent to world events of the magnitude of the Russian Revolution, was enthused by an ideology that paralleled sentiments concerning the masses he had expressed in the *Comedias bárbaras* and other works. But his interest was apolitical.[53] Just as earlier he had espoused the cause of Carlism in its aesthetic significance, Valle-Inclán turned to the communist ideal as the modern solution to man's inhumanity to man. The transition of this viewpoint is clear in the following statement:

In the nineteenth century, the history of Spain might have been written by Don Carlos; in the twentieth century, it is being written by Lenin.[54] (A171)

The communist outlook survived the vagaries of politics because it created a new way of life; and Valle-Inclán saw this as a necessity:

A government regime that has not created a new style and, consequently, a new way of life, fails to exist![55] (A172)

World War I inspired not only political evolution but also changes in artistic outlook that cut loose many and varied ideas previously repressed. The era of the "isms," begun earlier, was unleashed fully as a result of sensibilities shocked by the conflagration in Europe, and the postwar outlook came under the influence of its grotesque and horrible revelations. The onslaughts of reality drove creative minds to seek other than established forms to express their visions. The rationale of realism was no longer valid. Consequently, some individuals disguised reality in abstraction while others diffused it through distortion. It was the period of the *Avant-garde*.

In the opening chapter of an anthology of articles and plates on Spanish Basque art, Valle-Inclán expressed in 1919 his own *vanguardist* views, many of which had been promulgated for years in the cafés of Madrid:

The region of Castile manifests a mystical expression, an expression of termination, an expression of exhaustion. It has existed and, in order to exist again, looks back, like men who have had full lives and, seeing a future without recourse, seek to find themselves in their consciousness . . . Our Mediterranean is not the Eastern Mediterranean, nor is it the one that benefited from Greece; it is the African Mediterranean, the sad Semitic Mediterranean, the sad deceptive Mediterranean. Such are the two revered expressions of Spanish art to date: the Castilian of exhaustion and the Levantine of deceitfulness . . . Castile is dead because Castile looks back and, on looking back, one can't view the present; in so doing, one can't acquire consciousness. And the person who acquires consciousness of his acts, together with awareness of what he has experienced and the pain of having lived—because on looking back and seeing oneself in one's consciousness, we all feel the sorrow of not having achieved something intense—that person becomes a mystic and consecrates himself to knowing how to die. But the Basque people, and with it all those who look on the Cantabrian Sea, have yet to evolve and are unable to look back to a past, to a previous age, to conquests, to a geographic history—ever past, as is all history—nor does it possess knowledge learned from others: they are primitives; still possessed of a youthful sense, they look ahead and are driven by the Spermatic Logos, by the generative drive.[56] (A173)

Such concepts, although applied to art, continued to be valid in terms of "the problem of Spain," which had preoccupied the "Generation of '98" since its inception. Valle-Inclán, for one, was still struggling to find a perspective that would aid in resolving the problem.

While the war had not touched Spain directly, it did have an impact on the life of the nation. The creative sector of the country was impressed by the horrors of "the war to end wars," as President Woodrow Wilson had termed it, and sought to find new interpretations of existence in the light of the holocaust. While society turned its back on the recent realities, adopting a nervous giddiness that reached its height in the 1920s, its artists did not adopt such a fictitious attitude. They turned, instead, to the reinterpretation of the condition of humanity based on the recent disclosures of the war.

Tolling the death throes of Darío's *Modernismo*, a generation of new writers began to look for directions offering greater artistic freedom. The futurism of Marinetti and the Dadaism of Tristan Tzara had repercussions in postwar Spain. *Creacionismo*, elaborated by the Chilean Vicente Huidobro, found its most ardent Spanish voice in the poet Gerardo Diego. But it was *Ultraísmo* that became the focal movement at this time. Its tenets demanded that Spanish letters, particularly poetry, be purified by eschewing all that was considered nonpoetic, elements such as narrative, rhetoric, traditional forms, and cliché. The adoption of this purgative view would allow the poet, it held, to make image and metaphor the veins of poetic expression. Thus, the mechanics of the medium were realigned toward a new freedom, both visionary and interpretative.

Although he continued to have earlier works re-issued or translated,[57] it was the publication of *La pipa de kif*,[58] Valle-Inclán's second book of poems, that marked his creative reaction to the changing times. While he did not align himself with any of the new movements, he participated in their spirit through the renovation of his poetic stance. The poems in *La pipa de kif* lack the modernistic tone of earlier works and the strong Galician flavor of *Aromas de leyenda*, his first collection of poems. The vision that the poet versifies in the new book is encrusted with a cynicism and a stylization whose tendency is toward deformation; the tragic gesture is treated with satanic humour; the movement of life is seen in terms of its grotesqueness. In "Fin de carnaval," the poet notes wryly:

Dogs put their snouts together
In the darkness:
They lament all the better
Man's ineptness.

Absurd afternoon. Horrifying
Grimace of pain.
The Goat-Footed One is trying
The Prior's mane.[59] (A174)

Having observed daily life's absurdity, the poet decrees in "¡Aleluya!" that his poems will reflect that condition:

Through divine Spring inspired,
My mind has become riled

Writing teetering verses today—
Grotesque, a purist would say.[60] (A175)

And in "Garrote vil" the preparations for an execution reinforce a cynical social indifference toward death made all the more grotesque by the persistent hammering:

Tan! Tan! Tan! The hammer rings.
As the scaffold is erected,
In the field the cuckoo sings,
And the stars to leave elected
To the rhythm of the beat
which the hammer beats out neat:
Tan! Tan! Tan!

A lone gypsy hawks his fritters
From the shelter of a barn,
Braying donkeys thrust their ears
Over thatched walls in the yard,
And the circle of the clods
Hears the gypsy of the fritters
Loudly praise the guilty man.

In the chapel waits the culprit;
While a priest says Latin prayers,
Cries a single yellow candle

And the doomed man gulps his meal
Of a yellow herb tortilla
Which the small café had sent
To the chapel for the guest.

In the plaza rings the hammer
As the hangman earns his keep.
Cloth of mourning drapes the slammer.
Since the cloth is Catalan,
It's not strange to see it yellow
While the hammer sounds a bellow:
Tan! Tan! Tan![61] (A176)

In "Vista madrileña" the city is viewed in intimate detail, each observation casting its grotesqueness:

An ugly girl—
Whom typhoid left
Devoid of hair—
in the garret dances,
Dragging a chair,
And playing the man.
She peers from the window
And looks like the cuckoo
That peeps from the clock.

There's an iron fountain
And a dog in the fountain,
Taking a casual piss.[62] (A177)

And the poet ends the collection with the autobiographical sonnet "Rosa del sanatorio," written in 1919, about recovering from an operation:

Under the influence of chloroform,
I am made to quiver with inner alarm
By aquarian light in a modern garden
And the yellow smell of iodoform.

Cubist, Futurist, and Strident,
Through the feverish chaos of halfsleep
Sensation takes flight, blotted at last,
Green fly, on my forehead droning.

For my nerves, with joyous coldness,
The bowing of a frenzied violin.
From an A flat the clear peep

Quivers in the garden's aquarian light,
And my boat sails the wide river
That separates shore from shore.[63] (A178)

The expression of these poetic visions is the concretion of views founded in earlier writings, such as the *Comedias bárbaras*. The consequences of the war and the bold adventure of the Russian Revolution provided the proper setting in which Valle-Inclán could bring to bear with full impact his impression of society. The deformity and grotesqueness that the poet defines in the verses of *La pipa de kif* are the immediate antecedents of similar treatments he developed shortly thereafter in the novels and dramas he termed *Esperpentos*.

The third and final book of poems, *El pasajero. Claves líricas*,[64] is partially allied to the thematics of *La lámpara maravillosa*, but lacking in its poems is the joyful hope of the aesthetic treatise. *El pasajero* is largely pessimistic, for in this work the poet looks at his life with regret over some phases and with resignation to the inevitability of death; in "Rosa hiperbólica" he sees his illusions truncated in the process of living:

I dreamed of laurels, but no more,
And my soul is free from ire.
I lack envy, save for money's mire!
And won't call at glory's door!

I walk only with my lions now
And the knowledge of my self.
The Devil listens to my prayers.
My heart sings: Tomorrow's now![65] (A179)

Even more pointed is the pessimism evident in "La trae un cuervo" (A Raven Brings It), where the poet is obsessed with the thought of death because he believes that his life is drawing to a close:

My life is broken! Through the combat
Of so many years, my drive wears thin,
While haughtiness too soon's abated
By thoughts of death obsessing it.

Would I could enter, live within myself,
And cross my forehead once again.
And putting off both friend and foe,
Live out my life devoutly and alone.

Where is that green ravine on high
With flocks of shepherds playing songs?
Where to experience that vision pure

Which makes the soul and flowers one?
Where can I dig my sepulchre in peace
And knead the mystic bread from pain?[66] (A180)

The same idea presses him to write in "Rosa de Job":

All leads to death
As if in concert,
All life is change
Till dead we part![67] (A181)

And finally the poet asks in "Rosa deshojada" (Depetaled Rose) the only questions the individual can make in the context of life's absurdity:

The why of life?
What did I sow in it?
What unknown path
Did my tread make?

Farewell illusions!
My years at last attain
The placid reasons
For my disenchantment.

The laurels perish,
The days become extinct,
The only memories
Extinguished ash.[68] (A182)

Youthful illusion has become the stoic acceptance of the approaching end—death. From that moment on there is only mere existence in expectation of the final moment. In matching the tenor of the poems with the reality of the poet's life, this marked disillusionment can be seen to stem from such vital factors as the increasing ill health he was experiencing, his unstable economic condition, and the lack of "official recognition" of his artistic merits. Particularly, Valle-Inclán was enraged and then depressed by his continued exclusion from membership in the Real Academia Española. In 1919 Julio Casares, who had made his reputation with his scathing *Critica profana*, was elected to membership in that august body. That the Academy was unjust in its selection of a secondary figure when Valle-Inclán was an obvious choice cannot be denied; but in its history there had been many such omissions, often to the point that the membership frequently reflected a lesser level of achievement. Nonetheless, the admittance of Casares and the disdain of certain academicians toward Valle-Inclán never ceased to bother him, even if at times he acted otherwise.

There is no doubt that his personality, appearance, and attitudes toward the establishment contributed to Valle-Inclán's exclusion from the Academy. Furthermore, his espousal of socialist causes during this period probably added to the consternation, especially when his ideas saw expression in printed form. One such item was a brief note, "Ganarás el pan" (You Will Earn Your Bread), which appeared on May Day:

The Precept of the Celestial Father, dictated as a punishment, has the festiveness of Religion. It is the only feast of modern times in which the sacred sense of the new Humanities shines forth. An ardent wind of biblical intuitions shakes the conscience of men of good will. The genesis raises its mystic dawn above the numb West.

Hallelujah! Hallelujah!

The workers of the world celebrate and affirm the meaning of life: The Law of Human Effort. Man's religious sense again travels in the theological cavern with an echo of Eternity. The workers of the world break bread. And it manifests the harmony of evangelical admonitions, the bellowing breath of biblical punishment.

Humanity, in a festive mood, is on its knees before the precept of the Celestial Father.

Hallelujah! Hallelujah![69] (A183)

Another declaration appeared in an interview with Cipriano Rivas Cherif in an organ of the Spanish branch of the Third International:

What is art? The supreme game. When art attempts ends that are utilitarian, practical, immediate, it loses its excellence. Art is a game, and its norms are dictated by numerical caprice, thus its peculiar charm. Fourteen verses are said to make a sonnet, and art, therefore, is form.

What must we make? Not art. We shouldn't create art now because playing at this moment in time would be immoral, something vile. First, we must achieve social justice.[70] (A184)

"Social justice" was to be achieved not through words but through action. For Valle-Inclán the involvement with the Teatro de la Escuela Nueva, a socialist venture founded by Rivas Cherif, was one way of seeking to actualize his beliefs: the theatre was always, in his eyes, a place for experimentation and education. But Valle-Inclán's willingness could not overcome the lack of funds for the Teatro de la Escuela Nueva, and soon it became another noble but failed experiment.

In addition to his concern for the snub by the Academy, Valle-Inclán became concerned with the indifference to his creative merit as reflected in two of the important works published in 1920. In *Farsa italiana de la enamorada del rey* the playwright sets a dialogue in the second act between Don Bartolo, the king's chaplain, and Don Facundo, one of his Ministers:

D. Facundo: . . . It is time
    that I apprise you of a matter of personal import.
    I am a candidate for a chair in the Academy.
D. Bartolo: You wish to be immortalized in its chamber!
    I think that's good. What a fine day it'll be
    when I can welcome you as a colleague!

D. Facundo: And your vote?
D. Bartolo: It wouldn't change a thing.
I hope to cast it for you on another occasion.
Your opposition is too prestigious.
Don Santos Santos! Santos de las Heras,
who published the noble titles awarded
for services under the flag in Flanders!
And the *Centón erudíto*, which comments on
how many times the word "inn"
is mentioned in the *Quijote*!
. . . .
D. Facundo: Since you mention the *Quijote* in his praise,
remember that in that eighth wonder,
I counted every one of Sancho's belches,
highlighting them in italics.
And who provided the new etymologies
of "cadaver," "carnaval," and "hemlock,"
and paid first tribute to ironies of
Carbo Data Vermis?
D. Bartolo: You, without a doubt!
I don't deny your merits. But you must have
patience, my friend Don Facundo.[71] (A185)

The conversation has a cynical tone undoubtedly reflecting the election of Julio Casares; it also demonstrates, through the figure of Don Bartolo, the superior air characteristic of members of the Academy, according to Valle-Inclán, toward aspirants or nonmembers.

Other poignant statements on the Academy are found in the second of the plays published this year, the *Esperpento Luces de bohemia*, in which Max Estrella delivers the condemnation in the fourth scene:

I have more than enough merits! But that miserable press boycotts me. They hate my rebelliousness and they hate my talent. In order to get ahead one has to cater to all the Segismundos. Appis the Bull fires me as he would a servant! The Academy ignores me! And I'm the greatest poet in Spain! The greatest! The greatest! And I fast! And I don't stoop to begging! And I'm not accursed! I'm the true immortal, not the bastards in that minor academy! Death to Maura![72](A186)

The bitterness of Max Estrella is unequivocally that of Valle-Inclán. Even while the character portrays implicit aspects of Alejandro Sawa, the bohemian who had died in 1909, the playwright has chosen this figure to express many of his own ideas. The name of Galdós is brought into the discussion of the Academy by another character:

Precisely at this moment, the chair of Don Benito the chick-pea man is vacant. (A187)

And in reality Galdós had died earlier in the same year that *Luces de bohemia* was published. The personal animosity that the dramatist had come to feel for the noted novelist over the incident with his play *El embrujado* was in that statement cynically united with the insults heaped on the Academy. In both cases respect had become derision for Valle-Inclán's personal reasons.

Even if he was not given his due at home, his fame did reach across the ocean to America. In 1921 he received an invitation from the Republic of Mexico and its Universidad Nacional to participate in the country's Independence Day celebrations. It was his Mexican friend Alfonso Reyes who was charged to tender the government's invitation.[73] Valle-Inclán was pleased by the offer and accepted it rapidly and enthusiastically. He arrived in time for the Independence Day festivities on 28 September. During his stay in the Mexican capital he resided at the Hotel Regis and frequented cafés such as El Fénix, La Flor de Méjico, and Los Monotes. He visited anew the places he had seen in his youth, renewed acquaintances from that first journey, and was introduced to the political and artistic communities. Among those he met was Gerardo Murillo, the noted critic and painter who used the pseudonym "Dr. Atl"; the friendship between the two men must have been memorable, because Valle-Inclán later portrayed him sympathetically as a political prisoner in his novel *Tirano Banderas*.

While in Mexico, he participated in such varied activities as a literary gathering at the Teatro Principal and a banquet for the Delegados del Congreso Internacional de Estudiantes, held in the gardens of Chapultepec. He lectured to a large audience at the University of Mexico; during his talk he referred to his *Sonatas*, disclosing as a source of *Sonata de estío* a Mexican adventure novel entitled *Los bandidos de Río Frío*. While the statement pleased his Mexican audience, as Valle-Inclán knew it would, it was hardly convincing to those who knew his frivolity in such claims (he had stated earlier that Campoamor was the model for Bradomín).

Of particular note was the friendship quickly engendered between Valle-Inclán and General Alvaro Obregón, president of the Republic of Mexico. Each was impressed by the other, the one by the heroic visage of the popular leader, and the other by the legendary fame of the author. This mutuality resulted in an exchange of mementos, and Valle-Inclán was regaled with an autographed copy of Obregón's book, *Ocho mil kilómetros en campaña* (1917) and with a signed portrait of the revolutionary. Obregón had found in Valle-Inclán a strong sympathizer with his agrarian reforms and a powerful voice that preached the eradication of the plight of the masses. Valle-Inclán's Marxist leanings were well known abroad. Spanish and other non-indigent landowners were first mistrustful of Valle-Inclán and later vehement in their opposition to his stance. Aware that continued attacks on their position could result in major upheaval, the landed European gentry came to fear his pronouncements. But Valle-Inclán would not check his outspoken manner, even while visiting a foreign country.

The Mexican leadership, revolutionary and popular, espoused many of the causes that had inspired the Russian Revolution; it may be that recognizing Valle-Inclán's ideology as their own Obregón and his advisers invited him to Mexico as a formidable Spanish voice who favored their position. In any case, Valle-Inclán's unequivocal espousal of agrarian reform and other popular measures had a salubrious effect in the eyes of the Obregón regime:

The Indian in Mexico, whom Spain emancipated and to whom were granted all the rights of a free man after the conquest, has now lost his freedom and is the victim of an exploitation worse than that of the slaves.[74] (A188)

It was this condition that the government of Obregón tried to remedy. Valle-Inclán was to study carefully such inequities in *Tirano Banderas*, but his first reactions are evident in interviews and in poems such as "¡Nos vemos!" dated May 1922:

I

To your sad face, I bid farewell, Mexican Indian!
I say farewell, my hand in your hand!

II

Mexican Indian, made a beggar by the Land Commission!
Mexican Indian!
Rise up and burn the stores of wheat!
Rise up! brother.

III

Break the chain. Shatter the clique. And let the bronze
of your temples shake off its grim tangles.
The seer beheld you as a Prometheus, by the seven lights
of the Tenebrae, beneath the arcades of a new
Jerusalem.

IV

Mexican Indian,
My hand in your hand
I profess my faith.
First, you must
hang the Landowner
and then, reap the wheat.
Mexican Indian,
my hand in your hand,
God as witness.[75] (A189)

Crucial to the definition of this outlook on the condition of Mexico at this time was a letter he wrote to Alfonso Reyes, dated 22 December 1923, after his return to Puebla del Caramiñal:

But I seem to be straying from my initial purpose in writing to you. You can guess that it concerns the Mexican Revolution. Frankly, I expected that move by the landowners. Revolutions can't be half-hearted. The *gachupines* own seventy percent of the nation's land: They are the throwaways of the Iberian lowlife. In the hands of those foreigners, land is held in the most noxious manner. Worse yet than if in dead hands. In order to end revolutions, our Mexico must nationalize landholdings and landowners. Newspaper reports are rather confused but, beyond this chaos, I foresee the triumph of the federal government. General Obregón is destined to accomplish great things in America. His valor, serenity, military knowledge, intuitive sense of strategy, and his lucky star as one of the chosen will assure his success. More than just the revolution in Mexico, it is the revolution latent in all Latin America. A revolution for independence, which cannot be reduced to a mere change of viceroys but must lead to the cultural supremacy of the Indian race, to the attainment of its rights, and to the expulsion of Spaniards of Jewish and Moorish descent. It would be better, of course, if their throats were slit.[76] (A190)

In "Obligación cristiana de España en América" (Spain's Christian Obligation in America), a lecture delivered at the Ateneo in Madrid on 19 February 1922, he again stated his case:

The civilizing work of Spain was represented by the spirit of its law, by the imposition of its language, and by the founding of many cities . . . In America, the Spaniard ought to be a citizen of the country in which he resides, as should South Americans in Spain. . . . I'm a believer in the distribution of land according to the system devised by the Soviets to satisfy the Russian émigrés who accompanied Admiral Koltchak. They went from Japan to Mexico, joining Mexican and Spanish proletarians against the landowners.[77](A191)

Besides the attack on the corrupting influence of the *gachupines* and the disparate attitude of the official Spanish façade, he attacked the coalition of Spanish landlords and international interests, especially those based in the United States, which wrested from the Mexican Indian his rightful lands and deprived him of the self-respect necessary to rise economically, socially, and educationally.

Once the official festivities were concluded Valle-Inclán began a leisurely return to Spain. He stopped in Havana first, arriving 17 November 1921 aboard the "Zelandia." This second visit to Cuba was made as an international celebrity and, unlike the first, attracted attention in many quarters. He was greeted during the period of quarantine by a delegation from the Centro Gallego, the most important Spanish organization in Cuba at the time, and he was later given a reception at its impressive quarters (Valle-Inclán hesitated in attending, perhaps due to his anti-Spanish statements in Mexico). The press welcomed such a newsworthy visitor, publicizing his arrival and printing articles and interviews devoted to the controversial

Spaniard. Of particular interest are articles that appeared in *El Diario de la Marina* covering Valle-Inclán's recent visit to Mexico.[78] During his brief stay of several weeks the newspapers and magazines were full of his anecdotes. Meanwhile, he concentrated on rediscovering the Cuban panorama, both artistic and geographic. He traveled through the exotic countryside refreshing his mind and storing memories he would employ in future works. Together with his traveling companion, the Nicaraguan poet Salomón de la Selva, Valle-Inclán made the acquaintance of the Cuban vanguard. He was frequently accompanied by Félix Lizaso, José Antonio Fernández de Castro, and Luis A. Baralt, among others. In the literary periodical *Social*, which was the principal organ of the vanguard, Valle-Inclán was pictured with the editors of the magazine Alfredo T. Quiles and Conrado M. Míssaguer (also a caricaturist), Selva, the poets Alfonso Roselló and Federico de Ibarzábal, and the historian Emilio Roig de Leuchsenring.[79] Before he left the country he was interviewed by *España Nueva*, the article appearing with the drawing that Moya del Pino had done some years earlier of Valle-Inclán in turban as he perused his manuscript *La lámpara maravillosa*.[80] In that interview Valle-Inclán discussed the Russian Revolution in his favorable manner, commented on the unstable political situation in Spain, and added further statements to his position on the poor economic and social status of the Mexican Indian, the masses, in contrast to the well-being and affluence on all levels of the Spanish colonials, the elite.

Valle-Inclán departed from Havana harbor early in December. His ship took him to New York, where he spent the rest of the month before proceeding to Spain. On his arrival[81] he was interviewed by Tulio Cesteros, correspondent in New York for *El Diario de la Marina*, regarding the accusations made against him by Olaguibel and Lugo de Viña. The reply appeared in Havana in the 7 December issue of the newspaper, but while it did not contain a defense, Valle-Inclán did disavow his supposed words as alterations of his real statements. Years later, Valle-Inclán would comment:

I've never made a habit of rectifying the words that reporters put in my mouth. What's the point? Even if one denies the statement, there are always readers who believe that the words were really spoken and are being denied out of fear. The best thing would be never to allow a reporter in, but that is cowardice, and I always confront danger. I trust the professional honesty of those who come to see me. I'm accessible for any interview and therefore can't complain. For every unpleasantness, there have been many satisfactions. In general, reporters convey my words with discretion. But I remember one occasion in Mexico when a certain malicious Cuban journalist twistedly reported some declarations I'd made and created a problem for me with Argentina. I don't like to make generalizations. My work shows my discretion in this regard. I spoke of Argentina as any Argentinian would. Neither Argentina, nor Spain, nor Mexico, nor any other country in the world has only one face. As in the vineyard of the Lord, there is everything, good and bad. It's convenient to exalt the good, but one shouldn't ignore the bad. . . . But those statements brought me numerous letters of protest. Even the minister plenipotentiary protested. I wasn't about to demean myself by answering someone who, without asking if those were my words, allowed himself the luxury of pretending to argue the matter with me. . . . Fortunately, there is among the guiding principles of peoples an undisputed moral base and none of the sincere friends whom I had left there believed in the hoax.[82] (A192)

Of his residency in New York, almost nothing is known. Thanks to a chance encounter between him and José Juan Tablada, it is known that he stayed at the Hotel McAlpin, where the Mexican poet visited him one afternoon to hear Valle-Inclán's impressions of his friend's native country:

Beautiful . . . Enormous . . . Excessive. Tradition is reborn out of the ashes of the Revolution . . . The façades of churches are inlaid with glazed tiles . . . War is good . . . It is an incubator which accelerates progress.[83] (A193)

He said of the great Mexican painter Diego Rivera:

Beyond "the Cubist adventure," Rivera has become convinced that no other painting exists but that of our Goya and of the primitive Italians.[84] (A194)

Tablada, who had been exiled from Mexico during the Revolution, ended his visit with Valle-Inclán when the subject turned to Marxism and revolutionary confiscation of privately held lands. Valle-Inclán's fervor for the Mexican experiment led him also to lecture to a larger audience in New York City on the plight of the Mexican Indian. He was undoubtedly the observant tourist that he had been in Mexico, Cuba, and Argentina, or in Paris and other European cities, but the memory of the great metropolis that is New York did not have any known reflection in his later works. Yet, it was important in another way. The publishing firm Harcourt, Brace contacted him regarding the publication of the *Sonatas* in the United States;[85] Valle-Inclán welcomed the contract, but he waited until 1924 before the edition was released. Thus, while the visit to New York has not been recorded in his work, it opened a new field for his novels, supplementing the small inroad into the English-language market made earlier by the publication of *La cabeza del dragón*.

Valle-Inclán was back in Spain in the early part of 1922. He traveled immediately to "La Merced," where his family awaited him unaware of his exact arrival date.[86] Once again he devoted himself to the bucolic life with the dreams of a Virgil, but the administration of a farm would never be his forte. Eventually he gave up "La Merced" and moved back to Puebla del Caramiñal, living at 3 Calle de San Roque with his immediate family, where economic demands were not so great. It was to this that he referred when he had Bradomín say to Darío in *Luces de bohemia*: "¡No me han arruinado las mujeres, con haberlas amado tanto, y me arruina la agricultura!" (Despite my having loved women for so long, I've not been ruined by them, and now I'm ruined by agriculture!).[87]

The Spain to which Valle-Inclán returned had undergone alterations (the culmination of the process being noted by Ortega y Gasset in his *España invertebrada*, published in 1921). It was the era in which Guillermo de Torre published his periodical *Ultra*, organ of the vanguard and barometer of the rapidly moving times. Highly notable too was the political deterioration of the nation. The assassination of Eduardo Dato had brought on the ministries of Allende Salazar and Maura. Then, the situation in Morocco, quiet since 1910, had been catapulted into a major crisis when a great part of the Spanish army in Africa was destroyed at Anual and Monte Arruit during the Rif rebellion led by Abd-el-Krim; the slaughter was in retaliation for the insensate acts of General Silvestre, who was in command. The bitter struggle for domination over the Rifs was not palatable to Valle-Inclán, who saw in it the desire for personal aggrandizement:

The war in Melilla will end when the lieutenants become colonels.[88] (A195)

Valle-Inclán, aware of the torpid attitude of the Spanish military establishment in its relations with the colonies, as reflected in the history of Latin America, could laugh cynically at the prolongation of the conflict in Africa and suggest a solution not implausible in the context of the absurd attempts to end the war:

Gentlemen, I believe that the solution lies in arranging for Abd-el-Krim to marry the Infanta Isabel.[89] (A196)

But while he grinned sardonically, Valle-Inclán recognized the temper of the times. From this period on the political framework of Spain creaked endlessly, heralding the eventual collapse of the monarchy.

Valle-Inclán's political concern became more obvious at the same time, as he demonstrated in public statements and in lectures, such as two delivered at the Ateneo in 1922: the aforementioned "Obligación cristiana de España en América" and "Impresiones mejicanas." Together with Unamuno, Valle-Inclán used the platform of the Ateneo to hurl his vocal venom at the king and the entire governing structure,[90] giving credence to the anti-monarchical statements referred to by Olaguibel in his Méxican article.

Unamuno was again united with Valle-Inclán at a banquet in honor of the latter at the restaurant Fornos on 1 April 1922. The invitation, extended to the artistic colony of Madrid, bore many signatures headed by that of Unamuno;[91] the continued appreciation of Valle-Inclán by his contemporaries was again underlined, this time in one of the largest events of his career.

Both the colleagues of his generation and the young writers of newer affiliations were there to honor a major voice of Spanish letters. Those who could not attend sent their message to be read before Valle-Inclán; among the more impressive was the sonnet that Antonio Machado composed for the occasion.[92] Valle-Inclán received these tributes with satisfaction and with what Aristotle termed *megalopsychia*, just or aristocratic pride, that is, the consciousness of one's own worth. In his speech to the assembled celebrants Valle-Inclán conveyed the proper gratitude and then answered publicly those charges of plagiarism made by Casares years before:

If I utilized some pages of the *Memoires* of Casanova in my *Sonata de primavera*, it was to put the atmosphere of my work to the test. Had I not conceived it correctly, the interpolation would be terribly out of place. Shakespeare placed speeches in the mouth of his Coriolanus that he took from historians of antiquity, and the success of the tragedy is proved in that, far from rejecting such foreign texts, it demands them. If you add to any of the historical dramas currently on stage words or documents of the period, you will see how well they suit them.[93] (A197)

He insisted once more that he was a writer only because he could do nothing else and stated somewhat prophetically that the destiny of the Spanish intellectual was a life of persecution by the Guardia Civil. These words reflect the temper of the times and the insecurity of the political situation in Spain. The censorship that the banquet invitation noted was growing, and Valle-Inclán was to be one of its targets.[94]

Shortly thereafter Valle-Inclán's contract with the Sociedad General Española de Librería, begun in 1915, was allowed to lapse without renewal, and the author was forced again into the attempt to publish his own books. The last works of his "Opera Omnia" series under the care of that publisher appeared in June 1922.[95] It would be almost a year before his complete works began to appear under the aegis of a new firm. In the meantime he had to content himself with publication in periodicals, as, for example, the serialization of *Cara de Plata*, his last *Comedia bárbara*,[96] and with the continuation of his public life in the café. He frequented the Café Regina and Café Maxim along with, among others, Enrique Diez-Canedo, Icaza, Vegue y Goldoni, and Bagaría, who did numerous caricatures of Valle-Inclán in this period. From time to time he joined Ramón Gómez de la Serna's group at Pombo where, on one occasion in 1922, he was one of the forty-five persons attending the celebrated banquet for "Don Nadie," in the company of Zuloaga and Ricardo Baroja, as a group photograph attests.[97]

The enthusiasm for Valle-Inclán in Madrid among his contemporaries was again given public expression, early in 1923, with the publication of an entire issue of *La Pluma* in his honor.[98] In addition to the regular printing was a special edition of fifty copies with special paper and binding. The tribute consisted of articles by Eduardo Gómez de Baquero ("Andrenio"),

Enrique Diez-Canedo, Ramón Pérez de Ayala, Alfonso Reyes, Ramón María Tenreiro, Manuel Bueno, Ricardo Baroja, Corpus Barga, José Moya del Pino, Jean Cassou, Francis de Miomandre, Jorge Guillén, Ramón Gómez de la Serna, Manuel Azaña, and Cipriano Rivas Cherif. There were poems by Antonio Machado ("Iris de Luna" [Moon Iris] dedicated to the "Maestro Valle-Inclán") and Rivas Cherif ("Soneto Estrambótico" [Eccentric Sonnet] dedicated to "Don Ramón, en consonancia con sus últimas préd-icas de café" [Don Ramón, in Accord with His Latest Café Pronounce-ments]).[99] The issue was well illustrated, containing decorations at the head of each article, a whimsical caricature by Angel Vivanco of Valle-Inclán piping to serpents as he rides a llama, and the woodcut by Moya del Pino that starkly portrays a pensive Valle-Inclán. Also included in the edition are two facsimiles from the manuscript of *La reina castiza*. The first two pages of the magazine were devoted to a "Dedicatoria."[100] One would expect Valle-Inclán's reaction to be gratitude for the homage volume, but his letter to *La Pluma*'s editor, dated 21 February 1923 from La Puebla del Caramiñal, conveys a very different reaction:

The dead must feel a similar emotion on hearing the responsories sung on their behalf in this world. I felt something akin to reading an obituary when I read this issue of *La Pluma*. Only you dare confront a living man, uncovering his sorrow and his drama. But the others tell anecdotes of such a distant time that, truly, the one of whom they speak seems like a dead man to me. Dead and foreign. May God have forgiven them![101] (A198)

While Benavente had won the Nobel Prize in Literature in 1922, Valle-Inclán had also won the admiration and enthusiasm of colleagues in the artistic world, if on a less exalted scale. Along with their encouragement came support for his career; Gregorio Martínez Sierra made it possible for Valle-Inclán's "Opera Omnia" to continue when he brought the author and Renacimiento, the publishing house with which he was affiliated, together under a new contract. This occurred in 1923 and two titles issued that year began the association: a new printing of *Sonata de estío* on 30 April and the first book edition of *Cara de Plata* on 10 December.

The international reputation of Valle-Inclán took a definite upward swing in this era. Increasingly, his works were being translated into Italian, French, and English. *Romance de lobos* marked the beginning of a series of translations of plays, novels, and stories.[102] The volume of foreign versions remained fairly constant thereafter as the name of Valle-Inclán filtered slowly into the literary landscape of other nations outside the Hispanic sphere. As a consequence, the number of foreign articles assessing his work increased.

Throughout 1923 ill health continued to plague him. An aneurysm caused a pulsating tumor to develop in his bladder and in the fall Valle-Inclán had to return to Puebla del Caramiñal for rest and medical observation. Spending most of the day in bed, he had to forgo much of his social activity; the walks he enjoyed taking had to be curtailed and his attendance at the local café was postponed. But his intellect could not be stilled, as evident in a letter in *España*, which had published an article in favor of Spanish landholders in Mexico; despite his illness, Valle-Inclán reacted forcefully:

Our Ministry of State listened quite attentively to the wealthy of that colony. Diplomatic representatives left here bound to them and there's nothing secret about the shameful dealings that resulted from extending recognition to General Obregón's government. As a sign of gratitude, the Spanish colony expected payment of four hundred million pesetas, under the guise of indemnization. It was expected that the laws of the nation would be violated on behalf of the Spanish colony. That the political program would be put aside, as in Spain. "But, despite recognition having been extended, the confiscation continued," writes the anonymous reporter, adding: "What has the Government of Spain done in the meantime? Dispatch notes, many notes." It has certainly done that. It expected that the ongoing conflict with the United States would bring down General Obregón's Cabinet. The government of Spain, its vacuous diplomats, and the wealthy colonials have yet to realize that far above consideration for the estates of grocers and moneylenders stand the historical ties of culture, language, and blood.

The Spanish Colony of Mexico, forgetting all spiritual obligation, has conspired during this period with Yankee oil interests. And even now, their suit having been lost, when someone rends his clothing and scratches his face, no one can deny that the politics of Spain in Mexico has been imposed by those avaricious troglodytes.

It is time for our diplomats to have a vision that is less miserly than that of the emigrant who owns a seedy store in America.[103] (A199)

He maintained contact with the world through visitors. Among those in frequent attendance was Victoriano García Martí. During the autumn of that year the two writers conversed at length over the text of *De la felicidad (Eternas inquietudes)*, which García Martí was preparing for publication and for which Valle-Inclán was writing a prologue:

At the close of September, in afternoons already autumnal, like those of Verlaine, of a long, cadenced sadness both sensual and mystical, my friend read me the pages of this book. The two of us discussed it in a cordial colloquy at the end of the reading. We were alone in the nook where I isolate myself to smoke a pipe and build castles. . . . My friend read in slow rhythm, his voice accenting the words as if desirous of enjoying that implausible afternoon moment, of transposing to a spiritual plane that crystalline landscape full of irreality, yet existing, in an anguished, fleeting state, imbued with the emotion of death.[104] (A200)

That same "emotion of death" became personalized when Valle-Inclán had to undergo surgery in October at the clinic of Dr. Villar Iglesias in Santiago de Compostela. While his illness was serious enough to encompass the possibility of death, Valle-Inclán was bothered mainly by the deterrence of his activities. To overcome apathy he continued to involve

himself in his work and to correspond with friends in Madrid and elsewhere. His letters to Alfonso Reyes disclose his physical state as well as the
awareness of its gravity. In correspondence dated 14 November 1923, he
wrote:

I received your fine, touching letter while laid up in bed, to which I'm still confined,
although it appears that I am somewhat better. My illness is the same as that which
killed our poor Nervo . . . I've suffered it for a long time, but the surge of pain has
never been this great. I've been in bed more than a month, bored and sad. If I
recover, I hope to see you soon in Madrid.[105] (A201)

But even though he was bedridden for such an extended period, Valle-
Inclán's spirits did not sag. The same correspondence with Reyes discloses
that the sick body could not repress the creativity of the spirit:

Let's talk about our Mexico. I've been working during this time on an American
novel. *Tirano Banderas*. It's a novel about a tyrant with facets of Doctor Francia,
Rosas, Melgarejo, López, and Don Porfirio. The protagonist is a synthesis, while
the language is a sum of Americanisms from all the Spanish-speaking countries,
from the low class to the gaucho style. The Republic of Santa Trinidad de Tierra
Firme is an imaginary country, as are those European courts depicted by Abel
Hernant in some book or other. I lack some facts for this book and you, dear Reyes,
could provide them. As a foil to the tyrant, I've created and developed the figure of
an apostle, more like Savanarola than Don Francisco Madero, even when it has
something of this visionary saint. Where can I find a biography of "Blessed Don
Pancho"? I depict a great cataclysm like the earthquake in Valparaiso, as well as a
social revolution by Indians. The latter requires details about Teresa Utrera, the
Saint of Ranchito de Cavora. My memory fails me and I'd like to refresh it. Is there
anything written about the saint? The books you have for me can be sent here and,
if accompanied by *Visión de Anahuac*, will be doubly appreciated. (A202)

Another letter, dated 16 November, answered the reply by Reyes:

With great affection, I'll send the *Tirano Banderas* of which I spoke in my previous
letter.[106] (A203)

Also on that date, he wrote:

I've been in bed for a month with kidney pains, urinating blood. I've suffered less
in the last two days and want to distract myself from this tedium and sorrow by
conversing in writing. If I get well soon, I'll go to Madrid. Renacimiento is looking
for a way to keep my books. As you know, I have a contract with them for the
publication of my works. Their ploy is not to publish the manuscripts, holding
them as a lien on a debt. They recently put *Sonata de estío* on sale.[107](A204)

In his communications with Cipriano Rivas Cherif Valle-Inclán also commented on the status of his new work:

I have little to tell you about myself. My health has improved somewhat. I'm working on an American novel about Spanish bossism and avarice. It's entitled *Tirano Banderas*. Rather than in dialogue form, it's in an expressive, non-academic prose. Like all my books, it has something of the beginner about it, and, as always, I try to avoid being pedantic. My characters and I know nothing of encyclopedias. My belief grows stronger daily that man is not governed by his ideas or culture. I imagine a fatalism at work in the environment, in heredity, and in physiological defects, with conduct totally divorced from thought. And yet, dark motivating thoughts being the consequence of that fatalism of environment, heredity, and well-being, only man's pride leads him to the supposition that he is a rational animal.[108] (A205)

His illness had dulled neither his mind nor his appetite for controversy. But it did sap his strength and even writing letters to friends was a demanding task. On 20 December 1923 he wrote to Reyes again; the letter, which discusses the influence of Chateaubriand on the *Sonatas* and comments on the Mexican revolution, ends with a brief statement that defines his continuing weakness:

I've become tired and hardly have enough strength to finish. I'm still very weak.[109] (A206)

The long period of internment and convalescence was made more palatable by the publication of his works in Madrid. His play *La cabeza del dragón* was re-issued as the tenth volume of "Opera Omnia" on 12 January 1924 by his old publisher Perlado, Páez y Cía. The magazine *España*, which had been founded by Ortega y Gasset, printed his letter to the editor under the title "Autocrítica" on 8 March 1924. On 22 March two plays, *La rosa de papel* and *La cabeza del Bautista*, appeared in the "Colección *La Novela Semanal*."[110] Also published, on 30 June 1924, was the book edition of *Luces de bohemia*, the nineteenth volume of "Opera Omnia," now under the imprint of Renacimiento.

Valle-Inclán had recuperated sufficiently from his surgery to return to Madrid in July 1924. But because of his operation he was thereafter seen walking with a cane, as he had in earlier years after the accident involving his foot. Anxious to resume his interrupted public life, he left his wife and children in Puebla del Caramiñal and took up temporary residence in Madrid's Hotel Gran Via,[111] a first-class establishment. The return of Valle-Inclán to the capital was an event that did not pass unnoticed; besides the reception accorded him by his collaborators in the *tertulia*, he was welcomed by various articles, such as those by Rivas Cherif and Gómez de la Serna.[112] His arrival was properly heralded. It seemed as if he had returned to life having risen from death, once again overcoming forces beyond the reach of normal men. His mettle was tested many times afterward in yet another context.

Forces of a different nature were working on the structure of Spanish politics at this time. During Valle-Inclán's forced retirement from the arena of Madrid the political posture of the nation had been altered considerably.

On 13 September 1923, the Captain General of Cataluña, Miguel Angel Primo de Rivera, had efficiently taken over control of the government. Seeking to avoid a pending crisis of major proportions, Primo de Rivera had suspended the Constitution with the approval of Alfonso XIII and had established a directorate composed of military officers. The power was, in time, vested entirely in Primo de Rivera, who achieved dictatorial status.

Needless to say, the self-appointed government's authoritarianism was immediately unpopular although this ruling body attempted to terminate the war in Morocco and sought reforms to benefit the nation. The anti-monarchical campaign was given new fuel with the ascension of Primo de Rivera. The anathemas of the intellectuals spearheaded the attack; Miguel de Unamuno, then rector of the Universidad de Salamanca, led the vociferous opposition. The absence of Valle-Inclán had left the reins totally in the hands of his colleague in arms, Unamuno.

The relentlessness of Unamuno's pen and voice angered the new regime. On 21 February 1924 Unamuno was ordered exiled from the mainland of Spain to the Canary Islands. Divested of his post but not of his honor, which he carried with him as Ruy Díaz de Vivar had in his own exile from Castile by another Alfonso, Unamuno embarked in Cádiz for the town of Fuerteventura. During the months he spent there he refused to pay his expenses and continued to pen letters against the regime, sending them to willing friends who made the contents known throughout Europe and Latin America. His continued rebellion still touched Primo de Rivera, who wrote one of his celebrated "official notes," published in El Sol on 21 March, attacking the culture and the ability of his adversary.[113] Unamuno continued his verbal forays into the enemy camp from his island off the African coast until he found it more advantageous to escape from its confinement. With the assistance of literary friends in France and Portugal, particularly Dumay, editor of the Parisian newspaper Le Quotidien, he fled the island on the sailing vessel "L'Aiglon." On reaching Puerto de la Luz in Las Palmas he managed passage on the "Zelandia," which set out for Lisbon on 21 July 1924. After his stay in Lisbon through the month of August, the self-expatriate Unamuno arrived in Cherbourg and then went on to Paris. He settled ultimately in Hendaya, near the Spanish border, in the French Basque country close to his own native region. The love of Spain and the hatred of oppression characterizing Unamuno's life during the six years of his exile are reflected in De Fuerteventura a París (1925) and Romancero del destierro (1927).

The voices of writers in Spain, Latin America, and Europe were raised in protest over the exile of so prominent a figure as Unamuno. Valle-Inclán, still confined to his bed at the time, circulated a letter in strong opposition to the dastardly affair and spoke to his visitors against the regime of Primo de Rivera. His indignation over the Unamuno incident and similar abuses was explosive, and on his return to the cafés of Madrid he became militantly vociferous in the hope that the dictator would also try to punish his insubordination. He welcomed reporters who approached him for views ranging from the exile of Unamuno to the general condition of Spain; in these interviews Valle-Inclán always inserted quotable barbs that could not be more direct:

The king is a grotesque puppet. There are many who believe that some disagreement could arise between Alfonso and Primo de Rivera. It can't happen! The directorate was created to save the monarch. The drunkard and the cretin understand each other perfectly. Unamuno says that Primo de Rivera is our Bertoldo. Nonsense! Not even that! He's a good wine wino. The difference between him and the sinister Martínez Anido rests on the fact that the latter is from Galicia, a region whose wines are worthless. Primo has a spry personality, often goes on a spree, and knows how to lose his balance. A few nights ago, he fell very hard after a binge. The official story was that he had run into a door at the office after a sleepless night of hard work. Despite it all, I'm fond of the scoundrel. Without being aware of it, he's doing a lot of good for the country. I oppose him for reasons of social hygiene. But I realize that we Spaniards should request that he stay in power. He started out by keeping political parties away from the king. He divided the Army in an amusing way. He squanders funds so recklessly that the peseta will soon roll on the floor without value. He will destroy Catalan industry. Let Primo de Rivera stay on! Do you know how I see him? Well, as the master of ceremonies at a popular ball! (Keep on dancing, ladies and gentlemen!) He made a mistake and put on a military uniform. He and his directorate came to power like rats invading a sinking ship. The directorate flaunts its thievery, unlike the puritans of old. Those Tartuffes took everything in sight with the utmost furtiveness. Nowadays, there aren't as many evasions in plundering. Today, every Spaniard is afraid because in fact every Spaniard has a few pesetas and, along with them, he's acquired a bourgeois fear. That's why he doesn't react. But the most fearful are those who fear that they won't be able to declare their independence. Sánchez Guerra can do so because he doesn't have a fortune and won't suffer any consequences. I too can shout because I own nothing. All I possess is the cape on my back. I don't have a peseta. Having nothing, I'm like an anarchist. I can't conceive of anyone being an anarchist in any other way.[114](A207)

Ironically, while Valle-Inclán was uttering his anti-monarchical remarks and Unamuno was embodying the opposition to the regime in his exile, the Real Academia was admitting into its ranks a close associate of both. José Martínez Ruiz, who had years earlier adopted the pseudonym Azorín, became one of the "immortals" on 26 October 1924.

As if sensing a need to recoup the time he had lost during his convalescence, Valle-Inclán allowed himself to be lured out of Madrid for periodic visits elsewhere. In 1925 he traveled to various cities of the peninsula. During the early part of the year he settled for a time near Vigo, at a place named somewhat appropriately "El Calvario." He remained in the Galician seaport until March, when an invitation to the production of one of his plays in Barcelona took his interest. Prior to his departure the literary circle with which he shared his free hours in Vigo gave him a farewell dinner;

after the speeches in his honor Valle-Inclán spoke on the emergence of a new Spanish language:

The pampas are vast oceans of wheat that give birth to the bread of humanity and nurture a new Spanish language, one that will breach the hermetic prison of current Castilian, making itself more flexible, more vital, and more sonorous. God willing, the American tongue will be to Castilian what the romance languages of the Roman colonies were to the formal Latin of the world's Lord. Pity newly emancipated peoples who don't know how to renovate the tongue inherited from the metropolis, fashioning theirs according to the measure of their own soul and necessity! . . . Languages don't come from the streets and boulevards of cities: cities give birth only to the argot of the rabble and gypsies; languages, on the other hand, are born in full sunlight, in open fields, and are the expression of the collective soul of a people. Cities corrupt languages, while the countryside and light preserve, renew, and purify them.[115] (A208)

This conception of language, comparable to that expressed in other works, lectures, and interviews would find practical application in the chapters of *Tirano Banderas*, the homogenous novel he had described earlier to Reyes and Rivas Cherif, which began to appear that same year.[116]

Arriving in Barcelona, Valle-Inclán took up residence at the Hotel Oriente, where he stayed whenever he visited the city. The first-class hotel had a pleasant setting on the Rambla del Centro, affording easy access to the magnificent Cathedral, the Roman walls, the infamous "Barrio Chino" (Chinese Quarter)[117] and the harbor where Columbus was received by Fernando and Isabel after his historic first voyage. On Calle Conde del Asalto, which bordered the hotel on one side, was the splendid Casa-Palacio Güell that Antoni Gaudí, the great mystic architect, had designed in 1885; everywhere else throughout the city stood the imaginative creations of the great architect: Parc Güell, Casa Milá, Casa Batlló, Santa Coloma de Cervelló (chapel of the Colonia Güell), and the unforgettable Temple de la Sagrada Familia, the great church left unfinished since the accidental death of the architect in 1926.

Valle-Inclán took in the artistic wealth of Barcelona in the company of his future biographer Francisco Madrid. Together, they attended the presentation of *La cabeza del Bautista*, starring the Italian actress Mimí Aguglia and directed by Cipriano Rivas Cherif, at the Teatro Goya on 20 March 1925. As in its premiere in Madrid, the new presentation met with public and critical acclaim, although Valle-Inclán had been secretly apprehensive about the effect that his many cutting references to Cataluña in his talks and works would have on the reception of the play. But if such distractions were present, there was no indication in Barcelona. Instead, the play and its author were warmly received everywhere.

The publisher Maucci, who had commissioned Valle-Inclán to do the translations of Eça de Queiroz at the turn of the century, reissued his versions *El crimen del Padre Amaro*, *La reliquia*, and *El primo Basilio*. His stay in Barcelona culminated in a banquet in his honor, given by the leading writers and artists of the city, on 23 March 1925. The tribute was convened at "El Canari de la Garriga," a tavern on Calle de Lauria. Among those present were Melchor Fernández Almagro, Francisco Madrid, the politician Emilio Junoy, the art gallery proprietor Dalmau, José María de Sagarra, the sculptor Casanovas, the journalist Hermosilla, Doctor Borralleras, the businessman Plandiura (whose "Col-lecció Artística Plandiura" had been opened to Valle-Inclán by invitation), Rivas Cherif, and Mario Aguilar. After the dinner the group went to the Maison Dorée to join the *tertulia* of Santiago Rusiñol.[118] As a result of this visit Valle-Inclán became more aware than he had ever before been of the political and cultural reality of Cataluña; consequently, he began to feel a drive toward better involvement with the life of that region:

There's a Spanish way of life I don't know that would be very interesting to fictionalize. The social struggles of Barcelona. The type of the worker who, after having a peaceful dinner, takes up the *star*, and goes after the employer, manifests a psychological state that would be interesting to analyze, to study.[119] (A209)

But, unfortunately, pressing engagements elsewhere and projects demanding completion kept Valle-Inclán from ever fulfilling the indications made in that statement.

At the invitation of the Ateneo Burgalés, Valle-Inclán opened the formal series of lectures for 1925 with his discussion of "La literatura nacional española," delivered at Burgos' Teatro Principal. In spite of many controversial political comments, the lecture proceeded without incident. During his stay in Burgos he made some excursions into the surrounding areas famous in the history of El Cid and the Conde Fernán González. Valle-Inclán visited the Colegiata and the Torre de Doña Urraca, both in Covarrubias, as well as the nineteenth century Monasterio de Santo Domingo de Silos, one of the most interesting examples of Spanish Romanic art, run by Benedictine Monks, whose invitation to stay the night must have tempted the mystic in Valle-Inclán to partake of the community's life. But there were other things to see and do. Besides the monumental thirteenth-century Cathedral, Burgos itself offered the Cartuja de Miraflores and the Real Monasterio de las Huelgas, repositories of Don Juan II and Alfonso VIII, respectively. A few short miles outside the city Valle-Inclán visited the town of Vivar, birthplace of Ruy Díaz, El Cid Campeador.

Valle-Inclán had also been invited to lecture in Asturias by the Ateneo de Oviedo. Because the audience was expected to exceed the capacity of the auditorium on the premises, the event was scheduled at the Teatro Toreno. The only concern of the organizers was for Valle-Inclán's combative attitude toward the dictatorship of Primo de Rivera, which required that a representative of the government attend all public events. Valle-Inclán reacted as expected:

I won't allow any delegate to come to my lecture. I don't cast pearls, etc.[120] (A210)

The editor of the newspaper *La Voz de Asturias*, Antonio J. Onieva, went to see General Zuvillaga, the military governor, to arrange some way of meeting the spirit of the law without offending the guest speaker. Valle-Inclán gave his extemporaneous dissertation on the impact of classical culture on Spanish society without incident, unaware of the presence at the head table of the general's plainclothed representative.[121]

Once filled with the experience of Barcelona, Burgos, and Oviedo, Valle-Inclán returned to the Madrid ambient that was always his mainstay. The city bristled with activity and sights; the changing times were evident everywhere, and the promise of even greater political ambiguity made the atmosphere tense. All this formed the panorama in which Valle-Inclán moved. If at times he left Madrid for Galicia, it was only to return shortly with renewed intent and the weapons of combat at the ready. The grotesquery that he had traced in his works and annotated in his discussions was at hand.

In the same year, 1925, came the break with his publisher Renacimiento, and Valle-Inclán found himself once again burdened with the issuance and distribution of his books. Since such necessities were not new to him, he took the development in stride, philosophically, and kept to his otherwise normal pace. The café called him twice daily as usual and he continued to sit among old friends and younger admirers. Among the first was Ricardo Baroja, for whom Valle-Inclán wrote the prologue to a new book; recalling the many years since the turn of the century that they had been friends, he remarked at length on the merit of his companion:

Ricardo Baroja is loved by the Muses. Not one of the Nine Sisters has denied him her gift. Had he pursued the graphic arts, he would have outdone the best. I imagine him in an Italian city, a painter in the days of the Renaissance. That rare ability to conceive and to execute quickly makes him brilliantly capable of doing grand mural works. What paradoxical humor he would have shown in training his disciples from the scaffolding, in welcoming rulers, in having discussions with cardinals! Verbal grace, frank humor, pleasant laughter, paradoxical flights are also distinctive in Ricardo Baroja—beloved of the Muses—who, eschewing romantic sputterings, heads toward old age.[122](A211)

Among the newer acquaintances was Ramón J. Sender, then on the staff of *El Sol* in Madrid, who frequented Valle-Inclán's *tertulia*.[123] Sender became one of his companions in the capital, and through the constant association he was able to see Valle-Inclán in his multifarious facets rather than only as the anecdotal figure of the café. One of the most striking aspects he saw was the solitude of the Man.[124] This solitude, apparently denied by the Mask, was the sacrificial distance between the Artist and his surroundings, the aesthetic separation that Valle-Inclán had declared in *La lámpara maravillosa*:

Be like the nightingale, which never looks at earth from the green bough whereon it sings.[125] (A212)

Sender's comprehension of the basic nature of the Artist, as reflected in Valle-Inclán, brought the two men closer in friendship. In 1928 Valle-Inclán would sign the prologue of one of Sender's books.[126] The friendship between the two men, based as it was on mutual respect and understanding, was to remain unbroken until the death of Valle-Inclán.

Among other activities of the year, Valle-Inclán hosted a banquet in honor of Julio Alvarez del Vayo to celebrate the publication of his book *La nueva Rusia*, taking the occasion to affirm his ideological commitment to Marxism and to express an opinion:

Russia is the future of the world.[127] (A213)

Yet, despite what might appear to be a fixation on politics, Valle-Inclán carried out his aesthetic mission as well, continuing to involve himself with artists, as evidenced by his appearance in the Julio Romero de Torres's 1926 film *La malcasada*, where he appears in a scene in the painter's studio.[128] He also continued to issue his works with regularity. Among his publications of 1926 were three short novels, *Ecos de Asmodeo* (Echoes of Asmodeus), *El terno del difunto* (The Dead Man's Outfit), and *Zacarías el Cruzado, o Agüero nigromante* (Zacharia the Crusader, or Necromantic Omen).[129] This last novelette later formed part of the full-length novel *Tirano Banderas. Novela de Tierra Caliente* (The Tyrant Banderas. Novel of Tierra Caliente), published in that year. The clamorous success of this major novel was totally unexpected by Valle-Inclán, and he experienced all the headiness of success.[130] The reception accorded the book and the new prestige attached to its author led Valle-Inclán to the extreme of disparaging all his works produced before *Tirano Banderas*, claiming that his real creative work was still ahead of him:

What I've written prior to *Tirano Banderas* is minor violin music, and bad music at that. *Tirano Banderas* is the first work that I've written. My task begins now.[131] (A214)

Having appeared late in the year, *Tirano Banderas* began to receive critical attention in 1927, especially in Latin America. Despite Valle-Inclán's concentrated effort to amalgamate many strains of culture, history, and character, individual reviewers, their nationalism showing, extracted from the synthetic novel the circumstances depicting their own region. Since there were large influences from specific nations (Mexico, Cuba, Argentina), it was possible for a Mexican reviewer, for example, to find in the work great affinities to his homeland.[132] It was generally noted among the reviews in Spain that Valle-Inclán's novelistic technique had come a long way since the *Sonatas*.[133] The far-flung fame of *Tirano Banderas* is attested by the attention given the novel in the United States,[134] even though the English translation did not appear until several years later.[135] Among many critics

Tirano Banderas has come to represent the outstanding work produced by Valle-Inclán.

The success of *Tirano Banderas* brought both aesthetic satisfaction, which inspired further creative endeavors, and financial reward, through which he was able to continue issuing his "Opera Omnia." Another important credit was added with the publication of *La corte de los milagros*,[136] the first novel in the ambitious series of nine planned under the title *El ruedo ibérico*.[137] This initial volume had been announced earlier:

Another, first in the series I've entitled *El ruedo ibérico*, is *La corte isabelina*.[138] (A215)

In the year that intervened between the announcement and the publication of the novel the title had been changed to *La corte de los milagros*, because the author did not wish to alert the censor to its contents.

Valle-Inclán's concept of the expansive series on the late nineteenth century, supplementing his *La guerra carlista* trilogy, was marked by a collective rather than an individualized protagonist:

Throughout its various volumes, there will not be protagonists in *El ruedo ibérico*. Its great protagonist is the social medium, the ambient. . . . I want to infuse the novel with Spanish sensibility, as it's manifested in the reaction to events of some importance. For me, the sensibility of a people is reflected and measured by the way it reacts to such events. To view the reaction of Spanish sensibility in that rather interesting period from the Revolution of 1868 to the death of Alfonso XII in 1895 is what I propose to do in the new novel.[139] (A216)

While *La guerra carlista* generally demonstrated the heroic quality through individualization, *El ruedo ibérico* shuns the hero or single protagonist in order to permit a satiric portraiture of an era:

They are all equal. When their moment comes, they emerge from the background and attain maximum importance. I know that the reader resents the abandonment of characters that first caught his fancy, but I'm writing the novel of a people, of a period, not that of a few men. The great protagonist of my book is the *Ruedo Ibérico*. The others are useful only insofar as their function defines a national aspect. The external quality of the event or the anecdote do not concern me. What does interest me is their expressive quality . . . The foundation of my books is shaped by these elements: light and action. A people can be known through the setting that engenders it and through the environment that expresses it. The *Ruedo Ibérico* is engendered by light and is expressed by action.[140]

To mock, to mock everything and everyone . . . Truth, Justice are the only things worth respecting. This genre of literary satire has a grand tradition. . . . Satirical literature is one of the forms of the song of history that preys on the powerful who did not act according to their duty.[141]

My purpose in it was none other than to recreate the history of Spain from the fall of Isabel II to the Restoration, and rather than writing a novelesque fable, I seek the satire hidden beneath an almost theatrical fiction.[142] (A217)

In adopting this attitude the author reaffirmed his concept of deformation, already ably expressed in *Tirano Banderas*. *El ruedo ibérico*, therefore, was intended as a continuation of this point of view; the series attempts to place the era it examines in front of a fun-house mirror reflecting images grotesquely, as defined in *Luces de bohemia*. Valle-Inclán's contemporary attitude permits the author to stand above the history of the late nineteenth century and to make what was usual, even correct, at that time appear decadent and twisted. The process is one of concentrated depreciation.

Reassessment of the past also came into focus in another context with the tricentennial of Góngora, the great "Siglo de Oro" poet. Among the respondents to a query on how writers viewed the poet and his works in 1927, Valle-Inclán gave a brief and surprising reply:

I reread Góngora a few months ago—last summer—and it provoked a distressing reaction, one wholly divorced from any literary respect. Intolerable! A coldness, an unabated scavenging for precepts . . . I'm incapable of hedging the truth.[143] (A218)

Valle-Inclán's view must have been known prior to publication, for Gerardo Diego, a staunch supporter of Góngora, planned to stone Valle-Inclán's residence in protest (if he did, there is no record of it) and sent him a can of disinfectant to use on his beard. As a more public gesture, Diego wrote in the issue of *La Gaceta Literaria* devoted to Góngora that Valle-Inclán was not, and had never been, a poet.[144]

Just as he re-interpreted historical personages and eras, Valle-Inclán the Man concerned himself with what he termed the "hora dramática" (dramatic hour) of his own period. It was no figment of imagination that Spain was undergoing considerable political strain not unlike that depicted in Valle-Inclán's novels. The growing hostility to the Primo de Rivera government in 1928 expressed itself in student strikes and riots.[145] Disturbances of varying degree were commonplace throughout the nation as the growing oppressiveness of the dictatorship affected more and more people. Valle-Inclán took mental notes and continued to be outspoken despite the increasing threat of reprisal by the regime.

Spain was not the only nation whose internal troubles Valle-Inclán followed with interest and concern. Mexico in 1928 was a volatile country still experiencing the ferment of revolutionary activity. While Alvaro Obregón was serving his limited presidential term the unrest of the opposition had been restrained, if never completely eradicated. When he stepped down in 1924, Obregón supported Calles, his Minister of the Interior, for the presidency. A peaceful transition was not achieved due to charges of fraud hurled by the Huerta-led opposition, and Obregón once again had to take to the battlefields in a civil war. Defeating the rebels in a succession of brilliant battles through the rugged Mexican geography, Obregón drove Huerta into exile. On 1 July 1928 Obregón was again elected president. But before he could take office, he was assassinated by José de León Toral on 17 July. The impact of his death reached across the ocean to Europe, where he was admired by many and distrusted by an equal number for his role as a reformer. To Valle-Inclán he had always been an admirable man and leader whose ideals coincided with his own.

Problems of a more personal nature were never far from Valle-Inclán, even while he was concerned with international matters. Since the termination of his contract with Renacimiento in 1925 he had been negotiating the rights to his works, which were held by the publisher. In August 1928 a settlement was reached satisfying the demands of both parties equitably. Armed with the release, Valle-Inclán proceeded to sign an impressive new contract with the Compañía Ibero-Americana de Publicaciones. The new firm, financed by the Bauer banking house, representatives of the Rothschild financial empire, guaranteed him a monthly income of 3,500 pesetas to be drawn against his royalties. It was the best contract that Valle-Inclán ever signed.[146]

The economic security the new association guaranteed had an immediate effect on Valle-Inclán:

My books, published in economical editions, will sell by the thousands; as was the case with *La guerra carlista*, published by CIAP, despite the horrible edition.[147] (A219)

He moved his family once more from quarters on Calle Santa Catalina to 9 Calle del General Oráa, a residence reflecting his improved economic situation. There one of his neighbors was the famed Juan Belmonte, whom he had befriended years before. Belmonte, now a matador at the height of his career, continued to fascinate Valle-Inclán with his dazzling mastery:

You were magnificent! That is exactly your kind of encounter, one in which you elicit sublime sparks from your physical misery, blending with the bull in such a manner that there's no way of telling where the man ends and the beast begins. The only thing lacking is that someday, surpassing yourself in the meaning and quality of your tragic art, honoring the delirious fanaticism that the public has for you, and going beyond the limits of your human transfiguration to the divine, you remain still and, instead of assuring your own success with a swirl of the cape, the bull seals your fate by piercing your heart with a horn. Thereafter, bull and torero would never again be separated on the poster, as they are now each afternoon of the bulls, after the magical play of the cape.[148] (A220)

Belmonte could not consider it a bad omen that Valle-Inclán dwelt on the one topic, death, that bullfighters dread most. Belmonte listened attentively to the apotheosis Valle-Inclán described and did not resent the talk of death because he knew that his friend and neighbor's conception of the moment was an exercise of his aesthetic sense.

Such unquestionable aesthetic motivation was typical of Valle-Inclán, whether in the context of private gatherings or in the public atmosphere of the café. There was no place for hypocrisy in his makeup and this was obvious to those who gathered with him at the Granja El Henar or at the Café Regina. He had lived all his life in the showcase of cafés and would continue to do so, as he explained to Unamuno:

My favorite vice is the café, where I spent my youth and spend my life outlandishly.[149] (A221)

The Café Regina attracted the German Hispanist Hans Jeschke in 1928 because of the presence of Valle-Inclán and others of the "Generación de '98," which he was studying in preparation for a critical work.[150] Jeschke was hindered neither by the passage of time in espousing the continued existence of the Generation nor by factors such as political variance and aesthetic opposition that had created a breach between the highly individualistic writers. In many cases even friendship had ceased to be a bond. Valle-Inclán later commented on the situation in reference to Jeschke's point of view:

Like a good German, he has a rigid spirit; he has brought with him such a fixation with the 9 and the 8 that it's impossible to make him understand how things are. Naturally, I asked him "which room was it that the 98 was in?" and why I was a writer of '98. That writer would belong to '98 who found on that date his definitive mode of expression and a lasting reputation based on it, but the writer who changes and renews himself and is transformed belongs to 1898 and 1929.[151] (A222)

The politically turbulent years during which these reunions at the Regina and Granja El Henar occurred made them, unlike the literary *tertulias* at the Levante, centers of political discussion. Governmental activities were assessed, generally damned, and contrary measures proposed. While Valle-Inclán was not partisan to any single cause alone, his well-known opposition to the dictatorship of Primo de Rivera cast him in the role of leader of the dissident factions gathering at the cafés. He was not anti-dictatorship but was only against the inequitable use of dictatorial power, as in the case of Primo de Rivera. His political versatility was also demonstrated by his continued attention to Carlist protocol when in 1929 he was received by Doña Berta de Rohán, widow of Don Carlos de Borbón, at her regal residence in Madrid. In contrast to this conservative side of his political nature was his acceptance of the honorary presidency of the "Amigos de la U.R.S.S." during the period 1929–1930.[152] More evidence of his various political affiliations are his activities on behalf of the radical Federación Universitaria Española, for which Valle-Inclán, being a frequent speaker at its rallies, became a symbol to its membership. The arrest and fines he accrued by his activity with this group endeared him to the FUE, the militant group whose incitement of student riots forced the closing of universities in 1929.

It seems clear that Valle-Inclán opposed the Primo de Rivera government with any weapon at his command, be it Carlist, communist, socialist, or anarchistic. The incarceration of many intellectual leaders during this time added fuel to his protestations (the Cárcel Modelo in Madrid had already been nicknamed "Ciudad Universitaria"). Valle-Inclán joined his colleagues in the prison twice that spring. On the first occasion he spent three days in jail, detained by the Dirección General de Seguridad without being given a reason. The affair gained in notoriety when the press learned of the incarceration. As Valle-Inclán said:

The foreign correspondents couldn't believe that we had to speak through the bars.[153] (A223)

The second time, on 10 April 1929, he was incarcerated for fifteen days, under order of General Severiano Martínez Anido, the undersecretary of state. The reason for the sentence was given as Valle-Inclán's failure to pay a fine for one of his celebrated "disturbances" in Madrid's Palacio de la Música earlier that month. Valle-Inclán recognized the special gravity of this new arrest:

It was more serious than the previous time. The police had sinister intentions. Had I been a worker, an unknown person, only God knows what would have happened . . . But it's not easy to make me vanish.[154] (A224)

It was on this occasion that Primo de Rivera issued another of his celebrated and much-quoted "notes."[155] Valle-Inclán's commentary on the official attitude divulged in the communique was predictably satirical:

What that Primo de Rivera says is fitting since he doesn't know Castilian. He meant to say that I am an "outrageous" citizen, but said "extravagant" instead. I am indeed extravagant because I tend to take a path other than the one on which people travel.[156] (A225)

Having sought incessantly to stir the wrath of the government, Valle-Inclán had succeeded finally in making himself a public martyr, if only in a minor key that could not match Unamuno's exotic exile.

Jail was a learning experience for Valle-Inclán. As he told Sender, he met people of all types and social levels during the common hours:

There are hierarchies there as in the so-called free society. The most powerful is that of the racketeers. They're in for a short time: their lawyers visit them, put up bail, and they're released. The second is that of the killers. They strut through the patios like bullfighters on Seville Street. In third place, that of political prisoners. After that are those of the "regulars" and prisoners who committed social crimes. . . .

Among the latter can be found the best from each family. Honesty, intelligence, dignity, culture. Socialists, Communists, unionists—the last of the great individualists left in Spain. Almost all are in the fifth gallery, the worst, the unhealthiest. They are forced to go into the patio that faces the Guadarrama. A cold under those conditions is a certain and infallible start of tuberculosis. Those who leave are marked indelibly for annihilation. Some had been there eight months under those conditions. . . . There was a Romanian doctor in my gallery who had nothing to do with politics. They imagined that a Romanian doctor, due to his profession and nationality, could only have come to Spain to kill the queen of Romania; as long as she was in the country, they kept him in jail. . . . When they took him [the bookdealer Vila] prisoner, there were two customers with him: Sr. Botella and a friend from Alicante. The alchemy they were discussing must have seemed rather suspicious—a pact with the Devil?—and the three men were jailed. . . . People of all classes: street vendors, writers, journalists. From circumstantial "friends" who sell us newspapers on the sidewalk to the most representative figures of the aristocracy, of the intellectual world.[157](A226)

Valle-Inclán continued to do his part and to show his disdain for the government through incessant vociferation. Particularly effective were verses of his that made the rounds of the cafés and streets of Madrid; of these, one has survived in the oral tradition of the capital:

Neither bomb, nor bullet, nor rope
will end your despicable life.
Your death will be under a pile
of excrement!

And a huge national phlegm
will cover you up like a shroud.
Cuckold! Riffraff in royal guise!
Habitual thief! (A227)

The verses, directed at Alfonso XIII, one of his favorite targets, demonstrated to what extent the king had fallen in the eyes of the author. The fact that the verses have survived is indicative, too, that Valle-Inclán's words reflected the public disdain.

His unflinching attacks against authority and the established order had other repercussions as well. Valle-Inclán's physical condition had worsened during his incarceration, and shortly after he was freed from jail, he applied for permission to visit a Dr. Leguet in Paris. Being persona non grata, he was denied a passport, but as Valle-Inclán told Sender,

Naturally, I left without a passport. No one bothered me. (A228)

While such an independent attitude had its momentary satisfactions, it continued to have a negative effect on Valle-Inclán's acceptance by the Establishment, particularly the Academy. The death of Eduardo Gómez de Baquero ("Andrenio") in 1929 had left a seat vacant in the Real Academia, and the candidacy of Valle-Inclán was revived instantly by Benavente, Azorín, Antonio Machado, and Pérez de Ayala, among others. But as in past attempts, the efforts of his boosters were unsuccessful. The counter-candidacy of Luis Martínez Kleiser, a journalist with *ABC* and *Blanco y Negro*, was supported by a greater number of the membership. Instead of humbling himself to solicit votes, Valle-Inclán chose to publicize his irreverent opinions:

The Academy of Language is a social club. Constituted as it is, no one should be in it unless they have social status. It is a gathering of decorative figures. If not, why is there a bishop among the academicians? The Academy of Language has never been a habitat for writers. The exception confirms the rule . . . writers were generally excluded, many of the great talents having died without being admitted to its ranks. . . . I'm also of the opinion that the Academy is convenient for writers of a certain established literary ilk. Not for me. I wouldn't be a good academician. What would I do in the Academy? No sooner would the academicians see me in their midst than they would become very upset . . . I would be an intruder.[158] (A229)

Having voiced his general impression, Valle-Inclán went on to discuss his opponent's candidacy:

It seems improper to me for Sr. Francos Rodríguez to have nominated Sr. Kleiser. My lord Bishop is well suited to the Academy. But Sr. Kleiser is not a bishop. A bishop is a decorative figure. Sr. Kleiser, notwithstanding his noted clerical significance, could never be that.[159] (A230)

In a final, mocking tone, Valle-Inclán administered the master thrust:

Perhaps I would consent to becoming an academician if they wore a showy uniform that I could display around town. How amusing it would be to enter places, including the Academy, in an outfit loaded down with gold and embroidery! . . . It would be tantamount to proclaiming: "Can you tell? I'm an immortal. My uniform says so." . . . I know myself and I know them. Lastly, isn't it true that the Academy can't even publish a dictionary? They've had to employ a publisher.[160] (A231)

With such declarations he guillotined whatever chance he might have had. The rancor he excited with his words and acts overcame whatever admiration his creativity elicited. But undoubtedly the statements against the Academy were the result of an auto-defense mechanism triggered by past experience. Earlier rejection had conditioned him to expect more of the same, particularly since the leaders of the opposition still remained. Despite the increasing number of friends in the Academy, Valle-Inclán realized that even their untiring efforts on his behalf would not be sufficient to overcome the prejudice of his detractors.

The situation could not have been different for the man who mocked social convention all his life. Only through a denial of the truths he had uncovered in the course of his existence would it have been possible for

Valle-Inclán to have experienced unmitigated success with his books, or acclamation in the theatre, or acceptance by the socially august. But he had come to the conclusion long ago that each man must live as an individual, regardless of society's traditions or attractions; the matter of personal conscience must be uppermost, he thought. Consequently, he believed that by indiscriminate catering to social demands man surrendered a most precious possession: his individuality. Such self-disenfranchisement was absurd to Valle-Inclán. In creating himself, therefore, he chose to adhere to the guidelines proposed by his being. Ironically, it was he who always seemed absurd to society.

9 Absurdity

The third and final phase of Valle-Inclán's activity in the theatrical idiom began in 1920, the year that saw the publication of four important new plays: *Farsa italiana de la enamorada del rey*, *Luces de bohemia*, *Farsa y licencia de la reina castiza*, and *Divinas palabras*.[1] While the dates of completion have not been established in all cases, none of the works belong to the period before 1913. They were all written between the publication of *El embrujado* and the year 1920. Appearing suddenly as they did, the implication is that Valle-Inclán found it necessary to publish again his drama statements and to attempt a return to the mainstream he had deserted when he terminated his association with the Guerrero-Díaz de Mendoza company. But while these works bear witness to the reemergence of the playwright, Valle-Inclán was still a dramatist without a stage. It would be 1924 before any of his plays were produced.

La enamorada del rey is a poetic drama in three acts set in the eighteenth century. Two traditions—folk and courtly—are depicted in the work side by side, coexisting but unrelated. Each tradition takes its own course until the love of the young tavern-girl Mari-Justina for the elderly king inspires the possibility of a union. The first act frames the continuous statement of her love, a mixture of passion and innocence. The fantasy of the girl is contrasted with the facts told her by La Ventera, her grandmother: the king is on a lofty plane to which she cannot aspire, he is not about to condescend to her whims, and, lastly, he is much older than the girl. But Mari-Justina cannot be deterred by this rationale. She reiterates her feelings when Maese Lotario, a young troubadour, arrives at the inn. Convinced by her sadness and her pleas, he promises to communicate her love to the king when he performs at the court. Lotario, who is secretly in love with Mari-Justina, delivers his message. The king is incredulous; he assesses his possibility as a lover and as an object of love and decides that Lotario's story has been contrived. Amid the courtly atmosphere his assertion seems sound. But when Altisidora, a lady-in-waiting, reads Mari-Justina's letter in an impassioned voice, the king forgets his earlier impression and begins

160

to accept as true the declaration of love. Accompanied by Don Facundo, his doubting minister, the king arrives at the inn; as he observes Mari-Justina in her pensive state, he recalls fragments of her letter and the cynical Don Facundo footnotes each statement with its source: the reading by Altisidora. Unrecognized in their folk attire, they order food and learn at first hand the facts of Mari-Justina's enamoredness.

The sudden entrance of Maese Lotario discloses the masquerade. Mari-Justina sees the king she had loved from afar in his true humanity. Love disappears. But the magnanimous king understands only too well. He unites Lotario and Mari-Justina and rewards the troubadour by naming him adviser to the throne. The raising of the poet to the high position satisfies an ideal, especially since the king dismisses his previous counselors unceremoniously, placing the kingdom in plebeian hands. The dream the dramatist could not see fulfilled in his reality became an accomplished and salutory fact in his play.

The optimism of *La enamorada del rey* was but one point of view. Valle-Inclán, who had experienced Madrid's artistic life in all its complexity, could not have his writings imply solely a positive facet. The times had been too severe for reality to be relegated to a secondary role; consequently, he depicted the anguish and frustration as well. The poet had already made his statement on the absurdity of the period in *La pipa de kif*. Valle-Inclán found it necessary to depict it also in his drama:

There are three ways of seeing the world artistically or aesthetically: from the knees, standing, or from the air. When one adopts the kneeling position—and that's the oldest stance in literature—the characters, the heroes, are given a condition superior to that of human beings or, at least, to that of the narrator or poet. Thus, Homer attributes to his heroes qualities that humans only have in limited form. In other words, it is a way of creating beings superior to human nature: gods, demigods, and heroes. There is a second way, which is to consider fictional protagonists as if they were of our own nature, as if they were our brothers, as if they were us, as if the character duplicated our essence, with its very virtues and defects. This is, undoubtedly, the most successful approach. This is Shakespeare, all of Shakespeare. . . . And there is a third way, which is to see the world from a superior plane and to consider the characters of the plot as beings inferior to the author, with a touch of irony. The gods become characters in a skit. This is a very Spanish manner, the manner of a demiurge who cannot conceive of himself as made of the same stuff as his figurines. This is the manner of Quevedo. . . . This manner is definitive in Goya. And it was this consideration that moved me to take a new course in my literature and write the *Esperpentos*, the literary genre that I baptize with the name of *Esperpento*.[2] (A232)

Valle had already expressed a similar opinion as early as 1921, and it is interesting to note later statements emerging from the compact nucleus of that era:

Authors must be studied according to their three manners. First, the character is superior to the author. The manner of the hero. Homer, who doesn't have the blood of the gods. Second, the author who duplicates himself: Shakespeare. His characters are nothing other than duplications of his personality. Third, the author is superior to his characters and contemplates them as God does his creatures. Goya painted his subjects as inferior to him. As did Quevedo. This is bred in picaresque literature. The authors of such novels did not wish to be confused with their characters, whom they considered very inferior to themselves, and this spirit still persists, naturally, in Spanish literature. I too consider my characters as my inferiors. My work is an attempt at what I tried to accomplish.[3] (A233)

The natural procedure would be to apply these ideas beyond the limited scope of individual representatives. Valle-Inclán did not omit this process; he chose to make a comparative study of three closely interrelated literatures:

French authors always stand ecstatically before the events in their plays and the voices of their characters. They deify their heroes. They engender gods. In France, the author is the first vassal of his offspring. He exalts the protagonist and his drama well beyond human limitations. He serves his heroes in good times and in bad as he would extraordinary divinities. The English, workmen full of decorum and sociability, exercise club literature. Their characters move within a circle of friends, subject to the rights and duties of men-of-the-world. An author places his hero in a circle, gives him the proper credentials, and grants him the right to vote in its deliberations. When the time comes for rewards, respectful of class interests, he grants him the title of peer. The author and his character experience the same human protocol. The play is a purely social event, one hardly worthy of mention in *The Times*. Othello is a family member who commits the impropriety of showing exaggerated jealousy. We Spaniards always place ourselves above the drama and its interpreters. We are always aware of our capricious manipulation of the strings of the farce. Cervantes feels superior to Don Quijote. He mocks him a bit, sometimes shows pity over his sorrows and follies, forgives him his fits, and even grants him the boon of a final moment of lucidity before leading him, quite generously, to the gates of Heaven. We Spanish authors, haughty from our youth, like to sprinkle the life that we create with a touch of sorrow. Ours is a harsh paternity. By dint of caprice and blood. Because we are ever accompanied by indignation at what we see taking place around us fatally. Spain is a vast stage selected by tragedy. There's always a dramatic moment in Spain; a drama well beyond the capabilities of the participants. These, cardboard figurines, lacking ideality and courage, seem ridiculous to us in their heroic trappings. Like strolling players, they interpret the most sublime tragic situations clumsily. Don Quijote is represented as just another Quijote. Doctors diagnose Don Juan's dramatic escapades as ambiguous physiology. Our whole populace is seen to be worth less than a gang of trivial players set on staging the genial drama of Spanish life. The result, of course, is an *Esperpento*.[4] (A234)

Luces de bohemia, the first *Esperpento*, is a drama in fifteen scenes tracing the final moments in the bitter life of Máximo Estrella, a poet blinded by syphilis, who has struggled for recognition only to witness the deterioration of hope. His life moves steadily toward its tragic denouement while the grotesqueries of human existence become increasingly visible in the incidence of irony, cynicism, dissonance, satire, baseness, lewdness, opportunism, mockery, and alienation. The caricature of life becomes the reality of Máximo Estrella.

Luces de bohemia is the biography of the flamboyant bohemian Alejandro Sawa, who was born in Málaga in 1862 and died early in August 1909 under conditions not unlike those described by Valle-Inclán in the play. In a letter to Darío Valle-Inclán communicated the news of his tragic end:

Dear Darío:
I've come to see you having first been to the house of our poor Alejandro Sawa. I cried in front of the dead man, for him, for myself, and for all the poor poets. I can't do anything; neither can you, but if some of us got together, we could do something. Alejandro left an unpublished book. The best thing that he's written. A diary of hopes and tribulations. The failure of all attempts at publishing it, along with a letter from *El Liberal* reneging on a piece that would have brought sixty pesetas, drove him mad in his last days. A hopeless madness. He wanted to kill himself. He died like a king in a tragedy: mad, blind, and raving.[5] (A235)

All the tragic elements depicted in the play are present in the description of Sawa's last days.[6] Present, too, are Valle-Inclán's sympathy and sorrow, as well as his identification with Sawa. The life that the dead writer led had been Valle-Inclán's before his marriage; he could have ended as did his friend and that recognition was disturbing. The life and death of Sawa verified the absurdity of human existence for Valle-Inclán, and he created *Luces de bohemia* in that cast. He classified the play as an *Esperpento* and even had Máximo Estrella define and discuss the new aesthetics:

Our tragedy is not tragedy . . . The *Esperpento*. . . . Goya was the inventor of *Esperpentism*. Classical heroes have taken a stroll along Gato alley. . . . Classical heroes reflected in those concave mirrors manifest the *Esperpento*. The tragic sense of Spanish life can only be rendered through an aesthetic that is systematically deformed. . . . Spain is a grotesque deformation of European civilization. . . . In a concave mirror, the most beautiful images are absurd. . . . Deformity ceases to be that when it is subject to a perfect mathematical system. My present aesthetic is to transform classical norms through the mathematics of the concave mirror. . . . Let us deform expression in the same mirror that deforms our faces, and the whole miserable life of Spain.[7] (A236)

In the expression of this and other tenets Valle-Inclán united his ideas to the life of Sawa and the resultant was Máximo Estrella, the protagonist who not only embodies one example of life's absurdity but is also the representative of all men whose existence enfolds the struggle between practicality and ideality. Because the artist cannot achieve complete separation from the world and yet must, as he senses, the struggle is absurd and the absurdity is underscored by the inevitability of the outcome. The prison of the body and the prisons man creates for himself keep his spirit from full flight. And ironically, as in the case of Sawa-Estrella, a point is reached where the artist must look to these same hindrances for salvation.

The body must be cared for and society must be caressed. In the end, however, these attentions come too late. Sawa, who penned attacks on the press and the government, found himself without assistance when he needed it; Max died in the same abandonment.

The bitterness of *Luces de bohemia* is never repeated again in the same tone in the drama of Valle-Inclán. But the seed of the *Esperpento* remains visible in the rest of his production, even in those works outside that explicit designation. A case in point is *Farsa y licencia de la reina castiza*, the play in which Isabel II, the controversial Spanish monarch of the nineteenth century and grandmother of Alfonso XIII, is treated with venomous candor. The play is a tirade against the Bourbon monarchy, past and present, whose characteristics have been lack of dignity, abnormality, degradation, unscrupulousness, and a host of other qualifications toward depravity. Valle-Inclán interprets the reign of Isabel II as an absurd moment in Spanish history populated by grotesque cardboard figures. In effect, the play is an *Esperpento*. The fact that it is composed in verse cannot change the viewpoint of the dramatist nor steer the work from its implicit association with that denomination. If it needs to be stated, the presence of poetic form (with its intrinsic beauty, orderliness, dignity, and quality) serves effectively as a foil to the deformity of character and situation that the reign of Isabel II signifies to Valle-Inclán. Afraid that the repetition of history was occurring in the reign of Alfonso XIII, the dramatist sent a copy of the play to the monarch with an instructional note appended:

Sir: I have the honor of sending you this book, a stylization of the reign of your grandmother, Doña Isabel II, and I pray that yours will not suggest a similar stylization to poets of the future.[8] (A237)

Alfonso's reaction to the book, if he did receive it, has not been recorded, and there is no evidence of official intervention to suppress the play. But its premiere did not take place, for whatever reason, until 1931,[9] after the king's tenure terminated.

The fourth of the plays to appear in 1920 was *Divinas palabras. Tragicomedia de aldea*,[10] another play not designated *Esperpento* but governed by the same tenets expressed in *Luces de bohemia*. Valle-Inclán's semi-classic interpretation of rural Galicia's reality (sorrow, drudgery, death) encompasses the grotesque both in characterization and in situation. The bucolic, too, can be viewed in the distortive mirror. *Divinas palabras* is a story of sexuality told in terms of repressions and license. To this traditional framework has been added the element of farce; the result is the absurdity and displacement of reality that Valle-Inclán has baptized with the name *Esperpento*.

Divinas palabras is the culmination of a series of rural tragedies begun with *Aguila de blasón* and *Romance de lobos* and continued with *El embrujado*, and an impressive aside in prose fiction in *Flor de santidad* and an occasional story. The setting of these works is also Galicia, and the characters are founded on regional types. But it is in *Divinas palabras*, one of the master-works of Valle-Inclán's literature, that the traditions depicted earlier find their most perfect delineation through heightened sensitivity and mastery of style, as Juan Ramón Jiménez noted in a letter to the dramatist dated 2 July 1920 from Madrid.[11] *Divinas palabras* remains an important link in the chain of technical, thematic, and aesthetic development of Valle-Inclán.

In 1921 Valle-Inclán published yet another drama of note, the *Esperpento* entitled *Los cuernos de don Friolera*.[12] In this work, the dramatist expanded on his theory of the grotesque through the words of Don Estrafalario, an intellectual, at the beginning of the prologue:

I've also been concerned with the Devil's grimace before the Sinner. The truth is that I had a very different idea of infernal laughter; I'd always thought of it as mocking, supremely mocking, but no . . . Don't for a moment believe in the reality of a Devil who takes an interest in the human charade, enjoying himself like a shopkeeper. Tears and laughter are born out of the contemplation of things akin to ourselves, and the Devil has an angelic nature. . . . Those sentimentalists who express sorrow over the agony of horses in the bullring are incapable of feeling the aesthetic emotion of the bullfight: Their sensibility is manifestly parallel to equine sensibility and, through some subconscious process, they've come to believe that their fate will be akin to that of those disemboweled horses. . . . That's how it is. And there's a similar parallel with whatever makes us laugh: We reserve our jeers for whatever relates to us. . . . My aesthetic transcends pain and laughter, as must the conversations of the dead when they tell stories of the living. . . . All our art is born out of the knowledge that we will pass away some day. That knowledge makes men equal, more so than the French Revolution. . . . I would like to view this world with the perspective of the other shore. . . . I'm like that relative of mine who, when asked by his overseer what he would like to be, replied: "A corpse."[13] (A238)

Don Estrafalario, like Max Estrella before him, reveals the intent and point of view of the dramatist. These, however, are not presented in a thesis play. Instead, Valle-Inclán employs the traditional theme of the cuckold (*Commedia dell'Arte*, Molière, *Siglo de Oro*, Restoration Comedy) in union with a strong anti-militarism to depict the grotesqueries of contemporary life. The dramatist avoids the cliché, as he has consistently, and proceeds to demolish satirically the "sacred cows" before him. And in the process he succeeds in making *Los cuernos de don Friolera* both a social and a theatrical document, the first through the exposure of social conventions as ridiculous, and the second through the satirization of drama thriving on bastard thematics. The prologue and epilogue that frame the twelve scenes of the *Esperpento* make clear Valle-Inclán's attitude on the second point; the play proper discloses his social commentary.

The prologue commences with the peripatetic intellectuals Don

Estrafalario and Don Manolito conversing against the active background of a fair.[14] The aesthetic pronouncements of the former stand out in the popular setting, appearing as eccentric as his name. But his views are shortly reinforced through the fantasy created by a puppeteer and his creatures. Reality is eclipsed temporarily while the tale of the cuckold Friolera unfolds before an expectant crowd, prominent among whom are Don Estrafalario and Don Manolito. Friolera, the deceived lieutenant, is talked into killing his mistress as a point of honor despite his indifference to her affair. The prodding of the puppeteer brings on the indignation that leads to the act. But before Friolera can be imprisoned by society, he learns how to revive the fallen woman, an act completed as the playlet ends. This plot will be paralleled within the play proper; but the second version of the events will have its own variations, as will a third one narrated in the epilogue. Fantasy, reality, legend. Society will be served. But which of the three avenues will it call on? In the puppeteer's version both society and the individual are equally served: society (the insistence of the puppeteer) demands that the honor of the cuckold be avenged in the blood of the deceiver, and it is; the individual benefits from this purgation and is freed from legal consequences (also imposed by society) through the absurd resurrection of the victim. This is the world of fantasy and its absurd operations have an intrinsic logic, as Chesterton has stated in "The Logic of Elfland." It is this veracity that prompts the comments of Don Estrafalario on the status of the Spanish drama:

There's no doubt that the comprehension of such humor and morality does not come from Castilian tradition. It is Portuguese and Cantabrian, perhaps from the mountains of Catalonia as well. The other regions literally know nothing of such jests about cuckolds, of such witty good sense, so contrary to Castile's theatrical and African concept of honor. That puppet stage on the back of an old itinerant storyteller is more suggestive than the entire rhetorical Spanish theatre.[15] (A239)

Further, despite the qualifications to this statement suggested by Don Manolito, Don Estrafalario adds:

The cruelty and dogmatism of Spanish drama are found only in the language. Shakespearean cruelty is magnificent because it is blind, possessed of the greatness of natural forces. Shakespeare is violent but not dogmatic. Spanish cruelty has the entire savage liturgy of the *auto-de-fé*. It is cold and disagreeable. Nothing is more removed from the blind fury of the elements than Torquemada: His is a scholastic fury. If our theatre had the quaking of bullfights, it would be magnificent: Had it known how to convey that aesthetic violence, it would be a theatre as heroic as the *Iliad*. Lacking that, it has all the antipathy of codices, from the Constitution back to *grammar*.[16] (A240)

The opportunity to vent his views through one of his characters is not used in vain by Valle-Inclán. Estrafalario is made to express other expository ideas on the theatre:

Shakespeare rhymes to the beat of his heart, the heart of Othello: He is as one with the jealousy of the Moor: Creator and creature are of the same human stuff. As for that puppeteer, not for a second does he stop considering himself superior by nature to the puppets on his stage. He has a demiurgic dignity.[17] (A241)

It is this superior attitude, which obliterates sentiment and the melodramatic, that makes possible the *Esperpento*. As Don Estrafalario has pointed out, laughter and tears exist only where there is an identification. But such is not possible where puppets are concerned. Likewise, the *Esperpento* makes marionettes of the characters so that there can be no semblance of attachment. The dramatist achieves this end, just as the puppeteer does, by being superior to his creations. The dramatist considers them grotesque because their frame of reference is an absurd existence:

Life—its events, sorrows, loves—is always the same, fatally so. What changes are the characters, the protagonists of life. Those roles were previously played by gods and heroes. Today . . . well, what's the use of speaking? In the past, destiny fell on the shoulders—haughtiness and sorrow—of Oedipus or Medea. Today, destiny is the same, fate is the same, greatness is the same, pain is the same . . . But the shoulders that bear them have changed. Actions, concerns, recognition are the same as yesterday and forever. The shoulders are different, too miniscule to support that weight. Out of that are born contrast, disproportion, and the ridiculous. In *Los cuernos de don Friolera*, the sorrow of the protagonist is the same as Othello's and yet it lacks its greatness. Blindness is beautiful and noble in Homer. But in *Luces de bohemia* that same blindness is sad and lamentable because it concerns a bohemian poet, Máximo Estrella.[18] (A242)

With the publication of these five plays at the beginning of his third period of activity in the drama, Valle-Inclán made his most important statements in that idiom. The promise of his second era was being fulfilled amply. It should be noted that he completed his trilogy *Comedias bárbaras* in 1922 with the issuance of *Cara de Plata*. His accelerated productivity was accompanied by new activity in the theatre, but not on the professional level. Still smarting from his bouts, he sought out the Teatro de la Escuela Nueva, a group of semi-professionals with Marxist leanings founded under the auspices of the Ateneo de Madrid. With that group he resumed his sometime role of director.[19] But no matter how brief or lengthy it may have been, the important thing is that through such activity the playwright was committing himself to the theatre in an enthusiastic manner. Had this trajectory not been interrupted by illness and subsequent internment in 1923 and 1924, Valle-Inclán might have reached a higher plateau sooner. As it was, he returned to Madrid in July 1924 to be followed shortly by his family. His wife, Josefina, became active in theatrical circles once more, and Valle-Inclán benefited from his wife's efforts. Suddenly, in 1924, he was again a playwright with a professional stage at his disposal.

A new play, *La cabeza del Bautista* (The Head of the Baptist),[20] first subtitled *Novela macabra* but later called *Melodrama para marionetas*, premiered on 17 October 1924, accompanied by Valle-Inclán's earlier play *Cuento de abril* (April Tale),[21] at the Teatro El Centro in Madrid under the direction of Enrique López Alarcón; playing the principal roles were Gil Andrés, Alfonso Tudela, and Alfredo Gómez de la Vega. In this new drama Valle-Inclán showered scorn and heaped ridicule on social and moral values. Don Igi, the caricature of the avaricious Spaniard who made his fortune in America (prototype of other *gachupines* in *Tirano Banderas*), is the embodiment of corruption on both levels. La Pepona, who prostitutes love in order to assure her physical well-being, is a falsifier whose very sin becomes her punishment. El Jándalo, whose role as conscience would have made his death heroic and meaningful, is a deceiver who twists morality to serve his base purpose. The symbolism established in the title is a mockery. Man once again emerges as a grotesque being who must be portrayed in terms of puppetry. Such is the absurdity of the human condition that the dramatist perceives. Consequently, as in all his works designated as puppet plays, the reality of life is best portrayed on the stage by live actors acting in the context of the marionette theatre. It was in this manner that the dramatist interpreted his vision.

La rosa de papel (The Paper Rose), the other *Novela macabra* published with *La cabeza del Bautista*, also was given the later subtitle *Melodrama para marionetas*. It, too, demonstrates Valle-Inclán's intention to present human frailty in terms of the frailty of puppets. A macabre play of avarice and death, *La rosa de papel* is a powerful and sordid work with many theatrical possibilities within its grotesqueness. It is a piece worthy of the Grand Guignol, but it does not stop merely with the horrible. It continues into the realm of dehumanization and alienation explored later by Brecht in his doctrine. Valle-Inclán, too, presents motives and actions whose incomprehensibility makes the characters decrease in their humanity. But, as occurs in Brecht's theatre despite his theoretical "alienation effect," the audience reacts to the grotesque and the absurd by referring to its own humanity, as did the Greeks before their monumental theatre. The result of this introspection will be as varied as each individual, but the effectiveness and aesthetic efficacy of plays such as *La cabeza del Bautista* and *La rosa de papel* reside in the horrible awareness they bring to the conscious mind that mankind is possessed of terrible demonic powers and that these may rise from the caverns of the subconscious to change the course of existence.

Sacrilegio. Auto para siluetas, is a suggestive one-act play featuring another aspect of life's somber side in terms of deformity. The piece is set in a cave of thieves reminiscent of *Comedia de ensueño*. Being a play of shadows, light (or its absence) has an important role in the atmosphere and in the characterization. Identity is hindered by the half-light of the torch, by the darkness of covered eyes, and by the falsification that gives the plot its ultimate grotesqueness. It is fitting that identity be diffused in this manner for, as Dante has indicated, thieves lose theirs as punishment for the crime of depriving others of property (an extension of identity/personality). In paralleling the interpretation of Dante, Valle-Inclán has given his work deeper meaning.

Ligazón was the second work subtitled *Auto para siluetas*. More so than in *Sacrilegio*, the dramatist employs light and darkness to give his characters the quality of silhouettes. Against the brilliance of the moon, profiles inherit an aura of unreality that fits the mood of the work. The static luminosity of moon, stars, and objects reflecting their light contrasts with the dynamic shadowiness of characters moving in the night and the dramatic landscape set blackly against the moon. In this visual sensuality words seem like discordant echoes. The characters speak of marital arrangements, of passion, of love's prostitution, of devil pacts, of death, but it is action (movement, gesture, violence) that paces the play: the knife-sharpener's wheel in motion heralding a tragic action as scissors reflect the moon; the dazzle of a necklace in the night light; the ritual cadences of passion; the blood pact between lovers; the stroke of the scissors as a death weapon.

The power of such plays, and others that followed soon after, resulted from the complete mastery of dramatic form. That Valle-Inclán was aware of this can be seen in his attempt to redefine *all* his work in theatrical terms:

> I write in a scenic form, in dialogue, almost exclusively. But I'm not concerned whether or not the works are staged later on. I write in this form because it pleases me greatly, because it seems to me the best literary style, the most serene, the most impassive in conveying the plot. I love impassivity in art. I want my characters to present themselves and to be themselves without the commentary, the explication, of the author. Everything should be the plot itself.[22] (A243)

This principle, stated relatively late in his career, is evident in Valle-Inclán's earliest works. Regardless of what denomination it bore, the majority of his novels, stories, and, of course, plays showed that dialogue formed the core. Further, many of the themes, characters, and plots first employed in other genres found their concrete and definitive expression in the dramatic form.

Continuing his association with the non-professional theatre, Valle-Inclán discovered a new outlet in "El Mirlo Blanco," a group founded in Madrid on 34 Calle Mendizábal by Ricardo Baroja and his wife Carmen Monné. On 8 February 1926 they inaugurated their dining-room theatre with the prologue and epilogue of Valle-Inclán's *Los cuernos de don Friolera*, Ricardo Baroja's *Marinos vascos*, and Pío Baroja's *Adiós a la bohemia*. Many other works were presented in the months that followed, among them Claudio de la Torre's *El viajero*, Edgar Neville's *Eva y Adán*, and O. Henry's *Miserias comunes*. Pío Baroja also contributed *Arlequín, mancebo de botica o Los pretendientes de Colombina*, while Carmen Baroja de Caro gave her *El gato de la mère Michel*. So much did the small chamber theatre attract him that Valle-Inclán chose to premiere his play *Ligazón* there on 8 May 1926 and curiously, although Josefina Blanco was among the members of the cast, he did not attend.[23] In November, near All Saints' Day, when the group presented Zorrilla's *Don Juan Tenorio*, in which Ricardo Baroja played Butarelli and his wife played the role of the Comendador, the chamber performance was heightened by Valle-Inclán's characterization of Doña Brígida, in which he attempted to disguise his unruly beard behind a large tablenapkin. According to another Baroja family member, Valle-Inclán took the matter very seriously.[24] It was his first appearance on a stage as an actor since the days before the loss of his arm, in 1899.

Inspired by "El Mirlo Blanco," Valle-Inclán gathered together his own company,[25] at first under the name "Ensayo de Teatro" but later as "El Cántaro Roto." The company gave its first presentation on 19 December 1926 in the theatre of the newly inaugurated Círculo de Bellas Artes in Madrid. After some lengthy opening remarks by Valle-Inclán, two plays were presented: Moratín's *La comedia nueva o El café* and Valle-Inclán's *Ligazón*.[26] On subsequent evenings the group presented *El paso de las aceitunas* by Lope de Rueda; *El café chino* by Eduardo Villa-Señor, a Mexican writer whose play had been done previously at "El Mirlo Blanco"; *La cabeza del dragón* by Valle-Inclán; *El hombre que casó con mujer muda* by Anatole France, translated by Ceferino Palencia Tubau; and *Arlequín, mancebo de botica, o los pretendientes de Colombina* by Pío Baroja. Unfortunately, the venture did not extend beyond these samplings, although plans included presenting plays by many other dramatists. Not unexpectedly, Valle-Inclán found himself at odds with the administration of the Círculo de Bellas Artes over his complaint that his fifty percent allocation was not enough to cover production costs and about the restriction of the number of performances on every play. His first recourse was to write to the president of the Círculo de Bellas Artes, but, not receiving a reply from Fernández Rodríguez, Valle-Inclán characteristically made the issue a public one via interviews appearing on 1 January 1927 in *El Heraldo de Madrid* and on 3 January in *La Voz*.[27] The bureaucratic reply by Fernández Rodríguez in *El Heraldo de Madrid* on 4 January prompted Valle-Inclán's final statement, on the front page of the next day's newspaper:

Sr. D. Juan Fernández:
   My dear sir, you have committed a lamentable error in affirming in yesterday's *Heraldo* having answered two of my letters, wherein I stated that you should not disclaim responsibility for the single presentation of Anatole France's *El hombre que*

casó con mujer muda by El Cántaro Roto. Believe me, had your reply reached my hands, I would have been overjoyed in making it public. In any case, I trust that you'll be kind enough not to avoid sending a copy of the letter and, for my part, I promise to make it known immediately to the readers of the *Heraldo*.

Cordially,
Valle-Inclán
5 January 1927 (A244)

Valle-Inclán's impatience here, as in the past, had brought to a premature end what might have been a new, felicitous relationship with the theatre. However, the variety of works presented served to give a glimpse of Valle-Inclán's aspiration for a theatre to serve in the capacity of museum and laboratory. "El Cántaro Roto," with its pessimistic name, was the closest he came to achieving his desire.

Once more without a theatre in which to vitalize his ideas, Valle-Inclán began to collect his plays in several formats. *Ligazón* was one of the five plays included in *Retablo de la avaricia, la lujuria y la muerte*;[28] the others were *La rosa de papel*, *El embrujado*, *La cabeza del Bautista*, and *Sacrilegio*. It was curious to some that *El embrujado*, dating from Valle-Inclán's second period of theatrical productivity, was included in a collection dedicated otherwise to plays from a much later era.[29] A year later he published another collection, *Tablado de marionetas para educación de príncipes*,[30] which included *Farsa italiana de la enamorada del rey*, *Farsa infantil de la cabeza del dragón* and *Farsa y licencia de la reina castiza*.

Martes de carnaval (Shrove Tuesday), his final collection of plays, contained the *Esperpentos* entitled *Los cuernos de don Friolera*, *La hija del capitán* and *Las galas del difunto*.[31] When *La hija del capitán* was first published[32] it became notorious because of its unequivocal attack on the military regime of Primo de Rivera. Its potent satire, coming at a time when national defiance was increasing, proved an unsettling brew to members of the government who saw themselves in the grotesque characters created by Valle-Inclán. The laughter of Madrid was the last straw. Faced with the disruptive influence of the work and prompted to reprimand its author for his levity, Primo de Rivera ordered the confiscation of the edition.[33] Being an official statement and given the necessity of publishing the government's decrees, the notice appeared in all the Madrid newspapers. In effect, it served to propagandize the work even more and to aggrandize the popular image of Valle-Inclán, the author whose name had been omitted cunningly from the communique. This ordered repression of the original edition was never lifted, but shortly after the exit of Primo de Rivera, Valle-Inclán planned to include the play in *Martes de carnaval*:

This coming March I'll publish *Martes de carnaval*, which is a work against dictatorships and militarism. I had thought of publishing it in May when, given the climactic conditions of Madrid, the Cárcel Modelo, whose cells I know quite well from previous stays, is comfortable. Nonetheless, despite the prevailing cold, I won't hold back publication because I feel that the moment is opportune. Since the young keep silent, it is up to the old to act on their behalf.[34] (A245)

Even though the strong dictatorial hand of Primo de Rivera had been removed from the wheel of state, the military still controlled the government. Valle-Inclán's statement, therefore, was still valid. Added to the anti-militarism of the plays in the collection was the provocative title *Martes de carnaval*, suggesting unruly celebration underscored by the grim reminder that Ash Wednesday followed on the excesses with its somberness and privation. The grotesque and deformed life of the carnival symbolized the temper of the period, to which the title also adds the martial image of the military. In that context the book's meaning could not be missed.

La hija del capitán is an *Esperpento* in seven scenes, set in the Madrid of Valle-Inclán's time. The capital (locales, life, tempo, populace) plays an important role in the play, as it did in *Luces de bohemia*. Once more, the playwright distorts the already distorted cityscape and its inhabitants through the means of his convex and concave mirrors. The folklore of Madrid is viewed not as Mesonero Romanos saw it in his *cuadros costumbristas* but in the reflection of its decadence. Each character is the embodiment of a part of this vision; together, the characters constitute the city's depraved life. The externalization results from the reduction of each individual's personality to a caricatural state; in this condition, with his very being turned inside out to reveal its grotesque nature, the character becomes one more dot on the pointillistic canvas. The *Esperpento* functions within this aesthetic premise.

Las galas del difunto is another anti-militaristic *Esperpento* in seven scenes. While *Las galas del difunto* does not contain the unequivocal satire of the military, it does make its contribution. Juanito Ventolera is, after all, a soldier. Valle-Inclán employs this character as a voice for his own point of view regarding the conduct of Spain toward the American colonies. Juanito is direct in his condemnation. But Juanito is also a scoundrel and an insensate who defiles the grave's sanctity to steal a suit of clothes and then makes a mockery of the widow's grief. His diabolism, while *simpático* to an audience, is terrifying to Doña Terita. But Valle-Inclán's intent goes beyond either description. The behavior of Juanito is intended to depict the condition to which the "heroes" of the American campaigns are reduced on their return to society. His medals notwithstanding, Juanito Ventolera suffers the indifference of a crass public. He is reduced to grave-plundering and to intimidating women in order to survive. He is excellent in both roles because military life has given him good training. The fine sentiments Juanito Ventolera may have possessed at one time have been perverted during his military career. The man who returns to society is worse than the man it gave to the service of his country. Therefore, Valle-Inclán's condemnation of militarism is the same as in *La hija del capitán* and *Los cuernos de don Friolera*; only the targets of his satire are different.

Apart from his literary attacks on militarism, Valle-Inclán took every opportunity to fight any semblance of its patronage he encountered. One such example is particularly memorable. Shortly after the premiere in 1927 of García Lorca's *Mariana Pineda*, which had not met with the hoped-for public acceptance, the company of Margarita Xirgu and Alfonso Muñoz mounted the verse drama *El hijo del diablo*, about the supposed son of Don Juan Tenorio. The author of the play was Joaquín Montaner, a minor literary figure and a Catalan. Montaner held a semi-official post as secretary to the committee organizing the Exposición Universal de Barcelona. In this capacity he supervised a governmental subsidy to be paid to leading writers for their services in propagandizing the exhibit. While many renowned authors had been contracted, Valle-Inclán's name had not appeared on the list. The omission irked him doubly—he took it as a rebuff from the government, and as a negation of his right to the monthly income he thought he merited more than others. Despite his protest, he was not included on the payroll. Consequently, when the premiere of Montaner's play was announced, Valle-Inclán prepared himself for the encounter with the Philistine. On the evening of 27 October 1927, he entered Madrid's Teatro Fontalba accompanied by some friends, among them Cipriano Rivas Cherif. He brought all his resentment against the dictatorship of Primo de Rivera as well as his personal animosity toward Montaner. Before the second of the play's five acts was over, Valle-Inclán had had his revenge. At a moment when the *claque* was most active, the theatre resounded with Valle-Inclán's derogatory voice: "¡Muy mal!" He repeated this several times, and the play was effectively interrupted. When the crowd recognized Valle-Inclán as the protestor, the pandemonium increased. In due time, he was taken forcibly from his seat, removed from the theatre, and ushered, accompanied by Rivas Cherif, into the police precinct of Buenavista. There, he continued his performance, much like Max Estrella in *Luces de bohemia*, to the chagrin of his interrogator. He eventually was set free pending a hearing before a magistrate at a later date.

Rejoicing over his victory, Valle-Inclán entered La Granja El Henar to the ovation of his comrades. The news of the incident had circulated quickly through Madrid's artistic colony; the next morning, reviews of the play's premiere carried accounts of Valle-Inclán's performance.[35] His ardent interruption of the play became known through the press as "El grito del Fontalba," and the event became a *cause célèbre* all over Madrid. Eager for details, journalists interviewed the perpetrator of the fiasco unceasingly. He responded by explaining that his "shout in the Fontalba" was against the play, its production, and the excessive support of the audience:

Against everything. Because everything there was disastrous. The right to express an opinion had to be reaffirmed, openly, freely, in the face of the contrary and noisy opinions of the others; in the face of the attempt to make the Fontalba a preserve where a sincere voice cannot express its rebelliousness, a voice that doesn't wish to join the public in its support, expressly or tacitly. What I did, in fact, was to be the first in expressing what the audience was to do later: reject the play. I said in a loud voice what many were thinking and what, subsequently, in one way or another, everyone ended up saying. More intelligent, or more expert, or more sincere, I saw in the second act what the audience expressed at the end of the play.[36] (A246)

Appreciative of the spotlight into which he had cast himself, Valle-Inclán took the opportunity to express his opinions at greater length:

Not only is there the right to express an opinion, but also the duty to do so faithfully, nakedly. Who can take that right away from the person who has purchased his ticket? One must act against a mercenary audience that seeks to impose its paid applause—paid in one way or another—on free judgment and artistic independence. Of course, expressing an opinion in this way has its risks. That's the reason why there's a noticeable lack of expression and a complacent silence in theatrical life. But that risk can be a deterrent to those who live from the theatre: the Quinteros, the Marquinas, the Fernández Ardavíns . . . but not to me. . . . One has to speak out, express an opinion, and protest. One must always feel young; the cult of silence and prudence may be comfortable, but it is neither beautiful nor sincere. Spaniards are too inclined to that devotion to silence, to that fear of passing judgment in a loud voice . . . on the basis of my authority and prestige, I saw it as my duty to intervene, such is the purpose of my authority . . . If I have an obligation, it's that: to express an opinion, to warn the audience when something isn't as it should be, to tell it if something is good or not, because the audience can be baffled and must be told the truth.[37] (A247)

This concern for the inability of the audience to discern the quality of a play was characteristic of Valle-Inclán. Having suffered much at the hands of a public accustomed to mediocrity, he felt the need to clear the stage of what the audience regarded as good theatre. Likewise, in a positive way, the theatregoer had to be educated in what constituted a good play:

It can also be baffled by an out-of-the-ordinary play, one that isn't clear and open. Because, faced with Arniches's characters—a guard or a cook—everyone knows if the dialogue is suitable or not, dealing as it does with everyday life, where there's a guard on every corner and a cook in each house. But in a play in which ghosts appear and speak, how is the audience to know—not having family ghosts at home—if that spectral language is proper or not? And, furthermore, faced with a play in verse, people have no sure way of knowing if the lines are suitable. . . . They're happy if they sound right. And that can't be! One must express an opinion. And one must tell it to the public![38] (A248)

Valle-Inclán's trial for the celebrated incident was delayed until 2 February 1928. The prosecution demanded a fine of one thousand pesetas and a six-month imprisonment. Valle-Inclán, accompanied by a lawyer, sat indifferently as the courtroom filled with celebrities from the theatrical and literary worlds. Not willing to play a scene from Kafka, Valle-Inclán refused to stand when instructed, asked the magistrate's name when his own was requested, and protested the taking of the court oath, saying cynically that as a Catholic he was not allowed to do so. The trial became another vaudeville with Valle-Inclán as the master of ceremonies. In spite of the irregularities his individualism contributed, and perhaps due to his lawyer's perspicacity, Valle-Inclán left the courtroom a free man, having as the only burden the payment of a fine.[39] He had obtained his satisfaction by besting established authority.

But victories often carry a stigma. The controversial man that was Valle-Inclán often impeded the progress of the talented playwright. Perhaps due to his recent notoriety and to his radical stand against the government, he could not succeed in interesting Juan Bonafé, the prominent actor, in producing *Los cuernos de don Friolera* in 1929. This was the last-known attempt among several in his lifetime to premiere the play in Spain.

The uncertainty inspired by the ups and downs of his career in the theatre was reflected in Valle-Inclán's opinion of his role as a dramatist. Negatives and positives alternated in accordance with the temperature of theatrical acceptance or rejection. In a letter dated 5 May 1927 from Madrid to the editor of *La Voz*, Enrique Fajardo, in answer to a recent request for leading dramatists to discuss their craft, Valle-Inclán stated concretely:

My dear friend:
You ask me to participate in the poll by *La Voz* and I would gladly do so if I were a playwright. No doubt you place me in that category because I wrote some works in dialogue. But please note that I've always published them with sufficient notations to explicate them through reading rather than through the intervention of actors. If some of these works have been staged, I've given the matter so little importance that I never thought it worth remembering the lamentable accident by listing the cast and date of the production in the book edition. Consequently, I declare myself totally removed from the theatre and its desires, means, and rewards.[40] (A249)

As a follow-up, *ABC*, another Madrid newspaper, asked Valle-Inclán why he did not write for the theatre, to which he replied:

For the stage? No. I haven't written, do not write, nor do I intend to write for the stage. I'm very fond of dialogue, as my novels show. And, of course, I like the theatre, and have done theatre, always trying to overcome the difficulties inherent in the genre. I've done theatre taking Shakespeare as my mentor. But I haven't written, nor will I write, for Spanish actors. . . . Spanish actors haven't as yet learned to speak. They babble. And as long as there isn't one who knows how to speak, it seems to me ridiculous to write for them. It would be stooping to the level of illiterates.[41] (A250)

But such infrequent statements are traceable to moments of dissatisfaction with the theatre. In reality, Valle-Inclán believed that his plays represented an advance in the field, and he was impatient with a public that was not ready for his dramatic view. Too, he often castigated the structure of the theatre for fostering mediocrity instead of making progress through the presentation of innovative works. Thus, he could state:

I believe my plays to be perfectly stageable. . . . I feel that my *Esperpentos* could be done to perfection by our actors since the plays possess something akin to popular farce, between the tragic and the grotesque. . . . I can imagine Bonafé, for example, performing *Luces de bohemia*.[42] (A251)

If he couldn't pass up an opportunity to mock, he believed the talent was ready to be tapped, although the economics of the theatre prevented its renaissance. Nonetheless, Valle-Inclán's basic optimism made him continue to write for the stage; despite his meager denials, he was a playwright.

It must be remembered that from the very beginning of his career Valle-Inclán sought out the theatre—be it as actor, adapter, director, or playwright—and tried continuously to succeed in it. If there were interruptions in his activity therein, as the years between his three theatrical periods attest, these were caused by the theatre's rejection of him rather than the opposite. His advanced technique, which other segments of the European theatre were discovering and accepting through their own experiments, proved to be too radical for laggard Spain. He had to find satisfaction elsewhere. The dramatist was especially enthused by correspondence with Russia in 1931, which promised to open a new public not only to his novels but also to his plays:

They have just written from the USSR asking permission to translate my works into Russian. The State Publishing House wants to issue *Tirano Banderas* and *La corte de los milagros*. I don't know how they'll manage. I think they can't be translated. . . . They've also invited me to attend the premiere of *La reina castiza*, *Luces de bohemia*, and *Los cuernos de don Friolera*. . . . I may go. I'll see in Russian what I haven't been able to see staged in Spanish.[43] (A252)

Valle-Inclán was also pleased by the partial translation of *Divinas palabras* in English.[44] But while he had expressed his disappointment at not finding a stage for many of his works in Spain, the Spanish theatre recognized, in part, its neglect of Valle-Inclán and proceeded to remedy the situation. The company of Irene López Heredia and Mariano Asquerino produced two of his plays in 1931 at Madrid's Teatro Muñoz Seca: *Farsa y licencia de la reina castiza* on 3 June and *El embrujado* on 11 November.
Each production ran for several weeks at Madrid's Teatro Muñoz Seca, receiving critical acclaim.[45]

But these kudos were circumstantial and temporary. Only the passing of time and the change of artistic atmosphere could make possible the recognition of the great dramatist that was Valle-Inclán. Unfortunately, he did not live long enough to receive the full accolade.

III THE FINAL YEARS

1930–1936

10 Republic

The absurdity that became a principal ingredient in the novelistic and theatrical works of Valle-Inclán was a literary reflection of a political reality in Spain, which in turn was the precursor of the approaching chaos wherein all of Europe would be involved. The situation in Spain would become increasingly worse between 1930 and 1936; the latter year would see the outbreak of the Spanish Civil War, in one sense the dress rehearsal for World War II.

On 28 January 1930 Primo de Rivera resigned with the acquiescence of Alfonso XIII. The general who had brilliantly led major attacks ultimately ending the war in Morocco and had preserved the monarchy was the victim of both internal and external factors. The international economic crisis of 1929 had brought the peseta to its lowest level; military unrest among the Spanish cadre had manifested itself continuously in attempts to overthrow the dictatorship; stunted reforms at home failed to remedy many inequities; failure to achieve the desired status in the League of Nations caused Spain to lose face; dissension between the dictator and the sovereign was encouraged by influential ministers; the opposition of the intellectual community gathered momentum with the adherence of extremist factions, such as Catalonian nationalists, socialists, and communists. These combined forces rendered the dictator's position untenable, forcing him to disenfranchise himself. Primo de Rivera left Spain for a voluntary exile in France. Broken in health and in spirit, he died in Paris on 16 March of the same year. The king called on General Dámaso Berenguer to form a new government along less dictatorial lines, but the length of his tenure did not allow Alfonso XIII much time in which to implement his hope for a constitutional monarchy.

Valle-Inclán was not the only one whose writings and spoken comments depicted the unstable era. José Ortega y Gasset launched *La rebelión de las masas*, Rafael Alberti published "Elegía cívica," which heralded the end of the old order, and Unamuno, who had returned from his self-imposed

French exile on 9 February, shortly after the withdrawal of Primo de Rivera, wasted no time in denouncing Alfonso XIII for his suspension of civil rights in favor of the dictatorial regime. In lectures at the Ateneo and the Teatro Europa on 2 and 4 May, respectively, Unamuno delivered his most scathing attacks. There would be no let up, for as Valle-Inclán had stated, the old had to speak when the young would not. In greeting Unamuno's return, he expressed his sentiments:

At this moment of national decline, his superior literary category is obscured by his virtues as a citizen, and he appears to me as the only Grandee of Spain. Don Miguel de Unamuno, Prior of Iberia: Greetings![1] (A253)

The words could define the speaker as well, for Valle-Inclán helped lead the opposition in his own manner, as is evident in his interviews of this period, exemplified by his assessment of the new regime:

Berenguer, animated by the best intentions, has no supporters in the military, while those civil elements that wish to work with him are very suspect. While he orients himself, which he won't accomplish, he reiterates that his only goal is to facilitate the restoration of legality. But how? Without freedom nothing can be achieved, while with it the regime won't last a week.[2] (A254)

Besides his many lectures in which the problems of contemporary Spain were discussed, he dealt with the regime in works such as *Luces de bohemia*, *Los cuernos de don Friolera*, and *La hija del capitán*. But his end was never satire for its own sake. Like any fine satirist Valle-Inclán used his literary ability to attack for the purpose of pointing out flaws and bringing about the elimination of his target. And there was the hope that something better would follow. In *Divinas palabras*, Séptimo Miau says enviously of France:

That is a Republic, as Spain ought to be. In Republics, the people give the orders, you and I, my friend.[3] (A255)

But that desire could not be achieved without the abdication of Alfonso XIII. Valle-Inclán continued to do his part toward that end with every power at his command; his subversive attitude gave birth to verses that became part of the folklore of the period:

Alfonso, look out
and ready your flight,
for Spain is about
to see the light.

Or else you may find
that the sovereign mass
will take off your hind. (A256)

Another set of verses was also promulgated throughout Madrid:

Rise up, Spanish people
and hang him from a steeple!
Make him dance a jig up there
with his kinfolk in the air!
From the queen who rules Britannia
to that Spanish bitch, Eulalia.
From the prince who's hemophylic
to Fernando the amylic.
From the spindle-legged Infante,
who's a deaf-mute without ante,
to that Infanta Isabel
. . . quite a belle.

Make their tongues hang out in pain
in the people's sun of Spain! (A257)

But Valle-Inclán extended his activities beyond these spheres into areas where the repercussion would be greater. Joining with others whose sentiments were for the establishment of the Second Spanish Republic, Valle-Inclán signed the Pacto de San Sebastián on 14 October 1930. Among the effects of the Republican manifesto was the military revolt at Jaca on 15 December 1930 under the leadership of Fermín Galán and Hernández. Although it was aborted, the revolt indicated the tenor of the times and promised further acts of military and civil disobedience.

The outcome of the intensified anti-monarchical campaign was unavoidable. The government of General Berenguer resigned on 14 February 1931, and a new administration was convened under Admiral Juan Bautista Aznar. In order to achieve a more balanced representation on the local level, municipal elections were decreed. These were held throughout Spain on 12 April. While the official results were not made public, the key cities of Madrid and Barcelona, together with other important population centers, voted heavily for Republican candidates. One of these, Niceto Alcalá Zamora, an ex-monarchist minister who had led the polls in Madrid as representative of the revolutionary forces, chose the opportunity to deliver an audacious ultimatum addressed to the king seeking the abdication of Alfonso. In it he demanded that power be transferred to his committee. On 14 April 1931 Alfonso XIII decided on his own course. He left his Palacio de Oriente at night in a curtained automobile, traveled to Cartagena, and embarked for exile in France. His decision had negated the possibility of a civil conflagration. The Count of Romanones, writing a series of articles on the history of the monarchy, stated that Alfonso XIII could have abdicated in favor of his son. Valle-Inclán, who saw in Romanones the man who made possible the bloodless coup, attacked this particular concept:

How is it possible to talk about such a thing? Who was he to abdicate in any specific person when the right to name a successor and regent belongs solely to the Cortes? A king can step down at any time, but abdicate, no. One relinquishes something. . . . One abdicates in. . . . This "in" means that the heir to the royal power is to be selected, and that cannot ever be done by a constitutional monarch without the authority of the Cortes. Don Alfonso had committed many serious infractions of the Constitution; the one abdicating in favor of the Infante . . . would have been the most enormous of all.[4] (A258)

Alcalá Zamora was quick to fill the gap created by the absence of the monarch. He set up a provisional government, with himself at its head, and in effect established the Second Republic.

Learning of the king's departure from the capital, Valle-Inclán set out to demand of Alcalá Zamora that the injustice of the escape be rectified. But Alfonso had already separated himself from Spain, unknowingly forever. Like many of his contemporaries, Valle-Inclán saw the actions and the omissions of Alfonso as deserving public reprimand; moreover, he could not envision an effective revolution in Spain without the bloodshed that characterized other European upheavals:

I won't state that the ideal of the Spanish revolution should be that of a smooth transformation of the regime. On the contrary, I believe that there can't be a great revolution without war on the frontiers. Such was the case of the French Revolution and of the Russian Revolution. A revolution like the one I envision would, perhaps, provoke the arrival of a hundred thousand sons of St. Louis from the North and a hundred thousand sons of St. George from the South. There would be foreign vessels in all our ports. Don Alfonso would not have been allowed to leave Spain. In effect, that revolution would be the most fecund and, perhaps through its inspiration, we would create national unity. But the fact is that Spain opted for tactics that were possibly more normal and prudent, and they must be followed to the end. Nothing worse than to change tactics now. Let us continue, therefore, as we began. And to prevent the interruption of normalcy, let us place the government of the Republic in the hands of the great historical Republicans.[5] (A259)

Inspired by the opportunity of creating an ideal government, Valle-Inclán defined his conception of it and its leadership:

The Republic ought to be served by those capable of serving it. It's a matter of men. The most urgent matter, what I believe should preoccupy us immediately, is the structuring of the Republic. The Republic is not yet constructed. We are living in a provisional period. Spain has a pressing need of seriously structuring the Republic. To do so, men must be elected who ought to and can take on that responsibility. Who are they? Could they be the republicans who earlier served the monarchy and failed in that service? If those individuals did not know how to govern fruitfully in conditions much more favorable than those of the present, that is, within the political framework of a secular regime, what confidence could they instill in the people at this moment when an entirely new Spain must be created?[6] (A260)

The astute observations, based on historical reality, may have been reinforced in part by Alcalá Zamora's failure to detain Alfonso XIII in Spain. Continuing to discuss the role of the leadership, Valle-Inclán stated:

We must now consider that first great government, the one that will consolidate the Republic. When that day comes, those men who have a history that justifies them will assume power: individuals who can demonstrate a life of sacrifice, faith, and hope in the ideal of the Republic. Recognition must be given to Sr. Alcalá Zamora's high aspirations, to his noble ability to react irreproachably in the face of ethical matters; he has given himself to an ideal with dignity. But it is not enough. . . . Sr. Alcalá Zamora would be well-suited to the heights of the presidency of the Republic, where the functions are of a moderating nature. To lead the government, Spain will need other men, those individuals who, as I say, have the authority of their personal history.[7] (A261)

He went on to propose the candidates in whom he found the rare qualities he saw as necessary:

By the process of elimination, we must concur that all the conditions for a head of state (the first government of the Republic) are present in Don Alejandro Lerroux. Not merely by elimination, but by selection. He is the man who can go to the people . . . and the people will have confidence in such men because history gives them the necessary authority. . . . Don Alejandro Lerroux is a man who has led the masses since his youth. This experience gave him true mastery in knowing the people, in foreseeing its desires, and even in the interpretation of its instincts. In effect, it made him a leader. Everything, everything leads one to believe that Lerroux is the man, the only man, capable of heading the first government of the Republic. I, aloof from anything political, make such statements under the inspiration of a vast feeling of patriotism. I have not pursued, nor do I now seek, anything personal in politics. Anyone who knows me realizes that my opinion is always absolutely impartial. I view the republican spectacle as a deeply attentive spectator, and my assessment of the men and affairs of Spain at this moment convinces me that the nation's government must be placed in the hands of Don Alejandro Lerroux and his political colleagues, his ideological mates, among whom figures the minister who has achieved the most extraordinary and transcendent task: the Minister of War, Don Manuel Azaña. Those are the men for the first government! It is clear to me that we would all perform a patriotic deed in standing by, strengthening, and encouraging Don Alejandro Lerroux.[8] (A262)

The friendship between Valle-Inclán and Manuel Azaña gave added impetus to his words. These would be borne out in the months that followed.

Despite his disclaimer of personal interest in politics, Valle-Inclán continued to participate on its periphery. When the Bourbon dynasty fell on the exile of Alfonso XIII, he received a letter from Don Jaime, Carlist pretender to the throne, naming him "Caballero de la Orden de la Legitimidad Proscrita."[9] Shortly thereafter, he again entered the lists as a candidate. On 12 April 1931 his name appeared in the municipal elections, but his new bid for political status in Galicia ran the same course as his earlier endeavor.

While serving the old cause of Carlism with his political candidacy,

Valle-Inclán also functioned in the camp of the new republicanism. His first public manifestation of support came on 20 May 1931, when he spoke at a banquet in honor of Julio Alvarez del Vayo, Spain's new ambassador to Mexico. With Mexico as focus, Valle-Inclán integrated the revolutionary fervor of that nation with Russia's as catalysts for Spain's own radical turn:

Mexico may be one of the greatest countries in the world. Undoubtedly, it is the greatest in America. It is a bronze Republic, the one most resembling Russia. In Mexico, white men—Madero and Obregón—fought heroically for the redemption of the Indian, erasing some old hereditary laws that denigrated and debased him. Spain sends its first ambassador to Mexico after having completed an astonishing, genuinely Spanish revolution. And it did so after casting out the last of the Bourbons, who wasn't ejected for being a king but for being a thief. Spain has undergone the revolution of men of good will against thieves. And such is the embassy sent to Mexico, which itself underwent another great revolution: that of redeeming the Indian.[10] (A263)

Valle-Inclán's ongoing politically oriented speeches kept him in the arena of politics. The earlier defeat did not prevent his name from being entered again by his friends in June when the important election of deputies to the Cortes was held:

I believe I was put up as a candidate. I'm not certain because I haven't been to Galicia this season, nor have I shown the least interest in being a delegate.[11] (A264)

Valle-Inclán's independence made him unattractive to the *caciques*, and he again made a poor showing in the balloting. It was his second defeat within three months. While Unamuno and Azorín succeeded in their bids for parliamentary seats, Valle-Inclán shared defeat with Baroja. In the days that followed, Valle-Inclán's voice was heard in the La Granja El Henar reviling the political machinery that had maneuvered the elections:

In a province such as Pontevedra, the smallest in Spain, full of roads and railroads, the count has yet to be completed. The explanation is as follows: the "machine" has signed election certificates with the number of voters left blank, filling them in as they see fit, always higher in number than the unfavorable counts at the tables. There are other eloquent practices. Lerroux received two thousand votes in La Coruña, while a nobody who had at one time been a Gassetist delegate, then an Albaist, and was now a Republican autonomist, I believe, received twelve thousand. To wrap up the list of inequities, you should know that among the winners were four monarchists who couldn't even get elected in the days of the monarchy. . . . Only a people submissive to the most disdainful bossism can put on the display that Galicia has just evidenced. My Galicia has become docile before the wishes of the new lord, who is the same type as ever: the unscrupulous boss. . . . I believe that the elections in all four provinces must be annulled. By giving satisfaction to the people, superior in every way to the bosses, by declaring null and void such obscene maneuvers, the honest men of Galicia will know that their vote can't be cancelled by ministerial influence; the racial prestige of my land, lately evidenced in the protest against the men of the dictatorship who had gone there to campaign for seats on the Cortes, to what end is unclear, would be greatly boosted. . . . Galicia ought to restructure its personality federally, with no greater or lesser expectation than Catalonia. And, like Catalonia, it should seek to delimit the provincial borders of the region.[12] (A265)

The vocal indignation was transferred to the written page in a letter responding to an article by Ramón María Tenreiro, long a friend and an admirer as attested in his tribute to Valle-Inclán in *La Pluma* (1923). The letter stated in whole:

My dear and admired Sr. Tenreiro:
    You have made some statements in *El Sol* in which I feel that you have alluded to me, and so I am obliged to give a reply by reason of rights to truth and justice. You rashly attempt to deny the abuses of the Galician elections, hiding the fact that you owe your status as a delegate to those very abuses. You speak of "those who adopt a holy indignation when in fact their ire is due to having lost." Sr. Tenreiro, since I'm the one who will impugn the elections in La Coruña before the election board, you should have shown more restraint. Sr. Tenreiro, I am not a phariseean feigner of salubriousness or of indignant protests. The Galician elections are an affront to every honest person. Like you, I have been a candidate for La Coruña, but with a notable difference in conduct. While you traipsed through the Galician landscape for purposes of intrigue, in league with the old bosses, I stayed in Madrid. And when I was asked to help propagandize my candidacy, I knew how to say no and not beg my friends for their votes, even though I have many in that area. Clearly, my behavior cannot serve as a norm for you and your colleagues. I was able to tell those who requested my presence in the campaign: My name is well known, well-known too is my life, self-evident and significant in its works, resignation, and poverty. If Galicia doesn't know it, this is not the time to learn it. But that reply, which in my case shows moderation and dignity, would be outrageous boasting on the part of you and your colleagues. Sr. Tenreiro: representation in the way you have obtained it, when not relinquished, brings dishonor.[13] (A266)

Tenreiro replied to Valle-Inclán's letter with one of his own.[14] Valle-Inclán, in turn, wrote the punctuation to the celebrated incident with a precise statement and a controlled attack:

My dear and admired Sr. Tenreiro:
    You affirm that your person and those of your accomplices in the machinations of La Coruña's elections give way to no one in uprightness, nobility of character, and dignity. This being affirmed by the interested party, my commentary can only be a smile. Uprightness, nobility of character, and dignity are accredited by deeds. Mine are well known. No doubt you and your accomplices can say the same, and the arrogant statement you made leads me to assume as much. But my erudition is so limited that I am ignorant of them. I have given Galicia an aesthetic level—the highest—and have asked nothing of it, nor have I rendered it adulation. You, Sr. Tenreiro, have asked it for an election certificate, receiving it through means that I will never pursue. This is the ethical difference between us, Sr. Tenreiro.[15] (A267)

The elections of June 1931, notwithstanding the irregularities, brought to

Madrid the first constituent Cortes in many years. Of the 466 seats, 315 went to left-wing parties, the same who had fomented the overthrow of the monarchy. The new deputies met in July and enthusiastically began to create a new constitution. The deliberations extended into the final month of the year. The radicality of some proposals and the variety of political ideologies represented in the new Cortes were responsible for the extended delay. Luis Araquistain, for one, wanted the concept of a worker's republic included within the nucleus of the new constitution; he achieved his desire when the document defined the nation as "a democratic republic of workers of all classes" whose power and authority were derived from the people. Valle-Inclán saw the replacement of the previous oligarchy with another class as intolerable:

And it's absurd, ridiculously absurd, for any one to have thought of a socialist solution. . . . And in that vicious circle of absurdity, it is even more absurd to think of a government headed by Largo Caballero. It would be the last straw! Setting aside whatever virtues may adorn Largo Caballero, it is impossible to forget that Largo Caballero holds the position, and always will—for it's indivisible from his identity—of secretary of the UGT. . . . The socialists! . . . It is well to point out that the Socialist Party is named the Socialist Worker's Party. Let's not forget it! And it should be kept in mind because said party represents a caste; and a caste that is as odious as the ecclesiastical or military caste. . . . What angers me the most is the sorry group of people who glory in the title of intellectual worker. I don't understand. . . . What is that? There are three horrible topics making the rounds: feminism, unionism, and Americanism. My blood boils when I hear "intellectual worker." What tripe! The intellectual cannot be a worker. The exception might be an errand boy on an hourly wage at a newspaper, where concepts of creation and execution are so disparate that it's impossible to bring them together.[16] (A268)

The problem of autonomy for Galicia, Catalonia, and the Basque provinces was a hotly debated issue for the new Republic. Such a problem, which had troubled the nation for decades, could not be resolved quickly; its implications were too great. Valle-Inclán, too, had his view on the matter:

The peninsular spirit must be integrated in the way conceived by the Romans. It is the most fitting. Divide the peninsula into four departments: Cantabria, Bética, Tarraconense, and Lusitania. . . . There are only four large cities on the peninsula: Bilbao, which is Cantabria; Barcelona, which is Tarraconense; Seville, which is Bética; and Lisbon, which is Lusitania. Each large city to its own sea . . . [17] (A269)

The omission of Madrid, which did not exist in Roman times, is curious. But more to the point were other commentaries:

The problem of Galicia is the complete opposite of Catalonia's and, consequently, ought to be resolved with a different statute, not a Mediterranean but an Atlantic one. Catalonia needs a tariff that will favor its industry, while Galicia needs the creation of a free port in Vigo and the suppression of all tariffs. Everything produced by Galicia (people, salted fish, etc.) is sent abroad. Not so in Catalonia. From this it can be deduced that the problem of Galicia is the opposite of Catalonia's. The Catalan problem will cease to be a problem when it stops being dual and becomes plural, that is, when no longer limited to Madrid and Catalonia exclusively. Concretely: out of a third party in discord will surge concord. That's why I'm a federalist. No one who knows Spanish history could be anything else because Spain, seen historically, is an actual federation, wherein there are regions, such as Navarra, which others ought to emulate. Navarra is unique, not just in the history of Spain, but of the entire world. No region compares to the ancient region of Navarra, which, through the centuries, has preserved its independence, its personality, and its prosperous happy life without asking anyone for anything or counting on any official protection. And this despite Navarra's lack of access to the sea and its limited number of mines. But Navarra is Navarra and it has a historical consciousness that other regions lack. . . . Galicia too has the awareness of its personality, so vast, so unknown; that personality which has seldom been reflected here, not out of malice but due to a lack of knowledge of its character and true nature.[18] (A270)

Finally, basing its decision on the Pacto de San Sebastián, whereby Catalonian autonomists agreed to support Republican demands in return for concessions, the new Cortes voted limited autonomy to regions that could justify such a need and prohibited, at the same time, any federation of such autonomous states.

Among the other issues resolved by the assembly was the unicameral status of the Cortes, which was elected for periods of four years and had the power to appoint the president of the Republic. Valle-Inclán commented wryly on the issue of bicameral versus unicameral parliaments:

Nations resemble ruminant animals. They must chew the cud well in order to have good digestion. That's why I'm a believer in the senate system. The Congress of Delegates makes laws, a process similar to the first chewing; then they go on to the Senate, which is a second chewing. In this way, new reforms are absorbed perfectly and there's no chance of indigestion.[19] (A271)

Other problems were resolved with relative rapidity. General lines of foreign policy were drawn along the principles of respect for international law and the abhorrence of war as a means toward extra-national ends. The equality of women was established legally, and with it came the granting of the vote to all individuals over the age of twenty-three. Of this new universal suffrage, Valle-Inclán said:

Saint Paul took a great step on behalf of the dignity of woman; but there was another great step left and that has been taken by the Spanish Republic. In his famous *Epistle*, St. Paul had left woman—undoubtedly without intention—out of the electoral census. . . . For me, it would be more interesting to have a proportional vote according to the status of the marriage. The perfect marriage would have four votes, while the imperfect one, that is, the undesirable one, would have only one: that of the husband.[20] (A272)

Although Valle-Inclán saw the new law as a needed social advance, he felt the role of women was diminishing:

Women! The poor things can be given only the justice in Schopenhauer's renowned phrase. And now they no longer even have long hair! Women are left with nothing to do in this civilization.[21] (A273)

This new equality of women, however, became the basis for a new outlook on marriage, which could now be dissolved by mutual consent or by petition of one of the parties. The establishment of divorce in Spain was a shocking reality to a nation whose outward religiosity had maintained traditions from the Middle Ages in sacred prudery.

Other traditional concepts were swept away by the Republic with equal gusto. As Valle-Inclán had desired, the once inalienable rights of the nobility were severely curtailed or done away with completely through the abolition of titles and the expropriation of estates by the Cortes, subject to adequate reimbursement. The lands acquired under these statutes became the basis for the land reforms proposed by the Republic. It would attempt, often clumsily, to resettle large segments of the peasant population in land parcels carved from the nobility's former holdings.

Following the reforms begun by the monarchy, primary education continued to be free and compulsory. But the Republic made a major change in the educational system of the nation when it decreed that the task of educating the populace would rest entirely on the shoulders of civil authority. The Church was severed from its long-held role as educator in Spain. The Republic took the radical step because it saw the history of religious education in the country as inefficient and conservative. The many problems that the former system had created were analyzed by Ramón Pérez de Ayala in his novel *A.M.G.D.*, the story of a Jesuit school, which Cipriano Rivas Cherif produced in a dramatized version in Madrid shortly after the promulgation of the new decree.

The religious issue was the most difficult of all. The temper of the time was strongly anti-clerical, but there was a growing anti-Church feeling as well, as evidenced in the burning of churches in May 1931. Consequently, the issue created the greatest contention as traditionalists and liberals fought for their respective stands. Germinal to the argument was the historical affiliation of church and state, a condition the majority of the Cortes membership found intolerable. The new constitution ordered the severance of the oppressive relationship. The concept of an "official" religion was terminated, and freedom of conscience and of worship were declared. Further, all religious orders came under scrutiny and their privileges were revoked; they were forced to adhere to strict controls as well. The Jesuits, principal educators and most powerful religious order in Spain, were the prime targets of the new regime. Their lands were confiscated and placed in the public domain for distribution, their traditional importance was downgraded, and they were watched carefully. Valle-Inclán saw this process dispassionately:

Another trivial matter! The Jesuits fulfilled their destiny. They're like the Templars, who were through in the Middle Ages.[22] (A274)

Finally, on 23 January 1932, the Society of Jesus, founded in Spain by Ignatius Loyola in 1538, was ordered to disband and its members were ordered to leave the country. It was Manuel Azaña who, through impassioned oratory against the tentacles of religion, moved the Cortes to the actual abolition.

As a result of the heated deliberations on the role of religion under the Second Republic, the government of Niceto Alcalá Zamora and his Minister of the Interior, Miguel Maura, resigned on 14 October. This initial crisis brought Manuel Azaña forward as Prime Minister. Valle-Inclán saw the ascension to power of his friend Azaña as exemplary of the revolutionary process:

The revolution never had men. It's absurd to say that Spain lacks men for the revolution. The revolution is life and, as such, it creates what it needs. The example of Azaña is a clear one. Six months ago he was known only by his friends. In a heterogeneous government, replete with internal conflicts, he knew how to stand firm and proud with the maximum authority. Azaña had a sound background and was congenial. I'm not saying that the men who are needed can be created in six months; but in a year or two, there's no doubt that Spain will have them by legions.[23] (A275)

The *Constitución de 1931* was promulgated on 9 December, and later that month Alcalá Zamora was returned to the government in the relatively decorative but dignified position of first president of the Republic. Valle-Inclán's judgment on the matter of leadership had proven prophetic; the presidency had been filled as he had indicated while, in the absence of Alejandro Lerroux, Valle-Inclán's long-time friend Azaña, whom he had espoused as a second to Lerroux, emerged as the strong hand needed to guide the Republic. The broad-based socialism of the new leader was not unpalatable to Valle-Inclán:

For now, the socialists are a class party, an organization for the defense of workers. The evolutionary process will convert it into a great party of national governance, not just for workers, but for all Spain.[24] (A276)

By the final months of 1931 Valle-Inclán had come to realize that Lerroux was not the ideal leader he had supposed earlier:

What we can no longer afford is to continue thinking like Lerroux: restoring to the ranks those putrefied corpses of Alba and Don Melquiades. Is it possible that Lerroux believes that the wombs that produce such grotesques in Spain have dried up?[25] (A277)

Valle-Inclán recognized that the only way Spain could be ruled effectively during the trying period of adjustment was through the power of a government like Lenin's in Russia:

In Spain, the revolution must be achieved through a dictatorship. It is imperative. And not one like Primo's but like Lenin's. When Carlos III wanted to clean up Madrid, which was a latrine, he explicated the protest of the masses with a phrase: "The masses cry like children when one tries to wash their faces." Dignity is not acquired; it is imposed. Enslaved peoples accept it through being whipped. Whoever is used to being on his knees finds it difficult to stand. . . . In dictatorships, individuals are not needed; what governs is the concept, not the individual.[26] (A278)

Again, his admiration for resolute, strong leadership was in evidence:

The hero is what's important to me. Without heroes there's no history. Great things are achieved by superior men, not by gregarious masses. . . . What matters is the man who thirsts for power in love, in politics, in religion, in the world. And it's the same whether that man is named Lenin, or Don Quijote, the Marquis de Bradomín, or Christopher Columbus.[27] (A279)

By the beginning of 1932 the Republic had many of its social reforms well underway. Complementing the ambitious attempt to educate the populace and to eradicate illiteracy, the new Ministry of Culture and Public Education, headed by Fernando de los Ríos, had created cultural missions whose function it was to travel throughout Spain instructing the people in their common traditions through the use of exhibits, libraries, music, art, theatre. Alejandro Casona's "Teatro del Pueblo" was one of the latter instruments; another was "La Barraca," under the joint directorship of Federico García Lorca and Eduardo Ugarte. The Republic opened its arms to the arts through such ventures as well as through the employment of intellectuals in pertinent capacities.

Valle-Inclán was one of the individuals to be singled out at the outset. Late in August 1931, he had been named "Conservador General del Patrimonio Artístico Nacional" and appointed to head the palace-museum at Aranjuez, historic residence of the Spanish monarchy. Manuel Azaña had promoted his nomination to the post.[28] The announcement of the appointment appeared in the Gaceta de Madrid, but the notification of the authorities outside Madrid had not been simultaneous. When Valle-Inclán arrived in Aranjuez, he was hampered in his attempts to enter the palace. But such difficulties were resolved eventually, and he proceeded to his duties. He occupied himself with the inventory and other matters pertaining to the maintenance of the artistic and historic treasures in his care.[29] But soon Valle-Inclán was faced with another problem: the establishment of the so-called Museo de la República in another former palace.[30] Senseless proposals by various deputies, ministries, and organizations sought to convert the monuments technically in his charge into functional places, and Valle-Inclán reacted to the abominable suggestions with his usual unequivocal statement:

Converting what once were royal palaces into asylums, student cafeterias, reformatories, and hospices would be as great a barbarity as that foisted in Mendizábal's era, when churches were converted into barracks. If palaces are destined to become charitable institutions, my spirit would be shattered, for it would be a utilitarianism more repugnant than the destructive fury of Attila.[31] (A280)

Further, as director of the palace-museum at Aranjuez and the Casa del Labrador, he communicated with Marcelino Domingo, his immediate superior, in an attempt to save and to rescue both places:

The so-called Museum of Aranjuez is a lamentable hodgepodge of furnishings and paintings of varying artistic merit. There are good ones, reasonable ones, and some of the most sordid vulgarity. Some of the outstanding paintings have been used to decorate other palaces; such is the case with "The Cart of Eros" and "The Temptations of St. Anthony" by Hieronimous Bosch. No less lamentable is the transfer to the palace in Madrid of the lamp that graced the Salon of the Porcelains. A unique piece impossible to replace in that artistic whole, it is the most significant example of our nation's past ceramic heritage. The undersigned wishes to engage the aesthetic sensibility of your excellency toward the return of that lamp. . . . What was once the Royal Palace of Aranjuez lacks even the most rudimentary fire protection. The undersigned, indoctrinated by what took place in the Palace of La Granja and by the recently attempted arson at the Casa del Labrador, as well as by the still-smoking ruins at the University of Valencia, places the situation before the consideration of your excellency. Should the undersigned keep this matter quiet, his responsibility would be as great as it would be easy in effort and moderate in cost to provide reasonable fire protection. Your excellency should keep in mind that the waters of the Tajo lap at the walls of the palace. And the risk for the Casa del Labrador is no less. To fight fires, it has only one fire extinguisher and, as if in compensation, it is always under threat of flooding by the Tajo. Two lovely marble placards affixed to a pillar mark the flood levels of 1916 and 1924. Some dikes were erected in the days of the monarchy, but it would not be unreasonable for your excellency to order a technical inspection. It would be lamentable for the Republic to have to put up a third placard! It is the opinion of the undersigned that, as a first measure, the museum should be closed in order to reorganize it completely; to this end, the appropriate orders have been sent to the secretary of the museum, who has the double role of administrator of what was once the Royal Patrimony. Since the undersigned has seen his orders unheeded, I submit the matter to your excellency's consideration. Should the undersigned merit your excellency's confidence, he awaits respectfully the ratification of his orders and the demand for their implementation through your excellency. Should the decision be negative, and holding your excellency's view in the greatest esteem, I have the honor of offering your excellency my resignation.[32] (A281)

Valle-Inclán's efforts met with silence; his letter remained unanswered and his proposals unheeded. It would not be long before the matter would become intolerable.

Also difficult to bear, if for a very different reason, was the termination of his other source of income: the 3,500 pesetas a month guaranteed by his publisher, the CIAP. The backers of the firm, sidetracked into fruitless ventures and hampered by the increasing unrest in Europe, had gone into bankruptcy. The cessation of the CIAP's existence early in 1932 explains the abrupt end to book publication by Valle-Inclán; he could no longer raise the necessary funds to issue his "Opera Omnia" as in earlier days. During the unpleasantness, Valle-Inclán continued to live in the capital and to be active in its many activities. On 12 December 1931 Valle-Inclán recorded fragments of *Sonata de otoño* and *Claves líricas* for the "Archivo de la palabra," Centro de Estudios Históricos, in Madrid. These are the only known recordings of his voice. Then, on 3 March 1932 he was invited to speak at the Casino de Madrid; he chose as his topic "Capacidad del español para la literatura" but ranged over many areas in his usual impromptu manner. He spoke briefly on the Spanish capacity for the theatrical:

The entire art of style lies in substituting the spoken word. Style replaces tone, irony, and expression. The Spaniard has capability in the theatre due to the theatre's plasticity, because the Spanish Minerva is more plastic than literary. . . . Castilian lacks centuries of evolution. There is no style in Spanish. In Spanish, no one has said "his own," but rather that which belongs to all. There is a dumb adoration of the dictionary. And since style is not a necessity in the theatre, being replaced by tone and expression—the plastic—the Spaniard's capability is in the theatre.[33] (A282)

He ventured to trace aspects of his theme in an unusual parallel:

The line of Spain's literary capability could be traced in one of those works of simple perspective featuring hooded penitents holding candles. The first procession: that of the sentimental fledgling composers of carols and folk songs, crystal tears and "cante jondo," Murillo and Salzillo. The second procession: that which covers from Desdeñaperros to the Moncayo, from the Cervantes of Alcalá to the Goya of Aragón. They don't have curly manes but each carries a large yellow candle. The third procession: that of men from the Atlantic coast. They too carry a light, or seem to. But the sun will shine and their lights will be extinguished, not being of candles but of imagination. It was the light of the "holy souls." But the Spanish norm is that of the second procession, which treads Castile. That Castile which possesses the magical power of regeneration. Among those regenerated by Castile were the Flemish Carlos I, the Greek Theotocopulus, and the Basque Unamuno, perhaps more expressive than any other in the language of Castile because Don Miguel has penetrated into its depths, which means beyond its grammar. (A283)

Then, he went on to trace the basis of Spanish literature in realism:

The Castilian mode is realism, which is not a copy but the exaltation of spiritual forms and customs. The world's first epic poem that eschews the supernatural is the *Farsalia* by Lucan, a Spaniard. When the Castilian tongue begins its historical consolidation, it produces the poem of the *Cid*. The supernatural intervenes in all its French counterparts. Roland's Oliphant can be heard for a hundred leagues, and the hero splits a mountain with a blow of his sword. If anything supernatural occurs to the Cid, such as the apparition of the archangel, it is in dreams. Thus, the Spanish sense of truth is not an accident, neither is the incapacity for fantasy in inventiveness. The triad—the World, the Flesh, and the Devil—dominates Spanish art of all periods, especially literature. Out of the terror of the year one thousand emerges the sinful libertine who invites the dead to dinner, which is a rather serious matter. Satan, who is not an uncreated principle but a created one, and who is necessary so that sin will not cease to be, and with it the world, answers the call of the libertine. Later, Don Juan erupts on the frontier to do battle, in league with the world. And he ends up in Seville defiling maidens, a prisoner of the flesh. (A284)

Finally, he defined Spain in terms of the ethics demonstrated in its history:

Spain is an ethical force. Seneca was a scoundrel, but he had a great enthusiasm for good. Quevedo was not an innocent either, yet he wrote terrible moral epistles, "Hell-fire and exempla." Ethical furor is the characteristic of Spain. Through ethical furor Isabel the Catholic succeeded her brother before the crown could pass to an offspring of adultery. Through ethical furor Carlos IV abdicated, the Spanish King not wishing to know that his queen was having affairs. Ethical furor drafted the document that dethroned Isabel II. The latest Spanish revolution has been an ethical sanction. (A285)

Valle-Inclán always returned to the topic of his contemporaneity, tying in the historical with present reality. According to the newspaper accounts, his talk was interrupted several times by applause and was concluded with an ovation from the membership and friends of the Casino de Madrid.

When Manuel Azaña, burdened by the growing demands of his political office, announced in March 1932 that he would resign the presidency of the Ateneo, new elections were announced. Two important figures were among the candidates for the vacant office: Unamuno and Valle-Inclán, the latter's name having been proposed by Manuel Azaña and seconded by a hundred members of the Ateneo.[34] The amicable relationship that had matured since the two men had resolved their youthful incompatibility was not endangered by their opposing candidacies. But the supporters of each were very active and the halls of the Ateneo rang with praises and attacks on both sides. Valle-Inclán was denounced by some as not being a member of the organization because he had not paid his dues; others defended him, claiming that most of his detractors had not paid either. Unamuno was less attractive a candidate to the liberal membership because he had cast himself in the image of a mystic, although Valle-Inclán could have been seen in the same light because of his *La lámpara maravillosa*; some saw in Unamuno's election to the Cortes and the public homage he received a sufficient amount of honor. When the votes were totaled in

May, Valle-Inclán had been elected president of the Ateneo with a majority of 311 votes. Unamuno had received 146 but did not surpass the 285 of Hernández Pacheco, who assumed the vice-presidency. Those elected with Valle-Inclán were Agustín Millares Carlo (Librarian), Dubois (Second Director), Moreno Laguía (Trustee), and Victoriano García Martí (First Secretary). Together, they began to revitalize the organization and restore its physical quarters, as well as take the first inventory of its possessions in many decades.

Already involved with the Ateneo elections, Valle-Inclán found himself nominated and approved as the only Spaniard on an international committee convened to formulate the agenda for the "Grand Congrés Mondial contre la Guerre."[35] Romain Rolland sounded the famed call: "La guerre vient . . . Muselons la guerre!" (War is coming . . . Muzzle the war!).[36] But because of illness Valle-Inclán could not participate actively in the committee nor attend the event held in Amsterdam between 27 and 29 August 1932. Even if he had been in good health, it is doubtful that he could have afforded the journey to Holland.

These honors came at an opportune moment, helping to offset various affronts he received during this period. The first came that same month of May. Valle-Inclán had submitted three novels to the Academia de la Lengua for its "Premio Fastenrath," named after the noted German Hispanist Johannes Fastenrath (1839–1908). In an interview after the finalists were announced, Valle-Inclán declared his surprise over the selection of *Tirano Banderas*:

I don't know the details, but there was something strange about the notification. Please note. I submitted *Tirano Banderas, La corte de los milagros,* and *¡Viva mi dueño!* . . . Seeing that only the first is a finalist, along with the works of the other gentlemen, had I submitted the other two alone, they wouldn't even have made it to the final judging! As you see, the matter has some humor. . . . But I can't explain it. Unless the reason that they weren't mentioned, rather, proposed, was because they're anti-monarchical and the Academy has turned pro-monarchist without my knowing it . . . I myself took them with the three entry forms, meeting all the requirements. I turned them over personally to the secretary of the Academy, Sr. Cotarelo, who was very courteous to me and who I had not had the pleasure of meeting until that moment. He told me that my having brought them in person made it unnecessary to have entry forms, vouchers, or any formalities whatsoever. . . . I don't know if the gentlemen of the committee—I'm ignorant of who's on it—have recognized the intent in the work to create a Castilian not just of Castile, but of all Spanish-speaking peoples. It is a fusion of our language with the Spanish language, or languages, of South America.[37] (A286)

The decision of the Academy was to forgo awarding Valle-Inclán the "Premio Fastenrath" for his novel *Tirano Banderas*.[38] Apparently, the continued hostility of that organization could not be overcome even by the large number of Valle-Inclán supporters among the membership.[39] The action of the jury was prejudiced and the press did not permit the inequity to pass unnoticed,[40] but Valle-Inclán presented a calm face in an interview:

I hold no grudge against the Spanish Academy. I've sent works of a truly revolutionary nature, works against the old regime. So revolutionary in fact that the Soviet Library has published them. And the Academy, naturally, has rejected them. I didn't aspire to the prize itself. I had hoped that the Academy would take a definitive stand, and it has. The Academy is reactionary and monarchist. It's what I expected. What I didn't expect is the passivity of the Ministry of Public Education. The following day, the Minister of Public Education should have dictated a deposition denying the competence of the Academy to recommend works to be acquired by the Ministry, which is required to heed the Academy's judgment. The situation has very serious implications, not for me since, as I've said, I did not expect a prize and it wouldn't benefit me, but rather for the precedent that it sets. When the minister tries to acquire books and consults the Academy, it will forward its decision in favor of works of a reactionary type and against those of a liberal bent. . . . The Academy is an institution originated by the monarchy and it hasn't been able to purge itself of that damaging infirmity. It has kept to its role. Which doesn't surprise me. But the Ministry of Public Education is republican, and it ought to have acted, and always should act, in a republican manner.[41] (A287)

His friends, rebuking the Academy and celebrating his successful candidacy in the Ateneo, gave him a banquet on 7 June 1932 at Madrid's elegant Palace Hotel.[42] The event also commemorated the success of *Tirano Banderas* and *La corte de los milagros*. Unamuno gave the principal address, in which he lauded the celebrated guest and damned the Academy.[43] His words were seconded by the messages sent by notable figures who could not be present.[44] Valle-Inclán responded to the praises and camaraderie with gratitude and then reiterated many ideas; on the relationship between the writer from the provinces and the Castilian language, he stated:

Authors like us, who come from dialect-speaking regions, do battle with great enemies. Neither first nor last of these is the fact that we speak bad Castilian. Galicia doesn't speak Gallego, rather a tongue contaminated by Castilian. Learning Castilian is our greatest difficulty. When the young Galician, Catalan, or Basque aspires to write, a siren says to him: "If you speak in your regional tongue you will be a genius. In the regional tongue one doesn't have to struggle with twenty nations, only with four provinces." It's much too easy to be a genius in one's dialect. I opted not to follow that line, wanting to compete with a hundred million men, and what's more, with five centuries of heroism in the Castilian language. That's the great difficulty and the great virtue, as I have experienced. I've wanted to undergo the struggle and if I haven't emerged victorious, the dignity of the undertaking has saved me.[45] (A288)

Once again, he defined Spain in terms of its facets and related the nation to its former colonies in America.

Like coins, Spain has two faces: one, Roman and imperial, and another, Berber and Mediterranean. Spain goes to America like a daughter of Rome; but it takes the

Berber and Mediterranean facet along as well. As Rome's daughter, it takes the language, establishes a body of judicial doctrine, and founds cities. At present there is an intent to return to the barbaric Mediterranean Berberism. It is imperative that we turn the coin and keep only one face: the one that makes us sons of Rome. Spain is not here: it's in America. On the anniversary of the Constitution, we ought to bring the American Republics together, and to do that the Republic must create something to stimulate those nations. With those palaces and residences that belonged to the Crown, we could give their ambassadors an idea of Spain. But as long as the matter rests in the hands of the Directorate of Properties, there's no redemption. Spain must be created by those of us who know her.[46] (A289)

And referring to Unamuno, he added:

Who knows Spain better than those who have experienced sorrow and sleeplessness in order to express their feelings? How is it that we know about Russia? Because of the czar's laws or through the works of Tolstoy and Dostoievsky? And France? Do we know her because of the laws of Gambetta, Grevy, and Combes or through the works of Zola and Flaubert? Those of us who came from the provinces were captivated by the great power of Castile. Our maestro—Unamuno—is the best example. There's also that of Carlos I, who came to Spain without loving her, yet in his old age did not retire to any of the abbeys of his great empire but to a Spanish place: the monastery of Yuste. And El Greco, who came from lands rich in luminosity only to forget them when he reached Castile. This is what happened to our maestro, who came from his native region and turned into the greatest and most expressive of Castilian writers.[47] (A290)

Valle-Inclán's words were rewarded with the warm applause of friends and sympathizers.

Shortly after the tribute, Valle-Inclán was stricken by a serious bladder attack. This time he was taken to the Red Cross hospital in Madrid where his friend Dr. Salvador Pascual performed yet more surgery. His recovery was slow and painful, yet he continued to oversee his duties as "Conservador General del Patrimonio Artístico." He wrote again to his superior in an attempt to rectify the problems outlined in his unanswered first letter:

Enclosed anew herewith is a copy of a letter dated the sixth of this month, which was sent to your excellency, regarding the condition of the so-called Museum of Aranjuez. To the complaints lodged there must be added others of equal gravity, examples of the most shameful negligence and supine ignorance. The undersigned, alarmed by the clumsy way in which public visits are conducted in the Palace of Aranjuez and the Casa del Labrador, on Friday the third of this month, in his dual aspect as general conservator of the Artistic Patrimony and director of the Museum, telegraphed the secretary to cancel further visits. The rightness of this order, which has been wholly disobeyed, is patent in the fact—confirmed later by the secretary before witnesses—that more than six thousand people tramped through the Casa del Labrador on Sunday the fifth. The vandalism implied by such numbers does not require comment. The fragility of all that is housed in this small museum, its disposition, and the smallness of its rooms, call out in mute voices against the offense. And since the tourist caravans and free visits threaten to continue unabated, the undersigned, conscious of the responsibilities of his charge and reputation, respectfully places the matter before your excellency. Those who lack responsibilities and history, having emerged with a modest notoriety in the dawn of the Republic, may keep such a situation silent or even authorize it without being aware of its implications, since one cannot expect either sensibility or aesthetic culture from functionaries of the political administration. The undersigned wishes to close by urging your excellency to press for an opportune solution to the situation outlined. At the same time, and with all due respect, it is necessary to solicit from your excellency the moral support and the material means now lacking; should these not be forthcoming, it is requested that my resignation be accepted.[48] (A291)

This second letter was not answered either, and Valle-Inclán sent in his resignation:

Most exalted Sir:
   Faced with the eloquent silence with which your excellency has greeted the protestations and complaints that I had had the honor to make known to you, there remains to me only the presentation of my resignation as General Conservator of the National Artistic Patrimony and Director of the Museum of Aranjuez.[49] (A292)

Valle-Inclán had taken his office seriously and had tried to serve the nation to the best of his abilities in order to preserve for future generations the artistic and historic treasures in his charge. As Azaña's memoirs reveal, his appointment had not been made with serious intent but rather as a reward to a deserving individual. When Valle-Inclán realized this after six months in office, he could do no less than resign. It had been expected by the minister and all others involved that Valle-Inclán would be a mere figurehead, and finally the former took notice of his resignation and asked him to remain in the position:

The minister replied to my resignation in a letter, which I'm not at liberty to divulge. He urged me with amiable vagaries to withdraw my resignation. Having just received his letter, I read in the newspapers the following notice: "Proposed law regarding the protection of the national artistic heritage. The permanent Commission of Public Education agreed at yesterday's session to open proceedings on said project, to which all interested parties and entities may contribute in writing. The dates for the acceptance of such reports will be from today to the seventh of July, said reports to be addressed to the president of the Commission of Public Education." I clipped the notice, pasted it on a card and wrote below it: "My dear friend: I received your attentive letter and then read this notice. I feel that, as General Conservator of the National Artistic Patrimony, I should at least have been extended the courtesy of being informed. Faced with this situation, I can only reiterate my resignation."[50] (A293)

The introduction of a commission to investigate the very things that Valle-Inclán had suggested and the new affront of not notifying him of its creation proved that his resignation was the only possible course of action. While attempts were made to convince him to keep his post, if only as a

means of earning a much-needed income, Valle-Inclán refused such overtures with pride in his stance. The open letter he wrote to Manuel Aznar,
editor of *El Sol*, published 26 June, made public his resignation, explained
his dissatisfaction, and divulged the contents of the correspondence he
had sent to his superior. In it he rectified the statements, termed
erroneous, which had been published in *Informaciones* by an eager reporter
who had been turned away during Valle-Inclán's recovery:

It's no secret that some friends from the newspapers had visited me and that I had
begged them not to write about my resignation. Someone who has always shown
me the greatest courtesy, such as Montero Alonso, can verify it. After the apocryphal report in *Informaciones*, it is no longer valid to keep silent about the events or
to keep secret the exchange of documents.[51] (A294)

His closing statement to Aznar showed a bitter pessimism:

And to close, dear Aznar: Out of the apocryphal account published in *Informaciones*,
the only thing that coincides with the truth is my plan to undertake a trip to
America: not to Valparaiso, as the account has it, but to Rio de Janeiro. It is also
true, as I've said repeatedly to my friends, that, should I perish abroad, I am set
against any official tribute.[52] (A295)

His illness and the disgraceful treatment he received from the Republic
embittered Valle-Inclán. What should have been a peaceful old age became
a nightmare.

Engulfing financial difficulties arose as a result of his resignation of the
political appointment, which had brought him a substantial income. He
refused any such assistance thereafter. The only income he could muster
came from his occasional publications in periodicals. Through his friend
Aznar, he contracted with *El Sol* for the serialization of *La corte de los
milagros*,[53] but most noteworthy was the appearance of part of *Baza de
espadas*,[54] the third volume in the first series of *El ruedo ibérico*.

The growing problems made the home life of his family difficult. Ten-
sions seemed insurmountable and the relations between husband and wife
reached an impasse. The twenty-five years of their union terminated in
separation, and a judge ordered that half of Valle-Inclán's income be given
to his wife.[55] According to Azaña, Valle-Inclán's resentment of the court
order led to his resignation of his post as Conservador del Patrimonio
Artístico Nacional so that his wife would not have access to his salary as
ordered by the court. Josefina kept their youngest daughter, María
Antonia, while Valle-Inclán took care of the remaining children with the
exception of their eldest daughter, who had married earlier.[56] The
accumulation of woes was reflected in his statements:

I'm an old man, I'm ill, there is nothing more of me to give . . . I've had to resign from the post entrusted to me because I didn't want to give in to other criteria . . . There's nothing left for me to do than follow the path taken, I've written the mayor of Madrid asking for four places for my children in an asylum, and I will retire to the Instituto Cervantes.[57] (A296)

But his letter to his old friend Luis Ruiz Contreras, dated 27 July 1932, was even more revelatory of his pathetic condition:

My dear C:
I received your good letter. I'm overwhelmed. Yesterday I hocked my watch. I'll no longer be able to tell the hour of my death. Since I have to cook for the little ones, the heat of the stove has finally destroyed my gall bladder. I have neither health nor money, and friends are so scarce. That's why I'm doubly grateful for your letter. If in my experience, disillusioned, I find I can no longer hold on to hope, there is one consolation. Don't think for a minute that I despair. I surprise myself with what indifference I see the end approaching. I've called the children together and told them the situation. They too have Stoic souls. I've said to them: "My children, we're going to hock the watch. Once we've eaten those hundred pesetas, we will undergo a fast with no foreseeable end. It isn't a matter of buying a rope and hanging ourselves all in a row. I've never been a sponger and I want to die without stooping to that. I think that our friends will help, at least in finding us places in asylums. I'll retire to the Asilo Cervantes. I have a friend there: Don Ciro Bayo." Like little heroes, they swallowed their tears and have shown themselves ready to face the storm without giving it too much importance. In fact, it isn't very important and, if I made it seem so at times, it's because I forget that it's a daily occurrence for us to be a family without means and with a sick father. Such vulgar sorrow, repeated daily, isn't worth making a fuss over. My condition accentuates the episode, giving it importance; but that's in the face of public opinion, not to me. What obsesses me most is the thought of not being able to die in peace: seeing death come slowly during serene afternoons. To be able to close my eyes forever without being afflicted in the interim by the lack of money. Write me, dear friend.[58] (A297)

But his friends were not all indifferent to his plight. Fernando de los Ríos, for one, continued his attempts to procure for Valle-Inclán a government subsidy with which he could live out his days in comfort; in a letter to José Balseiro, dated 12 September 1932, he gave evidence of his efforts.[59] While this attempt was unsuccessful, other avenues were being sought. Gregorio Marañón, Azorín, Azaña, De los Ríos, Manuel Bueno, and Ignacio Zuloaga, among others, proposed in October that Valle-Inclán be considered to head the Academia Española de Bellas Artes in Rome.[60] But the candidate's controversial reputation again prevented an immediate approval of the petition. The matter would not be resolved until the following year. In the meantime, Valle-Inclán's pessimism was expressed in the poem "Requiem," published that same October:

I walk alone through refuse.
The baggage of misfortune
burdens my old shoulders.

Halo of trembling whiteness,
the oil lamp of the dead
lights my darkened night.

I move through mourning night,
mouth mute to protest,
eyes arid to tears.

Blessed, fortunate Death,
I concentrate all hope
on reaching your abode.[61] (A298)

But even this burdensome reality could not destroy the Man's sarcasm. In a companion poem entitled "Testamento," he lashed out at the crude reporters who waited eagerly for his demise:

Gentlemen, health and good fortune!
My candle has flickered its last.
Death's hand has reached up to place
its demands on my ivory tower.
I leave to the corner innkeeper
my laurels—decor for his door.
My palms, to a neighbor's veranda;
my tinsel, to a crazed local mask.
Reporter, to you, my cadaver.
(If the glory of life is but smoke,
you smoke all of mine in Havanas.)
My cadaver to you, mangy cur,
who, banquetting on my cold news,
spiced in newsmongering prose,
have sated yourself on my carcass,
and, reeking of smoke, ingenuously
state, while sipping bicarbonate:
"May Don Miguel not croak this way!"[62] (A299)

The year ended with the final decree of divorce, issued on 19 December 1932, under the *Constitución de 1931*. According to the provisions of that document, Valle-Inclán filed the necessary papers while he and his wife lived separately: he in quarters at 5 Calle del Progreso, and she in a *pensión* on Avenida Eduardo Dato. The lasting devotion that made them inseparable in the eyes of Martínez Sierra only four years earlier had now become ironic.[63] His penury made it impossible for Josefina to be given an income, and so she had to return to the theatre, accepting the opportunity presented by Tirso Escudero, who was then impresario of the Teatro de la Comedia where María Luisa Rodríguez headed the company. During this agonizing period, Valle-Inclán and his offspring lived on the subtle generosity of such friends as Zuloaga, Rodríguez Acosta, Marañón, and Ruiz Contreras. His old friend Luis de Hoyos showed particular concern over the children, outfitting them periodically with clothing they would not have otherwise. Valle-Inclán accepted this generosity with humility and gratitude. The frequent visits of Unamuno, Vighi, Ciges Aparicio, and others helped relieve the boredom of the long hours he was directed to spend in bed daily. In this manner, he and his younger children managed to survive one of the most trying periods of a turbulent life.

The first months of 1933 offered no relief. Sparse publications in periodicals continued to be his only source of personal income.[64] His candidacy for the post in Rome, supported by the Consejo de Cultura and the prestigious Museo de Arte Moderno,[65] was opposed by the Museo del Prado and the Academia de Bellas Artes de San Fernando, which nominated respectively Victorio Macho and Teodoro de Anasagasti. The discussions seemed endless, and as the possibility of his appointment fluctuated, Valle-Inclán entertained the idea of leaving Spain and expending his remaining time in America. The thought of joining Alfonso Reyes in Brazil had tempted him, but his thoughts also focused on Mexico, a country for which he continued to have great admiration. That Mexico, in turn, appreciated Valle-Inclán was shown when its Ambassador to Spain, Jenaro Estrada, extended on behalf of his government an invitation including traveling expenses for himself and his children, and the promise of a suitable post. The generous offer proved almost irresistible to the man who saw himself as forsaken by the Republic. But some uncanny hope was kept alive in Valle-Inclán. This was justified on 8 March 1933 when his nomination to head the Academia Española de Bellas Artes in Rome was finally approved; he received the news in a room at the Red Cross hospital, to which a new bladder attack had forced him to return.

Valle-Inclán was sufficiently well to give a reading of *Divinas palabras* to the company at Madrid's Teatro Español on 24 March 1933. This was a preliminary to the projected premiere of the work under the direction of Cipriano Rivas Cherif and starring Margarita Xirgu as Mari-Gaila and Enrique Borrás as the male lead, with Galician decor by Castelao. Valle-Inclán sat at a small table on the cavernous stage and read his tragicomedy to a fascinated audience.[66] When he had finished, he was asked if he would attend the opening and he replied:

I won't be able to. What's more, I may be unable to attend the rehearsals. I'm leaving immediately for Rome. I'm not concerned about the interpretation. I know that Rivas Cherif will lavish much love on it. Likewise, Xirgu and Borrás will be well suited to their roles. Castelao will provide the scenic design. On him depends the most pressing need in *Divinas palabras*, the visualization of Galicia on the stage. It has infinite hues. And, as you noted, it has varied rhythms, but within an indestructible melodic unity. The voices have an extraordinary value in it. That's why the play must be rehearsed as one would an orchestra.[67] (A300)

He arrived in Rome on 19 April to take over his duties as director of the Academy. His children accompanied him there with the exception of

Carlos, who had been sent to study in Santiago de Compostela, where he resided with the family of Andrés Díaz de Rábago, one of his father's oldest friends. Arriving in Rome, which Mussolini was in the endless process of renewing in his bizarre neo-Roman taste, Valle-Inclán went directly to San Pietro in Montorio, supposedly the site of the Apostle's execution, to the palace that housed the Academy. To his dismay, he found that the architecture of the building was its only recommendation; the neglect of the Spanish monarchy for this once-grand outpost of national culture was evident in its run-down condition and its lack of furnishings, as one of his memos, recently discovered, makes clear:

Excellent Sir:
  Informed by the secretary of this academy, Don Hermenegildo Estevan, of the protocol and admonition given him by the illustrious trustee Don Gonzalo de Ojeda regarding the prohibition against transferring furniture from one room to another, I seek your indulgence due to my ignorance that in so doing I was committing a breach. At present, I adhere to that prohibition with such strict respect that today, when six people were in my office, there being chairs for only three, I spread my cape on the floor and invited them to sit thereon.[68] (A301)

But Valle-Inclán, who had often lived with the barest of necessities, adapted himself to his lot, although he never ceased to petition for sufficient funds to refurbish the palace in the manner befitting its importance. Yet another memo describes his plight in sardonic terms:

It should be kept in mind that seven people require seven beds. According to the inventory, this address has the pleasure of owning five; if I'm not wrong, two are lacking to make seven. Seven beds, in turn, require fourteen sheets, counting two sheets to a bed. According to the inventory, this address has the pleasure of owning sixteen sheets. All beds made, there are two sheets left over. When the time comes to change the bedding, the replacement sheets being insufficient (these consist of two sheets, as stated), this office blushes with shame when it has to compel the laundress to wash sheets in the morning so that the presser can iron them in the afternoon. Seven beds require, quite fittingly, fourteen pillows; that is, two pillows per bed. According to the inventory, this address has the pleasure of owning nine pillowcases. At two pillowcases per bed, four and a half beds can be fitted. If the beds are seven in number, one doesn't have to be a Pythagoras to count two beds without pillowcases and one bed with half the allotment. It is not an exaggeration to say that the director of the Academy is living at present as if in a gypsy camp. Neither his health, nor his white hairs, nor his habits, nor the dignity of his office make it possible for him to continue under such conditions.[69] (A302)

Needless to say, such pleas achieved very little; but at least some essentials were obtained.
  First, he saw Rome, the city whose title of Eternal had been restored by Mussolini not only by his grandiose schemes but also by a concordat with Pope Pius XI that settled the Vatican problem. Valle-Inclán's letter to Dr.

Salvador Pascual, dated 27 April 1933, expressed the feelings that Rome evoked:

I've yet to visit a museum, church, or ruin. I see the city externally. It is marvelous and unique. The entire history of a two-thousand-year-old civilization. . . . What Mussolini has achieved has both amazed and kept me in suspense. Next to a dynamic fury, full of promise, there's the sacred sense of Roman tradition. There was a recent opening of a new Via—the Via Impero—which runs along the most significant ruins of the Latin world. This Via is decorated with four bronze statues brought from the Museum of Naples. That of Julius Caesar, with the most serene elegance; that of Octavian, expressive and having a captivating green hue. That of Trajan, with an inscription on its pedestal: "Principe Optimo." I confess that my heartbeat joyously before the bronze statue of this outstanding Cordoban. Come to Rome. I have never seen, nor can comprehend its equal.[70] (A303)

Valle-Inclán managed to procure an automobile and chauffeur, which permitted him to travel extensively through the Italian countryside. He saw Italy in terms of its fascinating history, and everywhere he traveled he was impressed by the mark of great events and men on the cities of the peninsula:

Whoever comes to Rome to view the city objectively, as I did, receives an enormous impression. Ostia Antica lies on the way from Naples to Rome. . . . In Capua, Hannibal tracks a long terrestrial line and it appears that the destiny of the European world will then be in Africa. But the Roman toys with the Carthaginian. And, while Hannibal remains in Capua, Scipio sets out with his triremes and conquers Carthage. There has come to the fore the great military concept of war on two fronts: the maritime and the terrestrial. The maritime triumphs. And the triumph of the ship is Italy's triumph.[71] (A304)

He communicated his enthusiasm to the many visitors he received. The Spanish poet Adriano del Valle was one of these. In 1933 he visited Valle-Inclán, finding him suffering from haematuria yet able to handle the numerous steps that led to his quarters and willing to express his realistic attitude toward the fascism of Mussolini:

Fascism? Fascism is neither a party of hoodlums, as Spain's radical imbeciles believe, nor a regime of the extreme right. It is an imperial drive toward universality, in its most ecumenically vertical and horizontal sense. From the stars to the little flowers of Saint Francis of Assisi. Here is Rome, below us, offering itself for our contemplation as a splendid paradigm of marble gloriously mutilated by the centuries, with her Imperial Via—Mussolini's Caesarean accomplishment—on which four statues have been raised as examples to all the peoples of the world: Julius Caesar, Augustus Octavian, Trajan, and Nerva. Because Trajan was a Spaniard and Nerva was elected emperor by the Hispanic and Gallic Legions. For such reasons, Spain was also Rome, as was the entire known world, to land's ends extending into unknown seas. And if Catholicism achieved universality and, along with spiritual power, its imponderable geographic holdings, it did so because it too was Rome. Because it was the voice and the arm of Rome in performing the tasks of the Catholic liturgy. And Fascism is that same continuity of the Roman plan, to the extent that if Briand's famous utopia, the United States of Europe, were to attain political reality, it would have its capital in Rome, since all that is modern in Europe is what was old in Rome.[72] (A305)

His views on Italian fascism were the result of his observations. In his view, Italy had benefited from the unifying vision of Mussolini and in that context fascism was a logical outgrowth of necessity:

Mussolini's work tends primarily to inculcate an ideal in his people, a concept of sacrifice; at a time so full of egoism, there is none in Rome and so the Italians are the people most willing to sacrifice themselves for a historical ideal, the only kind a people should have. . . . Like Hannibal, Caesar, and Napoleon, Mussolini always has a categorical and determined concept and goal. For that reason there is a sad historical experience loomimg near Mussolini. There's no room for class egoism in the dictatorship of an individual. Such was the case with Napoleon, such is the case with Mussolini, such is the case with any great ruler. Each attends to the needs of all sectors and, consequently, is able to achieve great results. There is a difference between Mussolini and Hitler: the former possesses something akin to a Platonic idea and has awakened a sense of universality in the poetic souls of all Italians, a people full of heroic expression; but in order to feel it, it has had to do the opposite of the Germans. While Hitler purges the German people of all elements not purely Germanic, Mussolini, like Caracalla, knows that the whole of cultured Europe has Italian citizenship. This sense of universality is explained by stating that Mussolini has erected four statues on the Imperial Via . . . of two emperors from Rome and two from the empire, that is, who were not born on Roman soil. Throughout Mussolini's politics there reigns that sense of universality.[73] (A306)

But while Valle-Inclán could express comprehension of Mussolini's political stance, he did not fail to detect the human weaknesses in the man; in a later conversation with another of his visitors, he referred to Il Ducce as:

. . . a buffoon who will fall very soon.[74] (A307)

And perhaps this change occurred because Valle-Inclán, a representative of Republican Spain, was merely tolerated by fascist Italy. Valle-Inclán detected the malice behind the formal attitude of Italian officials encountered in the execution of his duties:

They esteem and yet fear me. Both things. Are you aware that they're attempting to take the Academia de España from me? But as long as I'm its director, they won't succeed.[75] (A308)

Valle-Inclán, always the individualist, could not be classified politically with the ease with which some of his contemporaries placed him in one camp or another. Thus, while enjoying Mussolini's Rome, he maintained his communist contacts, as a letter dated in 1933 and written on his official Roman stationery attests:

Sr. Don Fedor Kelin.
My distant and good friend:
I can't begin to tell you the echoes that your letter has stirred in me. I'm a literary renegade. For some years now, I've lived apart from writers and books. You speak of mine, saying that I have some readers there, and I make a melancholy comparison between that good fortune and my failure in Spain. Clearly, my failure is the same as that of all writers worthy of respect. I was crazy enough to think that I could live from my writing and, after forty years of struggle—and so as not to end up in an asylum, at who's door I was already knocking—I've been able to remedy the situation through the directorship of this Academy.
I haven't received the issue of *Literatura Internacional* that you mention. I would like to send you some of my books but I don't have any. Most of them are out of print. I wrote to Madrid so that they would send you *Opera lírica*, *Martes de carnaval*, *Tablado de marionetas*, and any others of which they may have copies. Spanish literary life is so base that publishers don't chance their money on reprinting unavailable books.
Some time ago, I was invited to go to Russia and I received yet another invitation recently, but the obligations of this directorship prevent me from giving vent to that great desire of my heart. Let's see if I can do it in October. Surely by then diplomatic relations between Spain and Russia will have been re-established.
I fear that Spain will once more make a mistake in the choice of ambassador they send you.
And nothing more, my good friend, than to thank you for the affection of your letter and to shake your hand.
Valle-Inclán[76] (A309)

He was also an activist of sorts. In 1933 he was elected president of the Asociación de Amigos de la Unión Soviética, he convened the Primer Congreso de la Asociación de Escritores y Artistas Revolucionarios at the Ateneo de Madrid, and he became a correspondent of *Le Monde*, an international magazine "in the struggle against fascism and the white terror." Romain Rolland, who founded the journal, had earlier sounded the call for the "Grand Congrès Mondial contre la Guerre" (Great World Congress against War) to which Valle-Inclán had been nominated by Henri Barbusse, the editor of *Le Monde*.

From the beginning of his public career he demonstrated only a partial affinity to whatever ideology he espoused. While he adhered to some of the political tenets therein, his outlook was centered always on the concept of authoritarianism. But the force of this classification had to be tempered by enlightenment. Thus, in his first years as a journalist and a bohemian, he admired the cause of anarchy because it represented the autonomy and authority of the individual; during this Carlist period, he was attracted by the latent power of the classic king; when he declared himself a socialist, it was because the working classes were led by strong men like Lerroux. His communism was founded on the authority and order that Lenin had forged out of the chaos of the Russian Revolution. It was the same with his fascism. The Roman figure of Mussolini draining the Pontine Marshes, leading his people toward the conquest of lost prestige, and raising out of its ruins a new imperial Rome satisfied Valle-Inclán's concept of the hero and led him to admire the work of the man. But he saw also the eventual failure of the dream because the man was not large enough to rise above personal ambition. In time, the self-styled Caesar would become a grotesque figure worthy of one of Valle-Inclán's *Esperpentos*.

During the time spent in Italy, Valle-Inclán returned to Spain several times, either for reasons of health or to further some project. Among these visits was one in August 1933.[77] Once more in Madrid, he was witness to the flux of Spanish politics. Manuel Azaña resigned as head of the government that same autumn and the reins were entrusted to Alejandro Lerroux; a new political party, the Falange, was organized on 29 October under the leadership of José Antonio Primo de Rivera, son of the former dictator, and its proclamation was made in the Teatro de la Comedia; the 19 November elections gave a sizable margin to conservatives, composed of Acción Popular or of CEDA (Confederación Española de Derechas Autónomas), indicating increasing public dissatisfaction with the performance of recent administrations. The Republic was floundering. Valle-Inclán witnessed the spectacle and did not hedge in tracing the present condition to the inevitability of history:

Spain has suffered the dictatorship of its four different branches: that of the nobility, the military, the Church, and the populace. The first which Spain underwent was that of the nobility, the privileges of the nobles, and it wasn't the people alone who suffered but the monarchs as well, until the Catholic kings deposed the nobles and transformed them from dictators into courtiers. Immediately thereafter came the dictatorship of another social branch: that of the Church, with its Inquisition. It is the dictatorship of the Church over all other branches of society. That is, the dictatorship of a collective over the rest. And this theocracy establishes national unity under Catholic unity. The Church is succeeded by the Army. Spain suffers military dictatorship in the nineteenth century. O'Donnell represents the Liberal Union; Narváez, the moderates; earlier, Espartero represents the progressives; Prim is the September Revolution; the Restoration, Martínez Campos; while the most recent dictatorship is that of Primo de Rivera, under which Spain suffers the egoism of the class that is the Army, which violates and impoverishes the other three. Continuing the process, Spain is now experiencing a socialist dictatorship whose egoism also enslaves the other three classes. The fact is that there's no socialism here and it is . . . a fleeting class . . . I call it a fleeting class because it lacks the sense and desire for permanence. A noble doesn't aspire to be something else; a chaplain wants to be a bishop, who wants to be a cardinal, who later wants to be Pope; the soldier dreams of becoming a general; but the worker wants to become an owner. That is to say, that while the other three branches don't wish to leave their class, the populace does. For that reason, it is a class full of resentment and one with a lower status. The dictatorship that may be necessary is not that of a class but of an individual. It is sad to reach such a conclusion, but, unfortunately, that's reality. The outcome of all this would be the fusion of all classes into one, and that is communism. But to achieve it there would have to be the suppression of inheritance, as well as a nationalization of banks, land, industry, and mines. The tremendous omission is not having taken this path, thus making the proletarian class disappear through the suppression of the rest, making them all equal. To attain this, everyone must be made to work, and this can't be achieved simply by stating in the constitution that Spain is a Republic of workers of all classes, but by suppressing various things, uppermost of which is inheritance since I've never seen a rich heir working. Whoever works does so out of need. That's why Jehovah didn't say to Adam that he would earn his bread by the sweat of his brow until depriving him of that magnificent land grant that was Paradise.[78] (A310)

Besides concerning himself with the political front, he was cognizant of the changing cultural panorama of Madrid. He returned to favorite cafés to discuss the classic and Renaissance art he had seen in Rome; with Gómez de la Serna and his wife Luisa Sofovich, he attended the tribute to the painter Miguel Viladrich after a successful exhibition of his works; Sender and others walked with him through the streets of the capital; in the company of Benavente, he returned to the theatre for the rehearsals of *Divinas palabras*, which Margarita Xirgu and Enrique Borrás were preparing under the direction of Cipriano Rivas Cherif. He was much in demand.

Divinas palabras, in rehearsal since March, was premiered finally on 16 November 1933 under the scrutiny of the playwright. The long-awaited production of the controversial play met with mixed reaction from the public and apparent discomfort among some of the interpreters due to the play's sexual premise.[79] Nonetheless, the theatricality of the work was recognized by all, and the production was relatively successful in the economic sense. The renewed popularity of the play prompted a new edition.[80] *Divinas palabras* was to be the last of Valle-Inclán's plays to be performed in Spain during his lifetime. Of his large number of dramas, farces, and *Esperpentos* there remained to be presented on a Spanish stage the important works *Comedias bárbaras*, *Los cuernos de don Friolera*, *La enamorada del rey*, *Luces de bohemia*, *Las galas del difunto* and *La hija del capitán*.

Valle-Inclán returned to Rome to the leisurely life his few duties permitted, although his worsening health restricted his activities. Nonetheless, his life in the Italian capital was multifaceted.[81] As a tourist, he walked incessantly through the historic city, often in the company of his daughter Mariquiña, and observed the glories of the past surrounding him at every turn; as a member of the diplomatic corps, he attended important functions and received invitations to the homes of social and political leaders; as a cultural representative of Spain, he hosted many gatherings at the Academy, often debilitating the budget and requiring the fiscal assistance of the Embassy; as a noted novelist and playwright, he entered into the intellectual life of the city and made the acquaintance of many of its leaders. A profitable artistic association resulted from his introduction to Anton Giulio Bragaglia, the Italian director who had founded the Teatro Sperimentale degli Independenti and the Teatro delle Arti, the first Italian national theatre. Bragaglia discussed with Valle-Inclán the possibility of presenting one of his plays in Rome, and they agreed on *Los cuernos de don Friolera*, whose anti-militarism would be poignant in the Italian setting. But, as in Spain, the publicity given the project brought the intervention of the authorities:

Bragaglia is trembling. The censor has intervened. . . . I don't intend to attend its premiere.[82] (A311)

But the director stuck to his plans and the rehearsals continued. Censorship may have forced author and director to make some changes in the script and interpretation, but the *Esperpento* was permitted to make its premiere in 1934, at the Teatro dell Arti.[83]

Rafael Alberti, the poet who had won the Premio Nacional de Literatura in 1925, visited Rome in August 1934 in the company of María Teresa León with the express purpose of meeting Valle-Inclán and conveying to him messages from Russia, where he had been in attendance at an international meeting of writers.[84] Alberti was received in the impoverished surroundings of the Academy; he noted the decay into which the building had been allowed to lapse, but he perceived, as did Valle-Inclán, the possibility of restoring it as a center for Spanish artists.[85] The two men became friends immediately, and Valle-Inclán confided in the poet more than his plans for the Academy. He divulged that in spite of his divorce from Josefina, his former wife continued to harass him in the pejorative style she had learned from him. Her letters were full of accusations and sarcasm.[86] But Valle-Inclán thrived on controversy and his rage seemed to Alberti a cover for his enjoyment.

The romantic spirit of Rome must have acted strongly on Valle-Inclán because he let himself be enticed into a secretive relationship with a younger woman.[87] His recent divorce and a growing awareness that he did not have long to live undoubtedly disposed him to flirt with love one last time. The affair had all the trimmings of a Bradominesque adventure except that it was not a literary creation; Valle-Inclán was acting out in his reality the role he often assigned to grotesque characters in his *Esperpentos*. He must have realized this, but he permitted the affair to continue for several months. Its abrupt and unpleasant end made his age weigh even more heavily. While the spirit of youth had flared in him, it had not inspired the girl to think of him in terms beyond his physical age. While her flirtation was cruel, it awakened Valle-Inclán to reality and destroyed the spirit of Bradomín that he had seemingly attempted to transfer from the novel to the plane of his own life.

Eventually, as he revealed in a letter of 26 August 1934, Valle-Inclán became seriously ill:

Here I am with a hematuria of several days that has all the aspects of the one I had in Madrid, which required a transfusion to halt it . . . If the hematuria stops on its own, I'll have electrocoagulation immediately. If, as I fear, the hematuria is obstinate, I will have to undergo a transfusion.[88] (A312)

With the continuation of his malady, he had to seek medical attention in Rome; knowing the gravity of his illness, he decided to travel to Spain again. He did so that fall. He did not return to Rome again although he kept his directorship of the Academy.

While Unamuno had retired from the rectorship of the University of Salamanca at the age of seventy, delivering his final lesson ceremoniously on 30 September 1934 and receiving the accolades of the academic community together with official honors, Valle-Inclán returned to Madrid to face yet another rebuke by the Academia de la Lengua in its new rejection of his candidacy. Emilio Cotarelo, secretary of the organization, publicly denounced Valle-Inclán by stating that he was not a good writer and that he destroyed language, among other things. Valle-Inclán retorted, stating:

Sr. Cotarelo is right. The Academy is a temple. I am a heretic. Heretics cannot enter the temple. I'm not being ironic. I speak sincerely. It's a matter of a great truth. I'm an incorrigible heterodox, a rebel by nature.[89] (A313)

While he damned Valle-Inclán, Cotarelo praised José María Salaverría, who had been elected instead of him, as well as Muñoz Seca, the next prospect, and Pío Baroja, a recent inductee.

Unimpressed at this stage of his life and career by such pronouncements, Valle-Inclán continued to write, publish, and participate in the political life of Spain. In November 1934 he was a signatory of a pro-Azaña document,[90] and in late December he participated in a banquet in honor of the political prisoner Dr. Del Río Ortega, at which he said:

Along with all honest men, I want to remember that great intellectual, Dr. Del Río Ortega—and all who are jailed with him—and it is imperative that we take up a collection to make at least our small contribution to their Christmas dinner.[91] (A314)

He also continued to write segments of El ruedo ibérico. His old friend Luis Ruiz Contreras, no longer able to publish Valle-Inclán's work himself as he had in the past, contacted Juan Bergua, whose publishing firm was very prosperous, and asked him to assist the needy writer.[92] Bergua, who had been planning a new collection of books of modern literature, became interested in the proposal and agreed to visit Valle-Inclán to discuss a collection of his stories.[93] In the conversation recorded by Bergua, Valle-Inclán talked about his translations of Queiroz and of Ruiz Contreras's versions of Anatole France's work. But the main subject was the publication of his own writing in the collection proposed by Bergua:

It seems like a good idea. . . . And do you know what else I'd like you to bring together in another volume of my works? . . . The *Sonatas*. . . . Then, if this project turns out well for you, and it will, I guarantee it, we'll issue the *Sonatas*. . . . If I speak with such assurance it's because I have a basis for it. My books, in economical editions, will sell by the thousands . . . Don't harbor the smallest doubt. And following the *Sonatas*, we will issue a third volume, to include what I consider the best work I've written. . . . *Cara de Plata, Aguila de blasón*, and *Romance de lobos*. The three would be wonderful in one of your volumes.[94] (A315)

Valle-Inclán's enthusiasm and optimism belied his condition. Fired by the idea of collecting his best stories in a new volume, he sought an appropriate title:

We haven't spoken at all about a very important matter. What title will you give the book? Have you thought about it? . . . It's essential and shouldn't be put aside. Titles are the faces of books, and the best recommendation for men and books is a beautiful face. Titles always preoccupy me greatly, and if I told you that some took more effort to create than the books themselves it could be that I'm not exaggerating. . . . As I say, I worry a lot about such details. What effect would it have on you to see a blob of paint on a fine work? . . . That's the effect I feel a title that is bad, limp, or inexpressive would have. . . . Yes, we must deliberate on it until we come up with something suitable to all.[95] (A316)

From the thought that Bergua gave to the problem during a pause in the conversation came the proposed *Flores de almendro*, which Valle-Inclán accepted wholeheartedly. But the book, containing thirty-two stories, would not be published until a few months after the death of Valle-Inclán.

Despite his ill health, Valle-Inclán continued to be active. On 29 December 1934 he was the guest of Federico García Lorca at the premiere of *Yerma*. In a photograph taken that evening at the Teatro Español he is shown in the company of García Lorca and Pura de Ucelay, who directed the theatre club "Anfistora."[96] Margarita Xirgu portrayed the leading role under the direction of Rivas Cherif, but even with such expert interpretation and direction the play did not appeal to Valle-Inclán. He did not allow his friendship with the playwright nor the latter's admiration to temper his criticism of Yerma's depiction as a woman, wife, and frustrated mother.[97] Nonetheless, Valle-Inclán showed his admiration for the younger playwright in a written tribute in February 1935, to which he was a signatory with Victorio Macho, Juan Ramón Jiménez, Alejandro Casona, Adolfo Salazar, and others. Later that month he lectured on Spanish history and literature at the Ateneo in San Sebastián.[98]

Perhaps because of his indefatigable activity, in March 1935 Valle-Inclán was stricken again and had to enter the Sanatorio Médico-Quirúrgico of Dr. Manuel Villar Iglesias in Santiago de Compostela. The treatments he received restored his strength sufficiently so that he became an ambulatory patient and was permitted to visit El Derby and El Español, cafés where old friends gathered to converse with him and where young writers, painters, and students came under the spell of his ever-commanding personality. At other times, he walked the fabled streets of Santiago in the company of the admirers who were always at his side. Almost daily, he lunched at the restaurant intriguingly named "El Asesino," and sat facing the street at the table by the window in the innermost of the dining rooms. In this way the limits imposed by his illness seemed more bearable; as he wrote on 9 May 1935:

I have no idea how much longer I'll remain in this sanatorium. I was very ill when I came here; even when I said nothing about it, I knew it and had no hope of being cured. Having read something in books that deal with such illnesses, I suspected that the papilloma had degenerated into a carcynoma and that I had little time to live. It turned out differently and I'm cured of that apprehension. I'm undergoing radium treatment and believe that it will be effective. Along with my health, I've regained my optimism to a degree and even started a novel. It's well along.[99](A317)

That same month he was one of the signatories, along with Azaña and De los Ríos of an invitation to a banquet in honor of Bernardo G. de Cándamo, then librarian of the Ateneo de Madrid.

His energy seemed inexhaustible as he continued writing—almost as if he knew how little time he had left—and he visited Vigo on 29 June in the company of two doctors to view an exhibit of paintings by Manuel Colmeiro, and accepted positions, such as that of President of the Asociación Internacional de Escritores, Spanish section, as well as that of Honorary President of the national campaign against the death penalty, which resulted in a document signed by Valle-Inclán:

The death penalty, when instituted to drown in blood the protesting voice of the immense majority of people clamoring from the remotest corners for the cessation of a state of things that denies the most basic rights of citizenship, does not constitute an adequate corrective measure toward exemplariness and order, rather a way of imposing through terror that which the people, anxious for liberty and justice, repudiate with all the passion of its indignation. . . . Such are the antecedents that serve as a base for the death penalty and, as a result, we gauge the manifest monstrosity in the face of its total inefficacy. In cases such as the one at hand, penology itself has shown that the death penalty is wholly injurious and counterproductive. . . . For the state (which today does not represent the will of the people) to legalize, legitimize, and justify the premeditated killing of honest citizens, who risked their lives and spilled their blood while fighting for a social state that, in their judgment, was more just, is so terrible and monstrous, so unjust and arbitrary, that any individual aware of his rights and duties as such, and of the responsibility that affects each of us before society at any given moment of history, must reject and condemn. . . . The most fundamental humanitarian principles, the dictates of justice and law that are inherent, neither authorize nor can authorize that a minority institute, against the will of the majority, the act of taking the life of one's equals in the premeditated, reflective, and cold manner which the law makes evident. . . . This association, composed of numerous men of the law, who fight and wish to continue fighting so that justice may be resplendent (not that partial and privileged justice that has been established by those who do not represent or interpret the will of the people), hurls this challenge to all men who identify fully, to the most expressive and categorical extreme of how they think and feel, with a problem that so deeply affects the hearts of all citizens, men and women, without political labels, who, embedded in the intellectual camp, be it in the areas of science, law, or the arts, in their varied manifestations, keenly observe the social realities which surround us at this grave moment.—Don Ramón del Valle-Inclán.—Victoria Kent, President, A.S.O.—Vicente Riscos, Secretary, A.S.O.[100] (A318)

During his daily periods in bed, he wrote feverishly. He devoted his energy principally to the lengthy series *El ruedo ibérico*, demonstrating his uninterrupted interest in the political history of Spain during the nineteenth century by working on new episodes entitled *El trueno dorado*.[101] He had envisioned continuing the series belatedly by writing a novel on Cuba, of which he had personal knowledge from earlier times:

I would like my historical narratives to reach a work entitled *Los campos de Cuba* . . . my view of the *mambí* and of the Spanish volunteer will cause a commotion.[102] (A319)

This interest in politics was carried through in various articles he published during this period. His acuity was exemplified in one in which he grins at the hope of Bourbon supporters to restore the monarchy with Don Juan, the son of Alfonso XIII:

"In January, Juan the Third." This motto—undoubtedly more coarse than the usual heraldic and arms mottoes—held the prediction and promise of faithful monarchists not too long ago. That January passed and the prognostication came to naught, as is often the case with similar predictions of the true Zaragozan. Now the announcements are of Hymen. The nuptial motto has yet to be trocheed; but the cause has noted poets, so there will be no lack of inspiration in the hallelujah being readied for the occasion. It will be a motto, if not from an armoury, then from a candy shop, one of those found on the red and gold ribbons that enfold wedding sweets.[103] (A320)

His confinement notwithstanding, Valle-Inclán's interests still extended beyond Spanish borders. His involvement with international movements was reinforced during 1935. His importance in the world intellectual community led to his installation as one of the twelve praesidium members of the Association Internationale des Escrivains pour la Defense de la Culture, which had its first Congrés Internationale in Paris, 21–25 June.[104] His delicate health impeded his attendance, as it had in 1932 at the other international meeting of prominent writers.

But there were compensations. In July of that year, Victoriano García Martí organized Valle-Inclán's many friends in Galicia and elsewhere in an attempt to collect enough money to purchase an estate for him, hoping thereby to fulfill a dream the poet had expressed in "Karma," in his volume *El pasajero*:

I want to erect a house
Like the meaning of my life,
Leaving my soul in the stone
Edified.

I want to build my retreat
Centered in a Latin grove,
Horatian Latin and Byzantine
Grimoire Spells.

I want my honest manhood
To pass to son and grandson,
Restoring through my scepter
Its Respect.

Like a pyramid, my house
Will be a sanctum of death.
The breeze that furls my chlamys,
Tertiary.

I want my rustic retreat
With a patio facing East,
On which I can meditate
Devoutly.

I want a Stoic house
Walled in the stone of Barbanza,
Seneca's house, heroic
In Restraint.

And let it be built of stone.
My house, the Karma of clan,
With ivy one day entwined
On the dolmen of Valle-Inclán.[105] (A321)

On 2 August there was promulgated a statement regarding the intent of his friends to collect funds for the house; it was signed by outstanding writers, painters, politicians, and other citizens of Santiago de Compostela. The motion reached Madrid, where it received greater dispersion through *El Sol* than it had previously.[106] But the process of enlisting sufficient public support became involved and lengthy. The months of summer passed into those of fall and still the funds had not been raised. The projected gift was never realized.

In mid-September 1935 Valle-Inclán made a one-day excursion to the Galician city of Orense, which he had never visited. He was accompanied by his son Carlos and Joaquín Arias Sanjurjo. They were met by Ramón Otero Pedrayo, who was serving as Valle-Inclán's guide to the sights of the city that had once been the court of Suevian kings. After dining at Fornos, Valle-Inclán visited the Plaza Mayor and the Cathedral, joined by Julio Alonso Cuevillas, a companion in Santiago when both were students at the university. The day was spent between touring and conversing; with the approach of evening Valle-Inclán and his party returned to Santiago.[107]

Work continued to occupy him. Having published a series of studies on the nineteenth century in *Ahora*, he turned to contemporary matters. What was to be his last published article[108] dealt with Manuel Azaña's book *Mi rebelión en Barcelona*, in which the former Republican leader explained the incidents that led to his arrest and trial in connection with the Catalonian revolt of October 1934. Valle-Inclán's article was a tribute to a friend as well as to a man he respected; after citing an intrigue during the reign of Isabel II concerning an attack on one of the ministers by his political adversaries, he went on to draw a parallel with the accusations brought against Azaña. But Valle-Inclán also indicates that some good resulted from the evil that Azaña had suffered:

To one who is astute, jail is the mother of counsel. And, without even celebrating the fact that the enemies of the great Republican have honored him with such hard schooling, it could be considered a fortunate rigor on seeing the ripened fruit that is the book. If it's of great importance to one's regard for national affairs to have the knowledge obtained by tramping through sun and rain with seven-league boots, no less important is that derived from pacing back and forth, day after day, in a dungeon, contemplating the moon atop the barred skylight. When it is the result of unjust persecution, jail offers a noble laurel wreath.[109] (A322)

And, indeed, as Valle-Inclán estimated in his article, Azaña's arrest and trial (with its absolution) made the political leader a hero and gave him unquestioned control of the Frente Popular, a coalition of leftist groups. Eventually, this popularity and experience would lead Azaña to be chosen the second president of the Republic, as Valle-Inclán also predicted.

The thoughts of Valle-Inclán also turned to his own life. With a new attack of his old illness in November, he saw the quickly approaching end to his life and sought to review its pains and joys. And yet, he would remember the sorrow of others, as in the case of the family of Luis Bello, who died on 7 November 1935; Valle-Inclán sent a telegram to Manuel Azaña from the hospital in Santiago:

I beg you manifest deepest sorrow Bello family and represent me burial rite. Count on me for whatever may be necessary. Greetings. Valle-Inclán.[110] (A323)

He began what was to be his last year with his memories and the knowledge that he had been true to his ideals. These were his only possessions; he did not even own copies of his own books, everything having been sold during his most recent period of need. To reap once again the personal satisfaction of *Tirano Banderas*, which he considered his best novel, he had to borrow a copy from Dr. García Sabell. The generosity of friends made it possible for him to read those books that interested him; it was this reading that helped to distract him from his pain:

A recluse in a sanatorium and more ill perhaps than even I suspect, I distract myself from my illness and afflictions with amiable readings.[111] (A324)

Even the exercise of writing became protracted as his pain increased; often, he had to employ the aid of friends in dictating the occasional paragraphs of *El ruedo ibérico*. Nonetheless, he continued to write, aware that his time was limited and that death would arrive, as Keats said, "before my pen has gleaned my teeming brain." He was preoccupied, too, with the attitude of posterity toward his work and frequently instructed his son and friends to care for future editions so that they would represent him faithfully.

The pain he experienced was no longer bearable with the fortitude and heroism of youth. It had become a challenge to his prized serenity and endurance, as attested by a scribbled note to his doctor:

Come to see me. The terrible pains have returned and I'm on the verge of complaining like a woman.[112] (A325)

There was no need for him to hide his suffering any longer. In a letter to Fernández Almagro, dated 5 December 1935, Valle-Inclán gave yet another written notice of his condition:

The body is not lacking in pain nor the spirit in sorrow. Everything comes together at the end of my life.[113] (A326)

This time, Valle-Inclán knew, the macabre dance of death would accomplish its end. As he believed any Celt should intuit, Valle-Inclán knew that the moment of his death was at hand. Not raging "against the dying of the light," as Dylan Thomas would advise, Valle-Inclán gave himself gently, with dignity, and further instructed son and friends:

I want to purge my dying of any semblance of ceremony. . . . I don't want death notices published . . . Have my body placed in a modest coffin, and at no time should there be any ostentation in the funeral rites.[114]

Let it be a civil burial . . . no discreet priest, or humble friar, or know-it-all Jesuit.[115] (A327)

Listening to the plea for a simple, secular burial were his son Carlos, who was at the start of his medical studies at the Facultad de Medicina, the doctors Villar Iglesias, García Sabell, Manuel Villar Blanco, Ardicey, Castro, and Deveso, as well as many friends, among them Andrés Díaz de Rábago, Santiso Girón, Arturo Cuadrado, and Fernando Barros Pumariño. Valle-Inclán uttered his memorable sentences as they listened to his still resonant voice:

Look. Death is regal, dignified. Shortly before dying, the Lord arrives with candles, prayers, and processional canopies. My ancestors all had their rooms decked with flowers, the bedspreads with the best Caramiñas lace, the newest clothes, and received the Lord standing. It wouldn't do to await the Lord while lying on the bed of one's sins. . . . But, since I'm not a believer . . . [116] (A328)

Some, like Díaz de Rábago, were dismayed at his refusal to receive the sacraments of the Church, but Valle-Inclán had brought his body to die in Santiago de Compostela, the holy city, in what could be seen as a mystical pilgrimage reminiscent of that described in *La lámpara maravillosa*. In that work he also wrote of the moment of death:

How often the full secret of a life is disclosed in the rigor of death! There is an expression that is mine alone, only one, but it is effaced like the profile on a medal through the mundane passing of days and the vain flight of hours. My face wears a hundred fictional masks that succeed each other under the base dictates of an insignificant fate. Perhaps my true expression has yet to reveal itself; perhaps it cannot emerge from under the numerous veils accumulated day after day and interwoven by my many hours. I myself do not know who I am; perhaps I am condemned to suffer that ignorance forever. I ask myself frequently which among all the sins is mine and so interrogate the masks of vice: Arrogance, Lust, Vanity, and Envy have left their imprints on my carnal face as well as on my spiritual demeanor; yet I know that all but one will disappear in due course, that one to remain fixed on my features when death arrives. On that earthly day—when eyes with stiff lashes and wax lids sink into violet hollows, when the forehead raises its brow in seeming flight, when the nose is profiled in anguishing transparency, when the ligaments of the jaw slacken the lips into a smile they had never worn before—my unique expression, which perhaps had never been seen and yet was mine, will reclaim its dominion over the immobility of death. . . Let us contemplate ourselves within our very selves until we discover in our consciousness that virtue or sin which is the root of its eternal responsibility; we will find it stilled and substantiated in an expression. [117] (A329)

Nonetheless, to die in the gloom of the rain-washed mystical city was difficult and valorous:

"How terrible it is to die among these greys! . . . How hard it is!" [118] (A330)

His agony ended at 2:00 p.m. on Sunday, 5 January 1936. The tolling of the hour by the bells of the great Cathedral seemed to announce his death to the Galician landscape and its populace. He died in the same month as his father, nine days short of the day of his sire's demise.

Valle-Inclán's death had both predictable and unpredictable repercussions. The sorrow of his relatives and friends needs no notation, but the widespread response that his death elicited was unforeseeable in its full dimension. Local, national, and world presses carried the notice of his passing and followed it with countless articles on the man and his works. Galician nationalists, looking for a spark to assist their cause, attempted to add pomp and circumstance to his burial with the proposal that his remains be placed alongside those of Rosalía de Castro in the Iglesia de Santo Domingo. From Madrid came urgent requests to transfer the body into the care of the Republic for a fitting national tribute.[119] Officials of Santiago declared 6 January as a day of mourning. All of Galicia recognized the loss while Spain began to realize the real worth of the man and writer it had largely ignored.

The trustees of Valle-Inclán's last requests could not be persuaded to veer from his instructions; these were followed as literally as possible. On the day after his death, suitably the feast of the Magi, Valle-Inclán's body was placed in a simple coffin reputed to have cost twenty pesetas and was borne through the rain-swept streets to the cemetery of Boisaca on the outskirts of Santiago. Among the mourners were those who had been with Valle-Inclán at his deathbed, as well as Villar Ponte, Plácido Castro, Otero Pedrayo, Anxel Fole, Martínez López, Francisco Fernández del Riego, and many others.[120]

Newspaper accounts did not carry the complete story of the burial, however. At a plot donated by city officials, Valle-Inclán's coffin was readied for lowering into a wet and muddy grave. The setting was perfect for the gruesome episode that ensued. As the gravediggers were releasing slowly their burdened ropes one of the mourners, identified as a young sculptor named Modesto Pasín, hurled himself at the coffin trying to wrest from its lid a wooden cross placed there despite Valle-Inclán's wishes. His passionate attempt to carry out Valle-Inclán's request for a civil ceremony was successful, but not before he had tumbled into the grave atop a broken lid that exposed the body beneath it. The rain, the mud, and the darkness heightened the grotesqueness of the incident, which rivaled the spectral scene at the opening of Romance de lobos. Having emerged somewhat shaken but triumphant, Modesto Pasín disappeared while hasty repairs were made on the coffin. There were no words spoken over the body. The burial was concluded with dispatch.[121]

The most impressive of the tributes were convened by the Ateneo de Madrid under the direction of Rafael Alberti and María Teresa León, both of whom had been with Valle-Inclán in Rome. The affair was held at the Teatro de la Zarzuela on the evening of 14 February 1936. First, Federico García Lorca mentioned poems that Rubén Darío had written for Valle-

Inclán and then gave a dramatic reading of the prologue for *Voces de gesta*; Luis Cernuda read comments about Valle-Inclán written by Juan Ramón Jiménez; Rafael Alberti and Antonio Machado gave their tributes; and Francisco Vighi related many of the anecdotes that had made Valle-Inclán notorious. The highlight of the gathering was the Spanish premiere of *Los cuernos de don Friolera*, performed by the theatre group "Nueva Escena."

Not everyone was pleased by the homage to Valle-Inclán. His children and other relatives opposed the event, while his former wife, Josefina Blanco, produced a letter from Valle-Inclán that he had dictated a few days before his death, wherein he stated:

You know how it upsets me to have my works performed. I know no greater torment to my aesthetic sensibility than to see one of my plays produced.[122] (A331)

The matter of the production was moot since Valle-Inclán's presence was not germane.

The tribute arranged by the Ateneo had a double edge. While its sincerity was unquestionable, a secondary motive is entirely possible. Spain was again in the midst of political jockeying, with new elections scheduled for 18 February. The Ateneo, ardent supporter of the Frente Popular, led by its past president Manuel Azaña, wanted to stir Madrid into re-adopting the cause it had forsaken in the previous elections. The tribute to Valle-Inclán presented the ideal occasion for this, while the political satire of *Los cuernos de don Friolera* could not be more in point. The subsequent victory at the polls by Azaña would have pleased Valle-Inclán.

Valle-Inclán died on the eve of great upheavals on the Spanish scene. Civil disorders followed the election of the Frente Popular: land was seized by peasants; churches, seminaries, and other religious properties were looted and burned; prisoners were freed; an anti-capitalistic wave of terror swept the country, accompanied by murder and assassination. From February through July there were hundreds of strikes and cases of violence, particularly against the Church. The wave of illegality that characterized the period culminated in the ouster of the moderate President Alcalá Zamora and the election of Azaña to the leadership post on 10 May by near-unanimous concensus. But neither the conscientious Azaña nor his minister, Santiago Casares Quiroga, were able to stem the violence. On 13 July, José Calvo Sotelo, a monarchist minister during the Primo de Rivera regime and later a leader of the conservatives, was assassinated. The event touched off a series of reprisals that bloodied the Spanish political scene even more.

Meanwhile, the disorder that the Republic could not quell was swelling the ranks of the Falange with discontents. The party was fast becoming a new political force, finding its strength primarily among the military, which had seen vast downgrading of its traditional status under the

Republican policy of de-emphasis. Five days after the assassination of Calvo Sotelo, General Francisco Franco led the garrison in Spanish Morocco into rebellion. The following day Franco began to ferry his troops into the peninsula with planes and ships provided by Italy and Germany. Successful military coups took place all over Spain within a short time—in the important cities of Andalucia, throughout Galicia, in parts of Asturias and León, in the Basque provinces. Madrid and Barcelona alone remained secure strongholds of the Republic. Had these cities fallen, the conflagration that was the Spanish Civil War would have been averted. As it was, by the end of July the intervention of Russia and Mexico on behalf of the Republic and the support provided by Italy and Germany on the side of the Nationalists made Spain the rehearsal arena for a greater war. Extreme cruelty was the keynote of the hostilities, as evidenced by the mass murders of bishops and priests on the one hand, and the indiscriminate massacre at Badajoz and the bombing of Guernica, made memorable by Picasso, on the other hand.

In the wake of slaughter came death under many guises. Some died as a result of personal hatred; among these were Federico García Lorca and Ramiro de Maeztu. Still others died because their time had come: Pedro Muñoz Seca, Francisco Villaespesa, Emilio Cotarelo Mori. The demise of Miguel de Unamuno on 31 December closed 1936 on yet another tragic note. The death of Valle-Inclán at the very beginning of the year, of Ramiro de Maeztu on 11 November, and of Unamuno on the last day, making 1936 a year of losses and marking the erosion of the "Generación del '98," signaled an end to a way of thinking, living, and dying. Valle-Inclán, at least, did not have to witness the ultimate *Esperpento*: the spectacle of a Spain broken by the Civil War.

Coda

The death of Valle-Inclán brought an end only to the physical reality that was the Man. The works of the Artist and the anecdotal personality of the Mask remained behind to affect the reputation of the magnificent figure of Valle-Inclán. It remained for posterity to dilute the prejudice that clouded his career and to place him on a proper pedestal among the great. That judgment has been given at numerous international events in 1966 and 1986 honoring respectively the centennial of his birth and the semi-centennial of his death.

The complexity of Valle-Inclán has been made manifest in the facts of his life, in the development of his aesthetic, and in the creation of his personality. Each facet, distinct at first, moved steadily toward a merger with the others during mutual evolution. As the Man grew in age and in experience, he became more aware of the Artist that he contained (or the daemon that possessed him); he strove to create a Mask in conjunction with that discovery and to give expression in his writings to the ideology he envisioned. The process required the stirring of his latent individuality and metaphysics. His daemon began to emerge through this self-evaluation and declared itself forcibly in the context of thought, attitude, and action.

The earliest indication was the alteration of his physical appearance through the adoption of cape, beard, and mane, symbols of the romantic and of the bohemian. This was paralleled by changes in his point of view toward life and art. Valle-Inclán dedicated himself to the assimilation of the Man, the Artist, the Mask into a whole, the personification of his ideal. Although he knew that the accomplishment of his end (perfection) was impossible in the human context, he knew as well that unless the attempt were made life would have no meaning. Recognizing that veracity, he interminably revised and polished everything that concerned him so that the totality he sought might be approached in a complete lifetime. The Aristotelian concept guided his existence on the three levels.

Through the devices of imagination he fashioned a world in which he could exist more fully, more meaningfully, at the same time that he lived among other men. This was not mere escapism. It represented an aspiration to rise above his imprisoning humanity, the same desire that motivated the mystic. The seeming irrationality of such a quest is a denominator common to all men, although one that few recognize or dare permit more than dalliance. The man of vision, however, "sees" beyond his own poor humanity and aspires to possess apocalyptic rewards that he knows exist on a level awkwardly termed "the supernatural." How to acquire those rewards is the problem that the individual must resolve for himself in an aloneness that cannot be dispelled. Valle-Inclán understood this. Exactly mid-way in his literary career he produced *La lámpara maravillosa*, his apologia, wherein he allied all facets of his existence in the search for fulfillment. It is that revelatory work that best consolidates the Man, the Artist, the Mask in the oneness requisite for the attainment of the mystical experience.

Once the initiatory phase of his early career had been concretized in his auto-conception, Valle-Inclán could embark on the journey described in his aesthetic treatise. Like the Cartesian philosopher, he proceeded from his particulars to the whole. He thought first, "Cogito, ergo sum." And on this certainty he built a series of truths by which he guided his existence. In thinking he created himself. He became his own best character, a figure fashioned from the sinews and the marrow of a pure aesthetic, who played out his unequivocal and fascinating role on the theater of life, like a protagonist from Shakespeare or from Calderón's pen. He united Man, Artist, Mask in a figure larger than life. In so doing, Valle-Inclán emerged as an entity of memorable proportions.

Notes

Notes for Preface

1. The Library of Congress erroneously lists Valle-Inclán's year of birth as 1870 (see Cataloging-in-Publication Data) despite efforts by many to have them make the correction.
2. All translations from *La lámpara maravillosa* are from Ramón del Valle-Inclán, *The Lamp of Marvels*, trans. by Robert Lima (West Stockbridge, MA.: Lindisfarne Press, 1986). Note citations are to the Spanish only.

Notes for Chapter 1: Origins

1. *Obras completas de don Ramón del Valle-Inclán*, vol. 2 (Madrid: Talleres Tipográficos de Rivadeneyra, 1944), 1908–9. Unless otherwise indicated, all quotations from Valle-Inclán's works are from volumes 1 and 2 of this work, hereafter cited as *OC*. To date, there are no critical editions of the works of Valle-Inclán that establish definitive texts.
2. *OC*, 2:1897.
3. See Alvaro Cunqueiro, "Parentes de don Ramón por parte das estrelas," *Grial* 13 (July-September 1966): 347–51.
4. Folio 101, Book 7: "On the thirty-first of October of the year one thousand eight hundred sixty-six. . . . I, the undersigned Bachelor, Parish priest of San Cipriano de Cálago in Villanueva de Arosa, in that parish church solemnly baptized, anointed with the Holy Oils and named Ramón José Simón, a child born the previous day, twenty-eighth of the current month, at six in the morning, being the legitimate son of don Ramón Valle and doña Dolores Peña, residents of this town; the paternal grandparents: don Carlos, native of San Lorenzo de András, and doña Juana Vermudez, from the Puebla del Deán, parish of Caramiñal; the maternal: don Francisco, native of the Isla de Arosa, and doña Josefa Montenegro, from Santa María de Vigo. The godparents were don Francisco Peña and doña Josefa Montenegro, grandparents of the baptized and residents of this town, whom I informed of the relationship and other obligations that the Roman Ritual imposes. And so that it will be affirmed, I sign on the date listed above. Dr. José Bto. Rivas (Seal)."
Misreadings of the certification have created wrong impressions of the baptismal and birth dates. The entry was made on 31 October 1866. The text clearly states the child was born on 28 October, the date before the christening. More complications ensued when the entry appeared in Joaquín Pesqueira, "Don Ramón del Valle-Inclán," *El Correo Gallego* (12 January 1936); a typographical error gave the wrong year of birth.
This baptismal record was considered false when, in 1929, it was introduced to Valle-

Inclán's friends in Madrid; Enrique Diez-Canedo denied its validity most volubly. My own inspection of the document in the church records verified it without a doubt. Furthermore, Valle-Inclán's parochial and civil matrimonial records list his age as forty on 24 August 1907, months before his forty-first birthday. Nonetheless, Valle-Inclán himself compounded the error by insisting that he was born three years later, or four. On one occasion, in a letter to Tanis (Estanislao Pérez Rey) dated 25 October 1935, he asks for assistance to renew his expired passport with his legal name, place of birth, and age: "Ramón del Valle y de la Peña—native of Villanueva de Arosa. Age: 66 years. The priest who baptized me left out the Inclán, believing it to be the second name of my father and not one entire last name. Therefore, I require the document stating the wording of the baptismal certificate in order to validate a public document" (letter in my personal file; provided by Víctor Pérez Pita).

5. Carlos, Francisco, and María were the other children. Ramón del Valle Inclán Bermúdez had a daughter, Ramona, by a previous wife.

6. This period coincided with the European expansion of the Hallstatt Culture (ca. 900–400 B.C.) and the overlapping La Téne Era (ca. 500–15 B.C.).

7. Central to southern European Celts were characterized by a round head, broad face, broad and heavy nose, hazel gray eyes, chestnut-colored hair, medium height, thickset body. Nordic Celts were characterized by a long head and face, prominent and hooked nose, blue eyes, light-colored hair, great stature. These groups are intermixed in various shadings depending on period of migration and area settled. Both types appear in Galicia.

8. There is more than irony in the theory that the remains discovered in Iria Flavia were those not of St. James the Apostle but of Priscillian, the great heretic executed at Trier in 385.

9. Jerónimo del Hoyo, *Memorias del Arzobispo de Santiago* (1620?), ms. in the Archivo del Palacio Arzobispal, Santiago de Compostela: "There are in this town many noble persons and among the best in Galicia, as are . . . the Montenegros . . . who, although they possess houses in other parts, have owned property and lived in this town for a long time, some of them over two hundred years."

10. *OC*, 1:356.

11. José María Castroviejo, *Galicia—Guía espiritual de una tierra* (Madrid: Espasa-Calpe, 1960), 156–57, 161: "Almost nothing remains in Rua Nova of the ancient fortress that, besieged and annihilated in the XV century during the feudal struggles, was ultimately converted into an estate; it was entailed in 1740 to don Miguel Inclán (de los Santos) and doña Rosa Malvido (de la Rua). . . . The historic house was one of many fortresses of the Galician fiefdom; it belonged to the famous Grand Master of Ocampo; it was inherited by don Miguel de los Santos Inclán y Ocampo, Captain of Armored Cavalry, who died without heirs, being succeeded by his sister doña Antonia Inclán, married to don Luis Antonio del Valle (a nobleman). The academic Don Francisco del Valle-Inclán . . . descendant of this house, was the founder of the first Academia de la Lengua Gallega and of the first regional newspaper, *El Cantón Compostelano.*"

12. Ramón del Valle-Inclán, *Femeninas (Seis historias amorosas)*, prologue by Manuel Murguía (Pontevedra: Imprenta de A. Landín, 1895): "Nobility obliges. And the author of these pages knows it well. He is descended from a glorious family in which the illustriousness of blood, rather than a hindrance, was an inducement to great accomplishments. He has a double duty to accomplish. In the old days, his house included great captains and notable men of science and literature, the pride and glory of this poor Galicia. It is necessary, therefore, that he continue the uninterrupted tradition, and, as in the case of his predecessors, that he add one more laurel leaf to the crown of the homeland."

13. *OC*, 1:87.

14. Ibid., 127–28.

15. Ibid., 130, 131.

16. Ibid., 828–29.

17. *Escenas gallegas*, vol. 1 (Pontevedra: Tipografía de José Eiras García, 1894), 134 pp.

18. Murguía "How would it be possible to remain silent in the prologue to the son's book

about the intimate friendship that united me to his father? How could I not recall the old forgotten poet, that pure soul, that upright person, the one who bore the same names as the author of this book? It was only yesterday when, on the threshold of death, he extended his hand to me for the last time and we spoke of those things that were so dear to us for such a long time: the region of Galicia and the poetry that had enchanted his lonely hours. He knew that Death had already touched him; yet, that didn't mean that he felt so distant from the earth that he didn't think of his region or feel pained by the misfortunes of others. He who had known such misfortune himself! Rest, rest in peace, my good friend; your son follows the path you showed him through the example of a life more honest than most. Your son gathers on your behalf the laurels you might have earned had you not disdained them, content in the peace of the village. If you could see him now!"

19. Manuel Murguía, *España sus monumentos y artes. Su naturaleza e historia. Galicia* (Barcelona: D. Cortezo, 1888), 31–32.

20. José López Pinillos ("Parmeno"), "La vocación de Valle-Inclán," *Los favoritos de la multitud. Como se conquista la notoriedad* (Madrid: Editorial Pueyo, 1920), 153–60.

21. *OC*, 1:839.

22. See "Valle-Inclán y Góngora," *La Gaceta Literaria* (1 June 1927).

23. Interview with Juan López Nuñez, "Valle-Inclán," *Por Esos Mundos* (1 January 1915).

24. *OC*, 1:831.

25. Ibid., 243.

26. Ibid., 551.

27. The deep friendship between Valle-Inclán's father and the Muruaís family is evidenced in an elegy written by Valle Inclán y Bermúdez on the death of Andrés Muruáis, brother of Jesús, in 1882.

28. Record of the Universidad de Santiago de Compostela, No. 115. p.230. The left margin of the letter bears several notations in other hands; below one stating, "He provided proof," is written, "I know this student personally . . . A. Milón."

29. Díaz de Rábago had married a daughter of General Aguiar; the name Aguiar would figure prominently years later in the genealogy of the Marqués de Bradomín.

30. José Fernández Ferreiro, "Valle-Inclán, estudiante." *ABC* (2 November 1966): 63: "It is now recalled in café chats that when Valle-Inclán studied law at the University of Santiago de Compostela, he earned some money—of which he had very little—by giving private lessons in the homes of several noble families."

31. *OC*, 1:820–22.

32. It was Seoane to whom Valle-Inclán dedicated his first book, *Femeninas*, in 1895.

33. See Antonio Iglesias Laguna, "Valle-Inclán, La Restauración, El Ateneo," *La Estafeta Literaria* 274 (1963): 19.

34. López Pinillos, "La vocación," 154.

35. Francisco Madrid, *La vida altiva de Valle-Inclán* (Buenos Aires: Poseidon, 1943), 294.

36. Ibid., 293.

37. Among the works in which Zorrilla figures prominently are "En tranvía," *El Globo* (1 February 1892); "Los últimos versos del Duque de Rivas," *El Correo Español* (4 May 1892); "Como escribió Zorrilla *Don Juan Tenorio*," *El Universal* (7 June 1892); "El conspirador de las melenas," *El Universal* (17 July 1892).

38. In a lecture entitled "Semblanzas de literatos españoles," F. Madrid, *La vida altiva*, 293–94.

39. "En Molinares," *Café con Gotas* (4 November 1888); "Babel," *Café con Gotas* (11 November 1888); "A media noche," *La Ilustración Ibérica* 7, 317 (26 January 1889): 59, 62. This last story contains the first-known mention of the word "Bradomín," as the name of a church. Two accounts of Valle-Inclán's earliest writings appeared in *Bulletin Hispanique* 58, 4 (1955): Charles V. Aubrun, "Les débuts littéraires de Valle-Inclán," 331–33, and Simone Saillard, "Le premier conte et le premier roman de Valle-Inclán," 421–29. The latter critic reprinted "Babel," generally considered to be Valle-Inclán's first published work. However, José Caamaño Bournacell,

Por las rutas turísticas de Valle-Inclán, states: "Number 21 of *Café con Gotas*, dated April 15, 1888, is dedicated to the memory of the chemist Antonio Casares, who had died two days earlier, and it would appear that its pages contain an unsigned article by Valle-Inclán. According to references which we have been unable to verify, Valle-Inclán was submitting contributions during this period to *El País* and *Barcelona Cómica*." Domingo García-Sabell, "El gesto único de Don Ramón," *Insula* 236–37 (July-August 1966), 31, adds, "I also possess the original of a ballad in Castilian, dated 1888, most likely written in Santiago during his student days, no doubt unpublished. But all these things, which certainly lend themselves to interesting literary speculation, are but an outline, a fragmentary sketch of what is to come."

40. *Indice de Armas y Letras* (May-June 1954).
41. López Pinillos, "La vocación," 154–55.
42. *OC*, 1:778.
43. Ramón Gómez de la Serna, *Don Ramón María del Valle-Inclán*, 23.
44. López Pinillos, "La vocación," 155.

Notes for Chapter 2: Emergence

1. "Psiquismo," *El Universal* (7 August 1892). William L. Fichter, *Publicaciones periodísticas de Don Ramón del Valle-Inclán anteriores a 1895*, 26, attempts to deny the visit: "But it is almost unbelievable that he could have attended. . . . This is, certainly, nothing more than another example of Don Ramón's habit of imagining experiences and adventures for himself."
2. Gina Lombroso Ferrero, *Cesare Lombroso, storia della vita a delle opere* (Turin: 1915), 301–2.
3. "El Mendigo," *El Heraldo de Madrid* (7 June 1891). This is a short story.
4. There is a total of six articles and two stories: "A media noche" (30 July 1891); "Angel Guerra, novela original de D. Benito Pérez Galdós" (13 August 1891); "Una visita al convento de Gondarín" (22 September 1891); "Cartas galicianas: De Madrid a Monforte—El último hidalgo de Tor" (2 October 1891); "Cartas galicianas: Pontevedra—Una visita a Echegaray" (13 October 1891); "Cartas galicianas: Por la tierra saliniense—El castillo de Lobeira" (4 November 1891); "El rey de la máscara" (20 January 1892); "En tranvía" (1 February 1892). Charles V. Aubrun, "Les débuts littéraires de Valle-Inclán," *Bulletin Hispanique* 58, 4 (1955), has pointed out the similarities between Valle's last "Cartas galicianas" and his father's "El castillo de Lobeira" (*Crónica de Pontevedra* [23, 25 August 1886]). In "El rey de la máscara" the author again uses the name Bradomín, this time referring to "the lord abbot of Bradomín." While these articles and stories are signed as indicated, it is curious that a caricature of Valle in *El País Gallego*, 1891, is accompanied by a short verse with an early reference to the name he adopted in April 1892: "His critical stance / turns into idolatry / at the very mention of Chateaubriand / who is an obsession / for Ramón del Valle-Inclán."
5. (3, 4, February 1892): 2458, 2459. These fragments, as stated in an editorial note, "will not permit a proper assessment of the novel *El gran obstáculo*, but will allow the reader to sample the fine style of the learned editor of *El Globo*." Simone Saillard, "Le premier conte et le premier roman de Valle-Inclán," *Bulletin Hispanique* 58, 4 (1955), has reprinted these excerpts and produced a study showing how this work is reflected in later ones.
6. (6 February 1892); first published in *El Globo* (1 February 1892).
7. Caamaño Bournacell, *Por las rutas turísticas de Valle-Inclán*, 78, gives a newspaper account of the lecture but does not cite the source.
8. José López Pinillos, "La vocación de Valle-Inclán," *Los favoritos de la multitud. Como se conquista la notoriedad* (Madrid: Editorial Pueyo, 1920), 157. The details of this trip have been difficult to establish and some remain unsettled. Valle arrived in Veracruz, Mexico, on 8 April 1892 aboard the *Havre*, as announced in *El Monitor Republicano* (12 April 1892): "Maritime activity. Veracruz, 8th of April of 1892. Passengers on the French ship 'Havre' from Amberes and other ports: Spaniards—Valle Pena . . . " Further evidence is the dating of Valle's story "La Generala" on board the *Havre* as April 1892.

My correspondence with Cie. Commerciale de Transports a Vapeur Français, owners of the ship in question, has not produced sailing date, verification of the place of embarkation, or itinerary, information necessary to clarify whether Valle visited Cuba *before* his arrival in Mexico (see fn. 41). He certainly could have embarked on the *Havre* in Cuba after a stay there, which, making the 1892 stay in Italy impossible, supports the 1891 visit.

9. Interview by Roberto Barrios in *El Universal* (19 September 1921).

10. *Obras completas de don Ramón del Valle-Inclán*, vol. 2 (Madrid: Talleres Tipográficos de Rivadeneyra, 1944), 1891. Unless otherwise indicated, all quotations from Valle-Inclán's works are from volumes 1 and 2 of this work, hereafter cited as *OC*.

11. *El Universal* (16 June 1892). This sketch may have been influenced by Bernal Díaz del Castillo's *Historia de la conquista de Nueva España* or by its French translation *La conque* by the Parnassian José Maria de Hérédia. "Bajo los trópicos" was incorporated into "La Niña Chole," where Valle reinforced the view of Veracruz: "The 'Dalila' anchored in the waters of Villa Rica de Veracruz. With my soul captivated by religious emotion, I contemplated the scorching beach. . . . O! How beautiful those tropical countries are! Whoever sees them will never forget them. . . . My thoughts are rejuvenated today remembering the immense silvery reach of that Mexican gulf, which I haven't experienced again. The towers of Veracruz pass through my memory; the forests of Campeche; the sands of Yucatan; the palaces of Palenque; the palm trees of Tuxpan and Laguna."

12. López Pinillos, "La vocación," 157–58.

13. Melchor Fernández Almagro, *Vida y literatura de Valle-Inclán* (Madrid: Editora Nacional, 1943), 25, states that Valle used "some relatives of his who had a business in Veracruz" as a pretext to emigrate. He continues, "During the trip Valle struck up a friendship with an Asturian named Menéndez Acebal, who lived in Veracruz, where he had a printing shop and published a daily newspaper entitled *El Veracruzano Libre*, or something along those lines." According to the biographer, Valle accepted a position offered on this newspaper. While the first statement seems plausible enough, the one affirming Valle's association with the newspaper has to be denounced. Fichter, *Publicaciones periodísticas*, 28–29, indicates there was no periodical by that name; and there is no record of Valle's affiliation with a newspaper in Veracruz. In fact, Valle could not have stayed in Veracruz for more than a few weeks because his journalistic career in Mexico City began in April, the month he arrived in Mexico. These errors are not corrected in Fernández Almagro, 2d ed. (Madrid: Taurus, 1966). Even though I refer to the 1966 edition here, all references to Almagro's work are to the 1943 edition.

Fernández Almagro also errs in claiming Valle held an editorial post in Mexico City with *El Imparcial* (26). Fichter again points out the discrepancies in this statement (28); in another context, he quotes a letter dated 15 May 1892 supporting Valle's early appearance in the capital: "Sr. Valle-Inclán is a young, already-known Spanish journalist. . . . He has been in Mexico for a month and is an editor of our colleague *El Correo Español*" (34).

14. "Consejos de la musa" (17 April 1892); "Adiós para siempre" (24 April 1892); "En el tranvia" (24 April 1892), previously published in *El Globo* and in *Diario de Pontevedra* as "En tranvia"; "Tristana" (27 April 1892); "A Maximina" (1 May 1892); "Los ultimos versos del Duque de Rivas" (4 May 1892); "A una mujer ausente por la muerte" (8 May 1892), a poem that Aubrun, "Les débuts," has shown to be a slight revision of one written by Valle-Inclán's father.

15. Stories: "Zan el de los osos" (8 May 1892); "Bajo los trópicos" (16 June 1892); "Caritativa" (19 June 1892); "Los caminos de mi tierra" (22 June 1892), a revision of "A media noche;" "El canario" (26 June 1892); "¡Ah! de mis muertos" (3 July 1892); "La confesión" (10 July 1892); "El conspirador de las melanas (Histórico)" (17 July 1892). Articles: See J. Rubia Barcia, *A Bio-bibliography and Iconography of Valle-Inclán (1866–1936)*, 93–94. See also Javier Serrano Alonso, ed., *Ramón del Valle-Inclán. Artículos completos y otras páginas olvidadas* (Madrid: Ediciones Istmo, 1987), 54–58.

16. Salvador de Madariaga, *De Galdós a Lorca* (Buenos Aires: Editorial Sudamericana, 1960), 169–71, states, "A good name is as necessary for a writer as a good frame is for a painting. . . .

Don Ramón María del Valle-Inclán is a poet with an excellent ear for the sounds and rhythms of the language. It is fitting, therefore, that his name naturally evoke a heroic hendecasyllable, if one with a modern turn. . . . This name is representative of our poet for other of his aspects, no less typical—thus, the sense of form that it discloses . . . thus, its chivalric sonority . . . thus, the symbolic María . . . the audacity of such a high-sounding name . . . which indicates that Don Ramón María del Valle-Inclán is not afraid to be unique and unfashionable."

17. In his "Estudio preliminar," Fichter, *Publicaciones periodísticas*, 13–15, points out some of Valle's stylistic leanings in works published before Mexico: "A note of mystery . . . pairs of adjectives . . . the dialogue is still sufficiently natural.· . . . The setting is Galicia—another typical touch . . . there appears for the first time an example of two adjectives followed by a comparison, as if in anticipation of the formula that would later be so characteristic . . . he hasn't learned as yet how to avoid overly long sentences."

18. Barrios, Interview in *El Universal*.

19. *El Pais Gallego* (1891) and *El Universal* (15 May 1892).

20. Ramón del Valle-Inclán, "Autobiografía," *Alma Española* 1, 8 (27 December 1903). This material, with variations, also appears in *Sonata de estío*, which, in turn, used sections published earlier in "Bajo los trópicos" and in "La Niña Chole." For the factual side of this autobiography see the end of Chapter 3.

21. Francisco Madrid, *La vida altiva de Valle-Inclán*, 160.

22. Angel Sol, "Aventuras novelescas de Valle-Inclán" *Excelsior* (19 January 1936).

23. Ricardo Baroja, "Valle-Inclán, en el café," *La Pluma* (January 1923): 51.

24. F. Madrid, *La vida altiva*, 163, quotes from an article published by Valle-Inclán in Mexico: "how beneficial is the tyranny of certain dictators to some peoples."

25. "Gachupín" is a derisive term used by Mexicans to refer to Spaniards. Here, the use is playful since he was a defender of Mexico. Ramón Gómez de la Serna, *Don Ramón María del Valle-Inclán*, 25.

26. F. Madrid, *La vida altiva*, 164.

27. *El Tiempo* (12 May 1892): "Being a Mexican, I love my country and note with sadness that a large number of the Spaniards who come here now do so to demoralize the country, and that is why I will impugn with my entire being all that may tend to defend, not the mother country, which I will always revere, but the trash that she constantly heaps upon us and that comes here solely motivated by personal gain, trampling whatever we hold dear and sacred."

28. "Duelo pendiente. Don Ramón del Valle-Inclán y don Victoriano Agüeros," *El Universal* (15 May 1892).

29. "Lance terminado," *El Correo Español* (18 May 1892). The letter by Agüeros reads, in part: "I am unable to disclose the name of the author of the Letter, unless that person authorizes me to do so. And, insofar as my responsibility for having published it in *El Tiempo*, I assume it, but refusing any solidarity with the ideas expressed therein, which, well or badly, I have refuted. Lastly, I make it clear to you so that you can convey it to Sr. Valle-Inclán, that his name is not among those suppressed in the published letter, nor can I assume that he is included in the generality alluded to in the letter since I have no motive whatever to doubt his honorability." The facts of the event have been garbled in conflicting reports having their basis in anecdotes, such as those promulgated by Valle-Inclán himself, mildest of which is, "On disembarking, I went from the dock to a newspaper office, having just read an insult directed at all Spaniards, from Hernán Cortés to the latest arrival . . . that is, me. What a commotion I stirred up! But had I been Hernán Cortés, I would have finished all of them off" (Gómez de la Serna, *Don Ramón María del Valle-Inclán*, 25). Such tales led to the erroneous statements by his biographers that the incident occurred in Veracruz; the correct and complete statement is found in Fichter, *Publicaciones periodísticas*, 29–35. A version of the "duel" appeared in "Un periodista gallego en México," *Diario de Pontevedra* (15 June 1892).

30. *El Universal* (20 May 1892). The previous day this newspaper announced, "To all Spaniards. The noted writer D. Ramón del Valle-Inclán has joined our Editorial Staff to write about Spain in our pages. . . . Our intent is that *El Universal* deal with matters pertinent to Spain—

political, literary or social—from a Spanish perspective, and that is the charge given to Sr. Valle-Inclán. We believe that the Spanish readers of *El Universal* will be very pleased by the addition of such an elegant writer to our staff."

31. Writing in a Latin American periodical on his friendship with Valle-Inclán, the Mexican poet José Juan Tablada (author of *Bestiario*) gives his impressions of him when they first met in Mexico in 1892: "Ah, Don Ramón del Valle-Inclán! Mage, demiurge, friend of Rubén Darío . . . ; upholder of immortal Spain amidst Floral Games weakened by rhetorical vanities! . . . To me, you are more! . . . Because you have fraternally partaken of our *mole*, have smoked our marijuana, and have loved our Niña Chole! And have taken into your extraordinary heart the juice of the maguey, the fruit of the nopal and the heat of our sun . . . You were then part of . . . Mexico." The article was reprinted as "Una bella excitación al recuerdo de José Juan tablada a Don Ramón del Valle-Inclán," *Cosmópolis* 43 (1922): 265–68.

32. López Pinillos, "La vocación," 159.

33. Fernández Almagro, *Vida y literatura*, 29: "He returned with a clear perception of his literary destiny and with that world created by his pipe of marijuana." Gómez de la Serna, *Don Ramón María del Valle-Inclán*, 103: "He acted as if he were a fakir, not only because he hardly ate but also because he smoked hashish." Ramón Pérez de Ayala, *Divagaciones literarias* (Madrid: Biblioteca Nueva, 1958), 203: "He doesn't smoke in public. It would appear that when he's alone, he smokes marijuana, the grass of dreams." Francisco Villaespesa, "Tertulia," *Obras completas*, vol. 2 (Madrid Aguilar, 1954), 979–80: "And there is no other palette, / nor will another be as rich and sovereign, / as that of his passionate fantasy / as visionary and poet, / toxin of sun and marijuana." Ramón Sender, *Examen de ingenios: Los noventayochos* (New York.: Las Américas, 1961), 79, 80: "I recall an afternoon in his quarters on Progreso Street in Madrid . . . in the days of the Republic . . . While lying on an enormous bed, Valle-Inclán smoked his pipe of kiff, a habit from the good old Modernist days. . . . Under the blue smoke of the kiff, Valle-Inclán recalled the stages in the approach to God."

34. *OC*, 2:1966–67.

35. Ramón del Valle-Inclán, *La media noche. Visión estelar de un momento de guerra* (Madrid: Imprenta Clásica Española, 1917), 8.

36. Buenos Aires, Teatro Nacional, 28 June 1910. Cf. F. Madrid, *La vida altiva*, 193–94.

37. "Psiquismo," *El Universal* (7 August 1892), in which he promises to discuss the subject further "in another article." Undoubtedly he planned to continue on the staff of *El Universal*.

38. Juan Naya Pérez, "Valle-Inclán y Murguía. El prólogo de *Femeninas" Boletín de la Real Academia Gallega* 29 (1959): 53–54.

39. Ibid. Fernández Almagro, *Vida y literatura*, 28, does not accept this dating: "Without going through Paris—as he would have it by dating 'La Niña Chole' there—he finally returned to Spain—Spring of 1893." Rubia Barcia, *Bibliography and Iconography*, 7, echoes in fn. 22: "He dated 'La Niña Chole' in Paris in spite of the fact that he had not been there." Neither biographer gives any reason for denying the locale. Both, however, accept the dating of the other stories in the collection without question. A piece of information, though hardly conclusive, in support of Valle's stay in Paris can be found in Benavente's *La comida de las fieras*, where he says of Teófilo Everit, a character patterned on Valle-Inclán: "He was a smash in Paris; we met him in a cabaret in Montmartre."

40. There is no doubt that he visited Cuba during this journey to America. But there is conjecture as to when this visit took place (see fn. 8). Fernández Almagro, *Vida y literatura*, 28, asserts: "When Valle considers his Mexican stay over, he decides to return to Spain. But not until he stops for a time in Cuba, as the guest of the González de Mendoza family at their San Nicolás plantation in the province of Matanzas." This is the most plausible conclusion within the scheme of events and evidence indicated in the text. However, there is one version that presents the occurrence of the visit to Cuba in 1892, before Valle-Inclán's arrival in Mexico. In "Las dos visitas de Valle-Inclán a Cuba," *El Nacional* (11 April 1957), Salvador Bueno quotes from a letter published in *ABC* by an old Cuban employed at the plantation where Valle-Inclán stayed, supposedly in 1892 prior to his arrival in Mexico: "When the ship docked in Havana,

Valle and González de Mendoza took the train to Güines, up to the switching point for the sugar plantation, where the author of the *Sonatas* stayed for some three months." There is no other affirmation of this view. But it might be possible that the letter-writer erred in the date of the visit. Valle-Inclán did not publish any articles or date any stories in Cuba. No mention of his visit to the island has been uncovered in his writings. This lacuna makes it difficult to verify either version. But the weight of circumstances is on the side of the visit in 1893.

41. "X" (8 July 1893); "Páginas de Tierra Caliente" (20 August 1893); "Un cabecilla" (16 September 1893); "Octavia Santino" (28 October 1893). These are not listed in Fichter's list of publications by Valle-Inclán before 1895.

42. "Páginas de Tierra Caliente" was derived from "Bajo los trópicos," published in Mexico; "Octavia Santino" was based on "La confesión," published in *El Universal* (10 July 1892) and in *El Globo* (10 July 1893). "X" was collected after Valle-Inclán's death in *Flores de almendro* (Madrid: Bergua, 1936) under the title "Una desconocida;" in it the author again uses an Italian motif—the brother and sister, Count and Countess De Lucca—and has his narrator refer to his own visit to Italy. "Un cabecilla" had appeared previously in *El Globo* (29 September 1893). This last story may have been inspired in Alphonse Daudet's "Le cabecilla."

43. A., "Pasado mañana lunes—¡Cáa, señor!" *El Español* (1943). The article refers to these friendships.

44. The library of Jesús Muruáis was inherited by the Instituto de Pontevedra. Among the many French and Italian authors represented are Théodore de Banville, Barbey d'Aurevilly, Gabriel D'Annunzio, Théophile Gautier, Emile Zola, Guy de Maupassant, Leconte de Lisle, Giacomo Leopardi, José Maria de Hérédia, Paul Verlaine, Gustave Flaubert, the Goncourts, René Ghil, Victor Hugo, Paul Bourget, Honoré de Balzac, Giosué Carducci. The library also contained Greek, Latin, and oriental works translated into French, among them many titles of erotica, mysticism, and philosophy.

45. Simone Saillard, *Le cercle de Muruais et les influences françaises sur les premiers essais littéraires de Don Ramón del Valle-Inclán*, Mémoire pour le Diplôme d'Etudes Supérieres (Paris: Institut d'Etudes Hispaniques, 1955).

46. Valle-Inclán's physical appearance at this time has been described by Joaquín Pesqueira, "Don Ramón del Valle-Inclán," *El Correo Gallego* (12 January 1936): "A very long beard, long hair, a long smock, a broad-brimmed hat, and large tortoise-shell glasses. Everything was black: black hair, black clothing, black glasses. On the quiet streets of Pontevedra, his presence had the impact of a strange occurrence. . . . (I can report that I, then a mischievous lad, felt respect and awe before that haughty and extravagant figure of the frail man who, daily in the afternoon, came out of a house facing mine in that outfit.)"

47. The six tales are "La Condesa de Cela," "Tula Varona," "Octavia," "La Niña Chole," "La Generala," and "Rosarito."

48. *Blanco y Negro* (1 June 1895): "The distinguished Pontevedran poet Ramón del Valle-Inclán has gathered in a beautiful tome, which is a credit to the publishing house of Landín in Pontevedra, an exquisite selection of stories, all of them elegant and of such exquisite crafts manship that they prove their author, influenced by French novelists, to be a figure of great prestige." Writing in *Madrid* (Buenos Aires: Losada, 1952), 93, Azorín added a comment to the lack of receptiveness: "He had given . . . his book *Femeninas* to the publisher. But, having been published in the provinces, not having reached Madrid, its existence was unknown to the critics."

49. Dionisio Gamallo Fierros, "Aportaciones al estudio de Valle-Inclán," *Revista de Occidente* 15 (October-November-December 1966): 348.

50. *Helios* 1, 2 (May 1903): 246–47: "I believe that such evocation of past greatness, of ancient chivalry, of romantic emotions, is, in Valle-Inclán, the fortunate melody that displays the total assurance of his mind. Throughout his work can be seen the tendency to caress that which is ancient and noble; already in *Femeninas*, a very beautiful first book, can be found the themes and characters that will continue to appear in all the pages by the admirable writer."

51. F. Madrid, *La vida altiva*, 110. Valle erroneously gives the date of the book as 1902.

52. "The book at hand is one that could be said to be entirely the work of youth. It is that because of the nature of its topic, because the author wrote it in the prime of life, because it merits being considered a fortunate beginning, and, lastly, because the entire book is new, with all the charm and originality that the term implies. . . . On speaking of what is new in the book—both in theme and form—I do so in relative terms and without saying that the author has forged a new path; I speak solely in the context of the place in which it appeared. This qualification of the statement is not damaging because the author, nonetheless, presents his own personality in it, . . . whosoever believes that this is just another book among many would be wrong. . . . Just the opposite. . . . He would have written the same book had he never read others. It is totally his and only its brevity gives it a resemblance to those the current literary scene produces with such unfortunate prodigiousness."

53. Article by Darío cited by Gamallo Fierros, "Aportaciones," 362: "*Femeninas* is another book of stories—real or imagined—in which plot and style are merged in a plausible manner. It is the first instance in which the shadow of a flock of French birds is cast over the purity of Castilian narrative. It is the heraldic birds of Constable D'Aurevilly that fly close to that beautiful and tragic 'Rosarito.' "

54. "Un cabecilla," *El País* (27 May), and *Don Quijote* (13 August); "X," *El País* (19 July); "Ivan el de los osos," *Blanco y Negro* 5, 238 (23 November 1895). The last story was illustrated by Huertas. This version and the original "Zan el de los osos" were reprinted by Fichter, *Publicaciones periodísticas*, to contrast the variants.

55. The document outlining his duties and salary stated in part, "Under the budget for the restoration of the cathedral of León, Don Ramón Valle y Peña is named inspector . . . with the annual salary of two thousand pesetas" (Cf. F. Madrid, *La vida altiva*, 52). Such appointments would occur from time to time in Valle-Inclán's career, causing the envidious comment of Pío Baroja, *Memorias* (Madrid: Minotauro 1955), 1160: "He was employed during most of his life; according to the talk, he had never had a goal or a job."

56. Apart from his many political activities, González Besada authored various works, among them *Historia crítica de la literatura gallega*, translated into French and German. Antonio Iglesias Laguna, "Valle-Inclán, La Restauración, El Ateneo," *La Estafeta Literaria* 274 (1963), states, "González Besada had won his girlfriend away when both were studying law in Santiago; but in 1896, as compensation, he got him a post in the Ministry of Development. He was generous to his compatriot. (There exists a curious unpublished correspondence between them, from which can be deduced that biographers are in error when they assert that Valle never resorted to the charity of others.)" Contrary to Iglesias Laguna's assertion is the statement by Luis Ruiz Contreras, *Memorias de un desmemoriado* (Madrid: Marzo, 1917), 191. "No matter what the circumstances, he would never have asked me for money. His dignity, which he considers essential, would not have allowed it."

57. Gómez de la Serna, *Don Ramón María del Valle-Inclán*, 26: "He arrived with a Mexican hat, wearing the long hair of an explorer and a red scarf, saying that he disliked Madrid because he was fond of walking with his two lions and he wasn't allowed to get on the trolley with them. . . . Shortly thereafter, he was wearing a high hat, a pointed black beard, long hair that curled around the velvet collar of his MacFarland, and glasses tied with a long black ribbon. He was the best mask on foot along Alcalá Street." In "Lances y recuerdos de don Ramón del Valle-Inclán," *La Prensa* (15 January 1967), Pedro Massa quotes a conversation he had in the 1930s with Luis Ruiz Contreras, who stated, "One night there came into the pub on Carrera de San Jerónimo a bearded, long-haired, vine-like young man with a black suit, silk hat, and cape: Valle-Inclán. No one knew him. A bit later, he told us that he was from Galicia, had fought outrageously in Mexico for the sake of love and literature, and that among his intellectual baggage, almost exclusively in portfolios, he already had a beautifully printed book: *Femeninas*." Rubén Darío, having met Valle-Inclán at Ruiz Contreras's house, commented on his appearance in an article cited by Gamallo Fierros, "Aportaciones," 362–63: "Ramón del Valle-Inclán is a writer who could easily be accused of being a *poseur* due to his bizarre garb.

Undoubtedly, Valle-Inclán is 'odd,' but underneath it all lies the artistic ardor of one of the chosen, with books of exquisite prose—crafted, illuminated, incised; it is difficult to listen to him for any length of time, but it is even more difficult to give up reading one of his pages, in which the musicality of the word is enchantingly enveloped within a harmonious organism of gold. . . . A curious, a curious life of adventure! Valle-Inclán is of Galician origin; today, he lives in the capital after traipsing around half the world. He has been an actor, journalist, Trappist monk, Mexican soldier. He's a philosopher who smiles sadly, having hardly passed his youth, and who has found the divine refuge of art under the winds of life. On the journey to his ideal city, he has passed through La Mancha; he will never be able to hide his points of contact with the sublime Knight. His Quixotism is exceptional, made more complex by the Renaissance and a millenary mysticism."

58. Ruiz Contreras, *Memorias*, 200–201: "He never belonged to the so-called bohemian group . . . Valle-Inclán was always . . . a loner among the others . . . and he always had his own home . . . his intimate life was orderly . . . he paid his monthly rent punctually, as well as the gratuity to the gatekeeper (who attended to his needs), and his provisions: a liter of alcohol, a kilo of sugar, a package of tea." Antonio Machado, writing in the prologue to Valle-Inclán, *La corte de los milagros* (Madrid-Barcelona: Ed. Nuestro Pueblo, 1938) 9, states, "Don Ramón was never, not even in the worst moments of his penury, a bohemian in the dissolute, fetid, and alcoholic style of his age. Don Ramón drank only water, without pride in his abstinence (he knew very well that mere absence of vice does not indicate virtue), and without letting his being *dry* interfere with his dealings with the *wet*, especially when the *wet*, as in the case of the great Rubén Darío, possessed greatness. . . . No one bore the poverty and misfortune of Spanish writers with greater dignity and less mendacity than our Don Ramón."

59. Manuel Bueno, "Días de bohemia," *La Pluma* 44.

60. Ibid., 41–42: "Calvo Asensio Street, opened at that time through an extensive barren area and lacking easy access to the center of the city, was impossible by day and dangerous by night due to the darkness. The door to Valle-Inclán's dwelling was always open. . . . The apartment had only the indispensable furnishings: a bed, a side table, and two chairs of a light-colored wood, while in an adjoining room there were a table, a small cupboard with no aspect of family life, the dining table, and four chairs. I seem to remember that the entire wall decor consisted of a panoply with two rusty fencing foils and a mask." In *Estampa* (11 January 1936), Pío Baroja is quoted on this subject: "One day we went to his lodgings, out there on Calvo Asensio Street, and saw that he had nothing more than a dark apartment with a miserable bed and a box. . . . On the wall hung a wrinkled garment and a hat."

61. Ruiz Contreras, *Memorias*, 191: "There were many days when he had to rely solely on a very hot cup of tea and a few lumps of sugar, his indispensable subsistence." Antonio Machado, prologue, *La corte de los milagros*, 9: "The voluptuousity of fasting! Our great Don Ramón experienced it often, although he never boasted about it. The reason for it being that Valle-Inclán, consecrated at the start of his literary career to a task of self-development and apprenticeship that was constant and profound, to the creation of a new form of expression, to the total rupture with the commonplace, to what he called 'the union of words for the first time,' could only achieve such ends by renouncing all the material advantages available to mercenary writers at the time."

62. "Los excitantes," lecture in Buenos Aires, Teatro Nacional, 28 June 1910. See F. Madrid, *La vida altiva*, 190–91; Gómez de la Serna, *Don Ramón María del Valle-Inclán*, 109.

63. "*Angel Guerra*, novela original de D. Benito Pérez Galdós," *El Globo* (13 August 1891).

64. Pedro Massa, "Lances y recuerdos": "Antonio Palomero brought him to my *tertulia* on Madera Street. Already gone were Ricardo Fuentes, Delorme, Alejandro Sawa—all of whom had been brought to my house by Joaquín Dicenta, the author of *Juan José*—but among the friends still gathered in my 'romantic' study were Azorín (then still Martínez Ruiz), Benavente, and Rubén Darío, with all of whom the new arrival immediately struck up friend-

ships." Azorín, "Aquella generación," *La Esfera* (1914), also has data on these *tertulias*: "We would sit in ample armchairs; we conversed in shouts; we discussed new books; we rebuked the maestros—from afar."

65. Baroja's relationship to Valle-Inclán was very equivocal, at least from Baroja's viewpoint, as his *Memorias* indicate: "Someone with whom I've lived for a long time, in spite of seldom being in accord with him on literary matters, was Valle-Inclán. Valle was a friend of several Galicians who were also my friends, among them Portela Valladares, Camilo Bargiela, and Trillo" (417); "As with his physical aspect, so too did he change his moral aspect. According to his fellow students in Galicia's Santiago—Bargiela, Trillo, Portela, and others—his name was Ramón Valle y Peña and he transformed himself into Ramón María del Valle-Inclán y Montenegro" (1160). Throughout the *Memorias* Baroja adopts a disdainful attitude toward Valle-Inclán, basing his antipathy on physical grounds (the episode of Baroja's dog being kicked by Valle-Inclán) and intellectual differences (according to Baroja, Valle-Inclán feared that Baroja would do something worthwhile, but he never felt such jealousy about Valle-Inclán's work, only alienation). These memoirs date from the 1940s; in *Aventuras, inventos y mixtificaciones de Silvestre Paradox* (Madrid: Caro Raggio, 1901), Baroja created the "simpático" bohemian Juan Pérez del Corral in the mold of Valle-Inclán, but had him die ignominiously.

66. *Estampa* (11 January 1936), quotes Baroja on this project: "I remember that four or five— Bargiela, Maeztu, Valle, I don't know if someone else, and I—went to propose to the publisher González Rojas that he issue a serial to be entitled *Los misterios del Transvaal*, in which Valle-Inclán proposed that Bargiela be concerned with diplomatic secrets, that I deal with poisons, and that he be in charge of matters dealing with America. . . . Of course, González Rojas did not deem the project feasible and we had to abandon it."

67. Ibid.: "All of us in that group were going to create those *Misterios del Transvaal*, which, later, I published by myself in forty-odd sections in *El País*." See Van Poel Krupp, *La guerra del Transvaal y los misterios de la banca de Londres*, ed. E. Inman Fox (Madrid: Taurus, 1974). Maeztu commented in his introduction to Valle-Inclán in 1897: "I was walking with Manolo Bueno along La Equitativa, when we saw a young man with a long beard and hair down to his shoulders, forcibly arguing with three students . . . 'That's Valle-Inclán!' Bueno told me. And we approached. Don Ramón, on seeing us, faced me: 'Hidalgo!' he yelled. 'Take a step back and stand firm against these villains!' "

68. Ruiz Contreras, *Memorias*, 185.

69. Ibid., 186. "What has been lost of Valle-Inclán's passing conversations is possibly worth as much as what has been preserved in his works."

70. Important cafés in Valle-Inclán's early life in Madrid: Café de Madrid (Calle de Alcalá, near La Puerta del Sol), Café de la Montaña (between Calle de Alcalá and Carrera de San Jerónimo), Horchatería de Candelas (across from the Escuela de Bellas Artes de San Fernando), Nuevo Café de Levante (on Calle del Arenal), and Lion d'Or (Calle de Alcalá, across from the convent of the Calatravas). Maxim, Gato Negro, Luna, Colonial, Universal are cafés of lesser renown.

71. Ricardo Baroja, *Gente del 98* (Barcelona: Juventud, 1952).

72. Manuel Bueno, "Días de bohemia," *La Pluma* 42: "From afternoon to afternoon, Joaquín Dicenta would show up at our *tertulia*, and, of course, he monopolized the conversation. . . . The dialogues between him and Valle-Inclán were incredible. Two aesthetics were face to face. Dicenta possessed a natural talent that everyone recognized, while Valle, besides being very intelligent, embellished his ideas with a cultural richness exempt from pedantry that was dazzling. . . . When Valle expounded his aesthetic tenets, Dicenta—unable to contradict him in the domain of criticism—would turn the situation to his favor by thrusting on us half a dozen literary dogmas that Zola had placed in circulation. Those were conversations! Generally, they ended with a clever witticism by Palomero, which would make us all laugh, or with an opportune and caustic phrase by Benavente. With the passing of time, and obedient to the inflexible rule of exhaustion, the gathering would break up, but somewhat later we would regroup in Fornos, in the Café de Levante . . . or in the 'Gato Negro.' "

73. Benavente continued to be a friend and admirer of Valle-Inclán, as attested by his moving prologue in *OC*, 2:7–16.

74. In *Estampa* (11 January 1936), Ricardo Baroja recalled, "A very attractive model named Dora, whom we all knew, used to frequent the Café Madrid. The girl had a single curious avocation: cleaning. Since she knew that Valle-Inclán lived alone, she felt that his dwelling would present many opportunities to display her talent and she showed up there ready to scrub everything in sight. But Valle-Inclán fell in love with her and told her so constantly. Dora never paid any attention to him and one day they argued; she never returned after that. One day he ran into her in front of Fornos. Valle-Inclán began to shout: 'Indecent beggar, you've stolen the silver utensils I had at home!' Had it not been for us, he would have given her a beating." Pío Baroja, in *Memorias*, also refers to this episode: "Dora had no sympathy for Valle-Inclán, who used to court her and give her gifts; she didn't even like his writings. . . . Valle-Inclán and Dora had a falling out and argued, even insulting each other."

75. Ruiz Contreras, *Memorias*, 193: "Since Valle-Inclán promoted himself as a *preciosista*, I realized that he was writing a brief book and enthused him with the plan of publishing it in a Colección Flirt."

76. Ibid., 195–96: "Undoubtedly Valle-Inclán thought it indispensable to follow the friendly counsel of Murguía ('You need only to discipline your style somewhat in order to become a great prose writer'), and when he decided to write *Epitalamio*, he exaggerated his meticulousness to the point of spending hours poring over a phrase or word. I can still see him in the spacious salon of my house as he paced back and forth, totally immersed in his illusory difficulties, more attentive to form than to theme, more to sound than to expression, repeating two or three words a hundred times with different modulations."

77. *Epitalamio (Historia de amores)*, Colección Flirt (Madrid: Imprenta A. Marzo, 1897), illustrated by Sánchez Geroña. Ruiz Contreras, *Memorias*, 196, commented: "At last, we gave the printer the manuscript, very few pages indeed. The work ends on page 107. Each page has eighteen lines of twenty-four letters; with covers, chapter headings, etc., there are thirty-five pages without text! Consequently, there are only seventy-two with reading matter, totaling five thousand words." The projected Colección Flirt contains only this one title, as Ruiz Contreras, *Memorias*, 193, explains: "Because when this book reached the public, there was no longer a reason to ask Benavente for his *Cuentos*, which had been announced, nor did I have further interest in collecting my *Amores crueles* in a frivolous volume."

78. Ricardo Fuente, "Un escritor mundano," *De un periodista* (Madrid: 1897). Azorín, in the prologue to *OC*, 1:9–10, states, "The book, his second, has been printed in an exquisite manner; the author wanted the delicacy of the work to be reflected in the exquisiteness of the book. The book is small; one cannot measure the transcendence of a work by its dimensions. Out of this minute work will stem an entire original mode in Spanish literature. The author already senses it and he has a singular affection for the book he has just published at his expense." In "Aquella generación," *La Esfera* (25 April 1914), Martínez Ruiz commented, "For us, he possesses the sorcery of style: a style that is refined, elegant, attic, full of illusion and poetry, as we have never experienced before." Rubén Darío added, "He is respected as a newcomer in literature for the imposition of his own style and his fervent thirst for beauty." Cited in Gamallo Fierros, "Aportaciones," 363.

79. Azorín, prologue to *OC*, 1:10: "And when making his rounds of Madrid, from bookseller to bookseller, he has experienced the brutal harsh contrast between his illusions and reality. . . . He ends up saying that he refuses to do anything else; he wants nothing to do with booksellers or with his small book. And with a definitive gesture, he hurls the book he had been holding out the window. . . . It doesn't imply that the author repudiates his creation; he doesn't hurl it because he finds it repugnant; the fact is that in hurling *Epitalamio* to the street, he throws his gauntlet before all industrial literature."

80. "Clarín," "Palique," *Madrid Cómico* (25 September 1897), 315. In "Valle-Inclán en 1897," Valle-Inclán, *Obras completas* (Madrid: Editorial Plenitud, 1954), xix, Azorín states, "Dedicated in its entirety to Valle-Inclán . . . Clarín's 'Palique' was published in the *Madrid Cómico* issue of

September 25, 1897. . . . Clarín, in Oviedo, did not know Valle-Inclán except by the laudatory words of Palacio Valdés; he says so himself. . . . The critic sees in Valle-Inclán a writer with 'imagination' and one capable 'of achieving a style.' But the tone of the article is one of irritation. Clarín is irritated by a writer like Valle-Inclán, whom he judges to be a belated follower of French modes: the fashions of twenty-five years earlier. . . . The critic believes that the writer is looking back, when, in reality, he's looking forward." In *Madrid* (Buenos Aires: Losada, 1952), 93, Azorin gives the erroneous date of Clarín's "Palique" as "25 octubre de 1897."

81. Francisco Navarro Ledesma, (*"Epitalamio"*) *El Globo* (3 April 1897). Fernández Almagro, *Vida y literatura*, 98: "Navarro Ledesma had published a negative review of *Epitalamio*, also in *El Globo* (3 April 1897), expressing judgments such as: 'An exotic writer, and we're not certain if one shouldn't say affected, is this Sr. Valle-Inclán. The story or, better, *nouvelle*—the name that best suits it—*Epitalamio* is conceived in the French manner and written as the author has conceived it. *Epitalamio* seems to have an excess of intellectual elegance or decadent refinement, more or less forced, the rest being subtle as a consequence.'" Curiously, Rubén Darío was similarly reserved toward the book: "And he has written *Epitalamio*, a *bijou* of a little book, whose defect is, perhaps, that it pays too much homage to D'Annunzio and the exaggeration of delicacy."

82. In Gamallo Fierros, "Aportaciones," 355.

83. "Clarín," "Palique," *Heraldo de Madrid* (9 October 1897). Reproduced in Gamallo Fierros, "Aportaciones," 356–58.

84. In Gamallo Fierros, "Aportaciones," 360–61.

85. Juan López Nuñez, "Valle-Inclán," *Por Esos Mundos* (1 January 1915).

86. *Corte de amor, Historias perversas, Flores de almendro.*

87. *Germinal* (24 May 1897).

88. Cf. Guillermo de Torre, "La generación española de 1898 en las revistas del tiempo," *Nosotros* 6, 15, 67 (October 1941): 14.

89. R. del Valle-Inclán, "Lluvia," *Almanaque del Don Quijote* (1897), 10–12.

Notes for Chapter 3: Absorption

1. *La España Moderna* (June 1895): "Spanish society is undergoing a profound crisis. . . . Its mental and moral condition provides a depressing spectacle. . . . All of us are enveloped in an atmosphere of shame."

2. *Anarquistas literarios (Notas sobre la literatura española)* (Madrid: Fernando Fe, 1895): "Our backwardness becomes obvious when we compare ourselves to other nations. . . . There is doubt that the law of progress can be verified in Spain. . . . Apathy ties our hands. . . . Militarism chokes us; the tide of reactionary religion is welling up. . . . Taxes increase, industry dies, agriculture decays. The worker agonizes. . . . Periodicals, books, and public performances are censored in the name of morality. . . . Politics is a school for criminals. . . . Suffrage is a lie. . . . Public education hardly has a foothold."

3. *Hacia otra España* (Bilbao: Biblioteca Bascongada de Fermín Herrán, 1899): "*Progressive paralysis* . . . The sickness that Spain is experiencing. . . . There is no other way to qualify that continuous erosion of collective national life. . . . Paralysis . . . is the term that explains the frightful indifference of the nation. . . . Intellectual paralysis . . . Moral paralysis . . . Creative paralysis."

4. *El tablado de Arlequín* (Madrid: Caro Raggio, 1903): "We have purged the error of having discovered America . . . we have lost our colonies. . . . Spain stands like the blackened trunk of a mutilated tree."

5. Jorge Guillén, "Valle-Inclán y el 98," *La Pluma* 70: "Don Ramón del Valle-Inclán is, perhaps, the only writer of the Generation of '98 who hasn't written anything on 'The

Problem of Spain.' Let's state it openly: that empty nave becomes one of the firmest of the beauties in the grand edifice erected by the great builder. . . . For Valle-Inclán was at that time, the only one at the time, already erecting his houses of prose and building his bridges of verse within his ideal perennial Spain." While Guillén's observation is true in a strict sense, it does not account for Valle-Inclán's socio-political views as expressed in many of his works, as well as in his *tertulias*.

6. Francisco Madrid, *La vida altiva de Valle-Inclán*, 54.

7. *Obras completas de don Ramón del Valle-Inclán*, vol. 1 (Madrid: Talleres Tipográficos de Rivadeneyra, 1944), 795, 796, 797. Unless otherwise indicated, all quotations from Valle-Inclán's works are from volumes 1 and 2 of this work, hereafter cited as *OC*.

8. Amores García de la Barga ("Corpus Barga") has referred to these important members of the Generation with the composite word VABUMB (Valle-Inclán, Azorín, Baroja, Unamuno, Machado, Maeztu, Benavente). Azorín's appellation became the most widely accepted because it resolved the incongruity of grouping all the young writers together as "Modernistas," a term applicable in Spain only to some followers of Darío. See Guillermo Díaz-Plaja, *Modernismo frente a 98* (Madrid: Espasa-Calpe, 1951).

9. *Madrid* (Buenos Aires: Losada, 1952): 61, 64, 71, 76: "The 'Generation of 1898' is a historical generation and, therefore, traditional. Its concern is with continuity. And out of its attempt to achieve it emerges the conflict between the past and the proposed superimpositions. . . . The Generation of 1898 condemned qualifying epithets and relied on authentic details. . . . Color attracts the writers of 1898. Those writers live in an atmosphere of painting . . . they have seen color where it hadn't been noticed before. And they have seen the violent chiaroscuro of Spain. . . . We were concerned over foreign relations. . . . Spain needed to have close communication with Europe."

10. *Obras completas 9* (Madrid: Aguilar, 1954), 1136: "Around 1896 there came to Madrid from the provinces some young men with literary ambitions; they joined others here who were starting to write. They were all part of the group that soon began to publish in small newspapers and magazines of scant circulation."

11. *Clásicos y modernos* (Buenos Aires: Losada, 1959), 186–191: "In Spanish literature, the Generation of 1898 represents a renaissance. . . . A renaissance is simply the fertilization of the national mind by foreign thought. . . . A spirit of protest, of rebellion animated the youth of 1898. Ramiro de Maeztu wrote impetuous and ardent articles . . . Pío Baroja, with his cold analysis, depicted the landscape of Castile and introduced a profound spirit of alienation into the novel . . . Valle-Inclán, with his great lordly haughtiness, with his disheveled long hair, and his refinement of style, had a great appeal to new writers, awing them with his vision of landscapes and characters out of the Italian Renaissance. . . . The Generation of 1898 loves old villages and the landscape; it attempts to revive the old poets (Berceo, Juan Ruiz, Santillana); it fosters a new fervor for El Greco; it rehabilitates Góngora; it declares itself romantic; it is enthused by Larra . . . in effect, it makes an effort to approximate reality and to free the language, making it more intense and restoring to it old words . . . while intellectual curiosity over what is foreign, as well as over the spectacle of the disaster—the failure of the whole of Spanish politics—has intensified its sensibilities and given a variant never before found in Spain." First published in *ABC* (10 February 1913).

12. Ramiro de Maeztu, "El alma de 1898," *Nuevo Mundo* (March 1913).

13. Miguel de Unamuno, "Nuestra egolatría," *El Imparcial* (31 January 1916).

14. *Divagaciones apasionadas* (Madrid: Caro Raggio, 1924): "I do not believe that there has been, nor that there is, a Generation of 1898; if there is, I do not belong to it. In 1898 I had published very little, was not known, and didn't even have the smallest reputation. . . . It has never seemed to me a fortunate thing for Azorín, the baptizer and almost inventor of that generation, to have associated the names of a few writers with the date of the country's defeat, in which they didn't have the slightest role" (27). "Neither through political or literary tendencies, nor through our conceptions of life and art, nor even through age, could there be

seen in us the semblance of a group. The only thing we had in common was our protest against the politicians and writers of the Restoration. A generation that lacks common points of view, common aspirations, spiritual solidarity, and doesn't even have the bond of age, is not a generation; thus, the so-called Generation of 1898 is more an invention than a fact" (30).

15. Domingo García-Sabell, "Españoles mal entendidos, II: Don Ramón del Valle-Inclán," *Insula* (July-August 1961): 19.

16. F. Madrid, *La vida altiva*, 102.

17. "Modernismo," lecture in Buenos Aires, Teatro Nacional, 5 July 1910. See F. Madrid, *La vida altiva*, 200–201.

18. *OC*, 1:xx: "Generations are distinct from one another for that reason: the concept of perfection. . . . The concept of perfection in 1897, in the era which began with that year, is found equally in a page by Valle-Inclán, in a lyrical passage by Baroja, and in a scene by Benavente."

19. Luis Granjel, *Panorama del la Generación del 98* (Madrid: Guadarrama, 1959), 88: "The weekly *Germinal* . . . a poorly printed magazine of confused ideological and literary orientation, in which only its advanced republicanism is unequivocal, was published for two years and its issues had as contributors, among others, . . . Ricardo Fuentes . . . Antonio Palomero . . . Delorme . . . Benavente, Villaespesa, and Valle-Inclán, who used the pseudonym *Bladamín* . . . Maeztu . . . and Pío Baroja."

20. "We have come to promote and defend THE NEW, what the public desires, THE MODERN, what is commonplace throughout Europe but is lacking here due to the vice of routine and the tyranny of habit. And so we posit that *VIDA NUEVA* will be not the periodical of TODAY but the periodical of TOMORROW."

21. *Vida Nueva* 71 (15 September 1899). He was also the subject of an article by P. González in the 3 December 1899 issue.

22. *La Vida Literaria* 11 (18 March 1899): 187, and 15 (20 April 1899): 244, respectively. Melchor Fernández Almagro, *Vida y literatura de Valle-Inclán* (Madrid: Editora Nacional, 1943), 233, states, "Returning to the marionette theatre that Valle-Inclán had always wanted to create, he indicates the desire in his distant *Reina de Dalicam*." However, the supposed play is a short-short story about Rosita Zegrí, the king of the islands of Dalicám, and the Duquesito de Ordax; it was later amplified as "Rosita" in *Corte de Amor* (1903).

23. *Don Quijote* (1899): 16–17.

24. "We belong to the generation that was downtrodden by the conceited conquerors; usurping power under the guise of innocent freedoms, they imposed their blind tyranny on us, making themselves odious. . . . Educated in the school of suffering, we learned resignation and pity." In the "Epílogo": "This is the end of the tenacious effort and the unrecognized sacrifice. Epilogue of sorrows and hopes, our work is offered to the humble and aspires to the attention of the exalted. We are living in a difficult period that is at once epilogue of a war, of a nation, of an ethic, of a century, and of a world."

25. F. Madrid, *La vida altiva*, 111.

26. Luis Ruiz Contreras, *Memorias de un desmemoriado* (Madrid: Marzo, 1917), 196–197: "The sixth issue of *Revista Nueva* included the first chapter and the rest appeared successively during two months; but in all that time he failed to write the seventh episode." The chapters appeared as follows: 1, 6 (5 April 1899): 255–59; 7 (15 April 1899): 305–10; 8 (25 April 1899): 343–47; 9 (5 May 1899): 425–28.

27. Ibid.: "And instead of confessing his ineptitude to me . . . he stopped seeing me, and with a cynical brazenness would say in the café that he could not resign himself to continue writing for a magazine in which his prose was displayed with multiple errors. . . . Because of *Adega*, our friendship was interrupted." Valle-Inclán's reason was valid, however. Magazines of the period were notorious for their lack of professional finish; Valle's meticulous attention to detail in his published works since 1895 was well known, as José Moya del Pino notes in *La Pluma* 65: "Valle-Inclán's influence has been most evident and best defined in the art of the book. All of the current editions that have artistic merit are derived from the designs of his

early books." Obviously, Valle-Inclán would have resented flagrant errors due to carelessness in the preparation of magazines; this is evidenced further in comparing typographical errors in his pre-1895 stories and articles with the same writings published later, which are free of those errors.

28. Pío Baroja, *Memorias* (Madrid: Minotauro 1955), 300: "One evening, in the ale house on Alcalá Street, where, as I said earlier, some of us who were budding authors would meet, words were spoken against the editor-owner of *Revista Nueva* because he made some of those published in its pages contribute money. The one who satirized him the most was Valle-Inclán, who created a sort of grotesque historical document on that gentleman with great burlesque solemnity."

29. Rubén Darío, in Dionisio Gamallo Fierros, "Aportaciones al estudio de Valle-Inclán," *Revista de Occidente* 15 (October-November-December 1966): 363: "He's working on two pieces that will appear shortly: *Tierra Caliente*, memoirs and impressions of travels in America, and *Adega*, a long story, or *nouvelle*, some of whose chapters have appeared in magazines. They manifest the same qualities of style, the same preoccupation with plasticity and rhythm, the well-known procedures and the charm of a melody by D'Annunzio."

30. In *Juventud* 1, 1 (1 October 1901); and *Juventud* 1, 3 (30 October 1901), respectively.

31. Pedro Salinas, *Literatura española—Siglo XX* (México, D.F.: Seneca, 1941), 29–30: "We do not encounter the entire group in any of these publications until, in 1903, *Alma Española* appears. The whole list of the new literary generation is there, offering itself to the public at large. Can't we deduce from this that the individuals of '98 have come closer and closer bit by bit; that, even if apart at first in groups or *tertulias*, they come to feel the mandate of community, as expressed in the publication of *Alma Española*, where all are present?"

32. Rubén Darío, in Gamallo Fierros, "Aportaciones," 362: " . . . and in *Niña Chole*, an intense feeling of tropical life, emanations of the torrid Americas, the voluptuous and fiery soul of the hot land (keep in mind that the ultramarine nature of the writer of these lines validates what has been said) expressed in an artistic style foreign to Castilian, yet without abandoning the noble qualities of the golden Spanish of better days. I would say that he is an *arabesque* author, in both senses of the word, in terms of ornamentation and of fantasy."

Notes for Chapter 4: Early Stages

1. Ricardo Baroja, "Valle-Inclán, En el café," *La Pluma* 51: "One evening, in the Plaza de Oriente, Valle-Inclán did something extraordinary. . . . He went around the Plaza and, in front of each statue, recited parts of ballads, scenes of plays, segments of history, or anecdotes that referred to that king or queen."

2. Francisco Madrid, *La vida altiva de Valle-Inclán*, 124.

3. Sebastián de la Nuez y José Schraibman, *Cartas del archivo de Pérez Galdós* (Madrid: Taurus, 1967), 27–28.

4. Jacinto Benavente, *Obras completas*, 1:311–64 (Madrid: Aguilar, 1950).

5. Pedro Massa, "Lances y recuerdos de don Ramón del Valle-Inclán," *La Prensa* (15 January 1967), presents a long account of this episode by Ruiz Contreras.

6. F. Madrid, *La vida altiva*, 125. See also Massa, "Lances y recuerdos," for Ruiz Contreras's account.

7. Caricature by Cilla, reproduced in Azorín, "Un cincuentenario," *ABC* (1948).

8. Pío Baroja, *Memorias* (Madrid: Minotauro 1955), 568: "Señor Benavente is a fine *litterateur*. S— on the Spanish aristocracy."

9. See Massa, "Lances y recuerdos," in which Ruiz Contreras recounts: "Opening night arrived. The first act well under way, I was in my seat waiting with fearful impatience for Valle-Inclán's appearance on stage. Who knows what I imagined: that he would stumble on entering, that he would drop the silk hat, that everyone would learn that the magnificent frock coat that was his costume had cost fifty pesetas a day earlier at a second-hand store on

Gato Street. But, oh, the power of genius! Valle-Inclán carried himself that evening as if he were the most accomplished actor and, despite his brief appearance in the play, the best applause in the house was for the author of *Epitalamio*."

10. *La Epoca* (8 November 1898).

11. F. Madrid, *La vida altiva*, 142.

12. Ibid., 142–43.

13. See Massa, "Lances y recuerdos," in which Ruiz Contreras recalls: "*La comida de las fieras* was followed by the premiere of *Los reyes en el destierro*, by Alphonse Daudet, and, in playing the role of the old general, Valle had his worst failure."

14. Ricardo Baroja, *Gente del 98* (Barcelona: Juventud, 1952), 146–50.

15. Prior to the production, *El Globo* (1899) commented, "In honor of Valle-Inclán. A group of literary figures, which feels an admiration as sincere as it is justified for the gallant author of *Femeninas*, has organized a theatrical event that will be held very shortly to benefit him.

The event, which, first of all, will be a fortunate occasion for the public to appreciate the talent of Sr. Valle-Inclán as a dramatist, has been organized by Jacinto Benavente, that genial and gentlemanly writer who is an honor to our theatre. Needless to say, the author of *La comida de las fieras* has had the collaboration toward that endeavor of lesser-known but equally fine writers who know how to appreciate the value of a literary artist of Sr. Valle-Inclán's substance.

The play to be performed is *Cenizas*, a work which the author of *Femeninas* wrote recently; it is a meritorious work in the human psychology the characters manifest and in the serene naturalness in which they die.

We don't wish to offer the public more concrete references regarding *Cenizas* because whatever officiousness we show in this regard will deprive it from penetrating independently in the depths of the drama when presented.

The organizing committee for the theatrical event, which will be held at the Lara, has decided, for reasons which do not need to be specified since they can be surmised, that no free tickets will be issued. It is a matter of making a contribution toward the betterment of the condition of a talented but poor writer; it shouldn't surprise anyone that the organizers of the event desire the greatest possible income for the beneficiary.

On the other hand, those who write theatre criticism for our newspapers are excellent people who will gladly attend this opportune calling to their impartiality."

Benavente's one-act comedy, *Despedida cruel* (Cruel Farewell), was premiered on that same evening to complete the program. Besides its author and Martínez Sierra, the cast included Josefina Blanco. See Melchor Fernández Almagro, *Vida y literatura de Valle-Inclán*, 69, and Diego San José de la Torre, *Gente de ayer* (Madrid: Reus, 1952), 147–48: "With his patriarchal beard, long cape in winter, and his lisping, shrill voice, Don Ramón María del Valle-Inclán was a figure out of another age in the cafés of Madrid and in the literary circles he frequented, always surrounded by friends and partisans; it brought to mind the Athenian philosophers, accompanied by disciples who listened to their lessons with religious silence, as if they were dogmas of faith toward salvation, be they irrefutable truths or the errors of their own theories.

There also comes to mind the first memory I have of him during my own literary beginnings. . . . In the studio of Saint-Aubin. . . . That artistic grouping was composed of ladies and gallants; I have no memory of the ladies, nor did any besides Josefina Blanco, later to be his wife, ever attain Fame as an actress; . . . among the gentlemen, I seem to remember Benavente, Martínez Sierra, Pío Baroja, Pérez de Ayala, Enrique Amado, Nilo de Fabra, Enrique de Mesa, and a tall, bearded *garon* with long hair like an old Christ, who covered his myopic eyes with frameless lenses and who was the author and protagonist of the work being rehearsed.

The play in question was entitled *Cenizas* and the author was called Valle by his cronies. It was he who, as father of the 'creature' and artistic director, was conducting the rehearsal, not always with cordiality, due to which the affair came close to ending on more than one occasion . . . but when it was over, everyone left singing the praises of the play, cast in a new mold, in which, of course, they were to make their first outing in the scenic art.

The play finally opened—I don't recall in what theatre, although I believe it was the Comedia—in one of those evening events for amateurs involving no risk for the impressario."

16. R. del Valle-Inclán, *Cenizas* (Madrid: Bernardo Rodríguez y Perma, 1899). This melodrama indicates the evolution of Valle-Inclán from short-story writer to playwright; its origin can be traced to "¡Caritativa!" *El Universal* (19 June 1892) and from there to "La confesión" *El Universal* (10 July 1892) and to "Octavia Santino" in *Femeninas*. The definitive form of the play would be achieved in *El yermo de las almas* (1908), with variants such as the exclusion of Don Juan Manuel and the addition of the role of Doña Soledad.

17. F. Madrid, *La vida altiva*, 56. Manuel Bueno's account of the incident has been recorded in *Estampa*, 5: "The conversation took a bad turn because in those days Valle was a sour man, and, suddenly, he threw a pitcher of water at me. I tried to defend myself with my cane, but, as bad luck would have it, one of his cuff links became embedded in his arm." The version given by Gómez de la Serna, *Don Ramón María del Valle-Inclán*, 97, based on the testimony of other witnesses, particularly Francisco Sancha Lengo and José Ruiz Castillo, differs as to who initiated the fracas: "Manuel Bueno . . . took a step backward and raised his cane, which had a metal shaft. Valle grabbed a bottle of water by its neck . . . and, soaking everyone, instigated Manuel Bueno to land a blow with his cane."

18. F. Madrid, *La vida altiva*, 56.

19. Ibid.

20. Gómez de la Serna, *Don Ramón María del Valle-Inclán*, 47: "Don Ramón was consulted and he agreed to the amputation, but without anesthesia; there are even those who say that he trimmed part of his beard so that he could watch the operation, adding in greater exaggeration yet that a mistake was made and another cut had to be made higher, with Don Ramón also witnessing the second surgical procedure while smoking a cigar! The fact is that he fainted during the operation and, on coming to, already armless and bandaged, he said to Don Jacinto: 'How this arm hurts!' And Benavente replied: 'Not that arm anymore, Ramón'."

21. Alberto Ghiraldo, "Como perdió su brazo D. Ramón María del Valle-Inclán," *Diario de La Plata* (9 September 1923).

22. Syndicated in many periodicals; See *The Washington Post*, 14 January 1979. Manuel Bueno, *Estampa*, 5: "From that moment on, our friendship became closer, perhaps. We started frequenting the Café Inglés with Dicenta, Palomero, Ricardo Fuente. . . . Later, when he married, I would go to his house with my wife and they would come to mine."

23. Marqués de Bradomín, in *Sonata de invierno, Obras completas de don Ramón del Valle-Inclán*, vol. 1 (Madrid: Talleres Tipográficos de Rivadeneyra, 1944), 432. Unless otherwise indicated, all quotations from Valle-Inclán's works are from volumes 1 and 2 of this work, hereafter cited as *OC*: " . . . the loss of my arm. If only I had attained that state in the most glorious occasion ever! I confess that at that time I envied the divine soldier that achievement more than the glory of having written the *Quijote*."

24. F. Madrid, *La vida altiva*, 59.

25. Ramón Gómez de la Serna, "Algunas versiones de cómo perdió el brazo D. Ramón Ma del Valle-Inclán," *Muestrario* (Madrid: Artes Gráficas [Biblioteca Nueva], 1918), 273–87. See also Gómez de la Serna, *Don Ramón María del Valle-Inclán*, 48–54.

26. José Rubia Barcia, "Valle-Inclán y la literatura gallega," *Revista Hispánica Moderna* 21 (2 April 1955) 117–18, makes an interesting observation: "It has been believed, naturally, that the description of the loss of the Marquis's arm was inspired in the author's similar occurrence in his own life. But the coincidences with the pages in Vicetto are too frequent to cast aside such a probable literary inspiration." He refers to Vicetto's *Los hidalgos de Monforte* (Seville, 1851). Undoubtedly, Valle-Inclán was inspired in Benito Vicetto's novel, as Rubia Barcia points out, but it is likely the particulars relating to the loss of an arm became important to Valle-Inclán only after he suffered the same misfortune. The incident gained personal meaning thereafter and was added to his *Sonata de invierno* because of that connotation even though the author may have interpreted it in terms of Vicetto's novel.

27. *OC*, 1:432.

28. Ramón del Valle-Inclán, *Obras Completas*, 2:330 (Madrid: Editorial Plenitud, 1954).

29. *La lámpara maravillosa*, *OC*, 1:778. Once again, Valle-Inclán tampered with his chronology, this time in dating the loss of his arm.

30. In José Brissa, ed., *Parnaso español contemporáneo* (Barcelona: Maucci, 1914). Among the many examples of one-armed characters of minor stature in the works of Valle-Inclán are two soldiers, one in ¡*Viva mi dueño*! and the other in *Divinas palabras*.

31. Ruiz Contreras, *Memorias de un desmemoriado* (Madrid: Marzo, 1917), 188: "I had introduced him to María Tubáu and Ceferino Palencia, both of whom delighted in his highly original conversation."

32. Vol. 1 (Madrid: Nueva Editorial de J. García, 1900), 688 pp. In "El gesto único de Don Ramón. (En torno a una obra ignorada de Valle-Inclán)," *Insula* 236–37 (July-August 1966): 4, Domingo García-Sabell writes, "It was published with both color and black-and-white illustrations; the cover said: '*La cara de Dios* / Novel / Based on the Celebrated Play / of / Don Carlos Arniches / by Don Ramón del Valle-Inclán / First Volume.' The second volume never appeared, nor, in fact, was it foreseen since the novel concludes, unequivocally, in the first volume. The second page of the book reprints a letter from Arniches, which states: 'Sr. Dr. Ramón del Valle-Inclán. / My distinguished friend: Of course you can count on my authorization to make a novel out of my modest play *La cara de Dios*. / And highly honored thereby, I take this occasion to reiterate the assurances of my affection. / Carlos Arniches / 27 of December 1899.'"

33. García-Sabell, "El gesto único," 31: "*La cara de Dios*, at the same time that it represents a scornful gesture by the writer in the face of an ignorant contemporary public, is also a compendium of his total personality and, consequently, of his entire work. In *La cara de Dios* are the *Sonatas*, the *Comedias bárbaras*, *La lámpara maravillosa*, the *Esperpentos*, and *El ruedo ibérico*. *La cara de Dios* is, definitively, an anticipatory and premature anthology of Valle-Inclán." The article continues, "But besides this, there is in *La cara de Dios* a procedure that will be repeated over and over throughout Valle-Inclán's work, to wit: the transfiguration of the immediate surrounding world into a world of fantasy, or the appropriation of names and toponyms to serve either the needs of plot or of aesthetics. Thus, there appear in the drama, the Marquis de Bradamín (*sic*), the knight Don Pedro Aguiar y Mendoza, the healing woman of Céltigos, the shepherdess Adega, the mysterious pilgrim, and even Marela and Bermella, two cows 'as ponderous as two abbesses.' On the other hand is the Socialist-worker atmosphere of turn-of-the-century Madrid. Similarly, we encounter the surprising revelation that the judge who presides over the investigation dealing with the assassination of modern Madrid is named, of all things, Don Máximo Baroja. And the Police Inspector is named Bargiela. There even appears a French Governess, 'Señorita Cornuty,' while a friend of Víctor Rey, the protagonist, answers to the name Antonio Palomero. Is it necessary to list the comparable characters in *Luces de bohemia*?"

34. Ricardo Baroja, *La Pluma*, 55.

35. Ibid.

36. Luis Granjel, *Panorama del la Generación del 98* (Madrid: Guadarrama, 1959), 86: "The troubled premiere of Benavente's *La gata de angora*, the night of April 1, 1900; the initial hostility of the audience that filled the Comedia theatre, born in the recognition of its author as the principal representative of Modernism, the symbolic catcalls of someone in the audience, immediately provoked a reaction from Valle-Inclán and Cornuty that culminated in their arrest, the latter charged with insulting Echegaray."

37. Ibid.: "Under the auspices of those apprentice writers, then under the leadership of Valle-Inclán, spread the noisy stomping that destroyed a poor comic piece on the day of its premiere in the Zarzuela theatre." Baroja, *Memorias*, 326, discusses Valle-Inclán's hostility toward López Pinillos, an Andalusian playwright. In 1901 a play of his was to be premiered at the Teatro Español; Valle-Inclán, in the presence of Baroja, schemed with two actors to ruin the performance.

38. Baroja, *Gente del 98*, 119–23, discusses this fully.

39. H. Chonon Berkowitz, *Pérez Galdós, Spanish Liberal Crusader* (Madison: University of

Wisconsin Press, 1948), 350–51: "The tumultuous reception of *Electra* . . . The disillusioned Spanish realists of 1901 experienced something comparable to the frenzy of the French romanticists of 1830 . . . And Valle-Inclán, sworn enemy of emotion in art, was seen crying behind his shell-rimmed glasses. . . . In the afternoon before the premiere they gathered in a famous *cervecería* . . . where they gave vent to their emotions and exultation. Valle-Inclán set the pace with impassioned volubility . . . Everyone revealed by word and gesture the hypnotic effect of *Electra*."

40. Azorín, *Madrid*, 92: "We had no relations . . . with Benito Pérez Galdós. The premiere of *Electra* increased the aloofness. Baroja opposed it in private conversations. I opposed it in print, when everyone else was applauding."

41. Berkowitz, *Pérez Galdós*.

42. Juan López Nuñez, "Valle-Inclán," *Por Esos Mundos* (1 January 1915).

43. Quoted in Cristóbal de Castro, "El monumento a Galdós," *Nuevo Mundo* (1 March 1918).

44. In *Luces de bohemia*, published in 1920.

45. *OC*, 1:818, 819, 820.

46. Azorín, *Madrid*, 41: "Before Larra's niche, next to Espronceda's, in the lowest row of niches, we held a funerary testimonial in honor of the individual who possessed so much of our own spirit."

47. Ibid.: "On several nights, after the *tertulia* at the café, we went to one of those abandoned cemeteries around Fuencarral gate. We entered through a breach in the wall. We wandered around the old tombs in the silence of the night. We were drawn by the mystery. The vague melancholy which impregnated that generation was one with that which emanated from those sepulchres."

Notes for Chapter 5: Recognitions

1. Juan Ramón Jiménez, in *Renacimiento* 2 (1907): 422, stated:, "I received letters from young writers inviting me to come to Madrid and to publish a book of poetry. Being young, I gave in to temptation. . . . And I came to Madrid, for the first time, in April of 1900, with all of my eighteen years and a deep spring melancholy. . . . Valle-Inclán gave me the title for one book—*Ninfeas*—and Rubén Darío for another—*Almas de violeta*—while Francisco Villaespesa, my then inseparable friend, wrote some symbolic prose so that we could be together as brothers in those sentimental pages fastened with violets."

2. Baroja had published *Estudio sobre el dolor* earlier; *Vidas sombrías* and *La casa de Aizgorri* appeared in 1900. Valle-Inclán noted the appearance of the latter in an article in *Electra* 3 (30 March 1901). See Pío Baroja, *Memorias* (Madrid: Minotauro, 1955), 412.

3. The works, respectively, were "Las tres cosas del tío Juan" and "La Chucha." According to a rumor at that time Pardo Bazán and Blasco Ibáñez switched entries; if so, the winning story was really written by the latter. See Fernández Almagro, *Vida y literatura de Valle-Inclán*, 71.

4. Francisco Madrid, *La vida altiva de Valle-Inclán*, 111.

5. Juan Valera, *Obras completas*, vol. 44 (Madrid: Alemana, 1916); the letter reads, in part: "Perhaps it deserved the prize as much or more than any of the others. . . . However, the Jury refrained from awarding it because of the hair-raising, frightening or scabrous nature of the story. . . . Be that as it may, 'Satanás' is written with energetic conciseness of style, with great richness of color, and with the enviable power of giving life to the characters, etching deeply into the readers' memory their aspect and personality. . . . The story 'Satanás,' worthy of praise in my opinion, is the work of D. Ramón del Valle-Inclán, a young writer yet, as it would seem one of the so-called Modernists, whose art of writing I do not reprove when it is exercised with moderation and skill, and when the one who employs it has talent."

6. Ricardo Baroja, *El Pedigree* (Madrid: Caro Raggio, 1926). The "G.P." referred to by Valle-Inclán stands for "gran puta" (great whore).

7. F. Madrid, *La vida altiva*, 61–62. Fernández Almagro, *Vida y literatura*, 73, quotes a letter

he received from Dr. Goyanes in reference to the aftermath of the incident: "The maestro—Dr. San Martín—was at that time serving as surgeon of the Press Association and was a friend of Valle-Inclán and a frequenter of his circle at the café. He verified that the accident had been a casual one, but it was still murmured about that there had been a duel with ladies involved. The fact is that he had a bullet lodged not too deeply in a foot. Valle-Inclán was then living in a miserable garret on Argensola Street and, for financial reasons, had to be operated on at home. He underwent the surgery with a local anesthetic (not easily obtained at that time), stoically, the extraction of the bullet and his recovery being without complications."

8. Eduardo Marquina, *Obras completas*, vol. 8 (Madrid: Aguilar, 1951), 362–63, contains a poem, "A Don Ramón del Valle-Inclán," which ends: "And whenever the banal and inane accost him, / He, who can make of his hut a palace, / cradles his lost arm and, laughing like / Lord Byron, makes game of his lameness."

9. The theme of blindness appears on various levels of importance in novels and plays particularly. Electus, the blind man of Gondar, makes frequent entrances in *Flor de santidad, El Marqués de Bradomín, Cara de Plata, Divinas palabras*, and *Romance de lobos*; but his crowning role is in *El embrujado*. The blind man of Flavia is another recurrent character. Máximo Estrella, another blind man, is the protagonist of *Luces de bohemia* and Ginebra is the sightless protagonist of *Voces de gesta*. Valle-Inclán's preoccupation with eyes can be seen also in "Geórgicas," "¡Malpocado!" *La reina castiza*, and *Sonata de primavera*, as elsewhere, in a minor key. Some poems, like "En el camino" from *Aromas de leyenda*, also reflect variations on the theme. See E. Segura Covarsi, "Los ciegos de Valle-Inclán," *Clavileño* 3, 17, (1952): 49–52.

10. José María Eça de Queiroz, *El crimen del Padre Amaro*, Versión castellana de Ramón del Valle-Inclán, 2 vols. (Barcelona: Maucci, 1901).

11. "Un cabecilla," reprinted in *La Ilustración Artística* 20 (1 July 1901). The story had been published first in *Extracto de Literatura* (16 September 1893) and in *El Globo* (29 September 1893). Fichter does not include the present publication in his notes to the text.

12. F. Madrid, *La vida altiva*, 62. Barbey d'Aurevilly's *Le rideau cramoisi* has been indicated as another possible influence on *Sonata de otoño*. See Julio Casares, *Crítica profana: Valle-Inclán, Azorín, Ricardo León* (Madrid: Imprenta Colonial, 1916).

13. F. Madrid, *La vida altiva*, 114.

14. "Sonata de otoño," *Los Lunes de El Imparcial* (9 September 1901); "Don Juan Manuel," *Los Lunes de El Imparcial* (23 September 1901), not to be confused with "Rosarito," which bears that title in *Jardín novelesco* (Madrid: Tipografía de *Revista de Archivos, Bibliotecas y Museos*, 1905); "Hierba santa," *Juventud* 1, 1, (1 October 1901); "Corazón de niña," *Juventud* 1, 3, (30 October 1901); "El palacio de Brandeso," *Los Lunes de El Imparcial* (13 January 1902); "El miedo," *Los Lunes de El Imparcial* (27 January 1902), which was only part of a story with the same title he had tried to publish unsuccessfully in *La España Moderna*.

15. The polemic begun by Casares and continued by later critics, with reference to the background of the first *Sonata* to be published, has been resolved by Emma Susana Speratti Piñero, "Génesis y evolución de *Sonata de otoño*," *Revista Hispánica Moderna* 25, 1–2 (January-April 1959): 57–80. The article includes the full texts of "Sonata de otoño," "Don Juan Manuel," "Corazón de niña," "El palacio de Brandeso," and fragments of "El miedo." Her notations indicate the many variants between these "excerpts" and the subsequent book editions of *Sonata de otoño*.

16. *Sonata de primavera. Memorias del Marqués de Bradomín* (Madrid: Imprenta de Antonio Marzo, 1904), 195 pp., dedicated to José Ortega Munilla in a prologue whose pages are unnumbered.

17. (Madrid: Imprenta de Ambrosio Pérez, 1902), 177 pp., dedicated to "Don Armando Palacio Valdés. Homenaje de admiración. Valle-Inclán." Shortly after publication appeared what must be the first critical mention of the novel, in Julio Burell, "Escritores jovenes—Noticia de un libro," *Los Lunes de El Imparcial* (17 March 1902): "Valle-Inclán labors over, enlivens and refines his *Sonata de otoño*, like an ancient craftsman embossing marvelous triptychs, monstrances, and chalices."

18. Valentín de Pedro, *España renaciente. Opiniones, hombres, ciudades y paisajes* (Madrid: Calpe, 1922), 63–68, refers to Valle-Inclán and quotes Ricardo Calvo: "Publishers were not interested in a new book of his, which I had read in its original form and thought stupendous: it was *Sonata de otoño*. Valle despaired over not being able to have it published; all his friends were supportive of his diatribes against publishing houses—and how he ranted!—but the book remained unpublished. But one day when I had funds, I let him know through a mutual friend who had told me how frustrated Valle was, that he shouldn't worry any longer because I would issue his book; that's how I became his publisher. It could be said that I was the one who thrust him into the literary marketplace because *Sonata de otoño* had the splendid success that all of us expected."

19. José Ortega y Gasset, "Glosa," *Faro de Vigo* (28 August 1902).

20. The poem reads: "Marquis (like the divine one titled), I greet you. / 'Tis autumn and, saddened, I come from Versailles. / 'Twas cold and the vulgar masses tramped through it. / The stream of Verlaine's fountain was mute. Facing a nude marble, I stood pensive / on seeing a dove that flew by without warning, / and, in an unconscious cerebral way, / you came to mind. An exegesis is to be avoided. / Autumnal Versailles; a dove; a striking / marble; roaming crowds, urban, dense; / prior reading of your subtle prose; / your recent triumph still in mind . . . I leave / details aside in explicating how I came / autumnally, to send this rose bouquet to you."

21. See Valle-Inclán's interesting appraisal of Don Juan in Ramón Gómez de la Serna, *Don Ramón María del Valle-Inclán*, 63–64.

22. Francisco Luis Bernardez, "Valle-Inclán en la Puebla del Caramiñal," *La Nación* (30 January 1955).

23. "Semblanzas de literatos españoles," lecture by Valle-Inclán. See F. Madrid, *La vida altiva*, 291–92.

24. J. Rubia Barcia, "Valle-Inclán y la literatura gallega," *Revista Hispánica Moderna* 21, 2 (April 1955): 102–3.

25. *La Ilustración Española y Americana* 46, 7 (22 February 1902). Note that views on modern art will be repeated in the prologue to *Sombras de vida* (see fn. 27).

26. Ibid.

27. See citations from the prologue by Valle-Inclán in Melchor Almagro San Martín, *Sombras de vida* (Madrid: A. Marzo, 1902), 11–21. This same prologue was the basis for Valle-Inclán's "Breve noticia de mi estética cuando escribí este libro," which prefaced the second edition of *Corte de amor* (1908).

28. "Modernismo," lecture by Valle-Inclán in Buenos Aires, Teatro Nacional, 5 July 1910. See F. Madrid, *La vida altiva*, 196–201.

29. "La adoración de los Reyes," *El Imparcial* (1 January); "El palacio de Brandeso," *El Imparcial* (13 January); "El miedo," *El Imparcial* (27 January); "Su esencia," *La Correspondencia de España* (9 February); "Egloga," *El Imparcial* (10 February); "Modernismo," *La Ilustración Española y Americana* (22 February); "Corazón de niña," *Diario de Pontevedra* (28 February); "Sonata de otoño," *El Liberal* (5 March); "A media noche," *La Ilustración Artística* (7 April); "Tierra Caliente," *La Correspondencia de España* (8 April); "A ras de tierra," *El Imparcial* (9 June); "Las tormentas del 48," *La Correspondencia de España* (6 July); "Tierra Caliente. Los tiburones," *La Ilustración Artística* (7 July); "Rosita Zegrí" *El Imparcial* (14 July); "La reina de Dalicám," *Revista Ibérica* (15 July); "Tierra Caliente. A bordo de la fragata Dalila," *La Correspondencia de España* (3 August); "Eulalia," *El Imparcial* (18, 25 August; 8, 15, 22 September); "¡Malpocado!" *El Liberal* (30 November); "¡Malpocado!" *La Correspondencia Gallega* (3 December).

30. "A media noche," *La Ilustración Artística* 21 (7 April 1902); "Tierra Caliente," *La Ilustración Artística* 21, 1071 (7 July 1902).

31. Paul Alexis, *Las chicas del amigo Lefèvre*, trans. by R. del Valle-Inclán (Valencia: Imprenta de El Pueblo, 1902).

32. José María Eça de Queiroz, *La reliquia*, trans. by Ramón del Valle-Inclán (Barcelona: Maucci, 1902). The first edition of the novel had been translated by Carmilo Bargiela, who did

the literal version using his knowledge of *gallego*, and Francisco Villaespesa, who composed the final draft. The inadequacy of that first version prompted the publisher to seek Valle-Inclán's rendition; this was successful for it proved worthy of being used for the third edition (Barcelona: Maucci, 1925). Casares, *Crítica profana*, 95, has commented on Valle-Inclán's translation by pointing to some variants of miniscule importance between the original and the Spanish versions: "It is obvious that Valle-Inclán translated *saudoso* (nostalgic) with *suave*, something unpardonable in a Galician writer." He adds in the footnote attached to the criticism: "This and similar blunders lead me to wonder if Valle-Inclán translated Eça from the French."

33. F. Madrid, *La vida altiva*, 111.

34. *Insula* 176–77 (July-August 1961): 9, cites these comments by J. R. Jiménez: "I recall that in the short-story contest held by *El Liberal*, it was not seen fit to award the first prize to the story "¡Malpocado!" I became indignant because I knew that the gem was well worth five hundred pesetas, and found it typically Spanish for it to be said that the story was worth *only two hundred and fifty*."

35. Joaquín Pesqueira, "Don Ramón del Valle-Inclán," *El Correo Gallego* (12 January 1936): "'Malpocado' (*sic*) is an imperishable page in Spanish literature. 'Malpocado' is the living soul of Galicia. With 'Malpocado,' Don Ramón del Valle-Inclán became a sudden celebrity and was proclaimed, by unanimous consensus, the 'magical prose stylist of Spain.'" But José Ortega y Gasset, "*La Sonata de estío* de don Ramón del Valle-Inclán," *La Lectura* 4, 1 (February 1904): 227–33, criticizes, "Valle-Inclán neither stirs up emotions nor wishes to do so. Only in 'Malpocado' do a few definitive lines move the reader. The rest of the piece is inhumanly devoid of tears. He writes in a manner that decries fresh sentimentalism, nor is there a page devoted to a last-minute inspiration. The artist jealously hides man's bitterness and misfortunes: there is an excess of art in this writer. He becomes as disagreeable as a man who never drops his guard by abandoning himself to passion, exhaustion, or weariness."

36. "Cartas galicianas: Pontevedra—Una visita a Echegaray," *El Globo* (13 October 1891). According to the evidence in the article Valle had been introduced to Echegaray by Torcuato Ulloa.

37. F. Madrid, *La vida altiva*, 297–98; Gómez de la Serna, *Don Ramón María del Valle-Inclán*, 78–79.

38. Francisco Villaespesa, *Obras completas*, vol. 2 (Madrid: Aguilar, 1954), 879–80: "One-armed like Cervantes, / with bearded face and mien of wax, / like an ascetic in Ribera's oils, / in lisping phrases, Valle-Inclán / proffers the strangest paradoxes / to a group of bearded painters, / listening religiously, / or tells them of the deeds / and the romantic quests / Tierra Caliente saw him do."

39. J. Moya del Pino, "Valle-Inclán y los artistas," *La Pluma* 63, 65: "The influence of Valle-Inclán's aesthetic norms on contemporary Spanish art has been extensive. All the artists mentioned—among whom are many who have attained solid, well-deserved prestige—were influenced, to a greater or lesser degree, by his doctrines, which they diffused through their own works. . . . I believe that in some future time, when the painting, sculpture, and applied art produced today is studied in depth, the role of Valle-Inclán in this regard will achieve an extraordinary prominence." See also Robert Lima, "Hacia una exégesis de las ediciones de Valle-Inclán tras su diseño," in Juan Antonio Hormigón, ed., *Valle-Inclán y su tiempo hoy*, Actas del simposio internacional en el cincuentenario de su muerte (Madrid: Ministerio de Cultura, 1988).

40. *La Pluma*, 56, 57: "It was a festive night whenever Don Ramón would read us his latest work. In the center of the group, Don Ramón would remove his glasses, leaning over the manuscript; we listened in silence, and out of that circle of attentive heads and bent backs would come the metallic voice of the maestro . . . Our gatherings took on special importance whenever the Exhibition of Fine Arts was held . . . we came to have correspondents in London, Paris, Munich, Basel, Rome."

41. Ibid., 57.

42. Gómez de la Serna, *Don Ramón María del Valle-Inclán*, 88.

43. Interview with C. Rivas Cherif, *El Sol* (3 September 1920).

44. Gómez de la Serna, *Don Ramón María del Valle-Inclán*, 136.

45. C. Rivas Cherif, "Los españoles y la guerra. El viaje de Valle-Inclán," *España* (11 May 1916).

46. "Modernismo," lecture by Valle-Inclán, in which he refers at length to the example of the old masters (Raphael, Velázquez, El Greco) and proceeds to delineate how certain of his contemporaries (Sorolla, Rusiñol, Romero de Torres) have learned from them.

47. Gómez de la Serna, *Don Ramón María del Valle-Inclán*, 95.

48. Ibid.

49. Ibid., 100.

50. "Breve noticia acerca de mi estética cuando escribí este libro" (August 1903), *Corte de amor* (Madrid: Imprenta Balgañón y Moreno, 1908). The quotation is exactly as it appears in the text in regards to spelling (Rimbaut) and misquotation of part of Rimbaud's sonnet "Voyelles," which should read: "A noir, E blanc, I rouge, U vert, O bleu."

51. See the important catalog *Exposición Valle-Inclán y su tiempo* (Madrid: Ministerio de Cultura, 1986).

Notes for Chapter 6: Continuation

1. "Concurso de críticas," *El Globo* (1 April 1903); "Una lección," *El Globo* (6 April 1903); "Crónica. Un Retrato," *El Liberal* (7 February 1903); "El Modernismo en Literatura," *Album Americano* (22 August 1903).

2. Juan Cuesta y Díaz, ed., *Colección de frases y refranes en acción* (Madrid: Bailly-Baillière, 1903); "Corte de amor," *Los Lunes de El Imparcial* (9 March 1903); "Por Tierra Caliente," *La Correspondencia Gallega* (27 May 1903); "Jardín umbrío (un cabecilla)," *Los Lunes de El Imparcial* (1 June 1903); "Su esencia," *La Correspondencia Gallega* (10 July 1903); "Satanás," *Nuestro Tiempo* 3, 25 (1903); "Sonata de estío," *Los Lunes de El Imparcial* (20, 27 July; 3, 10, 24, 31 August; 14, 21, 28 September 1903); "Hierba santa," *La Ilustración Artística* 22 (7 September 1903); "Sonata de estío," *El Heraldo de Madrid* (3 October 1903); "Sonata de estío," *El Liberal* (9 October 1903); "Rosarito," *La Ilustración Española y Americana* (30 October; 8 November 1903); "Ano de hambre (Recuerdo infantil)," *El Heraldo de Madrid* (28 November 1903); "Tragedia de ensueño," *La Ilustración Artística* (7 December 1903); "Noche buena (Recuerdo infantil)," *Los Lunes de El Imparcial* (24 December 1903); "Autobiografía," *Alma Española* 1, 8 (27 December 1903).

3. Pedro Massa, "Lances y recuerdos de don Ramón del Valle-Inclán," *La Prensa* (15 January 1967). Also see Ramiro de Maeztu, "¡Adios, Bohemia!" *El Pueblo Vasco* (9 August 1903): "Each paragraph that he writes represents a week of work; each story a trimester. At the end of a year, he earns a total of two hundred and twenty pesetas. Yesterday he spoke to me of his firm resolve to have himself tonsured and to enter an asylum." The lengthy process indicated by Maeztu resulted not from inability of expression but from a meticulosity demanded by his aesthetic. In later years, when he had mastered his art, Valle-Inclán declared that writing came easily to him. See Francisco Madrid, *La vida altiva de Valle-Inclán*, 108–9.

4. (Madrid: Vda. de Rodríguez Serra, 1903 [Biblioteca Mignón, xxxiii]), illustrated by José Sánchez Gerona, who had designed *Epitalamio*; the cover was adorned with the sketch of a romantically evocative garden scene. *Insula* 16, 176–77 (July-August 1961): 9, quotes Juan Ramón Jiménez's criticism of the book: "Knowing that Don Ramón del Valle-Inclán was enamored of this beautiful title, I immediately sent for the book when its publication was announced . . . I have enjoyed anew these stories, admirable stories that I already knew . . . I felt again that these writings of Valle-Inclán ought to be engraved in enduring letters, in large, clear letters on impressive folios, letters that would permit the appreciation of the exactness and delicacy of phrasing, the marvelous way of narrating beautiful things without recourse to artifice or base rhetorical devices . . . And yet, I feel that this was not the proper title for these

stories. This title well deserves an entirely new book, which would elaborate a new tenderness and sadness of the heart; some pages in which the pen would craft the golden and illusory lacework of the soul. Remember that divine *Sonata de otoño*." This advice may have been a reason why in later editions there is the explanatory subtitle, *Historias de santos, de almas en pena, de duendes y ladrones*. In 1905 the author used that subtitle after the title *Jardín novelesco*, apparently seeking to reconcile content and title as Jiménez had pointed out.

5. (Madrid: Imprenta de Antonio Marzo, 1903), dedicated to José Ortega Munilla.

6. *Helios* 1, 2 (May 1903): 246–47: "That evocation of past greatness, of ancient courtliness, of romantic emotions, is what I believe to be the felicitous melody, the total self-assurance of thought in Valle-Inclán. . . . Being of a refined carnal sensuality himself, Valle-Inclán's women are either sensual or victims of the sensuality of others . . . Valle-Inclán's entire sensual refinement is a type of romanticism. He is a romantic: a soul like that of Espronceda, of Zorrilla, and a rich phraseology full of exquisite ondulations. The rest—the moonlight, the sad nights of breezes and whimpers, the black dogs full of evil—has something of Musset, Heine, and Bécquer; better said, it contains something of that deep flowery shadow out of which have always emanated so much fragrance, cadences, and tears."

7. Antonio de Hoyos y Vinent, "El cine mudo . . . Los Banquetes," *Ahora* (28 January 1936): 11.

8. Melchor Almagro, *Sombras de vida* (Madrid: Imprenta de Antonio Marzo, 1903), ix-xxii. An article entitled "Prólogo al libro *Sombras de vida* de Melchor Almagro," appeared in *El Imparcial* on 28 May 1903, reproducing Valle-Inclán's prologue.

9. "Modernismo," *La Ilustración Española y Americana* 46, 7 (22 February 1902).

10. Melchor Almagro, *Sombras de vida*, ix-xiii.

11. Serialized version: *Los Lunes de El Imparcial* (20, 27 July); (3, 10, 24, 31 August); (14, 21, 28 September 1903). The subsequent book: (Madrid: A. Marzo, 1903). The antecedents for this work can be found in "Bajo los trópicos" and "La Niña Chole," the former published on 12 June 1892 being incorporated into the story from *Femeninas*, whose date of composition was April 1893. Fernández Almagro, *Vida y literatura de Valle-Inclán*, 217, refers to Valle-Inclán's statement in a lecture (1921) that an episode in *Sonata de estío* was inspired in *Los bandidos de Río Frío*, a Mexican novel.

12. La *Sonata de estío* de don Ramón del Valle-Inclán," *La Lectura* 4, 1 (February 1904): 227–33. Historicity: "Don Ramón del Valle-Inclán is a 'Renaissance' man. The reading of his books makes one think of the names and great moments of that era of human history. . . . Yes: the author of the *Memorias del Marqués de Bradomín* is a man from another century, a stone from a geological era that lies forgotten on the face of the earth"; aesthetic sense : "Sr. Valle-Inclán's literature . . . is agile, without transcendence, beautiful like useless things . . . resembling the craft of a metalsmith more than that of a writer . . . But, above all, his is an exquisite and perfect art: the artist keeps vigil in his spirit, with the solicitude of a prudent virgin, over that first lamp of which Ruskin speaks: the lamp . . . of sacrifice"; literary technique: "There are pages in *Sonata de estío* that must have cost their author more than a week of struggling with words and turning them over. He has worked very hard, as is obvious, to grasp the technique of composition that provides the greatest intensity and descriptive power to adjectives. Valle-Inclán has a sincere and true affection for them; in some cases, he demonstrates a veritable cult and handles them sensually, now placing them before, now after the noun, not on a whim, but because in that particular position, rather than in another, they convey their full expressiveness and appear in full relief: he shuffles, multiplies, and caresses them"; character: "In order to capture that charming and pleasant aspect of persons and things, it is necessary to have had a full life, to have pried into many corners and—who knows?—perhaps to have had little love for one's home and have knocked about often in odd places."

13. Ibid.: "If Sr. Valle-Inclán were to enlarge his frame of reference, his style would benefit from sobriety, losing its imaginary and musical illness, that preciosity that is sometimes cloying but almost always charming. Today, he is a very personable and interesting writer; then, he would become a great writer, a master among writers. . . . Among our contemporary

writers, he is one of those I read with great pleasure and greater attentiveness. I believe that, better than any other, he manifests certain knowledge of phraseological chemistry."

14. Ibid.: "When I've finished reading this potential book and patted it with pleasure, I'll exclaim: 'Here at last is the book in which Valle-Inclán has abandoned fanciful themes and given us human stories, wholly human stories, in the noble style of a well-born writer!'"

15. "Sonata de primavera," *Los Lunes de El Imparcial* (22, 29 February; 7, 14, 21, 28 March; 11, 18, 25 April; 30 May; 6, 13, 20, 27 June 1904); "Fué Satanás," *Galicia* (13, 14 July); "La confesión," *Por Esos Mundos* 114 (July 1904); "Geórgicas," *Los Lunes de El Imparcial* (15 August 1904); "Un cuento de pastores," *Los Lunes de El Imparcial* (19 September 1904); "Santa Baya de Cristamilde," *Los Lunes de El Imparcial* (26 September 1904); "Flor de santidad," *El Gráfico* (13 October 1904); "Flor de santidad," *Los Lunes de El Imparcial* (17 October 1904).

16. "Prólogo (Crónica: Un retrato)," Augusto Riera, *Aventuras del bandido gallego Mamed Casanova* (Barcelona: Maucci, 1904). José María Eça de Queiroz, *El primo Basilio*, trans. by Ramón del Valle-Inclán, 2 vols. (Barcelona-Buenos Aires: Maucci, 1904). A second edition of this translation was issued by the same publisher in 1925.

17. (Madrid: A. Marzo, 1904).

18. Valle-Inclán, *Flores de almendro* (Madrid: Librería Bergua, 1936), 221, contains a footnote on "¡Malpocado!": "This same story, with slight variants, can be found as an episode of *Adega*, in chapters 1, 2, and 3 (fourth section). Still another of the chapters of that work (3 of the second section), is 'Egloga,' published separately by the author."

19. Antonio Machado, *Poesías completas* (Madrid: Espasa-Calpe, 1928), 239–40: "This simple legend in sage country tongue, / not old or new, composed by Valle-Inclán, /. uncovers through the pleasant breath of evening wind, / that sacred flower, the soul, that will not die. // The legend's field on field. A pilgrim / returning from the Holy Land alone, / where Jesus lived, now wanders aimlessly / through the Galician sierra's rough terrain. // Spinning silently, the distaff at her waist, / eyes resplendent with an azure flame / born of humble piety, Adega sees the pilgrim's / pallid figure, set against the waning light, / his face resplendent with the glory and the gall / of love which once belonged to Christ the Lord."

20. (Madrid: A. Marzo, 1904). The description relates the atmosphere: "An old bed with a silk canopy . . . old curtains of crimson damask . . . paintings hanging on the wall. They were old canvases of the Florentine School . . . The salon was golden, French in style, feminine and luxurious. Little Cupids with garlands, nymphs dressed in lace, gallant hunters, and stags with proliferous horns covered the tapestry on one wall, while on the console could be seen charming porcelain groups of ducal shepherds . . . country marchionesses."

21. J. Moya del Pino, "Valle-Inclán y los artistas," *La Pluma* 6, 32 (January 1923): 65 : "His taste for plasticity always led him to a preoccupation with the beauty of furnishings and interior decor; the current renaissance of the sumptuous arts in Spain is due, in great part, to his ideas on these subjects."

22. For example, the parallelism between D'Annunzio's Maximila and Valle-Inclán's María Rosario in several minor details. See Julio Casares, *Crítica profana: Valle-Inclán, "Azorín," Ricardo León* (Madrid: Imp. Colonial, 1916), 99.

23. For example, the episode of the monk who tells the protagonist that in a portentuous dream he has seen death being plotted against Bradomín and that he must seek the help of a witch if he is to survive the attempt, is common to both Casanova and Valle-Inclán's work (see Casares, *Crítica profana*, 101–9). But the author acknowledges his source when Bradomín refers to the *Mémoires* as "mi lectura favorita" and to Casanova as his teacher.

24. F. Madrid, *La vida altiva*, 109–10. See also Fernández Almagro, *Vida y literatura*, 220.

25. (Madrid: Tipografía de la *Revista de Archivos, Bibliotecas y Museos*, 1905). Chapters of the novel also appeared separately: "La corte de estella," *Los Lunes de El Imparcial* (15, 22, 29 May; 19, 26 June; 31 July; 7 August 1905); "Sonata de invierno. Texto del capítulo final de la obra," *El Imparcial* (16 November 1905).

26. "La misa de San Electus," *Los Lunes de El Imparcial* (6 February 1905); "La misa de San Electus," *La Correspondencia Gallega* (13 February 1905); "A media noche," *La Ilustración*

Española y Americana (8 March 1905); "Una desconocida," *La Ilustración Artística* (13 March 1905); "Una desconocida," *La Correspondencia Gallega* (21 July 1905).

27. *Jardín novelesco—Historias de santos, de almas en pena, de duendes y ladrones* (Madrid: Tipografía de la *Revista de Archivos, Bibliotecas y Museos*, 1905), 267 pp.

28. Azorín published his evocative *La ruta de Don Quijote*; Unamuno analyzed *La vida de Don Quijote y Sancho*, beginning his study with the word *Nada*; Marcelino Menéndez y Pelayo published three essays: "Cultura literaria de Cervantes," "Interpretaciones del Quijote," and "El Quijote de Avellaneda"; Julio Cejador issued *La lengua de Cervantes*; F. Navarro Ledesma published *El ingenioso hidalgo Miguel de Cervantes Saavedra*; Francisco Rodríguez Marín's first critical edition of the *Quijote* came out that year; and abroad, J. Fitzmaurice Kelly published *Cervantes in England*.

29. Interview with José Montero Alonso, *La Novela Semanal* 6 (1926).

30. In these essays he viewed first "La psicología de Echegaray," as expressed in the recent play; in "La obra del diablo" he saw the awarding of the Nobel Prize and the proposed homage as the result of the Devil's intervention; in "Examen del programa" he chastised the association that arranged the tribute; and in "La cuestión del día" he made a resumé of the entire career of Echegaray as one filled with awards, praise, and honor that had not been earned or otherwise deserved.

31. Ramón Goméz de la Serna, *Azorín* (Buenos Aires: Losada, 1957), 156, cites a letter signed by Grandmontagne and Valle-Inclán: "Dear Azorín: Valle-Inclán and I came by the editorial offices last night in order to give you the list of signatories. We discussed the manner of publication for that small protest. We wanted to consult you about it. We concluded that the most opportune way was for it to be included in one of your articles. We feel that we owe you that satisfaction since you're the only one who has faced the issue in writing. So, you can write a few pages as you see fit and publish the signatures of the protestors with the text agreed upon by all."

32. "La protesta," *La Farándula* (1905), published by Azorín as a postscript to his articles in *España*. In the essay accompanying the declaration he noted that Echegaray should not be the only recipient of the young intellectual's ire: "There must also be a protest against the many others who, like him . . . stand for a Spain that is long past, dead, corroded by prejudice and deceit, assaulted by despots, exploited by an extortive bureaucracy."

33. F. Madrid, *La vida altiva*, 247.

34. Ricardo Baroja, *Gente del 98* (Barcelona: Juventud, 1952), 79: "Valle-Inclán dictated to an improvised secretary. The draft was read; it was discussed; some slight corrections were made. It was translated into French (by Oroz). I don't remember what was in it, but I do recall that it sounded like a choice passage from an anthology of Chateaubriand. The waiter brought writing materials and the one in our group with the best penmanship copied the missive. Without a thought to the consequences for falsifying a signature, he signed Anita Delgado, the Camelia. There were five of us in the café at that time (Valle-Inclán, Baroja, Julio Romero de Torres, Leandro Oroz, and Anselmo Miguel Nieto). Each of us placed five *céntimos* on the writing desk. We went into the street. At the Puerta del Sol . . . the five of us bought a postage stamp . . . We wanted to share equally in the glory that our intervention would undoubtedly bring."

35. There are as many variations on the details of the story as there are recorders of the events concerned: Fernández Almagro, *Vida y literatura*, 128: "Valle-Inclán came up with the jest of writing a clever letter, in which she declares her love for the maharajah, that he composed and signed with Anita's name. The joke had an unexpected outcome, with events taking such a turn that the Indian ruler took the Malagueñan dancer of the Central Kuursal with him to Paris, put her in school so she would have a modicum of social graces, and, eventually, married her. Satisfied with his accomplishment, Valle-Inclán told Leandro Oroz: 'Try to get that man to grant me a Kaputalan decoration with the right to wear a turban, kaftan and cutlass.'" Gómez de la Serna, *Don Ramón María del Valle-Inclán*, 86: "The maharajah fell in love with a dancer, Anita Delgado . . . and wrote her a letter, which her prudent mother

gave to Valle-Inclán to see if it was a serious matter. 'Of course this is serious!' replied Don Ramón. 'Go to the Café Levante after tonight's performance and I'll write the reply.' Valle-Inclán's letter was effective, and . . . the beautiful Anita, after spending some time in a school in England, married the maharajah. Half in jest, Valle-Inclán asked only: 'Try to get me a Kapurtalan decoration with the right to wear a uniform.'" F. Madrid, *La vida altiva*, 253–58, gives details about Anita and her family, their financial condition, and the overtures of the maharajah: "He wants to be her protector, but Anita rejects the offer. She insults the interpreter and the prince. The following day, the maharajah sends a bouquet of camelias and a message. He asks her forgiveness and bids her farewell. Then, several days later, when the matter is all but forgotten, the messenger reappears . . . This time he brings a letter from the prince's secretary in which she's offered one hundred thousand pesetas to spend a friendly period in Paris with the maharajah. . . . It was mandatory to reply to the prince's letter, which was full of gallantries. Valle-Inclán is chosen for the task. His flowery style will create a masterpiece. Valle-Inclán writes the reply in a highflown, grandiloquent language." The outcome of the marriage is discussed in Gómez de la Serna, *Don Ramón María del Valla-Inclán*, 86; Ricardo Baroja, *Gente del 98*, 82–84, mentions the dissatisfaction of the participants with the "embassy" of Oroz in regard to obtaining recognition of their part in the accomplishment of the affair.

36. Antonio Iglesias Laguna, "Valle-Inclán, La Restauración, El Ateneo," *La Estafeta Literaria* 274 (1963).

37. "Autobiografía," *Alma Española* 1, 8 (27 December 1903).

38. Josefina Blanco was the ingenue in the company at the Teatro de la Princesa, following in the tradition of her aunt Concha Suárez. Her first meeting with Valle became part of her memoirs and appeared in Pedro Massa, "La ilustre actriz Josefina Blanco, esposa que fué de don Ramón del Valle-Inclán, refiere en este fragmento de sus Memorias, cómo concoció al glorioso escritor," *Crónica* (12 January 1936): "There, close by, in the balcony alcove, stood out the plain figure of an ageless man. . . . He seemed not to see or hear. But, suddenly, as in a collision, my eyes encountered his. I quickly avoided that look, but not so quickly that I avoided noticing the expression with which those two eyes fixed on me for the first time. Without seeing it, I could feel the weight of that look. . . . The odd stranger left me with a mixed impression of fear and a certain ineffable sweetness."

39. Sebastián de la Nuez and José Schraibman, eds., *Cartas del archivo de Pérez Galdós* (Madrid: Taurus, 1967), 30. Nervo attests to being introduced to Galdós by Valle-Inclán at this time in "Los Grandes de Espana," *Obras completas*, vol. 21 (Madrid: 1920–1928), 91: "Valle-Inclán and I did, indeed, make those observations one afternoon while walking to the house of Don Benito Pérez Galdós."

40. *Sonata de estío. Memorias del Marqués de Bradomín* (Madrid: Sucesores de Hernando, 1906), 261 pp. Other 1906 publications: "Un ejemplo," *El Liberal* (13 March); "Comedia de ensueño," *Por Esos Mundos* 135 (April), and *Revista Moderna de México* (May); "Del misterio," *Los Lunes de El Imparcial* (15 April); "Del camino (A media noche)," *Los Lunes de El Imparcial* (22 April), and *La Correspondencia Gallega* (30 May); "Aguila de blasón," *Los Lunes de El Imparcial* (28 May), *La Correspondencia Gallega* (4 June), *España Nueva* (17, 19, 22, 24, 30 September; 3, 5, 9, 12 October; 4, 7, 10 November; 23, 30 December); "Comedia bárbara," *Los Lunes de El Imparcial* (18 June); "Jornada antigua," *Los Lunes de El Imparcial* (2 July); "Lis de Plata," in *Los Lunes de El Imparcial* (16 July), *La Correspondencia Gallega* (20 July), and *Diario de Pontevedra* (23 July); "Un bautizo," *La Correspondencia Gallega* (27 September), *Galicia* (15 December); "Gavilán de espada," *Por Esos Mundos* 7, 140 (September): 194–201.

41. *Cartas . . . de Pérez Galdós*, 29.

42. Ibid., 30.

43. See Sebastián de la Nuez Caballero, *Tomás Morales* (Canarias: Universidad de la Laguna—Biblioteca Filológica, 1956), 167.

44. Matilde Serao, *Flor de pasión*, trans. by Ramón del Valle-Inclán (Barcelona: Maucci, 1907); *Historias perversas* (Barcelona: Maucci, 1907), 200 pp. Prologue by Manuel Murguía, as in

Femeninas; Aguila de blasón: Comedia bárbara dividida en cinco jornadas (Barcelona: F. Granada, 1907).

45. Alberto Ghiraldo, "Como perdió su brazo D. Ramón María del Valle-Inclán," *Diario de La Plata* (9 September 1923): 420.

46. I have personally verified the data in both the registry of the parish church (*Matrimonios—libro 58*—6 April 1904 to 6 July 1912—folio 160, vuelto 468) and in the civil register. The parish entry is as follows: "Number 468. Don Ramón Valle y Peña with Doña Josefina Blanco y Tegerina. Married and witnessed August 24, 1907. In the parish of St. Sebastian of Madrid, on the twenty-fourth of August of the year one thousand nine hundred and seven: I, Dr. Andrés Mª Mayor, in its charge, with an expedient from the Illustrious Vicar General of the Bishopric, dated the twenty-second of this month . . . married in person and immediately witnessed the joining of Don Ramón José Simón Valle y Peña—employed, single, forty years of age—with Doña Josefa María Angela Blanco y Tegerina—single, twenty-five years of age, a native of León, like her parents, domiciled at Santa Catalina, number eight . . . The witnesses were Don Manuel Zas y Estevez and Don Eugenio Morales y Vega, members of this parish. And to verify it, I affix my signature . . . Dr. Andrés Mª Mayor." It is interesting to note that F. Madrid, *La vida altiva*, 149, in the section of his book headed "Anecdotario viajero," has a subheading "Conflicto en Chile," which reads: "Honeymoon of Don Ramón. He was very much in love with his wife, Doña Josefina Blanco, who, as everyone knows, had a delicate and small figure . . . There was so little to her that she looked like a girl rather than a woman. Don Ramón was running about the street in despair. . . . 'I can't find shoes for Josefina. . . . There are only seven-league shoes, size thirty-five, or shoes for little girls, and my Josefina has doll's feet.' "

47. See photograph in *Primer Acto* 82 (1967): 10.

48. Cipriano Rivas Cherif, *La Pluma* 6, 32 (January 1923): 90. "Shorn of the romantic mane that, until recently, had provoked the curiosity of Madrid, odd eyeglasses replaced by normal ones, more solicitous and neat about his appearance than ever before, the figure of Valle-Inclán was still unmistakable."

49. F. Madrid, *La vida altiva*, 275.

50. Rivas Cherif, *La Pluma* 6, 32 (January 1923): 90: "Valle-Inclán received us in the dining-room of his home, where, at the foot of a red-hot stove, lay a naked baby only a few days old, since the mother was still convalescing. Don Ramón was contemplating his daughter while trying to act as if he had no paternal feelings." Darío, *Todo al vuelo* (Madrid: Renacimento, 1912), 58: "He has almost become a bourgeois, marrying a 'kindred spirit' who understands him and truly loves him. . . . In his home on Santa Engracia Street, which is a nest of art, a pink little girl is a rose crowning his glory; she is the princess." In all, Valle-Inclán and Josefina had six children, the others being Joaquín María, Carlos Luis, María Beatriz, Jaime Clemente, and María Ana Antonia. He also gave all his children the added name Balthasar, the name of one of the Magi. As the first names bear out, Valle-Inclán consciously paid tribute to the Carlist tradition through his offspring.

51. Victoriano García Martí, *El Ateneo de Madrid (1835–1935)* (Madrid: Dossat, 1948), 264: "Among the personalities who visited the Ateneo and occupied its rostrum in the early years of the twentieth century, were, among others: Marconi, Maeterlinck, Bergson, the Prince of Monaco, Einstein, Sarah Bernhardt." See p. 269: "While Don Ramón was still a young man, around forty-odd years of age and with a beard that was still black, he created great interest in one of his early lectures from the rostrum of the Ateneo when he presented a sort of auto-biographical talk; he began by saying: 'In Galicia there are two classes of people—the masters and the servants. I belong to the first class.'. . . The laughter and applause of the audience went on and on."

52. Valle-Inclán had already employed that phrase in *Sonata de invierno*, in a speech by Bradomín, in *Obras completas de don Ramón del Valle-Inclán*, vol. 1 (Talleres Tipográficos de Rivadeneyra, 1944), 456. Hereafter abbreviated *OC*: "I don't aspire to teach, but to entertain. My entire doctrine can be found in one phrase: 'Long live the bagatelle!' For me, the greatest

achievement of humanity is having learned how to smile." Writing in the prologue to Valle-Inclán's *Obras completas*, vol. 1 (Madrid: Plenitud, 1952), xxii. Azorín referred to another use of his phrase in *Luces de bohemia*: "That 'Long live the bagatelle,' coined by the author of these lines, is used here without notice of its paternity."

53. F. Madrid, *La vida altiva*, 326.

54. (Madrid: Vallavicencio-Tipografía de la *Revista de Archivos, Bibliotecas y Museos*, 1907), 99 pp. Two of the poems had appeared in periodicals: "Milagro de la mañana," *Los Lunes de El Imparcial* (15 May 1907); "Flor de la tarde," *Revista Latina* 1, 1 (September 1907): 43. The book is introduced by Rubén Darío's "Soneto iconográfico para el señor Marqués de Bradomín": "This grand Don Ramón of the billy-goat beard, / whose smile is the flower of his form, / seems like an old god, towering, evasive, / who has come to life from his sculpture's cold. // The copper of his eyes flashes furtively, / kindling a red flame in the olive sprig. / I sense that I live and experience with him / a life that is harder and much more intense. // Don Ramón del Valle-Inclán disquiets me; / and through the zodiac of my present verses / he's diffused in vibrant visions of the poet, // or else broken in a shattering of crystal. / I have seen him pull the arrows from his chest / shot at him by all the Seven Deadly Sins."

Darío adds this commentary in *Todo al vuelo*, 58: "These fourteen lines do not fully convey the complex figure of this grand Don Ramón."

55. "Auto-retrato," *El Nuevo Tiempo Literario*, vol. 6 (1907–1908), 362; "A Isabel Venegas," *El Nuevo Tiempo Literario*, vol. 7 (1908–1909), 405. See Donald McGrady, "Una poesía desconocida de Valle-Inclán," *Insula* 334 (September 1974): 4. Other 1907 publications in periodicals include: "Tragicomedia," *Los Lunes de El Imparcial* (11 March); "Milagro de la mañana," *Los Lunes de El Imparcial* (15 May); "Aromas de leyenda," *El Liberal* (30 June); "Flor de la tarde," *Revista Latina* 1, 1 (September): 43; "Jornada antigua," *Revista Moderna de México* (October); "Romance de lobos (Comedia bárbara)," *El Mundo* (21, 22, 24, 30 October; 1, 2, 3, 4, 6, 12, 14, 19 November; 2, 4, 11, 18, 20, 26 December); "El Marqués de Bradomín," *El Imparcial* (3 November).

56. Articles in *El Mundo*: "Exposición de Bellas Artes. La primera palabra" (29 April); "Notas de la Exposición. Las intrigas" (2 May); "Notas de la Exposición. Un pintor" (3 May); "Notas de la Exposición. Las tres esposas" (6 May); "Notas de la Exposición. Divagaciones" (11 May); "Notas de la Exposición. Santiago Rusiñol" (19 May); "Notas de la Exposición. Ricardo Baroja" (1 June); "Notas de la Exposición. Del retrato" (12 June); "Notas de la Exposición. Las hijas del Cid" (30 June); "Notas de la Exposición. La clausura" (4 July 1908).

57. (Barcelona: Maucci, 1907), 200 pp.

58. *Jardín novelesco* (Barcelona: Maucci, 1908). This second edition contained several stories not collected in the first edition: "Hierbas olorosas," "Fué Satanás," "Egloga," "Una desconocida," and "La hueste." Excluded, however, was "Don Juan Manuel," whose subject matter had been incorporated into *Sonata de otoño*; *Corte de amor* (Madrid: Imprenta de Balgañón y Moreno, 1908). The four stories collected under this title are "Augusta," "Rosita," "Eulalia," "Beatriz." Other 1908 titles include: "Poetas del dia en España," *Revista Moderna de México* (August), which published the poem "Auto-retrato"; "Drama vulgar," *Por Esos Mundos* 9, 164 (September): 227–30; "Autobiografía," *Revista Moderna de México* (October); "Geórgicas," *Galicia* (15 December).

59. (Madrid: Imprenta de Primitivo Fernández, 1909). The book was designated as "Obras completas de don Ramón del Valle-Inclán. Tomo primero." This collection contained "Tula Varona," "Octavia," "Mi hermana Antonia," "La Generala," "La condesa de Cela." The prologue is signed by M. Murguía but lacks the dating that accompanied it in *Femeninas*. Other 1909 titles include: "Sol de la tarde. Ave," *España Artística y Literaria* (28 February); "Un bautizo," *Gaceta de Galicia* (16 March); "Un bautizo," *La Correspondencia Gallega* (27 March).

60. Biblioteca de Escritores Gallegos, vol. 1 (Madrid: A. Marzo, 1910). The cover of the book bore a portrait of Valle-Inclán done by Anselmo Miguel Nieto.

61. *Cartas . . . de Pérez Galdós*, 31.

62. Ibid.

63. *OC*, 1:450.

64. F. Madrid, *La vida altiva*, 282.

65. *El Cuento Semanal* 3, 121 (23 April 1909).

66. *La guerra carlista: Los crusados de la causa* (Madrid: V. Suárez—Imprenta de Balgañón y Moreno, 1908). The novel also was serialized in *El Mundo* (21, 22, 25, 26, 30 November; 1, 3, 5, 7, 11, 13, 17, 26, 29 December 1908); *El resplandor de la hoguera* (Madrid: G. Pueyo—Imprenta de Primitivo Fernández, 1909). The novel also was serialized in *El Mundo* (17, 21, 23 January; 1, 8, 9, 21, 28 February; 6 March; 4, 17 April; 7 May 1909); *Gerifaltes de antaño* (Madrid: G. Pueyo—Imprenta de Primitivo Fernández, 1909). The novel also was serialized in *El Mundo* (17, 18, 22, 29 August; 14, 22 September; 5, 12, 14, 24 October; 7, 10, 17, 21, 25, 27 November 1909). See also "La corte de Estella," *Por Esos Mundos* 11, 180 (January 1910): 4–14.

67. *El Correo Español* (24 June 1909): "Our good friend Sr. Argamasilla de la Cerda and the brilliant writer Don Ramón María del Valle-Inclán left yesterday for Navarra to tour that most loyal of regions and to recall the epic deeds of our last crusade, so that the outstanding novelist may be able to trace out in admirable pages, and with full knowledge of people and terrain, the third of his novels on the Carlist war, which have achieved so much success. The excursion will last a month." *El Eco de Navarra* (June 26, 1909): "The great literary figure Don Ramón del Valle-Inclán was in Pamplona yesterday accompanied by our distinguished friend and countryman Don Joaquín Argamasilla de la Cerda. In the afternoon, they set out by automobile for Estella. Sr. Valle-Inclán intends to spend a period studying Navarra and gathering impressions for a novel that will be, as all of his are, a beautiful work. Welcome to the great stylist." Similar reports of Valle-Inclán's arrival and itinerary appeared in *La Tradición Navarra*, *El Diario de Navarra* (1 July 1909), and *El Pensamiento Navarro*. *El Eco de Navarra* had two other items, on 2 and 3 July 1909. Another report is included in "Fragmentos de una biografía inédita de don Ramón del Valle-Inclán, que prepara su hijo Carlos del Valle-Inclán Blanco," in *Gerifaltes de antaño* by Ramón del Valle-Inclán (Madrid: Espasa-Calpe, 1945), 7–13.

68. "Fragmentos . . . ," 10.

69. Pío Baroja, *Memorias* (Madrid: Minotauro, 1955), 127, asks: "How can the three novels of *La guerra carlista* written by Valle-Inclán please me when the author set them in the Basque Country never having been in it?" Baroja's error is obvious on the face of the facts and in the informed content of the last two novels of the series.

70. Jacinto Benavente, *De sobremesa* (Madrid: Fernando Fe, 1910), 119, states: "I don't know if some fossilized liberal on reading *El resplandor de la hoguera*, the latest of Valle-Inclán's novels, will judge him to be definitely allied to the Carlist faction and mourn his having died to literature, to liberal literature—which is not to say all literature since literature is, above all, freedom. As for me, I can state that I know no other narrative of our civil wars that is more artistically dispassionate about the entire concept of factions. In it, those of one party or the other are human beings full of humanity, over whom passes fatally that whirlwind of collective madness that periodically inflames peoples and makes them war against one another over things that were inconsequential earlier and, consequently, should not matter to them."

71. See José Extramiana, *La guerra de los vascos en la narrativa del 98. Unamuno—Valle-Inclán—Baroja* (San Sebastián: Haranburu, Editor, 1983), 414 pp.

72. Carlos del Valle-Inclán, who inherited his father's library, has listed sixty-five works in that collection dealing with the period of the Carlist wars, almost all contemporary accounts. Valle-Inclán also possessed nearly complete editions of several newspapers of that era. His notes and private papers further disclose that Valle-Inclán had access to many other works outside his own holdings. See Gaspar Gómez de la Serna, "El *Episodio Nacional* como género literario—II—Las dos Españas de Don Ramón María del Valle-Inclán," *Clavileño* 3, 17, (1952): 17–32. Valle-Inclán's interest in Carlism dated from his student days at Santiago and was, undoubtedly, fostered by his father's tutelage. Many of the books and newspapers of Valle-Inclán proceeded from his father's collection, which he inherited.

73. F. Madrid, *La vida altiva*, 181–82.

74. Ibid., 183: "Spanish Postal Service. Madrid. One hundred attendees Carlist Circle ban-

quet honoring Inclán, offer themselves unconditionally king to save Spain present sectarianism. Inclán-Alcaraz."

75. "Cartas galicianas: De Madrid a Monforte—El último hidalgo de Tor," *El Globo* (2 October 1891): "I had to interrupt my journey and spend several hours, attracted by the novelistic aspect of the city, ancient feudal holding of the Counts of Lemus. Seen at the close of day and for the first time, as I experienced it, it stirs a vague recall, with its sombre fortified tower, of illustrations in the novels of Scott that I had read in my youth, as well as the chivalric spirit of those works. Monforte awakens the remembrance of a dark past, of wars between guilds, of fires and castle ruins, of feudal strife, of free villages and of those in the royal patrimony, of something akin to melancholic nostalgia for the fifteenth century, but of that fifteenth century full of legends and ballads about Frouseira gold, of that which made poetic the cry 'Free Galicia.' In such cities one can more readily understand the *political regionalism* of some Galicians."

76. F. Madrid, *La vida altiva*, 174–75.

77. Santa Cara, Joaquín Argamasilla de la Cerda y Bayona, *El yelmo roto*, Prologue by Ramón del Valle-Inclán (Madrid: Imprenta La Editora, 1913), v-viii.

Notes for Chapter 7: Drama

1. Segments of this chapter appeared in Robert Lima, "Valle-Inclán: The Man and His Early Plays," *Drama Critique* 9, 2 (Spring 1966): 69–78; and in Robert Lima, "Valle-Inclán in the Theatre: The Second Phrase," *Hispania* 53, 3 (September 1970): 419–28.

2. Maetzu told an anecdote regarding these reunions, *Estampa* (11 January 1936): 4: "We were in María and Fernando's small salon in the Español. In those days, he was a frightening figure, what with his huge collars from-who-knows-where, his tremendous paleness, and the rest of his aspect: the long beard and the hair down to his shoulders. . . . An Andalusian came by the salon that evening and said: 'One has to come to Madrid to hear wax figures speak!'"

3. Oreste Macrì, ed., *Poesie, di Antonio Machado* (Milan: Lerici, 1959), 20. Either Calvo or Macrì mistitled the play, which was *Andrea del Sarto*: "Antonio went to Granada, invited by Valle-Inclán, for the presentation of his version of *Andrea Doria* (sic), according to the actor Ricardo Calvo; the troupe went to Cordoba afterward, as did Antonio, who later returned to Madrid around the start of 1904."

4. Sebastián de la Nuez y José Schraibman, eds., *Cartas del archivo de Pérez Galdós* (Madrid: Taurus, 1967), 28. See also H. Chonon Berkowitz, *Pérez Galdós, Spanish Liberal Crusader* (Madison: University of Wisconsin Press, 1948), 439: "[Galdós] himself had already begun the dramatization back in 1897, but had never got beyond a preliminary, partial outline. In 1904 the job was taken over by Valle-Inclán, who abandoned it two years later, however, when it was almost finished." As attested by Valle-Inclán in a letter to Galdós, dated in Granada, "30-X-1906": "I've almost completed *Marianela*." He also states: "At Galdós's suggestion the Quinteros revived the idea in 1914 as their contribution to the national subscription." See also Julio Casares, *Crítica efímera*, vol. 2 (Madrid: Biblioteca Calleja, 1919), 43: "It appears that a haughty stylist first took on the job of doing a version, that other engineers attempted the task, and that it was finally done by the brothers Alvarez Quintero."

5. *Jardín novelesco* (Madrid: Tipografía de la *Revista de Archivos, Bibliotecas y Museos*, 1905). The names employed by Valle-Inclán in *Comedia de ensueño* indicate his periodic excursion into medieval and Renaissance sources. Madre Silvia is inspired in Celestina, the "mother" of brigands and practitioner of the black arts; Ferragut is named after the character in Boiardo's *Orlando innamorato*, Turpin's *Chronicles*, and Ariosto's *Orlando furioso*. Galaor, another bandit, derives his name, if not his morality, from the gallant knight of the novels whose extraordinary deeds are depicted in the epic bearing his name (his name reappears in *La cabeza del dragón* as "El General Fierabrás"); Argilao may be a derivative from a character of the *Orlando innamorato*; Solimán's name is the same as that of a character in Tasso's *Gerusalemme liberata*,

Suleiman the Magnificent, a Turkish sultan; Barbarroja derived his name from several infamous pirates of the Mediterranean during the sixteenth century; Gaiferos's appelation stems from one of the Twelve Peers of Charlemagne who, along with Roland, met his death at Roncesvalles; Cifer bears the name of one of the great and oldest of chivalric heroes of Spanish literature, the protagonist of *El cavallero Cifar*.

6. Floridor, writing in *ABC* (26 January 1906), commented, "Premieres. At the Princesa. *El marqués de Bradomín*, romantic drama in three acts. Written by Don Ramón del Valle-Inclán. Although all four sonatas are equally beautiful, I have a special predilection for that of autumn, which is intensely poetic, vibrant, fragrant, idyllic.

To those of us who know *Sonata de otoño*, the ill-fated love of Concha and the Marquis of Bradomín has lost nothing of its intimate essence or of its complex psychological process in being transferred to the stage; to those meeting them for the first time, the characters might seem somewhat nebulous and confused for lack of antecedents and documentation, which are always lost in any attempt to go from novel to play. But if the process required such painful permutation, the landscape, on the other hand—the conception of the staging, especially in the first act with those troublesome beggars—is firmly and admirably depicted, while the limpid style, rich and copious, that flows throughout the play, is delightful in its exquisiteness."

7. *El Marqués de Bradomín. Coloquios románticos* (Madrid: Pueyo—Tipografía de la *Revista de Archivos, Bibliotecas y Museos*, 1907). The book contained an epilogue, "Elogio de Don Ramón María del Valle-Inclán," dated 1907 in Paris and signed by Vargas Vila: "Valle-Inclán's books are not bestsellers, but quite simply a triumph of Art . . . I haven't read a peninsular author who better or more highly represents the soul of his Homeland, or whose writings depict more pointedly *the color of the Spanish Soul*. . . . Like all young intellectuals of Spain, Valle-Inclán despises politics and politicians, isolating himself from them as from contagious leprosy . . . to me, the Trinomial of Latin Art in Europe is composed of these three names: D'Annunzio in Italy, Maeterlinck in France, and Valle-Inclán in Spain . . . his greatest merit is not so much in what he says but in what he suggests." This first edition of the play contained the following dedication: "These dialogues saw life in the theatre some time ago. That memory smiles at me on re-reading these pages: With them I send Matilde Moreno and Francisco García Ortega my greeting in acknowledgement, admiration, and friendship." The frontispiece to this edition noted that *Hernán Cortés*, a work which had been in preparation since Valle-Inclán's Mexican trip, was "En prensa," but the work never appeared in print and the manuscript is presumed lost. See Casares, *Crítica efímera*, 119: "Ask Valle-Inclán about *Hernán Cortés* and he'll tell you that it's been at the printer's for ten years, and he hasn't dared to publish it as yet." See also Andrés González Blanco, *Los contemporáneos*, 3d series (Paris: Garnier, 1910), 28, fn. 3: "Perhaps in a study devoted to Valle-Inclán's future work, *Hernán Cortés*, already at the printer's, I'll take as my topic 'Modern Prose in Valle-Inclán.'" The same frontispiece also noted that the editions of *Femeninas*, *Epitalamio*, and *Cenizas* were exhausted, contradicting the statements by Valle and others that these works had fared badly in distribution.

8. This character was founded partly on Don Juan Manuel Pereira, a Galician who had died in 1892 and to whom Valle-Inclán had referred as "mi tío" in a lecture at the Ateneo in Madrid. See Ramón Otero Pedrayo, "El viaje a Orense de D. Ramón del Valle-Inclán," *Insula* 236–37 (July-August 1966): 3.

9. *Comedias bárbaras: Cara de Plata* first published in installments in *La Pluma* 26–31 (July-December 1922); first book edition: "Opera Omnia," vol. 13 (Madrid: Renacimiento—Imprenta Cervantina, 1923). *Aguila de blasón: Comedia bárbara dividida en cinco jornadas* (Barcelona: F. Granada, 1907), was supposedly written in fifteen days, possibly during Valle-Inclán's stay in Barcelona in 1907. *Romance de lobos* first published in installments in *El Mundo* (21 October-26 December 1907); first book edition: (Madrid: Pueyo, 1908).

10. Francisco Madrid, *La vida altiva de Valle-Inclán*, 151. See also José Caamaño Bournacell, *Por las rutas turísticas de Valle-Inclán*, 22, where, speaking of Valle-Inclán's ancestors, the

author says, "His brother Don José also participated in these revels and relaxations. All this took place in the choice and fruitful years of the Valle-Inclán brothers—1773–1774—who, because of such activities, became the real archetypes of the loutish sons of Don Juan Manuel Montenegro—Don Mauro, Don Rosendo, Don Pedrito, Don Farruquiño, Don Gonzalito—created on the stage by his grandson Don Ramón."

11. C. Rivas Cherif, "La Comedia bárbara de Valle-Inclán," España (16 February 1924): 8.

12. "Autocrítica," España 10, 412 (8 March 1924): 6. See Eva Llorens, Valle-Inclán y la plástica (Madrid: Insula, 1975), regarding El Greco's impact on Valle-Inclán.

13. El yermo de las almas. Episodios de la vida íntima (Madrid: Imprenta de Balgañón y Moreno, 1908). At various times in his career Valle-Inclán thought of including this play and three others—El Marqués de Bradomín, Cuento de abril, La Marquesa Rosalinda—in one volume, to be titled Tramoya romántica. The plan never materialized. El yermo de las almas would be produced by Margarita Xirgu in 1915.

14. Ramón Gómez de la Serna, Don Ramón María del Valle-Inclán, 107.

15. See review by Alejandro Miquis, "La semana teatral," Nuevo Mundo 845 (1910): "The new season has brought only one interesting premiere, and that thanks to the Teatro de los Niños, which Benavente transferred to the Comedia, where it has given us a very welcome gift: Valle-Inclán's two-act play La cabeza del dragón." See also Floridor's review in ABC (6 March 1910): "The outstanding Company of the Teatro de los Niños, created and sustained with selfless devotion by the renowned Jacinto Benavente, yesterday gained new laurels with the presentation of a new play, an exquisite tale by Don Ramón del Valle-Inclán. This marvelous craftsman of our prose could not have remained indifferent to this appealing movement and, consequently, has joined it with all the splendor of his genius and all the finesse of his style, with a children's tale in two acts full of ingenuity, tenderness, charm, and irony. The eminent author of the Sonatas took an infinite number of bows. The interpretation was very proper."

16. Europa 1, 1 (20 February 1910): 4–5. An illustration by Anne Frenchi and a photograph of Valle-Inclán are included. The book edition: (Madrid: Imprenta de Primitivo Fernández, 1910).

17. Europa 1, 4 (13 March 1910). The book edition is La cabeza del dragón. Farsa (Madrid: Perlado, Páez y Cía., 1914), "Opera Omnia," vol. 10, 159 pp. Although this period was one of growing commitment to the drama, Valle-Inclán continued to publish stories and poems in 1910: "El miedo," La Voz de Galicia (3 January); "Beatriz," La Correspondencia Gallega (8 January); "El miedo," La Correspondencia Gallega (19 January); "El miedo," Gaceta de Galicia (5 March); "Las lumbres de mi hogar: 'Oraciones,' 'La puerta dorada,'" Europa (6 March); "Mendigos," Gaceta de Galicia (12 March); "Lirio franciscano," Revista Moderna de México (April); "Cantigas de vellas," El Noroeste (5 April); "Cantigas de vellas," La Correspondencia Gallega (16 July); "Pobre rapaza sin padres," La Correspondencia Gallega (20 July); "Mendigos," La Correspondencia Gallega (17 August); "Lis de Plata," La Correspondencia Gallega (6 October).

18. My attempts to clarify the details of this journey met with the following reply from the Royal Mail Lines, Ltd., in London, operators of the "Amazon": "We thank you for your letter dated December 6th (1966), but very much regret that we are unable to assist you with your research on Ramón del Valle-Inclán as our records going back as far as 1910 have been destroyed." Tracing the possibility that Valle-Inclán may have passed through New York during this trip, as he implied in an interview in Buenos Aires (F. Madrid, La vida altiva, 174), I corresponded with the National Archives and Records Service, Washington, D.C., and with the Port of New York Authority. Neither office found any evidence of Valle-Inclán's arrival in the United States at any time. See José Juan Tablada's account of a visit with Valle-Inclán at New York City's McAlpin Hotel December 1921, in Cosmópolis 43 (1922): 265–68.

19. F. Madrid, La vida altiva, 174, 175.

20. Ibid., 178, quotes the invitation to the banquet: "The undersigned editors of the magazine Nosotros, echoing the idea that Argentina's intellectual youth put forth of paying tribute to the illustrious writer Don Ramón del Valle-Inclán through a heartfelt demonstration of their esteem, invite you to a dinner in his honor on the 20th of this month, at 8 p.m., in the Aue's

Keller restaurant." The undersigned are Carlos Octavio Bunge, Ricardo Rojas, José Ingenieros, Eduardo Talero, Juan Pablo Echagüe, Emilio Becher, Robert F. Giusti, Alfredo A. Bianchi, Enrique J. Banchs, Joaquín de Vedia, Enrique García Velloso, Carlos de Soussens, Alberto Gerchunoff, Enrique Sachetti, Pedro J. Naón, Arturo Giménez Pastor, Alfredo L. Palacios, Alfredo C. López, Pedro Sondereguer, Emilio Suárez Calmagno, Rafael Ruiz López, Alfredo Costa Rubert, Marcelo del Mazo, Alvaro Melián Lafinur, Luis Ipiña, Hugo de Achával, Gastón F. Tobal, Gustavo Caraballo, Carlos Alberto Leumann, Carlos Atwell Ocantos, Miriano Antonio Barrenechea, Miguel Mastroggianni, Enrique Hurtado Arias, Edmundo Montagne, Emilio Ravignani, José H. Rosendi, Armando Chimenti, Julio L. Noé, Jorge Walter Perkins, Eloy Farina Núñez, Vicente Cuitiño, Rómulo D. Carbia, Julio Rinaldini, Salvador Boucau, Alberto Ghiraldo, Guillermo Achával, Arturo Vázquez.

21. Azorín, *Madrid* (Buenos Aires: Losada, 1952), 36: "If Valle-Inclán found generally supportive elements in Buenos Aires, there was also a sour note. He says it in one of his letters. Certain isolated individuals opposed him. This deviation or dislike was occasioned by, among other things, the political ideology of the speaker. As Valle-Inclán writes: 'But these attacks were due—more than to the reasons stated earlier—to others. My stature as a traditionalist. . . . '" Azorín also notes on the previous page, "Valle-Inclán has always shown concern over our impact on America. In that letter, he expressed a vehement desire that our relations with our sister nations from across the sea—the American nations—be improved. Among other procedures that could approach that goal, he suggested sending to America spiritual missions made up of individuals who would be acceptable to the Americans. At that time, the Infanta Isabel had traveled to Argentina and, accompanying her as an exalted retinue, were four to six literary personalities of Spain. In Valle-Inclán's view, not all those individuals had stirred the enthusiasm of the Argentinians."

22. F. Madrid, *La vida altiva*, 176: "That night the theatre was filled with that cordial and impassioned public that makes up the Spanish colony. . . . It gave itself easily and Valle-Inclán's success was immediate and secure. There were delirious ovations at the end of each act, as well as during the play itself on the conclusion of particularly brilliant and juicy sets of verses. Doña Josefina Blanco received so much applause in the third act that Don Ramón had to share in them, taking bows in the middle of the act due to the audience's insistence."

23. The Uruguayian critic "Urgonif" (anagram of Frugoni) wrote in *El Día* (17 June 1910): "Those who, too accustomed to feelings of a secondary nature brought on exclusively by the the efficacy of scenic effects, are incapable of finding delight in elevated verbal harmonies that evoke a superior beauty, or of following the poet to uncontaminated regions of art, should not bother to visit the Cibils when Valle-Inclán's play is repeated—if it is—because they will not enjoy themselves. . . . Did our public like this gem, acclaimed in Madrid and, recently, in Buenos Aires? I wouldn't think of affirming or denying it for the simple reason that the public . . . was notorious by its absence. Some passages were applauded, but such signs of approval could not reach the level possible only in well-attended theatres. It is common to hear the praises of our cultural life and to be told that Montevideo has hundreds of people of taste and cultural awareness. Where were those hundreds the night before last that they didn't attend the theatre on Ituzaingó Street?

24. "Andanzas de un español aventurero. Hojas de mi cartera. De viaje por las Indias, Buenos Aires, 18–05–1910," *El Mundo* (12 June 1910); "Andanzas de un español aventurero. La señora Infanta en tierra argentina. De viaje por las Indias, Buenos Aires, 24–05–1910," *El Mundo* (19 June 1910).

25. Valentín de Pedro, *España renaciente. Opiniones, hombres, ciudades y paisajes* (Madrid: Calpe, 1922): "attached to the retinue of the Infanta Isabel, whether in the role of official playwright or not we don't know, was Eugenio Sellés, survivor of a theatrical aesthetic that Valle-Inclán found abominable. To his chagrin, we might add, because the producer of the Cómico, looking to bolster the season (*Cuento de abril* had been well received but hadn't brought in money), decided to pay tribute to the author of *Las vengadoras* by returning Sellés' play to the stage, despite Valle-Inclán's angry protests."

26. Azorín, *Madrid*, 35–36.

27. Ibid.

28. F. Madrid, *La vida altiva*, 183–184.

29. In *La cabeza del dragón*, in *Obras completas de don Ramón del Valle-Inclán*, vol. 2 (Madrid: Talleres Tipográficos de Rivadeneyra, 1944), 573. Unless otherwise indicated, all quotations from Valle-Inclán's works are from volumes 1 and 2 of this work, hereafter cited as *OC*. This statement seems to indicate that the lecture contract was signed while Valle was still in Spain and that this was one of the reasons for his trip to Argentina. This assumption can be made because *La cabeza del dragón* had been written and premiered prior to his departure; however, the lines cited may have been added to the text later, after the fact of his lecture contract.

30. F. Madrid, *La vida altiva*, 186–90. The lecture transcribed by Madrid consists of major excerpts derived from newspaper accounts following its presentation.

31. F. Madrid, *La vida altiva*, 194–95; see Gómez de la Serna, *Don Ramón María del Valle-Inclán*, 109–10, for variations on the quote (for example, instead of citing "removing from them" he cites "adding to them," which makes more sense in the context).

32. It appears that another lecture had been prepared to precede both this and the one on "Los excitantes." Azorín, *Madrid*, 35, quotes Valle-Inclán's letter to him dated 1910 in Buenos Aires: "Now I find myself giving lectures here. Today, the fourth, has been on Modernism in Europe; I covered painting and literature, trying to reestablish the parity of their values. I spoke of you, Benavente, and Unamuno, the only writers of books who are really known and esteemed here." The implication, if Valle-Inclán did not err, is that three and not two lectures preceded the one on "Modernismo." But in fact only the two others cited were delivered. The enigma can be resolved easily by tying in Valle-Inclán's statement in a conversation quoted in Gómez de la Serna, *Don Ramón María del Valle-Inclán*, 199: "'Did the bomb in the Colón interrupt your lectures?' 'Yes. I was going to deliver my second lecture that day, but I couldn't.'" The second lecture, therefore, never took place because of the bomb that exploded on 26 June during a performance of *Manon Lescaut* at the Teatro Colón (see F. Madrid, *La vida altiva*, 173). Consequently, Valle-Inclán could correctly refer to what was the third lecture he delivered as his fourth because it was indeed the fourth that he had prepared. The subject matter of the missing lecture has yet to be determined. However, Valle-Inclán did publish "Cosmogonía," *La Nación* (29 June 1910), an essay with ideas similar to those developed fully in *La lámpara maravillosa*. Published three days after the bombing, this article may in fact be the text of the lecture he could not deliver.

33. Jesús Arraco, *Don Ramón del Valle-Inclán* (Mexico, D.F.: Secretaría de Educación Pública, 1947), 27, 28. The critic Joaquín de Vedia has referred to Valle-Inclán in Argentina and to this lecture in particular. He is quoted in F. Madrid, *La vida altiva*, 202: "I met him during his visit to Argentina. He was enveloped by the reputation of his slander and rancor. I had just the opposite impression. It's always the case with individuals who are said to be of a sour disposition or malicious. In one of his lectures on important Spanish writers of the period, he praised Benavente, Ciges Aparicio, Baroja, that is, writers foreign to his way of thinking, of seeing, alien to his own sensibilities. . . . And he spoke of them with respect, exalting their merits and shunning their defects. . . . He spoke well of true writers, even if these were not of his spiritual persuasion. He was a total gentleman."

34. F. Madrid, *La vida altiva*, 201.

35. The anonymous review in *ABC* (27 May 1912) read in parts: "And the curtain falls slowly, while the play still rings in our ears like the echo of a divine melody that is being extinguished. The theatre fills with light and the audience, in an explosive, clamorous applause, insistently demands, as in the previous acts, the appearance of Valle-Inclán. And Valle appears, at last, to an effusive tribute, acclaiming his illustrious name. This pastoral tragedy—powerful, vibrant, and nobly entoned, if lacking the primitivist emphasis—is, in terms of style, D'Annunzian, and as admirable as *Romance de lobos* in its verve and vigor. Valle's triumph was great, enormous even, as was that of the amazing María Guerrero. One must look back to the most accomplished creations of the great artists in order to find some-

thing similar. In the role of the shepherdess Ginebra, María Guerrero was both the lightning and explosive element in the tragedy. Her attitude, bearing, and voice were ever attuned to the impression and the moment, attaining through the arrogance of her words and the energy of her expression the highest pinnacle of her art. She was colossal, stupendous."

36. *Mundial* 3, 7, 16 (1911–1912). On 2 August 1911, Amado Nervo wrote to Darío regarding *Mundial*: "Valle-Inclán's work is fine, very fine; he's every bit a poet surging." Undoubtedly he was referring to the first act of *Voces de gesta* (See Alberto Ghiraldo, "Como perdió su brazo D. Ramón María del Valle-Inclán," *Diario de La Plata* [9 September 1923]: 153.

37. Dictino Alvarez Hernández, S.J., *Cartas de Rubén Darío (Epistolario inédito del poeta con sus amigos españoles)* (Madrid: Taurus, 1963), 187.

38. Ghiraldo, "Como perdió su brazo," 420.

39. Alvarez, *Cartas*, 187. Apparently, Valle's letter was searching for an acknowledgment. That he had not received one is explained by the following letter to Darío by Josefina Blanco, dated 11 September 1911: "On returning from Santander, your letter of September 2 was waiting for me at home. My husband did indeed ask me to make a copy of *Voces de gesta*, but since I didn't know your address I sent the copy of the second act to Ramón so that he could forward it to you. That was about fifteen days ago, so I'm surprised that you haven't received it. Write and ask him for it again. His address is: Mira-Concha, 15, San Sebastián."

40. Alvarez, *Cartas*, 188.

41. Ibid., "My distinguished friend: On Ramón's behalf, I enclose the original that you need for the Christmas issue. As to the receipt, my husband has already written to you and now asks me to mention it again: you should write in the amount that you deem proper, taking into account the means of the Magazine and the way they normally do things." The letter is dated 24 September 1911 in Valladolid. From Burgos, on 5 October, Josefina wrote again to Darío: "I sent from Valladolid an original that you needed for the issue of *Mundial* scheduled to appear at Christmas. Since I haven't had a reply from you, I fear that it may have been lost; I beg you, therefore, to let me know if that's what happened so that I can file a claim. I'll be in Zaragoza until the twenty-third of the month and will await your ever-welcome news."

42. Ghiraldo, "Como perdió su brazo," 421. There is a possibility that the summer trips Valle-Inclán refers to, besides those indicated by the dating of his correspondence with Darío, included a journey to Brussels. See G. Campos, "Hablando con Valle-Inclán," *Chronique d'Egypte* (4 November 1911). He must have also returned to Villanueva de Arosa the year in which his mother died.

43. Alvarez, *Cartas*, 190. *La marquesa Rosalinda* was serialized in *Por Esos Mundos* 12, 202 (December 1911): 965–71.

44. *Voces de gesta. Tragedia pastoríl* (Madrid: Imprenta Alemana, 1912). The cover bears the date 1911 to indicate the date of completion of the play. The book was dedicated to María Guerrero. The ballad reads: "From the land of dreams, darkness and splendor, / where wild plants and strange flowers grow / through the debris of castles in ruin, / alongside the slopes of the mountains; / where shepherds pray in their huts / while their dogs sleep by the fire, / where ancient shadows still flit / through the caves of the wolf and the fox, / things of great mystery were borne by / Don Ramón María del Valle-Inclán. // Mysterious, tragic and strange things, / out of the dark tales of old, / harrowing love, criminal deeds and harm / nurtured as if in volcanic fumes, / Bloodthirsty faces, faces that pale, / shrieks in the night, sorrow and fear, / accursed spells, birds that fly / under the gerfalcon's threatening might, / are told in the gold and enamel poems of / Don Ramón María del Valle-Inclán. // Great Will would give full approval / and praises the great Don Miguel, / to him who writes tales of Springtime / or poems of blood and of gall. / For him, the palm and the laurel / that await in the hands of Spain, / for thousands of noble voices attest / they've been won in the fiercest jousts / by that other one-armed man of Madrid, / Don Ramón María del Valle-Inclán. // Missive / Milord, who in Galicia was cradled, / my two hands gladly give you these flowers, / beloved of the Moon and Apollo, / may their sacred essences bind us forever, / Don Ramón María del Valle-Inclán." /

45. Arturo Marasso, *Rubén Darío y su creación poética*, 3d ed. (Buenos Aires: Kapelusz, 1954).

46. See the interview by Luis Antón del Olmet, *El Debate*, in Fernández Almagro, *Vida y literatura*, 161.

47. "Autocrítica," *España* 10, 412 (8 March 1924): 6. The poet Xavier Bóveda published three poems on *Voces de gesta* in *Epistolario romántico y otros poemas* (Madrid: 1926). He later collected them in *Poemas iniciales* (Buenos Aires: Caubet, 1935).

48. "Richardus Baroia, Angelus Vivanco, Raphael Penagos, Joseph Moia, Anselmus Michaelis, Aurelius Arteta, Julius Romero, ornaverunt."

49. See review by "Mutis," *La Ilustración Española y Americana* (22 March 1912). An anonymous review appeared in *ABC* (6 May 1912). It read in part: "Theatrical notes. Last night our ears were entertained by the caressing music of flowery madrigals and courtly whisperings; our sight by the contemplation of that dreamlike garden where laugh, love, and weave garlands of illusion beautiful porcelain figures, for such the characters seem to be in this farce, at once sentimental and grotesque, conceived by the exquisite author of the *Sonatas*. . . .

La marquesa Rosalinda gave us that sensation . . . This sentimental and grotesque farce, exquisitely delicate, wrought by the dexterous hand of a goldsmith, is a gallant evocation of the eighteenth century. Its characters seem to draw life and emerge from the etchings of Watteau, from the tapestries of Versailles, from the lands of fans, snuff boxes, from display cabinets themselves. . . . Throughout the verses, . . . there flows the sap of Rubén Darío, devotedly proclaimed by Valle as the highest of our poets.

Maestro Valle-Inclán did not wish to accede to the repeated calls by the audience at the end of each act, withdrawing instead from their enthusiastic applause. But Valle-Inclán avoided the opportunity so as not to go against his belief that authors should never take bows; and, in fact, he did not.

Fernando Díaz de Mendoza had selected Valle's play for his own benefit performance."

50. See Robert Lima, "The *Commedia dell'Arte* and *La marquesa Rosalinda*," Anthony Zahareas, ed., *Ramón del Valle-Inclán: A Critical Appraisal of His Life and Works* (New York: Las Americas, 1968), 386–415.

51. *La Pluma* 6, 32 (January 1923): 94.

52. Ibid., 95.

53. Fernández Almagro, *Vida y literatura*, 167.

54. The facsimile of Valle-Inclán's handwritten original, from the papers of Tórtola Valencia in the Museo de Arte Escénico in Barcelona, is reproduced in José Amor y Vázquez, "Valle-Inclán y las musas: Terpsícore" in *Homenaje a William L. Fichter*, edited by A. David Kossoff and José Amor y Vázquez (Madrid: Castalia, 1971), between pp. 32 and 33. "A Tórtola" would appear as "Rosa de Oriente," first in *El pasajero* (1920) with minor changes and with the title "Rosa de Oriente," and in the 1930 edition, collected under *Claves líricas*, with major variants in the first stanza.

55. Caamaño Bournacell, *Por las rutas turísticas de Valle-Inclán*, 22–23: "In 1912, on the very day of his forty-sixth birthday, while in the area of Villajuan—a few days before moving to Cambados—Don Ramón went on foot, accompanied by his wife, on the pilgrimage to the shrine of Saint Simon, in the parish of Bayón—seven long kilometers wending through the foothills of Mount Lobeira—where he heard a maliciously philosophic blind man, astute and well-versed in true and invented tales, standing before a highly adorned poster and accompanying himself on an out-of-tune violin, narrate the parricide that took place on the night of August 23–24 of that year, when Ramón Cores, 'The Hopper,' was killed by his wife and children: jealousy, avarice, old resentments, all in one scenario of superstition and afflicted souls. . . . A few meters from the circle around the blind man, women dragged themselves on their knees to the nearby hermitage, carrying votive offerings in gratitude to Saint Simon for having freed them from 'the evil eye' or for restoring the health of 'the yellow woman,' bewitched through the hatred of a jealous female neighbor who had thrown some hairs in the water trough where she drank. . . . Faced with such scenes and hearing that narrative, Don Ramón's mind conceived *El Embrujado. Tragedia de Tierra de Salnés*, whose outline he began

that same night in his house in Villajuan, and whose plot he developed and wrote shortly afterwards in Cambados."

56. Schraibman, *Cartas. . .de Pérez Galdós*, 32–33. The proximate publication of the play was announced in *El Mundo* in late November: "Our serial. An unpublished novel by Valle-Inclán. *El Embrujado*. In a few days, *El Mundo* will begin publishing in serial form the new *Comedia bárbara* by D. Ramón del Valle-Inclán, titled *El Embrujado*. Everyone knows the insuperable beauty of Valle-Inclán's style, and the reach of that extraordinary originality in whatever he writes. *El Embrujado*, like the previous works of the great artist, evolves in an atmosphere of mystery, witchcraft, and superstition. Valle-Inclán has, in this new novel, reached the heights of perfection in the art of writing, as well as the level of tragedy regarding that inspiration that makes fecund the masterly works of the admirable writer." *El Embrujado. Comedia bárbara* appeared in *El Mundo* (25 November; 3, 7, 12, 15, 17, 23, 26 December 1912; 7, 19 January 1913).

57. Schraibman, *Cartas. . .de Pérez Galdós*, 33, fn. 23.

58. Ibid., 33–34.

59. Victoriano García Martí, *El Ateneo de Madrid (1835–1935)* (Madrid: Dossat, 1948), 269–70: "He went to the rostrum to make certain accusations against the company of an actress working at the Teatro Español, as well as against the director, Don Benito Pérez Galdós, for not having premiered his dramatic work entitled *El embrujado*. He said such things about each of them that a member of the board took the rostrum to state that the Ateneo was not responsible for anything that was being said by Don Ramón del Valle-Inclán. . . . The lecture continued and he read his play, but when someone in the audience coughed because it was winter and there were many with colds, he asked haughtily: 'Do some of you have whooping cough? . . . If you continue to cough, I'll stop reading.' There were unanimous protests and Don Ramón was forcibly removed from the rostrum by a member of the board; a ruckus ensued that in his heart greatly pleased Valle-Inclán." While *El embrujado* would not be produced until 1931, the play was published in book form in 1913 (Madrid: Perlado, Páez y Cia.—Imprenta de J. Izquierdo), "Opera Omnia," vol. 4.

60. Diego San José de la Torre, "Valle-Inclán," *Gente de ayer. Retablillo literario de los comienzos del siglo* (Madrid: Instituto Editorial Reus, 1952), 154–55.

Notes for Chapter 8: Panorama

1. Valle-Inclán contributed four articles on the 1912 National Exhibition of Painting, Sculpture and Architecture, held in Madrid, which he must have attended. The articles appeared in *Nuevo Mundo* as follows: "Notas y comentarios de arte. Divagación," 959 (23 May); "Julio Romero de Torres," 960 (30 May); "Santiago Rusiñol," 961 (6 June); "Notas de la Exposición," 963 (20 June). Parts of these articles would be used in *La lámpara maravillosa*, published in 1916.

2. José Caamaño Bournacell, *Por las rutas turísticas de Valle-Inclán*, 52: "On March 29 of that year of 1913, the Círculo Jaimista of Santiago organized a social in his honor, presided over by the distinguished poetess Filomena Dato Muruáis, and with the participation of the gentlemen Portal Fradejas, Martín Losada, and Remuñán García, the latter with a magnificent lecture entitled 'The Life and Works of Don Ramón del Valle-Inclán,' which prompted Don Ambrosio Borobio Díaz, pastor of the church of San Andrés, to send to *Diario de Galicia*, in that same city, several pieces, which were published on the 2d and 8th of April, entitled: 'Remitido. De cosecha ajena. Juicios sobre Valle-Inclán.' In these he collects opinions of the Rev. Ladrón de Guevara, from his 'Novelistas malos y buenos,' and of the Rev. Burguera, from his 'Representaciones escénicas malas, peligrosas y honestas,' as well as fragments by Don Severino Aznar published in *El Correo Español*, in which he takes issue with Don Ramón's literary production."

3. R. Carballo Calero, "A temática galega na obra de Valle-Inclán," *Grial* 3 (January-March 1964): 4.

4. Ramón Gómez de la Serna, *Don Ramón María del Valle-Inclán*, 182. See photograph of Valle-Inclán, Miranda, Pérez de Ayala, and Belmonte at Miranda's house in 1915, "Sección escolar," *Revista Hispánica Moderna* 2, 4 (July 1936): 58. See also Sebastián Miranda, "Recuerdos de mi amistad con Valle-Inclán, *Cuadernos Hispanoamericanos* 67, 199–200 (July-August, 1966): 5–21.

5. Melchor Fernández Almagro, *Vida y literatura de Valle-Inclán*, 173–74, records the announcement: "Since Juan Belmonte is among us, we have deemed it propitious to honor him with a fraternal dinner in the Gardens of Retiro Park. Fraternal because the arts are equal sisters of the same mother, so much so that cape, banderillas, muleta, and sword, when held by such hands as Juan Belmonte's and when they give sentient, purified form to a heroic heart such as his, are not instruments of an aesthetic order lower than that of pen, brushes, and chisel; rather, they surpass these, because the genre of beauty they create is sublime by being momentaneous. And if the artist, whatever the genre, is supposed to give his life to the work itself, only the torero makes a total abdication and sacrificial offering; this could be compared to that of the ideal statesman, according to the maxim of D. Antonio Maura. But, unfortunately, the maxims of our politicians merit little credit. We consider tauromachy more noble and enjoyable, although no less tragic, than logomachy—that is, Spanish politics—and Juan Belmonte more worthy of popular favor and the laurel of the chosen than the greater part of those dexterous types who have won their ears in Parliament."

6. Ramón Pérez de Ayala, *Troteras y danzaderas* (Madrid: Pueyo, 1923), 31–32: "Don Alberto del Monte Valdés, like Spaniards of old, had given the nervous years of youth to adventures in the lands of New Spain, in whose discovery and conquest, according to him, his ancestors had a glorious hand . . . he arrived at the capital and court in outlandish garb and proclaiming the good news of a strange art. Passers-by laughed at his appearance; literary figures opposed his writings with ridicule. . . . A skinny, bearded, and sombre man. At first glance, this man seemed to be the most perfect corporeal image of Don Quijote de la Mancha. Thereafter, it became evident that he was more heavily bearded than the ancient knight, this person's beard being like that of a Capuchin; similarly, the hawkish nose of Don Quijote had abandoned its hump on passing to the new face and, although it protruded, had become more like an awl."

7. Mauricio Bacarisse, "Dedicatoria," *Mitos* (1930).

8. José Brissa, ed., *Parnaso español contemporáneo* (Barcelona: Maucci, 1914), 167–70 "Versos de Job" was published later as "Rosa de Job" in *El pasajero* (1920); "Paisaje" appeared in the same collection as "Rosa vespertina."

9. (Madrid: Perlado Páez y Cía., 1914), "Opera Omnia," vol. 12, which includes the stories "Juan Quinto," "La adoración de los Reyes," "El miedo," "Tragedia de ensueño," "Un cabecilla," "La misa de San Electus," "El rey de la máscara," "Rosarito," "Del misterio," "A media noche," "Mi bisabuelo," "Comedia de ensueño," "Millón de Arnoya," "Un ejemplo," and "Nochebuena." The text is followed by "Oración."

10. Alberto Ghiraldo, "Como perdió su brazo D. Ramón María del Valle-Inclán, *Diario de La Plata* (9 September 1923): 419.

11. "La geste des loups: Comédie barbare en trois journées," *Le Mercure de France* 108 (16 March-16 April 1914): 325–49, 525–59, 773–803.

12. Caamaño Bournacell, *Por las rutas turísticas*, 57.

13. Ramón del Valle-Inclán, "Epistolario," *Revista de Occidente* 15, 44–45 (October-November-December 1966): 129–30.

14. Ibid., 130. Valle-Inclán had been publishing parts of what was to be *La lámpara maravillosa* in *Los Lunes de El Imparcial* as follows: "La lámpara maravillosa" (9, 16, December 1912); "La lámpara maravillosa: Ejercicios espirituales" (6 January); "La lámpara maravillosa. Ejercicios espirituales" (3 February); "El matiz (Ejercicios espirituales)" (5 May 1913); "La lámpara maravillosa (Guía)" (28 September); "Los tres tránsitos de la belleza" (7 December 1914). Since the letter to Ortega is dated 29 October 1914, Valle-Inclán was probably refering to the 28 December article.

15. Pío Baroja, *Memorias* (Madrid: Minotauro, 1955), 182: "I named Valle-Inclán and Azorín.

The two met with the reporters from *El Liberal* in the Café Suizo. Valle-Inclán called Carrillo aside and told him that to challenge me to a duel over a phrase said in jest was a stupid, unamusing thing to do, and that all our fellow writers and friends who knew what happened agreed that it would be inane. 'I'll duel all the writers who said that,' shouted Carrillo. 'Not me you won't,' replied Valle-Inclán. Such a fracas ensued over this that the affair came to naught."

16. Juan López Nuñez, "Valle-Inclán," *Por Esos Mundos* (1 January 1915): 54.

17. Ibid., 56.

18. Ibid.

19. "El verbo de la noche y el verbo del sol," *Nuevo Mundo* 1095 (2 January 1915); "Quietismo estético," *La Esfera* 1, 66 (April 1915); "Las tres rosas estéticas," *Summa* (15 October; 1, 15 November; 1 December 1915).

20. F. Madrid, *La vida altiva de Valle-Inclán*, 346, states that Valle did not complete the play. In fact, while it never appeared under this title, the work was finished by 1920 and, published under the title *Divinas palabras*, and later performed by Margarita Xirgu in 1933. My suspicions about the relationship of the two titles was corroborated by replies to my inquiries, particularly the one by Ramón Sender, dated 9 August 1965: "Yes, the play for Xirgu was *Divinas palabras*."

21. "Ministerio de Gracia y Justicia. Títulos del Reino. Relación de instancias presentadas en este Ministerio durante los meses de enero, febrero y marzo," *Gaceta de Madrid* (14 April 1915).

22. Julio Casares, "Ramón del Valle-Inclán," *Crítica profana: Valle-Inclán, Azorín, Ricardo Léon*, 15–130.

23. (Madrid-Barcelona-Buenos Aires: Compañía Ibero-Americana de Publicaciones—Renacimiento, 1931).

24. What may be the earliest published antecedents of *La lámpara maravillosa* are two prose pieces that appeared together in 1910: Ramón del Valle-Inclán, "Las lumbres de mi hogar: 'Oraciones,' 'La puerta dorada'" *Europa* 1, 3 (6 March 1910): 20.

25. "Opera Omnia," vol. 1 (Madrid: Sociedad General Española de Librería—Imprenta Helénica, 1916), 258 pp. Containing drawings by Moya del Pino, including one as a frontispiece of Valle-Inclán in a turban holding the manuscript of *La lámpara maravillosa*, this work is dedicated to Joaquín Argamasilla de la Cerda.

26. *The Lamp of Marvels*, trans. by Robert Lima (W. Stockbridge, Mass.: Lindisfarne Press, 1986), 106–7; *Obras completas de don Ramón del Valle-Inclán*, vol. 1 (Madrid: Talleres Tipográficos de Rivadeneyra, 1944), 823–24. Unless otherwise indicated, all quotations from Valle-Inclán's works are from volumes 1 and 2 of this work, hereafter cited as *OC*.

27. *Indice de Artes y Letras* 74–75 (April-May 1954): 23, quotes a letter from Machado: "My thanks and congratulations for that extraordinary *Lámpara maravillosa*, which I have read and re-read with delight, having known it first in segments. As ever, the professional critics are silent, and not exactly in a Pythagorean manner, about your book. It's better that way. In any case, you don't need intermediaries. . . . I hold you as a poet philosopher, contrary to opinion, as a man capable of seeing and assessing intuition under rational norms. . . . I am very much in accord with your poetics, marvelously explicated in your 'Milagro musical'; no matter its daring, it seems perfectly justified, and, like you, I believe, have always believed, in the aphorism that 'each day we should open in our soul a chasm of emotions and intuitions into which the human voice has never penetrated, not even in its echoes'; the musical miracle of St. Bernard of which you speak. In effect, I could say much more about your work, which I keep on my table and re-read, always finding something new in it."

28. Letter in the collection of the Biblioteca y Archivo de Unamuno, Salamanca.

29. Anxelo Novo, "Rubén en la Cacharrería," *La Estafeta Literaria* 360–61 (31 December-14 January 1967): 9. See variants in Dionisio Gamallo Fierros, "Aportaciones al estudio de Valle-Inclán," *Revista de Occidente* 15, 44–45 (October-November-December 1966): 363–64.

30. Domingo García Sabell, "Valle-Inclán y las anécdotas," *Revista de Occidente* 15 (October-November-December 1966): 320.

31. Ibid., 321.

32. Fernández Almagro, *Vida y literatura*, 178–79, quotes Valle-Inclán: "It is composed of D. Enrique Gómez Carrillo, D. Rufino Blanco Fombona, D. Pedro Emilio Coll, D. Amado Nervo, and another writer, me, although unworthy. . . . No doubt on naming me they took into account, more than my merit, the memories I have of the poet, the admiration I feel for his work, and the friendship I had in life with that grand child."

33. *OC*, 2:1924–25.

34. Cipriano Rivas Cherif, "Los españoles y la guerra. El viaje de Valle-Inclán," *España* (11 May 1916): 11.

35. Ibid.

36. Ibid.

37. Ibid.

38. Ibid.

39. Ibid.

40. Corpus Barga, "Valle-Inclán en la más alta ocasión," *Revista de Occidente* 15, 44–45 (October-November-December 1966): 288–89. The author makes reference to Valle-Inclán's statement that this was his first visit to Paris, adding: "Although one of his early Modernist books was dated in Paris, it's possible that he made the statement so as not to spoil the initial joy Chaumié felt on Valle-Inclán's arrival."

41. Fernández Almagro, *Vida y literatura*, 188–89, fn. 1. Corpus Barga, "Valle-Inclán en París," *La Pluma* 6, 32 (January 1923): 60–62, gives further details on Valle-Inclán's activities: "We sat around the table in the Chaumié household during his first evening in Paris. . . . The next day we strolled through Paris. . . . What he liked most were the views of the Seine. . . . He breathed through his eyes there. . . . In Paris, Don Ramón spoke only in Spanish. . . . Maurice Barrés gave a dinner in honor of Valle-Inclán. Chaumié was the interpreter. They spoke of Santiago de Compostela and of the French pilgrims who walked from their cities along Santiago Street. On leaving, Don Ramón made the customary remarks in praise of Barrés . . . adding, 'He looks like a wet crow.' . . . The impression that Valle-Inclán made on those he met in Paris was well summed up by Jacques Chaumié's father . . . who, if someone spoke of Don Ramón in front of him, always said: 'There's someone who isn't trivial.'"

42. Fernández Almagro, *Vida y literatura*, 180. The first communique indicated generally the type of individual desired for the position: "A literary figure and publicist of renown who is sanctioned by the critics and public opinion." The second communique contained the direct appointment: "H.R.H. the king—may God protect him—has seen fit to name as special Professor of the Aesthetics of Fine Arts D. Ramón del Valle-Inclán, in whom are personified the avowed requisites."

43. Leal da Camara, "Um plano que falhou!" *Miren ustedes* (Porto: Livraria Chardron, 1917), 199: "The French government extended Don Ramón an official invitation to visit the battlefront, and, at this moment, the writer is in the trenches of Verdun, having visited the almost sacred sites of Ypres and Rheims, as well as having flown—which has been verified—in an airplane over the German lines of Alsace, dropping from his high observatory a hundred calling cards meant to give the Germans who read them an idea of Latin bravery and irony. Printed on the cards was the following: 'Ramón del Valle-Inclán. Professor of Aesthetics.'"

44. Corpus Barga, "Valle-Inclán en la más alta ocasión," 297.

45. (Madrid: Imprenta Clásica Española, 1917), 113 pp.

46. Ibid., 5.

47. Ibid., 6.

48. Ibid., 7.

49. Fernando de la Quadra-Salcedo, *El Versolari*, prologue by D. Ramón del Valle-Inclán (Madrid: Imprenta del Patronato de Huérfanos de los Cuerpos de Intendencia e Intervención Militares, 1917), ix-xiii.

50. *Páginas escogidas de A. Palacio Valdés* (Madrid: Editorial Calleja, 1917).

51. Ramón del Valle-Inclán, "Epistolario," *Revista de Occidente* 15, 44–45 (October-November-December 1966): 131.

52. Mário Roso de Luna, *De gentes del otro mundo* (Madrid: Biblioteca de las Maravillas, 1917):

"To Don Ramón del Valle-Inclán—prodigious stylist: the mystic bard of *La lámpara maravillosa* and orchestrator of the *Sonatas* of the seasons, his admirer, Mario Roso de Luna."

53. Writing in *El Sol* (3 September 1920), Rivas Cherif commented, "Is Don Ramón a convert to socialism? No. Don Ramón is a Bolshevik or, if you wish, a Bolshevist in that he feels great sympathy for the anti-democratic, dictatorial proceedings that the Bolsheviks employ toward a humanitarian ideal, which, as they see it, only a minority can impose on the world."

54. Fernández Almagro, *Vida y literatura*, 218.

55. F. Madrid, *La vida altiva*, 261.

56. *La pintura vasca, 1909–1919. Antología* (Bilbao: Sociedad Económica de Amigos del País, 1919), 135–38.

57. See *Mi hermana Antonia* (Madrid: José Blass, 1918), and *The Dragon's Head: A Fantastic Farse*, trans. by May Heywood Broun, in *Poet Lore* 29 (1918): 531–64. This translation was also published the following year in *Poet Lore Plays. Series* 2 (Boston: R. G. Badger, 1919); and in Spanish in Guillermo Jiménez, ed., *Cuentos, estética y poemas de don Ramón del Valle-Inclán. Cultura* 9, 2 (Mexico: 1 October 1919). The contents include "Eulalia," "Rosarito," "La Niña Chole"; "El milagro musical," "Los monstruous clásicos," from *La lámpara maravillosa*; "Preludio," from *La marquesa Rosalinda*; "La tienda del herbolario," from *La pipa de kif*; and "Los pobres de Dios," "Geórgica," "Flor de la tarde," "Prosas de dos ermitaños," "Ave Serafín," "Estela de prodigio," "Página de misal," "Lirio franciscano," and "Sol de la tarde," from *Aromas de leyenda*. Also included was Darío's "Soneto iconográfico."

58. (Madrid: Sociedad General Española de Librería—Imprenta Clásica Española, 1919). The cover reproduces a pelican by A. Vivanco.

59. *OC*, 2:1929.

60. *OC*, 2:1924.

61. *OC*, 2:1951, 1952–53.

62. *OC*, 2:1957, 1958.

63. *OC*, 2:1967.

64. (Madrid: Sociedad General Española de Librería—Tipografía Yagües, 1920).

65. *OC*, 2:1891. This poem, with slight variants, was also printed in *Farsa de la enamorada del rey* as "Canción," sung by Maese Lotario.

66. *OC*, 2:1917.

67. *OC*, 2:1918.

68. *OC*, 2:1920.

69. *España* 6, 261 (1 May 1920): 5.

70. *La Internacional* 46 (3 September 1920). Rivas Cherif comments, "To what extent is the social betterment that Valle-Inclán desires compatible with the Carlism of earlier times? . . . The patriarchalism of a Tolstoy, of a Leo XIII, together with the catechetical word of a St. Paul, of a Fray Diego de Cádiz, of a Lenin, and the military spirit of an Italian *condottiero*, or of a Porfirio Díaz, make up the political ideology of this man, perhaps to his chagrin magnificently quixotical and anarchic." Another identification of Valle-Inclán with Bolshevism occurs in the sonnet dated 26 September 1920 that Luis Araquistaín, editor of *España*, sent from Milan: "Italy 1920. / To Don Ramón del Valle-Inclán / The air of Italy's replete with acrid smells / of human blood. A wind of social cataclysm / whips through factories and souls. Ancient Rome, / the old she-wolf, attacks her son: Capitalism. / Once more out of the East, the Gospel dawns, / as Christianity once did some twenty centuries before, / and once again this land, within its magical retort, / fuses feeling, norms, law, and Bolshevism. / Life here has dashed its secular roughness / and, as in the Renaissance, has but one dike / of grace, perfection, equilibrium, beauty. / You, Don Ramón, being the first Bolshevik / and last Christian—both fire and justice— / permit me to convey this news to you." The poem appeared in *La Pluma* 1, 5 (October 1920): 194.

71. *OC*, 2:507–8.

72. Ibid., 1528.

73. Alfonso Reyes, *Obras completas*, vol. 4 (Mexico, D.F.: Letras Mexicanas—Fondo de

Cultura Económica, 1956), 278–79, states, "I was in San Sebastián when I received the request to invite Valle-Inclán to the celebration of the Centennial of Mexican Independence, as guest of honor of the Republic. I sent him a telegram at Puebla del Caramiñal. I did so with a certain vague fear. . . . But Don Ramón came through. When he was perhaps most involved with his family and the pleasures of country life, rusticating through picturesque Galicia, he heard the call of adventure. And, by return wire, he conveyed the decision to set out."

74. From a lecture in New York (December 1921); see *Repertorio Americano* (9 January 1922).

75. *México Moderno* (1 September 1922), 67–68. This poem was reprinted in *Repertorio Americano* 4, 17, (1922). Both Speratti Piñero and Díaz-Plaja cite this poem with numerous omissions and mistakes. My source is the periodical in which the poem was first issued. See Robert Lima, "Valle-Inclán, Obregón and the Mexican Indian: A Basis for the Autograph Poem '¡Nos Vemos!'" *Revista de Estudios Hispánicos* 4, 1 (April 1970): 19–26.

76. Emma S. Speratti Piñero, *La elaboración artística en "Tirano Banderas"*, 148–49. The rest of this letter has been quoted in Chapter 5, in regard to influences on the *Sonatas*.

77. F. Madrid, *La vida altiva*, 161.

78. *El Diario de la Marina* (26 November 1921) reprinted an interview by Francisco Manuel de Olaguibel written for *El Universal* decrying the "intemperate actions taken by Don Ramón del Valle-Inclán against Spain, its king, and its people when he was in the Aztec republic." A few days later the same newspaper published the anonymous "La hispanofobia de Valle-Inclán." Both articles showed Valle-Inclán in a bad light. However, it was Ruy Lugo de Viña, writing in *Excelsior* (December 1921) well after Valle-Inclán's departure, who created the most ill will by misquoting and twisting statements made in reference to Argentina, Spain, and Mexico. Valle-Inclán did not attack his willful misinterpreter, but he did deny the statements in a later interview with Julio Cesteros, *El Diario de la Marina* (7 December 1921).

79. *Social* (December 1921).

80. *España Nueva* (30 November 1921).

81. Interested in establishing exact dates of arrival and departure, I contacted the National Archives, Washington, D.C., and the Port of New York Authority, as well as steamship lines. The agencies did not possess any record of Valle-Inclán's entry into the United States, while company records could not establish on which ship he may have arrived. That he was in New York for several weeks is established by the Cesteros interview; by Helen Bullitt Lowry, "Don Ramón of Spain," *The New York Times* (1 January 1922): "So it is that Don Ramón del Valle Inclán has come out of Spain . . . lingers for a week or two in New York—and now plans to return . . . whence he has come"; and by José Juan Tablada in an untitled article reproduced in *Cosmópolis* 43 (1922): 265–68.

82. F. Madrid, *La vida altiva*, 207–8.

83. *Cosmópolis* 43 (1922): 265–68: "A sense of unreality . . . welled up in me on seeing Don Ramón del Valle-Inclán in an absolutely 'standard' room of the Hotel McAlpin . . . white and cold, despite the radiators. . . . Don Ramón had kept vigil and he stood before me in the doorway of the 'refrigerator' wearing his morning pajamas . . . at one in the afternoon! I beheld the image that recent iconography has substituted in my head for that of Valle-Inclán in younger days. . . . Don Ramón walked with uncertain gait, and seemed to be cold. . . . He was coming out of the depths of trance. The city noises had lacerated his being. . . . Don Ramón had the immature intent of discussing Russia and its revolution . . . agrarian reform in Caesar's Rome and in Navarra . . . I bid him farewell. Don Ramón's own *Esperpentos* were on their way. . . . I left before discussing marijuana and other topics of the tropics."

84. Ibid.

85. Lowry, "Don Ramón of Spain," states, "Now Don Ramón is to be translated into English by a linguist who suits his taste, by the publishing house that brought out *Main Street* . . . The four novels called his *Sonatas* will be out now in six or eight months." This article is accompanied by a painting of a *tertulia* at the Café Regina in Madrid, with Valle-Inclán as the focal point. The translators were May Heywood Broun and Thomas Walsh.

86. Gómez de la Serna, *Don Ramón María del Valle-Inclán*, 129–30: "He arrived at night and

the mother was asleep in the marriage bed with two of the children. Not wanting to awaken them under the circumstances, Valle carefully slipped into bed with the youngest. The next morning, when the child opened her eyes . . . and beheld that long-bearded man in her bed, she ran out of the room in a terrible panic and screaming."

87. OC, 2:1625 (scene 14).

88. F. Madrid, La vida altiva, 265.

89. Ibid., 266.

90. Victoriano García Martí, El Ateneo de Madrid (1835–1935) (Madrid: Dossat, 1948), 268–69: "Around the time when a definite anti-monarchic campaign was started, Valle and Unamuno seemed like rivals in their attacks on the king, as if one were trying to outdo the other in his statements. Shortly after Don Miguel gave a lecture that caused a great deal of comment and, I believe, brought the intervention of the authorities, Valle gave one in which he also attacked the king's person. He alluded to a diplomat, a minister in an American nation, who had protested some statements made by Valle-Inclán in America, and Don Ramón, recounting the incident, said that the minister had sent said protest to the Ministry of State written in a good hand but with poor spelling . . . signed 'Minister of His Majesty, the King of Spain!' And in a brief aside added: 'He may represent the King, but he doesn't represent me.' He continued in this tone, and other aggravating comments led a Madrid court to institute judicial proceedings against Don Ramón; but Valle refused to reply during the judge's hearing, positing the outlandish theory that the court was powerless because only the judge of Cambados had jurisdiction over him."

91. This reads, "Academies, those factories that expedite patents of ephemeral immortality, fend him off with the cross as if he were the devil; the great colosseums, zealous over the support of their patrons and institutions, cast him aside as if he were a gypsy, yelling: 'Lizard! Lizard!' Newspapers, with few exceptions, fear that the chaste nudity of his language will make the Tartuffian mask of their readers blush; the general sordidness and hypocrisy of publishing houses have forced him to become his own publisher; having no official status, he hasn't even been elected representative."

92. Antonio Machado, Poesías completas (Madrid: Espasa-Calpe, 1928), 309–10: "In my dreams, Don Ramón, I traveled / rough paths, while you were a Charon / with eyes aflame, funereal bargeman / on the turbulent waters of Acheron. / A fullness of beard fell to your chest. / (I'd sought your armlessness in vain.) / Over the black barge there hovered / your green senescence of pagan god. / 'Speak,' you said, and I: 'I wish to / praise your landscape, your Don Juan, / upon this moment for the honest truth.' / Because your homage lacked my voice, / permit that from this palid shore I may / repay my passage with a golden verse."

93. Fernández Almagro, Vida y literatura, 220; compare with F. Madrid, La vida altiva, 109–10. Perhaps to show his disdain for the charge, Valle-Inclán used Casanova as a character in Farsa italiana de la enamorada del rey (1920).

94. The quest for artistic freedom at this time was not repressed only in Spain. James Joyce had to publish his work in Paris because of hostility in the English-speaking world. Valle-Inclán, then active in various international organizations, signed a writer's protest published in 1922 against the prohibition of Ulysses. Funds were solicited for a special edition to commemorate the solidarity of writers with Joyce. Díaz-Plaja, Las estéticas de Valle-Inclán (Madrid: Gredos, 1965), 255, fn. 197, states that Valle-Inclán's name appears among the list of writers within the covers of said special edition. But the librarian of the Joyce Collection at Yale University has stated in a letter to me: "There are critical comments, but none by Valle-Inclán, inside the front covers of the Odyssey Press edition of Joyce's Ulysses (1932). The Slocum and Cahoon bibliography doesn't mention Valle-Inclán." I have checked all pertinent editions of Ulysses (1922, 1928, 1932, 1934) to no avail.

95. Corte de amor, Aguila de blasón, La lámpara maravillosa.

96. La Pluma 26–31 (July-December 1922).

97. Luis S. Granjel, Retratos de Ramón (Madrid: Guadarrama, 1963), illus. 8.

98. La Pluma 6, 32 (January 1923): 96 pp.

99. Ibid., 40: "I'm not requesting of the Numen either / goat-shod Pan's seringa or the poetic / and rhetoric lyre that academic laurels / seem to place around your worthy works. / A pounding heart within the breast / stirs a fest that doesn't stir the air; / and if the gold I pay in friendship / appears base, it hides pure sentiment / beneath the torpid way in which I speak. / I do not need the shade of famous Greece / to cast its mantle on my hymn to you. / Let but your Muse's charm embrace my word. / Let the Galician bagpipes sound. And Time, / in motion a long while, may long await your *miserere*."

100. Ibid., 5–6: "We will discuss among friends the noble things accomplished by another, who precedes us, and we will erect a stele in his honor, as a trophy. This does not imply the evocation of a shadow, the rekindling of past fame, nor giving the poet a decree of retirement; . . . we gather around a still unfinished body of work, which brings us bright images of life through a poetical transposition of the many delusions of our age. . . . He's more our contemporary for giving perfect expression to certain feelings that we possess. . . . Speaking of the poet elicits the joy, the serene conviction of one who deals with eternal values. . . . Maestro, such is the spirit that we bring to this tribute."

101. Caamaño Bournacell, *Por las rutas turísticas*, 101.

102. Italian translation *La novelle dei lupi*, by A. De Stefani (Milan: Piantanida Valcarenghi, 1923); French translations include *Sonates de printemps et d'été*, by A. Glorget (Paris: Les Editions de France, 1924); *Mémoires aimables du marqués de Bradomín: Sonate de printemps, sonate d'été, sonate d'automne, sonate d'hiver*, by C. Barthez (Paris: Ambert, 1924), 2 vols; "Rosarito," by A. Francastel, *La Revue Politique et Littéraire* 62 (1924): 505–13; English translation *The Pleasant Memoirs of the Marquis of Bradomin: Four Sonatas*, by May Heywood Broun and T. Walsh (New York: Harcourt, Brace, 1924; London: Constable, 1925).

103. "Méjico, los Estados Unidos y España," *España* (20 October 1923).

104. Prologue by Valle-Inclán in Victoriano García Martí, *De la felicidad (Eternas inquietudes)* (Madrid: Editorial Mundo Latino, 1924).

105. Speratti Piñero, *La elaboración artística*, 147.

106. Ibid., 148.

107. Caamaño Bournacell, *Por las rutas turísticas*, 111.

108. C. Rivas Cherif, "Apunte de crítica literaria: La *Comedia bárbara* de Valle-Inclán," *España* (16 February 1924): 8. The article begins with a reference to Valle-Inclán's long absence from Madrid: "For some time now the august figure of Don Ramón del Valle-Inclán has been missing from the literary world of Madrid. Retired for long periods from the bustle of cafés, his habitual *tertulias* have languished as if orphaned. Meanwhile, in his Galician manor, he corrects the proofs of the edition of his *Obras*, re-issued by Renacimiento, and prepares some new novel or other. Never lazy, not even on those occasions when he seemed to waste his genius on mere chats with friends in the capital, the withdrawal that he imposes on himself now, too long for our liking, is, fortunately, beneficial to literature. From time to time, news of him reaches us, nourishing our hopeful expectations. We would like to transcribe a segment of a personal letter that would be of interest to his assiduous readers because of its welcome announcement and justifiable autocriticism. The fact that he didn't know it would be made public gives it the added value of spontaneity, while corroborating the indissolubility of man and writer in the person of Valle-Inclán."

109. Speratti Piñero, *La elaboración artística*, 150.

110. Both plays were subtitled "Novelas macabras."

111. That autumn his family joined him at a new residence at 10 Calle Santa Catalina, in a house owned by the Ateneo.

112. Rivas Cherif, "Bradomín en la Corte," *Heraldo de Madrid* (4 August 1924); Gómez de la Serna, "El escritor en la enfermería," *Nuevo Mundo* (18 July 1924): "He has returned to Madrid cured, full of vitality, declaiming with his one hand, showing us his strange striated head, ashen as if dusted by the memory of all Ash Wednesdays. . . . The lyrical basilisk who was consumed for many days in a hospital bed—it would have been more pleasant in one of those hospitals for pilgrims!—has flung aside the robe (partly of madman, partly of the wounded)

worn by the sick in the sanatorium; he returns to the lists of literary jousts, engaging the characters of his novels in friendly battle. . . . The writer has returned from the infirmary."

113. "To me, Unamuno is not a wise man, or anything resembling it, as everyone in Spain is aware, and it's imperative to unmask him here. . . . We must recognize what Unamuno is. I don't believe that a smattering of Hellenic culture gives one the right to meddle in everything human and divine, or to talk rubbish about all other matters."

114. Interview by the Argentinian journalist Edmundo Guibourg; see F. Madrid, *La vida altiva*, 264–65. He had made similar condemnations of Spanish politics in a controversial interview by Ruy Lugo de Viña in *Excelsior* (December 1921).

115. F. Madrid, *La vida altiva*, 205.

116. The following articles appeared in *El Estudiante* in 1925: "El jueguito de la rana," 8–13 (June-July) and 1–2 (6, 13 December); "El honorable cuerpo diplomático," 3–4 (20, 27 December); and in 1926: "Esperpento de los cuernos de don Friolera. Epílogo," 5 (3 January); "El honorable cuerpo diplomático," 6 (10 January); "Mitote revolucionario," 7–9 (17 January, 11 February); "La mueca verde," 10 (28 February); "El Congal de Cucarachita," (21 March, 4 April); "Final de la Farra," (18 April); "El fuerte de Santa Mónica," (1 May).

117. Valle-Inclán showed a great interest in this section of the city that Francisco Madrid had baptized in a series of articles, making the notorious neighborhood known throughout Europe.

118. Melchor Fernández Almagro, "De banquete a banquete," *Insula* 176–77 (July-August 1961): 3. See also Antonina Rodrigo, "Valle-Inclán en Barcelona," *La Vanguardia Española* (28 February 1976), which has a photograph of those attending the banquet and reproduces Valle-Inclán's signature in the restaurant's guest book.

119. F. Madrid, *La vida altiva*, 151.

120. Antonio J. Onieva, "Valle-Inclán en Asturias," *La Estafeta Literaria* (30 November 1945).

121. Ibid. "The auditorium filled with a select audience; Don Ramón spoke (he didn't read) about the transcendence of classical culture, of Rome in Spanish society; he said beautiful things, half true, half invented; the audience constantly rewarded him with applause; the lecture was an undeniable triumph, and one of the first to congratulate him was the government's representative, who otherwise remained anonymous. Don Ramón made a circuit of other Asturian Atheneums and, at night, after dinner, he would stop in my newspaper office, where a *tertulia* of friends and admirers awaited him. Our guest felt at home in the vacant easy chair that was always there for him. He was the only one who spoke, which is what we wanted, and he said incredible things that, due to their causticity, were constant invitations to laughter. One evening he told us how Alejandro Sawa had died . . . when he finished, it was four in the morning and we accompanied him to his lodgings. . . . From Gil de Jaz Street to the Hotel París—six hundred meters—took us two long hours. Valle would lean against the stone abutment of a house and, prodded by one of our group, told us some of his adventures in Mexico."

122. Prologue to Ricardo Baroja, *El Pedigree (Tres jornadas y un epílogo)* (Madrid: Caro Raggio, 1926), 9–15.

123. In his letter to me, dated 9 August 1965, Sender writes, "I met Valle-Inclán in the Granja del Henar, in the inner patio of the columns where, in 1926, he held his *tertulia*. I don't think that anyone introduced me. I had friends there, such as Luis Bello, an important contributor to *El Sol*, the Portuguese journalist Novais Teixeira, the poet Francisco Vighi— who, with modest, humorous pride, termed himself the eleventh great poet of his generation—and others. I simply appeared there and without realizing it entered into a friendship with Don Ramón, who quickly honored me with his confidences."

124. Ramón J. Sender, *Valle-Inclán y la dificultad de la tragedia* (Madrid: Gredos, 1965), 9–10: "If I were to say that Valle-Inclán lived alone most of his life, readers would be scandalized. But it's the pure truth. Daily, at four in the afternoon, he attended a *tertulia* in a café, and another at night. The greater part of the year, summer and winter, he spent afternoons and early evenings surrounded by ten or twelve persons, but Don Ramón was alone. . . . I again

recognized Don Ramón's immense solitude while walking with him one day on his way home. . . . On that occasion I spoke to him of his novels on the Carlist war, of his *Comedias bárbaras*, and of his *Esperpentos*. When I started to speak I saw his face light up . . . Since Valle-Inclán never spoke of his own works in the *tertulia*, I had to take advantage of such moments in the street or in the Ateneo or at his house. And Valle-Inclán, pleased to know that someone penetrated joyfully into those small secrets, urged me to continue speaking. . . . I was amazed by the pleasure Don Ramón seemed to get from conversing with me, and I realized that he needed to discuss such things with others. . . . He had no one to talk to . . . because everyone preferred the picturesque side of Don Ramón: the phantom, the outlandish mask." See my review of Sender's book in *Hispania* 50, 2 (May 1967): 388–89.

125. *OC*, 1:779.

126. Ramón J. Sender, *El problema religioso en México* (Madrid: Editorial Cenit, 1928). In his letter to me, Sender explained, "Don Ramón's prologue to my book (a series of editorials for *El Sol*, retouched and 'enlarged') was not written by Don Ramón but by the publisher and was benevolently signed by Don Ramón, who, through the use of his prestigious name, sought to help a company founded by friends." Díaz-Plaja, *Modernismo frente a noventa y ocho* (Madrid: Espasa-Calpe, 1951), 153, fn. 4, cannot understand Valle-Inclán's failure to discuss the political aspects of the period in the prologue and uses this as a basis in demonstrating the apolitical attitude of Valle-Inclán. Díaz-Plaja did not know that the prologue had not been written by Valle-Inclán.

127. Juan Antonio Hormigón, *Valle-Inclán. Cronología y documentos* (Madrid: Ministerio de Cultura, 1978), 45. In 1931 Julio Alvarez del Vayo was named ambassador of the Republic. See Ramón J. Sender, "Despedida de un embajador. Banquete A Julio Alvarez del Vayo," *La Libertad* (21 May 1931): 4.

128. Juan Antonio Hormigón, *Valle-Inclán y su tiempo* (Madrid: Compañía de Acción Teatral, 1982), 46.

129. *Ecos de Asmodeo* (Madrid: La Novela Mundial, 1926), illus. by F. Pozio, a novelette that forms the second chapter of *La corte de los milagros* (*El ruedo ibérico*, vol. 1), published in 1927; *El terno del difunto* (Madrid: Imprenta Rivadeneyra, 1926), illus. by Masberger, was the predecessor to the *Esperpento Las galas del difunto*; *Zacarías el Cruzado, o Agüero nigromante*, in *La Novela de Hoy* 225 (3 September 1926) is preceded by Mariano Tornar, "A manera de prólogo Hablando con Valle-Inclán."

130. *Tirano Banderas. Novela de Tierra Caliente* (Madrid: Imprenta Rivadeneyra, 1926), "Opera Omnia," vol. 16, 362 pp. All the works with the Rivadeneyra imprint are addressed "12 Santa Catalina. Madrid," indicating that Valle-Inclán was publishing and distributing those works. See F. Madrid, *La vida altiva*, 113: "On seeing it in bookstore windows, people bought up the first and second editions. It was one of the greatest literary successes that Spain had seen up to that time. . . . Don Ramón received every conceivable popular and critical accolade. The critics, commentators, interviewers, etc., praised the work. It was again mentioned that Don Ramón should be named to the Academy as quickly as possible, and an attempt was made to promote a national tribute."

131. F. Madrid, *La vida altiva*, 113–14.

132. Martín Luis Guzmán, "Tirano Banderas," *Repertorio Americano* 14, 13 (2 April 1927): 196.

133. Enrique Diez-Canedo, "Tirano Banderas," *El Sol* (3 February 1927): 2. Other important reviews of the novel are Gabriel Miró, "Valle-Inclán," *Heraldo de Madrid* (18 January 1927); R. Blanco-Fombona, "En torno a Tirano Banderas," *La Gaceta Literaria* (15 January 1927); E. Goméz de Baquero, "La novela de Tierra Caliente," *El Sol* (20 January 1927); Antonio Espina, "*Tirano Banderas*," *Revista de Occidente* 15 (1927): 274–79.

134. Harriet V. Wishnieff, "A Synthesis of South America: *Tirano Banderas*," *The Nation* (16 May 1928): 569–70; W. A. Drake, "Tirano Banderas," *The New York Herald-Tribune* (5 June 1927).

135. *The Tyrant*, trans. by Margarita Pavitt (New York: Henry Holt & Co., 1929). Reviewed by Angel Flores in *The New York Herald-Tribune* (20 October 1929); *Boston Transcript* (27 November 1929); *The New York Times* (22 December 1929).

136. (Madrid: Imprenta Rivadeneyra, 1927), "Opera Omnia," vol. 21. Reviews of the book

appearing earlier are E. Gómez de Baquero, "*La corte de los milagros*," *El Sol* (30 April 1927); R. Baeza, "La resurrección de Valle-Inclán," *Le Gaceta Literaria* (15 June 1927).

137. *El ruedo ibérico*—first series: *Los amenes de un reinado; La corte de los milagros* (originally, *La corte isabelina*), vol. 1; *¡Viva mi dueño!* (originally, *Secretos de estado*), vol. 2; *Baza de espadas*, vol. 3; second series: *Aleluyas de la Gloriosa: España con honra*, vol. 4; *Trono en ferias*, vol. 5; *Fueros y cantones*, vol. 6; third series: *La restauración borbónica* (originally, *Los cucos de El Pardo*): *Los salones alfonsinos*, vol. 7; *Dios, Patria, Rey*, vol. 8; *Los campos de Cuba* (originally, *La campaña de Cuba*), vol. 9. Only three volumes, those in the first series, ever appeared. Two were published during the author's life and the incomplete third after his death. "El trueno dorado," published in *Ahora* (19, 26 March; 2, 9, 16, 23 April 1936) was the last material in the series, published posthumously. See Gómez de la Serna, *Don Ramón María del Valle-Inclán*, 208–9: "(Valle) Pensaba que la última parte iba a llamarse *Los cucos del Pardo*" (The Cuckoos of the Pardo).

138. Mariano Tornar, "A manera de prólogo. Hablando con Valle-Inclán," *La Novela de Hoy* 225 (3 September 1926); Manuel Azaña, *Obras completas*, vol. 3 (Mexico, D.F.: Oasís, 1967), 878–79: "May 3 (1927). Have read the first volume of *Ruedo ibérico, La corte de los milagros* . . . this book cannot compare to *Tirano Banderas. La corte* suffers from lack of observation, and it isn't compensated by fantasy. Valle censors Galdós strongly because in his *Episodios* he wove a slight novelesque plot around invented characters, placing it more or less arbitrarily on an historical foundation. 'The novel must be structured with the historical personages themselves'—says Valle—'who are then set in motion.' Very well. But in *La corte de los milagros* the characters are invented figurines who make faces. They lack depth, they lack humanity. It is a vast descriptive painting, overly picturesque and superficial. . . . Didn't court, city, and countryside have other than grotesque beings?"

139. Interview with José Montero Alonso, *La Novela Semanal* 6 (1926).

140. Interview with Paulino Massip (see F. Madrid, *La vida altiva*, 106–7).

141. Ibid.

142. Gregorio Martínez Sierra, "Hablando con Valle-Inclán. De él y su obra," *ABC* (7 December 1928).

143. "Valle-Inclán y Góngora," *La Gaceta Literaria* (1 June 1927). Valle-Inclán's reply is dated 15 February 1927 from Madrid.

144. See Manuel Azaña, *Obras completas*, vol. 3, 883:

145. While the relationship between these occurrences and the centennial celebration of the death of Francisco José de Goya y Lucientes (16 April 1928) cannot be proved, it is curious that the condition of Spain at this time was not unlike that depicted by Goya in his *Caprices* and *Proverbs*; students may have been aware of the parallel, just as Valle-Inclán saw in Goya's attitude a kinship to his own.

146. The first title issued under the new agreement was *¡Viva mi dueño!* (Madrid: CIAP—Imprenta Rivadeneyra, 1928) "Opera Omnia," vol. 22. An excerpt appeared earlier as *Teatrillo de enredo*, in *Colección Los Novelistas* 1, 16 (28 June 1928). This novelette, derived from "¡Ah, de mis muertos!" published in 1892, became chapter seven, "El vicario de los verdes," of *¡Viva mi dueño!* These 1928 publications are the first of his works with a copyright.

147. Prologue to *Flores de almendro* (Madrid: Librería Bergúa, 1936), 10. *La guerra carlista*, to which he refers, was in *Colección Los Grandes Autores Contemporáneos* (Madrid: CIAP—Imprenta de Artes Gráficas, 1929).

148. Gómez de la Serna, *Don Ramón María del Valle-Inclán*, 165–166.

149. Ibid., 185.

150. Hans Jeschke, *Die Generation von 1898 in Spanien* (Halle: Niemeyer, 1934).

151. F. Madrid, *La vida altiva*, 245.

152. Sender, letter cited.

153. Ramón J. Sender, "Valle-Inclán, la política y la cárcel," *Nueva España* 3 (1930); 14–15. About this first occasion, Sender writes: "In the spring of last year, Valle-Inclán woke up one day under the sign of Martínez Anido. Very early that morning—the Dictatorship was an

early riser—two policemen turned up at the writer's home. Valle-Inclán rises late; he's unwilling to change his habits, and the police had to content themselves with waiting in the portal. They couldn't return to the *cosqui* without the *burno*—the *burno* being the author of *Farsa y licencia de la reina castiza*. They went back around midday. The writer has slept and could get up; but he doesn't want to. The rudeness with which the matter is again brought up irritates him even more. In the name of what law are they bothering him? His indignation is terrible, serene. . . . He refuses to get up although already half-dressed. The others insist. . . . They are being mocked and they won't permit that two servants of the law—of what law?—be mocked. The policemen vacillate, looking at each other for an answer. Finally, they resort to force: they put on his boots. Then Valle-Inclán, with a clear conscience, finishes dressing; he is then led to the General Security Office. . . . He spent three days in a cell. Solitude, the crash of bolts against armor-plated doors, bugle calls. Graffiti on the walls. . . . He was set free as he had been detained: without knowing the cause."

154. Ibid. Of this second encarceration, Sender writes: "Ten o'clock at night in an as yet indecisive April. Valle-Inclán was walking up Castellana with the painter Don Juan de Echevarría. . . . When they separated, policemen who were lying in wait, fell on Valle-Inclán. He ended up alone in a cell again. He stayed there for eight days, until they put him in the 'political' section. The cells there have room for two. Filth, misery, desolation, and, instead of a straw mattress, one of cornstalks and another of wool. At the head of the bed was a toilet without water or cover, from which sewer rats emerge at night. With his stomach illness, Don Ramón received his daily food ration at eleven in the morning. His wife's diligence was unable to prevent his having to eat cold meals, due to the wait in the visitors' center, the searches made by officials, the opening of thermoses and food containers. . . . Don Ramón missed his other arm more than ever. He couldn't prepare tea or coffee for himself with one hand. Although he proved that he was suffering from hematuria—Dr. Pascual attended to him—he had to remain in jail. The Dictatorship had its reasons."

155. Fernández Almagro, *La vida y literatura*, 233: "The eminent writer and extravagant citizen Sr. Valle-Inclán has also contributed to his arrest because, on deciding not to pay the 250 peseta fine levied for his governmental infraction to the end of keeping him from losing his freedom, he has proffered such insults against the authorities and such overwhelming attacks on the established social order that it has become impossible to exempt him from sanctions, as was intended."

156. José A. Balseiro, *Blasco Ibáñez, Unamuno, Valle-Inclán, Baroja. Cuatro individualistas de España* (New York: Torres, 1949), 182, fn. 8. See also Olaf K. Lundeberg, "An Evening with Valle-Inclán," *Hispania* 13, 5 (November 1930): 401: "The one trace of humor that escaped Don Ramón's lips while telling of the affair was in reference to his prison mates. It seems that he was unceremoniously dumped into a dungeon full of rabid communists, who welcomed him boisterously as one of their own. It was not clear whether their enthusiastic welcome pleased or disgusted the poet; we did have reason to feel that it amused him immensely."

157. Sender, *Valle-Inclán y la dificultad de la tragedia*, 14–15.

158. F. Madrid, *La vida altiva*, 334.

159. Ibid., 334–35.

160. Ibid.

Notes for Chapter 9: Absurdity

1. *Farsa de la enamorada del rey* (Madrid: Sociedad General Española de Librería—Gráfica de Ambos Mundos, 1920), 149 pp. *Luces de bohemia*, serially in *España* (31 July-23 October 1920), a version with twelve scenes; book edition: (Madrid: Renacimiento—Imprenta Cervantina, 1924), "Opera Omnia," vol. 19, 299 pp., a version with fifteen scenes. *Farsa y licencia de la reina castiza*, serially in *La Pluma* 1, 3–5 (August—October 1920); book edition: (Madrid: Talleres Tipográficos de Artes de la Ilustración, 1922), 156 pp. *Divinas palabras*, serially in *El Sol* (19

June-14 July 1919); book editions: (Madrid: Tipografía Yagües, 1920), "Opera Omnia," vol. 17, 286 pp., and (Madrid: Tipografía Europa, 1920), "Opera Omnia," vol. 18. Although published in 1919, the serialization omitted passages considered inappropriate and only the book edition contains the full text of the play. See the review of the seventeenth volume of "Opera Omnia" by Cipriano Rivas Cherif, "Libros y Revistas," *La Pluma* 6, 32 (January 1923): 137–38.

2. Interview with Martínez Sierra, "Hablando con Valle-Inclán. De él y de su obra," *ABC* (7 December 1928): 1. Lope de Vega's *Pedro Carbonero* mentions three ways in which an author can observe his creations; it is possible that Valle-Inclán derived his theory in part from this source.

3. F. Madrid, *La vida altiva de Valle-Inclán*, 104.

4. Ibid., 344–46. See also Ramón Gómez de la Serna, *Don Ramón María del Valle-Inclán*, 138, for other statements on the subject. Toward the end of *Niebla*, Unamuno and Augusto Pérez discuss the relationship of author and character in a similar manner.

5. Dictino Alvarez Hernández, *Cartas de Rubén Darío* (Madrid: Taurus, 1963), 70–71. The note is unsigned but bears a cross drawn by Valle-Inclán. Darío wrote the prologue to the posthumous book, *Iluminaciones en la sombra* (1910). In this context it is important to note Sawa's letter to Darío, dated 31 May 1908 from Madrid, as reproduced in Alberto Ghiraldo, *El archivo de Rubén Darío* (Buenos Aires: Losada, 1943), 214–15: "The only thing that you know of this latter part of my mortal life is that I've become blind. That would seem to be sufficient, but it isn't; besides being blind, I have also been so ill for nearly two years that the Trappist phrase of our great Villiers—'My body is already ripe for the grave'—has become one of the most frequent litanies in which my soul is diluted. And so, in my condition, in my being, I live in the middle of Madrid more forsaken yet and with less assistance than if I had set up my tent in the middle of barren lands away from all roads. Relying on my literary prestige, I've knocked on the doors of newspapers and publishing houses to no avail; relying on social contacts—I'm not an ogre or a wild beast—I've called on friends, insistently, again to no avail. Is it possible that someone like me can die this way, dismally, assassinated bit by bit by everyone, so that his death, like his life, has no more significance than that of a mere anecdote about solitude and rebellion in contemporary society?"

6. Pío Baroja also employed Sawa's last days in an episode in *El árbol de la ciencia* dealing with the character Rafael Villasús.

7. *Obras completas de don Ramón del Valle-Inclán*, vol. 2 (Madrid: Talleres Tipográficos de Rivadeneyra, 1944), 1597, 1598, 1599. Unless otherwise indicated, all quotations from Valle-Inclán's works are from volumes 1 and 2 of this work, hereafter cited as OC. Valle-Inclán's consistent identification of the *Esperpento* with Goya underlines the relationship of influences flowing from the painter to the writer. In 1928, Ramón Sender suggested emphasizing this relationship by publishing in *El Sol* one of the *Esperpentos* in honor of Goya's centennial. See Ramón J. Sender, *Valle-Inclán y la dificultad de la tragedia* (Madrid: Gredos, 1965), 42.

8. Melchor Fernández Almagro, *Vida y literatura de Valle-Inclán*, 206.

9. The play was first produced on 3 June 1931 at the Teatro Muñoz Seca in Madrid. It was designed by Bartolozzi. The cast was headed by Irene López Heredia and Mariano Asquerino, and included Francisco López Silva, Elías Sanjuán, Nicolás Perchicot, and Adela Carbone. The premiere was well-attended by the public and enthusiastically received by the knowledgeable critics, such as Rafael Marquina, "La reina castiza," *Gaceta Literaria* (15 June 1931): "With a theatrical goal in mind, *La reina castiza* tends to the satirical. It accentuates the grotesque profile of the caricature, and its dramatic impact is founded on one such by way of making a pejorative condensation of a period's symptomatic framework. A master at such definitive syntheses . . . Valle-Inclán has applied to the staging of his September farce his very typical process of verifying details toward the framing of the whole, and of using the fantastic and the abstract to underscore what is real and concrete. A humorous farce, the depth of his satire, artful in its human creation, takes root in the picturesque but functions on the national level. The reach is parabolic, although the aim may have been low. . . . Perhaps more evident here than in any other of his plays is the interaction between the purely scenic and the

essentially theatrical. Contributing to it is that coexistence on the stage of puppets or figurines (El gran preboste, Don Lindo, etc.) and real characters (La reina, el jorobeta, el estudiante papista, etc.), who are sketched and vitalized with identical criticism and due flippancy. Needless to say, were we to dig a little deeper, we'd find this to be one of the most revealing and typical of characteristics of Valle-Inclán's literature. In it, the world is viewed from above and projected onto the eternal. Perhaps this is why in some instances puppets are more human than the characters. All this aside, in *La reina castiza* the best literary qualities of Don Ramón attain an agile grace that doesn't impair its density. Jocund humor, audacious imagery, idiomatic pirouettes, verbal elegance, and that very typical mode of energizing the grotesque, of dramatizing the expressive, are resplendent in this farce through persuasive and exceedingly beautiful means."

See also Carlos Delgado Olivares, "Noción de *La reina castiza*," *Gaceta Literaria* (15 September 1931): "His plays are absolutely theatrical. . . . There's nothing more certain than the fact that the newest, most original, and timeliest theatre being created in Spain is that of Valle-Inclán." In a photograph dated 4 June 1931, Irene López Heredia and Mariano Asquerino are shown performing in *La reina castiza* (photograph by Alfonso, Collection Fundación Juan March, file F78).

10. Premiere: 16 November 1933 at the Teatro Español in Madrid. Cipriano Rivas Cherif directed the company of Margarita Xirgu and Enrique Borrás.

11. *Juan Ramón Jiménez. Cartas* (Madrid: Aguilar, 1962), 230–31: "My dear friend: many thanks for the copy of *Divinas palabras* that you were kind enough to send me. I'm rereading the marvelous tragicomedy, one of your works that I like best; and which, due to its convulsive power of invention, its multifaceted internal passion, its colors, its language and style, synthesis of the entire Spanish jargon—of all the Spains, is the only 'theatrical' play to be written in Spanish since the best—*Romance de lobos*—also by you. I've sent a copy of *Divinas palabras* to Lennox Robinson, one of the directors of the Abbey Theatre in Dublin, where, as you know, the famous and exquisite Irish Players perform regularly. I was telling our friend Alfonso Reyes the other day how some of your things are similar—this wonderful play in particular—to certain early works (by Yeats, Synge, Lady Gregory) of the modern Irish theatre; all of which makes sense after all since you are Galician, a Celt, and yourself. I believe that if they could read it in Spanish—because translating this splendid language of yours is, of course, impossible—they would really like *Divinas palabras* and include it in their repertory along with, for example, *In the Shadow of the Glen* or *The Well of the Saints* by the great Synge. When I see you I'll talk to you about the many theatrical possibilities of which your magical tragicomedy has made me think."

12. Serially in *La Pluma* 11–15 (April-August 1921). Book edition (Madrid: Renacimiento-Imprenta Cervantina, 1925), "Opera Omnia," vol. 17, 263 pp. The premiere occurred after Valle-Inclán's death: on 14 February 1936, at Madrid's Teatro de la Zarzuela, produced by the "Nueva Escena" group under the auspices of the Ateneo de Madrid, headed by Rafael Alberti and María Teresa León.

13. *OC*, 2:1697, 1698, 1699.

14. These characters represent the "Generación del '98," as is obvious in their conversation. Further, Don Estrafalario has certain traits that make him resemble Unamuno, as his companion asserts: "You're not a philosopher and, consequently, have no right to reply with pedantries. You're nothing more than a heretic, like Don Miguel de Unamuno." *OC*, 2:1706.

15. Ibid., 1704.

16. Ibid., 1705. "*Grammar*" refers to Nebrija's work, the first grammar in Europe since the Roman era.

17. Ibid., 1706.

18. F. Madrid, *La vida altiva*, 114.

19. Alfonso Reyes, *Obras completas*, vol. 4 (Mexico, D.F.: Letras Mexicanas—Fondo de Cultura Económica, 195X), 277. "In the mornings, he slept. He ate lunch around one and by three (he always walked, very fast) he was in the Ateneo directing the rehearsals of the Teatro

de la Escuela Nueva, counseling Rivas Cherif to show more energy and sobriety, or Magda Donato to demonstrate more charm and ease; taking on everyone's role; creating anew the plays with his personal interpretation." Fernández Almagro, *Vida y literatura*, 234, notes that Valle-Inclán was active as the director of this group in the spring of 1921. He mentions the success of the company with Ibsen's *The Enemy of the People*, but whether or not Valle-Inclán directed that production is not stated.

20. This work was first published with the subtitle *Novela macabra* in *La Novela Semanal* 4, 141 (22 March 1924). It was accompanied in the same issue by *La rosa de papel*, another play with the same subtitle.

21. Two other new short plays, *La rosa de papel* and *Sacrilegio*, appeared on the same program. See Robert Lima, "Melodramas for Puppets and Playlets for Silhouettes: Four Stageworks by Valle-Inclán," *Modern Drama* 13, 4 (February 1971): 374–81.

22. Interview by José Montero Alonso, *La Novela Semanal* 6 (1926).

23. Ricardo Baroja, *Estampa* 6: "One of his plays was first presented in my house: *Ligazón*. It was performed by his wife, Carmen Juan de Benito, Luis G. Bilbao, Isabel Palencia, and Cipriano Rivas Cherif. It's curious that . . . he was so afraid of openings that he stayed away, even though it was a performance for friends."

24. Julio Caro Baroja, "Recuerdos vallinclanescos—barojianos," *Revista de Occidente* 44–45 (October-December 1966): 309: "There weren't enough actors to fill all the roles, but it was decided that one of them, Don Ramón, should serve as prompter and general understudy. I remember, as if I were seeing her now, my mother in the role of the Mother Superior of the Calatrava convent and my uncle Ricardo's wife, dressed as the Knight Commander, stout and wearing a white cotton beard. . . . Small roles were easily filled. But the large roles put people off, except when Don Ramón would function as solicitor and motivator rather than as prompter. I don't recall who played the Tenorio role. But he performed it like Christian declaring his love in *Cyrano de Bergerac*. His soul was Don Ramón. Then came the moment for the entrance of whoever had the role of Doña Brígida. It was so badly done that Valle-Inclán couldn't stand the clumsy interpretation of the role; he called for a long black cape, wrapped himself in it fully, tucked in his beard, and removed his glasses. And he began to perform with the most commonly used affectations, inflections of voice, and conventions of the role. To see and to hear him recite the lines . . . was to witness a unique spectacle. I don't believe that Don José Zorrilla has ever received a better or greater tribute than that one on a November afternoon close to All Saints' Day. He then went on, indefatigably, to perform the roles of the sculptor, of Captain Centellas, of all the others imaginable; the verses flowed from him in torrents, with that peculiar lisp of his, so distant from the Andalusian, of course."

25. Among the members were Josefina Blanco, Herminia Peñaranda, Isabel O. de Palencia, Carmen Juan de Benito, Cipriano Rivas Cherif, Fernando G. Bilbao, García Heredia, Calibán, Salvador Bartolozzi, and José Robledano. See "¿Un teatro escuela? Los ensayos de Valle-Inclán en el Círculo de Bellas Artes," *El Heraldo de Madrid* (18 December 1926). See also "Informaciones teatrales: Valle-Inclán y su 'Cántaro Roto,'" *La Voz* (20 December 1926); and Floridor, "Ensayo de teatro," *ABC* (21 December 1926).

26. E. Diez-Canedo, "Información teatral. Círculo de Bellas Artes. Ensayos de teatro dirigidos por D. Ramón del Valle-Inclán," *El Sol* (21 December 1926): "*Ligazón*, the 'play for shadows,' by Valle-Inclán, was performed earlier in the home of the Barojas and published in a popular series; well-known, it concluded the program. It is a painting with energetic hues, in which the young woman, rebellious against the Celestinesque plot that threatens her romantic needs, evades its machinations by giving in to her desire, embodied in the convincing young man whom fate has brought to her doorstep. Its atmosphere of mystery, witchcraft, bribery, crime depicted with the vigorous brush that created the *Comedias bárbaras*, the play presents a dramatic jolt through skillful dialogue. Josefina Blanco, Carmen Juan, Isabel Palencia, Fernando Bilbao were the speaking shadows of this play, for which Bartolozzi and López Rubio have created a schematic design to be viewed, as are the figures, in a tenuous light."

In his "Diarios íntimos y cuadernillos de apuntes," *Obras completas*, vol. 3, 890, Manuel Azaña states, "The theatrical enterprise that he undertook at the start of the year at the Círculo de Bellas Artes did not turn out well. Valle, who directed the affair alone and despotically, dragging in all his friends and disinterested parties, ended up at odds with them, especially with Cipriano, since he couldn't admit his personal failure nor blame the Círculo, nor provoke a scandal through which he could acquit himself and emerge haughtily. 'They've abandoned me!' he would say to café companions, referring to Cipriano and other friends. He adopted an infantile anger that was indelicate, considering that his friends had given the project an enormous amount of effort, some money, and chanced failure—its success would have bene-fitted only Valle. For three or four months he's avoided places where he could run into Cipriano. Some were very scandalized over what Valle did and said. Cipriano, full of common sense, didn't pay any attention. He knows what he must do from now on. 'He'll get over it,' he would say. And, in effect, he has. When Cipriano's mother took ill, Valle went to visit the house. He went with me and Luis Bello. He was as affectionate as if Cipriano had never behaved badly. This is typical of Don Ramón."

27. Entitled respectively "Pleito artístico. Por qué suspende su actuación la compañía del Cántaro Roto. Valle-Inclán contra el presidente del Círculo de Bellas Artes" and "El Cántaro Roto. Ha suspendido sus representaciones. Una conversación con Valle-Inclán."

28. (Madrid: Imprenta Rivadeneyra, 1927), "Opera Omnia," vol. 4.

29. J., (On *Retablo de la avaricia* . . .) *La Gaceta Literaria* (1 February 1928) noted: "But some scrupulous soul could impute a lack of inventiness to that tendency to mix periods of art. The man rich in creative potential is known by his fixation in going beyond aged works, by disdain toward any of his work that doesn't stem from the drive of the present. It is sad to encounter an author without periods, one who seems paralyzed. That is in lamentable discord with his own vital evolution. Or, worse yet, so slow, so enervated an evolution that it makes possible the inclusion of works from different periods in the same volume without a hint of any transition." The review continues in its negative tone. But there is no criticism of the contents, only of the coherence of the collection.

30. (Madrid: Imprenta Rivadeneyra, 1926), "Opera Omnia," vol. 10.

31. *Martes de carnaval* (Madrid: Pueyo—Imprenta Rivadeneyra, 1930), "Opera Omnia," vol. 17. *Las galas del difunto* was first issued as *El terno del difunto*.

32. *La Novela Mundial* (28 July 1927).

33. F. Madrid, *La vida altiva*, 71; the text of the decree is as follows: "The Directorate General for Security, following the government's mandate, has ordered the withdrawal of a pamphlet passing itself off as a novel, entitled *La hija del capitán*, which the author labels an *Esperpento*, there being in it no line that doesn't wound good taste or fails to denigrate highly respected social classes through the most absurd of fables. If it were possible to publish some segment of the aforementioned pamphlet, it would suffice to show that the governmental determination is not based on narrow and intolerable criteria, but solely on the need to impede the circula-tion of those writings that can only succeed in prostituting good taste, thus committing an outrage against respectability."

34. F. Madrid, *La vida altiva*, 73.

35. See F. Madrid, *La vida altiva*, 364. Enrique de Mesa, reviewing the play on 28 October 1927, stated, "It was buried through an adverse criticism expressed in a loud voice by the noted poet Don Ramón del Valle-Inclán, who last night at the Fontalba was the only repre-sentative of the lineage, as well as the most loyal and fervent admirer of, the young Sevillan Zorrilla."

36. F. Madrid, *La vida altiva*, 365.

37. Ibid.

38. Ibid.

39. F. Madrid, *La vida altiva*, 361–69, and Gómez de la Serna, *Don Ramón María del Valle-Inclá*, 162–65.

40. *La Voz* (1927).

41. "¿Por qué no escribe usted para el teatro?" *ABC* (23 June 1927).

42. T. Ortega, "El teatro futuro según las actuales generaciones," *La Gaceta Literaria* (15 October 1930).

43. F. Madrid, *La vida altiva*, 78. The translations of *La corte de los milagros* (José Rubia Barcia, *A Bio-Bibliography and Iconography of Valle-Inclán. 1866–1936* [Berkeley: University of California Press, 1960], 60) and *La reina castiza* (Rafael Alberti, *Imagen primera de . . .* [Buenos Aires: Losada, 1945], 78) have been verified. Alberti adds that the *Sonatas* also appeared in Russian. My correspondence with Soviet ministries on this matter has not produced new information, but in his article "Valle-Inclán y la Unión Soviética," *La Literatura Internacional* 1, 2 (1944): 50–54, F. V. Kel'in states, "As we will see, Valle-Inclán's work was known by the Russian reader long before the revolutionary era, on the eve of the First World War. . . . How could the Soviet reader not love him when, in 1935, he had become familiar with the first part of *El ruedo ibérico*, *La corte de los milagros*, published in Russian by the Literary Editions of the State (Moscow-Leningrad). We stated earlier that the work of the 'great Don Ramón' was given to the Russian reader well before the revolutionary period. At first, he was able to read fragments of Valle-Inclán's books (especially his *Sonatas*) that appeared from time to time in the Russian press after 1908. Thus, Valle-Inclán's renown among us has the respectable antiquity of thirty-five years. Around 1912 to 1913, the Russian reader's interest in the works of Valle-Inclán was clearly obvious. This made possible the start of a complete collection of his works. Of course, the idea was not realized because the outbreak of the 1914–1918 war impeded it. The sole fruit of that intent was the edition of *Sonata de primavera* in Russian, in an excellent translation and with a prologue written by one of Valle-Inclán's Russian friends. *Sonata de primavera*, after which were to follow the others, was published by V. Z. Ziamenski and Co. in Moscow in 1912. . . . Valle-Inclán was the first of the writers of that old generation in his country—the Generation of '98—to touch the popular heart, the first to manifest his hatred for the imperialist war, and the first to create a series of grotesque novels and plays against violence and the clerico-feudal yoke, against that putrid Spanish reactionism. This is how Soviet critics view the works of Valle-Inclán and his role in the development of contemporary Spanish literature. This new perspective of the Soviet reader toward the works of the 'great Don Ramón' was strongly manifested on the publication of *Tirano Banderas*, issued by the Literary Editions of the State (Moscow-Leningrad) in 1931."

44. In Samuel Putnam, *The European Caravan* (New York: Brewer, Warren and Putnam, 1931), 332–36.

45. See "Muñoz Seca: *La reina castiza*," *ABC* (5 June 1931); also see Enrique Díez-Canedo, "*Farsa y licencia de la reina castiza*," *El Sol* (6 June 1931): "*Farsa y licencia de la reina castiza* has had to wait nine years on the printed page before it could be put on stage. It was on the verge of it at publication thanks to the enthusiasm of an independent theatre group, but its plan was frustrated by circumstances that were not propitious. This writer had the satisfaction of reviewing the book in this column, pointing out its perfect suitability for the theatre. Permit me to quote from the 1922 article: 'We don't feel that the book can be fully assessed if one loses sight of its ever-present scenic potential. The dramatist should always have it in mind; he should make it evident to the reader. And *Farsa y licencia de la reina castiza* is, above all, theatre.' . . . Today it is Valle-Inclán, tomorrow Unamuno, who comes to show us that in contemporary Spanish theatre there is more than the public suspects. My conscience is clear; rather than keep it to myself, I always proclaimed the fact. . . . *La reina castiza*, received by the audience at the premiere not just with merited applause, which was substantial, but with a sensibility that rang through the house in murmurs and laughter demonstrating the interaction of audience and the stage. . . . Valle-Inclán did not attend. After the second act, Asquerino read a letter in which the noted writer explained his absence with sound reasons. The applause, enthusiastic and ongoing, turned his absence into presence." On *El embrujado*, see reviews by Floridor, *ABC* (12 November 1931), and by Enrique Díez-Canedo, *El Sol* (12 November 1931). In a photograph dated 4 November 1931, Valle-Inclán is shown reading to Irene López Héredia and Mariano Asquerino at the Teatro Muñoz Seca (photograph by

Alfonso, Collection Fundación Juan March, file F81). Other photographs of the production appear in Pedro Massa, "Lances y recuerdos de don Ramón del Valle-Inclán," *La Prensa* (15 January 1967).

Notes for Chapter 10: Republic

1. *La Gaceta Literaria* 78 (15 March 1930): 4.
2. Ramón J. Sender, "Valle-Inclán, la política y la cárcel," *Nueva España* (March 1930): 15.
3. *Obras completas de don Ramón del Valle-Inclán*, vol. 2, (Madrid: Talleres Tipográficos de Rivadeneyra, 1944), 1222. Unless otherwise indicated, all quotations from Valle-Inclán's works are from volumes 1 and 2 of this work, hereafter cited as *OC*.
4. "Palabras de un gran poeta de España. Don Ramón del Valle-Inclán nos cuenta sus impresiones y sus inquietudes republicanas," *El Sol* (6 June 1931).
5. Ibid.
6. Ibid.
7. Ibid.
8. Ibid.
9. Letter published in "Valle-Inclán en ocho paginas," *Indice de Artes y Letras* 9, 74–75 (1954).
10. *El Liberal* (21 May 1931).
11. F. Madrid, *La vida altiva del Valle-Inclán*, 278. In his *Obras completas*, vol. 4 (Mexico, D.F.: Oasís, 1967), Manuel Azaña notes in his diary on 2 June 1931: "Guzmán tells me the doings of Valle-Inclán, who has just been defeated as a candidate in Galicia. We recall Valle's old furor against Lerroux and his theme: that only scoundrels could be republicans. . . . Cipriano came after dinner. Among other things, he tells me that Valle-Inclán, who had always treated me with respect, has had a falling out with Unamuno and Luis Bello because Valle told them that I was a mediocre person, that I have always been that, and that I lack imagination, as shown by my writings, which have gone unnoticed until now that I'm in the government. Unamuno replied that he didn't have to wait for that in order to read them, etc., etc. Bello replied in kind. Perhaps this change in Valle derives from Lerroux, of whom he is now a close friend, telling him my views on that friendship. All these back and forth stories don't bother me. Valle-Inclán could never be made over into a respectable person unless he were recast."
12. F. Madrid, *La vida altiva*, 278.
13. "Las elecciones en Galicia," *El Sol* (22 July 1931).
14. "Las elecciones de Galicia—Una carta de D. Ramón María Tenreiro a don Ramón del Valle-Inclán," *Heraldo de Madrid* (23 July 1931): "My much admired maestro: God knows that in my electoral note, as published in *El Sol*, there wasn't the slightest allusion to your exalted and venerated person since you, as far as I know, were not trounced in April's municipal elections, as was the individual clearly alluded to there, nor could I give credence to the notion that the Marquis de Bradomín would descend from that pure framework of the *Sonatas* to give himself over to the lowly business of challenging some election certifications. If, instead of attempting to be elected a delegate without leaving your ivory tower, you had made the rounds that I did, along with all those who wanted to get to know the needs and desires of the Galician people, who wanted to bring to the Cortes the direct and living impression of their lives, of the hamlets and towns of our land, speaking at dozens of meetings, you would be aware of the fact that in the province of La Coruña the votes were cast with an intensity, faith, and enthusiasm never before seen there, the proof being the enormous vote count we received. But, rather than visiting the land and informing yourself personally about Galician concerns, you preferred to echo the base gossip of those who were defeated, putting your pen at the service of a cause you know only in a partial way, which is incomplete and emotional. That's between you and your conscience. You are far above me in merit as a writer, as I acknowledge here and everywhere. But you are not in a similar position insofar as upright-

ness, nobility of character, and dignity, in which I and my fellow delegates are the equals of the most irreproachable individuals in Spain. The derogatory tone of the words you address to us is, therefore, unworthy of a response. Never have the new delegates of La Coruña felt so honored, as you would have in our place, as in having been made representatives in the Cortes by thousands upon thousands of Galicians, and we desire only that our entire energy permits us to respond to the generous popular drive that has brought us where we are."

15. "La réplica de D. Ramón del Valle-Inclán a D. Ramón María Tenreiro," *Heraldo de Madrid* (23 July 1931). In his *Obras completas*, vol. 4, Manuel Azaña comments on the exchange: "Valle-Inclán has published a letter insulting his friend, countryman, and admirer Ramón Tenreiro, elected delegate from La Coruña. Tenreiro replies. Valle answers him. Fernández Almagro thinks that Valle is right, but I deny it. And, furthermore, I believe that when one is old and missing an arm, one shouldn't antagonize anyone."

16. Francisco Lucientes, "Don Ramón del Valle-Inclán daría todos los derechos por una sola ley: supreción de la herencia," *El Sol* (20 November 1931).

17. Ibid.

18. F. Madrid, *La vida altiva*, 276–77.

19. Ibid., 275.

20. Ibid.

21. Lucientes, "Don Ramón del Valle-Inclán."

22. Ibid.

23. Ibid.

24. F. Madrid, *La vida altiva*, 272.

25. Lucientes, "Don Ramón del Valle-Inclán."

26. Ibid.

27. F. Madrid, *La vida altiva*, 79.

28. Manuel Azaña, *Obras completas*, vol. 4. Entry for 22 August 1931: "I've asked Guzmán to undertake a diplomatic mission on behalf of Valle-Inclán during the trip. Valle is in dire straits due to the suspension of payments by the CIAP, which had been giving him three thousand pesetas a month. He's been thinking of going to America, having arranged for his passport and ticket. At this afternoon's council meeting, I explained the situation and expressed the opinion that it wouldn't be fitting to have Valle go to America under the decorous pretext of giving lectures in order to make ends meet. Everyone agreed. While trying to come up with a way of helping him, with everyone convinced that to give him a position of responsibility would be dangerous due to his character, I proposed that we invent a post—Conservator General of the Artistic Patrimony of Spain, with a salary of twenty-five thousand pesetas—to be filled by Valle. Everyone in agreement, they wanted to issue the decree immediately; but I told them to wait until we had the assurance that Valle would accept, for should the decree be made public without that assurance, Don Ramón would take pleasure in refusing the appointment and would insult the government. I've asked Guzmán to handle the matter" (pp. 99–100). Entry for 24 August: "I've wasted the afternoon on three visits: by Vicente Gaspar, who comes to discuss the Republican Action Assembly; by Valle-Inclán and Guzmán; and by Commander Pastor. Valle has come to tell me that he accepts the post for which I nominated him 'if I believe that it won't create difficulties or protests.' We've conversed for over two hours, making me lose precious time. Politics, art, plans that he hopes to develop, etc., etc. All of which will no doubt conclude with a sensational resignation" (p. 101). Entry for 25 August: "I inform them that Valle-Inclán accepts the post I invented for him, and they agree to publish the decree. Curiously, this afternoon in the Congress, Marcelino Domingo asks if I had told Valle the salary. I said I had. Domingo laments the fact because he finds it difficult to accept that Don Ramón will receive a larger salary than the subsecretary. This must have been brought up by someone in the ministry. But since Valle knows it, the minister doesn't dare to modify the salary" (p. 102). Entry for 26 August: "Valle-Inclán became furious on speaking with the director of Fine Arts (Orueta), who has had the tactlessness of telling him that his fine post as Conservator General, etc., has as its principal duty the writing of monographs.

'That's what you give failed writers.' He left shouting, saying that he's not a beggar from the Republic, etc. I take Valle to see the Minister of Public Education and everything is resolved. He will be in charge of organizing the Museum of the Republic in the Royal Palace. Valle describes it as if he were looking at it" (p. 104).

29. Ibid., 141–42. Entry for 22 September 1931: "While in Congress, I stepped into the hallway during a discussion of some article or other because Valle-Inclán had called me. He was with Fernando Salvador, Amós' brother. They came to tell me that Fernando Salvador, an architect in the Ministry of Governance, had received an order from the subsecretary to remove the large shield of the Bourbons from the façade of the Ministry. It appears that the order came out of a communique from the mayor to all the ministries, asking that all royal emblems be removed. Fernando Salvador has seen fit to consult Valle-Inclán, with his resonant title of Conservator General of the National Artistic Patrimony. And Valle and Fernando have come to ask that I intervene. We speak in the anteroom of the minister's offices and I propose that we ask Maura to resolve the matter. While awaiting his arrival, I tell them that I'm opposed to acts of vandalism and that royal shields ought to be respected when they have a value that is artistic, historical, or monumental; it shouldn't come to ruining the Gate of Bisagra in Toledo by ripping out the shield of Carlos V, for example, nor chipping away the façade of the monastery in El Escorial, etc. Valle lets his fancy take wing and, giving himself to 'conserving,' opines, among other things, that the Palace of Riofrio should be restored as a hunting lodge, with the hills stocked with packs of mastiffs, beagles, and bloodhounds, etc., etc. Maura arrives and tells Fernando not to remove the shield from the Ministry under any circumstances. Maura enters the ministers' offices; Valle and Fernando leave."

30. Ibid. Entry for 29 October 1931: "Marcelino Domingo returns to his ministry to work on the budget and, shortly thereafter, Valle-Inclán arrives. He comes to show me a newspaper insert announcing Monday's inauguration of the Museum of the Republic in what had been the Royal Palace. He has a right to protest; nothing has been organized seriously. I tell him that I've heard nothing of such a museum and I arrange to meet him in the presidency the next morning during council hours" (p. 204). Entry for 30 October: "In the presidency, Valle-Inclán, waiting for Domingo. It turns out that Domingo is also unaware of the famous Museum of the Republic. And a bit later in the council, it comes out that the Minister of Finance, who provides the funds for the patrimony, knows nothing of it either." (p. 206).

31. F. Madrid, *La vida altiva*, 74–75.

32. Letter published by Valle-Inclán within "La riqueza artística nacional—Don Ramón del Valle-Inclán explica en una carta las causas y el trámite de su dimisión," *El Sol* (26 June 1932).

33. "Una conferencia de don Ramón del Valle-Inclán," *El Sol* (4 March 1932). See also photograph of Valle-Inclán, et al., in *Ahora* (4 March 1932). The following three extracts are from the same source.

34. Azaña, *Obras completas*, vol. 4. Entry for 31 May 1932: "I placed Valle-Inclán's name in nomination as my successor. Valle won't last long in the presidency because he alone is sufficient to start a commotion where none exists. But that's their concern" (p. 395). See also *Luz* (27 May 1932), which lists the signatories, who proposed, "Nothing better for the Ateneo than an exclusively literary presidency, and no better figure for that than Don Ramón del Valle-Inclán."

35. *Le Monde* (28 May 1932), listed the following other members of the committee: Mme. Sun Yat Sen, Theodore Dreiser, Upton Sinclair, John Dos Passos, Maxim Gorki, Heinrich Mann, Albert Einstein, Romain Rolland, Franz Masereel, Paul Langevin, Paul Signac, Henri Barbusse, Karl Kraus, Félicien Challaye, Michel Karolyi, Victor Margueritte, and Sandine.

36. *Le Monde* (17 June 1932). The "Appel" by Rolland had been preceded by one by him and Henri Barbusse, issued in *Le Monde* (4 June). The attempts to avert another world war were praiseworthy, but the organization was accused of being communist inspired and financed. See André Gide, *Littérature engagée* (Paris: Gallimard, 1950), 15.

37. Interview by Manuel Pérez Ferrero, in *Heraldo de Madrid* (16 May 1932).

38. Emilio Cotarelo, perpetual secretary of the Academy, made the following remarks years

later, which were reprinted in "La Academia de la Lengua no acepta a Del Valle-Inclán," *La Prensa* (11 December 1934): "This Valle-Inclán person entered in the Fastenrath Prize a novel about some revolution in some country or other of America. He had the audacity to think that it would win. . . . The novel was pure extravagance."

39. Corpus Barga, "Entre dos luces—La Academia española se ha cortado la lengua," *Luz* (21 May 1932): "The Spanish Academy was unable to gather enough votes to award a prize to one of Valle-Inclán's novels. What kind of a situation is this? Is it possible that Don Ramón must still go hat-in-hand to the Academy for a prize? Why hasn't he been made a member of the Academy yet, being the only one in Spanish literature who belongs there on his own merits? Of imaginative writers, only one has a seat in the Academy and is on a par with Valle-Inclán: Azorín. The rest are sunk in their academician's armchairs, deeply sunk in before the erect figure of Valle-Inclán. It was sufficient for him to have written one tale, *Flor de santidad*, for his influence in writing to have been felt in the Hispanic world. *Flor de santidad* marks a point of departure in the Castilian literatures of Spain and America. It marks an era, so to speak. When no one remembers the names of those who competed with Valle-Inclán for the prize, nor of those members of the Academy who did not vote for him, Valle-Inclán's will be a name of continuing importance in literature. It would be understandable, desirable even, for writers of more modern sensibilities to be antagonistic to the work of Don Ramón; but the Academy, not knowing how to render due homage to a stylist who has influenced the way of writing, is making a tacit confession that it is on the road to extinction. The Republic ought to create and intensify centers for philological study; but if it wants to assist in the renovation of the spirit, it will have no recourse but to suppress the Academies, the false values." Also Cipriano Rivas Cherif, in *El Sol* (21 May 1932): "It would appear (I don't have precise knowledge of the prize rules) that a preliminary committee [composed of Francisco Rodríguez Marín, Emilio Cotarelo, and José Alemany] and subsequently the Academy as a whole must approve it with sufficient votes for the contestants to guarantee an absolute majority. Neither I, nor the vast number of readers of newspapers and novels, know three of those in the running. Outstanding among them, Valle-Inclán entered one of his best—to me and to others his best—novels: *Tirano Banderas*, recently translated into Russian and published officially by the Soviets, as well as the work in which the great novelist Wells, at present a guest of Madrid, is learning Spanish. Nonetheless, this year the academicians have agreed not to award the Fastenrath Prize, which unanimous opinion had already bestowed on Valle-Inclán. Why? Because, despite the very real literary merits of a minority in the Academy, the rest have a social stance openly enemical to Republican institutions and their representatives."

40. Javier de Izaro, "La revancha de Argamasilla contra Valle-Inclán," *El Sol* (24 May 1932): "If there's such satisfaction around over a certain affront perpetrated, out of clumsiness or rancor, against one of the best living writers in the Castilian language, no one knows the reason. No need to assess why the resentment of a rather substantial and anticipated number of uncouth types should fall into that shameful, awkward form of expression; such emotions are normally kept prudently hidden rather than bravely flaunted to one's public shame. D. Mariano Tomás, one of the entrants, has nobly declared that had he known that one of the indisputably great figures of our literature, as is D. Ramón del Valle-Inclán, was in the competition, he would have withdrawn humbly. This attitude honors the conduct and culture of its exponent; unfortunately, it is wholly different—in its recognition founded on the acknowledged public stature of national literary figures—from that other stance, that taken jointly by the jury of the Academy and a sector of the public against D. Ramón del Valle-Inclán. Of course, no one has dared deny D. Ramón's stylistic and creative merits, celebrated and established in all countries where the language of Cervantes is spoken, as well as in others where it isn't . . . the name of D. Ramón del Valle-Inclán is one of those without which one couldn't explain the many orientations of contemporary Spanish prose. . . . Normal people—who have a good literary education, whose tastes are well-founded and secure, whose souls are free from the shameful pettiness that has led many, nonetheless, to display their satisfaction—believe that the Spanish Academy has rarely sunk so low."

41. *La Voz* (31 May 1932): 3.

42. "El homenaje a Don Ramón," *El Sol* (8 June 1932): "More than three hundred came to dine with Valle-Inclán. Joining the guest of honor at the main table were Sres. Ros, Suazo, Juan Cristóbal, the Mayor of Madrid, Maestro Vives, Unamuno, the Minister of Justice, Américo Castro, Jiménez de Asúa, Estrada, the Mexican ambassador; Cortesao, the ex-minister of Portugal to Madrid; Victorio Macho, and Del Río Hortega; at other tables were: Beatriz Galindo, Magda Donato, Natividad Zaro, Josefina Carabías, subsecretario de Comunicaciones, doctor Marañón, Royo Villanova, Ortiz de Zárate, Martín Puente, Salazar (Adolfo), Armasa, Hoyos y Vinent, Sassone, Hernández Catá, Blanco Fombona, Suárez de Deza, Hernández Barroso, García Martín, Alvarez (D. Basilio), Anselmo Miguel Nieto, José Pla, Julio Moisés, Pascual, Hoyos (D. Luis), Vegue Goldoni, Chaves, Nogales, Dionisio Pérez, Darío Pérez, Quintín de la Torre, Angel Segovia, Artigas Arpón, José Ballester, Emiliano Iglesias, Abad Conde, De Benito, Carral, Espinosa, Martínez de la Fuente, Yagües, Oteyza, Montero Alonso, etc."

43. Francisco Madrid, *Genio e ingenio de don Miguel de Unamuno* (Buenos Aires: Aniceto López, 1943), 180–81. Also, short quotes in "El homenaje a Don Ramón," *El Sol* (8 June 1932).

44. "El homenaje a Don Ramón": "Numerous communiques of support were received, among them those of Sres. Ramón Menéndez Pidal, the president of the Council of Ministers, the Minister of Public Education, D. Juan Madinaveitia, D. Ramón Pérez de Ayala, Lerroux, Benavente, Salinas, D. Manuel Aznar, Arteta, D. Emiliano Barral, Bello, Ricardo Calvo, Zamacois, D. Pedro Mourlane Michelena, Fernández Almagro, Eduardo Marquina, Vicente Sánchez Ocaña, Fernández Flórez, Giménez Caballero, Gerardo de Diego, Zubianrre (D. Ramón), Verdes Montenegro y Sender."

45. F. Madrid, *La vida altiva*, 101–2. Valle-Inclán had uttered similar ideas on other occasions, since his early days as a writer. That he had practiced what he preached is evident in his separation from the opportunities he had in Galicia to follow a career in journalism or literature.

46. "El homenaje a Don Ramón." See F. Madrid, *La vida altiva*, 102, for a variant on this segment of Valle-Inclán's speech.

47. F. Madrid, *La vida altiva*, 102–3.

48. "La riqueza artística nacional," *El Sol* (26 June 1932). Ramón Gómez de la Serna, *Don Ramón María del Valle-Inclán*, 191, states that Valle-Inclán tendered his resignation because his charges brought against the socialist deputy Bujeda for hunting on the royal estates in his charge were not taken seriously. While that episode may have taken place, Valle-Inclán's letters offer the best evidence of his tenure and its problems.

49. "La riqueza artística nacional," *El Sol* (26 June 1932).

50. Ibid. Azaña, *Obras completas*, vol. 4. Entry for 21 June 1932: "Valle-Inclán has resigned from the post that we gave him last year. He was penniless and didn't even have enough to eat. I created a post for him: that of Conservator of the Artistic Patrimony, with a salary of 24,000 pesetas [*sic*]. The government approved him and he was named to the post. He never even thanked me. He had nothing to do and so a few months later we had to assign him a function. He was told to attend to the palace at Aranjuez. He immediately had an argument with the commission of what had once been the patrimony of the crown and, acting like an autocrat, began giving arbitrary and senseless orders that no one was obliged to follow. Because of this, many picturesque things have occurred, as in any situation in which Valle-Inclán figures. At the same time, his wife sued him for divorce, and the judge has ordered that half his salary be held back. Furious at this, Valle has resigned, alleging that he hasn't been allowed to function properly in his post; but the truth is that he did so to prevent his wife from collecting anything. That's how Valle is, and, since he likes playing the victim, he sent his watch to be pawned on the same day that he showed his resignation to some friends. Now he goes around the cafés speaking against the government. I don't think he's attacked me verbally as yet, but he will. He goes around saying that my colleagues are setting me up like Prim, and that Casares and Menéndez will assassinate me" (p. 407).

51. Ibid.

52. His interest in Río de Janeiro was founded on the reports of Alfonso Reyes, who was then serving as a diplomat in that city.

53. *El Sol* (20 October-11 December 1931). Several changes differentiated this new edition from that of 1927: a section corresponding to book 2, chapter 21, was amplified slightly; to the original edition's content was added an entirely new book, "Aires nacionales," which preceded the others as book 1. Curiously, posthumous editions of *La corte de los milagros* do not include these changes but rather reproduce the 1927 edition. "La rosa de oro," first chapter of *La corte de los milagros*, appeared as "The Golden Rose" in W. B. Wells, *Great Spanish Short Stories* (Boston: Houghton-Mifflin, 1932), 47–84.

54. *El Sol* (7 June-19 July 1932). "Vísperas septembrinas," divided into five sections, formed the first part of *Baza de espadas*. This is as much of the novel as Valle-Inclán published in *El Sol*. Several of these sections had appeared earlier with different titles in *La Novela de Hoy* 392 (15 November 1929), and 408 (16 May 1930). The first edition of the novel, reproducing those sections issued in *El Sol*, appeared posthumously (Barcelona: Editorial AHR, 1958). An interesting antecedent of the novel was Valle-Inclán's article "El anarquismo español" in *El Universal* (2 June 1892): it discussed Fermín Salvoechea, a character in *Baza de espadas*.

55. The following item appeared in *Heraldo de Madrid* (14 December 1932): 15: "Valle-Inclán's wife has instituted the dissolution of the matrimonial bond. Mutual separation and other causes are the motives behind this matrimonial suit. The hearing will be behind closed doors, and the writer has not appeared in person. . . . The rest is of a personal nature and it would be indiscreet to comment on it."

56. Sender's letter to me, previously cited, states, "She married a young professor whose name, I believe, was Toledano. The marriage was not to Valle-Inclán's liking, but the writer did not formally oppose it." Gómez de la Serna, *Don Ramón María del Valle-Inclán*, 162: "His older daughter is going to marry young professor Toledano. The daughter fights with her father because, for no apparent reason, he won't give his consent, and she's heard to say: 'What can one expect from a father whose name isn't Valle-Inclán but Valle y Peña!'" Toledano was fond of saying that his father-in-law tested words as did people who distrusted coins and bounced them on a slab of marble, judging their worthiness by the sound they made (as told to me by the playwright Lauro Olmo).

57. F. Madrid, *La vida altiva*, 75.

58. Melchor Fernández Almagro, *Vida y literatura de Valle-Inclán*, 269–70; Gómez de la Serna, *Don Ramón María del Valle-Inclán*, 171–72. *Informaciones* (19 August 1977) refers to an article by Rosa Arciniega in *Nuevo Mundo* regarding Valle-Inclán's ordeal.

59. José A. Balseiro, *Blasco Ibáñez, Unamuno, Valle-Inclán y Baroja: Cuatro individualistas de España* (Chapel Hill: University of North Carolina Press, 1949), 464: "Precisely at this moment we are involved in petitioning the Cortes for a pension that will allow him to live in total dedication to his literary endeavors."

60. "La Dirección de la Academia de España en Roma. Ignacio Zuloaga defiende la candidatura de Valle-Inclán," *El Sol* (21 October 1932).

61. *Blanco y Negro* (30 October 1932). The autograph of this poem and another, "Testamento," written on stationery bearing the imprint "El Presidente del Ateneo de Madrid," were reproduced in *Indice de Artes y Letras* 9 (1954), 74–75. The latest assessment of these appears in Ramón del Valle-Inclán, *Artículos completos y otras páginas olvidadas*, edited by Javier Serrano Alonso (Madrid: Ediciones Istmo, 1987), 420–23.

62. Gómez de la Serna, *Don Ramón María del Valle-Inclán*, 200. Other versions of "Testamento" vary greatly. The autograph poem reproduced in *Indice de Artes y Letras* contains three stanzas of four lines each, roughly equivalent to the last twelve lines quoted above; the version published by Gaspar Gómez de la Serna in Valle-Inclán, *Obras escogidas* (Madrid: Aguilar, 1958), 11, has five stanzas of four lines each, with the two first stanzas exactly equal to those quoted, but the last three with extensive variations. In all, there are three versions of the last twelve lines of the poem.

63. Gregorio Martínez Sierra, "Hablando con Valle-Inclán . . . " *ABC* (7 December 1928): "an uncommon loyalty to each other has joined them in a lasting mutual bond. . . . They are unvarying . . . inseparable . . . "

64. Among them "Correo diplomático" (two publications with the same heading), *Ahora* (13, 20 March 1933).

65. An impressive portrait of Valle-Inclán by Juan de Echevarría is displayed prominently in the permanent collection of this museum.

66. Present at the reading were, among others, Margarita Xirgu, Enrique Borrás, Aguirre, Guitart, López Lagar, Enrique Alvarez Diosdado, Porredón, Ortíz, Pilarín Muñoz, Alberto Contreras, Cipriano Rivas Cherif, Juan Chabás, Angel Lázaro, Alberto Marín Alcalde, Victorino Tamayo, and Castelao.

67. "En el Español—Don Ramón del Valle-Inclán lee su tragicomedia *Divinas palabras*," *El Sol* (25 March 1933).

68. *El País* (9 November 1985).

69. Ibid.

70. Fernández Almagro, *Vida y literatura* 272.

71. F. Madrid, *La vida altiva*, 215.

72. Adriano del Valle, "Valle-Inclán vivió en Roma en olor de santidad fascista," *España* 1, 44 (14 December 1938): 3.

73. F. Madrid, *La vida altiva*, 281–82.

74. Rafael Alberti, *Imagen primera de* . . . (Buenos Aires: Losada, 1945), 80.

75. Ibid.

76. F. Kel'in, "Valle-Inclán y la Unión Soviética," *La Literatura Internacional* 1, 2 (1944).

77. Julián Marías, "Baza de espadas," *La Nación* (21 December 1958): "It was in Naples. . . . Toward the end of July 1933, the 'Ciudad de Cádiz,' on its return trip from a university tour through the Mediterranean organized by García Morrente, dean of the Faculty of Philosophy and Letters, arrived at the bay. Valle-Inclán, wanting to return to Spain, accepted our hospitality and sailed from the illustrious gulf, looking distractedly at the smoke emitted by Vesuvius, to Palma and Valencia. I recall him, old, tired, lounging on the deck, giving forth ingenuities, lyricism, mordacity, and disenchantment, his lisping words seemingly entangling themselves in his beard. We reached Valencia on the 1st of August and we began to disperse."

78. F. Madrid, *La vida altiva*, 279–81.

79. See reviews by M. Fernández Almagro in *El Sol* (17 November 1933); Juan Chabás in *Luz* (17 November 1933); and A. C. in *ABC* (17 November 1933).

80. *La Farsa* 327 (16 December 1933); the cover depicted Margarita Xirgu and Enrique A. Diosdado in their respective roles.

81. For anecdotes, see Gómez de la Serna, *Don Ramón María del Valle-Inclán*, 194–98, and F. Madrid, *La vida altiva*, 211–16.

82. Alberti, *Imagen primera de* . . . , 80.

83. A letter to me from Prof. Vittorio Bodini, dated 15 January 1967 from Rome states, "As a matter of fact, I'm pleased to be able to give you an item that may be useful: toward the end of 1934, Valle-Inclán had *Los cuernos de don Friolera* produced in Rome, under the direction of Bragaglia." Bragaglia again presented the play on two later occasions: as *Le corna del Sor Friolera*, Teatro delle Arti, 1937; as *Le corna del Don Friolera*, Teatro della Floridiana, Naples, 1950. See *Enciclopedia dello Spettacolo*, vol. 2 (Roma: Casa Editrice Le Maschere). Writing in *Valle-Inclán y su tiempo hoy—Catálogo General* (Madrid: Ministerio de Cultura, 1986), 38, Ignacio Hidalgo de Cisneros states, "In those days, Valle-Inclán's play *Los cuernos de don Friolera* was premiered in Rome. Fortunately, Don Ramón could not attend, being in Spain. I went to the premiere with Connie and Don Ramón's daughter Maruja, who lived in Rome with her father. The performance was a disaster. No one liked it. The audience did not hide its displeasure and we had a rather disagreeable time."

84. Alberti, *Imagen primera de* . . . , 77–78: "I was returning from Odessa. . . . I had come

from Moscow, having been invited to attend the First Congress of Soviet Writers, bringing Don Ramón from these individuals a warm, admiring greeting, still fresh due to the success of his *Sonatas* and *Farsa de la reina castiza*, translated into Russian."

85. Ibid., 79: "The Academy, poor Academy of Spain, with scarce support and bad directors, had been experiencing a dirty and uncomfortable life of disrepair, within a beautiful untended area with marvelous gardens and patios, one of these centered on a charming pavillion by Bramante. . . . He is obsessed with transforming the Academy, with turning it into a real home to Spanish artists. . . . He wanted to have, not beginners selected through some competition, but trained people, mature men who could benefit from the lesson of Rome in its immense amplitude." A photograph of Alberti and León flanking Valle-Inclán appeared in *Nueva Cultura* (January 1935).

86. Ibid., 82, refers to the envelope of one of Josefina's letters, which was addressed: "Sr. D. Ramón María del Valle-Inclán / Marquis de Bradomín / Author of *Divinas palabras* and other / words not as divine / Academy of Spain / Gianicolo, Rome."

87. Ramón J. Sender, *Valle-Inclán y la dificultad de la tragedia* (Madrid: Gredos, 1965), 146–48: "Valle-Inclán had his crisis of lecherous senility. . . . It was an unhappy adventure that ended in a few months. . . . I learned about it shortly thereafter through a diplomatic friend of Valle-Inclán, who intervened to avoid an uncomfortable aftermath and who was the confidante of 'the woman.' Incidentally, she was more beautiful than discreet. I also heard Don Ramón say something about the affair during his first return visit to Madrid. Naturally, Valle-Inclán did not disclose everything. But we tied up loose ends through the allusions and shadings of his words. . . . Don Ramón fell in love with a beautiful young woman from Naples. The first move . . . was made by her . . . Valle-Inclán did not fall in love immediately. . . . They became good friends. . . . The girl . . . on seeing her triumph, left Valle-Inclán in a fury. The old Bradomín bore the marks of her fingernails on his face for a few days. . . . The Neapolitan girl fled and the poet went after her through the south and north of Italy. People in Rome talked. The girl was well known and the incident reached . . . the seat of power on the Quirinal, where the Duce Benito heard the story. Mussolini asked Valle-Inclán's age and said: 'He ought to be congratulated.' These words reached the ears of the Marquis de Bradomín." This is the only mention of this incident that I have found.

88. Fernández Almagro, *Vida y literatura*, 275.

89. "La Academia de la Lengua no acepta a Del Valle-Inclán," *La Prensa* (11 December 1934). Cotarelo commented, "What rubbish! He hasn't been admitted, nor will he be. He's not a good writer. He's nothing but an inveterate gallicist. He destroys the Castilian language. He has no respect for the rules of the language. He's an extravagant character. Nothing more than a stray bullet. And this matters because the bylaws of the Academy require that an entrant be a person of good character."

90. Published in Manuel Azaña, *Mi rebelión en Barcelona* (Madrid: Espasa-Calpe, 1935). Others who signed the document were Azorín, Américo Castro, Federico García Lorca, Juan Ramón Jiménez, Eduardo Marquina, Gregorio Marañón, and Alejandro Casona.

91. *El Pueblo* (21 December 1934): 4

92. Juan B. Bergua, "El porqué de este libro," prologue to Valle-Inclán, *Flores de almendro* (Madrid: Librería Bergua, 1936), 5, quotes Ruiz Contreras: "I've just visited Valle-Inclán, who is ill. I don't know why he's still alive. Yet I do know: he lives on the strength of his spirit since he's only skin and bones. What's more, he has very little money. Why don't those of you who do well selling books publish something of his? Not only would you do him a favor, it would certainly be good business for you. Valle, as you know better than I, is one of the few authors who sell. . . . The problem is that if you want something as yet unpublished, I'm not certain that he can provide it. As he told me, he's working on something from the series *Ruedo ibérico*, but it's barely sketched out."

93. Ibid., 6–7: "He received me in the alcove. He had been in bed for several days. . . . One could discern the skeleton beneath the immaculate silk shirt that he wore. But the eyes, beyond the enormous glasses, possessed an incredible vitality."

94. Ibid., 8, 10.

95. Ibid., 11.

96. José Luis Cano, *García Lorca—Biografía ilustrada* (Barcelona: Ediciones Destino, 1962), 87.

97. Ramón J. Sender, letter to me dated 9 August 1965: "Valle-Inclán was in the audience at the Teatro Español—as was Unamuno—and expressed a dislike for the play, not as a work of art, but in terms of the way in which Lorca interpreted the feminine feeling of maternity."

98. *La Voz de Guipúzcoa* (20 February 1935). On 17 February the same newspaper carried the notice of the lecture.

99. José Caamaño Bournacell, *Por las rutas turísticas de Valle-Inclán*, 113–14.

100. *Política* (26 September 1935): 2.

101. Parts of these episodes appeared posthumously in *Ahora* (19 March-23 April 1936). They are an unincorporated fragment of the series.

102. F. Madrid, *La vida altiva*, 88. See variant in "Recuerdo de Don Ramón," *La Voz* (6 January 1936): 2.

103. "Epitalamios napolitanos," *Ahora* (2 June 1935). Other articles in *Ahora*: "Codex Calixtinus" (14 June); articles on Romanones's *Amadeo de Saboya* (18, 26 June; 2, 11, 19, 25 July); articles on Paúl y Angulo (1, 12, 16, 29 August; 19 September). The articles published in *Ahora* about the nineteenth century were undoubtedly to be related to *El ruedo ibérico*, perhaps as a continuation of *Baza de espadas*, *El trueno dorado*, or another part of the series.

104. André Gide, *Littérature engagée* (Paris: Gallimard, 1950), 83: "The Congress was held in Paris, at the Palace of Accord, from the 21st through the 25th of June 1935. Thirty-eight countries were represented by two hundred and thirty delegates. There were sixty-one speeches followed by discussions on the following major topics: The Individual, Humanism, Nation and Culture, Problems of Creation and the Dignity of Thought, the Defense of Culture. The opening session of the Congress took place on Friday evening, the 21st of June, presided over by André Gide and André Malraux, with an 'Address' by André Gide, whose text will be found immediately preceding his own major statement on the Defense of Culture, delivered at the midday meeting of Tuesday, the 25th of June; it was André Gide who translated the discourse by the German writer Klaus, who had come directly from Germany with the purpose of bringing to the Congress many manuscripts by German writers who, under threat of death, illegally continue to write. Before departing, the members of the Congress decided to continue the work begun there, establishing an International Association of Writers for the Defense of Culture, under the direction of a permanent International Bureau of one hundred and twelve members, headed by a praesidium of twelve members: Henri Barbusse, Romain Rolland, André Gide, Heinrich Mann, Thomas Mann, Maxime Gorki, Forster, Aldous Huxley, Bernard Shaw, Sinclair Lewis, Selma Lagerf, Valle-Inclán."

105. *OC*, 2:1921.

106. "El homenaje de Galicia a D. Ramón del Valle-Inclán," *El Sol* (10 August 1935). The article quotes the statement: "Here in Santiago de Compostela . . . brought together in a tight bond of admiration for the noblest figure of our literature, D. Ramón del Valle-Inclán, there ignited the desire to honor the venerable maestro of aesthetics, Spain's greatest writer, in a way that would at once eternalize his works and the lyric soul of Galicia. . . . To that end, a select group came up with the idea of making Don Ramón del Valle-Inclán the gift of a *pazo*, the definitive manifestation in stone of the Galician home, as well as the romantic setting for the most beautiful literary creations by the illustrious author of the *Comedias bárbaras*. It would be a noble manse situated in the peace of an old maritime hamlet or on the high summit of a Virgilian landscape, proclaiming the glory of this great lord of literature through its cresting tower . . . We want Valle-Inclán to be alive for Galicia in the exalted Galician context that befits him . . . we want our voice to spread throughout Spain and reach the nations of Hispanic America on the Atlantic wind . . ." The statement was signed by Ricardo Montequi, José Arias Ramos, Vicente Varela Radio, Fernando Alsina, Joaquín Arías Sanjurjo, Francisco Asorey, Ramón Baltar, Fernando Barros Pumariño, Ricardo Bescansa, Manuel Devesa, Andrés Díaz de Rábago, Ramón Díaz Varela, Eduardo Dieste, Domingo García Sabell, Antonio Martínez de la

Riva, Juan Luis López, Manuel Losa Alvarez, Carlos Maside, Santiago Montero Díaz, Vicente Otero Garrido, Angel Pedreira Ladadíe, José Puente Castro, Enrique Rajoy, Manuel Remuñán, Francisco Romero Molezún, Celestino Sánchez Rivera, Laureano Santiso Girón, and Manuel Villar Iglesias. The commission was headed by Manuel Devesa, Manuel Remuñán, and Fernando Barros Pumariño. See also M. Portela Valladares, "Una idea en marcha: El pazo para Valle-Inclán," *El Pueblo Gallego* (27 July 1935).

107. Ramón Otero Pedrayo, "El viaje a Orense de D. Ramón del Valle-Inclán," *Insula* 236–37, 3. In his "Mi Valle-Inclán. . . ¡Cuánta bondad y cuanta paciencia!" (Premio "Mariano de Cavia"), in *La Vanguardia Española* (27 October 1966), José María Castroviejo recalled his meeting Valle-Inclán in Santiago de Compostela in 1935: "Don Ramón's magical words, enlightened and perfect, evoked Priscillian—about whose extraordinary life he planned to write a treatise, something like a new 'lámpara maravillosa,' a project cut short by death—Gnosis, Plotinus . . . His words fell on the awestruck ears of this young man, almost an adolescent, like tongues of flame; like a breath of spirit. Time and space were eradicated, everything occurring at once, when, facing the already shadowy Cathedral, he told us why it possessed the divine golden number sacred to the Pythagoreans."

108. Valle-Inclán, "*Mi rebelión en Barcelona* (Nota literaria)," *Ahora* (26 September 1935); reprinted in *Política* (3 October 1935). His last published poem had appeared earlier that year: "Rosa de Zoroastro," *Ciudad* (23 January 1935). Another poem with this title had appeared in Valle-Inclán's book *El pasajero*, but there is no relation between them. The present poem, however, derives from "Rosa de oriente," another sonnet from *El pasajero* written under the inspiration of the famed Tórtola Valencia who had brought her exotic dances to Madrid.

109. Ibid.

110. *Política* (7 November 1935): 3.

111. F. Madrid, *La vida altiva*, 29.

112. To Dr. García Sabell. See *Insula*, 176–77 (July-August 1966): 19.

113. Fernández Almagro, *Vida y literatura*, 276.

114. F. Madrid, *La vida altiva*, 88.

115. Arturo Cuadrado, "Agonía y muerte de Don Ramón María del Valle-Inclán," *Galicia* 27, 330 (June 1940): 46–48. In his article "Cartas a *Nueva Cultura*. Desde Santiago de Compostela," *Nueva Cultura* (January 1936), J. Parrado gives a variant of these last instructions: "He died reminding his son Carlos (a militant in the Communist Youth, as well as a student at the university) of the following phrases from one of his books: 'I want the door shut to the ambitious priest, the humble friar, and the astute Jesuit since these are not suitable times for making investments, considering that the return is only three percent.'"

116. Cuadrado, "Agonía y muerte."

117. *The Lamp of Marvels*, 119–20. La lámpara maravillosa, "El quietismo estético, 9."

118. Cuadrado, "Agonía y muerte."

119. Later, the Republic granted Josefina a pension in honor of Valle-Inclán; this caused Pío Baroja, *Memorias* (Madrid: Minotauro, 1955), 1157 to sneer: "In the era of the Republic, it was said that he was a Communist and he was honored publicly as a revolutionary; and the Red Government gave his widow a pension."

120. *ABC* (7 January 1936): "Santiago, the 6th, 8 p.m. The burial of the body of D. Ramón del Valle-Inclán took place at five o'clock in the afternoon. Thousands of people from all walks of life participated in the funeral procession. Presiding were his relatives, the Governor of the province, the president of the Delegation, the Mayor of Santiago, Sr. Deveza who represented the Ateneo of Madrid, members of the Seminar on Galician Studies, as well as other individuals and representations, who accompanied the body to the cemetery. Expressions of condolence have been received from many, among them a very warm tribute from the Minister of Public Education offering to underwrite the funeral costs on behalf of the Government. The internment has been funded by the City Council of Santiago. The sculptor Azoreg (sic) made the plaster cast of the dead man's face." Francisco Asorey, the Galician sculptor who created impressive monuments to St. Francis in Santiago de Compostela, to Christ in Cuntis, and to

Feijóo in Samos, made the death-mask. Carlos Maside and Castelao did drawings of Valle-Inclán's head; Juan Luis López did a portrait. See also J. Parrado, "Cartas a *Nueva Cultura*": "The funeral was an immense mass of people; there would have been more, as it would have been fitting, but the hurricane-force rain and wind prevented the presence of the entire population of the city, especially of the workers. In any case, many people were present. By express order of the deceased, neither wreaths nor other manifestations of grief were permitted; nonetheless, the workers' parties—of the Republican left and the pro-Galicians—sent a collective bouquet; the C.P. sent another bouquet and, at the last minute, there came from Madrid a great wreath from its Ateneo, of which he had been a member and Honorary President. Had not the weather been bad, there would have been a huge popular manifestation for the man who, in Spain, incarnated the intellectual struggle against Fascism and war, the man who was Honorary President of the Committees for Assistance, etc."

121. Accounts of the incident appear in Gómez de la Serna, *Don Ramón María del Valle-Inclán*, 211; F. Madrid, *La vida altiva*, 94–95; Arturo Cuadrado, "Agonía y muerte," 46–48; Rubia Barcia, *A Bio-Bibliography and Iconography of Valle-Inclán. 1866–1936* (Berkeley: University of Caslifornia Press, 1960), 24. F. Madrid, *La vida altiva*, 95, adds that Pasín was shot later that year: "The go-between who asked the name of the gilder of statues who had wrested the cross from Don Ramón's coffin has not forgotten the name. And Modesto Pasín is the first to be executed by firing squad in Santiago de Compostela. He loses his life in that same cemetery, his fist held high."

122. José Luis Salado, "Velada en honor de Valle-Inclán," *La Voz* (15 February 1936). The article continues: "Despite the circumstances, yesterday we saw on the stage of the Zarzuela one of the most characteristic of Valle's plays: *Los cuernos de don Friolera*, an *Esperpento* undoubtedly not written to be performed. However, it took on some life yesterday thanks to the effective scenography of Fontanals and the actors of the New Stage company, which was full of youthful vigor . . . Sufficient, in fact, for Don Ramón's relatives to overcome their pious fear, which was absolutely unjustified." This "pious fear" led his son Carlos, years later, to order the etching of a cross on Valle-Inclán's monolithic tomb-cover against his father's death wish to have no religious symbols on his grave.

Selected Bibliography

Balseiro, José A. *Blasco Ibáñez, Unamuno, Valle-Inclán y Baroja: Cuatro individualistas de España*. Chapel Hill: University of North Carolina Press, 1949.

Barbeito, Clara L. *Epica y tragedia en la obra de Valle-Inclán*. Madrid: Editorial Fundamentos, 1985.

Borobó. *Papeles de Borobó. 1. El fantasma de Valle-Inclán*. Sada-A Coruña: Ediciós do Castro, 1986.

Caamaño Bournacell, José. *Por las rutas turísticas de Valle-Inclán*. Madrid: Privately published, 1971.

Cardona, Rodolfo, and Anthony N. Zahareas. *Visión del esperpento. Teoría y práctica en los esperpentos de Valle-Inclán*. Madrid: Castalia, 1970.

Casares, Julio. *Crítica profana: Valle-Inclán, Azorín, Ricardo León*. Madrid: Imp. Colonial, 1916.

Cuadernos Hispanoamericanos 67, 199–200 (July-August 1966).

Díaz Migoyo, Gonzalo. *Guía de "Tirano Banderas"*. Madrid: Fundamentos, 1985.

Díaz-Plaja, Guillermo. *Las estéticas de Valle-Inclán*. Madrid: Editorial Gredos, 1965.

Dougherty, Dru. *Un Valle-Inclán olvidado. Entrevistas y conferencias*. Madrid: Fundamentos, 1983.

Durán, Manuel. *De Valle-Inclán a León Felipe*. Mexico, D.F.: Finisterre, 1974.

Fernández Almagro, Melchor. *Vida y literatura de Valle-Inclán*. Madrid: Taurus, 1966.

Fichter, William L. *Publicaciones periodísticas de Don Ramón del Valle-Inclán anteriores a 1895*. México, D.F.: El Colegio de México, 1952.

Gómez de la Serna, Ramón. *Don Ramón María del Valle-Inclán*. Buenos Aires: Espasa-Calpe, 1944; rpt. Madrid: Espasa-Calpe, 1964.

Gómez Marín, José A. *La idea de sociedad en Valle-Inclán*. Madrid: Taurus, 1967.

González López, Emilio. *El arte dramático de Valle-Inclán (del decadentismo al expresionismo)*. New York: Las Américas, 1967.

———. *La poesía de Valle-Inclán. Del simbolismo al expresionismo*. San Juan: Universidad de Puerto Rico, 1973.

Greenfield, Sumner M. *El Teatro de Valle-Inclán*, Madrid: Fundamento, 1972.

Guerrero, Obdulia. *Valle-Inclán y el novecientos*. Madrid: Magisterio Español, 1977.

Guerrero Zamora, Juan. "Ramón del Valle-Inclán." *Historia del teatro contemporáneo*, I. Barcelona: Juan Flors, 1961.

Gullón, Ricardo, ed. *Valle-Inclán Centennial Studies*. Austin: University of Texas Press, 1968.

Hormigón, Juan Antonio. *Ramón del Valle-Inclán: La política, la cultura, el realismo y el pueblo*. Madrid: Alberto Corazón, Editor, 1972.

_____. *Valle-Inclán. Cronología y documentos*. Madrid: Ministerio de Cultura, 1978.

_____. *Valle-Inclán y su tiempo*. Madrid: Compañía de Acción Teatral, 1982.

_____. *Valle-Inclán.* Madrid: Fundación Banco Exterior, 1987.

Insula 16, 176–77 (July-August 1961); 21, 236–37 (July-August 1966).

Lado, María Dolores. *Las guerras carlistas y el reinado isabelino en la obra de Ramón del Valle-Inclán*. Gainesville: University of Florida Press, 1965.

La Pluma. vol 6, 32 (January 1923).

Lavaud, Eliane. *Valle-Inclán. Du journal au roman (1888–1915)*. Dijon: L'Université de Dijon, 1979.

Lima, Robert. *Valle-Inclán: Autobiography, Aesthetics, Aphorisms*. Limited Centennial Edition. Privately published, 1966.

_____. *Ramón del Valle-Inclán*. N.Y.: Columbia University Press, 1972.

_____. *An Annotated Bibliography of Ramón del Valle-Inclán*. University Park: The Pennsylvania State University Libraries, 1972.

_____. Translator. *The Lamp of Marvels*. West Stockbridge, MA: Lindisfarne Press, 1986.

Lima, Robert, and Dru Dougherty. *Dos ensayos sobre teatro español de los veinte*. Murcia: Universidad de Murcia—Cátedra de Teatro, 1984.

Llorens, Eva. *Valle-Inclán y la plástica*. Madrid: Insula, 1975.

Lyon, John. *The Theatre of Valle-Inclán*. Cambridge: Cambridge University Press, 1983.

Madrid, Francisco. *La vida altiva de Valle-Inclán*. Buenos Aires: Poseidón, 1943.

Maldonado Macías, Humberto A. *Valle-Inclán, gnóstico y vanguardista*. Mexico, D.F.: UNAM, 1980.

March, María E. *Forma e idea de los esperpentos de Valle Inclán*. Madrid: Castalia, 1969.

Paz-Andrade, Valentín. *La anunciación de Valle-Inclán*. Buenos Aires: Losada, 1967.

Primer Acto 28 (November 1961); 46 (October 1963); 82 (February 1967).

Ramón M. del Valle-Inclán, 1866–1966. Estudios reunidos en conmemoración del centenario. La Plata: Universidad Nacional de la Plata, 1967.

Revista de Occidente 15, 44–45 (November-December 1966).

Risco, Antonio. *La estética de Valle-Inclán en los Esperpentos y en "El ruedo ibérico."* Madrid: Gredos, 1966.

_____. *El demiurgo y su mundo. Hacia un nuevo enfoque de la obra de Valle-Inclán*. Madrid: Gredos, 1977.

Rubia Barcia, José. *A Biobibliography and Iconography of Valle-Inclán (1866–1936)*. Berkeley: University of California Press, 1960.

Sender, Ramón J. *Valle-Inclán y la dificultad de la tragedia*. Madrid: Gredos, 1965.

Serrano Alonso, Javier, ed. Ramón del Valle-Inclán: *Artículos completos y otras páginas olvidadas*. Madrid: Ediciones Istmo, 1987.

Schiavo, Leda. *Historia y novela en Valle-Inclán*. Madrid: Castalia, 1980.

Servera Baño, José. *Ramón del Valle-Inclán*. Madrid: Ediciones Júcar, 1983.

Smither, William J. *El mundo gallego de Valle-Inclán*. Sada-A Coruña: Ediciós do Castro, 1986.

Speratti Piñero, Emma S. *La elaboración artística en "Tirano Banderas."* México, D.F.: El Colegio de México, 1957.

_____. *De "Sonata de otoño" al Esperpento (Aspectos del arte de Valle-Inclán)*. London: Tamesis Books, 1968.

_____. *El ocultismo en Valle-Inclán*. London: Tamesis Books, 1974.

Tucker, Peggy Lynne. *Time and History in Valle-Inclán's Historical Novels and "Tirano Banderas"*. Valencia: Hispanófila, 1980.

Umbral, Francisco. *Valle-Inclán*. Madrid: Unión Editorial, 1969.

Ynduráin, Francisco. *Valle-Inclán—Tres estudios*. Santander: La Isla de los Ratones, 1969.

Zahareas, Anthony, ed. *Ramón del Valle-Inclán: An Appraisal of His Life and Works*. New York: Las Américas, 1968.

Zamora Vicente, Alonso. *Las "Sonatas" de Valle-Inclán*. Madrid: Gredos, 1955.

————. *La realidad esperpéntica (Aproximación a "Luces de bohemia")*. Madrid: Gredos, 1969.

Appendix

Chapter 1: Origins

A1

¡El gato que runfla! ¡La puerta que cruje!
¡La gotera glo-glo-glo!
¡Solos en la casa! A la puerta ruge
La bestia abortada cuando nací yo.

¡La noche de Octubre! Dicen que de Luna,
Con un viento recio y saltos de mar:
Bajo sus estrellas se alzó mi fortuna,
Mar y vientos recios me vieron llegar.

A2

Esta emoción divina es de la infancia,
Cuando felices el camino andamos
Y todo se disuelve en la fragancia
De un Domingo de Ramos.

A3

Los Montenegros de Galicia descendemos de una emperatriz alemana. Es el único blasón español que lleva metal sobre metal: Espuelas de oro en campo de plata.

A4

Tenía mi abuela una doncella muy vieja que se llamaba Micaela la Galana: Murió siendo yo todavía niño: Recuerdo que pasaba las horas hilando en el hueco de una ventana, y que sabía muchas historias de santos, de almas en pena, de duendes y de ladrones. Ahora yo cuento las que ella me contaba, mientras sus dedos arrugados daban vueltas al huso. Aquellas historias de un misterio candoroso y trágico, me asustaron de noche durante los años de mi infancia y por eso no las he olvidado. De tiempo en tiempo todavía se levantan en mi memoria, y como si un viento silencioso y frío pasase sobre ellas, tienen el largo murmullo de las hojas secas. ¡El murmullo de un viejo jardín abandonado! Jardín Umbrío.

A5

Antonia tenía muchos años más que yo. Era alta y pálida, con los ojos negros y la sonrisa un poco triste. Murió siendo yo niño. ¡Pero cómo recuerdo su voz y su sonrisa y el hielo de su mano cuando me llevaba por las tardes a la Catedral!

A6

Nuestra madre era muy piadosa y no creía en agüeros ni brujerías, pero alguna vez lo aparentaba por disculpar la pasión que consumía a su hija. . . . Mi madre era muy bella, blanca y rubia, siempre vestida de seda, con guante negro en una mano por la falta de dos dedos, y la otra, que era como una camelia, toda cubierta de sortijas. Esta fué siempre la que besamos nosotros y la mano con que ella nos acariciaba.

A7

Yo conocí a una santa siendo niño, y nunca me fué acordada mayor ventura. . . . Aún recuerdo como me sentí penetrado de la gracia de su mirar ideal y cándido. Aún evoco y revivo en mí la emoción sagrada. Otras muchas veces había visto a mi Madrina en igual actitud, . . . solamente en aquella tarde de leyenda piadosa gusté tan inefable alegría al contemplarla. Bajo la sombra de los viejos cipreses, mi alma de niño enlazaba la emoción estética y la emoción mística, como se enlazan en la gracia de la rosa color y fragancia. Acaso fué aquella mi primera intuición literaria. Yo había llegado a encarnar en la sustancia de la vida y en sus sombras más bellas las historias piadosas y los cuentos de princesas que me contaba mi Madrina. La tarde azul en el huerto de rosales fué el momento de una iniciación donde todas las cosas me dijeron su eternidad mística y bella. . . . A los nueve años me enamoré de mi madrina. . . . desde aquel momento todos sus actos se me aparecieron llenos de un divino significado.

A8

Lo único de mi infancia digno de mención es el asesinato de un lobo. Era un valiente lobo que se comía nuestros corderillos. Yo, junto a mi abuelo, que preparó la celada, le aguardé oculto, le disparé a bocajarro y tuve el desdichado acierto de partirle el corazón. Desdichado, porque entonces, como hoy, creía yo que traidoramente no se debía matar ni a los lobos. . . . El animal, que era de un grandor desmesurado, tenía el hocico y las patas llenas de sangre de recental, y, furioso por esta roja prueba de su crimen, le cogí por el rabo y le arrastré hacia casa. Pero pesaba mucho, y me detenía frecuentemente, con gran regocijo de mi abuelo, varón de una gracia un poco socarrona. "¡Ah, cobarde, que no puedes con él de miedo!" ¡Miedo! . . . Bien sabía él que yo no le temía a los lobos. ¡Si se hubiese referido a los ratones! . . . Y de mi infancia no quiero decir nada más. Fuí orgulloso, travieso, camorrista, soñador, desaplicado.

A9

Alboreando a mozo, estuve lleno de violencia y desamor. Fui lobo en un monte de ovejas.

A10

Yo nunca experimenté ese irresistible amor, esa vocación decidida de los predestinados al cultivo de las letras. Leí para educar mi espíritu, libros clásicos, especialmente; de historia, por lo general.

A11

Aún recuerdo la angustia de mi vida en aquel tiempo, cuando estudiaba latín bajo la férula de un clérigo aldeano. Todos los sucesos de entonces se me aparecen en luz de anochecer y en un vaho de llovizna. Nos reuníamos en la cocina: El ama, con el gato en la falda, asaba castañas, el clérigo leía su breviario, yo suspiraba sobre mi Nebrija.

A12

Era en la montaña gallega. Yo estudiaba entonces gramática latina con el señor Arcipreste de Céltigos, y vivía castigado en el rectoral. Aún me veo en el hueco de una ventana, lloroso y suspirante. Mis lágrimas caían silenciosas sobre la gramática de Nebrija, abierta encima del alféizar. Era el día de Nochebuena, y el señor Arcipreste habíame condenado a no cenar hasta que supiese aquella terrible conjugación: "Fero, fers, tuli, latum."

A13

Exm. Sr. El alugno Ramón del Valle y de la Peña natural de Villanueva de Arosa provincia de Pontevedra a VE. suplica que habiendo estudiado privadamente las asignaturas de *Literatura General y Española, Derecho Natural y Economía Política y Estadística*, le sea concedido permiso para ser de ellas examinado por enseñanza libre. Gracia que espera obtener de la reconocida rectitud de VE. Ramón del Valle y de la Peña.

A14

De todas las rancias ciudades españolas, la que parece inmovilizada en un sueño de granito, inmutable y eterno, es Santiago de Compostela. . . . Rosa mística de piedra, flor romántica y tosca, como en el tiempo de las peregrinaciones, conserva una gracia ingenua de viejo latín rimado. . . . En esta ciudad petrificada huye la idea del Tiempo. No parece antigua, sino eterna. Tiene la soledad, la tristeza y la fuerza de una montaña . . . Compostela, inmovilizada en el éxtasis de los peregrinos, junta todas piedras en una sola evocación, y la cadena de siglos tuvo siempre en sus ecos la misma resonancia. Allí las horas son una misma hora, eternamente repetida bajo el cielo lluvioso.

A15

Entonces leían con delectación *Los Lunes de El Imparcial* todos los estudiantes, y varios compañeros míos se pasmaban del mérito de sus colaboradores. "Son maravillosos, ¿eh?", Y yo, con un soberbio desdén de joven iconoclasta, votaba en contra: "Esas tonterías las hace cualquiera. Mis artículos valdrían mucho más." Y para demostrarlo, escribí un cuento—"A media noche"—, que recientemente publiqué en *Jardín sombrío* [sic].

A16

La veneración casi religiosa que yo sentía por la figura de don José Zorrilla, poeta de largos cabellos y de barba señoril . . . aumentó en mi perplejidad infantil ante la presencia del ídolo, al llegar a Santiago como un peregrino de ensueño en el prestigio de sus canas y de sus melancolías. Yo formaba en las columnas de estudiantes que fueron a recibirle. Era de los primeros y cuando Zorrilla dirigiéndoseme me preguntó: "Tú, ¿También eres poeta?", sentí la frase sobre mi espíritu como una verdadera consagración. ¿Poeta? Sí; yo ya había visto en el fondo de las cosas la distinción de la tristeza, había dialogado con la luna y comenzaba a descubrir que las rosas guardan el encanto de haber sido mujeres.

A17

Zorrilla acabó sus días entre la miseria más trágica. Un editor poco escrupuloso, aprovechándose de la miseria del poeta, le decidió a escribir una geografía en verso, y así compuso algunas poesías dedicadas a Madrid, Barcelona, Cádiz, Alicante, etc. . . . Otro editor le encargó un poema para aprovechar las ilustraciones de Gustavo Doré sobre *La Divina comedia.* Así nacieron *Los ecos de las montañas.* Zorrilla vivía entre la desesperación y el hambre. . . . Y más tarde llegó la muerte y el entierro popular y multicolor. Nadie tuvo como Zorrilla un entierro más vibrante y sugestivo. . . . Y a pesar de la grandeza del poeta y de lo que había hecho por España, el Gobierno se negó a rendirle honores "por no haber precedentes," como dijo, en forma pintoresca, el Presidente del Consejo.

A18

Cuando estuve en México visité la hacienda de Zorrilla, en los llanos de Apam, y revisé bastantes manuscriptos del poeta. En *La siesta,* por ejemplo, y en su composición dedicada a la Medinaceli, podía descubrirse la virtud que poseía el artista de unir dos palabras convirtiéndolas en un nuevo valor estético. . . . Y sobre todo soñé pensando que en la estancia mexicana había nacido don Juan Tenorio.

A19

¡Qué había de conquistarme! ¡Si yo despreciaba la literatura con todo el vigor de mi espíritu! . . . Y, para meditar seriamente y escoger un camino, me retiré a un caserón ruinoso que, abandonado por mi familia, se desmoronaba con serena lentitud en el bosque.

A20

Cuando yo era mozo, la gloria literaria y la gloria aventurera me tentaron por igual. Fué un momento lleno de voces oscuras, de un vasto rumor ardiente y místico, para el cual se hacía sonoro todo mi ser como un caracol de los mares. De aquella gran voz atávica y desconocida sentí el aliento como un vaho de horno, y el son como un murmullo de mares que me llenó de inquietud y de perplejidad. Pero los sueños de aventura, esmaltados con los colores del blasón, huyeron como los pajaros del nido.

A21

Cuando se me planteó el problema de tener que escoger una manera de vivir, pensé en seguida: "Yo tengo que buscar una profesión sin jefe." Y me costaba trabajo. Pensaba en ser militar, y se me aparecían los generales déspotas, dándome ordenes estúpidas. Pensaba en ser cura, y en seguida surgían el obispo y el Papa. Si alguna vez pensé en ser funcionario, la idea del director me preocupaba. . . . Sin jefe sólo existe el escritor.

A22

No había nacido yo para picapleitos, ni para registrador, ni para juez, ni para notario. . . . Defender a bandidos sin grandeza y a labriegos embrollones, ser un zorro a la devoción de otros zorros, . . . ¡no, no!

Chapter 2: Emergence

A23

En otro artículo, hablaré de los fenómenos que producen los "medium" y muy particularmente de Eusepia Paladino, que fué el "medium" de quien Lombroso se ha servido para sus experiencias, a las cuales he tenido el honor de asistir en Nápoles.

A24

Y, reflexionando en mi lecho-hamaca, resolví dejar los libros y marcharme a América. Por muchas razones, y una de ellas de gran importancia romántica para un mozo de veinte años que pretendía bullir en una revolución y ser general. Verá usted. Yo tenía una torre en Santa María del Caramiñal, de la que salió, para contribuir a la conquista de las Indias, mi antepasado Gonzálo Domínguez, capitán de caballos, que en la batalla de la Noche Triste murió a la vista de Cortés y por defenderle. Los indios le agarraron la lanza, le derribaron del caballo y, vivo todavía le extrajeron del pecho el corazón, que después fué arrojado, como ofrenda, en el gran Teocalí. Según Bernal Díaz, a Cortés "le causó esto mucha grima y disgusto," porque Domínguez era tan formidable capitán como Gonzalo de Sandoval y Pedro de Alvarado. Pues bien; leyendo yo esta muerte bárbara y gloriosísima, y deseando conocer el país que vió la empresa más heróica realizada por hombres, planeé mi viaje a México. Se escribe asi: México. No hay que cambiar la dulzura de la equis por la aspereza de la jota.

A25

Mis padres allá en España querían que yo me recibiese de abogado, es decir, que yo terminase esa carrera espantosa a la cual no tenía ninguna inclinación, a pesar de que sólo me faltaba el último examen. Pues bien para no terminarla me trasladé a México con el dinero que me dieron para recibirme.

A26

Echéme al mundo de un salto loco;
Fui peregrino sobre la mar,
y en todas partes, pecando un poco,
dejé mi vida como un cantar.

No tuve miedo; fui turbulento;
miré en las simas como en la luz.
Di mi palabra como mi alma al viento.
Como una espada llevo mi cruz.

A27

Acabamos de anclar. El horizonte ríe bajo el hermoso sol. Siéntese en el aire extremecimientos voluptuosos. Ráfagas venidas de las selvas vírgenes . . . contemplo con emoción profunda la abrasada donde desembarcaron, antes que pueblo alguno de la vieja Europa, los aventureros españoles . . . Recuerdo lecturas casi olvidadas que niño aún, me han hecho soñar con esta tierra hija del sol. . . . ¡Era verdad que iba a desembarcar en aquella playa sagrada! . . . Veracruz, vista desde el mar . . . una ciudad que sonríe . . . un poco extraña . . .

A28

Desembarqué en Veracruz y, como en peregrinación, fuí a caballo desde La Antigua, donde Cortés hizo que diesen de través sus naves, hasta México. . . . El árbol de la Noche Triste. Sí. Y jamás he sentido una emoción más aguda, más socarradora, más fiera y más tierna a la vez que la que me invadió ante el coloso. Era por la tarde. . . . De las ramas, que son de un oscuro verdor melancólico, lo mismo que las de los cipreses, le cuelgan unas a manera de telarañas que hacen el efecto de pobladísimas y sedosas barbas sucias. Y a estas telarañas les dicen los indios barbas de españoles. ¡Barbas de españoles! Tan inmensa fué mi conmoción ante el gigante decrépito, herido por el rayo y vestido de viejas barbas españolas, que nunca la he podido describir.

A29

(México) en donde encontré mi propia libertad de vocación. Debo, pues, a México, indirectamente, mi carrera literaria . . . aquí empecé a seguir mi propio camino, es decir, el literario.

A30

Estuvo el comienzo de mi vida lleno de riesgos y azares. Fuí hermano converso en un monasterio de cartujos y soldado en tierras de la Nueva España. . . . Apenas cumplí la edad que se llama juventud, como final a unos amores desgraciados, me embarqué para México en "La Dalila", una fragata que al siguiente viaje naufragó en las costas de Yucatán. . . . A bordo de "La Dalila"—lo recuerdo con orgullo— asesiné a sir Roberto Yones. Fué una venganza digna de Benvenuto Cellini. . . . Aquel mismo día la fragata dió fondo en aguas de Veracruz . . . Uno de mis antepasados, Gonzalo de Sandoval, había fundado en aquellas tierras el reino de la Nueva Galicia. Yo, siguiendo los impulsos de una vida errante, iba a perderme, como él, en la vastedad del viejo imperio azteca, imperio de historia desconocida, sepultada para siempre con las momias de sus reyes . . .

A31

Fuí soldado del 7° de Caballería durante cinco años. No podía dejar de ser militar en México. Todo huele a guerra, a muerte y a aventura, y a mí me encantaba ese perfume.

A32

Era un hombre con cara de león, que bebía aguardiente con pólvora, y que salía a caballo por las calles en cuanto había *mitote*. . . . Tiempos aquellos, cuando en México había un "güero" Poucel, que de un mordisco le quitó un dedo al gigante Zetina; y salimos a perseguir a Catarino Garza, el de la pandilla de Hipólito Cuellar . . .

A33

Creo que los dos más grandes diplomáticos del siglo XIX han sido León XIII y don

Porfirio. Porfirio Díaz tuvo su conciencia por encima de la ley, no a la manera de Julio César, que afirmaba la licitud de conculcar la ley, sino para mejorarla.

A34

. . . el cáñamo índico, que le hace vivir en una exaltación religiosa extraordinaria. . . . Así se explica ese desprecio a la muerte que les da un sobrehumano valor.

A35

¡Verdes venenos! ¡Yerbas letales
De Paraísos Artificiales!

A todos vence la marihuana,
Que da la ciencia del Ramayana.

¡Oh! marihuana, verde neumónica,
Cannabis índica et babilónica.

Abres el sésamo de la alegria,
Cáñamo verde, kif de Turquía.

Yerba del Viejo de la Montaña,
El Santo Oficio te halló en España.

Yerba que inicias a los fakires,
Llena de goces y Dies Ires.

¡Verde esmeralda - loa el poeta
Persa - tu verde vistió el profeta!

(Kif - yerba verde del persa - es
El achisino bhang bengalés.

Charas que fuma sobre el diván,
Entre odaliscas, el Gran Sultán)

A36

Yo, torpe y vano de mí, quise ser centro y tener de la guerra una visión astral, fuera de geometría y de cronología, como si el alma, desencarnada ya, mirase a la tierra desde su estrella. He fracasado en el empeño, mi droga índica en esta ocasión me negó su efluvio maravilloso. Estas páginas que ahora salen a la luz no son más que un balbuceo del ideal soñado.

A37

Hablemos ahora de la influencia del haschisch, Cáñamo índico, en la literatura y, especialmente, en mi obra. Confieso que lo he tomado, en abundancia, sin saber, sus consecuencias, y por prescripción médica. Los efectos fisiológicos producen una gran duración de frío interior, un hambre voraz y los síntomas de envenenamiento, pero analicemos los efectos anémicos del excitante. . . . Mi individualidad llegó a descomponerse en dos distintas. Comencé por ver en las cosas condiciones nuevas: como se creaba una desarmonía y otras veces una afinidad quimérica. Algo que podía decirse "la armonía de los contrarios" . . . Luego todas las cosas adquirían para mí un prestigio de misterio como los ruidos de la noche, mis recuerdos volvían a la infancia y establecí semejanzas extrañas como la de una flor a una colina. Lo más espantoso en esas alucinaciones era el recuerdo de todas las personas muertas, que desfilaban por mi memoria como una cinta cinematográfica. Y este fenómeno fué el que me decidió a abandonar el haschisch.

A38

La Crónica Mercantil /Veracruz /Apartado núm.
19./Administración Sr. D. Manuel Murguía.
Mi siempre querido amigo y respetable maestro.

Al escribirle a usted paréceme que me dirijo a toda nuestra Galicia, pobre, pensativa y sola, que dijo el poeta, de tal modo encarna usted para mí el espíritu regional, y el amor de la tierra, que, en forma de hondísima *saudade*, sentimos acá, en América, los que como una herencia sagrada, conservamos, al través de los siglos, un dejo de *celtismo*, que nos hace amar los robles carcomidos y las rocas vetustas, de nuestras *gándaras*. Sensaciones *meigas*, que se aspiran en la *Historia* de usted, y derraman una suave claridad de *lunar*, sobre las viejas razas que encendieron el primer fuego en el gran lar gallego.

Si, mi querido amigo, usted es nuestro gran *Vate*, en el más arcaico y puro sentido de la palabra, y por eso me dirijo a usted en demanda de unas cuantas líneas que poner al frente de mi primer libro.

El afecto que usted siempre me ha profesado, me hace creer que, apesar de sus muchas ocupaciones literias (sic), no dejará de tener un momento de vagar, para presentar al público al más humilde de sus admiradores, pero quizá el más leal y más entusiasta.

Mi hermano, entregará a usted los originales, y dará más explicaciones, si, como espero, se digna usted atender mi demanda.

Reciba usted con estos renglones, querido amigo y maestro, el testimonio de mi más respetuoso cariño, y mande, en cuanto guste, a este su errante discípulo que, donde quiera que los vientos, inclementes y contrarios, de la fortuna le arrastren, conserva, entre muchas cenizas, vivos como siempre los sentimientos de respeto y cariño hacia usted.

Ramón del Valle-Inclán.
Villa Rica de la Veracruz, 2-3-93.

A39

Señor don Leopoldo Alas.
Señor y maestro de mi mayor respeto:

Nuestro amigo Luis París, me ha dicho ayer, que usted debía ya tener noticia de mis "Femeninas"—libro de principiante descorazonado, que por azares de la fortuna ha vivido siempre alejado del trato de los hombres de letras—. Harto se me alcanza lo poco que mi libro vale, y aún para estimar eso poco, han de tenerse en cuenta la inexperiencia y la mocedad. Con el mayor gusto, envío hoy a usted un ejemplar, al cual he cuidado de cortar las hojas; no porque sea a usted más fácil el leerlo—que no le supongo ni tanto vagar ni tanta paciencia—, sino el hojearlo.

Entiendo yo que los libros de *estreno*, rara vez valen por sí. El crítico que habla de ellos, más lo hace como *profeta*. Mi libro, podrá ser algo así como una *esperanza*, que no es una *realidad*, lo sé yo mejor que nadie. ¡Cómo no he de saberlo, si tengo, —y guardo para mostrar a mis amigos—un ejemplar de "Femeninas" donde no hay página sin tachón!—Es un libro, que antes de salir a luz me hastiaba ya.

¡Oh! si tuviese tiempo, y un poco de estímulo, creo que sería capaz de hacer algo un poquillo mejor . . . Pero por Dios no me juzgue usted definitivamente, por esas *seis historias amorosas*.

Mi única aspiración, es que mi nombre le suene a usted a algo, cuando le envíe algún otro libro—suponiendo que no cuelgue la pluma, convencido al cabo, de que no me llama Dios por el camino de las letras.

Aprovecho gustoso esta ocasión, para ofrecer a usted respetabilísimo maestro, el testimonio más entusiasta de mi admiración y mi amistad—. De usted affmo. s.s.q.b.s.m.

Ramón del Valle-Inclán.

A40

De mi primer libro sólo pude vender cinco ejemplares . . . Cinco lectores. Todo mi público. Pues bien, seguí escribiendo para esos cinco lectores. Yo no fuí a buscar a los que se sumaron más tarde. Porque mi manera de escribir no gustase a unos yo no iba a escribir como aquél o como el de más allá . . . Eso es robar el público a los colegas y yo no soy ladrón. Hay que imponerse con lo que uno tiene y da. Y si no se logra es que no se tiene personalidad.

A41

La prensa avillana el estilo y empequeñece todo ideal estético. Las reputaciones que crea la prensa son deleznables. Hay que trabajar en el aislamiento, sin enajenar nada de la independencia espiritual.

A42

Hay excitantes poseesores de un prestigio moral, como el ayuno . . . Entre los antiguos el ayuno fué considerado como el sendero para llegar a la exaltación y a la perfección mental y moral. El hombre que más comprende es el que más ama y el amor es la flor de la moral. Por eso Jesús ayunó en el desierto y los fakires ayunan para desarrollar su poder, casi milagroso.

El ayuno del estilista es de pasiones y de ambiciones de todas las cosas del mundo, con el contraste de los días abrasados de sol y de las noches húmedas de rocio siempre en gran soledad de seres vivos. El ayuno en el desierto, en la orilla de un lago o en la orilla del mar. Allí donde los ojos pueden hundirse en la curva del horizonte y sentir la sugestión del infinito. Es una adivinación del placer que existe en la gran monotonía, tomada esta palabra en su más alto sentido de unidad, que equivale a eternidad.

Los segundones condenados a perpetuo ayuno conquistaron América; si no, no hubiesen sido héroes.

Hoy el ayuno sólo lo practican aquellos artistas bohemios que tienen la bolsa vacía.

Pienso en la regeneración de España por el ayuno, pero voluntario puesto que sin tal convicción no entrañaría virtud alguna. Antes es el germen de todas las rebeldías y de todas las anarquías.

El ayuno en el retiro de la celda es donde nace esa suprema excitación que tiene ocho estados anteriores, a saber: oración, meditación, edificación, contemplación, aridez, tránsito, deliquio, éxtasis.

A43

. . . hay un cierto *realismo superior* que el público español, que come bien y goza de excelente salud, no suele entender. Sería necesario someter a estos felices lectores, a ayunos como los de Angel Guerra . . .

A44

Los literatos, en lo por venir, vivirán en las antologías por una página bien escrita.

La belleza solo está en la forma. El que no cincele y pula su estilo, no pasará de ser un mal escribiente.

A45

Señor don Leopoldo Alas.
Señor de mi mayor y más distinguida admiración y respeto:
Doy a usted gracias muy sinceras por el Palique que en "Madrid Cómico" le dedica a mi libro "Epitalamio". Los reparos que usted pone al libro, y los consejos que da al autor los acepto y agradezco de muy buena gana. Pero todavía agradezco más la bondadosa parquedad con que usted acota defectos de estilo, y de lenguaje. No se me oculta que en esa tarea pudo usted haber ido lejos, muy lejos . . . ¡Si usted viese que de tachas y enmiendas tengo yo hechas en un ejemplar de "Epitalamio". . . !
Dice usted que puedo arrepentirme y trabajar en la verdadera viña—con toda el alma agradecí a usted ese final alentador. En cuanto a "arrepentido" ya lo estoy; pero lo otro . . . ¡lo otro es tan difícil . . . !
Reciba usted con estas líneas la expresión más sincera de mi reconocimiento, de mi admiración, y mi amistad.
Tiene el honor de ofrecerse de usted affmo s.s.q.b.s.m. Madrid, s/c Calvo Asensio, 4
Ramón del Valle-Inclán

A46

Sr. don Leopoldo Alas.
Mi distinguido amigo y maestro:
Doy a usted gracias por su bondadosa carta. No he podido hacerlo antes, porque la *influenza* me tubo (sic) quince días en cama. Todavía hoy muevo la pluma con bastante trabajo.
La publicación de su carta de usted en *El Heraldo* ha sido un trágala para ciertos caballeros, que se regodeaban asegurando no me dejaba usted hueso sano en el palique de *Madrid Cómico*. Esta pobre gente no quiere convencerse de que un poco de justicia administrada por usted, puede ser más agradable que el bombo anónimo de los periódicos, o los elogios de Burell.
Me dice usted que huya de cierta literatura socialista que ahora se estila. Ya he huido. Mejor dicho, nunca quise ser de esa *escuela*. Las razones que así me lo aconsejan son casi las mismas que usted puntualiza en su carta.
Crea usted en mi amistad, y disponga de su afectísimo amigo s.s.q.b.s.m.
Madrid-18–X-97.
Ramón del Valle-Inclán.

A47

. . . cuando llegué a Madrid, vi que todo cuanto se escribía era muy malo. Decíalo así a mis amigos. Y como ellos, incrédulos, lo atribuyesen a un inmoderado afán de crítica, yo les replicaba manifestándoles que aquellos libros detestables podría escribirlos cualquiera. E hice uno: *Epitalamio*, que edité por mi cuenta.

Chapter 3: Absorption

A48

La guerra de Cuba la ganamos los cubanos en su patria y yo en las calles de Madrid.

A49

"¡Cobardes! Eso hay que decirlo desde tierra cubana . . . A luchar, a luchar . . . ¿Por qué no vais?"

A50

Ya no somos una raza de conquistadores y de teólogos, y en el romance alienta siempre esa ficción. Ya no es nuestro el camino de las Indias, ni son españoles los Papas . . . Ha desaparecido aquella fuerza hispana donde latían como tres corazones la fortuna en la guerra, la fe católica y el ansia de aventuras; pero en la blanda cadena de los ecos sigue volando el engaño de su latido . . . Ya nuestro gesto no es para el mundo. Volvamos a vivir en nosotros . . . Desterremos para siempre aquel modo castizo, comentario de un gesto desaparecido con las conquistas y las guerras. Amemos la tradición, pero en su esencia, y procurando descifrarla como un enigma que guarda el secreto del Porvenir.

A51

Mi generación, a través de la cultura, ha hecho Historia. La literatura es más operante de lo que la gente supone. Y Azorín—el Bautista del grupo—ha tenido un gran acierto al llamarnos "la generación del 98."

A52

Me han adscrito a la generación del 98. ¿Qué representa y vale la generación del 98? Don Manuel Azaña ha hablado de una digresión monstruosa de la historia de España. Pues bien, la generación del 98 vino a luchar contra ella y lo que representaba en el ambito del idioma. Hasta el siglo XV, el castellano escrito y el hablado tenían los mismos ritmos, y el mismo sentido de la respiración. Vino el Renacimiento, y por una moda se apartó el castellano escrito del castellano hablado. La generación del 98 quiso volver a unirlos, huyendo del párrafo largo que venía desde Cervantes a Ricardo León. A los del 98 nos llamaban modernistas, porque no seguíamos el castellano del siglo XIX. Rubén Darío y yo quisimos volver el castellano a las normas tradicionales que estaban detrás de la feliz pareja de los Reyes Católicos.

A53

En la literatura, Unamuno, Benavente, Azorín, Ciges Aparicio, Baroja, los Machados, Marquina y Ortega y Gasset tienen un sentimiento nuevo de patria. Aman la novela regional, en su tradición, no en aquellos de sus hombres que nada valen y que nada representan. El patriotismo consiste en imponer lo grande y no en dejar que la audacia vanidosa se imponga. Tal fuerza anima y vive en la obra de los nuevos escritores. Aparecen en un momento agitado en España y traen el sentimiento de la patria, no la patria bravucona y pendenciera que oculta los defectos y se lía la manta a la cabeza, sino la de los que se imponían con criterio único ser los mejores. Su patriotismo no es el de la ascensión. . . . Los pueblos son grandes por la comunidad de un mismo sentimiento en la Historia.

A54

Todos los diarios me habían cerrado sus puertas. Mis artículos eran acogidos como cosas extrañas . . . En vista de ese cerco decidimos fundar la *Revista Nueva*, Azorín, Baroja, Benavente, yo y cuantos hallábamos cerrados los periódicos.

A55

Este que veis aquí, de rostro español y quevedesco, de negra quedeja y luenga barba, soy yo: don Ramón del Valle-Inclán. . . . tengo una divisa, y esa divisa es como yo, orgullosa y resignada: "Desdeñar a los demás, y no amarse a sí mismo." . . . Yo, que en buena hora lo diga, jamás sentí el amor de la familia. . . Apenas cumplí la edad que se llama juventud . . . me embarqué para México . . . Por aquel entonces era yo algo poeta, con ninguna experiencia y harta novelería en la cabeza. Creía de buena fe en muchas cosas que ahora pongo en duda, y, libre de escepticismo, dábame buena prisa a gozar de la existencia. Aunque no lo confesase, y acaso sin saberlo, era feliz: soñaba realizar altas empresas, como un aventurero de otros tiempos, y despreciaba las glorias literarias.

Chapter 4: Early Stages

A56

En vista de que las letras no me dan para comer pienso trabajar como actor . . . No voy a tener otro remedio que meterme a cómico . . . Al fin y a la postre es lo que hacen en España todos los que no sirven para otra cosa.

A57

Sr. Don Benito Pérez Galdós

Mi querido amigo y maestro: Desde hace mucho tiempo acaricio la idea de dedicarme al teatro, como actor, para lo cual he estudiado un poco, y creo tener algunas disposiciones. Pero usted sabe las dificultades con que aquí se tropieza para todo. Necesito el apoyo de una gran Autoridad, y ruego a usted que me preste el suyo, recomendándome a Carmen Cobeña, a Emilio Thuillier y a Donato Gimenez—empresa nueva y flamante que acaba de tomar "La Comedia"—. Si usted echa mano de toda su respetabilidad, yo sé que la recomendación de usted será para ellos un "hukasse."

Perdone usted, don Benito, que le moleste, y sírvame de disculpa sus amabilidades para conmigo.

Anticipándole las gracias, le saluda con afectuoso respeto su admirador y su amigo Q.L.B.L.M.,

     Madrid, 5–IX-98
     Ramón del Valle-Inclán
     S/c Calvo Asensio, 4

A58

Así no se puede trabajar . . . Don Emilio dirige esto como si fuese una marcha fúnebre . . . Los actores pierden vivacidad . . . Usted no puede tolerar que su comedia se la haga fracasar el director.

A59

Parece ser que ayer lo hice muy mal y he decidido no trabajar nunca más. . . . Yo no puedo trabajar. Lo hice muy mal. Y no quiero repetir la suerte. No se debe reincidir en las cosas, cuando se hacen mal no deben repetirse.

A60

Está bien. Trabajaré porque usted me lo pide y para evitar un descalabro económico a la empresa. No me gusta perjudicar a nadie. Pero conste que tiene usted muy poco amor por sus obras. Yo no toleraría jamás que las mías las interpretasen actores que las estropean. Allá usted con su conciencia.

A61

Manuel Bueno me sujetó la mano y al apretar me clavó el gemelo aquí, en el mismo canto de la muñeca.

A62

No le di importancia al rasguño pero una semana más tarde se fué hinchando la mano y los dolores que esa hinchazón producían eran espantosos.

A63

Una noche leí en *Heraldo de Madrid* que el torero Angel Pastor había muerto de un flemón semejante al mío, y cuando me entrevisté con el médico le dije que cortara.

A64

¿Sabe usted por qué quise quedarme solo? Pues porque tenía ganas de llorar. Y lloré, sí, lloré, como lloran los hombres por un brazo perdido, lloré hacia el hombro huérfano del brazo . . . Por eso no quise que nadie me viera . . . Después de mis lágrimas, se acabó el drama. A los demás no debía importarles mi dolor.

A65

Zeñores, yo antes decía que valía mucho más que Cervantes. Acaso esto no era verdad . . . Pero de ahora en adelante no me negarán que, manco como estoy, por lo menos me le parezco bastante.

A66

. . . sólo pensé en la actitud que a lo adelante debía adoptar con las mujeres para hacer poética mi manquedad.

A67

Lloro haberlo perdido en un encuentro oscuro. Magnífico hubiera sido ver caer la mano al sacar la espada para defender a los niños Príncipes y a su madre la Reina.

A68

Al cumplir los treinta años, hubieron de cercenarme un brazo, y no sé si remontaron el vuelo (los sueños) o se quedaron mudos. ¡En aquella tristeza me asistió el amor de las musas! Ambicioné beber en la sagrada fuente, pero antes quise escuchar los latidos de mi corazón y dejé; que hablasen todos mis sentidos. Con el rumor de sus voces hice mi Estética.

A69

Tengo un lebrel,
Se llama Carabel,
—Es un caro recuerdo de Marquina.—
Nada le agrada tanto
Como dormir debajo de mis pies.

Cuando me enoja
Y le largo de mí,
Vuelve sumiso
A lamerme la mano.
Como sé que lo estima, se la entrego,
Busca después mi mano cercenada
Y, hocicando en la manga, da un gemido.
¡Llora por una mano que lamer,
Y yo lloro, Señor, porque quisiera
Darle una parte de mi humano ser!

A70

Retorciendo la Filástica,
un cordelero enfermó
pero al punto se curó.
¿Cómo? Con la Harina Plástica.

A71

¿La pesadilla fantástica
os agobia en invernales
noches? ¡Los estomacales
jugos con la Harina Plástica
reconfortad, animales!

A72

Toledo es una vieja cuidad alucinante. . . . Toledo es alucinante con su poder de evocación. . . . Estas piedras viejas tienen para mi el poder maravilloso del cáñamo índico . . . Toledo tiene ese poder místico. Alza las losas de los sepulcros y hace desfilar los fantasmas en una sucessión más angustiosa que la vida. . . . Toledo es a modo de un sepulcro. . . . Toledo sólo tiene evocaciones literarias, y es tan angustioso para los ojos, como lleno de encanto para la memoria.

Chapter 5: Recognitions

A73

En el primer concurso Valera se negó a firmar el acta, creyendo que el premiado debía ser uno mío . . .

A74

¡Grotescas horas españolas, en que todo suena a moneda fullera! Todos los valores tienen hoja: la Historia, la Política, las Armas, las Academias. Nunca había sido tan mercantilista la que entonces empezó a llamarse la Gran Prensa: G. P. ¡Maleante sugestión tiene el anagrama!

A75

Como todos los aventureros sentí la quimera del oro . . . En vista de que la literatura no me producía lo necesario para vivir me dediqué a buscador de minas . . . También lo había sido Balzac que soñaba con minas de plata y también lo fué nuestro Gustavo Adolfo Bécquer, quien pensó que en el monasterio de Veruela había un tesoro enterrado . . . Yo creí que la minería era un negocio fabuloso y me dediqué a él. Los romanos, careciendo de los medios que la industria y la ciencia proporcionan actualmente, abandonaban aquellas en que se presentaba unido el mineral buscado, azafre, fósforo o cualquier otra materia distinta a la que se quería extraer . . . Yo hice un estudio minucioso del asunto y deduje que en la Mancha había minas en esas condiciones. Una noche de enero, fría, muy fría, cuando recorría solitario montado en mi caballo el campo nevado, se me disparó una pistola. Me atravesé un brazo y una pierna. Estaba lejos de la estación de Valdecampo. Me hice una cura provisional con la misma nieve y resistiendo el dolor de las heridas, a campo traviesa, me dirigí a Almendralejo. Llegué a la estación y esperé el ferrocarril, pero éste no venía. En aquel lugar desmantelado estuve cerca de doce horas. Cuando llegó el tren no tenía más que vagones de carga y unos miserables vagones de segunda. "¿Dónde están los vagones de primera clase?" pregunté. "No los hay, señor," se me contestó. Protesté por esa falta y cuando mayor era mi indignación apareció un caballero alto, delgado, enfundado en un gabán pieles. Inquirió lo que me sucedía y cuando lo supo me invitó a subir a su departamento particular. Era don Segismundo Moret. El jefe político me atendió. La fiebre me consumía y el dolor me atenazaba, pero no salió de mis labios una palabra de queja. Cuando llegué a Madrid me entregué a aquel santo varón que fué el doctor Alejandro San Martín, que me hizo las primeras y dolorosas curas . . . Por entonces le servía de ayudante el doctor Goyanes . . . Estuve tres meses en cama, me olvidé de las minas de la Mancha . . .

A76

. . . escribí unas *Memorias* . . . Se las leí a Antonio Machado y a Francisco Villaespesa. Este, no bien hube terminado la última cuartilla dijo alborozado: "¡Eso se parece a *La Virgen de la Roca*, de D'Annunzio." Y Machado añadió: "¡Es magnífico!" Antonio me aconsejó que publicase mis cuartillas cuanto antes. Aquellas *Memorias* son *Sonata de otoño*. Escribí con facilidad. Tenía sentido literario y sentía un vivo desprecio por quienes escribían sin saber hacerlo y a quienes los diarios trataban de "maestros."

A77

Antes de ponerme a escribir necesito ver corporeamente, detalladamente, los personajes. Necesito ver su rostro, su figura, su atavío, su paso. Veo su vida completa anterior al momento en que aparecen en la novela. De esa vida completa que yo veo primero en el pensamiento, muchas veces es muy poco lo que utilizo luego, al llevar el personaje a las cuartillas, donde a lo mejor sólo aparece en una escena. Cuando ya lo he visto completamente, lo "meto," lo "encajo" en la novela. Después la tarea de escribir es muy fácil.

A78

No hace todavía tres años vivía yo escribiendo novelas por entregas, que firmaba orgulloso, no sé si por desdén si por despecho. Me complacía dolorosamente la oscuridad de mi nombre y el olvido en que todos me tenían. Hubiera querido entonces que los libros estuviesen escritos en letra lombarda, como las antiguas ejecutorias, y que sólo algunos iniciados pudiesen leerlas. Esta quimera ha sido para mí como un talismán. Ella me ha guardado de las competencias mezquinas, y por ella no he sentido las crueldades de una vida toda de dolor. Sólo, altivo y pobre he llegado a la literatura sin enviar mis libros a esos que llaman críticos, y sin sentarme una sola vez en el corro donde a diario alientan sus vanidades las hembras y los eunucos del Arte.

De alguien, sin embargo, he recibido protección tan generosa y noble, que sin ella nunca hubiera escrito las *Memorias del Marqués de Bradomín*. Tal protección, única en mi vida, fué de un gran literato y de un gran corazón: he nombrado a Don José Ortega Munilla. Hoy quiero ofrecerle este libro con aquel ingenuo y amoroso respeto que, cuando yo era niño, ofrecían los pastores de los casales amigos, el más blanco de sus corderos, en la casa de mi padre. V.-I. Real Sitio de Aranjuez. Mayo de 1904.

A79

Pero si además de la sensación material se hace preciso transmitir una imagen más o menos psíquica de tal, o cual sujeto . . . quizá resulte mejor proceder como yo procedí al decir que mi Marqués de Bradomín era un Don Juan feo, católico y sentimental, esquema en el cual el primer adjetivo define, con nota pintoresca, la exterioridad física de la criatura, mientras el segundo y el tercero señalan, por orden de importancia, los aspectos fundamentales de su persona interior.

A80

Y confieso que mi Marqués de Bradomín está inspirado en Campoamor y muchos de sus rasgos no son autobiográficos como creen algunos, sino que pertenecen al autor de las *Doloras*.

A81

Si en la literatura actual existe algo nuevo que pueda recibir con justicia el nombre de "modernismo," no son, seguramente, las extravagancias gramaticales y retóricas, como creen algunos críticos candorosos, tal vez porque esta palabra "modernismo," como todas las que son muy repetidas, ha llegado a tener una significación tan amplia como dudosa. Por eso no creo que huelgue fijar en cierto modo lo que ella indica o puede indicar. La condición característica de todo el arte moderno, y muy particularmente de la literatura, es una tendencia a refinar las sensaciones y acrecentarlas en el número y en la intensidad. Hay poetas que sueñan con dar a sus estrofas el ritmo de la danza, la melodía de la música y la majestad de la estatua.

A82

Y ya dentro de mi alma, rosa obstinada, me río de todo lo divino y de todo lo humano y no creo más que en la belleza. Sobre todas las cosas bellas amo la música, porque es una fragancia de emoción . . . ¡Oh, la emoción! Un libro en donde todo— idea, sentimiento, ritmo, rima—sea entrañable y tibio, sin más decoración que la necesaria y sin palabrería. Odio el palacio frío de los parnasianos. Que la frase esté tocada de alma, que evoque sangre, o lágrimas, o sonrisa; que en el vocablo haya siempre un subvocablo, una sombra de palabra, secreta y temblorosa, un encanto de misterio, como el de las mujeres muertas o el de los niños dormidos. . . . Poeta ultralírico, no creo, sin embargo, en lo sobrenatural; en mi obra he procurado únicamente hacer jardín y hacer valle; y entiendo que unos colores, unos sonidos, unas claridades de esta vida son más que suficientes; las armonías, las melodías, he ahí todo. Dadme siempre una mujer, una fuente, una música lejana, rosas, la luna—belleza, cristal, ritmo, esencia, plata—y os prometo una eternidad de cosas bellas. He sido niño, mujer y hombre; amo el orden en lo exterior y la inquietud en el espíritu; creo que hay dos cosas corrosivas: la sensualidad y la impaciencia; no fumo, no bebo vino, odio el café y los toros, la religión y el militarismo, el acordeón y la pena de muerte; sé que he venido para hacer versos; no gusto de números; admiro a los filósofos, a los pintores, a los músicos, a los poetas, y, en fin, tengo mi frente en su idea y mi corazón en su sentimiento.

A83

La juventud debe ser arrogante, violenta, apasionada, iconoclasta. . . . Hay en el mundo muchos desgraciados, víctimas del demonio, que discuten las parábolas de Jesús y no osan discutir una mala comedia de Echegaray o de Grilo . . . Esta adulación por todo lo consagrado, esa admiración por todo lo que tiene polvo de vejez, son siempre una muestra de servidumbre intelectual, desgraciadamente, muy extendida en esta tierra. Sin embargo, tales respetos han sido, en cierto modo, provechosos, porque sirvieron para encender la furia iconoclasta que hoy posee a todas las almas jóvenes. En el arte, como en la vida, destruir es crear. El anarquismo es siempre un anhelo de regeneración, y, entre nosotros, la única regeneración posible. . . . El autor de *Sombras de vida* ha hecho su profesión de fe modernista: buscarse en sí mismo y no en otros. Porque esa escuela literaria tan combatida no es otra cosa. . . . Por eso, sin duda, advertimos en los escritores jóvenes más empeño por expresar sensaciones que ideas. Las ideas jamás han sido patrimonio exclusivo de un hombre, y las sensaciones sí. . . . La condición característica de todo el arte moderno, y muy particularmente de la literatura, es una tendencia a refinar las sensaciones y acrecentarlas en el número y en la intensidad. . . . Esta analogía y equivalencia de las sensaciones es lo que constituye el modernismo en la literatura. . . . Hoy percibimos gradaciones de color, gradaciones de sonido y relaciones lejanas entre las cosas que hace algunos cientos de años no fueron seguramente percibidas por nuestros antepasados. En los idiomas primitivos, apenas existen vocablos para dar idea del color. . . . Y sabido es que la pobreza da el color . . .

A84

Yo creo que un buen diccionario de sinónimos hubiera establecido el paralelismo, la íntima relación entre joven modernista y perro judío. . . . El modernista es el que inquieta . . . es el que busca dar a su arte la emoción interior y el gesto misterioso que hacen todas las cosas al que sabe mirar y comprender. No es el que rompe las viejas reglas, ni el que crea las nuevas, es el que siguiendo la eterna pauta interpreta la vida por un modo suyo: es el exegeta.

A85

Triunfé con mi cuento "¡Malpocado!" pero se produjo un gran revuelto . . . por las decisión absurda del jurado que otorgó al que yo presenté y obtuvo el primer premio, la mitad de lo convenido en las bases . . . Y conste que gané en un concurso en el que se presentaron más de mil setecientos trabajos.

A86

El viaje a Marín—que hice no ha muchos días con objeto de visitar al autor insigne de *El Gran Galeoto*—es lo que en frase vulgar y un tanto arcaica se llama un encanto. . . . No recuerdo escritor alguno, que así, visto por fuera, aparezca menos en consonancia con el carácter de sus obras. Mientras hablaba el maestro, oíale yo maravillado, y sin poder comprender cómo hombre tan amable y tan afectoso, que tan enemigo de la sangre se muestra y en quien la lenidad parece ser la condición primera, puede, en la esfera literaria, ser forjador de los trances más dolorosos y sangrientos y de los conflictos pasionales más trágicos. Es esta, en mi opinión, la prueba más palmaria de lo artista que Echegaray es en sensaciones. Naturaleza privilegiada y múltiple, que sabe sugestionarse a voluntad y desenvolver en sí las personalidades más distintas y contradictorias, las cuales por un fenómeno de *polarización psíquica* y por la fuerza misma de lo que se llama *ley del contraste*, propenden a desemejarse lo más posible de la personalidad ordinaria del poeta.

A87

El Café de Levante ha tenido más influencia en el Arte y la Literatura contemporánea que un par de Universidades y de Academias.

A88

. . . parece una gacetilla de carreras de caballos . . . Dos o tres destacados y después se puede escribir como en esos sueltos, "tomarán parte cinco o seis animales más."

A89

El arte es un juego—el supremo juego—y sus normas están dictadas por numérico capricho, en el cual reside su gracia peculiar. Catorce versos dicen que es soneto. El Arte, es, pues, forma.

El arte exige la espera. Puede estar uno esperando toda la vida para sólo lograr el verso de la despedida, un adiós verdadero y sencillo.

El arte es siempre una abstracción. Si mi portera y yo vemos la misma cosa, mi portera no sabe lo que ha visto porque no tiene el concepto anterior.

En arte cuando no se es un genio, lo mejor es imitar al pueblo.

El arte es estar pidiendo limosna al cielo a la puerta del templo.

Los cuadros tienen que ser vistos hacia abajo, para que el asunto no estorbe a la percepción del color en sí mismo.

El arte no se acaba nunca y no se acaba nunca porque el arte sirve para pasar el invierno, ya que el arte es siempre primavera.

A90

Hay poetas que sueñan con dar a sus estrofas el ritmo de la danza, la melodía de la música y la majestad de la estatua. Teófilo Gautier, autor de la *Sinfonía en blanco mayor*, afirma en el prefacio a las *Flores del mal*, que el estilo de Tertuliano tiene el negro esplendor de ébano. Según Gautier, las palabras alcanzan por el sonido un valor que los diccionarios no pueden determinar. Por el sonido, unas palabras son como diamantes, otras fosforecen, otras flotan como una neblina. Cuando Gautier habla de Baudelaire, dice que ha sabido recoger en sus estrofas la leve esfumación que está indecisa entre el sonido y el color; aquellos pensamientos que semejan motivos de arabescos y temas de frases musicales. El mismo Baudelaire dice que su alma goza con los perfumes, como otras almas gozan con la música. Para este poeta, los aromas no solamente equivalen al sonido, sino también al color: "Il est des parfums frais comme des chairs d'enfants, Douces comme les hauts bois, verts comme les prairies." Pero si Baudelaire habla de perfumes verdes, Carducci ha llamado verde al silencio, y Gabriel d'Annunzio ha dicho con hermoso ritmo:

"Canta la nota verde d'un bel limone in fiore." Hay quien considera como extrava-gancias todas las imágenes de esta índole, cuando, en realidad, no son otra cosa que una consecuencia lógica de la evolución progresiva de los sentidos. Hoy per-cibimos gradaciones de color, gradaciones de sonidos y relaciones lejanas entre las cosas, que hace algunos cientos de años no fueron seguramente percibidas por nuestros antepasados. En los idiomas primitivos apenas existen vocablos para dar idea del color. En vascuense el pelo de algunas vacas y el color del cielo se indican con la misma palabra: "Artuña." Y sabido es que la pobreza de vocablos es siempre resultado de la pobreza de sensaciones. Existen hoy artistas que pretenden encontrar una extraña correspondencia entre el sonido y el color. De este número ha sido el gran poeta Arturo Rimbaut (sic), que definió el color de las vocales en un célebre soneto: "A—noir, E—bleu, I—rouge, U—vert, O—jaune." Y más moder-namente Renato Ghil, que en otro soneto asigna a las vocales, no solamente color, sino también, valor orquestal: "A. claironne vainquer en rouge flamboiement." Esta analogía y equivalencia de las sensaciones es lo que constituye el "modernismo" en literatura. Su origen debe buscarse en el desenvolvimiento progresivo de los sen-tidos, que tienden a multiplicar sus diferentes percepciones y corresponderlas entre sí, formando un solo sentido, como uno solo formaban ya para Baudelaire: "Oh! Métamorphose mystique / De tous mes sens fondus en un: / Son haleine fait la musique, / Comme sa voix fait le parfum." Los cuadros tienen que ser vistos hacia abajo, para que el asunto no estorbe a la percepción del color en sí mismo.

El arte no se acaba nunca y no se acaba nunca porque el arte sirve para pasar el invierno, ya que el arte es siempre primavera.

Chapter 6: Continuation

A91

¿Cómo dice? . . . . ¿Reducir, cortar cuarenta y ocho páginas a mis obras? . . . ¿Pero usted sabe lo que está diciendo? . . . ¡Cortar, mutilar, sólo para que el libro tenga el tamano que a usted le dé la gana! ¡No! ¡No! ¡Y hemos terminado, señor mío! ¡Hágame el favor de salir inmediatamente de aquí! . . . ¡Antes muero de hambre que mutilar una sola página porque a un editor se le antoje!

A92

Hay en todas sus páginas no sé qué alegre palpitar de vida, qué abrileña lozanía, qué gracioso borboteo de imágenes desusadas, ingenuas, atrevidas, detonantes. Yo confieso mi amor por estos libros, cuando descubro en ellos exubeberancia y emo-ción. Los amo tanto como aborrezco esa otra literatura, timorata y prudente, de algunos antiguos jóvenes, que nunca supieron ayuntar dos palabras por primera vez. . . . Amparándose en la gloriosa tradición del siglo XVII, se juzgan grandes sólo porque imitan a los grandes, y presumen que hicieron como ellos el divino Lope y el humano Cervantes. Cuando algunos espíritus juveniles buscan nuevas orientaciones, revuélvense invocando rancios y estériles preceptos. Incapaces de comprender que la vida y el arte son una eterna renovación, tienen por herejía todo aquello que no hayan consagrado tres siglos de rutina. . . . No haya de entenderse por esto que proclamo yo la desaparición y muerte de las letras clásicas, y la hoguera para sus libros inmortales, no. Han sido tantas veces mis maestros, que como a nobles y viejos progenitores los reverencio. Estudio siempre en ellos y procuro imitarlos, pero hasta ahora jamás se me ocurrió tenerlos por inviolables e infalibles.

A93

En mis narraciones históricas la dificultad mayor consiste en incrustar documentos y episodios de la época. Cuando el relato me da ocasión de colocar una frase, unos versos, una copla o un escrito de la época de la acción me convenzo que todo va bien. Eso suele ocurrir en toda obra literaria. Cuando escribía *Sonata de primavera*, cuya acción pasa en Italia, incrusté un episodio romano de Casanova para convencerme de que mi obra estaba bien ambientada e iba por buen camino. El episodio se acomodaba perfectamente a mi narración. Shakespeare pone en boca de su Coriolano discursos y sentencias tomadas de los historiadores de la antigüedad; su tragedia es admirable porque, lejos de rechazar esos textos, los exige. Póngase en cualquiera de esas obras históricas de teatro que se estrenan en nuestro tiempo, discursos y documentos de la época, y se verá cómo les sientan.

A94

El *Quijote* es un admirable ejemplo de la reacción del pueblo, de la gente, ante un hecho, ante las divinas locuras del "Señor de los tristes;" es una reacción de burla y de desdén, de engaño y de risa. Es una reacción de pícaros. Apenas hay en las páginas del libro una compensación, una ternura para el idealismo del caballero. España no es un país de Quijotes, porque don Quijote fue derrotado. No puede ser ese su país porque en él—sobre su tierra, entre sus gentes—no logró ser planta el anhelo de justicia y de amor que hubo en el hidalgo de la Mancha. No, el español no es don Quijote, ni siquiera Sancho, que alguna vez sabe tener para los sueños y aventuras de su señor una amorosa piedad. El español es Ginesillo de Pasamonte, es los galeotes.

A95

Parte de la prensa inicia la idea de un homenaje a don José Echegaray, y se abroga la representación de toda la intelectualidad española. Nosotros, con derecho a ser comprendidos en ella—sin discutir ahora la personalidad literaria de don José Echegaray—, hacemos constar que nuestros ideales artísticos son otros y nuestras admiraciones muy distintas.

A96

Apenas cumplí la edad que se llama juventud, cómo final a unos amores desgraciados, me embarqué para México.

A97

Querido Don Benito:
    Si a las dos está usted en casa, iré a saludarle con el secretario de Legación de México, y poeta Amado Nervo, que desea mucho conocerle. Siempre suyo su amigo que le quiere,
        Valle-Inclán

A98

Querido Don Benito:
    Antes se salir de Madrid fui a despedirme de usted, pero no lo hallé.
    Aquí tenemos en ensayo *Alma y Vida* que estrenaremos el domingo. Están muy bien en los protagonistas Josefina y Ricardo Calvo. Los demás tampoco descomponen, y saldrán vestidos con bastante propiedad, pues les hice hacerse los trajes con arreglo a figurines dibujados *por mí*.

Lo que andará un poco mal es el decorado, pues como estamos empezando no he podido mandar pintarlo. Si usted pudiese hacer que nos alquilasen el decorado con que se estrenó sería una gran cosa para hacer la obra en Las Palmas.

Tengo casi terminada *Marianela*.

De todo le tendrá al corriente su amigo que le quiere tanto como le admira,

Valle-Inclán

Dirección: Teatro Cervantes-Granada.

A99

A Don Benito Pérez Galdós
Paseo de Areneros, 46. Madrid.
Teatro Cervantes. Granada

Querido Don Benito:

Se han extraviado hojas del ejemplar de *Alma y Vida* correspondiente al segundo apunte, y le agredecería que me mandase uno.

Suyo siempre su amigo que le quiere,

Valle-Inclán

A100

Querido Rubén: Supe hace tiempo por *El Imparcial* que estaba usted en Mallorca, pero las señas exactas no las tuve hasta ahora. Deseaba mucho saber de usted y también contarle algo de mi vida. Ante todo le diré que me he casado, y que falto de Madrid desde hace seis meses. Nada sé de aquella gente y a fe que no lo siento. De su vida, ¿qué es? ¿Cuándo nos da el regalo de unos nuevos versos? Yo estaré en Barcelona hasta mediados de marzo . . .

A101

. . . es perfecto aquél en que la mujer acepta íntegramente la interpretación del marido para toda cuestión política y literaria.

A102

Yo quisiera ser orador. Se calumnia y envilece a la oratoria pero se es injusto. La primera condición de la oratoria es la generosidad. Y la suprema belleza está en el desinterés. Hay falsificadores que la degradan con su baja ambición de medro personal, pero el orador ideal es el que habla artística y bellamente para distraer a sus oyentes e interlocutores. Fíjese usted bien que el orador, el verdadero, convence por el gesto, el ademán, el tono. San Bernardo predicando la cruzada en Alemania, desconociendo el idioma, y conmoviendo, sin embargo, a las muchedumbres crédulas y persuadidas es sugestivo. La elocuencia es como la Eucaristía, que no necesita nada de externo. Todo espíritu, bendito, y generoso desprendimiento. Acude a mi memoria Hernán Cortés. Fué un orador maravilloso. Descalificado como lo estaba por sus vicios y pasiones, siempre lograba captarse las simpatías de cuantos hablaban con él hasta el punto de que Bernal Díaz del Castillo cuenta que habiendo ido a visitarle unos cuantos capitanes predispuestos en contra suya, logró atraerlos, a sabiendas todos ellos de que Hernán Cortés les engañaba. Tal era su poder.

A103

¡Oh, lejanas memorias de la tierra lejana,

olorosas a yerbas frescas por la mañana!
¡Tierra de maizales húmedos y sonoros
donde cantan del viento los invisibles coros,
cuando deshoja el sol la rosa de sus oros,
en la cima del monte que estremecen los toros!

¡Oh, los hondos caminos con cruces y consejas,
por donde atardecido van trenquando las viejas,
cargadas con la leña robada en los pinares,
la leña que de noche ha de ahumar en los llares,
mientras cuenta una voz los cuentos seculares,
y a lo lejos perros ladran en los pajares!

A104

Auto-retrato

Mi ensueño de poeta, que floreció en un canto,
a mi Psiquis dos alas le dio para volar
—una ala de anarquista y otra ala de santo—
a mi diestra, un puñado de trigo que sembrar.

. . . Había yo nacido para ser un hidalgo
de aldea, con un pazo, con un rocín y un galgo;
pero quise del mundo correr la vastedad,
y de mi viejo pazo dejé la soledad,
soñando con empresas tan sonoras y grandes,
que tuviesen los ecos de México o de Flandes.

Fuiste de la lujuria la esclava, y a su imperio,
alma mía, rendiste tu virginal misterio;
y ella te dio el secreto de la melancolía,
el divino secreto que te obsede, alma mía.
Alma mía, que tiemblas en tu oscura caverna,
como tiembla en las aguas negras de la cisterna
la rosa misteriosa de una estrella lejana,
¡Oh, alma mía, la rosa del azul es tu hermana!

¡Y mi amor de soldado y mi amor de poeta! . . .
Hoy me queda en recuerdo de aquella vida inquieta
una gran cicatriz al costado derecho,
un brazo cercenado y un pie medio deshecho.
Mas tengo la virtud de la renunciación,
y supe ser asceta después de ser león.

A105

Las historias que hallaréis en este libro tienen ese aire que los críticos españoles suelen llamar decadente, sin duda porque no es la sensibilidad de los jayanes. A ese gesto un poco desusado debieron su malaventura, cuando por primera vez quise hacerlas conocer. Si exceptuáis "Eulalia," todas ellas fueron condenadas a la hoguera, en alguna de esas redacciones donde toda necedad tiene su asiento. . . . "Augusta" no pareció bien . . . "Rosita" escandalizó . . . y "Beatriz" cayó en un concurso de *El Liberal* . . .

A106

Querido D. Benito:
  Estuve a verle con Gabriel Miró que quería agradecerle su carta.
  Un abrazo,
    Valle-Inclán

A107

Querido don Benito:
  Mañana volveré a verle para darle la enhorabuena por *Pedro Minio*.
  Un abrazo,
    Valle-Inclán

A108

Yo hallé siempre más bella la majestad caída que sentada en el trono, y fuí defensor de la tradición por estética. El carlismo tiene para mí el encanto solemne de las grandes catedrales, y aún en los tiempos de la guerra me hubiera contentado con que lo declarasen momumento nacional.

A109

Soy carlista solamente por estética. Me agrada la boina. Es una cresta pomposa que ennoblece. La blanca capa de los carlistas me retrotrae al imperio de una corte arcaica. Es, sin duda, el más bello disfraz político que ha existido.

A110

¡Si hubiera venido antes, querido Argamasilla, le habría dado otro ambiente a *Los cruzados*!

A111

Afirmo, señoras y señores, mi abolengo y filiación tradicionalista. Mi abolengo y filiación tradicionalista nació en circunstancias adversas para la causa carlista. . . . Mis primeras producciones literarias fueron alabadas por la prensa en general, porque no eran carlistas; pero tan pronto como empecé a escribir en la carlista, todos mis lectores anteriores dejaron de serlo. No me importa . . . No obstante, al convencerme que el que tiene un ideal debe trabajar por él . . . puse mi pluma al servicio del mío . . . Y el único brazo que tengo lo dedico a manejar la pluma en defensa de mis ideas, y si es necesario, ese brazo lo pondré a disposición de la causa para manejar otras armas . . .

A112

Tengo grandes compromisos en España. No sé cómo he podido dejarlos. Hasta última hora no tenía la seguridad de embarcarme para acompañar a mi amigo García Ortega. Mi viaje ha tenido muchos contratiempos. Esos compromisos que me ataban a España eran de índole muy seria. Compromisos políticos . . . He debido activar mi candidatura de diputado con que me disponía a intervenir en la próxima renovación de las Cortes. No era por mi voluntad que iba a la legislature nacional. Era un mandato imperativo de quien puede hacerlo. Al realizarse las listas de candidatos don Jaime de Borbón quiso premiar mis esfuerzos señalándome la candidatura por el distrito de Monforte. Pero surgieron dificultades inesperadas y en la revisión de la lista se me honró al designárseme por el distrito de Estella. Naturalmente, yo debía excusarme con razones poderosas; decir que mi anhelo mayor era el de visitar Buenos Aires, no bastaba. Hube de escribir al rey . . . Y él me concedió el permiso para retirar mi nombre. Otro me suplirá con ventaja.

Chapter 7: Drama

A113

Querido y admirado don Benito:
   Aquí, an Aranjuez, a donde llego después de una excursión por varios pueblos de Castilla, recibo su carta con la natural vergüenza, y el natural retraso. No crea usted que no he trabajado en *Marianela*, pero me contentaba muy poco lo hecho y lo rompí.
   Ahora vuelvo a tenerla entre manos. Creo que muy pronto le enviaré algo.
   Disculpe mi pereza, y mande a su admirador y su amigo que le quiere,
      Ramón del Valle-Inclán

A114

Mi obra viene a reflejar la vida de un pueblo en desaparición. Mi misión es anotarla, antes que desaparezca. En mis *Comedias bárbaras* reflejo los mayorazgos que desaparecieron en el año 1833. Conocí a muchos. Son la última expresión de una idea, por lo que mis comedias tienen cierto valor histórico.

A115

En esta Comedia Bárbara (dividida en tres tomos: *Cara de Plata*, *Aguila de blasón* y *Romance de lobos*), estos conceptos que vengo expresando motivan desde la forma hasta el más ligero episodio. He asistido al cambio de una sociedad de castas (los hidalgos que conocí de rapaz), y lo que yo vi no lo verá nadie. Soy el historiador de un mundo que acabó conmigo. Ya nadie volverá a ver vinculeros y mayorazgos. Y en este mundo que yo presento de clérigos, mendigos, escribanos, putas y alcahuetes, lo mejor - con todos sus vicios—era los hidalgos, lo desaparecido.

A116

He querido renovar lo que tiene de galaico la leyenda de Don Juan, que yo divido en tres tiempos: impiedad, matonería y mujeres. Este de las mujeres es el último, el sevillano, la nostagia del moro sin harén. El matón picajoso es el extremeño, gallego de frontera. El impío es el gallego, el originario, como explicaba nuestro caro Said-Armesto. El Convidado de Piedra es, por sólo ser bulto de piedra, gallego. Aquí la impiedad es la impiedad gallega; no niega ningún dogma, no descree de Dios, es irreverente con los muertos. Fatalmente, la irreligiosidad es el desacato a los difuntos. Estas ideas me guiaron con mayor conciencia al dar remate a *Cara de Plata*. Es un juego con la muerte, un disparar pistolones, un revolverse airado de unos a otros, una mojiganga de entregar el alma que hace el sacristán . . . Pero, a fuerza de hacer el fantasma, se acaba siéndolo. A fuerza de descreer de la muerte, de provocarla y de fingirla, la muerte llega. Y comienza *Romance de lobos*. La muerte llega con sus luces, con sus agüeros, con sus naufragios y orfandades, con sus castigos y arrepentimientos. Este fondo del primer Don Juan—Don Galán en el romance viejo—es lo perseguido con mayor empeño, porque lo tengo por la última decantación del alma gallega.

Hace usted una observación muy justa cuando señala el funambulismo de la acción, que tiene algo de tramoya de sueño, por donde las larvas pueden dialogar con los vivos. Cierto. A este efecto contribuye lo que pudiéramos llamar angostura del tiempo. Un efecto parecido al del Greco, por la angostura del espacio. Velázquez está todo lleno de espacio. Las figuras pueden cambiar de actitud, esparcirse y hacer lugar a otras forasteras. Pero en el *Enterramiento* sólo el Greco pudo meterlas en tan angosto espacio; y si se desbarataran, hará falta un matemático bizantino para rehacer el problema. Esta angostura de espacio es angostura de tiempo en las *Comedias*. Las escenas que parecen arbitratriamente colocadas son las consecuentes en la cronología de los hechos. *Cara de Plata* comienza con el alba y acaba a la media noche. Las otras partes se suceden también sin intervalo. Ahora, en algo que estoy escribiendo, esta idea de llenar el tiempo como llenaba el Greco ese espacio, totalmente, me preocupa. Algún ruso sabía de esto.

A117

A mi no me gusta un teatro de esta manera. Con los recursos de presencia que el teatro tiene nos echan a la cara trozos de realidad. El arte no existe sino cuando ha superado sus modelos vivos mediante una elaboración ideal. Las cosas no son como las vemos, sino como las recordamos. La palabra en la creación literaria necesita siempre ser trasladada a ese plano en que el mundo y la vida humana se idealizan. No hay poesía sin esa elaboración.

A118

La impresión primera que produce Buenos Aires es la de asombro. He podido ver que es una ciudad grande y, probablemente, una gran ciudad. . . . Siento, por lo que me han dicho y por lo que veo, que Buenos Aires será el futuro gran centro de la raza latina. . . . Conocer Buenos Aires del que tanto se habla en España, era una perpetua tentación para mi espíritu. Y la oportunidad me ha sido doblemente favorable, pues me permite conocer la gran ciudad cuando se preparan las fiestas del Centenario. Hay aquí millares de compatriotas, y esto me halaga. Algunos me estiman y es un placer conocerlos de cerca. . . . En el tiempo que me lo permitan mis labores de director artístico teatral visitaré la Argentina, sin propósitos de conquistador, sencillamente, como un curioso cualquiera. Bien puede haber por aquí algún hijo descamisado de don Juan Manuel Montenegro, ¿verdad? Por de pronto la ciudad me seduce y encanta. No podía concebir nada tan inagotable ni arrollador . . . Lo único que me ha impresionado es no haber oído en las horas de mi llegada una sola canción. . . . Dejaré también un poco de mi alma en esta tierra . . .

A119

He visto llegar a la Señora Infanta de España y a su cortejo . . . recibida con una declaración de huelga general y la ciudad en estado de sitio. . . . No hay aquí un solo hombre culto que no comente la torpeza de los gobernantes españoles enviando una dama de estirpe regia a la ciudad donde hay . . . más de 50.000 anarquistas.

A120

La Señora Infanta salvó la vida por milagro ayer en la catedral. . . . La policía detuvo a un anarquista que llevaba escondido un puñal en un número de *La Nación*. . . . Dicen que Doña Isabel advirtióla detención y que mostró verdadero ánimo real.

A121

Conmigo se molestó un poco, porque yo, habiendo salido de Espāna sin anuncio y sin jaleo de Prensa, era aquí un poco más conocido. En la intimidad, según me contaron, protestaba de que la intelectualidad argentina me hubiese dado una fiesta, porque yo en Espāna no era nadie.

A122

¿Ha visto usted qué tierra es ésta? Los que nada son en España parece que aquí son algo, y a las eminencias de España aquí nadie las conoce.

A123

No pensaba yo ser conferenciante en Buenos Aire. No soy orador. El orador no titubea, y yo titubeo; porque sé que las cosas tienen cien diversos matices y pueden ser expresadas de cien diversas maneras. Pero, en fin, daré conferencias. . . . A ello me he comprometido con el Conservatorio Labardén. Pienso volver a Buenos Aires, tal vez pronto, y entonces traeré preparadas desde Madrid unas cuantas conferencias sobre héroes y santos de la España vieja, sobre Santiago, Patrón de aquella península; sobre Fray Diego de Cádiz, sobre héroes olvidados de Galicia. Ahora improvisaré. Aunque no quisiera parecerme a Blasco Ibáñez, que también improvisó aquí.

A124

Cuando la música de los versos y la música de los cascabeles no basta aquí para llenar la bolsa, bufones y poetas nos embarcamos para dar conferencias en las Indias.

A125

El arte de escribir es un largo y penoso aprendizaje con dos caras: el aprendizaje para ver lo que todas las cosas tienen de bello, y el aprendizaje para expresar. Uno y otro deben hacerse unidos . . . Ha de estar hecho todo el aprendizaje antes de entregarse a la obra de arte; que la idea salga vertida sin esfuerzo; que el vestido sea parte de su esencia como la luz a la estrella. En la obra de arte no debe advertirse nunca el esfuerzo, porque no olvidéis que ocultar la fuerza es doblarla. . . . Jamás el artista debe proponerse la imitación de un modelo, por levantado que éste se halle. Es preciso cavar en el huerto propio para obtener nuestras flores y nunca imitar la manera que decimos 'clásica' porque es casi siempre una mala compresión de la literatura latina. Huir siempre de ese largo período, tan perjudicial a nuestro idioma castellano . . . . Trabajar en pro de la lengua de Castilla para vosotros y para nosotros es levantar un fuerte e inexpugnable muro en las patrias fronteras. ¡Ay de todos el día que perdáis el idioma o lo evolucionéis para las necesidades del comercio, solamente! Lo haréis más apto pero lo haréis menos bello. No olvidéis que ninguno de los romances nacidos del latín pudo igualar a la lengua materna; ninguno de los idiomas que nazcan del nuestro tendrá su noble y sonora austeridad, que es la austeridad del espíritu castellano. Y vosotras, señoras, amad las bellas y sonoras palabras, porque ellas tienen una augusta eternidad. Bautizad con sonoros nombres a vuestros hijos, bautizad con sonoros nombres vuestras estancias y vuestros quinteros, vuestras aldeas y vuestras villas. Poblad la pampa de altos y significativos nombres; recordad cómo los antiguos bautizaron a los ríos con las más sonoras voces, que parecen correr en nuestros labios como bajo el cielo el cristal de las aguas. Tal manera la tuvieron los antiguos porque juzgaban a los ríos, divinidades. Juzgad vosotros divinidad todo aquello que haya de nacer y merecer un nombre.

A126

La nada engendra el tiempo, de donde nace el presente, para lo inmutable. Por otra parte, el tiempo es la polarización de dos infinitos: el de la negación y el de la afirmación, los que a su vez nos dan la noción eterna del centro. Todo conocimiento está en Dios que no conoce el mal y como Dios es el centro, aproximarnos a él debe ser la suprema ambición humana. El que más ama, más goza. Universalicemos nuestra conciencia para ser mejores. En la tierra el hombre sólo puede ser centro de amor como lo fué Glarís. Esta teoría o sensación del centro me lleva a pensar que el artista debe mirar el paisaje con "ojos de altura" para poder abarcar todo el conjunto y no los detalles mudables. Conservando en el arte ese aire de observación colectiva que tiene la literatura popular, las cosas adquieren una belleza de alejamiento. Por eso hay que pintar a las figuras quitándoles aquello que no hayan sido. Así un mendigo debe parecerse a Job y un guerrero a Aquiles.

A127

No niego la tradición; pero aceptándola solamente en lo que puede tener de vital y de útil, y hago notar la necesidad de un ritmo interno sosteniendo las fórmulas. . . . Tantos corazones, tantas maneras de expresión. En arte, las reglas y los preceptos pueden ser variables como variables son las esencias, pero la medida en que cada una habrá de intervenir cambia por la manera personal del sentimiento. . . . En toda la obra de arte está el germen de otra distinta, y todo está en todo . . .

A128

España no ha sido nunca un país de guerreros. Uno sólo fué grande: don Gonzalo de Córdoba, llamado el gran capitán, que supo vencer ejércitos poderosos con su talento estratégico. Los conquistadores españoles no fueron guerreros sino moralistas. Llegaron a América con afán fundacional. Hernán Cortés y Pizarro tuvieron éxito en sus empresas, más por espíritu guerrero, por el conocimiento que tenían los hombres, por su perspicacia y por su fe. Los fundadores fueron más grandes que los guerreros y que los literatos. De ahí que todas las guerras emprendidas por España Antigua tuvieran un fin moral.

A129

Mañana saldrá original el título es *Voces de gesta*. Valle-Inclán.

A130

Querido Rubén: Supongo habrá recibido la primera jornada de *Voces de gesta*. La obra está ya terminada. Voy a publicarla tan luego usted lo haya hecho en su revista, y deseo una *Invocación* en versos de usted. La edición será con ilustraciones, imitando viejos grabados en madera, algo como la *Figlia di Iorio*, pero a dos tintas. Como en todo esto se tarda mucho, y los versos de usted deben ir en el primer pliego, con una orla en cada página, tienen una rabiosa e imperiosa urgencia.

A131

Querido Darío: Supongo que habrá recibido el segundo acto de *Voces de Gesta* que le mandé hace días. No dejen de enviarme las pruebas para corregir deficiencia que no he podido subsanar en la copia. ¿Y mi prólogo en verso?

A132

He recibido de la Administración de la revista *Mundial* la cantidad de . . . . . francos por la primera y segunda jornada del poema trágico *Voces de gesta*. Madrid, 8 de septiembre, 1911. Ramón del Valle-Inclán.

A133

Querido Darío: No se olvide de mi prólogo. De lo que me dice en su telegrama haga usted lo que le parezca. Usted conoce la situación financiera de la Revista y lo que acostumbra a pagar. A su arbitrio queda pues encomendado.

A134

Querido Darío: He recibido un cheque de 150 pesetas, importe de la Jornada publicada. Le agradeceré mucho que al publicarse la Segunda me envíen a Madrid un giro. Y mejor si esos señores de *Mundial* se dignasen pagar los dos trabajos entregados, aun antes de publicarse. Una gestión de usted, en este entido, podría allanarlo, y yo se lo agradecería mucho, pues en el momento ando escaso de dinero, que los viajes del verano me han costado un platal. Escríbame a Madrid. No olvide mi prólogo.

A135

Querido Darío: Estoy esperando con ansia su Introducción a *Voces de Gesta*. Tengo ya impresa la obra y solo falta tirar el primer pliego. En estos tiempos he terminado *La Marquesa Rosalinda*. Toda ella en rimas un poco estrafalarias como usted habrá visto por el prólogo publicado en *Mundial*. Por cierto que han hecho ustedes un número muy bello tipográficamente y literariamente. Mis felicitaciones de año nuevo y un abrazo.

A136

Será un libro de leyendas, de tradiciones, a la manera de *Cuento de abril*; pero más fuerte, más importante. Recogeré la voz de todo un pueblo. Sólo son grandes los libros que recogen voces amplias, plebeyas. *La Ilíada*, los dramas de Shakespeare . . . *Voces de gesta* es un libreto wagneriano.

A137

Estaba yo pensando, sin saber a qué atribuirlo, lo bien que se está en Madrid los sábados por la noche . . . Ahora he caído en la cuenta: todos los imbéciles están abonados a la Princesa. Pero el sábado que viene voy a interrumpir mi costumbre de no salir a escena, para decirle al abono cuántas son dos y dos, ea; ya estoy cansado de oir insensateces.

A138
Como que han reforzado ustedes la *claque* . . .

A139

Tiene al andar la gracia del felino

Es toda llena de profundos ecos,
Anuncian sus corales y sus flecos
Un ensueño oriental de lo divino.

    Los ojos negros, cálidos, astutos,
Triste de ciencia antigua la sonrisa,
Y la falda de flores una brisa
De índicos y sagrados institutos.

    Cortó su mano en un jardín de Oriente
La manzana del árbol prohibido,
Y enroscada a sus senos la serpiente

    Decora la lujuria de un sentido
Sagrado. En la tiniebla transparente
De sus ojos, la luz pone un silbido.

A140

Mi muy querido y admirado don Benito:
    Comienzo a publicar en el folletín de *El Mundo* una comedia bárbara al modo de otras que ya escribí, como *Romance de Lobos*. Si sus ocupaciones le dejan vagar, yo le agradeceré que lea el folletín. Acaso haya en esa mi comedia bárbara de *El Embrujado* una comedia capaz para el teatro, reduciéndola en alguna parte. Usted juzgará.
    A Matilde le tengo hecha promesa de alguna cosa para fin de temporada. Por eso tengo un doble interés en conocer su opinión sobre *El Embrujado*.
    Con el cariño de siempre le saluda el más devoto de sus amigos. Un abrazo de,
    Valle-Inclán

A141

Muy querido y admirado don Benito:
    Dos mañanas estuve a verle en su casa, y no le hallé porque ya era tarde para encontrarle en ella.
    Me dijeron que después de las diez no era posible verle, y como yo vivo muy distante de la casa de usted tendría que levantarme de víspera.
    Tengo muchos deseos de abrazarle y consultarle mi *Embrujado*. ¿Sería usted tan bueno que me señalase día y hora, procurando que también Fuentes lo pudiese oír? Aún cuando esto no es absolutamente preciso, pues ya conoce la obra.
    Le abraza, y le quiere tanto como le admira,
    Valle-Inclán
    Febrero-3.
    S/c. Santa Engracia, 23.

Chapter 8: Panorama

A142

Enfermo y decaído hasta el punto de valerme de mano ajena para escribir estas líneas, envío mi saludo de admiración, de afecto y de respeto al partriarca de las letras castellanas, al que siempre tuve por maestro, al primero y al mejor que en la tradicional aridez de la prosa castiza, hizo cantar, para regalo de todos, las líricas alondras. Fue el primero en su época. Era estelar la distancia que de los hombres y las cosas de su tiempo le separaba. Y no podía ser comprendido.

A143

Los toros son la única educación que tenemos. Y una corrida de toros es algo muy hermoso. Por ejemplo, hay que admirar el tránsito: Juan Belmonte. Juan es hombre pequeño, feo, desgarbado, y si se me apura mucho, ridículo. Pues bien, coloquemos a Juan ante el toro, ante la muerte, y Juan se convierte en la misma estatua de Apolo. Los griegos no nos dejaron mejor escultura . . . que la que representa Balmonte en la Plaza, prendido en el aire, junto a un toro bravo. Desde hace muchos años repito en mis clases de Estética que el verdadero artista se caracteriza por esa armonía de contrarios. Eso lo de Belmonte mejor que ningún otro artista. Y no se puede comparar esa maravillosa transfiguración con nada.

A144

Hace tiempo le escribí encareciéndole hablase a M. Remy de Gourmont para la publicación en el *Mercurio* de *Romance de lobos*. Hoy tengo el gusto de hacerle la presentación del autor de esta traducción incomparable: M. Chaumié Consul General de Francia en España, en quien hallará usted un profundo conocedor de nuestras letras, que sabe buscar hasta el fondo esotérico de los versos de usted, que tan arcanos se le presentan a tantos de nuestros académicos, críticos y poetas. M. Chaumié es el único capaz de hacer conocer el valor estético de España en la hora de ahora. Yo deseo vivamente que usted nos ayude e interponga su amistad con M. Remy de Gourmont para dar comienzo a la obra.

A145

¡Josefina, mis pecados fueron la causa de la muerte de nuestro hijo; voy a Santiago a postrarme a los pies del Penitenciario!

A146

Queridísimo Ortega:

No le escribí antes, porque no han faltado dolores y desazones. Hace dos días enterré a mi hijito. Dios Nuestro Señor me lo llevó para sí. Ha sido el mayor dolor de mi vida. Yo no sé qué cosa sea la muerte, que se la siente llegar: Mi niño estaba sano y yo esperaba una desgracia como algo fatal. Ya llegó, y sea sola. Estoy acabado. Esto es horrible, ¡Qué no sepa usted nunca de este dolor! La casa se me viene encima, y tampoco quiero, por ahora, volver a Madrid, donde nació mi niño hermoso que se me murió. Quisiera ir a Italia, pero con los míos: Mi mujer y mi hija: Ello es caro. Mi pobre Josefina que está tan muerta como yo, ha tenido una idea. Ella me inspira que le escriba a usted, para saber si podrían concederme una pensión de la Junta de Estudios para estudiar alguna cosa en Italia. Cosa para la cual, en conciencia, sea yo capaz. De pintura, de literatura: Una visión de Cervantes, de Lope, de Quevedo, en Italia: Diálogos de soldados, jugadores, mujeres, pilotos catalanes y de Valencia. Una visión estética de Italia. No sé si algo de esto podrá ser, ni tampoco si es ocasión. Usted, mi querido amigo (a quien libre de esta pena mi Dios Cristo Jesús, en quien usted no cree), verá lo que puede hacerse. Se lo agradecerá infinitamente su infortunado

Valle-Inclán

A147

Queridísimo Ortega:

Vivamente le agradecí su carta. Ya sabe usted que le di toda mi amistad desde el momento que le conocí. A su serenidad y a su gran talento, que yo advertí desde el primer día, unía usted el nombre. Yo hice mis primeras y últimas armas en *Los Lunes*, sintiendo el calor, la efusión y el aliento, del más grande corazón de hombre y de poeta que hallé en mi camino.

En un número de *El Imparcial* he visto que ha publicado usted un libro (acaso el que en su carta me promete), y estoy deseando leerlo. En un artículo donde Gómez Baquero capea su insignificancia, hallé estas palabras de usted: La filosofía es la ciencia general del amor. Tan conforme estoy, que en el mismo periódico escribía yo: El amor de todas las cosas es la cima de la suma belleza, y quien lo alcanza penetra el significado del mundo, tiene la Ciencia Mística: ¿Pero el amor, cuando es olvido de nuestro egoísmo, no es una divina intuición? Mándeme su libro. Un abrazo de su invariable

Valle-Inclán

A148

Con mi rebeldía creo que soy el más patriota de todos mis contemporáneos. Y creo que siendo la gobernación actual cosa tan detestable y aborrecible colaborar a la obra del Estado, es contribuir con nuestro esfuerzo a la perdición de España. Yo, cuando alguno de mis amigos se hace político—¡político!—, y como tal se encumbra y medra, dejo de saludarle.

A149

Treinta y cinco o cuarenta mil pesetas anuales . . . Y fíjese usted, me producen más las obras antiguas que las recientes. Esto demuestra que el tiempo es para los libros lo que para el oro: lo avalora más.

A150

No me gusta la literatura. Soy un forzado que escribe por inercia. Por consiguiente, no estoy contento de ella. Creo que equivoqué el camino . . . Sí, yo soy un equivocado. Yo quisiera ser orador. ¡La oratoria! ¡Cuánto se la calumnia y envilece!

A151

En los comienzos de mi iniciación estética sólo tuve ojos para gozar y amar el divino cristal del mundo, ojos como los pájaros que cantan al alba del sol. Todas las formas y todas las vidas me decían el secreto inefable del Paraíso, y me descubrían su lazo de hermandad conmigo . . . En esta ansia divina y humana me torturé por encontrar el quicio donde hacer quieta mi vída, y fuí, en algún modo, discípulo de Miguel de Molinos: De su enseñanza mística deduje mi estética. . . . Estaba solo, sin otra alma que me adoctrinase, y caminaba en noche oscura. Solamente me guió el amor de las musas.

Ambicioné que mi verbo fuese como un claro cristal, misterio, luz y fortaleza. En la música y en la idea de esta palabra cristal, yo poníá aquel prestigio simbólico que tienen en los libros cabalístícos las letras sagradas de los pentáculos. . . . Y años enteros trabajé con la voluntad de un asceta, dolor y gozo, por darles emoción de estrellas, de fontanas y de hierbas frescas . . . Me torturé por sentir el estremecimiento natal de cada una . . . Fué un feliz momento aquel en que supe purificar mis intuiciones de lo efímero, y gozar del mundo con los ojos divinizados. . . . En estas horas fue mi maestro Pico de la Mirándola.

A152

Siempre fueron pocos los hombres con quienes se pudiese tratar de negocios espirituales, pero cada día son menos. Las gentes temen hablar de la muerte, y son como los niños asustados de los fantasmas, que de noche, en la cama, se tapan la cabeza con las cobijas. Yo quisiera hablar a todas horas de la vida de nuestras almas a través de las estrellas, y de la compresión sideral de nuestras acciones. El dolor de haber vivido debe ser horrible. ¡Si ahora nos acaban los remordimientos, qué no será después! ¿Puede compararse la purificación de los años, con la purificación de la muerte?

A153

Darío era un niño. Era inmensamente bueno. Vivía en un santo temor religioso. Sin cesar, veía cosas del otro mundo. No había cosas, mejor dicho, que no se le proyectaran allá. Repito que era un niño. Ni orgulloso, ni rencoroso, ni ambicioso. No tenía ninguno de los pecados angélicos. Lejos como nadie de todo pecado luzbélico, él no conocía otros pecados que los de la carne. Era goloso, a veces glotón, era sensual, era muelle. Todo eso muere con la carne. Su alma era pura, purísima.

A154

No haga usted caso. Eso . . . no tiene importancia. Unamuno ahora habla así y mañana puede decir lo contrario. Vámonos a tomar el aire.

A155

El suceso, amigo don Miguel, no tiene nada de notable y mucho menos de desconcertante. Es, sencillamente, el resultado del enfrentamiento de dos sujetos diferentes y opuestos. Es una realidad natural. Ustedes no han nacido para entenderse porque Rubén y usted son antípodas. Vera usted: Rubén tiene todos los defectos de la carne: es glotón, es bebedor, es mujeriego, es holgazán, etc., etc. Pero posee, en cambio, todas las virtudes del espíritu: es bueno, es generoso, es sencillo, es altruista, es humilde, etc., etc. En cambio usted almacena todas las virtudes de la carne: es usted frugal, es usted abstemio, es usted casto, es usted infatigable. Y tiene usted todos lo vicios del espíritu: es usted soberbio, es usted ególatra, es usted avaro, es usted rencoroso, etc., etc. Por eso, cuando Rubén se muera y se le pudra la carne, que es lo que tiene malo, le quedará el espíritu, que es lo que tiene bueno, ¡y se salvará! Pero usted, cuando se muera y se le pudra la carne, que es lo que tiene bueno, le quedará el espíritu, que es lo que tiene malo, ¡y se condenará! . . . Desde entonces, Unamuno anda muy preocupado.

A156

Darío me alarga en la sombra
Una mano, y a Poe me nombra.

Maga estrella de pentarquía
Sobre su pecho anuncia el día.

Su blanca túnica de Esenio
Tiene las luces del selenio.

¡Sombra del misterioso delta,
Vibra en tu honor mi gaita celta!

¡Tú amabas las rosas, el vino
y los amores del camino!

Cantor de Vida y Esperanza,
Para tí toda mi loanza.

Por el alba de oro, que es tuya
¡Aleluya! ¡Aleluya! ¡Aleluya!

A157

En el año de 1616 y a 23 de abril, murió Miguel de Cervantes de una enfermedad del corazón. Para recordar aquella fecha y los tres siglos que hoy se cumplen, se hace la edición de este entremés de LA GUARDA CUIDADOSA. Fué, sin duda, escrito para un público ingenuo y representado por farsantes acaso más ingenuos. Los farsantes de la corona de papel dorado y las barbas de estopa. En los niños revive siempre la ingenuidad de los siglos pasados, y para entender y alcanzar el encanto de las literaturas viejas, no hay cosa mejor que saber hacerse niño. Por conservar la virtud cristalina de este encanto, no lleva ahora notas, glosas ni apostillas el entremés de LA GUARDA CUIDADOSA. Se imprime para los niños y ellos lo pueden entender mejor que los hombres.
    Valle-Inclán

A158

Escribiré un libro que tengo ya visto en concepto. Ese libro se irá publicando a medida que lo vaya escribiendo en varios periódicos franceses, ingleses y argentinos.

A159

Yo quisiera dar una visión total de la guerra; algo así como si nos fuera dado el contemplarla sin la limitación del tiempo y del espacio. Yo sé muy bien que la gente que lee periódicos no sabe lo que es la fatalidad de esta guerra, la continuación de la historia y no su interrupción . . . La guerra es fatal. Es fatal para que haya amor. El roce engendra calor y luz. La luz es amor. El hombre no es sino el producto del connubio del sol y la tierra, y así como el girasol obedece en el movimiento rotatorio de la tierra que lo sustenta a la fascinación del sol, así la humanidad sigue la ruta solar de Oriente a Occidente para renacer de nuevo en el punto de partida.

A160

Nuestra civilización recogió en Grecia toda la fuerza primitiva de la India; el Mediterráneo fue el mar *civilizado* de Roma, hasta que España, heredera de ese pasado greco-latino, fundó la civilización atlántica con el descubrimiento de América. La civilización atlántica tiene su punto de apogeo en el esplendor de Inglaterra . . . Inglaterra perecerá como perecieron los imperios de Grecia y Roma y España . . . Inglaterra perecerá; pero nunca a manos de Alemania, síno fatalmente a manos de los Estados Unidos de América, que están en la ruta del sol. Y una nueva aurora se encenderá en el Japón al ocaso del sol americano, y entretanto florecerá la civilización del mar Pacífico, y Panamá será el ombligo del mundo y el camino de la India, es decir, el retorno a la quietud donde se engendra el movimiento.

A161

Tiene papel y muy importante. El mismo de siempre: En la tragedia humana los caracteres son sostenidos. El alemán ahora como antes es el scita semental. Está demostrado que las razas mediterráneas pierden fuerza a medida que los cruces originarios se diluyen con la acción enervadora del tiempo. La sabia naturaleza dispone de vez en cuando las invasiones bárbaras que vigorizan nuestra sangre. Entonces el alemán, el scita semental, baja hacia el Sur, irrumpe en las tierras de sol y al par que purifica las razas demasiado espiritualizadas, se deja conquistar y dominar a su vez por el espirítu vivificador. En esta guerra Alemania, símbolo del materialismo de Jehová, será vencida en su fuerza.

A162

Debiéramos haber entrado en guerra contra Alemania. Se nos ofreciá por los aliados una compensación en el Mediterraneo oriental; hubiera sido continuar nuestra historia y algo más que un eco sonoro el grito de Lepanto . . . Pero los políticos españoles no saben a punto fijo hacia donde cae Constantinopla. En España aun se podría hacer algo, sin contar con los políticos, claro está. El rey . . . el rey tiene buena voluntad, un rey por sí solo, puede salvar un país, es cierto; pero . . . ¿y la dinastía?

A163

Yo tengo un concepto anterior, yo voy a constatar ese concepto y no a inventarlo. El arte es siempre una abstracción. Si mi portera y yo vemos la misma cosa, mi portera no sabe lo que ha visto porque no tiene el concepto anterior. La guerra no se puede ver como unas cuantas granadas que caen aquí o allá, ni como unos cuantos muertos y heridos que se cuentan luego en estadísticas. Hay que verla desde una estrella . . . fuera del tiempo y del espacio.

A164

Querida Josefina:
   Solamente podré ponerte dos letras, porque espero la visita de un americano, y creo que está llamando a la puerta. No era el americano. Sigamos. Esta tarde vendrá a verme un redactor de *Les Temps* que desea publicar una entrevista conmigo. Ahora creo que llama el americano. Espera en el salón y voy a terminar. Mañana me recibirá Briand, el presidente del Consejo de Ministros, y el hombre que pesa más en los destinos del mundo. Ha significado el deseo de conocerme. El martes de la semana próxima seré recibido en la Sociedad de Gentes de Teatro, que me han invitado muy cortésmente, para asistir a una sesión. Creo que quieren pedir que me condecoren con la Legión de Honor . . . Yo pienso que la condecorada eres tú, pues es a quien halagan estas cosas.

A165

El vuelo de noche ha sido una revelación. Será el punto de vista de mi novela, la visión estelar.

A166

Era mi propósito condensar en un libro los varios y diversos lances de un día de guerra en Francia. Acontece que, al escribir de la guerra, el narrador que antes fué testigo, da a los sucesos un enlace cronológico puramente accidental, nacido de la humana y geométrica limitación que nos veda ser a la vez en varias partes. . . . El narrador ajusta la guerra y sus accidentes a la medida de su caminar: Las batallas comienzan cuando sus ojos llegan a mirarlas: El terrible rumor de la guerra se apaga cuando se aleja de los parajes trágicos, y vuelve cuando se acerca a ellos. Todos los relatos están limitados por la posición geométrical del narrador.

A167

Pero aquel que pudiese ser a la vez en diversos lugares . . . de cierto tendría de la guerra una visión, una emoción y una concepción en todo distinta de la que puede tener el mísero testigo, sujeto a las leyes geométricas de la materia corporal y mortal. . . . Esta intuición taumatúrgica de los parajes y los sucesos, esta comprensión que parece fuera del espacio y del tiempo, no es sin embargo ajena a la literatura.

A168

Cuando los soldados de Francia vuelvan a sus pueblos . . . cada boca tendrá un relato distinto, y serán cientos de miles los relatos, expresión de otras tantas visiones, que al cabo habrán de resumirse en una visión, cifra de todas. Desaparecerá entonces la pobre mirada del soldado, para crear la visión colectiva, la visión de todo el pueblo que estuvo en la guerra, y vió a la vez desde todos los parajes todos los sucesos.

A169

Desde mis tiempos de estudiante, mucho antes de soñar con ser literato, profeso por don Armando Palacio Valdés una profunda admiración, cada día más grande, porque con los años lo comprendo mejor. Pero con ser tanta mi admiración al escritor, casi la supera mi admiración al hombre grave y esquivo ante el frágil y adocenado aplauso de la crítica y de la prensa.

A170

Mi querido Ortega:
   No sé si cometo una incorreción al escribirle en estos momentos, cuando el asunto de *El Imparcial* debe tenerle preocupado con la intensa y ética preocupación que usted sabe poner en todo. Le ruego me perdone. Ante todo mi más cordial felicitación por la actitud de ustedes. Y ahora una demanda: Nilo Fabra, muy querido amigo mío, que trabajó muchos años en *El Imparcial*, desea volver a aquella casa cuando ustedes vuelvan a ella. Creo que se le debe de justicia, y ustedes hallarán en él un colaborador inteligente y un corazón leal. Mucho le agradeceré querido Ortega, que usted le ayude en su empeño.
   De nuevo mi más efusivo saludo por su actitud. Le abraza su viejo
      Valle-Inclán

A171

En el siglo XIX la Historia de España la pudo escribir Don Carlos; en el siglo XX la está escribiendo Lenín.

A172

Un régimen de gobierno que no haya creado un nuevo estilo y, por consiguiente, un nuevo estilo de vida, ¡no existe!

A173

La región Castellana tiene una expresión mística, una expresión de acabamiento, una expresión de cansancio. Ha sido, y para volver a ser mira atrás como los hombres que han vivido mucho y que viendo cerrado el porvenir se buscan en su conciencia. . . Nuestro Mediterráneo no es el Mediterráneo Oriental, no es el que tiene la ciencia griega, es el Mediterráneo africano, el triste Mediterráneo semita, el triste Mediterráneo engañoso. Estas son las dos expresiones consagradas hasta ahora del arte español: la castellana de cansancio y la levantina de ciencia engañosa . . . Castilla está muerta, porque Castilla vive mirando atrás, y mirando atrás no se tiene una visión del momento; no se puede adquirir conciencia, y el hombre que adquiere conciencia en sus actos, y conciencia de lo que ha vivido y dolor de haber vivido—porque al mirar atrás y verse en su conciencia todos sentimos el dolor de no haber realizado una obra intensa—el hombre se hace místico y se consagra a saber morir. Pero el pueblo vasco, y con el pueblo vasco todos los que se asoman al Cantábrico, no se han desenvuelto aún, no pueden mirar atrás, a un anterior, a una época anterior, a unas conquistas y a una historia geográfica, y siempre pasada como toda la historia, ni tiene tampoco una ciencia aprendida de ajenos: son primitivos, éstos tienen todavía un sentido juvenil, miran adelante y son impulsados por el logos espermático, por la razón generadora.

A174

Juntan su hocico los perros
    En la oscuridad:
Se lamentan de los yerros
    De la Humanidad.

Absurda tarde. Macabra
    Mueca de dolor.
Se ha puesto el Pata de Cabra
    Mitra de Prior.

A175

Por la divina primavera
Me ha venido la ventolera

De hacer versos funambulescos.
—Un purista diría grotescos—.

A176

¡Tan! ¡Tan! ¡Tan! Canta el martillo.
El garrote alzando están,
Canta en el campo un cuclillo,
Y las estrellas se van
Al compás del estribillo
Con que repica el martillo:
¡Tan! ¡Tan! ¡Tan!

Un gitano vende churros
Al socaire de un corral,
Asoman flautistas burros
Las orejas al bardal,
Y en el corro de baturros
El gitano de los churros
Beatifica al criminal.

El reo espera en capilla,
Reza un clérigo en latín,

Llora una vela amarilla,
Y el sentenciado da din
A la amarilla tortilla
De yerbas. Fué a la capilla
La cena del cafetín.

Canta en la plaza el martillo,
El verdugo gana el pan,
Un paño enluta el banquillo.
Como el paño es catalán,
Se está volviendo amarillo
Al son que canta el martillo:
¡Tan! ¡Tan! ¡Tan!

A177

Una chica fea
—Que la tifoidea
Pelona dejó—
Baila en la guardilla,
Arrastra una silla,
Y ella es el gachó.
Sale al ventanuco
Y parece el cuco
Que habla en el reló.

La fuente de hierro,
En la fuente un perro
Lanzando su orín.

A178

Bajo la sensación del cloroformo
Ma hacen temblar con alarido interno
La luz de acuario de un jardín moderno,
Y el amarillo olor del yodoformo.
Cubista, futurista y estridente,
Por el caos febril de la modorra
Vuela la sensación, que al fin se borra,
Verde mosca, zumbándome en la frente.

Para mis nervios, con gozoso frío,
El arco de lunático violín.
De un sí bemol el transparente pío

Tiembla en la luz acuaria del jardín,
Y va mi barca por el ancho río
Que separa un confín de otro confín.

A179

Soñe laureles, no los espero,
Y tengo el alma libre de hiel.
¡No envidio nada, si no es dinero!
¡Ya no me llama ningún laurel!

Yo marcho solo con mis leones
Y la certeza de ser quien soy.
El Diablo escucha mis oraciones.
Canta mi pecho: ¡Mañana es hoy!

A180

¡Tengo rota la vida! En el combate
De tantos años ya mi aliento cede,
Y al orgulloso pensamiento abate
La idea de la muerte, que lo obsede.

Quisiera entrar en mí, vivir conmigo,
Poder hacer la cruz sobre mi frente.
Y sin saber de amigo ni enemigo,
Apartado, vivir devotamente.

¿Dónde la verde quiebra de la altura
Con rebaños y músicos pastores?
¿Dónde gozar de la visión tan pura
Qué hace hermanas las almas y las flores?
¿Dónde cavar en paz la sepultura
Y hacer místico pan con mis dolores?

A181

¡Todo hacia la muerte avanza
            De concierto,
Toda la vida es mudanza
            Hasta ser muerto!

A182

¿Por qué de la vida?
¿Qué fin truje a ella?
¿Qué senda perdida
Labré con mi huella?

¡Adiós ilusiones!
Ya logran mis años
Las quietas razones
De los desengaños.

Perecen las glorias,
Se apagan los días,
Quedan por memorias
Las cenizas frías.

A183

El Precepto del Padre Celestial, dictado a modo de castigo, tiene fiesta de Religión. La única fiesta de los nuevos tiempos, donde alumbra el sentido sagrado de las nuevas Humanidades. Un viento encendido de bíblicas intuiciones, estremece la conciencia de los hombres de buena voluntad. El génesis levanta sus místicas auroras sobre el aterido Occidente.
    ¡Aleluya! ¡Aleluya!

Los trabajadores del mundo celebran y confirman el sentido de la vida: La Ley del Esfuerzo Humano. El sentido religioso de los hombres vuelve a rodar en la teologal caverna con un eco de Eternidad. Parten el pan los trabajadores del mundo. Y tiene la armonía de las amonestaciones evangélicas, el aliento rugiente del bíblico castigo.

La Humanidad, en gozo de fiesta, está de rodillas ante el precepto del Padre Celestial.

¡Aleluya! ¡Aleluya!

A184

¿Qué es el arte? El Supremo juego. En cuanto el arte se propone fines utilitarios inmediatos, prácticos, en fin, pierde su excelencia. El arte es un juego y sus normas están dictadas por el numérico capricho, en el cual reside su gracia peculiar. Catorce versos dicen que es soneto, y el arte, por lo tanto, es forma.

¿Qué debemos hacer? Arte, no. No debemos hacer arte ahora porque jugar en los tiempos que corren es inmoral, es una canallada. Hay que lograr primero una justicia social.

A185

D. Facundo: . . . Apremia
    que os ponga en autos de algo que me importa.
    Me presento a un sillón de la Academia.
D. Bartolo: ¡Queréis ser inmortal en su retorta!
    Me parece muy bien. ¡Feliz día
    en que pueda abrazaros, compañero!
D. Facundo: ¿Vuestro voto?
D. Bartolo: Con él no decidía
    la elección. Otra vez dároslo espero.
    Se contraponen méritos muy grandes.
    ¡Don Santos Santos! ¡Santos de las Heras,
    que publicó los títulos de Flandes
    dados por los servicios en banderas!
    ¡Y el *Centón erudito,* que comenta
    cuántas veces en letras del *Quijote*
    puede leerse la palabra "venta"!
    . . . .
D. Facundo: Pues mentáis el *Quijote* en su alabanza,
    sabed que en esa octava maravilla
    los regüeldos conté de Sancho Panza
    y los saqué a la luz con bastardilla.
    ¿Quién dió las nuevas etimologías
    de "cadaver," de "antruejo," de "cicuta,"
    y al Carbo Data Vermis ironías
    primero tributó?
D. Bartolo: ¡Vos, sin disputa!
    No niego vuestros méritos. Esperas
    debéis tener, amigo Don Facundo.

A186

¡Me sobran méritos! Pero esa prensa miserable me boicotea. Odian mi rebeldía y odian mi talento. Para medrar hay que ser agradador de todos los Segismundos. ¡El Buey Apis me despide como a un criado! ¡La Academia me ignora! ¡Y soy el primer poeta de España! ¡El primero! ¡El primero! ¡Y ayuno! ¡Y no me humillo pidiendo limosna! ¡Y no me parte un rayo! ¡Yo soy el verdadero inmortal, y no esos cabrones del cotarro académico! ¡Muera Maura!

A187

Precisamente ahora está vacante el sillón de Don Benito el Garbancero.

A188

El indio en Méjico que España emancipó y a quien se concedieron,   después de la conquista, todos los derechos del hombre libre, ha perdido ahora su libertad y sufre una explotación peor que la de los esclavos.

A189

I

¡Adios te digo con tu gesto triste, indio mexicano!
¡Adios te digo, mano en la mano!

II

¡Indio mexicano, que la Encomienda tornó mendigo!
¡Indio mexicano!
¡Rebélate y quema las trojes del trigo!
¡Rebélate, hermano!

III

Rompe la cadena. Quebranta la peña. Y la adusta greña
sacuda el bronce de tu sien.
Como a Prometeo te vió el visionario, a las siete luces
del Tenebrario, bajo las arcadas de una nueva
Jerusalén.

IV

Indio mexicano,
Mano en la mano
Mi fé te digo.
Lo primero
Es colgar al Encomendero
Y después segar el trigo.
Indio mexicano,
Mano en la mano,
Dios por testigo.

A190

Pero advierto que me aparto del ánimo primero que me movía para escribirle. Ya usted adivina que es la revolución de México. Si he de ser franco le diré que esperaba ese intento de los latifundistas. No pueden hacerse revoluciones a medias. Los gachupines poseen el setenta por cien de la propiedad territorial: — Son el extracto de la barbarie ibera—. La tierra en manos de esos extranjeros es la más novica forma de poseer. Peor mil veces que las manos muertas. Nuestro México para acabar con las revoluciones tiene que nacionalizar la propiedad de la tierra, y al encomendero. Las noticias de los periódicos son harto confusas pero a través de este caos presiento el triunfo del Govierno Federal. El General Obregón está llamado a grandes cosas en América. Su valor, su ánimo sereno, su conocimiento del tablero militar, su intuitiva estrategia, y su buena estrella de pre-destinado, le aseguran el triunfo. A más que la revolución de México, es la revolu-ción latente en toda la América Latina. La revolución por la independencia, que no puede reducirse a un cambio de visorreyes, sino a la superación cultural de la raza india, a la plenitud de sus derechos, y a la expulsión de judíos y moriscos gachupines. Mejor, claro está, sería el degüellen.

A191

La obra civilizadora de España estaba representada en el espíritu de las leyes, en la imposición del idioma y en la creación de muchas ciudades . . . El español debe tener en América la nacionalidad del país en que se encuentre, lo mismo que los sudamericanos en España. . . . Soy partidario del reparto de tierras según el sistema de los soviets para satisfacer a los emigrados rusos que acompañaron al almirante Koltchak. Estos pasaron del Japón a México y se unieron a los proletarios mexicanos y españoles contra los latifundistas.

A192

Nunca he tenido por costumbre rectificar lo que me hayan hecho decir los periodistas. ¿Para qué? Aunque se desmientan las declaraciones, siempre hay lec-tores que creen que se han dicho y que por temor se rectifican. Lo mejor sería no recibir a ningún periodista, pero eso es una cobardía y yo afronto siempre el peligro. Me fío a la honradez profesional de quienes vienen a verme. Soy asequible a toda entrevista y no me puedo quejar. Por un disgusto que me haya llevado he tenido muchas satisfacciones. En general, los periodistas trasladan con discreción mis palabras. Pero, recuerdo que una vez en México, cierto periodista cubano y malintencionado me metió en un lío con la Argentina por unas declaraciones mías que interpretó torcidamente. No me gusta generalizar. Mi obra está llena de cuidado en este sentido. Hablé de la Argentina como un argentino más. Ni la Argentina, ni España, ni México, ni ninguna nación del mundo tiene una sola cara. Hay de todo como en la viña del Señor, bueno y malo. Conviene reoaltar lo bueno pero no está de más hablar de lo malo. . . . Pero aquellas declaraciones me valieron no sé cuantas cartas de protesta. Hasta el ministro plenipotenciario protestó.   No iba a rebajarme contestando a quien, sin preguntarme si eran ciertas mis palabras, se permitía el lujo de pretender discutir conmigo. . . . Menos mal que hay en los rectores de los pueblos un fondo moral indiscutible y ninguno de los sinceros amigos que había dejado pudieron creer en semejantes patrañas.

A193

Hermoso. . . Enorme. . . Desmesurado. De las cenizas de la Revolución resurge la Tradición. . . Chapean con azulejos las fachadas de los templos. . . La guerra es buena. . . Es una incubadora que al progreso acelera.

A194

Tras de la cubista aventura, Rivera se ha convencido de que no existe otra pintura que la de nuestro Goya y la de los italianos primitivos.

A195

La guerra de Melilla terminará cuando los tenientes lleguen a coroneles.

A196

Yo creo, señores, que la solución está en conseguir que Abd-el-Krim se case con la Infanta Isabel.

A197

Si aproveché unas páginas de las *Memorias* del caballero Casanova en mi *Sonata de primavera* fué para poner a prueba el ambiente de mi obra. Porque de no haber conseguido éste, la interpolación desentonaría terriblemente. Shakespeare puso en boca de su Coriolano discursos que tomó de historiadores de la Antigüedad, y el acierto de la tragedia se comprueba en que, lejos de rechazar tales textos ajenos, los exige. Pongan ustedes en cualquiera de los dramas históricos que ahora se estrenan palabras o documentos de la época y ya verán cómo les sientan.

A198

Los muertos deben sentir una emoción semejante al oír los responsos que aquí, en este mundo, les cantan. Yo sentía algo de necrológico leyendo este número de *La Pluma*. Sólo usted se encara con un hombre vivo y descubre su dolor y su drama. Pero los más cuentan historias de un tiempo tan lejano, que, de verdad, me parece un muerto aquel de quien hablan. Un muerto y un ageno [*sic*]. ¡Dios les haya perdonado!

A199

Harto oídos fueron los ricachos de aquella colonia por nuestros ministros de Estado. Consignados a los tales, salían de aquí los representantes deplomáticos, y no es un secreto el vergonzoso comercio que se intentaba reconociendo al gobierno del general Obregón. La Colonia Española esperaba, como prenda de gratitud, el pago de cuatrocientos millones de pesetas, en concepto de indemnizaciones. Se esperaba una violación de las leyes del país en pro de la Colonia Española. Un olvido del programa político al estilo de España. "Pero a pesar del reconocimiento, continuaron las confiscaciones"—escribe el anónimo articulista—, y añade: "¿Qué ha hecho el Gobierno de España entre tanto? Cursar notas, muchas notas". Eso ha hecho ciertamente. Esperaba que el conflicto en trámite con los Estados Unidos derribase al Gabinete del general Obregón. Los Gobiernos de España, sus vacuos diplomáticos y sus ricachos coloniales, todavía no han alcanzado que por encima de los latifundios de abarroteros y prestamistas están los lazos históricos de cultura, de lengua y de sangre.

La Colonia española de México, olvidada de toda obligación espiritual, ha conspirado durante este tiempo, de acuerdo con los petroleros yankis. Y aún cuando ahora, perdido el pleito alguno se rasgue las vestiduras y se arañe la cara, nadie podrá negar que ha sido imposición de aquellos trogloditas avarientos, la política de España en México.

Hora es ya de que nuestros diplomáticos logren una visión menos cicatera que la del emigrante que tiene un bochinche en América.

A200

Las últimas tardes septembrinas, ya otoñales, tardes verlenianas, de una larga y cadenciosa tristeza sensual y mística, mi amigo me leía las páginas de este libro. Los dos, en coloquio cordial al acaso de la lectura, íbamos comentándola. Eramos los dos a solas en el desvanillo donde yo me aislo para fumar la pipa y construir palacios. . . . Mi amigo leía con blanda cadencia y su voz acentuaba como un anhelo por gozar el momento inverosímil de la tarde, por transcender a vida espiritual el paisaje cristalino colmado de irrealidades y, sin embargo, existente, con una videncia angustiosa y fugaz, imbuída del sentimiento de la muerte.

A201

Recibí su carta conmovida y buena, enfermo en la cama, de la cual todavía no me levanto, aún cuando estoy, al parecer un poco mejorado. Mi mal es el que mató a nuestro pobre Nervo . . . Hace tiempo que sufro este achaque, pero nunca el ramalazo había sido tan fuerte. Pasa de un mes que estoy en la cama, aburrido, triste. Si me repongo, espero verle pronto en Madrid.

A202

Hablaremos de nuestro México.—Estos tiempos trabajaba en una novela americana. "Tirano Banderas." La novela de un tirano con rasgos del Doctor Francia, de Rosas, de Melgarejo, de López, y de don Porfirio. Una síntesis el héroe, y el lenguaje una suma de modismos americanos de todos los países de lengua española, desde el modo lépero al modo gaucho. La República de Santa Trinidad de Tierra Firme es un país imaginario, como esas cortes europeas que pinta en algún libro Abel Hermant. Para este libro me faltan datos, y usted podía darme algunos, querido Reyes. Frente al tirano presento y trazo la figura de un apóstol, con más de Savonarola que de Don Francisco Madero, aún cuando algo tiene de este Santo iluminado. ¿Dónde ver una vida de "El Bendito Don Pancho"? Trazo un gran cataclismo como el terremoto de Valparaíso, y una revolución social de los indios. Para esto último necesitaba algunas noticias de Teresa Utrera, la Santa del Ranchito de Cavora. Mi memoria ya no me sirve y quisiera refrescarla. ¿Hay algo escrito sobre la Santa?—Los libros que tiene para mí, puede mandármelos aquí, y si los acompaña una "Visión de Ana(h)uac" serán doblemente agradecidos.

A203

Con mil amores le enviaré este "Tirano Banderas" de que le hablaba en mi carta anterior.

A204

Desde hace un mes estoy en cama con un varetazo del riñón, orinando sangre. Hace dos días que sufro menos, y conversando por escrito quiero divertir el tedio y la tristeza. Si me repongo pronto, iré a Madrid. "Renacimiento" anda buscando quedárseme con los libros. Como usted sabe, yo tengo un contrato con esa gente para la publicación de mis libros. La jugada es no publicarlos y quedarse con ellos por una deuda. Estos días han puesto a la venta "Sonata de estío".

A205

De mí poco tengo que contarle. He recobrado un poco de salud. Trabajo en una novela americana de caudillaje y avaricia gachupinesca. Se titula *Tirano Banderas*. No es en diálogo, sino en una prosa expresiva y poco académica. Tiene, como todos mis libros, algo de libro de principiante, y, como siempre, procuro huir de la pedantería. Yo y mis personajes no sabemos que hay enciclopedias. Creo cada día con mayor fuerza que el hombre no se gobierna por sus ideas ni por su cultura. Imagino un fatalismo del medio, de la herencia y de las taras fisiológicas, siendo la conducta totalmente desprendida de los pensamientos. Y, en cambio, siendo los oscuros pensamientos motrices consecuencia de las fatalidades de medio, herencia y salud, sólo el orgullo del hombre le hace suponer que es un animal pensante.

A206

Me he cansado, y apenas tengo pulso para terminar. Aún estoy muy débil.

A207

El rey es un muñeco grotesco. Son muchos los que piensan que puede suscitarse algún desacuerdo entre Alfonso y Primo de Rivera. ¡De ningún modo! El Directorio se hizo para salvar al monarca. El beodo y el cretino se entienden perfectamente. Unamuno dice que Primo de Rivera es nuestro Bertoldo. ¡Quiá! ¡Ni eso! Es un borrachín de buen vino. La diferencia entre él y el siniestro Martínez Anido reside en que éste es gallego y el vino de Galicia no vale para nada. Primo tiene el carácter alegre, suele andar de juerga y sabe perder el equilibrio. No hace muchas noches, cayó, pesadamente, después de una mona. Se dijo que el general, en una noche de desvelo oficinesco, se había llevado una puerta por delante. En medio de todo, estimo a ese pillete. Sin quererlo ni saberlo está haciendo mucho bien al país. Lo combato por una razón de higiene social. Pero reconozco que los españoles debemos pedir que continúe en el poder. Empezó por apartar del rey a los partidos políticos. Dividió graciosamente el Ejército. Dilapida la hacienda de tal manera que en un día muy cercano la peseta rodará por el suelo desvalorizada en absoluto. Acabará con la industria catalana. ¡Qué se quede Primo de Rivera! ¿Saben ustedes cómo lo veo yo? Pues, ¡como un bastonero de baile popular! ¡Qué siga la danza, señores! Se equivocó de uniforme y vistió el militar. El y su Directorio llegaron al poder como las ratas cuando invaden un barco perdido. El Directorio roba abiertamente, no como los puritanos de antaño. Los tartufos robaron con todo disimulo. Ahora no se usan tantas vueltas en el despojo. Todo español tiene miedo hoy día porque resulta que todo español es dueño de cuatro pesetas y con ellas ha adquirido el miedo burgués. Por eso no reacciona. Pero los más miedosos son los que temen no puedan declararse independientes. Lo puede hacer Sánchez Guerra que no posee fortuna ni tiene cola de paja. Yo puedo gritar también porque no tengo nada. Todo mi haber consiste en esta capa que llevo puesta. No tengo una peseta. Como no tengo nada, soy como un anarquista. No concibo que se pueda ser anarquista de otra manera.

A208

Las pampas son un vasto océano de trigo donde nace el pan de la humanidad y donde se elabora el nuevo idioma español que romperá la cárcel hermética del castellano actual, que ha de hacerse más flexible, más vivo y más sonoro. El verbo de América será, quiéralo Dios, para el castellano lo que fueron los romances de las colonias romanas para el latin anquilosado del señor del mundo. ¡Pobres aquellos nuevos pueblos emancipados que no sepan renovar el verbo que les dió la metrópoli, y hacerse uno suyo a la medida de su alma y su necesidad! . . . Los idiomas no salen de las calles y los bulevares de las ciudades: en las ciudades solo nacen el *argot* de los canallas y las germanías; los idiomas, en cambio, nacen a pleno sol, en pleno campo, y son expresión del alma colectiva del pueblo. Las ciudades corrompen los idiomas, y solo el campo y la luz los conservan, los renuevan y los depuran.

A209

Hay una vida española que no conozco y que sería muy interesante novelar. Las

luchas sociales de Barcelona. El tipo del obrero que después de cenar tranquila-
mente coge la *star* y sale a por el patrono, obedece a un estado psicológico interesante para analizar, para estudiar.

A210

No admito que venga a mi conferencia ningún delegado. Yo no arrojo margaritas,
etc.

A211

Ricardo Baroja es el amado de las musas. Ninguna de las Nueve Hermanas le ha
negado su don. De haberse aplicado a las artes del diseño hubiera superado a los
mejores. Yo me lo imagino en una ciudad italiana, pintor en los días del Renacimiento. La rara condición para concebir y ejecutar con presteza, lo descubre genial-
mente dispuesto para las grandes pinturas murales. ¡Con qué paradójico humor
hubiera adoctrinado a sus discípulos, desde el andamio, y acogido a los duces, y
disertado con los cardenales! La gracia verbal, el humor franco, el placentero reír,
las fugas paradojales también son premios de Ricardo Baroja—amado de las musas,
que superando las hemoptisis románticas, va para viejo.

A212

Sé como el ruiseñor, que no mira a la tierra desde la rama verde donde canta.

A213

Rusia es el porvenir del mundo.

A214

Lo que he escrito antes de *Tirano Banderas* as musiquilla de violín . . . y mala
musiquilla de violín. *Tirano Banderas* es la primera obra que escribo. Mi labor
empieza ahora.

A215

Otra, primera de la serie que titulo *El ruedo ibérico*, se llama *La corte isabelina*.

A216

El ruedo ibérico no tendrá, a lo largo de sus varios volúmenes, protagonistas. Su gran
protagonista es el medio social, el ambiente. . . . Quiero llevar a la novela la
sensibilidad española, tal como se muestra en su reacción ante los hechos que
tienen una importancia. Para mi, la sensibilidad de un pueblo se refleja y se mide
por la forma de reaccionar ante esos hechos. Ver la reacción de la sensibilidad
española en aquel período tan interesante que va desde la Revolucíon, en el año 68,
hasta la muerte de Alfonso XII, en el año 85, es lo que me propongo en la nueva
novela.

A217

Todos son iguales. Cuando le llega su hora se destacan del fondo y adquieren la
máxima importancia. Ya sé que al lector le molesta que le abandonen el personaje
que ganó su primera simpatía, pero yo escribo la novela de un pueblo, en una
época, y no la de unos cuantos hombres. El gran protagonista de mi libro es el *Ruedo*

Ibérico. Los demás sólo sirven mientras su acción es definidora de un aspecto nacional. La calidad externa del suceso o la anécdota me tienen sin cuidado. Lo que me interesa es su calidad expresiva . . . La base de mis libros la forman estos elementos: la luz y la acción. A un pueblo se le puede conocer por el medio que lo engendra y por el medio que lo expresa. Al *Ruedo Ibérico* lo engendra la luz y lo expresa la acción.

Burlarme, burlarme de todo y de todos . . . La Verdad, la Justicia son las únicas cosas respetables. Este género de literatura satírica tiene una gran tradición. . . . La literatura satírica es una de las formas de la canción histórica que cae sobre los poderosos que no cumplieron con su deber.

Mi propósito en ella no es otro que hacer la historia de España desde la caída de Isabel II hasta la Restauración, y busco, más que el fabular novelesco, la sátira encubierta bajo ficciones casi de teatro.

A218

Releí a Góngora hace unos meses—el pasado verano—y me ha causado un efecto desolador, lo más alejado de todo respeto literario. ¡Inaguantable! De una frialdad, de un rebuscamiento de precepto. . . No soy capaz de decir una cosa por otra.

A219

Mis libros, en ediciones económicas, se venderán por millares; como se ha vendido *La guerra carlista*, publicada por la CIAP, a pesar de ser horrible la edición.

A220

¡Has estado magnífico! Es sencillamente ese tu toreo, en el que sacando chispas sublimes de tu miseria física, te fundes de tal forma con el toro, que no llega a saberse dónde acaba el hombre y dónde comienza la fiera. Sólo falta que un día, superándote en el sentido y en la calidad de tu toreo trágico, haciendo honor al fanatismo delirante que por ti tiene la afición, y sobrepasando los contornos de tu transfiguración humana hasta lo divino, te quedes quieto y en vez de rematar la suerte con un molinete, sea el toro quien la remate, clavándote un asta en el corazón. Así, en la estampa ya no podrán separarse nunca más toro y torero, como se separan cada tarde de toros, después de la mágica suerte de capa.

A221

Mi vicio predilecto es el café, donde perdí mi juventud y pierdo mi vida moliciosamente.

A222

Es un espiritu rígido, como buen alemán, y se ha traído clavados en la frente el 9 y el 8 y no hay manera de que comprenda las cosas. Yo le he preguntado, claro, que "qué cuarto era ése del 98" y por qué era yo un escritor del 98. Será del 98 el escritor que encontró en aquella fecha su definitiva expresión y la reputa a lo largo de los años, pero el escritor que cambia y se renueva y se transforma es del 1898 y del 1929.

A223

Los corresponsales extranjeros no podían creer que tuviéramos que hablar entre rejas.

A224

Era más serio que la vez anterior. Los agentes llevaban intenciones siniestras. Si hubiera sido un obrero, un desconocido, sólo Dios sabe lo que ocurre . . . Pero a mí no se me escamotea fácilmente.

A225

Está bien lo que dice ese Primo de Rivera, porque no sabe castellano. El ha querido decir que yo soy un ciudadano "estrafalario," y ha dicho "extravagante." Estravagante lo soy porque tiendo siempre a viajar fuera del camino por donde las gentes van.

A226

Hay allí jerarquías como en la llamada sociedad libre. La más poderosa la forman los estafadores. Suelen estar poco tiempo: los visitan sus abogados, depositan fianza y son puestos en libertad. La segunda los reos de sangre. Pasean por los patios como toreros por la calle de Sevilla. En tercer lugar, los presos políticos. Después los quincenarios y, finalmente, los presos por delitos sociales. . . . Entre estos últimos, se encuentra lo mejor de cada familia. Honradez, inteligencia, dignidad, cultura. Socialistas, comunistas, sindicalistas, las pocas grandes individualidades que quedan en España. Casi todos están en la quinta galería, la peor, la más malsana. Se les obliga a salir al patio que se abre hacia el Guadarrama. Un catarro es en esas condiciones el principio seguro e infalible de la tuberculosis. Los que salen quedan ya aniquilados para siempre. Había quien llevaba ocho meses en blanca. . . . Había en mi galería un médico rumano, ajeno por completo a la política. Pensaron que un médico rumano, por su profesión y por su nacionalidad, sólo podía haber venido a España a matar a la reina de Rumanía, y mientras ella estuvo aquí, lo tuvieron preso. . . . Al detenerlo se encontraban con él dos clientes: el señor Botella, un alicantino amigo suyo. Lo de la alquimia debió parecerles misterioso— ¿pacto con el diablo?—y los tres fueron encarcelados. . . . Gentes de todas clases: vendedores callejeros, escritores, periodistas. Desde los amigos circunstanciales que nos ofrecen periódicos en la acera, hasta las figuras más representativas de la aristocracia, de las ideas.

A227

Ni bomba, ni bala, ni cuerda
finarán tu vida canalla.
Morirás bajo una metralla
de mierda.

Y un gran gargajo nacional
te cubrirá como un sudario.
¡Cornudo! ¡Canalla real!
¡Quincenario!

A228

Yo me fuí, naturalmente, sin pasaporte. Nadie me molestó.

A229

La Academia de la Lengua es un centro social. Allí no deben ir, tal como está constituída, más que categorías sociales. Es una reunión de figuras decorativas.

¿Por qué, si no por eso, hay un obispo académico? La Academia de la Lengua no fué jamás albergue natural de escritores. Las excepciones confirman la regla . . . los escritores se quedaron ordinariamente fuera, y fueron muchos los de gran talento que murieron sin ingresar en ella. . . . También opino que la Academia es conveniente para los escritores de cierto y determinado tipo literario. Para mi, no. Yo no serviría para académico. ¿Qué haría yo en la Academia? Los académicos, apenas me vieran aparecer por allí, se llevarían un gran disgusto . . . Sería un intruso.

A230

Yo hallo mal que el señor Francos Rodríguez lance la candidatura del señor Kleiser. En la Academia está muy bien el señor Obispo. Pero el señor Kleiser no es Obispo. Un obispo es decorativo. El señor Kleiser, no obstante su acentuada significación clerical, no lo sería nunca.

A231

Tal vez yo consintiera en ser académico si los académicos tuvieran un vistoso uniforme que se pudiera lucir por ahí. ¡Qué gracioso sería entrar en cualquier sitio, y desde luego en la Academia, luciendo unas vestiduras recargadas de oro y bordados! . . . Tanto daría esto como ir diciendo: "¿No me véis? Soy inmortal. Mi uniforme lo dice." . . . Me conozco y los conozco. Por último, ¿es qué la Academia sirve siquiera para editar un diccionario? Ha necesitado una Editorial.

Chapter 9: Absurdity

A232

Hay tres modos de ver el mundo artística o estéticamente: de rodillas, en pie o levantado en el aire. Cuando se mira de rodillas—y ésta es la posición más antigua en literatura—, se da a los personajes, a los héroes, una condición superior a la condición humana, cuando menos a la condición del narrador o del poeta. Así Homero atribuye a sus héroes condiciones que en modo alguno tienen los hombres. Se crean, por decirlo así, seres superiores a la naturaleza humana: dioses, semidioses y héroes. Hay una segunda manera, que es mirar a los protagonistas novelescos como de nuestra propia naturaleza, como si fuesen nuestros hermanos, como si fuesen ellos nosotros mismos, como si fuera el personaje un desdoblamiento de nuestro yo, con nuestras mismas virtudes y nuestros mismos defectos. Esta es, indudablemente, la manera que más prospera. Esto es Shakespeare, todo Shakespeare. . . . Y hay otra tercer manera, que es mirar al mundo desde un plano superior, y considerar a los personajes de la trama como seres inferiores al autor, con un punto de ironía. Los dioses se convierten en personajes de sainete. Esta es una manera muy española, manera de demiurgo, que no se cree en modo alguno hecho del mismo barro que sus muñecos. Quevedo tiene esta manera. . . . Esta manera es ya definitiva en Goya. Y esta consideración es la que me movió a dar un cambio en mi literatura y a escribir los "esperpentos," el género literario que yo bautizo con el nombre de "esperpento."

A233

Hay que estudiar a los autores en sus tres maneras. Primera, el personaje es superior al autor. La manera del héroe. Homero que no es de sangre de dioses.

Segunda, al autor que se desdobla: Shakespeare. Sus personajes no son otra cosa sino desdoblamientos de su personalidad. Tercera, el autor es superior a sus personajes y los contempla como Dios a sus criaturas. Goya pintó a sus personajes como seres inferiores a él. Como Quevedo. Esto nace de la literatura picaresca. Los autores de estas novelas tenían mucho empeño en que no se les confundiese con sus personajes, a los que consideraban muy inferiores a ellos, y este espíritu persiste aún a traves de la literatura española, naturalmente. Yo considero tambíen a mis personajes inferiores a mí. Mi obra es un intento de lo que quise hacer.

A234

Los autores franceses se colocan siempre en éxtasis ante las peripecias del drama y las voces de los personajes. Divinizan sus héroes. Engendran dioses. Es el autor, en Francia, el primer vasallo de su prole. Exalta al protagonista y su drama por sobre lo más alto de los contornos humanos. Sirve a los héroes en el bien y en el mal como a divinidades extraordinarias. Los ingleses, obreros de corrección y sociabilidad, practican una literatura de club. El personaje de su obra se mueve dentro del círculo de sus amistades, sujeto a los derechos y a los deberes de los hombres de mundo. Al héroe lo inscribe en un círculo, le da carta de ciudadanía y le concede voto en los comicios electorales. A la hora de las exaltaciones, respetuoso de los intereses de clase, le otorga un título de par. El autor y el personaje viven el mismo protocolo de humanidad. El drama es un simple suceso social, apenas digno de una referencia en *The Times*. Otelo es un individuo de la familia que comete la incorrección de mostrarse exageradamente celoso. Los españoles nos colocamos siempre por encima del drama y de los intérpretes. Nos sabemos siempre moviendo a capricho los hilos de la farsa. Cervantes se siente superior a Don Quijote. Se burla un poco de él, se compadece, a veces, de sus dolores y locuras, le perdona sus arrebatos, y hasta le concede la gracia de una hora postrera de cordura para conducirlo, generoso, a las puertas del cielo. Los autores españoles, juvenilmente endiosados, gustamos de salpicar con un poco de dolor la existencia que creamos. Tenemos áspera la paternidad. Por capricho y por fuerza. Porque nos asiste la indignación de lo que vemos ocurrir fatalmente a nuestros pies. España es un vasto escenario elegido por la tragedia. Siempre hay una hora dramática en España; un drama superior a las facultades de los intérpretes. Estos, monigotes de cartón, sin idealidad y sin coraje, nos parecen ridículos en sus arreos de héroes. Gesticulan con torpeza de cómicos de la legua las situaciones más sublimemente trágicas. Don Quijote ha de encarnarse en un Quijote cualquiera. Los médicos diagnostican de fisiología ambigua los arrestos dramáticos de Don Juan. Todo nuestro censo de población no vale lo que una pandilla de comiquillos empecinados en representar el drama genial de la vida española. El resultado, naturalmente, es un esperpento.

A235

Querido Darío:
    Vengo a verle después de haber estado en casa de nuestro pobre Alejandro Sawa. He llorado delante del muerto, por él, por mí y por todos los pobres poetas. Yo no puedo hacer nada; usted tampoco, pero si nos juntamos unos cuantos algo podríamos hacer. Alejandro deja un libro inédito. Lo mejor que ha escrito. Un diario de esperanzas y tribulaciones. El fracaso de todos sus intentos para publicarlo y una carta donde le retiraban una colaboración de sesenta pesetas que tenía en *El Liberal*, le volvieron loco en los últimos días. Una locura desesperada. Quería matarse. Tuvo el final de un rey de tragedia: loco, ciego y furioso.

A236

La tragedia nuestra no es tragedia . . . El Esperpento. . . . El esperpentismo lo ha
inventado Goya. Los héroes clásicos han ido a pasearse en el callejón del Gato. . . .
Los héroes clásicos reflejados en los espejos cóncavos dan del Esperpento. El sentido trágico de la vida española sólo puede darse con una estética sistemáticamente
deformada. . . . España es una deformación grotesca de la civilización europea. . . .
Las imágenes más bellas en un espejo cóncavo, son absurdas. . . . La deformación
deja de serlo cuando está sujeta a una matemática perfecta. Mi estética actual es
transformar con matemática de espejo cóncavo, las normas clásicas. . . . Defor-
memos la expresión en el mismo espejo que nos deforma las caras, y toda la vida
miserable de España.

A237

Señor: Tengo el honor de enviaros este libro, estilización del reinado de vuestra
abuela Doña Isabel II, y hago votos porque el vuestro no sugiera la misma estilización a los poetas del porvenir.

A238

También a mí me ha preocupado la carantoña del Diablo frente al Pecador. La
verdad es que tenía otra idea de las risas infernales; había pensado siempre que
fuesen de desprecio, de un supremo desprecio, y no . . . No crea usted en la
realidad de ese Diablo que se interesa por el sainete humano, y se divierte como un
tendero. Las lágrimas y la risa nacen de la contemplación de cosas parejas a
nosotros mismos, y el diablo es de naturaleza angélica. . . . Los sentimentales que
en los toros se duelen de la agonía de los caballos, son incapaces para la emoción
estética de la lidia: Su sensibilidad se revela pareja de la sensibilidad equina, y por
caso de cerebración inconsciente, llegan a suponer para ellos una suerte igual a la
de aquellos rocines destripados. . . . Así es. Y paralelamente ocurre lo mismo con
las cosas que nos regocijan: Reservamos nuestras burlas para aquello que nos es
semejante. . . . Mi estética es una superación del dolor y de la risa, como deben ser
las conversaciones de los muertos, al contarse historias de los vivos. . . . Todo
nuestro arte nace de saber que un día pasaremos: Ese saber iguala a los hombres
mucho más que la Revolución Francesa. . . . Yo quisiera ver este mundo con la
perspectiva de la otra ribera. Soy como aquel mi pariente que . . . una vez, al
preguntarle el cacique, qué deseaba ser, contestó: Yo, difunto.

A239

Indudablemente la comprensión de este humor y esta moral, no es de tradición
castellana. Es portuguesa y cántabra, y tal vez de la montaña de Cataluña. Las otras
regiones, literariamente, no saben nada de estas burlas de cornudos, y este donoso
buen sentido, tan contrario al honor teatral y africano de Castilla. Ese tabanque de
muñecos sobre la espalda de un viejo prosero, para mí, es más sugestivo que todo
el retórico teatro español.

A240

La crueldad y el dogmatismo del drama español, solamente se encuentra en la
palabra. La crueldad sespiriana es magnifica, porque es ciega, con la grandeza de
las fuerzas naturales. Shakespeare es violento, pero no dogmático. La crueldad
española, tiene toda la bárbara liturgia de los Autos de Fe. Es fría y antipática. Nada
más lejos de la furia ciega de los elementos, que Torquemada: Es una furia

escolástica. Si nuestro teatro tuviese el temblor de las fiestas de toros, sería magníf-ico: Si hubiese sabido transportar esa violencia estética, sería un teatro heroico como la Ilíada. A falta de eso, tiene toda la antipatía de los códigos, desde la Constitución a la Gramática.

A241

Shakespeare rima con el latido de su corazón, el corazón de Otelo: Se desdobla en los celos del Moro: Creador y criatura son del mismo barro humano. En tanto ese Bululú, ni un solo momento deja considerarse superior por naturaleza, a los muñecos de su tabanque. Tiene una dignidad demiúrgica.

A242

La vida—sus hechos, sus tristezas, sus amores—es siempre la misma, fatalmente. Lo que cambia son los personajes, los protagonistas de esa vida. Antes esos papeles los desempeñaban dioses y héroes. Hoy . . . bueno, ¿para qué vamos a hablar? Antes, el destino cargaba sobre los hombros—altivez y dolor—de Edipo o de Medea. Hoy, ese destino el es mismo, la misma su fatalidad, la misma su grandeza, el mismo su dolor . . . Pero los hombros que lo sostienen han cambiado. Las acciones, las inquietudes, las coronas, son las de ayer y las de siempre. Los hombres son distintos, minúsculos para sostener ese gran peso. De ahí nace el contraste, la desproporción, lo ridículo. *En Los cuernos de don Friolera*, el dolor de éste es el mismo de Otelo, y, sin embargo, no tiene su grandeza. La ceguera es bella y noble en Homero. Pero, en *Luces de bohemia* esa misma ceguera es triste y lament-able porque se trata de un poeta bohemio, de Máximo Estrella.

A243

Yo escribo en forma escénica, dialogada, casi siempre. Pero no me preocupa que las obras puedan ser o no representadas más adelante. Escribo de esta manera porque me gusta mucho, porque me parece que es la forma literaria mejor, más serena, y más *impasible* de conducir la acción. Amo la impasibilidad en el arte. Quiero que mis personaje se presenten ellos solos y sean en todo momento ellos sin el commen-tario, sin la explicación del autor. Que todo lo sea la acción misma.

A244

Señor don Juan Fernández.

Padece usted, señor mío, un lamentable error al afirmar en el HERALDO de ayer haber dado respuesta a dos cartas mías, donde le decía no excusarse hacerse responsable de que El Cántaro Roto representase una sola vez la obra de Anatole France *El hombre que casó con mujer muda*. Crea usted que de haber llegado a mis manos la respuesta de usted, yo hubiera sentido un enorme regocijo haciéndola pública. En todo caso, espero que usted será tan amable que no esquive volver a repetir esa carta, y yo le prometo hacerla conocer inmediatamente a los lectores del HERALDO.

Le saluda,
Valle-Inclán.
5 de enero de 1927.

A245

Voy a publicar el próximo mes de marzo *Martes de carnaval*, que es una obra contra las dictaduras y el militarismo. Pensaba publicarla en el mes de mayo, pues entonces, dadas las condiciones climatológicas de Madrid, La Cárcel Modelo, cuyo interior conozco por mis permanencias en ella, está confortable. Sin embargo, a pesar de los fríos reinantes, no retrasaré la salida, porque considero que es un momento apropiado. Ya que los jóvenes callan, es cuestión de que lo hagan los viejos por ellos.

A246

Contra todo. Porque todo era allí desastroso. Había que afirmar el derecho de opinar airosamente, libremente frente a las opiniones contrarias y ruidosas de los demás; frente al deseo de hacer del Fontalba un sitio acotado, donde no se puede oír la rebeldía de una voz sincera, de una voz que no quiere unirse al asentimiento común, expreso o tácito. En realidad, lo que hice fué adelantarme a lo que luego iba a hacer el público: rechazar la obra. Dije en alta voz lo que pensaban muchos y lo que luego, de un modo u otro, acabaron por decir todos. Yo, más inteligente, o más experto, o más sincero, vi en el segundo acto lo que el público expresó al final de la obra.

A247

Hay no sólo el derecho de opinar, sino el deber de opinar lealmente, desnudamente. ¿Quién puede quitar ese derecho al señor que ha comprado su localidad? Hay que ir contra ese público mercenario que quiere imponer sus aplausos comprados—comprados de un modo u otro—, al juicio libre y a la independencia artística. Claro que el opinar de esta forma tiene su riesgo. Esa es la razón de la gran falta de opiniones y del silencio complaciente que hay en la vida teatral. Pero ese riesgo pueden tenerlo los que viven del teatro: los Quintero, los Marquina, los Fernández Ardavín . . . Yo, no. . . . Hay que hablar, opinar y protestar. Hay que sentirse siempre joven; el culto al silencio y a la prudencia podrá ser cómodo, pero no es bello ni es sincero. Los españoles sienten demasiado esa devoción del silencio, ese miedo del juicio en alta voz . . . por mi autoridad y prestigio, juzgué que era mi deber intervenir, mi autoridad es para eso . . . Si alguna obligación tengo yo, es ésa: la de opinar, la de advertir al público cuando se trate de algo que no debe ser, la de decirle si una cosa es buena o no, porque el público se desconcierta y hay que decirle la verdad.

A248

Y se desconcierta también ante una obra que no es su mundo habitual, que no es clara y sonriente. Porque, ante los personajes de Arniches—un guarda o una concinera—, todo el mundo se da cuenta si aquel lenguaje está bien o no; porque se trata de un mundo habitual, porque hay un guarda en cada esquina y una cocinera en cada casa. Pero en una obra en que aparecen y hablan fantasmas, ¿cómo va a saber el público—que no tiene en su casa fantasmas familiares—si aquel lenguaje de los espectros está bien o no? Y luego, ante una obra en verso, la gente tampoco sabe a punto fijo si los versos están bien o no . . . Le basta con que suenen bien. ¡Y eso no! Hay que opinar. ¡Y hay que decírselo a la gente.

A249

Mi querido amigo:
Me pide usted que tome parte en la encuesta de *La Voz* y lo haría con la mayor voluntad si fuese autor dramático. Sin duda me ha colocado usted en ese número

por haber escrito algunas obras en diálogo. Pero observe usted que las he publicado siempre con acotaciones que bastasen a explicarlas por la lectura, sin intervención de histriones. Si alguna de estas obras ha sido representada, yo le he dado tan poca importancia, que en ningún momento he creído que debía hacer memoria del lamentable accidente, recordando en la edición el reparto de personajes y la fecha de la ejecución. Me declaro, pues, completamente ajeno al teatro y a sus afanes, sus medios y sus glorias.

A250

¿Para el teatro? No. Yo no he escrito, escribo ni escribiré nunca para el teatro. Me gusta mucho el diálogo, y lo demuestro en mis novelas. Y me gusta, claro es, el teatro, y he hecho teatro, procurando vencer todas las dificultades inherentes al género. He hecho teatro tomando por maestro a Shakespeare. Pero no he escrito nunca ni escribiré para los cómicos españoles. . . . Los cómicos de España no saben todavía hablar. Balbucean. Y mientras no haya alguno que sepa hablar, me parece una tontería escribir para ellos. Es ponerse a nivel de los analfabetos.

A251

Yo creo que mi teatro es perfectamente representable. . . . Yo creo que mis "esperpentos," por lo mismo que tienen una cosa de farsa popular entre lo trágico y lo grotesco, lo harían a perfección nuestros actores . . . Yo me imagino a Bonafé, por ejemplo, representando *Luces de bohemia*.

A252

Me acaban de escribir desde la U.R.S.S. pidiendo autorización para traducir al ruso mis obras. La Editorial del Estado quiere publicar *Tirano Banderas* y *La Corte de los Milagros*. No sé como van a arreglarse. Me parecen intraducibles . . . También me invitan al estreno de *La reina castiza*, *Luces de bohemia* y *Los cuernos de don Friolera* . . . Es posible que vaya. Veré en ruso lo que no he podido ver representado en español.

Chapter 10: Republic

A253

En esta hora de mengua nacional su alta categoría literaria queda oscurecida por sus virtudes ciudadanas, y se me aparece como el único Grande de España. Don Miguel de Unamuno, Prior de Iberia: ¡Salud!

A254

Berenguer, animado de los mejores deseos, no cuenta con colaboradores en el ejército, y los elementos civiles que quieren colaborar con él son demasiado sospechosos. Mientras va orientándose, cosa que no conseguirá, repite que sólo se propone facilitar la restauración de la legalidad. Pero, ¿cómo? Sin libertad no se puede hacer nada y con élla el régimen no dura una semana.

A255

Allí es República, como debiera serlo la España. En las Repúblicas manda el pueblo, usted y yo, compadre.

A256

Alfonso, ten pestaña
y ahueca el ala,
que la cosa en España

se pone mala.
¡No sea que
el pueblo soberano
te dé mulé!

A257

¡Alzate, pueblo español
y cuélgale de un farol!
¡Qué baile la tarantela
con toda su parentela!
Desde la reina británica
a la Eulalia, cabra hispánica.
Desde el príncipe hemofílico
hasta Fernando el amílico
Desde el infante zancudo,
estúpido y sordomudo,
hasta la infanta Isabel
. . . de cartel.
¡Qué todos saquen al sol
la lengua, pueblo español!

A258

¿Cómo es posible que se hablara siquiera de semejante cosa? ¿Quién era él para
abdicar en una persona determinada, si la facultad de nombrar sucesor y regente
sólo corresponde a las Cortes? Un rey puede en cualquier momento renunciar;
abdicar, no. Se renunciá . . . Se abdica en . . . Este "en" significa que ha de elegirse
el heredero del poder real, y esto no puede hacerlo nunca un monarca constitucio-
nal sin que las Cortes se lo autoricen. Muchas y gravísimas infracciones de la
Constitución había cometido don Alfonso; esa, la de la abdicación en el infante . . .
hubiera sido la más enorme de todas.

A259

Yo no diré que el ideal de la revolución española fuera el de una suave y pacífica
transformación del régime. Creo, por el contrario, que no hay gran revolución sin
guerra en las fronteras. Así fué la Revolución Francesa y así la de Rusia. Una
revolución como la que yo sueño hubiera provocado, quizá, la llegada de cien mil
hijos de San Luis por el Norte y de cien mil hijos de San Jorge por el Sur. Tend-
ríamos barcos extranjeros en todos los puertos. No se habría permitido a don
Alfonso salir de España. Al cabo, esa revolución sería la más fecunda y acaso al
calor de ella pudiéramos crear la unidad nacional. Pero la realidad es que España
eligió tácticas más normales y prudentes quizá, y hay que seguirlas hasta el fin.
Nada más funesto que cambiar ahora de táctica. Sigamos, pues, como hemos
empezado. Y para que esa normalidad no se interrumpa, entreguemos el Gobierno
de la República a los grandes republicanos históricos.

A260

La República debe ser servida por los hombres que puedan servirla. Es cuestión de hombres. Creo que lo más urgente, lo que inmediatamente debe preocuparnos es hacer la República. La República no está hecha todavía. Vivimos en período de interinatura. España tiene necesidad apremiante de construir la República seriamente. Y para ello hay que elegir los hombres que deben y pueden asumir esa responsabilidad. ¿Cuáles son? ¿Acaso los republicanos que antes sirvieron a la Monarquía y que en ese servicio fracasaron? Si esos hombres no supieron gobernar victoriosamente en condiciones mucho más favorables que las actuales, o sea dentro del cuadro político de un régimen secular, ¿qué confianza podrán inspirar al pueblo en estas horas en que hay que crear toda una nueva España?

A261

Hay que pensar por hoy en ese primer gran Gobierno, que será el que consolide la República. Cuando llegue ese día habrán de asumir el Poder los hombres que tengan una historia justificativa: los hombres que puedan presentar una vida de sacrificio, de fe y de esperanza en el ideal de la República. Hay que reconocer en el señor Alcalá Zamora una gran elevación de miras, una noble capacidad de reaccionar irreprochablemente ante los estímulos de carácter ético; se ha entregado dignamente a un ideal. Pero eso no basta . . . Allá, en las alturas de la Presidencia de la República, donde se ejercen funciones de poder moderador, estará bien el señor Alcalá Zamora. Para la jefatura del Gobierno necesitará España otros hombres, esos hombres que yo digo tienen la autoridad de su historia.

A262

Por eliminación habremos de convenir en que todas las condiciones de un jefe de Gobierno (del primer Gobierno republicano) se hallan presente en don Alejandro Lerroux. No sólo por eliminación, sino además por elección. Es el hombre que puede dirigirse al pueblo . . . y el pueblo tendrá confianza en hombres así, porque la historia les da la autoridad necesaria . . . don Alejandro Lerroux es el hombre que desde la juventud ha vivido acaudillando muchedumbres. Ello le otorgó una verdadera maestría en el conocimiento del pueblo, en la adivinación de sus deseos y hasta en la interpretación de sus instintos. Le hizo, en fin, governante. Todo, todo hace pensar que Lerroux es el hombre, el único hombre indicado para presidir el primer Gobierno de la República. Yo, alejado de toda política, hablo así porque me lo inspira un vasto sentimiento de patriotismo. Nada he perseguido ni nada persigo en el orden personal de la política. Saben cuantos me conocen que mi opinión es siempre absolutamente desinteresada. Asisto al espectáculo republicano como un observador profundamente atento, y mi examen de hombres y de cosas de España en este momento me dicen que hay que poner el Gobierno de la nación en manos de don Alejandro Lerroux y de sus amigos políticos. De sus amigos políticos, de sus compañeros de ideal, entre los que figura el ministro que ha realizado una labor más extraordinaria y trascendente: el ministro de la Guerra, don Manuel Azaña. ¡Esos son los hombres del primer gobierno! Entiendo que todos haríamos obra patriótica rodeando, fortaleciendo y alentando a don Alejandro Lerroux.

A263

México es acaso uno de los países más grandes del mundo. Sin duda, el más grande de América. Es una República de bronce, la que más se parece a Rusia. En México, los hombres blancos, Madero y Obregón, lucharon heróicamente por la redención del indio, borrando algunas viejas leyes hereditarias que le denigraban y envilecían. España envíá México a su primer embajador, después de haber hecho una asombrosa revolución genuinamente española. Y hace esto después de arrojar al último de los Borbones, al que no se le echa por rey sino por ladrón. España ha hecho la revolución que hacen los hombres de bien contra los ladrones. Y ésta es la representación que se envíá México, que ha hecho otra gran revolución: la de redimir al indio.

A264

Creo que me incluyeron en una candidatura. No lo sé muy bien, porque no he ido a Galicia en esta temporada ni me he tomado la menor molestia para ser diputado.

A265

En una provincia como la de Pontevedra, la más pequeña de España, y tan nutrida de carreteras y ferrocarriles, aún no se ha terminado el escrutinio. La explicación es ésta: el caciquismo tiene actas firmadas y con el número de electores en blanco, y pone el que le da la gana, siempre superior al del escrutinio desfavorable de algunas mesas. Hay otros hechos elocuentísimos. Lerroux alcanzó 2.000 votes en La Coruña, y un cunero, que fué primero diputado gassetista, luego albista, y ahora creo que republicano autónome, ha obtenido 12.000. Para terminar de contar iniquidades, sepan que han salido cuatro monárquicos que ni en los tiempos de la Monarquía lo consiguieron. . . . Sólo un pueblo entregado al más bajo de los caciquismos puede dar el ejemplo que en esta hora ha dado Galicia. Mi Galicia se ha tumbado dócil a los deseos del nuevo amo, que es el de siempre: el cacique sin escrúpulos. . . . Creo que hay que anular las elecciones de las cuatro provincias. Dar satisfacción al pueblo, que es muy superior, a sus caciques, y con esta ejemplaridad, declarando nulas tan soeces maniobras, los hombres honrados de Galicia sabrán que su voto no puede ser anulado por la influencia ministerial, y el prestigio racial de mi tierra, últimamente evidenciado con la protesta a los hombres de la Dictadura, que fueron a hacer propaganda electoral de las Cortes, que no sé a efecto, recibiría un aliento . . . Galicia debe reconstruir la personalidad gallega federalmente, sin pretender más, pero tampoco menos que Cataluña. Y como Cataluña, abogar por que Galicia borre los límites provinciales de la región.

A266

Mi querido y admirado Sr. Tenreiro:
   Publica usted en *El Sol* unas lineas por las que me siento aludido, y a las cuales me obligan a responder fueros de la verdad y la justicia. Intenta usted temerariamente negar los atropellos de las elecciones gallegas y oculta usted su condición de diputado que a tales atropellos debe el acta. Habla usted de "los que simulan una santa indignación cuando su ira procede justamente de que no hayan triunfado." Por ser yo, Sr. Tenreiro, quien ha de impugnar en la Comisión de Actas las elecciones de La Coruña debió usted haber sido más comedido. Yo no soy, Sr. Tenreiro, un fariseo simulador de sanidades ni de indignadas protestas. Las elecciones gallegas son una afrenta para todo hombre honesto. Yo he sido, como usted, candidato por La Coruña, pero con notable diferencia en la conducta. En tanto usted se trasladaba a las tierras gallegas para intrigar, en contubernio con los viejos caciques, yo permanecía en Madrid. Y cuando fuí requerido para la propaganda electoral, supe negarme y no rogar el voto a ningún amigo, con ser tantos los que tengo en aquellas tierras. Cierto que mi conducta no puede ser una norma para usted y sus

compañeros. Yo he podido responder a los que me llamaban para la propaganda electoral: Notorio es mi nombre, notoria mi vida clara y significada de trabajos, de renuncia y pobreza. Si Galicia lo ignora no es ocasión de que lo aprenda. Pero la respuesta que en mí es mesura y dignidad, en usted y sus compañeros sería desaforada jactancia. Señor Tenreiro: representaciones como la que usted ha obtenido, cuando no saben renunciarse, son una deshonra.

A267

Mi querido y admirado Sr. Tenreiro:

Afirma usted que su persona y la de sus cómplices en el amaño electorero coruñés, a nadie ceden en hombría de bien, nobleza y dignidad. La afirmación la hace el más interesado en ella, y mi commentario sólo puede ser una sonrisa. Hombría de bien, nobleza y dignidad se acreditan por las obras. Las mías son bien notorias. Sin duda usted y sus cómplices podrán decir lo mismo, y la arrogante afirmación de usted me lo hace presumir. Pero mi erudición es tan corta que las desconozco. Yo he dado a Galicia una categoría estética—la máxima—y no le he pedido nada, ni le he rendido una adulación. Usted, señor Tenreiro, sin haber alcanzado lo primero, le ha pedido un acta y la ha logrado por caminos que yo no seguiré jamás. Esta es la diferencia ética que existe entre usted y yo, Sr. Tenreiro.

A268

Y es absurdo, ridículamente absurdo, que alguien haya pensado en una solución socialista . . . Y en ese círculo vicioso del absurdo, es más absurdo aún que se piense en un Gobierno de Largo Caballero. ¡Sería el colmo! Aparte las virtudes que adornen a Largo Caballero, no es posible olvidar que Largo Caballero actúa y actuará—eso es indivisible en su persona—como secretario de la U.G.T. . . . ¡Los socialistas! . . . Conviene advertir que el Partido Socialista se llama Partido Socialista Obrero. ¡No hay que olvidarlo! Y no hay que olvidarlo porque el tal partido representa una casta; una casta lo mismo de odiosa que la casta eclesiástica o la militar. . . . Lo que más me indigna es esa pobre gente que se vanagloria del título de obrero intelectual. No comprendo. . . ¿Qué es eso? Ahora ruedan por ahí tres tópicos horribles: el feminismo, el obrerismo y el americanismo. A mí se me subleva la sangre cuando oigo lo de obrero intelectual. ¡Qué cosas! El intelectual no puede ser obrero. A no ser que sea un faquín a sueldo de periódico donde encuentran tan dispares los conceptos de creación y de ejecución, que no hay modo de unirlos.

A269

Hay que integrar el espíritu peninsular como fue concebido por los romanos. Es lo acertado. Dividir la Península en cuatro departamentos: Cantabria, Bética, Tarraconense y Lusitania. . . . En la Península sólo hay cuatro grandes ciudades: Bilbao, que es Cantabria; Barcelona, que es la Terraconense; Sevilla, que es la Bética, y Lisboa, que es la Lusitania. Cada gran ciudad a un mar.

A270

El problema de Galicia es completamente opuesto al de Cataluña, y, por consiguiente, debe ser resuelto con un estatuto distinto, no mediterráneo, sino atlántico. Cataluña tiene necesidad de un arancel que favorezca su industria, y Galicia necesita la creación de un puerto franco en Vigo y la supresión de todo arancel. Todo lo que Galicia produce (hombres, salazones, etc.) lo manda al extranjero. Cataluña, no. De esto se deduce que Galicia, el problema de Galicia, es opuesto al de Cataluña. El problema catalán dejará de ser problema cuando deje de ser dual y se convierta en plural, o sea cuando no esté limitado a Madrid y a Cataluña exclusivamente. Concretado: de un tercero en discordia surgirá la concordia. Por eso soy federal. Nadie que conozca la Historia española dejará de serlo, porque España es, historicamente considerada, una federación de hecho, donde hay regiones, como Navarra, de las que debían tomar ejemplo todas las demás. Navarra es única en la Historia, no ya de España, sino de todo el mundo. Ninguna región se puede comparar con el antiguo reino navarro, que a través de los siglos ha conservado su independencia, su personalidad y su vida próspera y feliz, sin pedirle nada a nadie ni contar con protección oficial alguna. Y eso que Navarra no tiene mar y cuenta con poquísimas minas. Pero Navarra es Navarra y tiene la conciencia histórica que les falta a las demás regiones. . . . Galicia tiene también la conciencia de su personalidad, tan amplia, tan desconocida; esa personalidad que raras veces se ha reflejado aquí, no por mala intención sino por desconocimiento de su carácter y su verdadero espíritu.

A271

Los países se semejan a los animales rumiantes. Han de masticar bien para digerir mejor. Por eso, soy partidario del Senado. El Congreso de los Diputados hace las leyes que es como una primera masticación, luego pasan al Senado que es una segunda masticación. Así se digieren perfectamente las nuevas reformas y no puede haber indigestiones.

A272

San Pablo dió un gran paso en pro de la dignificación de la mujer; pero quedaba otro gran paso y ése lo ha dado la República Española. San Pablo, en su famosa Epístola había dejado a la mujer—por olvido, sin duda—fuera del Censo Electoral. . . . Para mi, lo más interesante sería el voto proporcional, según la modalidad del matrimonio. El matrimonio perfecto, con derecho a cuatro votos, y el imperfecto, o sea el indeseable, sólo con derecho a uno: el del marido.

A273

¡Las mujeres! A las pobres se las puede hacer únicamente la justicia de la conocida frase de Schopenhauer. ¡Y ahora ya ni siquiera tienen los cabellos largos! En la presente civilización no tienen que hacer nada las mujeres.

A274

¡Otro asunto sin importancia! Los jesuitas cumplieron su destino. Es como la Orden del Temple, que acabó con la Edad Media.

A275

La revolución no tuvo nunca hombres. Es un absurdo decir que en España no hay hombres para la revolución. La revolución es vida, y, por tanto, crea lo que le hace falta. Aquí tenemos bien palmario el ejemplo de Azaña. Hace seis meses sólo le conocian los amigos. En un Gobierno heterogéneo, colmado de conflictos interiores, supo afirmarse y erguirse con la máxima autoridad. Azaña tenía una preparación y muchas condiciones de genialidad. Yo no digo que en seis meses se creen los hombres que se necesiten; pero en un año o dos no hay duda de que España los contará por legiones.

A276

Los socialistas son, por ahora, un partido de clase, una organización de defensa obrera. La evolución les llevará a convertirse en un gran partido de gobierno nacional, de gobierno no sólo para los obreros, sino para España entera.

A277

Lo que no se puede hacer es seguir pensando a lo Lerroux: en reincorporar a esos muertos putrefactos de Alba y de don Melquiades. Pero, ¿se ha creído Lerroux que en España se han agotado las matrices que suelen producir tal clase de esperpentos?

A278

En España hay que hacer la revolución con la Dictadura. Se impone. Y no como la del pobre Primo, sino como la de Lenín. Cuando Carlos III quería adecentar Madrid, que era una letrina, justificaba los alborotos de la plebe con una frase: Los pueblos lloran como los niño cuando se les quiere lavar el rostro. La dignidad no se adquiere; se impone. Los pueblos esclavos la aceptan a latigazos. Quienes se hallan acostumbrados a estar de rodillas se les hace muy difícil ponerse en pie. . . . En las dictaduras, los hombres no son necesarios, lo que manda es el concepto y no el hombre.

A279

A mí lo que me importa es el héroe. Sin héroes no hay historia. Las grandes cosas las hacen los hombres superiores y no las masas gregarias. . . . Lo que importa es el hombre que tiene afan de poder en el amor, en la política, en la religión, en el mundo. Y ese hombre da igual que se llame Lenín que don Quijote, el marqués de Bradomín que Cristóbal Colón.

A280

Convertir lo que fueron Reales Sitios en asilos, cantinas escolares, reformatorios y hospicios constituiría una barbaridad sólo comparable con la que se cometió en tiempos de Mendizábal, transformando las iglesias en cuarteles. Si los palacios están llamados a convertirse en instituciones de caridad, mi ánimo se consterna, porque esto me parece un utilitarismo más repugnante que la furia destructora de Atila.

A281

El llamado Museo de Aranjuez es un lamentable hacinamiento de muebles y cuadros de muy diversa valoración artística. Los hay buenos, estimables y del más sórdido adocenamiento. Algunos cuadros muy señalados han ido a decorar otros palacios; tal acontece con el "Carro de Eros" y las "Tentaciones de San Antonio," de Jerónimo de Bosch. No es menos lamentable el traslado al Palacio de Madrid de la lámpara que decoraba el salón de Porcelanas. Pieza única y de imposible sustitución en aquel artístico conjunto, muestra la más significada de lo que fué la cerámica nacional. El que suscribe interesa la sensibilidad estética de V.E. para alcanzar la devolución de esa lámpara. . . . El que fué Palacio Real de Aranjuez no tiene ni el más rudimentario servicio de incendios. El que suscribe, adoctrinado por lo ocurrido en el Palacio de la Granja y por un conato de incendio iniciado no hace mucho en la Casa del Labrador, y, finalmente, por las ruinas que aún humean de la Universidad de Valencia, expone el hecho a la alta consideración de V.E. La responsabilidad del que suscribe, al silenciarlo, sería tanto mayor cuanto que las obras para dotar al Museo de un oportuno servicio de incendios son de fácil ejecución y moderado costo. Tenga en cuenta V.E. que el Tajo lame los muros de Palacio. Y no es menor el riesgo que corre la Casa del Labrador. Para extremos de incedios sólo tiene un equipo de extintores, y como compensación, está siempre amenazada por los desbordamientos del Tajo. Dos primorosas cartelas de mármol, adosadas a un pilar, conmemoran los límites que alcanzaron las riadas en los años de 1916 y 1924. Algunas obras de dique se han realizado en los tiempos monárquicos; pero no estaría fuera de propósito que V.E. dispusiese una inspección técnica. Sería lamentable que la República tuviese que poner una tercera cartela! Estima el que suscribe que, como primera providencia, debe clausurarse el Museo, para proceder a su completa organización, y a este fin se le han comunicado las oportunas órdenes al señor secretario del Museo, que tiene el doble carácter de administrador del que fué Real Patrimonio. Como quiera que el que suscribe ha visto desobedecidas sus órdenes, someto el hecho a la consideración de V.E. En caso de merecer la confianza de V.E., espera respetuosamente el que suscribe que V.E. ratifique sus órdenes y las haga cumplir. En el caso contrario, y acatando las decisiones de V.E., tiene el honor de ofrecer a V.E. su dimisión.

A282

Todo el arte del estilo está en suplir la palabra hablada. El estilo sustituye al tono, a la ironía, al gesto. La capacidad del español es para el teatro por lo que el teatro tiene de plástico, porque la Minerva española es más plástica que literaria. . . . A la lengua castellana le faltan siglos de evolución. En español no hay estilo. En español nadie ha dicho "lo suyo," sino lo de todos. Hay una tonta adoración al diccionario. Y como el estilo no es necesario en el teatro, porque lo sustituye el tono y el gesto— la plástica—, por eso la capacidad del español es para el teatro.

A283

La linea de la capacidad literaria de España se podría pintar en uno de esos cuadros de simple perspectiva en que se ven penitentes encapuchados con un cirio en la mano. Primera procesión: la de los literatizantes sentimentales del villancico y la petenera, lagrimitas de cristal y "cante jondo," Murillo y Salzillo. Segunda procesión: coge desde Desdeñaperros al Moncayo, desde el alcalaíno Cervantes al aragonés Goya. No llevan la melenita rizada, sino un gran cirio amarillo en la mano. Tercera procesión: la de los hombres atlánticos. También llevan una luz, o parece que la llevan. Pero saldrá el sol y se apagará la luz, que no era de cirio, sino de imaginaciones. Era la luz de la "santa compañía." Pero la norma española está en la segunda procesión, que es sobre Castilla. Castilla, que tiene ese poder maravilloso de recriar. Recriados de Castilla fueron Carlos I el flamenco, y Domenico el griego, y Unamuno el vasco. Unamuno, más expresivo que nadie acaso en la lengua de Castilla, en cuya entraña, que es más que en su gramática, ha penetrado don Miguel.

A284

La manera castellana es el realismo, que no es copia, sino exaltación de formas y modos espirituales. El primer poema épico del mundo en que se prescinde de lo sobrenatural es la *Farsalia*, de Lucano, un español. Cuando la lengua castellana empieza historicamente a consolidarse, produce el poema del *Cid*. En todos sus hermanos franceses, lo sobrenatural interviene. El Olifante de Rolando se oye a cien leguas, y parte el héroe un monte de un espadazo. Si al Cid le ocurre algo sobrenatural, la aparición del arcángel, es en sueños. No es, pues, un accidente el sentido español de la verdad, ni incapacidad de la fantasía para la invención. La tríada: el mundo, el demonio y la carne, domina todo el arte español de todos los tiempos, sobre todo en literatura. Del terror del año mil sale a pecar el burlador que convida a cenar a los muertos, cosa muy seria. Satán, que no es un principio increado, sino creado, y que es necesario, para que el pecado no se acabe, y con él el mundo, acude a la sugestión del burlador. Luego don Juan rompe en la frontera a pelear, en pacto con el mundo. Y acaba en Sevilla burlando doncellas, preso de la carne.

A285

España es una fuerza ética. Séneca era un granuja; pero se entusiasmaba con el bien. Quevedo no era una doncellica tampoco, y escribió terribles epístolas morales, "castigos y ejemplos." El furor ético es la característica de España. Por el furor ético, Isabel la Católica sucedió a su hermano, antes de que la corona fuera a una hija del adulterio. Por el furor ético abdicó Carlos IV, porque el español no quería saber que su reina andaba en frivolidades. El furor ético redactó el documento de destronamiento de Isabel II. La última revolución española ha sido una sanción ética.

A286

Yo no sé nada; pero sí me ha chocado una cosa en la noticia. Verá usted. Yo envié *Tirano Banderas, La corte de los milagros* y *¡Viva mi dueño!* . . . Al ver que sólo pasa al Pleno la primera de estas obras, con las de esos otros señores, pienso que si se me llega a ocurrir enviar solamente las dos no mencionadas, ¡pues ni al Pleno hubiesen pasado! Como verá, la cosa tiene su gracia. . . . Pues no me lo explico. Al no ser que no hayan sido mencionadas o mejor propuestas por su condición de antimonárquicas y sea la Academia monárquica sin yo saberlo. . . . Fui yo mismo a llevarlas con tres solicitudes con todos los requisitos. Se las entregué personalmente al secretario de la Academia, señor Cotarelo, quien estuvo amabilísimo conmigo y a quien hasta ese día no tuve el gusto de conocer. Me dijo que bastaba con llevarlas yo en persona para no hacer falta ni solicitudes, ni pólizas, ni formalidad alguna. . . . Yo no sé si esos señores que han formado la Comisión—no sé quiénes la componen—habrán visto la voluntad que hay en la obra de crear un castellano no sólo de Castilla, sino de todos los pueblos de lengua española. Es una fusión de nuestro idioma con el idioma o idiomas españoles que se hablan en Suramérica.

A287

No tengo ningún agravio de la Academia Española. Yo he enviado obras de carácter verdaderamente revolucionario, contra el antiguo régimen. Tan revolucionarias, que la Biblioteca de los Soviets las había publicado. Y la Academia, claro está, las ha rechazado. No aspiraba yo, ciertamente, al premio. Pretendía que la Academia se definiera, y la Academia, efectivamente, se ha definido. La Academia es reaccionaria y monárquica. Lo esperaba. Lo que no esperaba es la pasividad del Ministerio de Instrucción Pública. El Ministerio de Instrucción Pública ha debido dictar al día siguiente, sin esperar a más, una disposición negando competencia a la Academia para informar las obras que ha de adquirir el Ministerio, que necesitan, como es sabido, el requisito del dictamen académico. Porque esto entraña verdadera gravedad, no por mí, que ya digo que no pretendía un galardón que no había de servirme para nada, sino por el precedente que sienta. Cuando el Ministro trate de adquirir obras y consulte a la Academia, ésta emitirá dictamen favorable a las obras de carácter reaccionario y desaprobará las de índole liberal. . . . La Academia es una institución de origen monárquico, y no se ha podido limpiar de este morbo dañino. Ha estado en su papel. No me sorprende. Pero el Ministerio de Instrucción Pública es republicano, y ha debido y debe actuar siempre y por encima de todo en republicano.

A288

Nosotros, los autores castellanos que venimos de regiones dialectales nos batimos con grandes enemigos. No es el primero ni el mayor que hablamos un mal castellano. En Galicia no se habla gallego, sino una lengua contaminada de castellano. Llegar a saber castellano es nuestra mayor dificultad. Cuando el joven gallego, catalán o vasco siente la aspiración de escribir, aparece una sirena que le dice: "Si hablas en tu lengua regional serás un genio. En la lengua regional no hay que luchar con veinte naciones, basta luchar, simplemente, con cuatro provincias." Ser genio en el dialecto es demasiado fácil. Yo me negué a ser genio en mi dialecto y quise competir con cien millones de hombres, y lo que es más, con cinco siglos de heroísmo de lengua castellana. Esta es la extrema dificultad y la gran virtud, y yo la he tenido. He querido venir a luchar y si no he logrado vencer, me ha salvado la dignidad del propósito.

A289

España tiene, como las monedas, dos caras: una, romana e imperial, y otra, berberisca y mediterránea. España va a América como una hija de Roma; pero lleva también la faz berberisca y mediterránea. Como hija de Roma, lleva allí la lengua, establece un cuerpo de doctrina jurídica y funda ciudades. En la hora presente se quiere volver al bárbaro berberismo mediterráneo. Es necessario que volvamos la medalla y no tengamos más que una faz: la que nos hace hijos de Roma. España no está aquí: está en América. En el aniversario de la Constitución debemos convocar a las Repúblicas americanas, y para eso la República tiene que crear algo que estimule a aquellas naciones. Con los palacios y residencias que fueron de la Corona podiamos dar a esos embajadores una idea de España. Pero mientras eso esté en manos de la Dirección de Propiedades, no hay redención. España tenemos que hacerla nosotros que la conocemos.

A290

¿Quién puede conocer España mejor que los hombres que han sufrido sinsabores y desvelos para poder llegar a expresar su alma? ¿Por qué tenemos noticias de Rusia? ¿Por las leyes del zar o por las obras de Tolstoi y Dostoievsky? ¿Y Francia? ¿La conocemos por las leyes de Gambetta, Grevy y Combes o por las obras de Zola y Flaubert? Los que venimos de provincias hemos sido captados por la gran fuerza castellana. El maestro de todos—Unamuno—es el primer ejemplo. Y ahí está el de Carlos I que vino a España, sin amarla, y al final de su vida no fué a recogerse a ninguna de las abadías de su gran imperio, sino a un lugar español: al monasterio de Yuste; y el Greco, que vino de países ricos en luminosidades, y los olvidó todos cuando llegó a Castilla. Esto le ha ocurrido al maestro de todos, que vino de su país natal, Vasconia, y se hizo el más grande y expresivo de los escritores de Castilla.

A291

Con fecha 6 del actual he elevado a V.E. una relación, que nuevamente acompaña, del estado en que se encuentra el llamado Museo de Aranjuez. A los hechos consignados le urge añadir la referencia de otros, de tanta gravedad como aquéllos, muestras de la más vergonzosa incuria y de supina ignorancia. Alarmado el que suscribe de la forma cavernaria en que vienen realizándose las visitas de público al Palacio de Aranjuez y a la Casa del Labrador, el viernes, 3 del corriente, asistido por su doble carácter de conservador general del Patrimonio Artístico y director del Museo, telegrafió al señor secretario para que no fuesen autorizadas nuevas visitas. Lo acertado de esta prevención, que ha sido en absoluto desobedecida, queda patente en el hecho—confirmado más tarde ante testigos por el secretario—de haber desfilado más de seis mil personas por la Casa del Labrador el domingo 5 del corriente. El atentado vandálico que esto supone no necesita comentarios. La fragilidad de cuanto se encierra en este pequeño Museo, su disposición y lo reducido de sus estancias, claman con mudas voces denunciando el atentado. Y como quiera que las caravanas turísticas y gratuitas amenazan continuar en la misma forma, el que suscribe, consciente de las responsabilidades de su cargo y de su nombre, lo pone respetuosamente en conocimiento de V.E. Otras gentes sin responsabilidad y sin historia, nacidas a una modesta notoriedad con los primeros soles republicanos, pueden silenciar estos hechos y aun autorizarlos desconociendo su importancia, pues a funcionarios del orden político administrativo no hay razón para pedirles ni sensibilidad ni cultura estéticas. Termina el que suscribe encareciendo a V.E. el apremio de oportunas resoluciones sobre los hechos denunciados. Al mismo tiempo, y con todo respeto, se ve en el caso de solicitar de V.E. el apoyo moral y material que hoy le falta, y en el caso contrario, que le sea admitida la dimisión de sus cargos.

A292

Excelentísimo señor: Ante el elocuente silencio con que V.E. ha recibido las protestas y quejas que he tenido el honor de elevar a V.E., sólo me resta presentarle la dimisión de mis cargos de conservador general del Patrimonio Artístico Nacional y director del Museo de Aranjuez.

A293

A esta dimisión respondió el señor ministro con una carta que no publico por no creerme autorizado para ello. Me encarecía con amables vaguedades que retirase mi dimisión. Al mismo tiempo que recibía esta carta, leía en los periódicos la noticia que transcribo: "Proyecto de ley sobre protección al tesoro artístico nacional.—La Comisión permanente de Instrucción pública ha acordado en su sesión de ayer abrir información, por escrito, sobre el referido proyecto, a la que podrán concurrir, en la forma antes indicada, todos los individuos y entidades a quienes interese. El plazo para la admisión de las informaciones será a contar desde hoy hasta el 7 de julio próximo, y las mismas deberán ir dirigidas al presidente de la Comisión de Instrucción pública." Corté la noticia, la pegué en su tarjetón y escribí debajo: "Mi querido amigo: Recibo su antenta carta y leo esa noticia. Creo que, como conservador general del Patrimonio Artístico Nacional, cuando menos, debió haberse tenido conmigo la cortesía de darme cuenta. Ante lo hecho, sólo puedo reiterarle mi dimisión."

A294

No es un secreto que me habían visitado algunos amigos de los periódicos, y que a todos les había rogado que no hablasen del asunto de mi dimisión. Alguno que tiene siempre para mí las mayores atenciones, como Montero Alonso, puede atestiguarlo. Después del apócrifo relato de *Informaciones* no me parece oportuno silenciar la verdad de los hechos y mantener secreta su tramitación documental.

A295

Y para terminar, querido Aznar: De la apócrifa entrevista publicada en *Informaciones*, sólo responde a la verdad de mis pensamientos y propósitos el hecho de emprender un viaje a América: No a Valparaíso, como dice aquel relato, sino a Riojaneiro. Responde igualmente a una verdad que repetidamente he formulado entre mis amigos la repulsa a todo pésame oficial si está escrito que acabe de morirme por aquellas tierras.

A296

Soy viejo, estoy enfermo, no doy más de mí. . . . He tenido que dimitir el cargo que se me había confiado por no ceder a otro criterio. . . . Ya no me queda otro camino que hacer lo que he hecho. He enviado una carta al alcalde de Madrid pidiendo cuatro plazas para mis hijos en un asilo y yo me recogeré en el Instituto Cervantes.

A297

Mi querido C.:
Recibí su buena carta. Estoy abrumado. Ayer empeñé el reloj. Ya no sé la hora en que muero. Como tengo que cocinar para los pequeños, el fogón acaba de destrozarme la vejiga. Ni salud ni dinero, y los amigos tan raros. Por eso le agradezco doblemente su carta. Si en mi experiencia, desengañada, ya no puedo acogerme a ninguna esperanza, me trae un consuelo. No crea usted, sin embargo, que me desespero. Yo mismo me sorprendo de la indiferencia con que veo llegar el final. He convocado a los hijos y les he expuesto la situación. También ellos tienen el alma estoica. Les he dicho: "Hijos míos, vamos a empeñar el reloj. Después de comernos estas cien pesetas, se nos impone un ayuno sin término conocido. No es cosa de comprar una cuerda y ahorcarnos en reata. No he sido nunca sablista y quiero morir sin serlo. Creo que los amigos me ayudarán, cuando menos, para alcanzaros plazas en los asilos. Yo me acogeré al Asilo Cervantes. Allí tengo un amigo: don Ciro Bayo." Como pequeños héroes, se tragaron las lágrimas y se han mostrado dispuestos a correr el temporal sin darle demasiada importancia. En rigor, no la tiene, y si alguna vez yo se la he dado, es porque me salgo del hecho cotidiano de una familia sin recursos, con el padre enfermo. Tal dolor vulgar, repetido a diario, no merece sacar el Cristo de mi nombradía literaria. Esta condición mía acentúa el episodio dándole importancia; pero eso es ante la opinión ajena, no para mí. Lo que más me obsesiona es el pensamiento de no poder morir tranquilo: ver llegar despacio la muerte en las tardes serenas. Cerrar para siempre los ojos sin que en el ínterin me aflija e inquiete por carecer de algún dinero.
Escríbame, querido amigo.

A298

Voy caminando entre escombros.
La alforja del infortunio
agobia mis viejos hombros.

Halo de trémula albura,
un aceite de difuntos
alumbra mi noche oscura.

Voy en la noche de lutos,
la boca muda a la queja,
los ojos al llanto enjutos.

Muerte bienaventurada,
toda mi esperanza cifro
en llegar a tu posada.

A299

Caballeros, salud y buena suerte.
Da sus últimas luces mi candil.
Ha colgado la mano de la muerte
papeles en mi torre de marfil.
Le dejo al tabernero de la esquina,
para adornar su puerta, mi laurel.
Mis palmas, al balcón de una vecina;
a una máscara loca, mi oropel.
Para tí, mi cadáver, reportero.
(Si humo las glorias de la vida son,
tú te fumas mi gloria en un habano.)
Para tí, mi cadáver, perro ingrato,
que después de cenar con mi fiambre,
adobado en tu prosa gacetil,
humeando el puro, satisfecha el hambre
y harto de mi carroña, ingenuamente
dirás gustando del bicarbonato:
"¡Qué don Miguel no la diñe de repente!"

A300

No podré. Es más: quizá no pueda presenciar los ensayos. Me marcho en seguida a
Roma. Por la interpretación no temo. Sé que Rivas Cherif cuidará esto con mucho
cariño. Por otra parte, la Xirgu y Borrás han de estar muy bien en sus papeles. El
complemento lo dará Castelao. De él depende, en la estampa de *Divinas palabras,* lo
más inmediato para que Galicia esté en presencia en la escena. (Es) De infinitos
matices. Y como usted decía, de ritmos variados, pero dentro de una indestructible
unidad melódica. Las voces tienen aquí un valor extraordinario. Por eso habrá que
ensayarla como se ensaya una orquesta.

A301

Excelentísimo señor: Enterado por el secretario de esta academia, don Hermenegildo Estevan, de la advertencia y admonición que le ha hecho el ilustrísimo
señor consejero don Gonzalo de Ojeda referente a la prohibición de trasladar
muebles de una habitación a otra habitación, espero indulgencia, a causa de ignorar
que por tal hecho incurría en falta. Al presente me atengo a esa prohibición con tan
estricto respecto que hoy hallándose en mi despacho hasta seis personas, como sólo
hubiese asiento para tres, he tendido mi capa en el suelo y las he invitado a sentarse
en ella.

A302

No puede olvidarse que siete personas requieren siete camas. Las camas de que goza esta dirección son cinco, según reza el inventario; salvo error, hasta siete faltan dos. Siete camas requieren a su vez 14 sábanas, a razón de dos sábanas por cama. Las sábanas de que goza esta dirección son 16, según reza el inventario. Aparejadas las siete camas, quedan dos sábanas de repuesto. Cuando llega la hora de mudar las camas, como el repuesto no basta (el repuesto, ya queda dicho, son dos sábanas), esta dirección pasa por el sonrojo de apremiar a la lavandera para que las enjabone en la mañana y a la planchadora para que por la tarde las seque con la plancha. Siete camas requieren, corrientemente, 14 almohadas, a razón de dos almohadas por cama. Las fundas de almohada de que goza esta dirección son nueve, según reza el inventario. A dos fundas por cama se aparejan cuatro camas y media. Si las camas son siete, no es preciso ser un Pitágoras para sacar la cuenta de que quedan dos camas sin aparejo de almohadas y una cama con medio aparejo. Decir que el director de la academia vive hoy como en un aduar de gitanos no es expresión exagerada. Ni su salud, ni sus canas, ni sus hábitos, ni la dignidad del cargo, le permiten continuar asi.

A303

Todavía no he visitado ningún Museo, ni templo, ni ruina. Veo la ciudad por fuera. Es algo maravilloso y único. Toda la historia de una civilización de dos mil años. . . . Lo realizado por Mussolini me tiene asombrado y suspenso. Junto a una furia dinámica, colmada de porvenir, el sentimiento sagrado de la tradición romana. Recientemente se ha abierto una Vía—la Vía Impero—que avista las más insignes ruinas de la latinidad. Decoran esta Vía cuatro estatuas de bronce traídas del Museo de Nápoles. La de Julio César, de la más serena elegancia; la de Octavio, expresiva y de un cautivante tono verdino. La de Trajano, con una leyenda en el pedestal: "Príncipe Optimo." Le confieso que he sentido el latido gozoso ante el bronce de este insigne cordobés. Vengan ustedes a Roma. Yo no he visto ni comprendo nada igual.

A304

El que llega como yo a Roma para ver la ciudad con ojos desinteresados siente una enorme impresión. En el camino de Nápoles a Roma está Ostia Antica. . . . Aníbal en Capua traza una larga línea terrestre y parece que los destinos entonces del mundo europeo van a estar en Africa. Pero el romano entretiene al cartaginés. Y mientras Aníbal queda en Capua, Escipión parte con sus trirremes y conquista Cartago. Surge el gran concepto militar de la lucha de las dos líneas: la marítima y la terrestre. Triunfa la marítima. Y el triunfo de la nave es el triunfo de Italia.

A305

¿El Fascio? El Fascio no es una partida de la porra, como generalmente creen en España los radical-imbeciloides, ni un régimen de extrema derecha. Es un afán imperial de universalidad en su más vertical y horizontal sentido ecuménico. De las estrellas a las florecillas de San Francisco de Asís. Aquí está Roma, allá abajo, ofreciéndose a nuestra contemplación como un espléndido paradigma de mármoles gloriosamente mutilados por los siglos, con su Vía del Imperio—la obra cesárea de Mussolini—,donde se alzan cuatro estatuas ejemplares para todos los pueblos del orbe: Julio César, Octavio Augusto, Trajano y Nerva. Porque Trajano fué Español, y Nerva fué elegido Emperador por las legiones hispanas y galas. Por eso también España fué Roma, como lo era todo el mundo conocido, hasta los finisterres, que se adentraban en el mar tenebroso, y si el Catolicismo logró universalidad y, junto al poder espiritual, tuvo sus imponderables geográficos, fué por que era también

Roma. Porque era la voz y el brazo de Roma en un quehacer de católica liturgia. Y esta continuidad en los designios de Roma es el Fascio, hasta el punto de que si tuviera algún día realidad política aquella famosa utopía de Briand, los Estados Unidos de Europa tendrían su capitalidad en Roma, ya que todo lo moderno de Europa es lo viejo de Roma.

A306

La obra de Mussolini tiende principalmente a inculcar en su pueblo un ideal, un concepto de sacrificio; en esta hora tan llena de egoísmos es en Roma donde no existen, y por eso el pueblo italiano es el más dispuesto a sacrificarse por un ideal histórico, que es el único que pueden tener los pueblos. . . . Mussolini, como Aníbal, César y Napoleón, tiene siempre un concepto y un fin categórico y determinado. Por eso se pone cerca de Mussolini una triste experiencia histórica. En la dictadura de un hombre no puede haber egoísmos de clase. Es ya Napoleón, es ya Mussolini, es el caso del gran monarca. Atiende sin privilegios los intereses de uno y otro sector y puede hacer una gran obra. Existe una diferencia entre Mussolini y Hitler: el primero tiene como una idea platónica y ha despertado en las almas poéticas de todos los italianos, ese pueblo lleno de gestos heroicos, un sentido de universalidad, pero para sentirlo ha tenido que hacer lo contrario que el alemán. Mientras Hitler expurga al pueblo alemán de todos los elementos que no son puros germanos, Mussolini entiende como Caracalla, que toda la totalidad de la Europa culta, son ciudadanos italianos. Este sentido de universalidad queda explicado diciendo que Mussolini ha colocado en la Vía Impero, cuatro estatuas . . . dos emperadores romanos y dos del imperio, pero que ya no nacieron en el suelo de Roma. En toda la política de Mussolini impera el sentido de la universalidad.

A307

. . . un botarate que caerá muy pronto.

A308

Me estiman y me temen. Las dos cosas. ¿Sabe Ud. que intentan arrebatarme la Academia de España? Pero no será así, mientras yo sea su director.

A309

Sr. Don Fédor Kelin.
    Lejano y buen amigo: No acierto a decirle los ecos que su carta ha despertado en mí. Yo soy un renegado de la literatura. Hace algunos años que vivo en apartamiento de los escritores y de los libros. Usted me habla de los míos, y que tengo ahí algunos lectores, y comparo melancólicamente este buen suceso con mi fracaso en España. Claro que mi fracaso es el de casi todos los literatos que merecen respeto. Yo he sido tan loco que pensé vivir de la pluma, y al cabo de una lucha de cuarenta años,—para no acabar en un asilo, a cuya puerta ya estaba pulsando—, he podido remediarme con la Dirección de esta Academia.
    No he recibido el número que me anuncia de la *Literatura Internacional*. Quisiera poder enviarle alguno de mis libros, pero no tengo ninguno. La mayor parte están agotados. Escribí a Madrid para que le remitan *Opera Lírica, Martes de Carnaval, Tablado de Marionetas* y algún otro de que hay ejemplares. La vida literaria española es tan mezquina que los editores no aventuran su dinero para reimprimir los libros agotados.
    Hace tiempo he sido invitado para ir a Rusia, y he vuelto a serlo recientemente,

pero las obligaciones de esta Dirección me impiden dar cima a ese gran deseo de mi corazón. Veremos si para octubre puedo realizarlo. Para entonces, seguramente, se habrán restablecido las relaciones diplomáticas entre España y Rusia.

Mucho me temo que España se equivoque una vez más al enviarles un Embajador.

Y nada más, mi buen amigo, que agradecerle el afecto de su carta, y estrecharle la mano.

Valle-Inclán

A310

España he sufrido la dictadura de los cuatro brazos tradicionales: el brazo noble, el brazo militar, el brazo eclesiástico y el brazo popular. Primero sufrió España la dictadura de la nobleza, el privilegio de los nobles, y no los sufría sólo el pueblo, sino que también los sufrían los monarcas, hasta que los Reyes Católicos desasentaron a los nobles y de dictadores los convirtieron en cortesanos. Inmediatamente vino la dictadura de otro brazo social: de la Iglesia con la Inquisición. Es la dictadura de la Iglesia sobre los demás brazos sociales. Es decir, la dictadura de una colectividad sobre las demás. Y la teocracia funda la unidad nacional en la unidad católica. A la Iglesia sucede el Ejército. En el siglo XIX España sufre la dictadura militar. La Unión Liberal la representa O'Donnell; los moderados, Narváez; antes, Espartero a los progresistas; la Revolución de setiembre es Prim; La Restauración, Martínez Campos, y la última dictadura se ha llamado general Primo de Rivera, y España sufre los egoismos del Ejército, el egoísmo de esta clase, violentando y esquilmando a las otras tres. Siguiendo esta relación España sufre ahora la dictadura socialista y los egoísmos de esta clase esclavizan a las otras tres. El caso es que aquí no hay socialismo y es . . . una clase que está en fuga. Digo que es una clase en fuga porque carece del sentido y del afán de la permanencia. Un noble no aspira a dejar de serlo, un capellán aspira a obispo, éste a cardenal y después a Papa, el soldado sueña en llegar a ser general y el obrero aspira a ser patrono. Es decir, que mientras los otros tres brazos no quieren dejar su clase, la popular sí. Por eso es una clase llena de resentimientos y tiene una categoría menor. La dictadura que puede ser necesaria, es de un individuo, pero no de una clase. Es triste llegar a esta conclusión, pero es la realidad, desgraciadamente. El final de todo será fundir todas las clases en una, y eso es el comunismo. Pero para ello habría que suprimir la herencia y habría también que nacionalizar los Bancos, la tierra, las industrias y las minas. Lo tremendo es no haber seguido este camino, haciendo desaparecer la clase proletaria por la supresión de todas las demás, igualando a todas. Para ello hay que hacer trabajar a todos, y esto no se consigue diciendo en la constitución que España es una República de trabajadores de todas clases, sino suprimiendo varias cosas, y en primer lugar la herencia, porque yo no he visto trabajar a ningún rico heredero. Trabaja el que lo necesita. Por eso Jehová no dijo a Adán "ganarás el pan con el sudor de tu frente" hasta que le privó del magnífico latifundio del Paraíso.

A311

Bragaglia está temblando. Ha intervenido la censura. . . . No pienso asistir a su estreno.

A312

Aquí estoy con una hematuria que dura ya varios días y tiene todo el aspecto de ser como la última que tuve en Madrid e hizo necesaria la transfusión para cortarla . . .

Si la hematuria se corta por sí, me haré inmediatamente la electrocoagulación. Si, como me temo, la hematuria es rebelde, habrá que hacer la transfusión.

A313

Tiene razón el señor Cotarelo. La Academia es un templo. Yo soy un hereje. Los herejes no pueden entrar en el templo. No lo digo con ironía. Hablo con sinceridad. Se trata de una gran verdad. Soy un heterodoxo incorregible, rebelde por naturaleza.

A314

No quiero olvidar con ellos—todos los hombres honestos—a esa gran figura intelectual—al doctor Del Río Ortega—y a todos los que con él están en la cárcel, y es preciso que aquí recaudemos para enviarles nuestro pequeño óbolo, siquiera sea para la cena de Navidad.

A315

Me parece muy bien la idea. . . . ¿Y sabe usted lo que también me gustaría que reuniese usted en otro tomo de mis obras? . . . Pues las *Sonatas* . . . . Pues si este ensayo no le sale a usted mal, que no le saldrá, se lo garantizo, haremos las *Sonatas*. . . . Si le hablo a usted con esta certeza es porque tengo motivos para ello. Mis libros, en ediciones económicas, se venderán por millares . . . No le quepa a usted la menor duda. Y tras las *Sonatas* aún haremos un tercer volumen que reúna, a mi juicio, lo mejor de cuanto he escrito. . . . *Cara de Plata*, *Aguila de blasón* y *Romance de lobos*. Los tres quedarían a maravilla en un tomo de los suyos.

A316

No hemos hablado nada sobre una cosa importantísima. ¿Qué título le va usted a poner al libro? ¿Ha pensado usted en esto? . . . Pues no hay que echarlo en saco roto, porque es esencial. Los títulos son la cara de los libros, y una cara bella para hombres y libros es la mejor recomendación. A mí los títulos me preocupan siempre mucho, y si le dijese que algunos me han costado más que los libros mismos, puede que no mintiese. . . . me preocupo mucho de este detalle, como le digo. ¿Qué efecto le haría a usted en un buen cuadro un manchon de pintura? . . . Pues eso creo yo que hace un título feo, soso o inexpresivo. . . . Sí, tenemos que pensarlo despacio hasta dar con algo que les convenga a todos.

A317

No sé todavía el tiempo que permaneceré en este sanatorio. He venido aquí verdaderamente enfermo; aún cuando me lo callaba, yo lo sabía, y no tenía la menor esperanza de curarme. Por algo que había leído en libros que estudian estos males como el mío sospechaba que el papiloma había degenerado en carcinoma y que me quedaba poco de vida. No ha sido así, y de esa aprensión estoy ya curado. Me aplican el radium, y sus resultados creo que serán eficaces. Con la salud he recobrado un poco de optimismo y he empezado una novela. La llevo muy adelantada.

A318

La pena de muerte, cuando se instituye para ahogar en sangre la voz de la protesta de la inmensa mayoría de un pueblo, que desde los más apartados rincones exigen que cese un estado de cosas negativo de los más elementales derechos de ciudadanía, no constituye una adecuada medida correctiva de ejemplaridad y de orden, sino un modo de imponer por el terror aquello que el pueblo, con ansias de libertad y de justicia, repudia con todo el clamor de su indignación.

. . . Tales son los antecedentes que sirven de base a la implantación de la pena de muerte y, por todo ello, estimamos, tras su total ineficacia, su monstruosidad manifiesta. En casos como el que aquí se da, tiene demostrada la misma ciencia penal que la pena de muerte es totalmente nociva y contraproducente.

. . . Legalizar, legitimar y justificar el Estado (que hoy no es representación de la voluntad popular) la matanza premeditada de honrados ciudadanos, que expusieron su vida y derramaron su sangre, luchando por un estado social, a su juicio, más justo, es algo tan terrible y tan monstruoso, tan injusto y tan arbitrario, que todo hombre consciente de sus deberes y derechos como tal, y de la responsabilidad que ante la sociedad nos afecta en cada momento histórico a cada uno, tiene que rechazar y condenar.

. . . Los principios humanitarios más elementales, los dictados de la justicia y del derecho inmanentes, no autorizan ni pueden autorizar para que una minoría instituya, contra la voluntad de la mayoría, el acto de quitar la vida a nuestros semejantes de una manera premeditada, reflexionada y fría, como se manifiesta en la ley.

. . . Esta Agrupación, integrada por numerosos hombres de Derecho, que quieren luchar y luchan porque resplandezca la justicia, pero no esa justicia parcial y de privilegio estatuida por quien no representa o no interpreta la voluntad del pueblo, lanza este llamamiento a todos los hombres identificados hasta la saciedad, de la manera más expresa y categórica, como piensan y sienten, en relación con un problema que tan profundamente afecta al corazón de todos los ciudadanos, los hombres y las mujeres, sin distinción de matiz político, que, enclavados en el campo de la intelectualidad, en las esferas de la ciencia, del Derecho y del Arte, en sus múltiples manifestaciones, observan las realidades sociales que nos circundan en estos graves momentos.—Ramón del Valle-Inclán.—Victoria Kent, presidente de la A.S.O.—Vicente Riscos, secretario de A.S.O.

A319

Quisiera llegar en mi obra histórica hasta una descripción titulada *Los campos de Cuba* . . . mi interpretación del mambí y del voluntario español causará mucho ruido.

A320

"En enero, Juan tercero." Esta divisa—ciertamente, más ramplona que suelen serlo los lemas de heráldica y armería—era, no hace mucho, augurio y promesa de los fieles monarquizantes. Pasó aquel enero y quedó fallido el pronóstico, como acontece con tantos otros del verdadero Zaragozano. Ahora los anuncios son de Himeneo. Todavía no ha sido troquelado el lema epitalámico; pero insignes poetas tiene la causa, para que pueda faltar en la ocasión que se apareja la inspiración de la aleluya. Lema, si no de armería, de confitería, en los lazos rojo y gualdo que aten los dulces de la boda.

A321

Quiero una casa edificar

Como el sentido de mi vida,
Quiero en piedra mi alma dejar
Erigida.

Quiero labrar mi eremitorio
En medio de un huerto latino,
Latín horaciano y grimorio
Bizantino.

Quiero mi honesta varonía
Transmitir al hijo y al nieto.
Renovar en la vara mía
El respeto.

Mi casa como una pirámide
Ha de ser templo funerario,
El rumor que mueve mi clámide
Es de Terciario.

Quiero hacer mi casa aldeana
Con una solana al oriente,
Y meditar en la solana
Devotamente.

Quiero hacer una casa estoica
Murada en piedra de Barbanza,
La casa de Séneca, heroica
De templanza.

Y sea labrada de piedra;
Mi casa Karma de mi clan,
Y un día decore la hiedra
Sobre el dolmén de Valle-Inclán.

A322

La cárcel para el hombre cabal es madre de consejos. Y, aún sin celebrar que los enemigos del gran república lo hayan honrado con tan dura escuela, de ello pudiera decirse feliz rigor, mirando el fruto sazonado de este libro. Si para el recuerdo de los afanes nacionales es grande parte el conocimiento que promete el andar caminos bajo soles y lluvias con las botas de siete leguas, no es menor el que se saca de medir uno y otro día los cuatro pasos de un calabozo y de contemplar la luna sobre la altura del enrejado tragaluz. Noble laurel ofrece la cárcel cuando va acompañada de la persecución injusta.

A323

Ruégole testimonie profundo pésame familia Bello, y represénteme acto entierro. Contándose conmigo para cuanto sea necesario. Saludos. Valle-Inclán.

A324

Recluído en un sanatorio, y más enfermo acaso de lo que sospecho, distraigo mi mal y mis pesadumbres con amables lecturas.

A325

Venga a verme. Vuelven los terribles dolores y estoy a punto de quejarme como una mujer.

A326

No le faltan ni dolores al cuerpo ni penas al espíritu. Todo se me junta al final de la vida.

A327

Quiero despojar el acto de mi muerte de toda sombra de ceremonia. . . . Que no se publiquen esquelas . . . Que se deposite mi cuerpo en un féretro modesto y que en ningún momento haya ostentación en las exequias.
   Que el entierro sea civil . . . ni cura discreto, ni fraile humilde, ni jesuíta sabihondo . . .

A328

Mirad. La muerte es regia, digna. Un momento antes de morir llega el Señor, con luces, rezos y palios de fiesta. Todos mis antepasados ponían flores en sus habitaciones, las mejores colchas con encaje de Camariñas, el traje más nuevo y recibían al Señor de pie. No se puede recibir al Señor en el lecho de pecado. . . . Pero como yo no creo . . .

A329

¡Cuántas veces en el rictus de la muerte se desvela todo el secreto de una vida! Hay un gesto que es el mío, uno solo, pero en la sucesión humilde de los días, en el vano volar de las horas, se ha diluído hasta borrarse como el perfil de una medalla. Llevo sobre mi rostro cien máscaras de ficción que se suceden bajo el imperio mezquino de una fatalidad sin trascendencia. Acaso mi verdadero gesto no se ha revelado todavía, acaso no pueda revelarse nunca bajo tantos velos acumulados día a día y tejidos por todas mis horas. Yo mismo me desconozco y quizá estoy condenado a desconocerme siempre. Muchas veces me pregunto cuál entre todos los pecados es el mío, e interrogo a las máscaras del vicio: Soberbia, Lujuria, Vanidad, Envidia han dejado una huella en mi rostro carnal y en mi rostro espiritual, pero yo sé que todas han de borrarse en su día, y que sólo una quedará inmóvil sobre mis facciones cuando llegue la muerte. En ese día de la tierra, cuando los ojos con las pestañas rígidas y los párpados de cera se hundan en un cerco de sombra violácea; cuando la frente parezca huir levantando las cejas; cuando la nariz se perfile con una transparencia angustiosa; cuando la mandíbula, relajada en sus ligamentos, ponga en los labios una risa que no tuvieron jamás, sobre la inmovilidad de la muerte recobrará su imperio el gesto único, el que acaso no ha visto nadie y que, sin embargo, era el mío. . . Contemplémonos en nosotros mismos hasta descubrir en la conciencia la virtud o el pecado raíz de su eterna responsabilidad, y la veremos quieta y materializada en un gesto.

A330

¡Qué fuerte es morir entre estos grises! . . . ¡ Qué duro es esto!

A331

Tú sabes que me descompone que se hagan mis obras. Yo no conozco tormento mayor para mi sensibilidad estética que ver representáda una obra mía.

Index